Society for American Baseball Research, Inc.
Phoenix, AZ

Edited by Bill Nowlin
Associate editors
Len Levin & Carl Riechers
Foreword by Mike Gibbons

Baltimore Baseball
Edited by Bill Nowlin
Associate editors Len Levin and Carl Riechers
Foreword by Mike Gibbons

Copyright © 2021 Society for American Baseball Research, Inc.
All rights reserved. Reproduction in whole or in part without permission is prohibited.
ISBN 978-1-970159-55-4
Ebook ISBN 978-1-970159-54-7
Library of Congress Control Number: 2021915281

Book design: Jennifer Bahl Hron
Chapter fonts: Optima & Times New Roman | Cover fonts: CornerStore & Rockwell
Cover photo: Camden Yards is the first park to feature SABR member and architect Janet Marie Smith's hallmark retro style, combining elements from the great ballparks of the past with modern amenities.
Courtesy of the Baltimore Orioles.
Back cover photo: Nine-year-old Orioles fan Luke Millikin in front of Memorial Stadium before the last Orioles game played there on October 6, 1991. Courtesy of Mark Millikin.

Society for American Baseball Research
Cronkite School at ASU
555 N. Central Ave. #416
Phoenix, AZ 85004
Phone: (602) 496-1460
Web: www.sabr.org
Facebook: Society for American Baseball Research
Twitter: @SABR

Contents

Baltimore Baseball - A Foreword By Mike Gibbons — 8

A Preamble of Disconnections By Ken Mars — 10

Early Baltimore Ballparks By Ken Mars — 11

Early Black Baseball in Baltimore By Ken Mars — 18

Early Baseball Encounters in the West: The Yeddo Royal Japanese Troupe Play Ball in America
June 14, 1872: Dolly Varden Club 27, Yeddo Royal Japanese Troupe 23, at Newington Grounds By Bill Staples Jr. — 22

Union Park By David B. Stinson — 26

Seven Hits in Seven Tries for Wilbert Robinson
June 10, 1892: Baltimore Orioles 25, St. Louis Browns 4, at Union Park By Jimmy Keenan — 33

Baltimore Stuns the Champs, Scoring 14 Runs in the Ninth for the Win
April 24, 1894: Baltimore Orioles 15, Boston Beaneaters 3, at Oriole Park III By Mike Huber — 35

Birds Building to Sweep the Cup
October 5, 1896: Baltimore Orioles 6, Cleveland Spiders 2, at Union Park By Benjamin Sabin — 37

Hitting 'Em Where They Ain't 44 Games in a Row
June 18, 1897: Baltimore Orioles 11, Pittsburgh Pirates 9, at Oriole Park III By Kevin Larkin — 39

Good (Beaneaters) versus Evil (Orioles)
September 27, 1897: Boston Beaneaters 19, Baltimore Orioles 10, at Union Park By Bill Felber — 41

American League Park By David B. Stinson — 43

Baltimore Orioles Win Home Opener in a New Major League
April 26, 1901: Baltimore Orioles 10, Boston Americans 6, at American League Park By Jimmy Keenan — 51

Turkey Trots to a 6-6 Day at the Plate
June 24, 1901: Baltimore Orioles 17, Detroit Tigers 8, at Oriole Park IV By Kevin Larkin — 54

McGinnity Gives Two Spits over Umpire's Calls
August 21, 1901: Detroit 9, Baltimore Orioles 0 (Forfeit), American League Park By Chad Osborne — 56

Little Napoleon vs. the Czar
June 28, 1902: Baltimore Orioles 9, Boston Americans 4 (8 innings), at American League Park By Chris Corrigan — 59

Two Teams Going in Very Different Directions
Sept. 29, 1902: Boston Americans 9, Baltimore Orioles 5, at American League Park (Oriole Park III) By Bill Nowlin — 62

Bugle Field By Bill Johnson — 65

Terrapin Park/Oriole Park (V) By David B. Stinson — 68

Maryland Park – The Park that Time Almost Forgot By Steve Behnke — 77

Red Grier's Negro World Series No-Hitter
Oct. 3, 1926: Atlantic City Bacharach Giants 10, Chicago American Giants 0, at Maryland Park By Jim Overmyer — 80

Baltimore Black Sox Beat Lefty Grove and All-Stars Team
October 14, 1928: Baltimore Black Sox 9, All Stars 3, at Maryland Park By Bill Nowlin — 83

Municipal Stadium/Memorial Stadium By David B. Stinson — 85

Good Luck Birds: The Orioles Return to Baltimore After 52 Years
April 15, 1954: Baltimore Orioles 3, Chicago White Sox 1, at Memorial Stadium By Bob LeMoine — 97

• Baltimore Baseball •

Orioles Beat Red Sox In 17 Innings; Game Sets Records for Time And Players
June 23, 1954: Baltimore Orioles 8, Boston Red Sox 7 (17 innings), at Memorial Stadium By Bob Fleishman — 100

Celebrating the First Grand Slam at Memorial Stadium
July 30, 1954: Baltimore Orioles 10, New York Yankees 0, at Memorial Stadium By Cort Vitty — 103

Brooks Robinson's Debut Game
September 17, 1955, Baltimore Orioles 3, Washington Senators 1, at Memorial Stadium By Paul Scimonelli — 105

Dick Williams Homers to Tie Game at Curfew
May 18, 1957: Chicago White Sox 4, Baltimore Orioles 4, at Memorial Stadium By Tom Mank — 108

Billy O'Dell Pitches Three Scoreless Innings in American League All-Star Game Victory
July 8, 1958: American League 4, National League 3, at Memorial Stadium By Gary Sarnoff — 111

Orioles Knuckleballer Hoyt Wilhelm No-hits Yankees
September 20, 1958: Baltimore Orioles 1, New York Yankees 0, at Memorial Stadium By Mike Huber — 113

Time Runs Out for O's and Chisox in 18-Inning Marathon
August 6, 1959: Baltimore Orioles 1, Chicago White Sox 1, at Memorial Stadium By Richard Cuicchi — 115

Jerry Walker's Masterpiece
September 11, 1959: Baltimore Orioles 1, Chicago White Sox 0 (16 innings, game two of a doubleheader), at Memorial Stadium By Dave Moniz — 117

Umpire's "Time" Call Nullifies Ted Kluszewski's Apparent 3-Run Home Run
August 28, 1960: Baltimore Orioles 3, Chicago White Sox 1, at Memorial Stadium By Bob Brown — 119

19-Year-Old McNally Makes Quick Work of A's in Impressive Debut
September 26, 1962: Baltimore 3, Kansas City 0 (first game of doubleheader), at Memorial Stadium By Richard Cuicchi — 121

Wally Bunker Throws One-Hitter
May 5, 1964: Baltimore Orioles 2, Washington Senators 1, at Memorial Stadium By Joseph Wancho — 124

Rookie Orioles Pitcher Jim Palmer Hits First Career Homer and Earns First Career Win
May 16, 1965: Baltimore Orioles 7, New York Yankees 5, at Memorial Stadium By Mike Huber — 126

Frank Robinson's Home Run Out of the Ballpark
May 8, 1966: Baltimore Orioles 8, Cleveland Indians 3 (second game of doubleheader), at Memorial Stadium By Mark R. Millikin — 128

Wally Bunker Shuts Out Dodgers in Game Three of 1966 World Series
October 8, 1966: Baltimore Orioles 1, Los Angeles Dodgers 0, at Memorial Stadium By Austin Gisriel — 130

McNally Fires Orioles' Third Consecutive Shutout as Baltimore Sweeps Los Angeles
October 9, 1966: Baltimore Orioles 1, Los Angeles Dodgers 0, at Memorial Stadium By Frederick C. Bush — 132

Steve Barber and Stu Miller Combine for No-hitter in a Loss
April 30, 1967: Detroit Tigers 2, Baltimore Orioles 1, at Memorial Stadium By Jimmy Keenan — 136

5 Hours and 18 Minutes Later
June 4, 1967: Baltimore Orioles 7, Washington Senators 5 (19 innings), at Memorial Stadium By Gary Sarnoff — 138

Hard Slide Ends Weis's Season, Knocks Out Frank Robinson
June 27, 1967: Chicago White Sox 5, Baltimore Orioles 0, at Memorial Stadium By Laura H. Peebles — 141

Tom Phoebus Throws Orioles' Third No-Hitter
April 27, 1968: Baltimore Orioles 6, Boston Red Sox 0, at Memorial Stadium By Jimmy Keenan — 143

Orioles Blast White Sox, Setting Team Hits, Total Bases, and Runs Records
July 27, 1969: Baltimore Orioles 17, Chicago White Sox 0, at Memorial Stadium By Mike Huber — 146

Jim Palmer No-Hits the Athletics
August 13, 1969: Baltimore Orioles 8, Oakland Athletics 0, at Memorial Stadium By Jimmy Keenan — 148

Orioles Win First-Ever ALCS Game
*October 4, 1969: Baltimore Orioles 4, Minnesota Twins 3 (12 innings), at Memorial Stadium,
Game One, American League Championship Series* By Jimmy Keenan ... 151

Dave McNally Tosses 11-Inning Masterpiece in ALCS
October 5, 1969: Baltimore Orioles 1, Minnesota Twins 0 (11 innings), at Memorial Stadium By Brian M. Frank ... 154

Orioles Extend Their Winning Streak Against the Royals to 23 Games
August 2, 1970: Baltimore Orioles 10, Kansas City Royals 8, at Memorial Stadium By Sean Church ... 156

Orioles Clinch 1970 World Championship in Game Five
October 15, 1970: Baltimore Orioles 9, Cincinnati Reds 3, at Memorial Stadium By Jimmy Keenan ... 158

Frank Robinson Hammers His 500th Home Run
September 13, 1971: Detroit Tigers 10, Baltimore Orioles 5 (second game of doubleheader), at Memorial Stadium
By Joseph Wancho ... 161

Don Baylor Whacks Four Extra-Base Hits to Lead Orioles' Opening Day Rout
April 6, 1973: Baltimore Orioles 10, Milwaukee Brewers 0, at Memorial Stadium By Malcolm Allen ... 163

Jim Palmer Hurls 8 1/3 Perfect Innings
June 16, 1973: Baltimore Orioles 9, Texas Rangers 1, at Memorial Stadium By Brian M. Frank ... 165

Kaline Collects 3,000th Career Hit as Tigers Fall to Orioles, 5-4
September 24, 1974: Baltimore Orioles 5, Detroit Tigers 4, at Memorial Stadium By Jody Madron ... 167

Orioles Rally in Ninth – Lolich Reaches Wrong Side of 20; Stays in First Place
September 25, 1974: Baltimore Orioles 5, Detroit Tigers 4, at Memorial Stadium By Luis A. Blandon Jr. ... 170

Brooks Robinson's Last Career Home Run
April 19, 1977: Baltimore Orioles 6, Cleveland Indians 5 (10 innings), at Memorial Stadium By Bill Haelig ... 173

Orioles Magic Is Born
June 22, 1979: Baltimore Orioles 6, Detroit Tigers 5, at Memorial Stadium By Austin Gisriel ... 175

Tippy Martinez Retires 23 Consecutive Batters in Relief
July 23, 1979: Baltimore Orioles 7, Oakland Athletics 4, at Memorial Stadium By Brian M. Frank ... 177

Baltimore Sweeps Doubleheader to Extend Earl Weaver's Final Pennant Race
*October 1, 1982: Baltimore Orioles 8, Milwaukee Brewers 3; Baltimore Orioles 7, Milwaukee Brewers 1 (doubleheader),
at Memorial Stadium* By Rich Ottone ... 179

Brooks Robinson Celebration Night
August 5, 1983: Baltimore Orioles 5, Chicago White Sox 4, at Memorial Stadium By Austin Gisriel ... 182

Tippy Martinez Picks Off Three Blue Jays in One Inning
August 24, 1983: Baltimore Orioles 7, Toronto Blue Jays 4 (10 innings), at Memorial Stadium By Austin Gisriel ... 184

Fred Lynn Hits Walk-Off Home Runs in Back-to-Back Games
*May 10, 1985: Baltimore Orioles 6, Minnesota Twins 5, 1985; May 11, 1985: Baltimore Orioles 4, Minnesota Twins 2,
at Memorial Stadium* By Rich Ottone ... 186

Orioles "Slam" Rangers with Nine-Run Fourth Inning but Still Lose Game
August 6, 1986: Texas Rangers 13, Baltimore Orioles 11, at Memorial Stadium By Frederick C. Bush ... 189

Juan Nieves Throws No-Hitter Against Orioles
April 15, 1987: Milwaukee Brewers 7, Baltimore Orioles 0, at Memorial Stadium By John J. Burbridge Jr. ... 192

Orioles Soar to Victory on Mike Young's Two Extra-Inning Home Runs
May 28, 1987: Baltimore Orioles 8, California Angels 7, at Memorial Stadium By Gary Belleville ... 194

There's No Place like Home; There's No Place like Home; There's No Place Like Home!
May 2, 1988: Baltimore Orioles 9, Texas Rangers 4, at Memorial Stadium By Alan Cohen ... 197

• Baltimore Baseball •

New-Look Orioles Begin 1989 Season on Winning Note *April 3, 1989: Baltimore Orioles 5, Boston Red Sox 4 (11 innings), at Memorial Stadium By Jody Madron* — 200

"Untouchable" Wilson Alvarez Pitches A No-Hitter in Second Major-League Start
August 11, 1991: Chicago White Sox 7, Baltimore Orioles 0, at Memorial Stadium By Leonte Landino — 202

Orioles Play Their Final Game at Memorial Stadium
October 6, 1991: Detroit Tigers 7, Baltimore Orioles 1, at Memorial Stadium By Thomas J. Brown Jr. — 204

Oriole Park at Camden Yards By Curt Smith — 206

Orioles Play Their First Game in Oriole Park at Camden Yards
April 6, 1992: Baltimore Orioles 2, Cleveland Indians 0 at Oriole Park at Camden Yards By Thomas J. Brown Jr. — 219

Seven Suspended, Five Injured in Worst Brawl in Orioles, Mariners History
June 6, 1993: Baltimore Orioles 5, Seattle Mariners 2, at Camden Yards By Gary Belleville — 221

Remembering This Midsummer Classic: A Prodigious Blast and the Boo Birds
July 13, 1993: American League 9, National League 3, at Oriole Park at Camden Yards By Steven C. Weiner — 224

"Unbreakable" Record Passes: Gentleman to Gentleman
September 6, 1995: Baltimore Orioles 4, California Angels 2, at Oriole Park at Camden Yards By Ralph Peluso — 227

Hoiles Hits a Walk-off Grand Slam
May 17, 1996: Baltimore Orioles 14, Seattle Mariners 13, at Oriole Park at Camden Yards By Matt Clever — 230

Eddie Murray Clouts 500th Career Home Run During Rainy Evening
September 6, 1996: Detroit Tigers 5, Baltimore Orioles 4 (12 innings), at Oriole Park at Camden Yards By Gordon Gattie — 232

Mike Mussina Retires 25 Straight While Firing Brilliant One-Hitter
May 30, 1997: Baltimore Orioles 3, Cleveland Indians 0, at Oriole Park at Camden Yards By Gordon Gattie — 235

The Quiet Night at Camden Yards
August 12, 1997: Baltimore Orioles 8, Oakland Athletics 0, at Oriole Park at Camden Yards By Peter Coolbaugh — 238

Jeff Reboulet Delivers LDS to Baltimore
October 5, 1997: Baltimore Orioles 3, Seattle Mariners 1, at Oriole Park at Camden Yards By Joseph Wancho — 240

Cal Ripken's Consecutive Game Streak Comes to an End
September 20, 1998: New York Yankees 5, Baltimore Orioles 4 at Oriole Park at Camden Yards By Thomas J. Brown Jr. — 242

"They should have a mercy rule" Orioles Score Record 23 Runs in Blowout of Blue Jays
September 28, 2000: Baltimore Orioles 23, Toronto Blue Jays 1, at Oriole Park at Camden Yards By Mike Huber — 244

Nomo Joins Elite Company With No-Hitters in Both Leagues
April 4, 2001: Boston Red Sox 3, Baltimore Orioles 0, at Orioles Park at Camden Yards By Bill Staples Jr. — 246

Goodbye, Number 8
October 6, 2001: Boston Red Sox 5, Baltimore Orioles 1, at Oriole Park at Camden Yards By Peter Coolbaugh — 249

Orioles Lose 15-1 to Cleveland on Tuesday, Turn Tables and Score 18 on Wednesday
April 19, 2006: Baltimore Orioles 18, Cleveland Indians 9, at Oriole Park at Camden Yards By Mike Lynch — 251

Aubrey Huff's Milestone Cycle Not Enough to Help Orioles Beat Angels
June 29, 2007: Anaheim Angels 9, Baltimore Orioles 7, at Oriole Park at Camden Yards By Mike Huber — 253

Rangers Set Major-League Mark with 30-3 Victory
August 22, 2007: Texas Rangers 30, Baltimore Orioles 3, at Oriole Park at Oriole Park at Camden Yards By Thomas E. Schott — 256

One Sugarcoated Game
June 30, 2009: Baltimore Orioles 11, Boston Red Sox 10, at Oriole Park at Camden Yards By Thomas E. Schott — 258

Pie Cycles and Tillman Gets First Career Win for Orioles
August 14, 2009: Baltimore Orioles 16, Anaheim Angels 6, at Oriole Park at Camden Yards By Mike Huber — 261

Orioles Play Spoiler, Strike Midnight on Red Sox Season
September 28, 2011: Baltimore Orioles 4, Boston Red Sox 3, at Oriole Park at Camden Yards By Timothy Kearns   263

Orioles Lead Off Game with Three Consecutive Home Runs
May 10, 2012: Baltimore Orioles 6, Texas Rangers 5 (first game of two), at Oriole Park at Camden Yards By Bob Brown   266

Young's Pinch Hit Gives Baltimore Playoff Boost vs. Detroit
October 3, 2014: Baltimore Orioles 7, Detroit Tigers 6, at Oriole Park at Camden Yards By Robert Kimball   268

Orioles and White Sox Play for Normalcy in Empty Stadium
April 29, 2015: Baltimore Orioles 8, Chicago White Sox 2, at Oriole Park at Camden Yards By Mike Huber   270

Orioles Clout Franchise-Best Eight Homers in 19-3 Rout of Phillies
June 16, 2015: Baltimore Orioles 19, Philadelphia Phillies 3, at Oriole Park at Camden Yards By Mike Lynch   273

O's Exact Revenge on Royals with Pair of Eighth-Inning Grand Slams
September 11, 2015: Baltimore Orioles 14, Kansas City Royals 8, at Oriole Park at Camden Yards By Gary Belleville   275

Machado's Three Homers Include a Walk-Off Grand Slam
August 18, 2017: Baltimore Orioles 9, Los Angeles Angels 7, at Oriole Park at Camden Yards By Peter Seidel   278

Red Sox Defeat Orioles Behind Sale's Pitching, Benintendi's Home Run, and Bradley's Catch
May 8, 2019: Boston Red Sox 2, Baltimore Orioles 1 (12 innings), at Oriole Park at Camden Yards By John J. Burbridge Jr.   280

Contributors   282

Baltimore Baseball – A Foreword

The history of baseball in Baltimore is as deep-rooted and tradition-rich as anywhere in America. Long-time *Baltimore Sun* reporter and sports columnist John Steadman tellingly reflected on the genesis of our fabled legacy, calling the sport "the greatest game God ever invented!"

Chapter one of my lifelong love affair with our national pastime came on April 15, 1954, when my father fetched me from school midmorning and drove me to the first-ever home opener for our newly minted American League Orioles. Memories of the day are hazy; I was only 7. But walking up the ramp into the lower bowl of Memorial Stadium and taking in all that green grass remains a vivid recollection. That first game served as a springboard for dad and me, as we attended 20 or more home games a year, plus a few on the road, until I was in my late teens.

And so we saw many of the games expertly chronicled in this book, including two in 1958. In July we feasted on that year's All-Star Game, played in Baltimore, with the Orioles' Billy O'Dell pitching. Then, in September, we sat in Memorial Stadium's left-field bleachers for Hoyt Wilhelm's no-hitter against the Yankees, the first in franchise history. My childhood hero, Big Gus Triandos, generated the game's only run in the seventh inning, a monstrous clout that sailed directly over our splintery seats

Toward the end of our father-son-Orioles'-games experience, we attended Game Three of the '66 World Series, expertly portrayed herein by Austin Gisriel. But it was Game Four, which we did not attend, that is kept alive and vibrant in the Babe Ruth Museum archives by the baseball Frank Robinson hit in the seventh inning to give the Orioles a 1-0 victory and a series sweep of the favored LA Dodgers. "Would You Believe Four Straight!"

That leads me to chapter two of my connection to Baltimore baseball – my long association with the Babe Ruth Museum. In the early spring of 1982, I was a documentary producer working on a Babe Ruth biography, and had made an appointment to visit the Babe Ruth Birthplace Museum to research the mighty Bambino. That initial exposure led me to volunteer at the museum and to find a way to get greater numbers of Baltimoreans to visit the attraction. An Orioles presence, it seemed, might be the answer. I reasoned that Ruth had signed with the minor-league Orioles in 1914, so there was a connection to the big-league franchise.

Through the museum I met two gentlemen who knew as much as or more about Baltimore baseball and the Orioles than seemingly anyone, Jim Bready of the *Sun* and Bob Brown, PR director of the Orioles. They proved instrumental in securing me a meeting with Orioles GM Hank Peters. I explained the Ruth/Orioles connection and asked if the team had a museum or archive. Hank said, "No." I pitched a Museum/Orioles partnership, and right there and then the Babe Ruth Birthplace became the official museum of the Baltimore Orioles.

After gathering Orioles artifacts and audio and video highlights from the team, local media outlets and the general public, we opened an Orioles exhibit at the Birthplace in May of 1983. I was appointed the institution's executive director, and off the museum soared on a mission to preserve and maintain the proud heritage of Orioles baseball and, of course, Babe Ruth. Quickly, that mission expanded to include virtually all of Baltimore baseball, including the many iterations of the Orioles (1800s, minor-league era and the modern franchise), amateur ball, the industrial leagues, and Negro League play in Baltimore.

Early in my museum tenure I learned that the 1890s National League Orioles were/are considered by many to be baseball's first great dynasty. Catcher Wilbert Robinson's great-grandson gave me a glimpse of Uncle Robbie off the playing field, and shared with me an ancient telegram from September 1894 that read, "Cheer up, Mary, the flag is ours!" He also shared that Wilbert and Orioles teammate John McGraw in 1897 invented the game of duckpin bowling for their sports bar on Howard Street in Baltimore, aptly nicknamed "The Diamond."

Speaking of the Negro Leagues, Jim Overmyer and Bill Nowlin give us some great insight into Baltimore's rich contributions to Black baseball. In my early years at the museum I was fortunate to be able to interview historically significant players like Monte Irvin and Marylander Judy Johnson, as well as Sam Lacy, the renowned sports reporter for the *Baltimore Afro-American*, and Dick Powell, the last general manager for the Baltimore Elite Giants. Mr. Lacy shared with me his role in the 1947 breakdown of the color barrier, when he served as

• Baltimore Baseball – A Foreword •

Jackie Robinson's roommate on the road with the Dodgers. Mr. Powell helped me to better grasp the significance of Bugle Field in east Baltimore, where the game, played at its highest level, attracted huge, diverse crowds that helped our city soften the lines of segregation. An exact scale replica model of Bugle Field, brilliantly crafted by a museum volunteer, is an important part of our Negro League collection.

Jimmy Keenan's reflection on the 1970 World Series triumph over Cincinnati casts new light on a milestone in Orioles history, a time when I was overseas on a tour of duty with the US Navy. Years later, through the museum, I did get to know several members of that team, most notably World Series MVP Brooks Robinson, Boog Powell, Elrod Hendricks, Jim Palmer, Frank Robinson. and manager Earl Weaver, whose 1970 World Series ring (his only) remains on loan to the museum.

Thomas Brown covers the last game at Memorial Stadium, Detroit vs. Baltimore, October 6, 1991. The museum worked with the Orioles to plan a very special postgame ceremony. I remember meeting with O's PR director Bob Brown and Charles Steinberg, the team's director of public affairs. During spring training that year, we hatched a plan to have the dozens of former and current Orioles expected to participate in the ceremony make a circle around the pitcher's mound so that we could take a motorized, 360-degree panoramic photo to commemorate the event. It worked! Years later, Mike Flanagan, who struck out Travis Fryman for the last out at Memorial Stadium, presented us with the ball he threw for that last out.

We don't have anything representing Frank Robinson's 500th homer, but we do have the ball that Eddie Murray clouted for his 500th on September 6, 1996, a special moment recaptured herein by Gordon Gattie.

The museum was intricately involved in the planning and opening of Oriole Park at Camden Yards in 1992, leading hard-hat tours of the construction site, assisting architect Janet Marie Smith in uncovering photos of famous ballparks from the past to help give the ballpark that old-time feel, and producing the black-tie celebration of the park's opening on Saturday, April 4. I had the honor of writing the dedication speech for the evening ceremony … read by James Earl Jones.

Cal Ripken's streak, specifically the 2-1-3-1 game on September 6, 1995, has to be an all-time highlight. My wife, son, and I were seated down the third-base line in the upper deck at Camden Yards that night, the perfect vantage to take in the wonder of it all, especially Ripken's victory lap around the warning track before his adoring fans. Equally astonishing that evening was Cal's fourth-inning home run off the Angels' Shawn Boskie. Funny how the great ones come through when the lights shine brightest.

On September 20, 1998, my wife and I were seated behind the Orioles dugout. As the O's took the field in the top of the first, something seemed out of kilter, conjuring a low murmur from the large crowd. When the opposing New York Yankees climbed to the top of their dugout steps and started clapping we finally understood. Cal Ripken was not at third base. In his place, Ryan Minor! And so Cal's streak concluded at 2-6-3-2, a mark that will never be challenged.

Two other topics covered in this publication stirred personal memories; one very loud, the other all but silent. First, Delmon Young's pinch-hit double that propelled Baltimore past Detroit in the 2014 ALDS. The base-clearing blast generated the loudest crowd sound I'd ever heard at an Orioles game, comparable only to the ear-splitting decibel level every time John Unitas was introduced at Memorial Stadium.

Second, the April 29, 2015, game at Oriole Park that played out in the middle of the Freddie Gray riots. The game became the only major-league baseball contest ever played before *no* fans. Several of my museum colleagues and I camped out along Camden Street, taking in the contest through the fencing by Monument Park in right-center field. The only sounds wafting out from Camden Yards that day were generated by White Sox and Orioles players, or a batted ball. We watched and listened as Chris Davis's home-run clout cleared the flag court and bounced onto Eutaw Street. I called Orioles front-office friend Bill Stetka, who was in the press box that day, to try to fetch that ball for the collection. He did, and it is in the museum's archive.

If you are a fan of our national pastime, I am certain you will enjoy scrolling through this compelling chronicle of what makes Baltimore baseball unique. From Ruth to Ripken, from the Elite Giants to our Baltimore Orioles, there's nothing quite as intriguing as these tales of our orange and black.

April 2021

Mike Gibbons
Director Emeritus
Babe Ruth Birthplace Foundation

A Preamble of Disconnections

By Ken Mars

The history of baseball in Baltimore is largely one of disconnections, and the city has suffered many from the very beginning of the professional era.

The Maryland Base Ball Club of the original National Association of Professional Base Ball Players, imploded in 1870 when half the lineup abandoned the bankrupt team to join another in Fort Wayne, Indiana.

The National Association Lord Baltimores fell apart in 1874 after a massive fire downtown began a financial depression.

The 1881 American Association Baltimore Base Ball Club was historically terrible and replaced by the Orioles after one season.

The 1884 Baseball War claimed Baltimore's Union Association franchise and the minor-league Monumentals, leaving the Orioles the last team standing.

The National League Orioles were dissolved in 1899 mostly because of Harry Von Der Horst and Ned Hanlon's greed.

The American League Orioles were assassinated in 1902 as a casualty of the bitter feud between Ban Johnson and John McGraw.

The invading Terrapins of the 1914-1915 Federal League war exiled the Orioles for a season before folding themselves.

The Black Sox collapsed in 1934 after a long fight against the Great Depression.

The Oriole Park fire on July 4, 1944 robbed Baltimore of the last wooden major-league ballpark built, untold amounts of memorabilia, including Ned Hanlon's personal collection, and the club's complete archive.

The Elite Giants disbanded in 1950, because times had changed.

And finally, the end of the minor-league Orioles in 1953, partly because the St. Louis Browns were terrible.

Every time one of these teams went away and got replaced with another, hearts were broken, feelings were hurt, and the economy and landscape of baseball in Baltimore changed.

Our past got buried and forgotten, over and over and over.

Baltimore has a rich and complicated baseball history that is greatly misunderstood.

The time has come for that to change.

Early Baltimore Ballparks

By Ken Mars

#1 - Flat Rock (a.k.a Druid Hill Park) 1858-1859

When Baltimore grocer, George F. Beam, formed the Excelsior Base Ball Club in the summer of 1858, the choice for a practice space was imperative since ball playing within city borders was often impractical, and at times illegal. Just south of the Rogers family's Druid Hill plantation, there was an area originally called Flat Rock, named so for a large crop of stones near the road to the mansion. It's hard to imagine, but until 1888, Baltimore ended at North Avenue, and anything beyond was rolling farmland.

Beam and teammates chose the treeless and loosely graded site of the old Mount Vernon Cemetery, as it was the flattest, clearest land for play. The cemetery was dedicated in 1852, but the space quickly filled to capacity and became overgrown with neglect. Nicholas Rogers, whose land the graveyard bordered, sued the owner to have the corpses removed and reinterred in

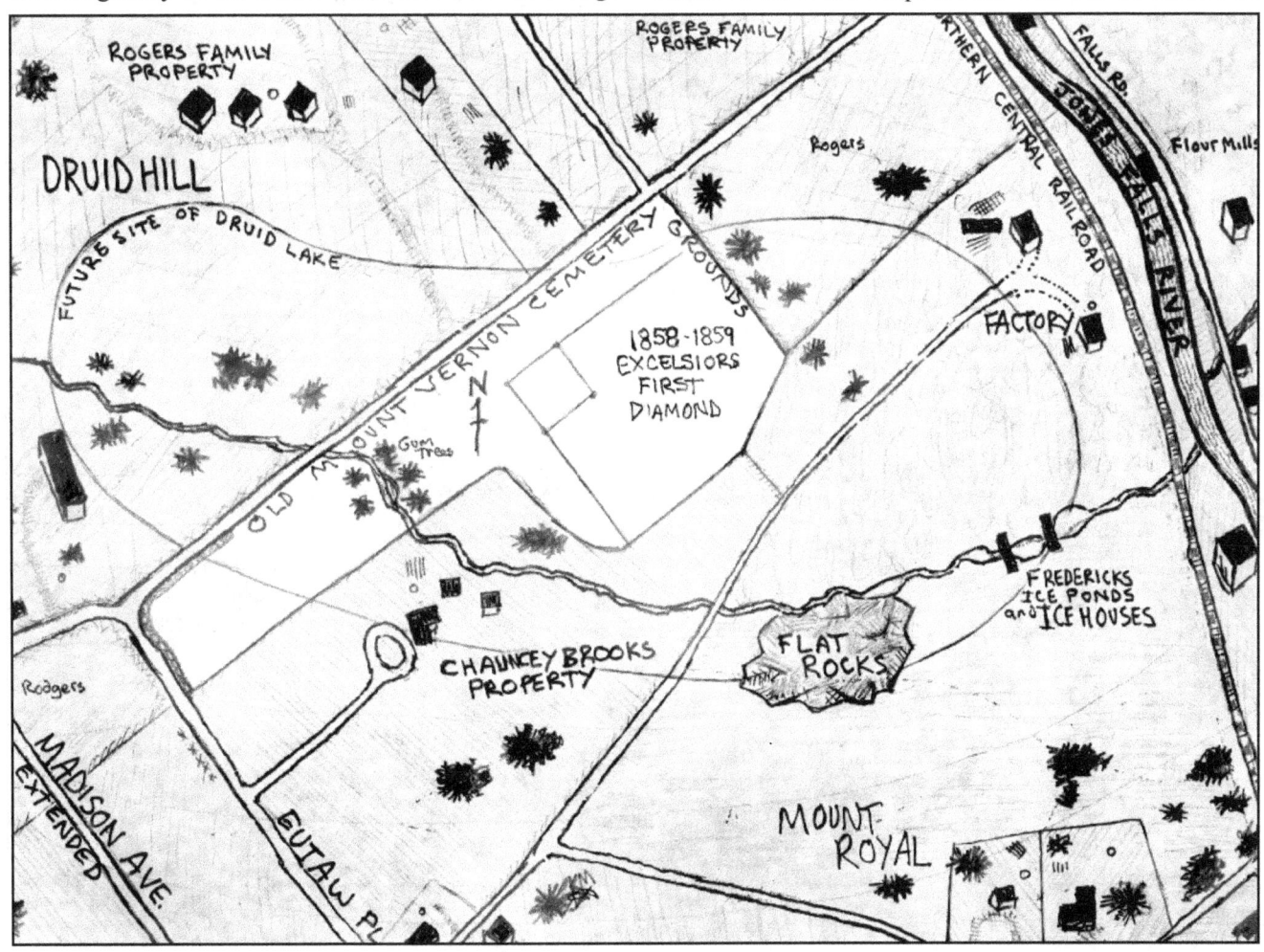

Map © Ken Mars 2016

• Baltimore Baseball •

Greenmount Cemetery to increase the value of his property, and the parcel went essentially unclaimed in 1858. It was an ideal location, with privacy and no neighbors to complain, but best of all, it was free.

It took some work, but once the men cut the weeds back and cleared out the debris, they laid out the very first baseball diamond in the State of Maryland. Home plate was surveyed with the batter facing east, and the pitcher facing the often-intrusive sun. Obviously, no local competitors existed at first, so they practiced and played inter-squad games on Wednesday and Saturday afternoons, though within a year, they would be joined by other clubs.

Close to Flat Rock was a saloon owned by Jacob Hartzell, called the Park House, which became a convenient meeting spot for refreshments before and after practice. In years to come, teams would build small clubhouses out back to change clothes and store equipment. The diamond on the old cemetery was only used by the Excelsiors for a few months in 1858 and the beginning of 1859 when it was announced that the City had completed the purchase of the Rogers' family lands to establish Druid Hill Park; the third municipal park in the country at the time. By 1870, the entire southeastern corner of the park was dug out, and a large retaining wall built up into the country's largest earthwork dam at 119 feet high. Once the reservoir was flooded, all trace of the first baseball field in Maryland history vanished and has been under a permanent rain out ever since.

#2 - Excelsior Field 1859-1860

In 1859 the Excelsiors rented a piece of land on the border of the city at the corner of Madison Avenue and North Avenue, with Gold Street on the south edge. Baltimore's public transit system was small and privately operated, but one route ran up Madison Avenue close to the ball fields, ending at the city boundary. This accessibility helped stimulate interest and the Continental, Druid, Oriental, and Peabody base ball clubs all came together over the next year, representing every corner of the city. The Baltimore Base Ball Club, a short-lived squad, made its mark on history on August 23, 1860, when they took on the Maryland Base Ball Club.

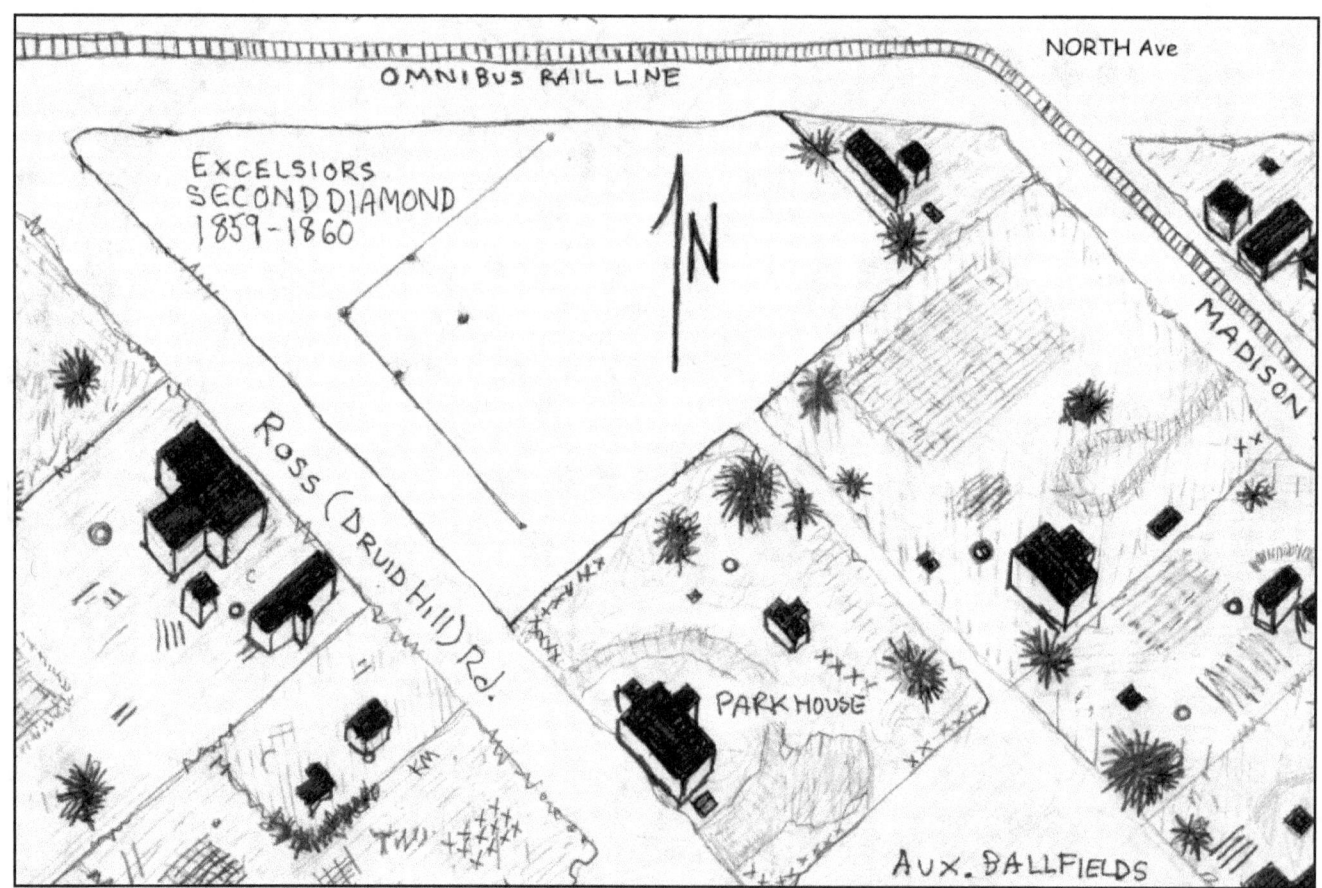

Map © Ken Mars 2016

• Early Baltimore Ballparks •

"BASE BALL- The first match game of base ball between rival clubs which has ever taken place in this city came off on the afternoon of the 23rd between the Baltimore and Maryland clubs. The game played on the grounds of the Excelsior club and was witnessed by about two hundred persons, a large portion of whom were ladies. The Maryland club have been playing but a very short time and the Baltimore for the last four months. The game was very well played, considering the disparity of ages between the members of the two clubs - the oldest members of the Baltimore club being but fifteen years of age, while those of the Maryland are all grown men. The playing of Master H. Vaughn of the Baltimore as catcher was very fine having caught four or five on the fly and as many on the bound. The batting of the Baltimore was better than the Maryland with but one exception, that done by Robert Green. The game was won by the Baltimore club with the following score: Baltimore 29, Maryland 11."[1]

The Brooklyn Excelsiors came to town on September 22, 1860, to play at the Baltimore Excelsiors diamond on North Avenue. During the pregame warmup the *Baltimore American* observed of the Brooklynites that, "the ball passed from one to the other with great precision, and seldom was it allowed to slip through the fingers of any of them. This little exhibition made it manifest that the Baltimore Club would learn a few new points before the game closed." The visitors took the field first, and crafty pitcher Jim Creighton retired the side in order, taking down George Beam on three pitches. Beam then took to the box and promptly gave up a bruising 16 runs in the first four innings. Brooklyn continued to pile it on while Creighton shut down Baltimore inning after inning, until he let a pitch slip and hit a batter in the head with a high fastball. Creighton was moved to the outfield, where in the late innings of the one-sided slaughter, he started what was likely the first triple play to occur in the State of Maryland. Baltimore had Samuel Patchen on second and John K. Sears on third with none out. Hervey Shriver got a hold of a good one and sent it soaring into the sky. The long fly ball drifted back on Creighton, who made a spectacular catch on the run for the first out. Without a pause, Creighton's cannon arm threw the ball in to third baseman, John Whiting, who tagged Sears for the second out. Whiting then relayed quickly to Asa Brainard waiting at second, just in time to nab Patchen for the third and final out. Deflated by their base running gaffe and inability to defend against their opponent's superior hitting, the home team was overwhelmed by a football-like score of 51-6.

#3 - Madison Avenue Base Ball Grounds 1860-mid 1870's

Early in 1860, William Clapham Pennington, a lawyer and future president of the Baltimore Fire Insurance Company, helped form the Waverly Base Ball Club. The Penningtons owned several plots near Flat Rock and took the initiative in establishing the Madison Avenue Grounds, the first formal baseball park in Maryland. With many players leaving to fight in the war, the Waverlys merged with the Excelsiors in 1861 to form the Pastimes. The venue itself evolved over a number of years, each season

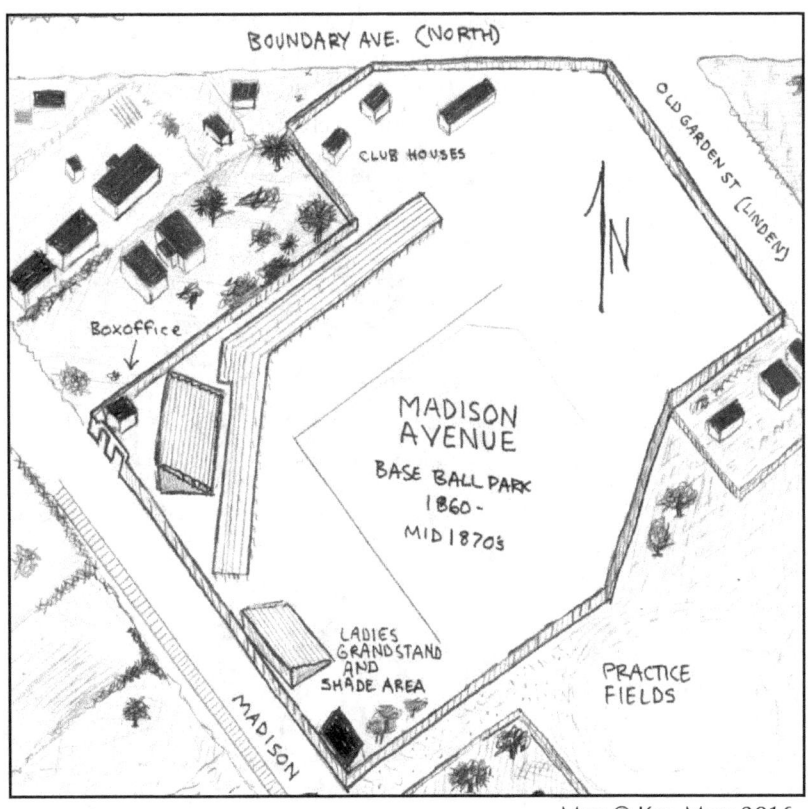

Map © Ken Mars 2016

• Baltimore Baseball •

bringing improvements and expansion: benches and grandstands, fences to enclose the area for privacy, and a section for women who wished not to mix with the foul-mouthed men. Most games cost 10 cents admission, and special events, such as out-of-town teams, cost as high as a quarter. The diamond was also rented out to other teams for practice and several clubhouses were built in the outfield to accommodate. In winter, the outfield was flooded, left to freeze, and turned into a skating rink. The location of the Madison Avenue Ball Grounds was just south of the corner of Madison Avenue and North Avenue. Eutaw Place, and Morris Street now cut through what had been the spacious outfield.

On August 27, 1867, the New York Mutuals, one of the best clubs in the country at the time, took on the Pastimes at Madison Avenue. When it came time to play the Pastimes, though, the Mutuals made a grave error and sent their "B" squad to Baltimore, thinking (correctly) that their amateur foes were pushovers. Madison Avenue was filled to capacity, but little was expected of the Pastimes, and the home crowd was shocked when Dick Thorn of the Mutuals gave up 14 runs in the first two innings. The New Yorkers switched positions several times with no improvement. In the ninth the Pastimes tacked on seven runs, including a three-run homer by Louis Mallinckrodt! When the dust settled, the lowly Pastimes of Baltimore had slain the mighty New York beast with a nice cushion, 47-31.

"In proportion to the elation and congratulation indulged among the Pastimes and their friends is the depression and mortification of the vanquished champions. Particularly was the victory of the Pastimes a source of jubilation from the fact that the Baltimore boys had not only to contend with the reputed best nine in the country, but also with a partial and biased umpire. Mr. Glover's decisions were frequently so reprehensible, so flagrantly partial and unjust, as not only to provoke the murmurs of the Pastimes, but to call forth the criticism of the fair-minded members of the Mutuals, in whose favor he constantly awarded… Whatever may be said by the interested, prejudiced or biased, it must be admitted that the playing of the Pastimes was up to the best and highest standard exhibited anywhere in the country. Where all played so well it would be invidious to commend individual action."[2]

4 - Newington Base Ball Grounds (a.k.a Newington Park) 1871-mid 1880's

In early November 1871, the Lord Baltimore Base Ball Club elected officers and began negotiating a 10-year ground rent on a plot of land off Pennsylvania Avenue at Gold Street for a new ballpark. By the end of the month, three covered grandstands had been built to seat 2,000, and an additional two-tiered stand was planned especially for stockholders. The final sale was delayed until just after the New Year, and by then primary investor Michael Hooper Sr. had withdrawn from the endeavor, leaving Alphonsus Houck and his brother George to purchase the property rights on their own. Samuel Snowden, chief litigator for the Newington Land and Loan Company, one of the largest public investment firms in the city facilitated the sale. In a very early example of corporate naming rights, the Pennsylvania Avenue Base Ball Park, was changed to the Newington Base Ball Grounds, to seal the deal.

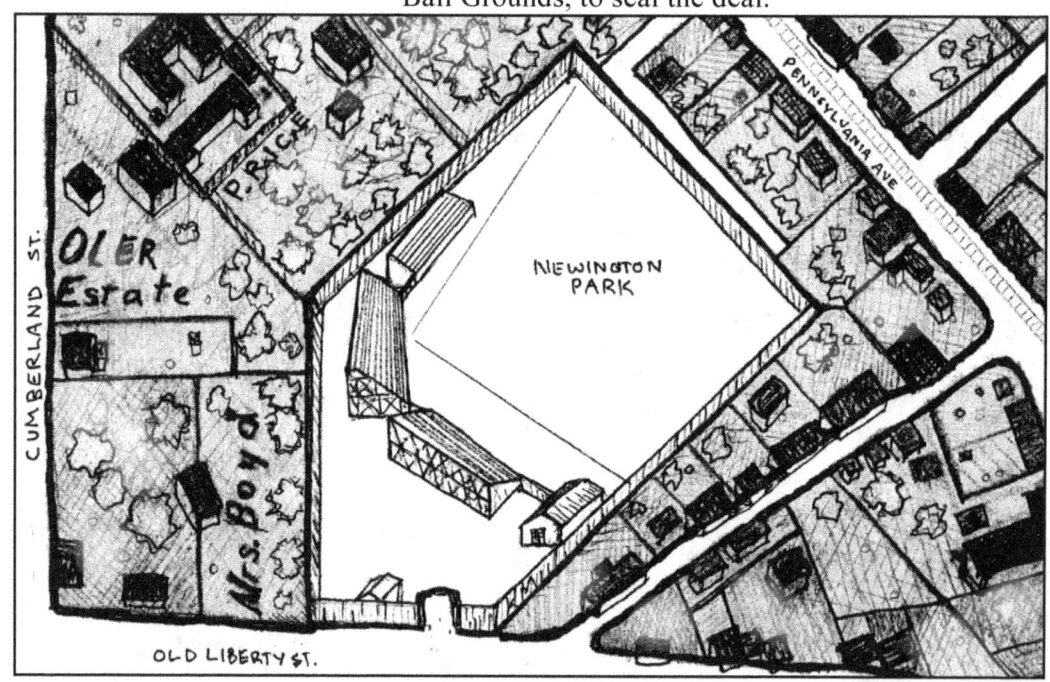

Map © Ken Mars 2016

Early Baltimore Ballparks

The Lord Baltimores National Association home opener at Newington on April 22, 1872, was a huge success. Bobby Mathews and the Lord Baltimores trounced the New York Mutuals, 14-8, in front of 2,500 screaming fans, and an estimated 1,500 more outside, standing on sheds and rooftops and the surrounding trees infested with children. It may not sound like a big crowd, but Baltimore's population was less than 40% of what it is now. Seizing upon local history, the Lord Baltimores sported specially-tailored white silk shirts emblazoned with the Calvert family arms, yellow and black argyle socks, and mustard gray knickers topped off with a white cap. It may sound acceptable on paper, but when the public saw them for the first time, they laughed. Nicknames were plentiful. Yellow Legs, Mustard Trousers, Dandelions, and Canaries. Not very flattering. The silk shirts were flimsy, and the men felt unprotected. Unfortunately, the Lord Baltimores collapsed after the 1874 season and Newington featured mostly amateur clubs for the remainder of the decade.

On Tuesday May 9, 1882, the American Association Baltimore Base Ball Club moved into Newington Park for their home opener. The Baltimores lost to the Athletics, 4-2, and would go on to compile a season so historically bad the franchise was taken away from owner/manager Henry Myers and given to Billy Barnie and Alphonsus Houck for a new club; the Baltimore Orioles.

5 - Huntingdon Avenue Base Ball Grounds (a.k.a Oriole Park I) 1883-1888

The search for a first nest led the Baltimore Orioles to an empty lot on the east side of Greenmount Avenue, south of Huntingdon Avenue, now known as 25th Street. Owned by the Sadtler family trust, the parcel was a wide-open field on the outskirts of town that had been used for over a decade by amateur clubs for practice. Unlike its predecessors, the ballpark was in a central location and readily accessible by public transportation. As soon as the ink was dry on the lease, construction began on the Huntingdon Avenue Grounds. Nestled in a residential area, the park used the space efficiently. Though smaller in acreage than previous ballparks in the city, the Orioles built upwards instead of spreading out. A central amphitheater style grandstand that sat 1,200 was raised above the field level with the bottom portion serving as the backstop. Along the right and left foul lines were two long sets of bleachers that held over 2,000 each, with space in the deep outfield for standing room only. A 10-foot-high wooden fence enclosed the entire perimeter to discourage onlookers. By comparison to Madison Avenue and Newington, the soon-to-be-nicknamed "Oriole Park" on Huntingdon Avenue was state-of-the-art.

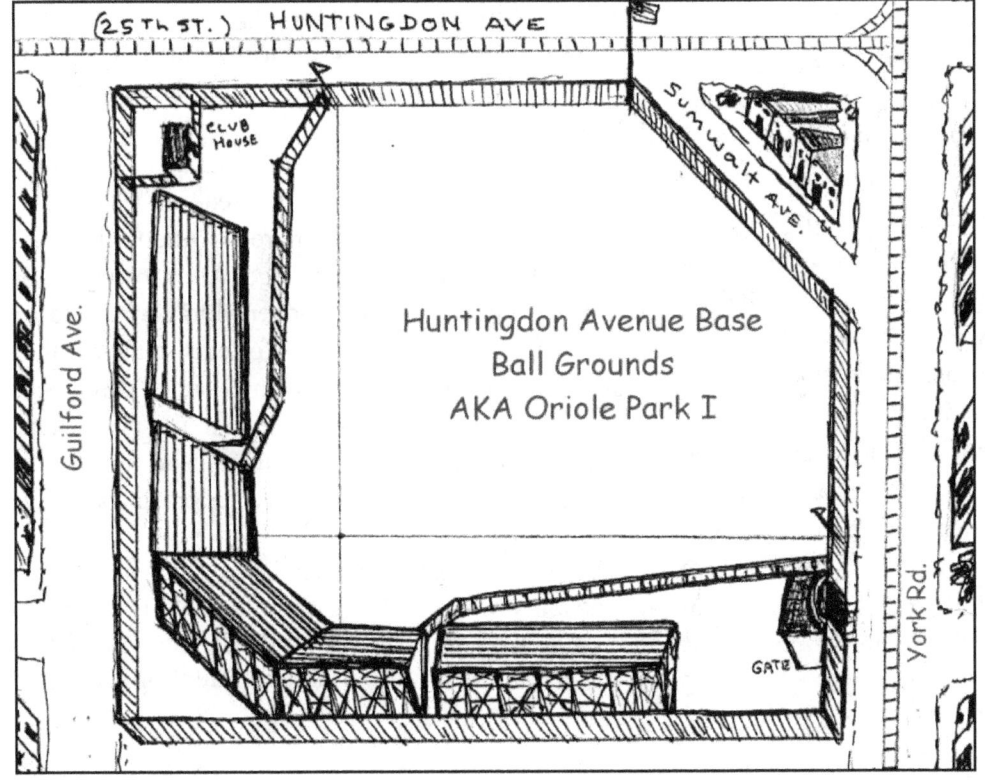

Map © Ken Mars 2016

On June 16, 1887, a rowdy crowd showed up at Oriole Park, eager to see the Birds best St. Louis and flirt with first place. Curt Welch of the Browns was one of the roughest and rudest of his era; often described as an illiterate and vulgar umpire baiter. Oriole fans had their eyes on him. The Birds and Browns were tied at eight in the ninth.

After scratching out a single, Welch tried to steal second. When he realized he was going to be thrown out by Chris Fulmer, Welch slammed into second baseman Bill Greenwood, who dropped the ball just after impact. Umpire John McQuade called Welch out - but not loud enough or gesturing clearly enough for anyone to get the call.

Greenwood had held on long enough to make the play, but no one was looking at McQuade - and Welch didn't immediately walk back to the Browns bench. Everyone thought Welch was called safe.

When Bill Barnie burst from the Orioles bench to demand judgment, Birdland turned into bedlam. The stands emptied. Men swarmed past the barbed wire lined picket fences and on to the field - straight toward Welch's throat!

Angry fans surrounded the Browns, pushing and shoving several to the ground. Barnie and Charlie Comiskey agreed to call the game a tie, in hopes it would disperse the furious fans. It didn't work. The police lost control of the situation. Browns ace and local boy Dave Foutz tried his best to calm the crowd, but when the throngs seemed uncontrollable, several Orioles smuggled Welch out of the park and off to Camden Yards Railway Station to catch the first train out of town.

However, when they got to the ticket office, there was already a small mob anticipating Welch's stealthy departure. With no escape, Welch hid in his hotel, waiting out the night with a growing crowd of irate Baltimoreans gathering outside his window. A court hearing was held in the morning in which a contingent of local fans banded together to bring assault charges against Welch. Greenwood was called in to testify, but pleaded Welch's innocence instead; stating that the play was nothing out of the ordinary.

Welch was released on a $200 ($5K) bond, paid in full by Orioles co-owner (with Barnie), Harry Von Der Horst, and wisely benched for the final game of the series. *The Sporting News* wrote, "The Baltimore audience displayed very little of the instincts of human beings, but on the contrary conducted themselves like idiots."

6 - Oriole Park (a.k.a. Oriole Park II) 1889-1891

At the corner of York Road and Tenth Street, (now 29th Street and Greenmount Avenue), Bill Barnie and Harry Von Der Horst built the second Oriole Park, though it is the first to have that name exclusively for its tenure. The main grandstand, elevated to form the backstop, could seat 2,000, and there was a second tier with private boxes for press and VIPs. Bleachers on the first-base side sat 3,500, and a covered pavilion along third for another 1,500. A passageway under the grandstand would join the two halves, with generous standing room for the biergarten between. The team clubhouse was tucked underneath the southern end of the covered pavilion.

One drawback to the new location on 29th Street was that only the York Road streetcar line ran up that far. Patrons coming from the west now had the option of transferring streetcars or walking 15 minutes north. General admission at the new park was held at 25 cents, but once inside a separate admission of another quarter would get you a grandstand seat, or 15 cents for the pavilion. The location was inconvenient and within a year the club would be forced to look for another location due to dwindling attendance. When construction on Union Park (Oriole Park III) lagged, Oriole Park (II) was used for the first home series of the 1891 season.

The 1889 Louisville Colonels were having the worst possible season imaginable. A streak of 18 straight losses brought them to Baltimore on Wednesday June 13, and their luck did not change. After losing to the Orioles, Colonels owner-manager Mordecai Davidson laid down a fine of $25 ($650) for each player if they lost again. The men brought up the issue of owed back pay and refused to take the field for the next game. A war of words escalated, and Davidson made legal threats. A cancellation was hastily issued, and a double header added to make up for it.

As the minutes ticked away towards the next game, Davidson waited at Oriole Park for his men to show up. Only six Louisville players did. The umpire was ready to call a forfeit, but in a moment of ingenuity,

Early Baltimore Ballparks

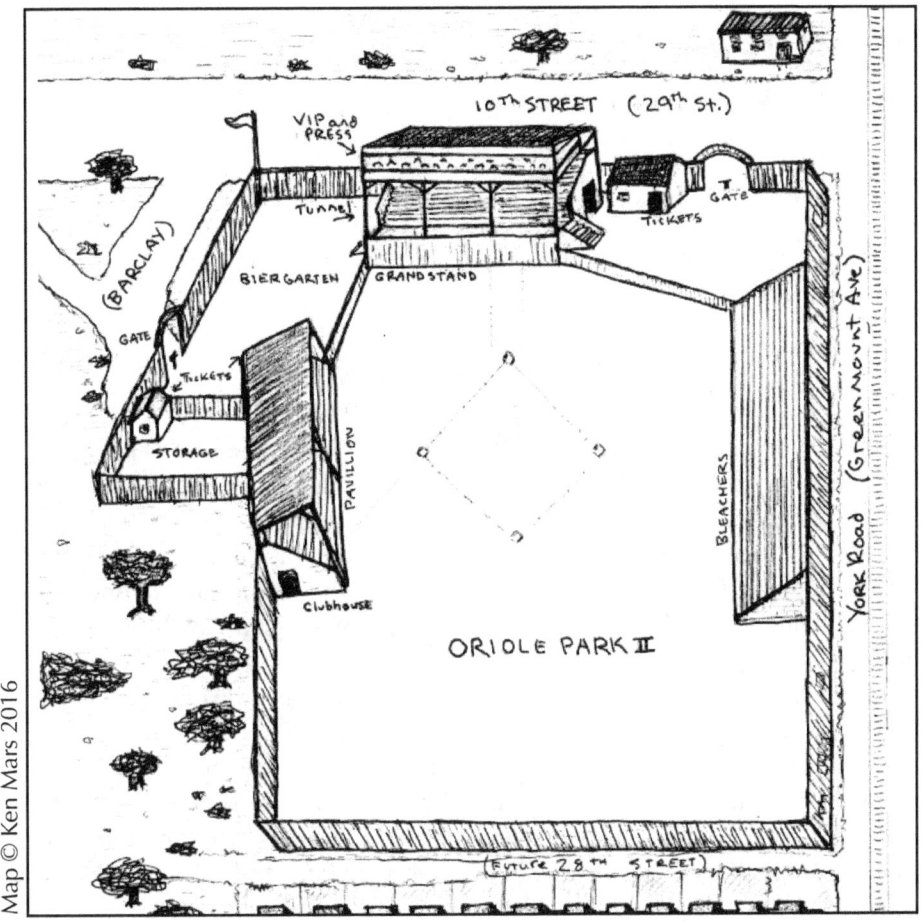

Davidson hired three replacements right out of the grandstand to fill out the roster for the day. Local boys Charles Fisher, John Traffley, and Mike Gaule were suddenly in the majors! Their stay would be short, barely a sip of coffee, as a rainstorm cut their debut at five innings and Louisville losing their 20th straight, 4-2.

Following the game, striking Colonels Guy Hecker, Pete Browning, and Harry Raymond, consulted with Bill Barnie, who convinced them to return to their club and assured them their grievances would be brought before the American Association. Before the first game of the Saturday doubleheader, Barnie made a roster move. To give the Colonels an even chance, he added local pitcher George Goetz to the Orioles roster to make his one and only professional start. And Goetz pitched a pretty darn good game for a first-timer, giving up just three earned runs through the first seven innings before allowing another in the eighth. Colonels pitcher Todd "Toad" Ramsey, a once dominant workhorse, had a sore arm and Baltimore came back to tie in the ninth and thus force extra innings.

The Orioles then knocked in four runs in the top of the 10th to win the game, 10-6. The night cap didn't go well for the Colonels either and were able to scratch out only one base hit against an ice-cold Frank Foreman. Louisville committed seven errors and Baltimore rolled to an easy 10-0 shutout. The Colonels losing streak would finally stop at 25 games.

Sources
Research for this article is based on the author's book, *Baltimore Baseball First Pitch to First Pennant 1858-1894*, Old Frog Publishing, 2018.

Notes
1 *Baltimore Daily Exchange*, August 29, 1860.
2 *Sunday Telegram*, September 1, 1867.

Early Black Baseball in Baltimore: 1865-1887

By Ken Mars

Baseball came to Baltimore in 1858 and grew in popularity over the next few years to become a genuine sensation. By the end of the Civil War, Baltimore had over 25,000 free African American residents, and therefore logical to believe that there were baseball games being played within their community. The game was too popular and evidence of black baseball clubs in other cities at the same time is well known. As the game grew during the post-war boom, Baltimore newspapers were slow to report on the progress of African American clubs, and the first reference to a game played by a Black baseball club comes from the *Evening Star* in Washington D.C., not a hometown source where the actual game took place.

On August 16, 1870, the Enterprise Base Ball Club played the Washington Mutuals at the Madison Avenue Base Ball Grounds, the premiere ballpark in Baltimore at the time. The Washingtonians out slugged their hosts by a good margin, 51-26. Charles Douglass, the son of Frederick Douglass, was the captain and star player for the Mutuals, one of the best Black clubs in the Mid-Atlantic at the time.

But, before a baseball club can start playing games, they have to have a place to practice, and back then Baltimore had very strict laws as to where and when such pastimes could occur. There are numerous accounts of ball players being arrested and fined for playing on the Sabbath, or on public property. The need for a wide-open space away from anyone who might complain about noise or broken windows, was crucial to even think about getting started. In the late 1860's, African American players established baseball diamonds in South Baltimore. The neighborhood had brick yards, factories, flat open fields, and very few residents. Land along the railway line in particular was open and undesirable because of the noise. There were two diamonds of note in this area: Stowman's Park, used primarily by White clubs and another on the opposite side of the B & O railway line, used by Black clubs. In between was the Bauernschmidt Brewery, a liberal supplier of libations to any who could pay. After hours or on the weekends, the neighborhood was mostly vacant of anyone who might complain about crowds or a rowdy game. As more businesses moved into South Baltimore, a large natural gas plant was built to meet the demand. The monstrous People's Gas Company became the main supplier for the area and the parcel adjacent to the plant remained empty for decades. For perspective: this location was less than a half mile from where the Baltimore Black Sox Maryland Park and Westport Park were, and about two miles from the Elite Giants Westport Stadium.

Throughout the mid 1870's the Lord Hannibal Base Ball Club grew to become the city's premiere black team, playing regularly at Newington Park, the successor to Madison Avenue. Newington was built in 1871 for the short-lived Lord Baltimores of the National Association. The Great Baltimore Fire of 1873 plunged the city into a depression and the club was gone soon after. However, in the absence of a major-league team, amateur and semipro baseball flourished. The Lord Hannibals were part of a surge of local black teams in the late 1870's and early 1880's, along with the Quicksteps, Mutuals, Atlantics, and Mansfields.

The *Baltimore Sun* reported in July 1883 that Baltimore had intended to form a league with other black clubs from Philadelphia, Washington, Richmond, and Norfolk for 1884. This did not come to pass as a formal arrangement, but as inter-city games increased over the next few years, it was a matter of time, trial, and error before professionalism would take hold. Circa 1884, professional baseball was still integrated, though on a very small scale. Catcher Moses Fleetwood Walker of the American Association Toledo Blue Stockings played in Baltimore twice in

Early Black Baseball in Baltimore: 1865-1887

1884. On June 4, the Orioles blanked Toledo, 8-0, at Oriole Park on 25th Street. Walker recorded 10 putouts and three errors while going hitless at the plate. And, on June 6, the Birds lost, 4-2. Oriole pitcher and future umpire Bob Emslie only gave up one earned run, with the other three scoring on errors. Walker again went '0-fer at the plate but caught Tony Mullane's pitching with ease. By 1886, integrated baseball clubs were growing scarce and skilled African American ballplayers went unsigned. In 1887, only five teams in the International League were integrated. It was a difficult time of backwards thinking and divisive arguments. With too much talent and desire to sit on the bench, the 1887 National Colored Base Ball League fought to establish itself in the wake of this social turmoil. But outside factors would conspire to make their inaugural season short.

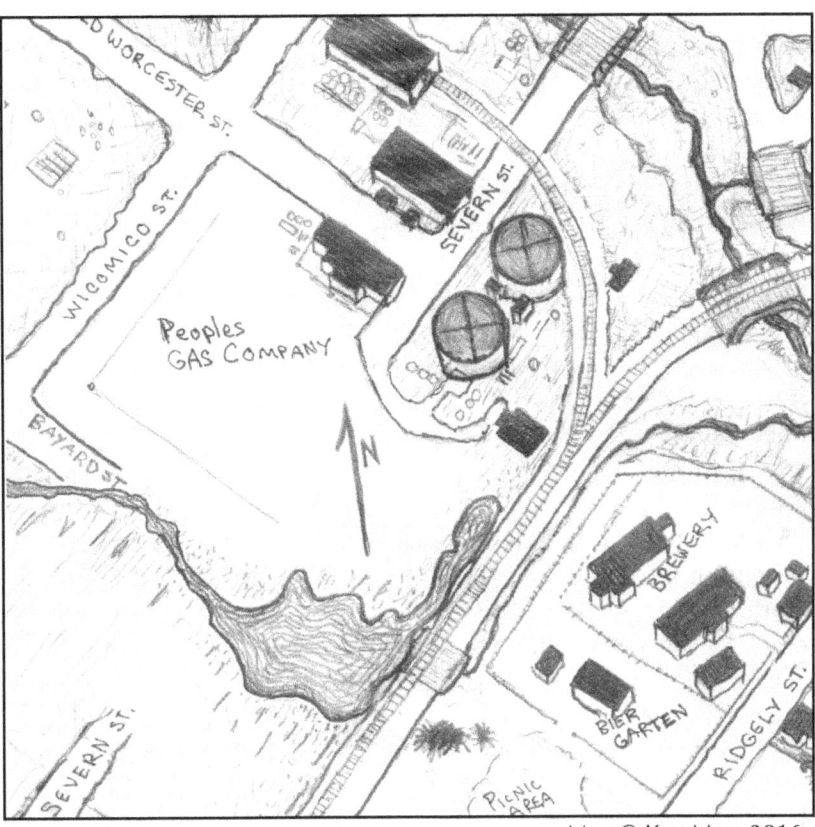

Map © Ken Mars 2016

After the Civil War, railway construction kicked into high gear. Small towns cropped up along every new line. Some thrived, but many failed. In a little over a decade, the boom went bust, and a national depression throughout the late 1870's was largely blamed on bad railroad investments. The railroads formed territorial monopolies and made their own rules, charging farmers in the west far more to ship east than their counterparts to ship west. Under pressure from citizens sympathetic to the farmers, in 1887, President Grover Cleveland signed the Interstate Commerce Act, which aimed to ensure fair rates and regulations. The railroad magnates, who had greased pockets in Washington for decades to get their way, were not pleased to be put under supervision and plotted revenge. Imagine for a moment planning a trip, months in advance and laying out a careful budget that normally would have been plenty - only to see your travel expenses double without warning. This is exactly what lay ahead for baseball clubs in the summer of 1887, when all group rates were repealed, and general fares went up.

A series of meetings throughout late 1886 culminated in February 1887, when representatives from the Philadelphia Pythians, Pittsburgh Keystones, New York Gorhams, Louisville Falls Citys, Boston Resolutes, and Lord Baltimores came together to finalize the schedule for the National Colored Base Ball League, the first professional baseball league owned, operated, and staffed by African Americans. Future Hall of Famer and author Sol White played second base for the Pittsburgh Keystones. Welday Walker, little brother of Moses Fleetwood, also played for Pittsburgh as catcher and outfielder. Arthur Thomas played third base for the Lord Baltimores and went on to have a great career with the Cuban Giants.

Another future Hall of Famer, Bud Fowler, would have played for the Cincinnati Browns, but they lacked funding and didn't enter the league in time. But possibly the most interesting player was James W. Wilson, left fielder for the Lord Baltimores. Wilson was born in Liberia and came to the States to study at Lincoln University. He is the first confirmed professional baseball player from the continent of Africa. The Lord Baltimore Base Ball Club could possibly be an evolution of the Lord Hannibals, taking the name of the old National Association club as their own. They lucked out and secured use of Oriole Park on 25th Street for over a month while the Orioles were on the road beginning their season. Lord Baltimore manager and National Colored League vice president Joseph Callis trained his men hard for the upcoming season, but bad weather cancelled several practice games with the Mutuals, another African American club from South Baltimore. Rain drenched their final weekend of practices and the two clubs had to play a short four innings the following Monday afternoon to make up for it.

On May 5, 1887, a cloudy Thursday afternoon with a chance of light rain, the NCL began official play. A work-day crowd of around 400 showed up at Oriole Park to see the Lord Baltimores take on the Philadelphia Pythians. Bowers, the Pythians' third baseman, got six hits as Philly jumped out to an early lead, but Baltimore was able to minimize the damage until the Lords could catch up and pull ahead. The crowd cheered when the Lord Baltimores took their bow at the end of the game to celebrate a hard fought, 15-12, victory. After a wild street parade and grand concert in Pittsburgh on Friday May 6, the New York Gorhams beat the Keystones, 11-8, before a big crowd of 1,200 Black and White fans. The game was a huge success for the new league and got them rave reviews in sports pages across the country. It was the kind of good press money can't buy.

The same day, the Lord Baltimores faced the Pythians again at Oriole Park. Hugh Cummings of Baltimore gave up only two hits but walked five and hit two batters. It wasn't the smoothest performance by any means, but the Lords made it work. The Pythians added to their own demise with a crippling 10 errors that led to an 11-3 Baltimore victory. Enthusiasm was high, but the league was quietly in desperate trouble.

The Boston Resolutes had been in operation since the late 1860's and were the best African American team in New England. To get to their first game against the Louisville Forest Citys, they scheduled several exhibitions along the way to pay for the trip. The excursion didn't go well. A huge storm system grumbled in from the west, cancelling games and stretching their budget. Travel expenses had gone through the roof as railroads lashed out with huge unannounced rate increases, sometimes doubling and even tripling overnight. The Resolutes failed to make it to Louisville in time for their first game. It was Kentucky Derby Week and railroads were taking advantage of the holiday crowds. Barely making it in time for their second scheduled game and winning before a sparse crowd, the gate wasn't enough compensation for the trip. The entire Boston club suddenly found themselves stranded without enough money to get to Pittsburgh, their next destination. The reality of the Interstate Commerce bill was becoming apparent to the baseball world just as the season got under way, and the American Association and National League struggled to adapt without discounted train fare. Some would use steamboats when possible to save money, but the havoc was unavoidable. Group rates would eventually return, but not in time to save the 1887 season from being a financial disaster for everyone.

The Lord Baltimores headed north to Philadelphia for a quick pair of games with the Pythians and lost twice. As they headed back home to meet their next foe, things had suddenly changed. The Pittsburgh Keystones received a telegram from A.A. Selden, manager of the Boston Resolutes saying that his team had been delayed and asked to reschedule for the next week. Boston had been on the road for 15 days already and had eight of them filled with rain. The one game in Kentucky was a disaster and the club was critically low on funds. The Resolutes sent telegrams home asking for more money, but it hadn't arrived yet. Selden advised Pittsburgh that the best thing for him to do was to pick up the Resolutes schedule in Baltimore. The Lord Baltimores met up at Oriole Park a few hours before their scheduled game versus the Boston Resolutes to stretch and have batting practice. Usually the visiting team would show up around noon and join in, but on Wednesday May 11, that was not so. The Lords practiced alone.

When fans showed up at the park at game time, they were told there was an unexpected delay, and to please be patient. The home team and umpire had been nervously waiting for Boston to arrive for a several hours now and no word of a cancelation had been sent. As the crowd grew restless and tired of waiting, the umpire declared a forfeit to Baltimore. Joseph Callis knew the Resolutes' predicament, and out of good sportsmanship, he declined to accept the victory. Instead of letting the fans go home disappointed, the Mutuals, who were all in attendance to root for their friends, volunteered to play. The Lords won, 10-8, but the victory was empty. As the sun went down and the crowd left to go home, the Boston Resolutes still had not arrived. The next day, the Lord Baltimores showed up early again to warm up, hoping that the Resolutes would be waiting at the gate, safe and sound, but no one was there. Joseph Callis hadn't heard anything overnight, either. The Baltimore men took their practice in eerie silence, the crack of the bat echoing lonely down York Road toward the harbor. Something had gone wrong and no one knew anything. Come game

Early Black Baseball in Baltimore: 1865-1887

time, a sparse and curious Thursday crowd filtered into Oriole Park. As they were seated, they were asked to be patient once again. The Lord Baltimores stood on the home side of the field waiting to play, while the visitors' bench remained empty. The umpire gave it a few minutes, but a second no-show seemed inevitable. A forfeit was issued to Baltimore and this time, it was accepted. As luck would have it though, the New York Gorhams reached Baltimore early and played a quick exhibition game to keep the fans happy.

The following morning it was discovered that the Resolutes were still stuck in Kentucky, and hope was fading that they'd be able to continue at all. The Gorhams beat the Lords, 15-3, in a poorly fielded contest in which Baltimore made 11 errors. The next day Baltimore rebounded to mangle the New Yorkers, 27-9, cranking out 20 hits in front of a good Saturday crowd. In Baltimore, at least, the NCBL was a success – as long as there was a visiting team to play.

Elsewhere, results were vastly mixed as news of the Resolutes misfortune circulated through the press.

The Lords played a thriller in Pittsburgh on May 16, coming from behind and scoring 15 runs in the ninth to beat the Keystones, 22-10. The next day, the tables were turned. Keystones second baseman Sol White recorded an unassisted double play. Pittsburgh rolled on to win the game and take another the following day. And then suddenly, the schedule ran out. The missing Boston Resolutes had caused panic among league owners. The Pythians and Gorhams announced they were both leaving the league. The Pythians couldn't afford the rent for the Athletics ballpark and suddenly had nowhere to play. Baltimore then refused to travel to Louisville after their poor treatment of the Resolutes was revealed. Despite best efforts to add Washington and Cincinnati as replacements. Five days later, the National Colored League ceased to exist. It would take the Boston men over a month to get back home, and the veteran club disbanded soon after. The 1887 National Colored League was a bold attempt with bad timing. Any other summer and they'd have had a much better shot. Though this league failed prematurely, it was the first big break for many players who would go on to great careers and form the first wave of barnstorming teams that would blaze a path to the first Negro Leagues in the early twentieth century.

Editor's Note

Based on a 2017 Jerry Malloy Negro Leagues Conference presentation by Ken Mars with contributions from Mark D. Aubrey and John Thorn, and new statistics by Larry Lester.

Further information can be found in the author's book *Baltimore Baseball History: First Pitch To First Pennant 1858-1894* (Old Frog Publishing, 2018), and a research guide to the 1887 National Colored League which can be found in SABR's Research Resources:

https://sabr.org/latest/mars-resource-guide-1887-national-colored-league

Early Baseball Encounters in the West:
The Yeddo Royal Japanese Troupe Play Ball in America

June 14, 1872: Dolly Varden Club 27, Yeddo Royal Japanese Troupe 23, at Newington Grounds

By Bill Staples Jr.

The Yeddo Royal Japanese acrobatic troupe toured America between 1871 and 1877. During their stops in the Washington/Baltimore area in the summer of 1872, they learned the finer points of baseball from a major leaguer and then competed in two exhibition games. Officials at the Japanese Baseball Hall of Fame in Tokyo call the acrobats' encounter with the national pastime in 1872 "an amazing discovery ... without a doubt, it's the oldest record of Japanese playing the game."[1]

Harue Tsutsumi, a Japanese researcher who specializes in kabuki (a classical Japanese dance-drama) in the Meiji Era (1868-1912), deserves credit as the first person to shed light on the Yeddo Royal troupe's historic involvement in baseball.[2] She discovered it while completing her doctoral thesis.[3] With a master's in theater history from Osaka University, she attended Indiana University and earned a doctorate in East Asian languages. In 2004 she concluded her studies at IU with the 331-page doctoral thesis titled *Kabuki Encounters the West: Morita Kan'ya's Shintomi-za Productions, 1878-79*. In her thesis, Tsutsumi also shared details of the Yeddo Royal Japanese troupe act:

Genjiro performed the traditional Japanese acrobatic stunt of putting a bamboo pole on his shoulder, then playing the shamisen [a three-stringed traditional Japanese musical instrument] while a boy balanced himself on the top of the pole. An acrobat called "Sunikechi" walked barefoot on a ladder of sharp-edged swords. The troupe also presented a tightrope walker called "Belle of Japan" ("Amusements" *Daily Morning Chronicle* [Washington] 5 June 1872), who was actually a man who specialized in walking on a tightrope in a woman's costume, a type of performance that was common in nineteenth-century Japan (Kodama 157). In his memoir, Kume recorded that a (male) troupe member called "Musume-san (girl)" walked the tightrope wearing woman's makeup and a fancy woman's kimono (Kume, *Kume hakase* 1: 251). According to Kurata, a tightrope walker called Yamamoto Kinjiro appears in a list of the members of Genjiro's original troupe (Kurata, *Kaigai koen kotohajime* 94). Although the original name of the "Belle of Japan" tightrope walker never appeared in newspaper articles, it is likely that he was Kinjiro.[4]

The 16-member troupe departed Yokohama on July 22, 1871, on the *SS Japan*.[5] They arrived in San Francisco on August 13, led by two British entrepreneurs known only as R. Mitchell and H.W. Welton.[6] Mitchell told the press that he had lived in Asia for eight years and persuaded the troupe to leave for the West after seeing them perform in Hong Kong.[7]

The *San Francisco Examiner* reviewed their first US performance, and declared it "the very best troupe that has ever visited the city."[8] After performing in California for two months, the acrobats ventured east, eventually reaching the Baltimore area in April 1872.[9]

The Yeddo Royal Japanese Troupe Play Ball

In Baltimore the troupe performed at Ford's Grand Opera House, a venue founded by John T. Ford, owner of Ford's Theatre in Washington, where President Lincoln was assassinated.[10]

On Friday, June 7, 1872, several members of the Yeddo Royal Japanese Troupe, along with their agent and an interpreter, played a baseball game against members of the Olympic Base Ball Clubs at Olympic Grounds in Washington. The *Daily Morning Chronicle* wrote, "This is to be a grand international game. ... [T]he Japs are not novices with the 'willow,' and some Americans are not without apprehension that the West will meet with a crushing defeat from the East."[11] The *Daily National Republican* reported that the game was competitive, and "came near being a victory for the Orientals. The style in which they (the Japanese) handle the ball and bat somewhat astonished our boys, and had not rain stopped the game" there was a chance that the Japanese might have won the game. The *Republican* listed the final score of 18-17, with a breakdown of runs by inning.[12] It reveals that the score was tied 15-15 going into the fifth inning, making for an exciting and entertaining finish.

The press reported that the Yeddo Royal Troupe practiced for two days to prepare for the game "under the guidance of Professor Brainard."[13] This "professor" for the Japanese was Asa Brainard, a pitcher for the Washington Olympics during the 1871 and 1872 seasons.

"Let's Play Two!" Another Game for the Japanese

A week after the game at Olympic Grounds, the *Baltimore Sun* announced that the "celebrated Royal Yeddo Japs … will play a game of base ball with a club of nine well-known Baltimoreans, at Newington Park, on Friday, June 14, at 3:30 p.m."[14]

Despite the fact that the game was billed as "Comic Base Ball," the Japanese tourists were serious in their approach to the game. The pregame advertisement read: "The Japs are desirous of learning our national game, and on their return to their far-distant homes will be the first to introduce it into the ancient Empire of Japan."[15]

The details of the Yeddo Royal game were published the following day.[16] According to the *Baltimore Sun*, the opposing Baltimoreans were replaced by a local nine known as the Dolly Varden Club. In this game, six innings were played and when it was over the Dolly Varden Club outscored the Japanese, 27-23.[17]

Three hundred fans witnessed the game at Newington Grounds, the home ballpark to the major-league Lord Baltimore baseball club of the National Association. The venue, which opened on April 22, about eight weeks before the game featuring the Japanese acrobats, seated up to 5,000, and was located in northwest Baltimore.[18] Today it is the site of Cumberland & Carey Park and multiple apartment buildings, businesses, and churches.[19]

Based on previous reports from other games and performances, below is a possible lineup for the Yeddo Royal Troupe:[20]

Position	Name
1B	Yannanowah
SS	Professor Gangero (Genjiro Hayakawa, troupe leader)
3B	Kingero (Kinjiro Yamamoto)
LF	Yoshi-Taro (Yoshitaro Takamori)
RF	Chonosuki
UNK	Quietaro ("best pop of the bunch")
UNK	Astaro ("extraordinary batter")
UNK	Buchuhami (10-year-old boy)
UNK	R. Mitchell (British manager)
UNK	Interpreter

The lineup for the Dolly Varden Club of Baltimore was not shared after the game against the Japanese. However, two weeks later the club competed in a Fourth of July contest and its lineup reflected the following names and positions:[21]

Position	Name
C	Miller
3B	Muller
RF	Martin
1B	Houser
P	Kinsley
CF	Lester
LF	Dew
2B	Dalrymple
SS	Bantz
LF	Jordan (substitute)

The Yeddo Royal Troupe left Baltimore and headed to Wilmington, Delaware, to perform at the Grand Opera House there. It appears that the troupe members were feeling confident about their newly developed ballplaying skills, as they challenged the Diamond State Base Ball Club of Wilmington to a game.[22]

After ads ran in both the *News Journal* and the *Wilmington Daily Commercial* promoting the contest, the game was canceled. Two members of the Yeddo Royal Japanese were unable to perform, so the game "was abandoned to the great disappointment of base ball fans."[23] After the attempted game in Delaware, there is no record of the Yeddo Royal Japanese Troupe competing on a diamond again.

Between 1873 and 1877, the acrobats zigzagged across the Midwest, the East Coast, and into Canada, never crossing west of the Mississippi River. In May 1875 the press reported that the troupe visited the baseball grounds of the St. Louis club. It was not

Of the 13 members of the Yeddo Royal Japanese Troupe, eight of them — including a 10-year-old boy — were among the first Japanese to play baseball in the U.S. Yamamoto Kinjiro, third from right, played third base for the Japanese team, and was called the "Belle of Japan" because he walked on a tightrope wearing a woman's costume, a common performance in 19th-century Japan. Courtesy of the Thanatos Archive.

specified if they visited the home of the St. Louis Red Stockings (Red Stocking Base Ball Park) or the St. Louis Brown Stockings (Grand Avenue Park), but their continued interest in the "national pastime" was noted.[24]

The Japanese acrobats journeyed south to the Caribbean and performed in Cuba in the fall of 1877, and in San Juan, Puerto Rico in 1878.[25] After that, there is no record of the Yeddo Royal troupe performing in the West.

Did they return to Japan in 1878? At this point, no one knows for sure. What we do know is that even though they were the first Japanese to play baseball, they did not fulfill their desire to become the "first to introduce it into the ancient Empire of Japan." That distinction belongs to American schoolteacher Horace Wilson, who is now enshrined in the Japanese Baseball Hall of Fame for his efforts.[26]

Editor's Note

An extended version of this article first appeared online at: "Early Baseball Encounters in the West: The Yeddo Royal Japanese Troupe Play Ball in America, 1872," by Bill Staples Jr., billstaples.blogspot.com, posted July 18, 2019.

Notes

1 "Baseball: Researcher finds earliest-recorded game involving Japanese," *Kyodo News*, July 18, 2019; english.kyodonews.net/news/2019/07/c8bd473c856b-baseball-researcher-finds-earliest-recorded-game-involving-japanese.html.

2 Harue Tsutsumi, *Kabuki Encounters the West: Morita Kan'ya's Shintomi-za Productions, 1878-79* (Bloomington: Indiana University, 2004).

3 Footnote 16, page 271, of her thesis features the Japanese baseball research discovery. She wrote: "In Washington, several members of this troupe, along with their agent and an interpreter, played a baseball game with selected members of the Olympic and National Base Ball Clubs. The names of the Japanese troupe members who participated in the game were Yannanowah (first b.), Professor Gangero (s.s.), Kingero (third b.), Yoshi-Taro (l.fi), and Chonosuki (r.f.) Base Ball." *Daily Morning Chronicle* (Washington) June 6, 1872: 4. Besides Genjiro, at least one likely member of Genjiro's original troupe, "Yoshi-Taro," who was probably Takamori Yoshitaro, the boy who performed on the top of the pole (Kurata, Kaigai koen kotohajime 94), appears on the list.

4 Harue Tsutsumi, 104.

5 *Daily Alta California* (San Francisco), August 14, 1871.

6 *San Francisco Chronicle*, August 30, 1871: 4.

7 "Japanese Performers," *National Republican* (Washington), May 31, 1872: 4.

8 "Yeddo Royal Japanese Troupe Gives First Performance," *San Francisco Examiner*, August 22, 1871: 3.

9 *Examiner* (Frederick, Maryland), April 10, 1872: 2.

10 *Baltimore Sun*, June 5, 1872: 2.

11 "Base Ball." *Daily Morning Chronicle*, July 6, 1872, 4.

12 *Daily National Republican*, June 8, 1872: 4.

Early Baseball Encounters in the West

13 "Base Ball Fun." *Chicago Evening Post*, June 14, 1872: 4.

14 Advertisement: Dual Ad Promoting both the Yeddo Royal Japanese Troupe Performances and "Comic Ball Game," *Baltimore Sun*, June 14, 1872: 1.

15 Knowing that Horace Wilson is in Japan and potentially introducing the game to his students around the same time makes the troupe's expressed desire to take the game back to Japan a significant statement. There is no documentation of Wilson traveling to Asia with an expressed desire or intent to introduce baseball "to the ancient Empire of Japan."

16 An additional article from the *Alexandria* (Virginia) *Gazette* that recaps the Yeddo Royal vs. Dolly Varden Club, reported that the final score of the game was 32-21. *Alexandria Gazette*, June 15, 1872: 2.

17 The opposing team's name, Dolly Varden, is inspired by a woman's outfit fashionable during the 1860s-70s in Britain and the United States. The name comes from a character in Charles Dickens's 1839 historical novel *Barnaby Rudge*, and the term was used at the time to describe anything that was fashionable. *Baltimore Sun*, June 15, 1872: 1.

18 *Baltimore Sun*, April 22, 1872: 1.

19 *Baltimore Sun*, April 9, 1981: 52.

20 Harue Tsutsumi, *Kabuki Encounters the West*.

21 "Base Ball," *Examiner* (Frederick, Maryland), July 10, 1872: 2.

22 *Wilmington* (Delaware) *Daily Commercial,* June 17, 1872: 5.

23 *News Journal* (Wilmington, Delaware) June 17, 1872: 2.

24 *St. Louis Post-Dispatch*, May 11, 1875: 4.

25 "Japoneses y Americanos," *Boletín mercantil de Puerto Rico* (San Juan, Puerto Rico), April 14, 1878: 3, and "Japoneses en Torrecillas," *Diario de la Marina* (Havana), November 25, 1877: 3.

26 Horace Wilson, Japanese Baseball Hall of Fame, Tokyo, Japan, english.baseball-museum.or.jp/baseball_hallo/detail/detail_148.html.

Union Park

By David B. Stinson

Union Park was the home of the National League Baltimore Orioles for the eight years of that team's existence, 1892 to 1899. Harry Von Der Horst, owner of the American Association Orioles and then the National League Orioles, opened Union Park in 1891 as home to his American Association franchise. Union Park was the third of three different ballparks he constructed for his Baltimore teams.[1] Von Der Horst's father, John H. Von Der Horst, owned Eagle Brewery and Malt House, at Belair Road and North Avenue in Baltimore.[2] In 1880 the son was given an interest in the brewery and the company renamed the J.H. Von Der Horst & Son Brewing Company. Harry's ownership of the Orioles certainly helped sell his father's product.[3]

The three ballparks were within four blocks of one another, in what were once the outer limits of Baltimore City. The first, Oriole Park (I), was home to the American Association Orioles from 1883 to 1888.[4] Also known as Huntingdon Avenue Grounds and American Association Park, it was at the southeast corner of what is now East 25th Street (formerly Huntingdon Avenue) and Barclay Street.[5] First base paralleled Greenmount Avenue (formerly York Road), right field paralleled East 25th Street, left field paralleled Barclay Street, and third base paralleled East 24th Street.[6] An apartment building and row houses now mark the site.[7]

Von Der Horst's second ballpark, Oriole Park (II), was home to the American Association Orioles from 1889 to 1891.[8] It was four blocks north of Oriole Park I at the southwest corner of what is now Greenmount Avenue and East 29th Street (formerly York Road and 10th Street).[9] First base paralleled Barclay Street, right field paralleled East 28th Street, left field paralleled Greenmount Avenue, and third base paralleled East 29th Street.[10] A McDonald's restaurant and row houses now mark the site.[11] In 1901 the site became American League Park, later known as Oriole Park (IV), and was the home of the first American League Baltimore Orioles franchise and later the Eastern League Orioles.[12]

Von Der Horst's third ballpark was Union Park, also known as the Baltimore Baseball and Exhibition Grounds and Oriole Park (III).[13] Union Park was the home of the American Association Orioles in 1891 and the National League Orioles from 1892 to 1899.[14] Von Der Horst chose the site for Union Park partly in response to complaints about the location of Oriole Park (II) and the difficulty fans experienced reaching it by streetcar.[15] Von Der Horst located Union Park adjacent to the site of Oriole Park (I), at the southeast corner of what is now Guilford Avenue and East 25th Street. First base paralleled Guilford Avenue, right field paralleled East 24th Street, left field paralleled Barclay Street, and third base paralleled East 25th Street.[16] According to baseball historian James Bready, Union Park's name may have derived from its association with the Baltimore Union Passenger Railway, a streetcar line that made trips to the ballpark.[17] Bready notes that "[a]s a business promotion, Union Passenger may have paid some of the new ballpark's construction costs."[18]

Union Park was Baltimore's first double-decker grandstand.[19] It also was the first ballpark to have lettered rows and numbered seats.[20] The outfield fence was 16 feet high, with the distance at 300 feet from home plate to the left-field corner and 350 feet to center field.[21] In May 1891, in preparation for the opening of Union Park, Von Der Horst sent engraved invitations to 1,000 people, including the governor of Maryland and the mayor of Baltimore.[22] As noted in the *Baltimore Sun*:

> It has been decided to have no street parade or other display, but twenty-one bombs will be fired at 3:30 o'clock on the day of the game. The field has been ploughed and

pressed with three rollers until it is level and hard. The diamond and part of the outfield are bare, and the surface has a slight slope to the west. The ticket office is up, and work on the stand and seats will be nearly finished today. Folding chairs with perforated seats will be put in the grand stand temporarily, but when the club leaves on its next trip those in use at the present grounds [Oriole Park (II)] will be transferred. The new boards will be painted dark green and red at the same time, and many changes made with a view to beautifying the grounds. Union Park has been selected as the name of the scene of the team's future games.[23]

Union Park opened on May 11, 1891, with a contest between the American Association Orioles and the St. Louis Browns, with the Orioles defeating the Browns 8-4.[24] As baseball historian Ken Mars noted:

It was a proud day for Harry Von Der Horst; the Orioles were his, as was the park, and also, the beer. It was the social event of the season, and a who's-who of Baltimore's finest clamored to attend. With 8,000 numbered seats, Union Park was the largest and grandest baseball park built in Maryland, eclipsing any previous diamond. A paid crowd of 10,412 flooded the seats and the outfield to see the unveiling, and were not disappointed. St. Louis committed ten errors that gave Sadie McMahon the entire buffer he needed to begin blanking batters.[25]

Work continued on Union Park, with the addition of a new grandstand entrance, and an uncovered, open-seating grandstand extending 120 feet to the south along the first-base line.[26] A new clubhouse was added in right field at the end of the grandstand.[27] In June, additional improvements were made:

Workmen are again busy at the Union Park grounds, and by the time the club returns it is expected they will have completed a number of improvements. More than an acre of the outfield has been plowed up for the purpose of lowering the left and centre fields and tilling in the right field until the entire playing surface is nearly level. Grass seed will be sown on the bare spots and when it takes growth the grounds will be attractive to the eye as well as suited for the best kind of ball playing. Rows of posts will be erected at intervals around the field. for stretching ropes to accommodate possible overthrows from the seats. They will be twenty feet from the boundaries of left and right fields and about thirty-five feet from the centre-field fence. With the added facilities 12,000 persons can be kept in order while a game is played.[28]

Union Park was built entirely of wood and, as such, fire remained a threat to the ballpark. The first reported fire at Union Park occurred soon after its opening, in June 1891:

The building used as a bar at Union Park and about thirty feet of the open stands at its north end were burned late Saturday night. The origin of the fire is not certain, but it is believed by some that the bar was rifled and then set in a blaze. No vestiges of it except the foundations and a pile of charred timbers remain. The fixtures belonged to Mr. John Kelly, of Kelly's hotel. The total loss was about $600.[29]

The 1891 Orioles were led by manager Billie Barnie, who was in his ninth and final year as Baltimore manager.[30] The Orioles finished the season with a record of 71-64, in fourth place in the American Association.[31] The team included future Hall of Famers John McGraw and Wilbert Robinson. On October 15, 1891, the Orioles hosted a "picked nine" team composed of former and current professional players, to honor manager Barnie:

Nearly all of the favorites who in days gone by filled the hearts of the Baltimore enthusiasts with pride and pleasure at the valorous deeds which they performed on the base-ball field as members of the Baltimore Club were seen at Union Park yesterday afternoon. It was the last game of the season, and was a testimonial to Manager Barnie. Over five thousand persons were present.[32]

The American Association folded after the 1891 season, and Baltimore received an expansion franchise (one of four) in the National League for 1892. At the start of the season, George Van Haltren was the player-manager, but he was replaced a month into the season by club secretary John Waltz on an interim basis.[33] Former Detroit Wolverines outfielder Ned Hanlon was named manager in May 1892 and set about changing the culture of the team, starting with the institution of morning practice at Union Park.[34] Soon after Hanlon's arrival, the Orioles played what would be one of their most memorable games at Union Park. On June 10, 1892, the Orioles defeated the St. Louis Browns 25-4 in the first game of a doubleheader, and catcher Wilbert Robinson collected a major-league record seven hits and 11 RBIs.[35] One of Hanlon's first acquisitions was Pittsburgh outfielder Joe Kelley, for whom he traded former manager Van Haltren.[36] By the end of the season, the Orioles found themselves in last place, with a record of 46-101. Hanlon had only begun to recast the Orioles into a competitive ballclub.

In 1893 Hanlon continued adding to the roster, acquiring future Hall of Famer Hughie Jennings in a trade with the Louisville Colonels. By the end of the 1893 season, the Orioles posted a record of 60-70, finishing in eighth place in the 12-team league. During the offseason, Hanlon added future Hall of Famers Dan Brouthers and Willie Keeler in a trade with the Brooklyn Bridegrooms.[37]

The Orioles began the 1894 season in front of 15,000 spectators (the ballpark seated 9,000) with an 8-3 home win over the New York Giants.[38] The Orioles surprised the baseball world that year with many decisive wins against the league's best clubs, and throughout the summer remained one of the top teams in the league.[39] The Orioles won 28 of their final 31 games, posting a record of 89-39 and bringing Baltimore its first baseball championship.[40] The team batted .343, with its starting lineup contributing a remarkable offensive output: 3B John McGraw, .340; RF Willie Keeler, .371; SS Hughie Jennings, .335; 1B Dan Brouthers, .347; LF Joe Kelley, .393; CF Steve Brodie, .366, 2B Heinie Reitz, .303; C Wilbert Robinson, .353.[41]

On January 14, 1895, during the winter after Baltimore's first championship, a fire swept through Union Park's grandstand and team clubhouses.[42] The open stands on the north side of the ballpark were spared, along with the ticket office.[43] The fire was discovered by groundskeeper Tom Murphy, who lived in a cottage in the northeast portion of the ballpark.[44] According to the *Baltimore Sun*, the destroyed grandstand was 300 feet long and seated 6,000.[45] The fire marshal determined that the fire "was the result of smoldering embers of the fire which Ground-Keeper Murphy discovered and supposed he had extinguished early Monday evening. ... The fire which burned the base-ball grand stand he believed to have been caused by mischievous boys or men. Malice or plunder, he said, had probably nothing to do with it."[46]

After the fire, it was uncertain whether the Orioles would return to Union Park or find a new ballpark site, a decision that was left up to manager Hanlon to decide."[47] The *Sun* reported that, regardless of where the ballpark was located, the grandstand:

> ...will be the best that has been known in Baltimore. It will, in the first place, be a double decker, with the private boxes and the press box on the second tier, and it will seat 4,000 persons. All the seats, too, will be opera chairs and the reserved seats will be better than those in the rest of the stand, though all the seats will be equally as good as any League grand stand.
>
> The structure will be ornamented, and it will have iron pillars instead of wooden ones, which will lessen the obstruction of view by the spectators. The stand will extend much farther toward right field than the old one did and will be divided off into sections. The clubhouses will be back of the grand stand, Manager Hanlon says, occupying much the position which the box office at Union park does now.[48]

Ultimately the decision was made to rebuilt at the site of Union Park, and work on the new grandstand began in March 1895.[49]

The Orioles again won the National League pennant in 1895, with a record of 87-43, and, in 1896, with a record of 90-39. In 1897 the Orioles posted a record of 90-40, but came in second, two games behind the Boston Beaneaters. On June 18, 1897, Willie Keeler posted the last hit of his 44-game hit streak at Union Park in a game against the Pittsburgh Pirates, which Baltimore won 11-9. (His streak reached 45 games if the last game of 1896 season is counted.) The streak ended the following day at Union Park, in a 7-1 loss to the Pirates.[50] On July 16, 1897, a team known as the Yanigans, begun by catcher Robinson and groundskeeper Murphy, played a game at Union Park against the Cuban Giants, a team composed of African-Americans.[51] The Yanigans won, 28-2. During the heat of the pennant race, on September 27, the Beaneaters defeated Baltimore 19-10 in one of the National League Orioles biggest losses ever.[52] In addition to its impact on the league championship that season, the

• Union Park •

"The Winning Team 1897, Boston (winners) versus Baltimore, played at Baltimore." On September 27, 1897, the Boston Beaneaters defeated the Baltimore Orioles, 19-10, in a match between the two top teams vying for the National League pennant. In the words of James Bready, it was *"the single most dramatic afternoon of the 19th-century major leagues. No 19th-century baseball crowd was larger." (Bready, p. 95).* Courtesy of Library of Congress Prints and Photographs Division.

game included the largest crowd ever to see a baseball game, one estimated at over 30,000.[53] The game, and crowd, is captured in a famous photograph of Union Park entitled, "The Winning Team."[54]

From 1894 to 1897, the first- and second-place National League teams played a best-of-seven series known as the Temple Cup, the brainchild of William Chase Temple, a lumber baron and part-owner of the Pittsburgh Pirates.[55] The Orioles played in all four Temple Cup Series during its four years in existence. They lost the first two series, to New York (4-0) in 1894, and to the Cleveland Spiders (4-1) in 1895.[56] In 1896 the Orioles won the Cup, sweeping the series against Cleveland (4-0), and won again in 1897, defeating Boston (4-1).[57]

The 1898 Orioles compiled a record of 96-53, and again placed second in the league, six games behind Boston. That season the Orioles set a record for victories thanks to the National League's expanded 154-game schedule.[58] Attendance at Union Park, however, dropped to less than half of what it was during the Orioles' glory years of 1894 to 1896.[59] In February 1899 the owners of the Orioles and the Brooklyn Bridegrooms agreed to an arrangement wherein Ned Hanlon and Harry Von Der Horst together purchased a half-interest in the Brooklyn franchise, and the Brooklyn owners, Gus Abell and Charles Ebbets, purchased a half-interest in the Baltimore team.[60] Known as "syndicate baseball," this arrangement allowed the two teams to act as one, often in the interest of one team over the other; the result being that Hanlon agreed to manage Brooklyn and took with him several of the Orioles' best players, including Keeler, Kelley, and Jennings.[61] McGraw and Robinson, who had a joint interest in the Diamond Cafe on North Howard Street, remained in Baltimore.[62] McGraw managed the 1899 Orioles and the team posted a respectable record (given the loss of some of Baltimore's best players to Brooklyn) of 86-62, finishing in fourth place, 15 games behind Brooklyn.

On October 10, 1899, the Orioles hosted the Washington Senators at Union Park, playing to a 5-5 tie before the game was called because of darkness.[63] It would be the National League Orioles' final game at Union Park; the league dropped the Baltimore franchise after the 1899 season.

During the winter of 1899-1900, McGraw and Robinson joined forces to bring about a possible Baltimore entry in the American Association, with McGraw as manager.[64] This possibility led to squabbles about the control and use of Union Park.[65] McGraw and Robinson helped form the Baltimore Baseball and Amusement Company and secured a lease on Union Park for the 1900 season.[66] Hanlon, still manager of the Brooklyn team, renamed the Superbas, disputed Baltimore's lease right.[67] On February 4, 1900, Hanlon and his Baltimore Baseball and Exhibition Company took control of Union Park.[68]

As reported in the *Baltimore Sun*:

> On Saturday the Amusement Company essayed to make entry upon Union Park "in a peaceable and easy manner and without a multitude of people," as prescribed by law, but the attempt was enthusiastically resisted, and in the end the manner of attack and repulse was neither peaceable nor easy, while more or less of a multitude of people became involved. With a strategic plan the invaders sought to gain admittance via the back fence while a feint attack and earnest parley were proceeding at the front door. The campaign so shrewdly conceived was rapidly executed, and the Amusement people succeeded in throwing a detachment into the disputed territory, but according to the Exhibition Company's general-in-chief the detachment afterward retired in good order.

Judge Henry Stockbridge on Saturday granted an injunction to the Amusement Company restraining the Exhibition Company from removing or destroying any of the fixtures at Union Park. The plaintiffs gave bond for $5,000. President Hanlon, Treasurer Vonderhorst, or Secretary Bormann, or all of them, will be served with a copy of the injunction today if they can be found.[69]

McGraw soon decided it was not possible to form an American Association team for the 1900 season and resolved instead to look to 1901.[70] On February 25, 1900, the two sides agreed on a compromise for use of Union Park under which the Exhibition Company paid the Amusement Company $3,500, the amount the Amusement Company paid for its lease of Union Park, plus $1,200 to $1,500 for expenses it incurred in its efforts to establish an American Association team in Baltimore.[71] Once the American Association efforts failed, and the National League officially abandoned Baltimore, the Eastern League considered a possible lease of Union Park for the 1900 season.[72] However, that possibility never came to fruition.[73] For the 1900 season, both McGraw and Robinson played (against their wishes) for the St. Louis Cardinals.[74]

In December 1900, as part of the search for a new ballpark site, Byron Bancroft "Ban" Johnson, the president of the new American League, along with McGraw and Robinson, toured Union Park and the former site of Oriole Park II on York Road and 29th Street.[75] After the tour, it was announced that the Union Park site was not in consideration, due in part to its short lease period. Ultimately, Baltimore chose the York Road site. Union Park continued to function as a ballpark during 1901, although the teams that played there were no longer major league. The Baltimore City Municipal League of Clubs took up residence at the ballpark.[76] The five teams in the league battling for the city municipal championship were the City Engineers, the Street Cleaners, the Water Department, the Subway Department, and the Health Department.[77] College baseball, football, and lacrosse teams also played in the ballpark, just as they had in previous years.[78]

In August 1902 the Chicago Stars, a female baseball club, "walloped" the Glendales, a local men's amateur nine at Union Park, with 1,500 spectators present.[79]

Game action at Union Park September 1899, one of the last professional games played at that ballpark. Courtesy of David B. Stinson.

• Union Park •

One of the last baseball games played at Union Park, as reported in the *Baltimore Sun*, was on August 16, 1902, with the Fulton Athletic Club defeating the combined Park Sparrows and Harlem Athletic Club, 8-5. Those two teams also were scheduled to play again on August 20; the *Sun* contains no report of the results of that game. Perhaps the last sporting event played at Union Park was a contest between the Park Athletic Club football team and the Indians, scheduled to be played on November 29, 1902.[80]

The National League retained the lease on Union Park throughout the 1902 season, presumably to prevent the American League from utilizing the ballpark.[81] The National League allowed the lease to expire in February 1903.[82] At the National League meeting that winter:

> Mr. Hanlon was appointed a committee of one to sell the old stands, lumber and all movable property belonging to the old club. He expects to sell the stands, etc., for the lumber in them, and they will probably be torn down. Thus will pass away the ball park that Hanlon's old champions made famous in the last decade.[83]

On December 27 the *Sun* reported that "[t]he lumber in the stands at Union Park baseball grounds has been sold and the stands will be torn down shortly."[84]

On October 2, 1905, the *Sun* reported the sale of Union Park to G. Howard White, noting that "[i]n a few months it is expected dwelling houses will occupy the site of the old Union Park on Twenty-fifth Street.[85] The *Sun* observed that, with nearly 1,800 building feet in the tract of land, about 120 dwellings could be erected on it.[86] On October 26, 1905, Mr. White finalized the sale of Union Park.[87] The former site of Union Park is now largely residential, with the St. Ambrose Housing Aid Center located in the building on 25th Street that once abutted the third base grandstand.[88]

Notes

1 Byron Bennett, "Union Park – Home of the World Champion National League Baltimore Orioles," DeadballBaseball.com, February 19, 2012, https://deadballbaseball.com/2012/02/union-park-home-of-the-world-champion-national-league-baltimore-orioles/ (accessed June 8, 2021).

2 "Local Matters, An Extensive New Malt Factory – How Malt Is Made, Baltimore Sun," February 12, 1875: 1; see generally, David B. Stinson, "Belair Road And North Avenue – The First Intersection Of Beer And Baseball in Baltimore," www.davidbstinsonauthor.com/2015/11/22/belair-road-and-north-avenue-the-first-intersection-of-beer-and-baseball-in-baltimore/ (accessed December 24, 2019).

3 "Local Matters."

4 "The Base Ball Season: A Good Team Secured for Baltimore, and Oriole Park Established," *Baltimore Sun*, March 24, 1883: 4.

5 Philip J. Lowry, *Green Cathedrals, The Ultimate Celebration of Major League and Negro League Ballparks* (New York: Walker and Company, 2006), 13; "Baltimore Club for 1887: Preparing for the Base-Ball Season – Sketches of the Home Players," *Baltimore Sun*, March 9, 1987: 6.

6 Byron Bennett, "The Six Different Ballparks Known As Oriole Park," DeadballBaseball.com, December 10, 2011. https://deadballbaseball.com/2013/12/the-six-different-ballparks-known-as-oriole-park/ (accessed June 8, 2021).

7 Bennett, "The Six Different Ballparks Known as Oriole Park."

8 Bennett, "The Six Different Ballparks Known as Oriole Park."

9 "Oriole Park II Baseball Today, Exhibition Practice Games, Association Against the League," *Baltimore Sun*, March 28, 1889: 4.

10 Lowry, 13; Bennett, "The Six Different Ballparks Known as Oriole Park."

11 Lowry, 13; Bennett, "The Six Different Ballparks Known as Oriole Park."

12 Byron Bennett, "Baltimore's First American League Park – Original Home of the Future New York Yankees," DeadballBaseball.com, August 23, 2012. https://deadballbaseball.com/2012/08/baltimores-first-american-league-park-original-home-of-the-future-new-york-yankees/ (accessed June 8, 2021).

13 Bennett, "Union Park."

14 Bennett, "Union Park."

15 Ken Mars, *Baltimore Baseball, First Pitch to First Pennant, 1858-1894* (Parkville, Maryland: Old Frog Publishing, 2018), 233.

16 Lowry, 14; see generally, Barnett, "Union Park."

17 James H. Bready, *Baseball in Baltimore, The First 100 Years* (Baltimore: Johns Hopkins University Press, 1998), 50.

18 Bready, *Baseball in Baltimore*, 50.

19 Bready, *Baseball in Baltimore*, 58.

20 Bready, *Baseball in Baltimore*, 57.

21 James H. Bready, *Home Team Our Orioles* (25th Anniversary Edition), (self-published, 1959), 26.

22 "Plans for Monday's Opening," *Baltimore Sun*, May 9, 1891: 6.

23 "Plans for Monday's Opening."

24 Bready, *Baseball in Baltimore*, 51.

25 Mars, *Baltimore Baseball*, 237.

26 "Talk of the Players," *Baltimore Sun*, May 18, 1891: 4.

27 "Talk of the Players."

28 More Changes at Union Park, *Baltimore Sun*, June 27, 1891: 5.

29 Talk of the Players, *Baltimore Sun*, June 29, 1891: 6.

30 baseball-reference.com/players/b/barnibi01.shtml (accessed December 24, 2019).31 baseball-reference.com/teams/BAL/1891.shtml (accessed December 24, 2019).32 "Ball-Players: Old Favorites Cheered by Baltimore Spectators – Barnie's Benefit," *Baltimore Sun*, October 16, 1891: 6.

33 Mars, 253.

34 "Hanlon in Charge: An Outline of His Methods for Winning Future Games," *Baltimore Sun*, May 10, 1892: 6.

35 Mars, 258.

36 Mars, 260.

37 Mars, 268.

38 Bready, *Baseball in Baltimore*, 61-62.

39 Bready, *Baseball in Baltimore*, 62-63.

40 Bready, *Baseball in Baltimore*, 66.

41 baseball-reference.com/teams/BLN/1894.shtml#all_team_batting (accessed December 30, 2019); Bready, *Home Team Our Orioles*, 28-29.

42 "Fire at the Ball Grounds: The Grand Stand and Clubhouses at Union Park Destroyed," *Baltimore Sun*, January 15, 1895: 7; Burt Solomon, Where They Ain't, the Fabled Life and Untimely Death ofThe Original Baltimore Orioles, the Team That Gave Birth to Modern Baseball (New York: Free Press, 1999), 87.

43 "Fire at the Ball Grounds"; Solomon, 87.

44 "Fire at the Ball Grounds"; Solomon, 87.

45 "Fire at the Ball Grounds."

46 "Base-Ball Fire-Bugs: Marshal Jackson Does Not Believe There Is an Organized Band of Them," *Baltimore Sun*, January 16, 1895: 6.

47 "World of Sport: Proposed Base-Ball Rules Which Will Not Be Adopted," *Baltimore Sun*, February 27, 1895: 6.

48 "World of Sport: Proposed Base-Ball Rules."

49 "Champion Base Ball Club: Men Who Signed and Men Who Didn't – Gleason's Good Intentions," *Baltimore Sun*, March 2, 1895: 6.

50 sabr.org/gamesproj/game/june-19-1897-wee-willie-keelers-44-game-hitting-streak-ends (accessed December 24, 2019).

51 "Yanigans, 28; Cuban Giants, 2: Captain Bobby's Aggregation Meets a Colored Club at Union Park to Play Ball," *Baltimore Sun*, July 17, 1897: 6.

52 Bready, *Baseball in Baltimore*, 94-95.

53 Bready, *Baseball in Baltimore*, 94-95.

54 Bready, Baseball in Baltimore, 94; loc.gov/pictures/item/2013646079/ (accessed January 1, 2020).

55 baseball-reference.com/bullpen/TempleCup (accessed December 24, 2019).

56 baseball-reference.com/bullpen/TempleCup.

57 baseball-reference.com/bullpen/TempleCup.

58 Bready, *Baseball in Baltimore*, 98.

59 Bready, *Baseball in Baltimore*, 98.

60 Bready, *Baseball in Baltimore*, 99.

61 Bready, *Baseball in Baltimore*, 99.

62 Bready, *Baseball in Baltimore*, 99; see generally, David B. Stinson, "The 500 Block of North Howard Street and the Diamond Cafe – Baltimore's First Sports Bar," April 19, 2019, davidbstinsonauthor.com/2019/04/09/the-500-block-of-north-howard-street-and-the-diamond-cafe-baltimores-first-sports-bar/ (accessed December 24, 2019).

63 "Last of the Season: Baltimore and Washington the Final Game at Union Park," *Baltimore Sun*, October 11, 1899: 6.

64 "Union Park: Manager McGraw Gets Lease for Association Club," *Baltimore Sun*, January 26, 1900: 6.

65 "Mr. Hanlon at Home: Refuses to Discuss Baseball Affairs, Will Play Here, He Says," *Baltimore Sun*, January 27, 1900: 6.

66 "The New Ball Club: Stockholders Organize With $20,000 Capital, Phil Peterson President," *Baltimore Sun*, January 27, 1900: 6.

67 "Reply from Mr. Hanlon: That Union Park Correspondence, Mr. Robison Still Here," *Baltimore Sun*, January 31, 1900: 6.

68 "Quiet Along the Fence: Association Men Make Entry at Union Park by Strategy," *Baltimore Sun*, February 5, 1900: 6.

69 "Quiet Along the Fence."

70 "Baseball Company Sticks: Regards American Association as Good for Next Year," *Baltimore Sun*, February 19, 1900: 6.

71 "Baseball Tempest Over: Compromise Agreed Upon for Use of Union Park by League," *Baltimore Sun*, February 26, 1900: 6.

72 "Baseball Interest Dead: Rooters Against Eastern League – McGraw and Robinson," *Baltimore Sun*, March 10, 1900: 6.

73 Hollow Baseball Talk: Hide and Seek by Powers And McGraw – Wants Baltimore Pair," *Baltimore Sun*, March 30, 1900: 6.

74 Solomon, 192-193.

75 "Picking a Ball Ground: McGraw, Robinson and Johnson on a Land Hunt, York Road Lot May Be Chosen," *Baltimore Sun*, December 20, 1900: 6.

76 "Washington Team Complete," *Baltimore Sun*, March 19, 1901: 6.

77 "Engineers, 6, Street Cleaners 5," *Baltimore Sun*, August 22, 1901: 6.

78 "'Meds' vs. Maryland A.C.: Great Scrap at Union Park for the State Championship," *Baltimore Sun*, November 15, 1902: 6; "Varsity Team at Union Park," *Baltimore Sun*, April 11, 1899: 6; "Football Comes Next: Local Teams That Will Jump Into Practice at Once," *Baltimore Sun*, September 11, 1900: 6; "J.H.U. Lacrosse Season Opens," *Baltimore Sun*, April 6, 1901: 6.

79 "Girls Play Good Ball: Chicago Stars Wallop Glendales 13 to 3 at Old Union Park," *Baltimore Sun*, August 13, 1902: 6.

80 "Fraudulent Football Tickets," *Baltimore Sun*, November 19, 1902: 6.

81 "Union Park Lease: Statement That National League Had Renewed It," *Baltimore Sun*, August 25, 1902: 6.

82 "Hanlon His Hopes: Feels Certain That Baltimore Will Have Baseball, Perhaps None Next Season," *Baltimore Sun*, December 15, 1902: 6.

83 "Hanlon His Hopes."

84 "Baseball," *Baltimore Sun*, December 27, 1902: 6.

85 "Old Union Park to Go: Scene of Baseball Glory to Be The Site Of Dwellings," *Baltimore Sun*, October 2, 1905: 12.

86 "Old Union Park to Go."

87 "Sale Of 50 Lots at Overlea Reported, Union Park Deal Is Closed by Howard White," *Baltimore Sun*, October 26, 1905: 9.

88 David B. Stinson, "A Room With A View Overlooking Baltimore's Union Park," April 4, 2014, www.davidbstinsonauthor.com/2014/04/04/a-room-with-a-view-overlooking-baltimores-union-park (accessed January 22, 2020).

The former site of Union Park, seen in this 2014 photograph by David B. Stinson. The peaked-roofed building to the right of the photo is 321 East 25th Street (currently St. Ambrose Housing Aid Center). The building was adjacent to Union Park's grandstand and its parking lot was once part of the playing field. It can be seen to the right of the grandstand in 1897 photograph on page 29 of Union Park entitled "The Winning Team." Courtesy of David B. Stinson.

Seven Hits in Seven Tries for Wilbert Robinson

June 10, 1892: Baltimore Orioles 25, St. Louis Browns 4, at Union Park

By Jimmy Keenan

Until Rennie Stennett matched the feat in September of 1975, only one man in major-league history had recorded seven hits in seven at-bats during a regulation nine-inning game. This rarest of batting achievements was accomplished on June 10, 1892, by Wilbert Robinson, later to become a Hall of Fame manager but at the time a portly catcher for the cellar-dwelling Baltimore Orioles.

The Orioles hosted the St. Louis Browns that Friday at their two-tiered wooden home ground, Union Park. Those who attended the scheduled doubleheader couldn't have expected anything approaching the history that would unfold before their eyes. The Orioles had won just 10 of their 42 games to that point. The Browns, like the Orioles a remnant of the recently disbanded American Association, stood at 16–27. Those clubs and their fellow Association adoptees to the National League, Louisville and Washington, had formed a cluster at the bottom of the standings where they would remain all season.

It was a cool, overcast summer day with a light breeze blowing in from the northwest when the Browns took the field in the first inning of the opening contest. St. Louis sent veteran pitcher Charlie "Pretzels" Getzien into the box to oppose the Orioles ace right-hander Sadie McMahon. McMahon, 24, was coming off 36- and 35-win seasons. But those victories had been posted in the disbanded American Association, and so far in 1892 McMahon had found the National League to be tougher. His record stood at just 3-10 as the game began.

Pretzels Getzien was at the end of a career that yielded 145 victories, 29 of them with the pennant-winning Detroit Wolverines in 1887. As recently as 1890, Getzien had won 23 games for Boston's National League team. But that had been his last strong season. Although just 27 years old, he started only 10 games in 1891, winning four and losing six. Nonetheless, in their desire for an experienced arm, the Browns had signed Getzien just a few days before, and he was 2-0 for them as he took to the pitcher's box in Baltimore.

Orioles batters, who exercised their right under the rules of the time to bat first, were all over Getzien's offerings from the outset. Billy Shindle led off with a blistering triple to left field, and by the time the first inning ended, the Orioles had sent 10 men to the plate and scored five runs. Robinson, the eighth hitter in the lineup, contributed a single.

Baltimore hitters continued to tee off on Getzien in the second inning, scoring five more runs, with Robinson adding a second single. The veteran hurler was removed at the end of the inning, his team trailing 10–1. He had given up seven hits and 10 runs in two innings of work. Getzien never recovered from the humiliation, losing eight of his final 11 starts before being released in late July.

Joe Young, making his major-league debut and, as it turned out, his only big-league appearance, replaced Getzien in the third inning. Young had been the star hurler for the Mount Carmel team in the Central Pennsylvania League before signing with the Browns, but he could do nothing to stop the Orioles' onslaught. The Baltimore club pounded him for 12 hits and 13 runs during his three innings in the pitcher's box. Amazingly, the leader of the Orioles assault was Robinson, a career .226 batter entering the season, whose third, fourth, and fifth hits were a single in the third inning, a double in the fourth, and a single in the fifth.

Besides being unable to stop Robinson or the Orioles, the visiting Browns had great difficulty catching up to McMahon's offerings. They managed only seven hits and four runs. Browns center fielder Steve Brodie, who later gained fame as an Oriole, was the only St. Louis player to make two hits off McMahon.

Left-hander Ted "Theo" Breitenstein came in to start the sixth inning, allowing the Orioles' 24th and 25th runs but avoiding Robinson, who did not come to the plate. Robinson batted in the seventh, collecting his sixth hit (a single), although the Orioles failed to add to their 25–2 lead. He batted again with two out in the ninth and produced a seventh base hit, his sixth single of the game. That seventh hit was harmless, but Robinson had already done enough damage, driving across 11 runs. The runs batted in were a single-game record that stood until 1924, and represented nearly 20 percent of the runs Robinson sent across the plate for the entire 1892 season.

Robinson was hardly alone in his offensive exploits that June day. The Baltimore lineup, despite the team's poor record, had its share of talented ballplayers. Future Hall of Famer John McGraw, playing second base in his sophomore season in the majors, connected for three singles in the opener, scored three runs, and stole a base. His double-play partner, shortstop George Shoch, connected for five hits, including a two-bagger, and he scored four runs. Baltimore's left-handed right fielder, George Van Haltren, swatted two base hits while crossing the plate five times. Third baseman Billy Shindle stroked a double and a triple. Jocko Halligan, Joe Gunson, and Curt Welch each came through with a pair of safeties for the Orioles in the lopsided victory. (Remarkably, despite 32 hits and seven bases on balls for both teams, the game took only an hour and 50 minutes to complete.)

Following his record performance, which included a stolen base, the durable Robinson caught the second game of the doubleheader, garnering two more singles. The result was a 9–3 Orioles victory that looked like a nail-biter in comparison with the opener. Robinson later told the press that his "lamps got tired during the second game" or he would have done better.

McMahon, who was coming off back-to-back 30-win seasons, fell off a bit in 1892, winning just 19 games. The Orioles played inconsistent ball for the rest of the 1892 season and finished with the worst record in the league. But on that one June day in Baltimore, Wilbert Robinson made baseball history.

Sources

In addition to the sources cited in the Notes, the author also consulted the *Baltimore Morning Herald, Sporting Life, St. Louis Globe Democrat,* and the *St. Louis Post Dispatch,* as well as Baseball-Reference.com and Jonathon Frazier Light's book *The Cultural Encyclopedia of Baseball* (second edition, Jefferson, North Carolina: McFarland, 2005).

Special thanks to Cynthia Millar, Subject Specialist, St. Louis Public Library. She generously provided me with articles and boxscores from the *St. Louis Dispatch* and *St Louis Globe Democrat* for this game.

Author's note

There is a discrepancy regarding St. Louis Browns pitcher Joe Young's statistics for this game. This article uses his pitching line from the Baltimore papers although it is by no means definitive. Baseball-Reference has Young pitching two innings, giving up 13 runs on 9 hits. This run total does not match up with inning-by-inning boxscores for the game. Baltimore scored twenty runs in the first four innings. If he pitched two innings, per Baseball-Reference, his total runs allowed would have been 10, not 13. The *St. Louis Globe Democrat* and the *St. Louis Dispatch* show Young pitching two innings, giving up 10 runs. Conversely the *Baltimore Sun* and *Baltimore Morning Herald* have him working three innings, allowing 13 runs on 12 hits.

An earlier version of this essay was originally published in Inventing Baseball: The 100 Greatest Games of the 19th Century, *published by SABR in 2013, and edited by Bill Felber.*

Notes

1 "St. Louis Knocked Out," *Baltimore Sun,* June 11, 1892: 8.

Baltimore Stuns the Champs, Scoring 14 Runs in the Ninth for the Win

April 24, 1894: Baltimore Orioles 15, Boston Beaneaters 3, at Oriole Park III

By Mike Huber

Just about every kid who has ever played baseball has had the dream about coming to bat in the ninth inning with his team down by a run or two and being the hero. The *Baltimore Sun* described this dramatic game with the same fairy-tale-type approach: "It was the beginning of the ninth inning. Mighty Boston was Baltimore's adversary and the score was 3 to 1. The three runs belonged to the visitors. Pent-up enthusiasm was at fever-heat and the 8,400 spectators were on the tiptoe of expectation, for it was the Oriole's [sic] last chance to turn defeat into victory. And they did it."[1] It seemed as if each Orioles batter played the hero, until the Beaneaters just gave up.

The Orioles had just swept three home games from the New York Giants to open the 1894 season. The defending champion Beaneaters had likewise swept the Brooklyn Bridegrooms. (The first game was played in Boston and the next two in Brooklyn.) In this contest, Baltimore, the home team, batted first. Jack Stivetts pitched for Boston and Sadie McMahon for Baltimore. Each pitcher had been the Opening Day victor. According to the *Boston Globe*, "What promised to end in a well-played game wound up in a burlesque."[2]

The first eight innings of the game between these top two contenders were close and exciting. Boston pushed across two runs in the second inning as Tommy Tucker singled, Jimmy Bannon reached on an error, Charlie Ganzel and Stivetts sacrificed the runners, and Bobby Lowe doubled. Baltimore answered with a solo run in the fourth when Joe Kelley singled, stole second, and scored on a single by Heinie Reitz. Stivetts and Lowe hit back-to-back doubles in the seventh inning for another Boston run. Both teams played with purpose and professionalism. The crowd was anxious that their Orioles might lose.

There was some cleverness in the third inning. With one out, Willie Keeler batted with Wilbert Robinson on second and John McGraw on first. Keeler lifted a routine fly ball to left field and the runners stayed near their bases, but left fielder Tommy McCarthy "purposely muffed the ball [and] with lightning quickness he picked it up and sent it to [Billy] Nash, who touched third and threw to Lowe on second" for a double play.[3] Beaneaters first baseman Tucker remarked, "That's a new one on you" to the Baltimore players as he passed them coming off the field.[4]

And then came the dramatics. According to the *Lowell Sun*, "Boston showed the white feather in the last inning and allowed Baltimore to win in a canter."[5] The excitement of the ninth inning started when Baltimore's third-base coach, Boileryard Clarke, in an effort to distract both Stivetts and umpire Tim Hurst, "walked out to the bleachers and raised his hands like a 'pop concert' leader, and a volume of sound filled the air, every man, woman and child yelling for all he or she was worth."[6] At first, Stivetts did not seem moved, but "Hurst became rattled at the awful noise."[7] Stivetts pitched to his catcher Ganzel's mitt, but Hurst kept calling them balls, and the crowd kept getting louder.

After Kelley drew a walk, Ganzel "made a vigorous protest"[8] and was fined 10 by the umpire. Reitz then stepped into the batter's box, "holding his bat on his shoulder without the least idea of striking at the ball."[9] He also walked on four straight pitches, at which point Stivett threw his cap to the ground. Hughie Jennings then stroked a single to short center, driving in Kelley. This brought the crowd to its feet. The first three pitches to Robinson were called balls, bringing thunderous roars from the crowd. With the third called ball, Stivetts again "acted like a wild man [and] he threw his cap upon the ground."[10] The Boston team gathered around home plate, offering Stivetts time to compose himself. Umpire Hurst then ordered Stivetts back to the mound. When he didn't comply, both the Beaneaters hurler and catcher were fined. A moment later, Stivetts was ejected.[11]

Beaneaters manager Frank Selee brought Kid Nichols on in relief. However, "he was refused the privilege of a little warming-up work by two big policemen, and went in cold and stiff."[12] Nichols threw one pitch, but it was wide, and Robinson trotted to first with an RBI walk. Suddenly the game was tied. Baltimore pitcher McMahon singled past Tucker at first, and two more runs scored. McGraw followed with a single, driving in Robinson. Then, according to the *Baltimore Sun*, the Beaneaters just quit; "the fielders acted like wooden soldiers when the Baltimore players sent the ball into their territory, and Nichols tossed the ball like a school boy."[13] Keeler singled, plating McMahon and McGraw, and advanced on a wild pitch. Steve Brodie tripled to the right-field fence and Dan Brouthers singled to left. One base hit followed another and the Baltimore squad batted around without making an out, scoring eight times.

Then, as Yogi Berra once said, "It was déjà vu all over again."[14] Kelley and Reitz once again reached via the base on balls. By now, the Baltimore fans were concerned that Boston would refuse to retire the side and the inning would be lost, due to darkness, giving the victory to Boston, so "the Baltimore players were loudly admonished by the spectators to be put out purposely."[15] Jennings popped out to second, but Robinson singled, driving in two more runs. McMahon laid down a sacrifice bunt, advancing Robinson to second, but Reitz held up at third. McGraw drew a walk to load the bases again. Keeler grounded back to Nichols, who threw wildly to first and two more runs came in. Keeler went to second on the error and then stole both third and home. The embarrassment finally ended when Brodie popped out to Nichols on the mound. The Beaneaters did nothing in the bottom of the ninth, making "no effort to get runs."[16]

Seventeen Baltimore players had batted in the final frame, scoring 14 runs. Had the Beaneaters batted first, the game could have been decided with a walk-off 4-3 victory for the Orioles. Instead, every Orioles player managed at least one hit and one run scored in the game. McGraw, Kelley, and Robinson led the Orioles offense with three hits each. McMahon pitched a good game, limiting the Beaneaters to three runs on eight hits, with the only strikeout of the game. Lowe shined for Boston with three hits, all doubles. There were eight sacrifices in the game. Amazingly, according to the *Baltimore Sun*, only four of the Orioles runs were earned.[17]

The two teams played again each of the next two days. Boston won both games, 6-3 and 13-7. For the season, Boston beat Baltimore eight of 12 matches, but the Beaneaters finished 1894 eight games behind the eventual champion Orioles.

Sources

In addition to the sources mentioned in the Notes, the author consulted baseball-reference.com and retrosheet.org. The author sincerely thanks Lisa Tuite of the *Boston Globe* for her assistance with providing sources.

Notes

1 "A Game From Boston: Something Dropped in the Ninth Inning, and Then, Oh, My!," *Baltimore Sun*, April 25, 1894: 6.

2 "Yelled Like Mad: Crowd Tried to Rattle Jack Stivetts," *Boston Globe*, April 25, 1894: 5.

3 "A Game From Boston: Something Dropped in the Ninth Inning, and Then, Oh, My!"

4 "A Game From Boston: Something Dropped in the Ninth Inning, and Then, Oh, My!"

5 "Badly Punished," *Lowell Sun*, April 25, 1894: 8.

6 "Yelled Like Mad: Crowd Tried to Rattle Jack Stivetts."

7 "Yelled Like Mad: Crowd Tried to Rattle Jack Stivetts."

8 "Yelled Like Mad: Crowd Tried to Rattle Jack Stivetts."

9 "Yelled Like Mad: Crowd Tried to Rattle Jack Stivetts."

10 "A Game From Boston: Something Dropped in the Ninth Inning, and Then, Oh, My!"

11 According to the *Boston Globe*, Boston pitcher Jack Stivetts and umpire Tim Hurst both hailed from Ashland, Pennsylvania. The *Globe* commented that it was "strange to say that every time that Tim umpires a game where Stivetts is pitching there is always trouble, and the Boston players claim that Mr. Hurst is not particularly stuck on his old townsman."

12 "Yelled Like Mad: Crowd Tried to Rattle Jack Stivetts."

13 "A Game From Boston: Something Dropped in the Ninth Inning, and Then, Oh, My!"

14 This Yogiism is attributed to Yogi Berra (date unknown). It is inscribed on the walls of the Yogi Berra Museum & Learning Center, Little Falls, New Jersey.

15 "A Game From Boston: Something Dropped in the Ninth Inning, and Then, Oh, My!"

16 "Yelled Like Mad: Crowd Tried to Rattle Jack Stivetts."

17 According to the *Boston Globe* and the *Lowell* (Massachusetts) *Sun*, Baltimore had six earned runs.

Birds Building to Sweep the Cup

October 5, 1896: Baltimore Orioles 6, Cleveland Spiders 2, at Union Park

By Benjamin Sabin

"Three games they lost for the Temple Cup;
Three games right at the start;
So Tebeau leaves with a pain in his back
And another in his heart.
Oh, where is Cleveland's pennant pole?
In the town of the oyster stew.
And where is the blooming Temple Cup?
I'm afraid they'll get that too."[1]

The Baltimore Orioles (90-39) of 1896 had finished first for the third straight year, previously having topped the National League in 1894 and 1895. But after losing the Temple Cup the last two seasons to the second-place teams, New York and Cleveland, they were poised for a much-needed victory in the competition for the Cup.

The Baltimore Orioles of the late nineteenth century were the dominating force in the National League. Baltimore was led by Ned Hanlon, a "short, stout manager who sat on the Orioles bench in a three-button Victorian suit."[2] Foxy Ned, as he was sometimes known, had just won the third of his five championships in a Hall of Fame career. The '96 Orioles were also led by five other future Hall of Famers: John McGraw at third, Hughie Jennings at short, Willie Keeler in right, Joe Kelley in left, and Wilbert Robinson behind the plate. It is no wonder that Hanlon and his boys are credited with perfecting the hit-and-run, bunting, the sacrifice, and the Baltimore chop, what came to be known as "inside baseball."[3]

The 1896 Cleveland Spiders (80-48), led by player-manager Oliver "Patsy" Tebeau, had finished second behind the overpowering Orioles. They had also finished second to Orioles in 1895, but had triumphed over Baltimore in the Cup series, and were not looking to relinquish what had "soothed the ruffled spirits of Tebeau when he thought of the pennant."[4] The Spiders were stacked with talented players, among them Cy Young, Nig Cuppy, Chief Zimmer, and Jesse Burkett. Although in the shadow of the Orioles, as was the rest of the professional baseball at that time, the Clevelanders were no slouches. Game Three of the Temple Cup took place on October 5, 1896, before a less-than-impressive crowd of 2,000. The interest in the Temple Cup had begun to lessen at this point and the turnout at Baltimore's Union Park was disappointing. Union Park was "fancier than most, a double-decked, 8,000 seat wooded stadium with a beer garden, picnic grounds and ladies grandstand."[5]

In the box for the Orioles was Bill Hoffer, who was coming off of a splendid season with a 25-7 record and a 3.38 ERA. Although he was pitching on just two days' rest – he had started in Game One of the series on Friday – and "had trouble in the earlier innings making his balls 'break' just right,"[6] he persisted and at "the proper moment, Hoffer became invincible."[7]

Pitching for the Spiders was Nig Cuppy, who had finished the season with a 25-14 record and a 3.12 ERA. He was the number-two starter for the Spiders behind Cy Young but was every bit as capable as the famous Cy.

The Orioles were the first to strike, in the bottom of the second. Cuppy had retired McGraw, Keeler, and Jennings in order in the first. Leading off the second for Baltimore was Joe Kelley, who topped the National League with 87 stolen bases in 1896.[8] He singled and was forced out at second on a groundball by Jack Doyle, the Orioles' first baseman. Doyle then stole second and was driven in by center fielder Steve Brodie. Brodie was the Cal Ripken of his day. He holds the nineteenth-century record for consecutive games played (727).[9] Cuppy then retired Baltimore catcher Robinson to put a stop to the blossoming rally.

Cleveland tied it in the top of the third. The Spiders had been hitting Hoffer well – "he was hit safely nine times in the first five innings" – but had nothing to show for it thus far. But three singles in the top of the third were enough to bring home a "tally."[10]

The Orioles jumped ahead in the bottom of the third. Hoffer helped his own cause by driving a triple past the scrambling Cleveland outfielders. Then he capitalized on a fly ball and "a poor throw by Burkett, which allowed Hoffer to score."[11] But Baltimore didn't hold the lead for long. In the top of the fifth inning, the Spiders took advantage of the only walk of the game and drove home another run on two singles.

Baltimore retook the lead in the bottom of the sixth. The pugnacious John McGraw manufactured a one-man rally. He led off the inning with a single off Cuppy, stole second, and went to third on a throwing error by catcher Zimmer. McGraw finally let someone else on the Orioles help with a fly ball. McGraw scored and Baltimore wouldn't lose the lead again.

Cleveland pitcher Cuppy "pitched a brilliant game up to the eighth inning, when the champions fell on him for three singles and a double."[12] Catcher Wilbert Robinson, who hit .312 over seven seasons with the Orioles,[13] started the rally with a double. McGraw's single drove in Robinson. Then McGraw stole second and was driven in on a single by Keeler, who in turn was then driven in by Kelley's single. The three runs seemed to seal the Spiders' fate. They left nine men on base in the game.

After two hours, Game Three of the Temple Cup was concluded. The Orioles won 6-2. The series traveled to Cleveland, but the Spiders were too far out of the race to come back. The Orioles won the fourth game at League Park and took the Cup home with them, along with $200 per player. The Temple Cup was played once more, in 1897, and the Orioles were victors again, but after that the Temple Cup series was scuttled for lack of interest by both fans and players.

Sources

Besides the sources cited in the Notes, the author consulted Baseball-Reference.com, the SABR Biography Project, and the following:

Eckhouse, Morris. *Legends of the Tribe: An Illustrated History of the Cleveland Indians* (Dallas: Taylor Publishing Company, 2000).

Thorn, John. "A Pictorial Chronology of Baseball in the 19th Century, Part 19: 1895-1896," ourgame.mlblogs.com, September 10, 2019. ourgame.mlblogs.com/a-pictorial-chronology-of-baseball-in-the-19th-century-part-19-1895-1896-8fa5370298cf.

Notes

1 "Clevelands Again Beaten," *Washington Evening Star*, October 6, 1896: 9.

2 Mike Klingaman, "In the Rough-and-Tumble Baseball of the 1890s," *Baltimore Sun*, July 7, 1996.

3 Edgar G. Brands, "Ned Hanlon, Leader of Famous Orioles and Noted Strategist of Game, Dies at 79," *The Sporting News*, April 22, 1937: 12.

4 "Clevelands Again Beaten."

5 Klingaman.

6 "Clevelands Again Beaten."

7 "Clevelands Again Beaten."

8 "Joe Kelley," National Baseball Hall of Fame, baseballhall.org/hall-of-famers/kelley-joe.

9 William Akin, "Steve Brodie," SABR.org, sabr.org/bioproj/person/cffef117.

10 "Clevelands Again Beaten."

11 "Temple Cup Contests," *Evening Bulletin* (Maysville, Kentucky), October 6, 1896: 4.

12 "Cleveland Defeated Again," *Daily Morning Journal and Courier* (New Haven, Connecticut), October 6, 1896.

13 Alex Semchuck, "Wilbert Robinson," SABR.org, sabr.org/bioproj/person/5536caf5.

Hitting 'Em Where They Ain't
44 Games in a Row

June 18, 1897: Baltimore Orioles 11, Pittsburgh Pirates 9, at Oriole Park III

By Kevin Larkin

Before Joe DiMaggio had his 56-game hitting streak in 1941, the major-league record for consecutive games with a base hit was the streak of 42 consecutive games achieved by Bill Dahlen of the Chicago Colts in 1894.

As the 1897 season began, the National League's Baltimore Orioles had just completed their third straight pennant-winning season. Prospects looked good for a repeat in 1897 with players like Hughie Jennings, John McGraw, Joe Kelley, and Wilbert Robinson returning for another shot at a pennant. Also returning to Baltimore for 1897 was the diminutive outfielder William Henry Keeler or, as he was better known, Wee Willie.

Keeler began as he so often stated, "hitting 'em where they ain't" in the first game of the 1897 season, a 10-5 victory over the Boston Beaneaters.[1] Through an eight-game homestand, Keeler got a least one hit in each game. Then, through a 25-game road trip in which the team visited nine of the other 11 National League cities, Keeler continued his streak. After the road trip Keeler kept right on hitting, passing Cal McVey (1876) and Dusty Miller (1895-1896), both of whom had hit in 30 straight games. Jimmy Wolf was the next name erased from the record books when Keeler crossed his mark of 31 straight games with a hit off the record books.

With a hit in his 37th consecutive game, Keeler passed Gene DeMontreville, who in 1896-97 hit in 36 straight games. After he broke Dahlen's record of 42 games with a hit, every game after that raised the number in the record book.

Preparing to face the Pittsburgh Pirates on June 18, the Orioles sat in first place with a record of 32-9, 1½ games ahead of the second-place Beaneaters. Pittsburgh, with a record of 20-22, was in eighth place, 12½ games behind the Orioles.

The visiting Pirates batted first, with Mike Smith grounding out to shortstop Hughie Jennings.[2] Second baseman Dick Padden missed the first two pitches from the Orioles' Joe Corbett (the younger brother of heavyweight boxing champion Jim Corbett), and then hit the next pitch over the fence for a home run.[3] Harry Davis and Steve Brodie singled, with Davis taking third on Brodie's hit. Patsy Donovan's infield out scored Davis. Brodie was out on an attempted steal of home and the half-inning ended with the Pirates leading 2-0.

For the Orioles, McGraw led off the first with a double but was out when a ball hit by Keeler struck him.[4] Jennings walked, then Keeler went to third on Jack Doyle's force-out grounder.[5] Keeler then stole home and the first inning came to an end with the Pirates on top 2-1.

The second inning was scoreless. In the Pittsburgh third, starting pitcher Pink Hawley led off with a single, Mike Smith walked, and Padden was hit by a pitch to load the bases. Davis hit a long fly ball to Tom O'Brien in left field, scoring Hawley and giving Pittsburgh a 3-1 lead.

In the bottom of the third inning, Orioles catcher Frank Bowerman and pitcher Corbett singled, putting runners at first and third. Corbett stole second and McGraw's second hit of the game scored both runners. McGraw was thrown out trying to steal third base. With the bases empty, Keeler doubled to center field and scored on a two-out triple by Doyle to give the Orioles a 4-3 lead.

Pittsburgh tied the game, 4-4, in the top of the fourth but the Orioles took the lead for good in the bottom of the inning. O'Brien, Joe Quinn, and Bowerman singled. Corbett doubled and McGraw reached on an error by Pirates catcher Joe Sugden. Keeler then tripled and Jennings singled. All this – six runs scored

– happened with nobody out, and it gave the Orioles a 10-4 lead.[6] The Orioles weren't done. Jennings stole second base and went to third after tagging up on a foul out. He scored the Orioles' seventh run of the inning on a long fly ball and Baltimore was now in command of the game, 11-4.

Pittsburgh got four hits in the sixth inning but just one run.[7] In the Pirates' eighth, singles by Donovan and shortstop Bones Ely combined with an out by Sugden gave Baltimore another run to make the score 11-6.

The Pirates rallied for three runs in their ninth inning, beginning with a walk to outfielder Mike Smith. Padden doubled and Davis's fly out scored Smith. Brodie singled and went to second on an out by Donovan. Ely's fourth single of the day scored Padden and Brodie to make the final score Baltimore 11, Pittsburgh 9.

The win gave the Orioles a two-game lead over the second-place Beaneaters. Pittsburgh was led by Ely's four singles and Donovan's three hits, which included a double.[8] Keeler, Bowerman, and Corbett each had three of the Orioles' 16 hits. "The Pirates slugged the ball yesterday as they have not done any other time this season," a Pittsburgh newspaper observed.[9] They made 16 hits and totaled 21 bases and yet could not win.[10]

Later in the season, the pennant race came down to two teams, the Orioles and the Beaneaters. The Beaneaters prevailed in the race and ended up the National League champions by two games over the Orioles.

Keeler's hitting streak of games ended at 44 in the Orioles' next game, a 7-1 loss to the Pirates, and he held the record until Joe DiMaggio bettered the mark, hitting in 56 games in 1941. Since DiMaggio, the only player to come close to DiMaggio, and for that matter Keeler's 44 were Pete Rose, who tied Keeler in 1978, and Paul Molitor, who hit in 39 straight games in 1987.

Sources

In addition to the game story and box scores cited in the Notes, the author consulted the Baseball-Reference.com and Retrosheet.org websites.

Notes

1   "The Throng at Union Park," *Baltimore Sun,* April 23, 1897: 6.
2   "Hot Batting Day," *Baltimore Sun,* June 19,1897: 6.
3   "Hot Batting Day."
4   "Hot Batting Day."
5   "Hot Batting Day."
6   "Hot Batting Day."
7   "Hot Batting Day."
8   "Donovan's Men Three Runs Shy," *Pittsburgh Daily Post,* June 19, 1897: 6.
9   "Pirates Batted Hard," *Pittsburgh Press,* June 19, 1897: 5.
10 "Pirates Batted Hard"

Good (Beaneaters) versus Evil (Orioles)

September 27, 1897: Boston Beaneaters 19, Baltimore Orioles 10, at Union Park

By Bill Felber

More than a battle for the 1897 National League pennant, the contest played out at Baltimore's Union Park was a living, breathing metaphor. To the 30,000 fans who literally broke down the park's gates and walls to see it, and to the thousands nationally who followed telegraphed accounts in locations as distant as Los Angeles, it was the real-world playing out of the eternal struggle of good vs. evil.

Few confused the assigned roles. Virtually across the nation outside Baltimore itself, the Orioles were the embodiment of all that was wrong with baseball. Led by third baseman John McGraw, shortstop Hughie Jennings, first baseman "Dirty Jack" Doyle and right fielder Wee Willie Keeler, the team managed by Ned Hanlon had since 1894 terrorized the rest of the league, sweeping to three successive pennants by both skill and intimidation. "The dirtiest ball ever seen in this country," Boston sports writer Tim Murnane lamented of the Orioles' style.[1] A reporter in New Orleans, commenting on a spring training exhibition, had characterized McGraw as having adopted "every low and contemptible method that his erratic brain can conceive to win a play by a dirty trick."[2]

Though hardly saints themselves, the Beaneaters—three-time champions from 1891–93 before being dethroned by the Orioles—assumed the mantle of fan favorites once it became clear in 1897 that either they or the Orioles would win the pennant. Between August 27 and September 26, they combined to win 39 of 49 decisions (three games ending in ties), neither team ever leading the other by more than one game in the standings. A fated schedule ordered the clubs together for three games the final week in Baltimore. As the series opened, the Orioles held a one percentage point lead over Boston, although thanks to having played three more games the Beaneaters were actually a half-game ahead in the standings.[3] The frantic first two games did nothing to resolve the tension. Boston won 6-4 on Friday behind ace pitcher Charles "Kid" Nichols with a throng of 13,000 overflowing onto the field. Another 14,000 turned out Saturday, again spilling onto the field and climbing atop the outfield fence, to watch the Orioles win 6-3 and draw the race back into a virtual deadlock. The illegality of Sunday baseball merely ensured that the drama would build one more day.

Despite the fact that Monday was a work day, fans overwhelmed the tiny baseball grounds to witness the decisive game. The attendance is commonly estimated at 30,000—easily surpassing the previous record for any game—but the truth is that nobody knows how many people watched. Fans broke through the outfield gate and knocked down part of the fence to get access. Others stormed the turnstiles, erected seats on the roofs of houses across the street, or perched themselves on telegraph poles.

A delegation of more than 100 fans from Boston—the genesis of the famed "Royal Rooters"—showed up complete with a brass band to challenge the home team's noise advantage. Thousands more crowded the streets of Boston's "Newspaper Row" to "watch" on large play-by-play boards in a scene repeated on smaller scales in cities across the country. Nichols, already a 30-game winner, returned to the rubber on two days' rest as did the Orioles' Joe Corbett, who was seeking his 25th victory.

But chance had it in for Corbett. The game's fourth batter, Chick Stahl, lined a drive off his hand that jammed several fingers. Hanlon was forced to remove his ace. The Beaneaters got a run out of that first inning, but Keeler's base hit led to two Oriole runs in the bottom half of the inning. The lead changed hands three more times by the end of the third inning, which ended with the score tied at 5-5. In the Boston fourth, Billy Hamilton, the era's premier baserunner, singled and stole second, Fred Tenney walked, and Bobby

Lowe singled to drive Hamilton across. Chick Stahl followed with a single that produced Tenney, and an error by Wilbert Robinson allowed Lowe to score an eighth run.

Bill Hoffer, whose 22nd victory had been Saturday's complete-game triumph, pitched scoreless ball from that point through the sixth. But by the beginning of the seventh inning Hoffer had worked 13 innings in less than two days against the league's best offense, and he was exhausted. What ensued turned the top of the seventh into one of the most productive (or, depending on your perspective, disastrous) half innings ever played.

Hugh Duffy opened for Boston with a solid base hit. Jimmy Collins drilled a fastball into the crowd in right field for a ground-rule double, and Dutch Long's double into the crowd in center scored both runners. When three more hits produced three additional runs, Hoffer did what in 1897 was the unthinkable: He motioned to team captain Robinson and manager Hanlon to relieve him. Both men ignored the gesture, imploring Hoffer to continue. He did, but by the time the slaughter had ended with Long's second double of the inning, nine Boston runs crossed the plate. The champion Orioles were, for the first time since 1893, effectively unseated.

When Nichols retired the last Baltimore batter and the final 19-10 score was posted, a remarkable scene ensued. Although the Baltimore and Boston fans had exchanged epithets all season long, they now joined on the field in a series of mutual salutes. Their bands serenaded each other with renditions of "Yankee Doodle," "Dixie," "There'll Be a Hot Time in the Old Town Tonight," and "Maryland, My Maryland."[4]

The nation treated the outcome as something of a purgative for what were widely perceived as the game's ills. "Never was interest keener in America's great national game than it is today," said the *Boston Globe*.[5] The outcome put Boston a game and a half in front with just three to play; two victories in Brooklyn the following weekend formalized the pennant that ended the pennant run of the 19th century's most feared and despised team at three.

Editor's Note

This essay was originally published in Inventing Baseball: The 100 Greatest Games of the 19th Century, *published by SABR in 2013, and edited by Bill Felber.*

Notes

1 T. H. Murnane, "The Champions," *The Sporting News*, June 30, 1894: 2.

2 Charles Alexander, *John McGraw* (Lincoln: University of Nebraska Press, 1988), 39.

3 The Orioles had four games remaining on their schedule compared to Boston's three. Due to travel problems, rained-out Orioles games in Cleveland and Louisville had not been made up.

4 "Boston On Top," *Baltimore Sun*, September 28, 1897: 6.

5 "Editorial Points," *Boston Globe*, September 28, 1897: 6.

American League Park

By David B. Stinson

American League Park was the home of the first American League Baltimore Orioles in 1901 and 1902.[1] From 1903 to 1914, the ballpark was known as Oriole Park (IV) and was home to the Eastern League Orioles and then the International League Orioles (when the league changed names in 1911).[2] The ballpark was located at the southwest corner of Greenmount Avenue (formerly York Road) and East 29th Street.[3] From 1889 to 1891, the site was the home of the American Association Baltimore Orioles; it was the second ballpark known as Oriole Park.[4] First base paralleled Barclay Street, right field paralleled East 28th Street, left field paralleled Greenmount Avenue, and third base paralleled East 29th Street.[5]

From 1892 to 1899, the National League Orioles played their home games four blocks south of American League Park at Union Park (Oriole Park (III).[6] When the National League departed after the 1899 season, Baltimore was left without a major-league franchise. The American League was formed during the following winter, 1900-1901, and Baltimore was granted one of eight franchises. John McGraw, the former National League Oriole, was chosen as manager of the new American League Orioles.[7]

Byron Bancroft "Ban" Johnson, president of the new league, visited Baltimore with McGraw in December 1900 to tour possible sites for the new American League ballpark, including Union Park.[8] After the tour, it was announced that the site at 29th Street and York Road was preferred, and that Union Park was not being considered for the ballpark site.[9] Of course, with Union Park still under the control of the National League, Ned Hanlon, a former Orioles manager and the current Brooklyn (NL) manager, had no intention of letting the American League utilize it as its home ballpark.[10] A third possible site was Electric Park, at Belvedere Avenue and Reisterstown Road near Pimlico racetrack.[11]

A five-year lease of the York Road grounds was signed on January 16, 1901, and the ballpark officially was named American League Park.[12] The cost of constructing the grandstands was estimated at between $15,000 and $20,000. The *Baltimore Sun* noted that "[t]he stands are to be of the most approved modern construction, and an effort will be made to have them as comfortable as possible."[13] One complaint about the York Road site, when it was used as the home field for the American Association from 1889 to 1891, was that train and trolley lines did not stop close to the ballpark and fans had to walk several blocks up York Road to reach the ballpark. The new American League ballclub made arrangements to fix that problem:

> The railway conditions are to be arranged shortly, and it is believed that the grounds can be reached from the center of Baltimore in 15 minutes, and probably 12 minutes can be made the limit. At present the only line going directly to the new ball park is the York road line.
>
> The St. Paul Street line, which runs over the elevated structure on North Street, goes close to the park, and passengers can go to York road and Waverly avenue or alight at St. Paul and Twenty-ninth streets as the line now runs. There would be little trouble, however, in running the line directly to the ground.[14]

Additional details concerning the grandstand and bleachers were announced on January 25, 1901:

> It was concluded to put up a single-deck grandstand, to be topped by a cupola, which will be divided into three sections – one for the press, one for the directors and one for the use of telegraph operators.
>
> The main floor will consist of a series of private boxes in front. Opera chairs will fill

American League Park / Oriole Park (IV), July 18, 1907. Courtesy of David B. Stinson and Bernard McKenna.

the remainder of the space. The grandstand is to seat 3,000 people.

An open, or bleacher, stand is to be built in the left field, and is to seat 3,000. In right field there is also to be an open stand, which is to seat 1,500.[15]

In February 1901, anticipating that American League Park would be used for more than just baseball, the Johns Hopkins Athletic Association agreed to raise $2,000 to install a quarter-mile running track and build a clubhouse.[16] Johns Hopkins agreed to a five-year subtenancy at American League Park.[17] Additional improvements by Johns Hopkins were:

In the deep center field there will be a clubhouse, built to harmonize with the other buildings on the grounds. In the clubhouse there will be a large ventilated locker room, a lounging room, a reading room, a "cooling off" room and baths of all improved kinds.[18]

Martin Lyston, the landscape gardener at Patterson Park, a popular public park in southeast Baltimore, was hired to install the grounds.[19] Leveling the grounds proved difficult as they previously had been used by circuses and were "gullied with ruts from the heavy wagons" and "stakes driven far into the ground."[20] About a month before Opening Day, the *Baltimore Sun* reported:

The fence at the ball park is practically finished, as are the bleachers. The grandstand is going up rapidly and the water pipes are being laid.

Builder Henry S. Rippel said last night that with the exception of the grandstand roof all the buildings will be complete by April 1, the date specified in the contract. The delay in finishing the roof of the grandstand will be caused by the fact that it became necessary to send South for the long timbers required in the construction. All the fencing is 14 feet high and double, so that peepers cannot get a quarter's worth through a knothole or a seam.[21]

On February 12, 1901, about 400 fans attended the groundbreaking for American League Park, which was held in the northeast corner of the plot, on which was being constructed an "Administration Building."[22] Used for the ceremony was a special silver spade, which the previous night was displayed at John McGraw's and Wilbert Robinson's Diamond Café on North Howard Street.[23] In attendance were McGraw, Col. J.P. Shannon, Johns Hopkins Professor Edward Renouf, and Sheriff John B. Schwatka, who "was the fortunate man to dig the first earth."[24] After the ceremony ended, "[t]he silvered spade was taken back to Robinson & McGraw's place of business with York road soil still adhering to it. It was hung up once more, and on a card depending from it are the words: 'I have done it.'"[25]

By the end of March 1901, final preparations were underway at the ballpark:

> A visit to the new grounds yesterday revealed a scene of activity which was crowded by all the men who could work comfortably in the space inclosed by the fences. Carpenters were busy preparing to put the roof on the grandstand, wagons were hustling in beams for the said roof and inside carpenters were putting finishing touches to the administration building, which is ready for the fittings.
>
> In the field a dozen horses were pulling around a varied assortment of agricultural instruments having for their object the leveling and packing of the outfield. On the diamond were about a score of rural-looking individuals with rakes, hoes and shovels making ready the sod and neatly adjusting any slight irregularities in the surface. These farmer folk allowed that the ground would not be ready for business for some ten days or more, but McGraw says that he will be ready to open there with Yale on April 5, and if there is any danger of the present force being inadequate he will find room for still more men.[26]

Several exhibition games preceded American League Park's major-league debut, including one on April 13, with the Orioles hosting the Maryland Athletic Club at 2:45 P.M., followed by a lacrosse match between Johns Hopkins University and the University of Pennsylvania at 4 P.M.[27] American League Park debuted on April 26, 1901, with the Orioles taking on the Boston Americans. The *Baltimore Sun* noted that many of the Boston players were well known to Baltimore fans: "Manager Collins and Outfielder 'Chick' Stahl were members of the Boston team of 1897, that defeated Hanlon's Champions and kept them out of their fourth successive championship in that famous series at Union Park, which was witnessed by nearly 50,000 people for the three games, and which decided the pennant fight."[28]

"A parade preceding the game began at the Eutaw House on North Eutaw Street (now the site of the Hippodrome Theater) at 12:30 P.M., and proceeded [f]rom Eutaw House down Baltimore Street to Holliday, passing the City Hall to Lexington Street, to Calvert, to Fayette, to Howard, to Monument, to Charles, to Huntingdon avenue, to the York road, and thence to the grounds."[29] The *Baltimore Sun* elaborated:

> With a big parade, with appropriate ceremonies and with hearty enthusiasm will Baltimore welcome today the return of baseball to this city, after an absence of 18 months. The discredited and unpopular National League moved out of the city in October, 1899 – today the young giant of baseball, the American League, escorted by popular players – McGraw and Robinson – will make its first bow to the Baltimore baseball loving public. That the new major league and the new Orioles will receive a hearty welcome goes without saying.[30]

The parade consisted of "25 open carriages in line, besides two tallyho coaches and a phaeton, all of which will be used to transport baseball club presidents, managers, directors, the ballplayers themselves and members of local athletic and ball clubs, as well as lovers of the sport in general."[31] The Fourth Regiment Band, some 40 strong, provided music for the parade and, as a "notable feature." the parade included "50 butchers, wearing white aprons and mounted on horses," headed by Baltimore butcher George Wannensvetsch.[32]

As for the game itself, 10,371 tickets were sold in what was a standing-room-only sellout, with Ban Johnson throwing out the first pitch.[33] The Orioles defeated the Boston Americans 10-6, with Joe McGinnity on the mound for the Orioles.[34] John McGraw had Baltimore's first American League hit (a double) and scored the first run.[35] Boston's Cy Young pitched the second game at American League Park and the Orioles won that game too, 12-6.[36] Improvements to American League Park continued during the inaugural season. In June a "big blackboard" was painted on the center-field fence and arrangements were "made to have the scores of all the American League games bulletined there by innings while the local game is in progress."[37] In August the Orioles held a Ladies' Day at American League Park and declared it a "great success," as the Orioles defeated the Cleveland Blues 1-0.[38] The *Baltimore Sun* noted, "[T]he ladies' stand presented a very pretty picture yesterday," with 2,566 in attendance.[39]

In the waning days of the 1901 season, the *Baltimore Sun* looked back on the first year of the American League:

> The American League Season closes next week. After Milwaukee, Cleveland and Detroit will come to Baltimore, and with Detroit the season ends.
>
> The American League has had a successful season, contrary to the predictions of the National League and its friends, who said it would not last six weeks. The American has the distinction of being the only organization that ever made a successful fight against the National League.
>
> Manager McGraw is not ready to announce his team for next year, but expects to have something interesting to tell shortly.[40]

That first year, the Orioles placed fifth in the American League with a record of 68-65, 13½ games back.[41] Attendance for the season totaled 141,952 and the Orioles claimed to have lost only $8,000.[42]

In addition to college baseball, American League Park also was home to city Municipal League of Clubs during the 1901 season. In one such match, on May 19, the Park-Street Cleaning Department defeated the Subway Department 10-9.[43] On May 30 the Yanigan baseball team (begun by Orioles catcher Wilbert Robinson in the 1890s) played the Cuban Giants, a team composed of African-American players.[44] On July 4 about 1,400 spectators filled the ballpark to watch three games played between the Yanigans and the Lafayettes, a team composed of white players, and the Baltimore Giants and the Norfolk Red Stockings, both teams of African-American players.[45] On July 22 the Baltimore Giants played the Lafayettes in the deciding game of the championship of Baltimore City.[46] The Lafayettes defeated the Giants 17-7.[47] Sporting events at the ballpark during the fall of 1901 included a college football game between Maryland Agricultural College (the University of Maryland) and Johns Hopkins University.[48]

In March 1902 John Murphy, brother of the former Union Park groundskeeper Tom Murphy, was hired as groundskeeper at American League Park.[49] Murphy added to the ballpark "marking of the batsmen's positions with a sod line instead of a line of lime" and "[t]an bark walks about three feet wide" leading "from the players' benches to home plate."[50] Murphy likewise added "the words American League Park in sod" and "[c]ircles of tan bark near the players' benches that designate those stations by the words 'Home Club,' and 'Visiting Club' in letters of sod."[51] In addition, he installed a large horseshoe of tanbark and turf near home plate "with the words 'Good Luck' under it."[52]

Improvements to the ballpark structure included a space "opened between the grandstand and the boardwalk to the ladies stand which acts as a huge ventilator for the grandstand."[53] In addition:

> To accommodate the large numbers expected at the Baltimore grounds, there will be four entrances to the grounds. Two of these will lead to the grand stand; and two to the bleachers. The seating capacity at the park is over 7,000.
>
> Places in the infield are to be roped off so that be the crowd never so large all are to be properly cared for.
>
> When the gates are thrown open tomorrow, visitors will see some new and original features in the way of beautifying the grounds and arranging them for the convenience of the players.[54]

Opening Day 1902 was April 23, with a parade leaving Eutaw House, "preceded by mounted police and the officials of the clubs."[55] As they had before the opening of the ballpark in 1901, the players rode in carriages "to North street, to Lexington, to Calvert, to Fayette, to Howard, to Madison, to Charles, to Huntingdon avenue, to the York Road and thence to the grounds at York road and Twenty-ninth street."[56] By May the wheels of the Orioles season and ultimately its existence in Baltimore began their detachment from the carriages. On May 5 McGraw was suspended by Ban Johnson for "trouble which occurred at American League Park" during the final game of a series with Boston.[57] While McGraw was suspended by the league, groundskeeper Murphy continued his beautification of the ballpark.[58] To a new design of sod "in front of the grandstand with the names McGraw and Robinson worked in sod," he added the words "Keep Off."[59] Murphy's design proved both ironic and prophetic. In

• American League Park •

July 1902 McGraw departed for New York to become the player-manager of the National League Giants.[60] With him went groundskeeper Murphy and several players, including Joe McGinnity.[61]

After McGraw's departure, the Orioles lacked a sufficient number of players to field a team and Ban Johnson "declared Baltimore's franchise forfeited to the league."[62] Wilbert Robinson was named manager of the team and "a ragtag of utility men from other teams" were added "to play out the season."[63] As the 1902 season wound down, Robinson reported on the state of the league and the Orioles, stating, "I tell you the American League teams are playing great ball, and our team, with little to spur them on and the uncertainty of next year, was simply outclassed."[64] Attendance at American League Park plummeted, and at the end of the season Baltimore was in last place with a record of 50-88, 34 games behind the Philadelphia Athletics.[65] The Orioles faced Boston in the last game of the season at American League Park, with Boston winning 9-5 before a paid attendance of 138.[66] It was the last American League contest at that site.

In October 1902 Ban Johnson consented to the sale of American League Park as part of the property formerly owned by Baltimore's American League franchise.[67] As observed by the *Baltimore Sun*:

> This means the selling of all the stands and buildings at the new American League Park, at York road and Twenty-ninth street, and President Ban Johnson's attorney, Mr. Olin Bryan, formally consented to the receivership.
>
> The latter fact would seem to indicate that the American League had given up all idea of having a club here next year, though not necessarily, as it is barely possible, though highly improbable, that the American League expects to buy from the receivers.[68]

In November 1902 the grandstand chairs at American League Park were sold, conditionally, by an appointed receiver for 50 cents each.[69] In December Ned Hanlon, the Brooklyn manager and former Orioles manager, placed a bid to purchase American League Park.[70] Hanlon had toured the facility with National League President Harry Pulliam on December 15.[71] The sale of the property was held up momentarily, at least in part to await completion of a joint peace committee between the National and American Leagues.[72] According to the *Baltimore Sun*:

> In the interim local lovers of the national game will be kept in doubt as to whether Baltimore is to have a big league club in 1903. That it will have such a club either in 1903 or the next year is believed by everybody who takes any interest in the question, and Mr. Hanlon says that it is sheer nonsense to think that a city of 600,000 inhabitants can be ignored as a home for a big league team.
>
> The Union Park site must undoubtedly soon go as a baseball landmark and what has been known as American League Park will probably be available for years.[73]

Hanlon purchased American League Park from the receiver on December 31, 1902, for $3,000, with the hope of securing a franchise from another National League city or a possible expansion franchise.[74] Another option Hanlon considered was a franchise in the Eastern League.[75] In purchasing the ballpark contents, Hanlon gained ownership of the opera chairs that the receiver had conditionally sold for 50 cents apiece.[76] According to the *Baltimore Sun*, "Hanlon is believed also to have got a bargain, as $15,000 would be required to erect buildings similar to those now on the grounds and to put any grounds in condition."[77] According to Hanlon, "[c]hances are that this city will have a good club in a big league, but much will depend upon the joint peace committee of the American and National League."[78]

Hanlon's prophecy proved incorrect, with the exception of a Federal League franchise in 1914-1915, which Hanlon helped bring to Baltimore and install in a new ballpark built next to American League, Park across 29th Street. It was not until 1954 that Baltimore received its second American League franchise (the original 1901 Milwaukee franchise, which moved to St. Louis in 1902).

In 1903 Hanlon acquired an Eastern League franchise from Montreal and moved it to Baltimore.[79] Hanlon renamed the team the Orioles and the team moved into the former American League Park, now Oriole Park (IV), installing Wilbert Robinson as manager.[80] Opening Day included a parade to the ballpark and a first pitch by Henry Chadwick, the New York baseball scribe and inventor of the box score.[81] Former Orioles shortstop Hughie Jennings joined the team in July, playing first base for the Orioles. The team played respectable baseball during its first few years in existence, placing fourth, second, second, and third from 1903 to 1906.[82] In 1906 Hanlon purchased the grounds on which the ballpark sat, as well as a parcel adjoining the ballpark, in hopes of bringing a major-league team to Baltimore.[83]

In October 1907 many of the former National League Orioles returned to Baltimore to celebrate their 1894-1896 championship seasons.[84] A game was played at Oriole Park (IV), preceded by a parade commencing at Eutaw House.[85] As noted by the *Baltimore Sun*, the event was a huge success for the city:

> Never has Baltimore been more enthusiastic over a baseball game than yesterday, when, after a parade through the principal streets of the city, witnessed by thousands of homecomers and faithful rooters, the three-time champions and the present Orioles played an interesting game at Oriole Park.

The festivities began Sunday night, when the old idols of the diamond arrived at the Eutaw House, where they gathered in a crowd and exchanged reminiscences of the days that used to be.[86] The "old Orioles" who played the game at Oriole Park included John McGraw, Willie Keeler, Hughie Jennings, Kid Gleason, Joe Kelley, Jack Doyle, Dan Brouthers, Steve Brodie, Heinie Reitz, Wilbert Robinson, Boileryard Clarke, Bill Hoffer, Sadie McMahon, George Hemming, and Tony Mullane, with Ned Hanlon as manager.[87]

Hanlon's hopes of bringing a major-league team to the former American League Park did not materialize and, in 1908 he sold the team and the ballpark to Jack Dunn, a former American League and Eastern League Oriole, for $70,000.[88] In 1909 "Dunn moved home plate from near Greenmount Avenue (where batters faced into the afternoon sun) to the lot's northwest corner."[89] He also scheduled games on Sundays in a ballpark he built in Baltimore County at Back River Park, to avoid Baltimore City's blue laws.[90] In 1914 Dunn famously acquired Babe Ruth, who pitched in Oriole Park (IV) as a member of the International League Orioles, until he was sold in August to the Boston Red Sox, and then played for their International League affiliate in Providence.

Dunn needed the money, for earlier that year, Hanlon had helped bring to Baltimore a new Federal League franchise, the Terrapins, who played in a new ballpark next to Oriole Park (IV) across 29th Street.[91] The Terrapins and the Federal League lasted just two seasons, 1914 and 1915, and after the league's demise, Jack Dunn purchased Terrapin Park from Hanlon and moved his International League Orioles to the former Federal League ballpark.[92]

Beginning in January 1916, Billy Sunday, an evangelist and former baseball player, erected a tented tabernacle on the site of the former ballpark.[93] As of April 1919, baseball still was played at the former site of Oriole Park (IV), with the Oriole Athletic Association sponsoring games there.[94] A McDonald's restaurant and two-story row houses fronting both sides of LIchester Road, constructed after the demise of American League Park/Oriole Park (IV), now cover the former ballpark site.[95]

Notes

1. Byron Bennett, "Baltimore's First American League Park – Original Home of the Future New York Yankees," https://deadballbaseball.com/2012/08/baltimores-first-american-league-park-original-home-of-the-future-new-york-yankees/ (accessed June 8, 2021).

2. Bennett, "Baltimore's First American League Park."

3. Bennett, "Baltimore's First American League Park."

4. Byron Bennett, "The Six Different Ballparks Known as Oriole Park," DeadballBaseball.com, December 30, 2013. https://deadballbaseball.com/2013/10/bugle-field-home-of-the-baltimore-elite-giants/ (accessed June 8, 2021).

5. Bennett, "The Six Different Ballparks Known as Oriole Park."

6. Bennett, "The Six Different Ballparks Known as Oriole Park."

7. "Baseball Directors Meet: J.J. McGraw Made Manager of the Team – Now to Get Grounds," *Baltimore Sun*, January 15, 1901: 6.

8. "Picking a Ball Ground: McGraw, Robinson and Johnson on a Land Hunt," *Baltimore Sun*, December 20, 1900: 6.

9. "Picking a Ball Ground."

10. James H. Bready, *Baseball in Baltimore, The First 100 Years* (Baltimore: Johns Hopkins Press University Press, 1977), 105.

11. Bready, 105.

12. "Ball Ground Leased: American League Park Is to Be the Name of It, Old Site on the York Road," *Baltimore Sun*, January 17, 1901: 6.

13. "Ball Ground Leased."

14. "Ball Ground Leased."

15. "Plans For Ball Park: Trip to American League Meeting, McGraw Signs Bresnahan," *Baltimore Sun*, January 26, 1901: 6.

16. "Athletic Funds For J.H.U.: Students to Equip Ball Ground with Lot," *Baltimore Sun*, February 15, 1901: 6.

17. "Ball Club and Varsity: Johns Hopkins Gets Fine Campus and Orioles a Gym at American League Park," *Baltimore Sun*, February 5, 1901: 6.

18. "Ball Club and Varsity."

19. "At American League Park: Liston's Good Work on Diamond – Double Fences Boys!" *Baltimore Sun*, March 19, 1901: 6.

20. "At American League Park."

21. "At American League Park."

22. "In Goes Silver Spade: Crowd Cheers When Ground Is Broken for Ball Field at American League Park," *Baltimore Sun*, February 13, 1901: 6.

23. "He'll Use a Silver Spade: Will Sheriff Schwatka in Breaking

American League Park

American League Park / Oriole Park (IV). Schedule for International League Orioles, June 8 to June 22, 1912, published by the United Railways and Electric Co., Trolley News. Courtesy of David B. Stinson.

Ground for Baseball Park," *Baltimore Sun*, February 12, 1901: 6.

24 "In Goes Silver Spade."

25 "In Goes Silver Spade."

26 "Orioles to Practice: McGraw to Have Them at Electric Park on Monday," *Baltimore Sun* March 30, 1901: 6.

27 Classified ad, *Baltimore Sun*, April 13, 1901: 1.

28 "Now, Play Ball! American League Season Opens with a Hurrah Today: Boston Against the Orioles," *Baltimore Sun*, April 24, 1901: 6.

29 "Now, Play Ball!"

30 "Now, Play Ball!"

31 "Thus Baseball Starts: Big Band, Four-Horse Carriages and Joyful Rooters," *Baltimore Sun*, April 22, 1901: 6.

32 "Thus Baseball Starts."

33 Bready, 107.

34 Burt Solomon, *Where They Ain't, the Fabled Life and Untimely Death of the Original Baltimore Orioles, the Team That Gave Birth to Modern Baseball* (New York: The Free Press, 1999), 207.

35 Solomon, 207.

36 Bready, 107; baseball-almanac.com/teamstats/schedule.php?y=1901&t=BO1.

37 "Notes of the Diamond," *Baltimore Sun*, June 11, 1901: 6.

38 "It Was Ladies' Day: One Reason Suggested Why the Birds Play

Great-Ball," *Baltimore Sun,* August 17, 1901: 6.

39 "It Was Ladies' Day."

40 "Baseball's Waning Season: Double-Headers with Brewers, Then Cleveland, Then Detroit," *Baltimore Sun,* September 21, 1901: 6.

41 Bready, 107.

42 Bready, 107.

43 "Maryland Contests," *Baltimore Sun,* May 20, 1901: 6.

44 "Sporting Miscellany," *Baltimore Sun,* May 30, 1901: 6; "Yanigans, 28; Cuban Giants, 2: Captain Bobby's Aggregation Meets a Colored Club at Union Park to Play Ball," *Baltimore Sun,* July 17, 1897: 6.

45 "White Players and Black: Yanigans Beat Norfolk Reds Badly, Lafayettes and Giants Even," *Baltimore Sun,* July 5, 1901: 6.

46 Sporting Miscellany, *Baltimore Sun,* July 22, 1901: 6.

47 "Lafayettes, 17; Giants, 7," *Baltimore Sun,* July 23, 1901: 6.

48 "Good for Farmers: Johns Hopkins Able to Score but Six Points on Them, Agriculturals Fight Hard," *Baltimore Sun,* October 20, 1901: 6.

49 "Jennings Not to Play Here: Secretary Goldman Says Rumor Is Untrue – Plans For Opening," *Baltimore Sun,* April 12, 1902: 6.

50 "Ready for the Game: American League Park Spruced Up for the Opening, Unique Designs in Flowers," *Baltimore Sun,* April 22, 1902: 6.

51 "Ready for the Game."

52 "Ready for the Game."

53 "Ready for the Game."

54 "Ready for the Game."

55 "It Comes Off Today: Band Will Play and the Orioles Will Hustle for Runs," *Baltimore Sun,* April 23, 1902: 6.

56 "It Comes Off Today."

57 "John McGraw's Suspension: Friends Nettled at Johnson's Act – Manager Refuses to Talk," *Baltimore Sun,* May 6, 1902: 6.

58 "Beauties of American League Park," *Baltimore Sun,* May 10, 1902: 6.

59 "Beauties of American League Park."

60 Bready, 108-109.

61 Bready, 108-109.

62 Bready, 110.

63 Bready, 110.

64 "Orioles at Home Again: Manager Robinson Says American League Is a Wonderful Success," *Baltimore Sun,* September 12, 1902: 6.

65 Bready, 110.

66 Bready, 110.

67 "Will Old League Buy? Receivers Appointed to Sell the Stands at New Baseball Park," *Baltimore Sun,* October 21, 1902: 6.

68 "Will Old League Buy?"

69 "Grandstand Chairs Sold, American League Park Receivers Get 50 Cents Each for Them," *Baltimore Sun,* November 8, 1902: 6.

70 "Hanlon Still Waiting, Regarded as Bidder for American League Park," *Baltimore Sun,* December 21, 1902: 6.

71 "Pulliam in Baltimore, He Looks Over Ball Parks With Manager Edward Hanlon," *Baltimore Sun,* December 16, 1902: 6.

72 "Skirmish for Ball Park, Local Promoters Waiting for the Outcome of Peace Negotiations," *Baltimore Sun,* December 23, 1902: 6.

73 "Skirmish for Ball Park."

74 "Hanlon's Ball Park Now, Brooklyn Leader Buys American League Club Out, Gives the Receivers $3,000," *Baltimore Sun,* January 1, 1903: 9.

75 "Hanlon's Ball Park Now."

76 "Hanlon's Ball Park Now."

77 "Hanlon's Ball Park Now."

78 "Hanlon's Ball Park Now."

79 "Promise a Good Team: Hanlon to Have One in the Eastern League, Gets the Baseball Park," *Baltimore Sun,* January 30, 1903: 9.

80 "Promise a Good Team."

81 Bready, 116.

82 Bready, 116.

83 "Now Owns Oriole Park, Mr. Hanlon's Purchase May Mean Big-League Ball Here Soon," *Baltimore Sun,* November 23, 1906: 9.

84 "Big Baseball Games, All the Old and New Players Are Rounded Up, a Luncheon to Homecomers," *Baltimore Sun,* October 13, 1907: 10.

85 "Big Baseball Games."

86 "Lovefeast for Old Ones, Banquet Precedes the Parade of the Rival Teams," *Baltimore Sun,* October 15, 1907: 10.

87 "Lovefeast for Old Ones."

88 Bready, 116-117

89 Bready, 116-117; "Dunn as Team Owner: Jack Wants to Buy Local Club's Franchise, Hanlon Says He Will Sell, but the Manager Declares He Must Get 'Proper Price,'" *Baltimore Sun,* October 8, 1909: 10; "Hanlon Is Sole Owner," *Baltimore Sun,* November 11, 1909: 10; Jack Dunn Buys Orioles: Former Manager Is Sole Owner of Baltimore Baseball Club, Old Robbie Is a Director, Charles H. Knapp Is Third Director and Secretary and Treasurer – New Faces to Be Seen," *Baltimore Sun,* November 17, 1909: 10.

90 Bready, 118.

91 "Big League Plan Launched: Articles of Incorporation of Federal Club Sent to Annapolis," *Baltimore Sun,* October 28, 1913: 16.

92 Byron Bennett, "Baltimore's Other Major League Ballfield – Terrapin Park/Oriole Park,": DeadballBaseball.com, December 6, 2012. https://deadballbaseball.com/2012/12/baltimores-other-major-league-ballfield-terrapin-parkoriole-park/ (accessed June 8, 2021); Bennett, "The Six Different Ballparks Known as Oriole Park."

93 "Paving Way for Sunday: Evangelist's Constructor and Advance Agent Arrive, Work on Tabernacle to Begin, Season of Neighborhood Prayer Meetings Starts This Evening – Registering Choir Members," *Baltimore Sun,* January 4, 1916: 3.

94 "Will Use Old Oriole Park," *Baltimore Sun,* April 13, 1919: CA15.

95 Bennett, "Baltimore's First American League Park – Original Home of the Future New York Yankees."

Baltimore Orioles Win Home Opener in a New Major League

April 26, 1901: Baltimore Orioles 10, Boston Americans 6, at American League Park

By Jimmy Keenan

In late January of 1901, American League President Ban Johnson convened a series of organizational meetings at the Grand Pacific Hotel in Chicago. The purpose of the gatherings was to iron out the final details in preparation for the launching of his new major league. Seven years earlier, Johnson, a Cincinnati sportswriter, had become president of the Western League, a very competitive minor circuit. In 1900, Johnson changed the name of the loop to the American League. The following year, claiming major-league status, he added teams from Baltimore, Boston, Philadelphia, and Washington.

A few weeks before Johnson's Chicago sessions, the Baltimore contingent elected its own officers and directors and authorized the construction of a ballpark. Third baseman John McGraw, one of the club's stockholders, would serve as the player-manager.

McGraw's Orioles, named after two previous major-league franchises in Baltimore, held spring training at Hot Springs, Arkansas. After a few weeks of practice and signing additional players, McGraw's squad came back to Baltimore in early April to take part in a series of exhibition games.

The Orioles' Opening Day opponent, the Boston Americans, led by player-manager Jimmy Collins, held their preseason workouts in Charlottesville, Virginia.

Following two consecutive rainouts, the Orioles finally crossed bats with the Americans on April 26, 1901. The game was played at American League Park (Oriole Park IV), located at what is now the southwest corner of Greenmount Avenue and 29th Street.

Beginning at 1 P.M., a procession of nearly 50 carriages started out from the Eutaw House Hotel at the northwest corner of Baltimore and Eutaw streets. American flags were draped from buildings along the parade route as fans of all ages lined the streets. Led by a detail of mounted policemen, the caravan of horse-drawn conveyances included team executives, players from both teams in uniform, sportswriters, politicians, union leaders, and other local baseball enthusiasts.[1]

More than 10,000 fans, a good-sized crowd for an early twentieth-century major-league game, were waiting at the ballpark. Ropes were strung along both foul lines to hold back the overflow of spectators. Lavish floral arrangements, which would be presented to the players at various stages of the game, lined the perimeter of the grandstands.

After a short practice session followed by the pregame festivities, Ban Johnson tossed out the ceremonial first pitch. Then the Orioles took their positions on the diamond. Joe "Iron Man" McGinnity, recovering from a recent bout of malaria, was the starting pitcher for the Orioles. (He reportedly earned the nickname due to his previous employment in an iron factory.) Beginning his third year in the majors, McGinnity was coming off back-to-back 28-win seasons and a total of more than 700 innings pitched. This durability would be a common theme throughout his career.

McGinnity's batterymate was Wilbert Robinson. The reliable backstop for Baltimore's National League champion Orioles, Robinson once caught 26 innings in one day during a tripleheader sweep of the Louisville Colonels in 1896. It would have been 27 except that the third game was called in the eighth inning because of darkness.

Boston's leadoff hitter, Tommy Dowd, started the contest with a bounder up the middle that McGinnity snagged for the first out. The next batter, Charlie Hemphill, swung down on a ball that landed in front of home plate before bouncing straight up in the air. McGinnity ran in from the pitcher's box, fielded the ball, then fired to first to catch Hemphill by a step.

Hemphill may have been taking a page from the 1890s Orioles playbook by attempting the famous "Baltimore Chop" to get on base.[2]

McGinnity, using to great effect the side-arm rising curveball he called "Old Sal," held the opposition scoreless for the first three frames. On the Boston side, pitcher Win Kellum was making his major-league debut. The southpaw hurler had been a 20-game winner with the Western League's Indianapolis Hoosiers in 1900. Baltimore's first batter, McGraw, received a three-minute ovation as he walked to the plate. The tough New Yorker acknowledged the crowd and greeted Kellum with a double off the top of the right-field fence.

Turkey Mike Donlin followed with a three-base hit over center fielder Chick Stahl's head that scored McGraw. (Donlin's turkey-like gait earned him the barnyard moniker.) After a walk to Jimmy Williams, Bill "Wagon Tongue" Keister smacked a double to right that scored Donlin and Williams.[3]

"A great ovation was given to Robbie and Mac when they stood together in the second inning and were presented with a beautiful floral tribute. Their names were inscribed on yellow and black ribbon which hung from the design" was how one local sportswriter described the tribute the two Orioles received from the fans.[4]

Baltimore added another run in the bottom of the third on Donlin's second triple of the game and a fly ball by Williams.

Boston scored in its half of the fourth. Jimmy Collins got things started with a liner between short and third that was good for two bases. With Buck Freeman at bat, Wilbert Robinson tried to pick Collins off second but nobody was covering the bag. The ball sailed into center field, and Collins scampered to third. Freeman knocked Collins in with a base hit to left. Robinson made amends soon after by throwing out Freeman by 10 feet on an attempted steal of second.

In the sixth, Keister drove a triple through the gap in right-center. After a walk to Cy Seymour, the Orioles reverted to some inside baseball. Seymour took off for second as Kellum released his pitch. The batter, Jimmy Jackson, playing in his first major-league game, protected the runner with a swing and a miss. Keister, on third, headed for home as Boston catcher Lou Criger unleashed his peg to second. Criger's throw was high, allowing Seymour to slide in safely while Keister crossed the plate. Jackson followed with a double that knocked in Seymour for the Orioles' sixth tally of the game.

After enduring seven innings of one-run ball, the Boston bats began to show signs of life in the eighth. With McGinnity tiring, Criger and Kellum reached base via a double and an infield hit. An RBI single by Dowd and a fly ball by Collins accounted for a pair of Boston runs before McGinnity retired the side.

In the Orioles' half of the inning, Keister ignited the offense again with a single to center. The next batter, Seymour, bunted for a base hit. Jackson followed with an RBI double. After a walk to Frank Foutz, Robinson swatted a grounder to third that Collins missed, allowing two runs to score. A pair of force outs pushed Foutz home with the Orioles' final run of the game.

Things got a bit dicey for Baltimore in the top of the ninth. With one out, Hobe Ferris hit a ball past first baseman Foutz. Williams, at second, backed up the play, but threw wildly to first, allowing Ferris to advance a base. After Criger got a hit, rookie catcher Larry McLean pinch-hit for Kellum and smacked a two-bagger that scored Ferris. Dowd followed with a grounder that Keister fumbled, and Criger came home. McLean scored on a fly ball before Stahl grounded out to end the game. Baltimore had won its first American League game, 10-6.

There were many defensive standouts that day. The Boston outfield of Dowd, Stahl, and Hemphill played too shallow on several occasions, but otherwise made some stellar grabs. For Baltimore, center fielder Jimmy Jackson hauled in everything in his territory, including a sensational shoestring catch off the bat of Collins in the sixth. The best play of all was made by McGraw in the third inning. Dowd sent a towering fly ball close to the third-base grandstand. McGraw, weaving his way through the blue-coated policemen stationed along the rope line, kept his concentration and gathered in the tough popup.

In regard to the Orioles' starting pitcher the *Baltimore American* wrote, "For seven innings McGinnity fooled the heavy hitting Bostonians, which was doing so well for a sick man that people are apt to wonder what the Iron Man will do when he quite recovers his health."[5]

After the game Boston player-manager Jimmy Collins told reporters, "Our boys will do better work after they get into the strides. You couldn't judge much by today's game."

Baltimore Orioles Win Home Opener in a New Major League

Although the 1901 season started off on a good note for Baltimore, the relationship between the manager and Ban Johnson deteriorated rapidly. Due in part to his contempt for Johnson's American League umpires, McGraw left the Orioles in July of 1902 to join the National League's New York Giants.

A mass player exodus soon followed, leaving Baltimore unable to put nine men on the field. Johnson asked other American League clubs to send players to Baltimore so the Orioles could play out the schedule. At the end of the 1902 campaign, Baltimore's American League franchise was transferred to New York. Originally called the Highlanders, this team is now known as the New York Yankees.

Author's Note

The Baltimore newspapers have varying accounts of what Boston runner was thrown out stealing by Wilbert Robinson for the third out in the fourth inning, Buck Freeman or Freddie Parent. By comparing the game accounts in the Boston and Baltimore newspapers Freeman was on first base when Parent was put out on a fly ball for the second out in the fourth. Freeman was then caught stealing for the last out of the inning.

Sources

In preparing this game account, the author consulted contemporary newspaper articles from the following newspapers: *Baltimore American, Baltimore Morning Herald, Baltimore Morning Sun, Boston Globe, Boston Herald, Boston Journal,* and *Sporting Life.*

Notes

1. The cavalcade traversed the principal streets of the city—Baltimore, Holliday, Lexington, Calvert, Fayette, Howard, Monument, Charles, Huntington Avenue, then finally out to York Road (present-day Greenmount).

2. Baltimore groundskeeper Tom Murphy was known to pack hard clay around the plate at Union Park, the home grounds of the great National League Orioles. When the Orioles batters chopped at the ball it would bounce high off the clay. By the time the opposition could make a play, the runner was usually safe. Whether the team's groundskeeper in 1901, Marty Lyston, employed the same tactic at American League Park has been lost to history.

3. The true origins of Keister's unusual nickname are up for debate. Was it his use of the Wagon Tongue model bat or his propensity for salty language? It was quite possibly a combination of the two.

4. "Orioles Made An Easy Start," *Baltimore American*, April 27, 1901: 10.

5. "Orioles Made An Easy Start,"

Turkey Trots to a 6-6 Day at the Plate

June 24, 1901: Baltimore Orioles 17, Detroit Tigers 8, at Oriole Park IV

By Kevin Larkin

John McGraw, the third baseman-manager of the Baltimore Orioles, led a team that included future Hall of Famers Wilbert Robinson, Roger Bresnahan, and Joe McGinnity as well as himself. Also a member of the team was Turkey Mike Donlin. Donlin got his nickname because of his strutting walk and red neck.[1] Donlin had played for the St. Louis Perfectos/Cardinals in his first two major-league seasons, 1899 and 1900, batting .323 and .326 and hitting a total of 16 home runs in baseball's Deadball Era.

Baltimore was hosting the Detroit Tigers in the third game of a four-game series. The Orioles had eked out a 4-3 win in the first game came away with a 10-3 victory in the second game.

As the 24th dawned, the Orioles, with a record of 22-20, were in fifth place in the American League, 4½ games behind the first-place Boston Americans (28-17). Detroit (27-23) was in third place, 3½ games behind Boston.

On the mound for George Stallings' crew in game three was right-hander Roscoe Miller, who had debuted in the major leagues on April 25. In his rookie year Miller would lead the Tigers in wins (23), winning percentage (23-13, .639), shutouts (3), and innings pitched (332).

Getting the start for the Orioles was right-hander Frank Foreman, who had made his major-league debut in 1884 for the Chicago/Pittsburgh franchise in the Union Association. The highlight of his career came in 1889 when he won 23 games for the Baltimore Orioles of the American Association, the only time in his career that he won 20 or more games.

After the game was over, the headlines in the paper could have read "Miller's Massacre" or perhaps "Detroiters Demolished," because Baltimore had beaten Detroit 17-8, with Donlin the chief tormenter, with a 6-for-6 day.[2]

Before Donlin was an Oriole he had acquired a reputation for demolishing pitchers' self-esteem and his performance in this game might have made people forget about all of his previous performances.[3] Against the Boston Beaneaters on June 2, 1900, Donlin reached Boston twirlers for three singles, a triple, and a home run as he and his St. Louis teammates went down to defeat at the hands of the Beaneaters, 17-16.[4]

On June 24 Orioles got four runs in the first inning, thanks to hard hitting and a couple of errors by the Tigers.[5] They scored six more runs in the second inning to take a 10-1 lead. Inning three saw Baltimore score three runs on a triple, a double, and two singles and go ahead 13-1.

Foreman allowed just one run in the first five innings, but the Tigers bats came alive for six runs in the sixth.[6] Foreman was driven out of the game. Third-year right-hander Joe McGinnity replaced Foreman and held the Tigers to one run the rest of the way.[7]

In the bottom of the sixth Baltimore added two runs to make the score 15-7. In the eighth inning Detroit plated its eighth run and Baltimore got two to come away with a 17-8 victory.

The 22 hits in eight innings by the Orioles for 35 total bases set an American League record.[8]

The Tigers were led on offense by Ducky Holmes, catcher Al Shaw, and Roscoe Miller, who each had two hits in the loss. Miller took the loss on the mound going the full nine innings, allowing all 17 runs and all 22 hits. He walked three batters, and hit two. The game was witnessed by just 2,000 spectators.

The only player who did not have a hit for Baltimore in the game was McGinnity, who had only one at-bat. Starting at the top of the lineup, John McGraw had one hit as did Roger Bresnahan (triple), first baseman Jimmy Hart, and Foreman (triple). Jimmy Williams (triple), Jack Dunn (the same Jack Dunn who would

Turkey Trots to a 6-6 Day at the Plate

discover a young left-hander by the name of George Ruth), and catcher Wilbert Robinson all had two hits. Those with three hits for the Orioles were Cy Seymour (double) and outfielder Jimmy Jackson.

Another feature of the game was the play at first base of the Orioles' Hart, who handled 13 chances without an error.

Donlin's six hits included two triples and two doubles. He scored five runs. Before this game a player had collected six or more hits in a game 49. Fred Tenney on May 31, 1897, and Barry McCormick on June 29, 1897, each had eight hits in a game.

After the loss, Detroit (27-24) and Baltimore (23-20) were tied for third place in the American League standings, 4½ games behind the Chicago White Sox, who had moved into first place past the Beaneaters.

The colorful Donlin[9] finished his 11-year major-league career in 1914 with the New York Giants, after playing for the Cincinnati Reds, the Beaneaters, and the Pittsburgh Pirates. His .333 career batting average placed him 28th on the all-time list, just behind Eddie Collins and Paul Waner and just ahead of Stan Musial and Wade Boggs.

At the end of the inaugural American League season, the Tigers were in third place with a record of 74-61, 8½ games behind the first-place White Sox. The Orioles (68-65) were in fifth place, 13½ games behind Chicago.

The Orioles played just the 1901 and 1902 seasons in the American League before league President Ban Johnson decided to move the team to New York to compete with the National League Giants. The Orioles became the New York Highlanders, and later the Yankees. Except for the upstart Federal League in 1914 and 1915, Baltimore remained a minor-league city until 1954, when the St. Louis Browns relocated there.

Sources

In addition to the game story and box-score sources cited in the Notes, the author consulted the Baseball-Reference.com and Retrosheet.org. websites

Notes

1 Michael Betzold and Rob Edelman, "Mike Donlin," SABR Biography Project, sabr.org, accessed June 2, 2019.

2 "Orioles Now Third," *Baltimore Sun,* June 25, 1901: 6.

3 "Orioles Now Third."

4 "Orioles Now Third."

5 "Miller an Easy Mark," *Detroit Free Press.* June 25, 1901: 10.

6 "Orioles Now Third."

7 "Orioles Now Third."

8 "Orioles Now Third."

9 He was cocky and self-assured, and when he wanted to be, also a damn fine ballplayer who appreciated his own worth. He once asked McGraw for a $500.00 raise, and when the manager refused, he "retired" and went on the road with his wife, actress Mabel Hite, as part of a husband/wife act. Thedeadballera.com/BeerDrinkersMikeDonlin.html. See also Donlin's biography at the SABR BioProject: sabr.org/bioproj/person/3b51e847#_edn1.

McGinnity Gives Two Spits Over Umpire's Calls

August 21, 1901: Detroit 9, Baltimore Orioles 0 (Forfeit), American League Park, Baltimore

By Chad Osborne

"Game forfeited to the Detroits," umpire Tommy Connolly shouted as a band of policemen whisked him off the field, away from the angry mob and into his dressing quarters.[1]

The room had become a familiar place for Connolly in Baltimore, and the yawps of impassioned players and fans a familiar tune.

Connolly, they surmised, missed an easy call in the fourth inning on this Wednesday afternoon when Orioles third baseman Jack Dunn zipped down the first-base line on an infield grounder. Dunn's foot touched the first-base bag just before the throw arrived, Orioles players and their fans thought. Dunn was safe, they believed, but Connolly called him out.[2]

"It was the spark that started the blaze," the Baltimore Sun reported the next day.[3]

The Baltimore players voiced their frustration to Connolly. Most demonstrative, it turned out, was Orioles star pitcher Joe McGinnity. As players argued with the arbiter, fans poured out of the American League Park grandstand and bleachers wanting – again – a piece of Connolly. His umpiring had been suspect the entire game, and during Monday's and Tuesday's contests, and a few other games in the last couple of weeks.

In the heat of the fuss, McGinnity stomped at Connolly's feet and spewed two shots of tobacco juice directly into Connolly's face, the umpire claimed.[4]

Spectators in the new ballpark on the corner of Baltimore's 29th Street and York Road had grown tired of Connolly's inconsistencies. They had seen enough, and wanted another word with the ump. The scene soon turned chaotic. Baltimore Police Captain Charles W. Gittings[5] and about 40 other officers quickly moved to surround and protect Connolly. They knew the routine. This was the fifth time Connolly needed protection from the Baltimore crowd in six games over a two-week span.[6]

Most of the attacks on Connolly were verbal, but 25-year-old Frank J.T. Allen, a clerk and loyal Orioles supporter, struck the umpire. Sergeant Max Mauer arrested Allen, who later in the day was fined $20 plus court costs.[7]

A couple of players – one from each side – also found themselves in police hands. One eager patrolman arrested Orioles shortstop Bill Keister for breach of peace although Keister was merely looking on, the *Sun* reported.[8]

Detroit's Kid Elberfeld, for some unexplained reason, ran toward Connolly as the mess was beginning, but not meaning to get involved. Rushing by him was an Orioles player who nudged the diminutive Tiger into one of the rookie police officers. "The new 'sleuth' seemed bent on doing something heroic, and when he rushed up, Elberfeld was the first who came within reach," the Sun reported. "Grabbing the inoffensive little shortstop by the collar, he trotted him off across the field at double-quick. The prisoner protesting volubly."

Later that day, Justice White at the Northern Police Station fined Keister $1 and court costs for his charge of disturbing the peace. The judge dismissed Elberfeld's case.[9]

Despite minor disturbances – if you can call getting tobacco juice in your face minor – Connolly escaped unharmed as police rushed him to his dressing area. As he left the field, he yelled the forfeit announcement, giving Detroit, which was already winning the contest 7-4, the victory.

Connolly stayed in the dressing room, with a policeman guarding its door, recovering from the ruckus and likely wiping tobacco juice from his mug. Police guarded Connolly for more than an hour, waiting for the offended to disperse.

They didn't budge.

So Gittings and his crew cleared the ballpark. As the

crowd walked away, police officers ushered Connolly to a carriage, which had been ordered by Orioles President Sidney Frank. The carriage, flanked by mounted policemen, hurried away carrying Connolly, Frank, and club director Miles Brinckley. Connolly's carriage could not, however, escape the hisses and hollers from fans still in the streets.

The *Baltimore Sun* reporter covering the game suggested that Connolly's delusions extended beyond the baseball field and that he, perhaps, had a greater impression of himself than was deserved. He wrote: "Some wag suggested that in his coach with outriders Connolly would more than ever imagine himself a czar and the crowd outside a band of nihilists."[10]

Orioles players, fans, and even the press felt they had legitimate gripes with Connolly. The umpiring throughout the season, the Sun surmised, had been "remarkably good."

"But in these last two series, Connolly's work has been so flagrant as to incense the spectators beyond control," the newspaper wrote. "Whether right or wrong, players and spectators believe that Connolly has intentionally given Baltimore the 'worst of it,' and every close decision against Baltimore lately, whether right or wrong, has added fuel to the flame."[11]

Earlier in the August 21 contest, with Baltimore leading 3-2, Detroit loaded the bases. Doc Casey smacked a long fly ball off Orioles pitcher Harry Howell. Everyone in the park, it seemed, saw the ball fly foul. Tigers baserunners stopped running, thinking they needed to retreat to their bases and await the next pitch to the switch-hitting Casey.[12]

Connolly, however, saw the ball's flight differently and barked, "Fair ball."[13] His judgment gave Casey a grand slam and it boosted Detroit to a 6-3 advantage. The call made the crowd furious and added another spark that soon ignited the blaze.[14]

Some criticism of the umpire came, too, from the Detroit players. The *Baltimore Sun*'s game stories of the previous two days were littered with details of ways Connolly blew calls.[15]

A day before Wednesday's game, Orioles Secretary Harry Goldman suggested to Connolly that he ask American League President Ban Johnson to move him out of Baltimore for his safety. Connolly refused. That same day, Baltimore player-manager John McGraw, who suffered a season-ending knee injury that same day,[16] wired a letter to Johnson. If Connolly stays, the letter read, he could cause tremendous tumult.[17]

Johnson stuck up for his umps, and that included suspending McGinnity indefinitely for his actions against Connolly.[18] "His alleged offense," the *Baltimore Sun* reported, "expectorating in Umpire Connolly's face." The *Sun* fearfully speculated that the suspension, which was thought then to possibly be for the remainder of the season, would drive McGinnity, who the paper said was "never a 'rowdy,'" out of Baltimore and back to Brooklyn's National League team, where he had played the year before. It would kill what small chances the "Orioles had to win the pennant."[19]

Johnson, meanwhile, had plenty to say to the press regarding players' and fans' treatment of umpires, claiming arbiters could benefit from words of encouragement and less criticism.

"The vaporings of a partisan press, and the wild utterances of a disgruntled manager or player should not be taken seriously," Johnson told the *Chicago Record-Herald*. "The best means to secure good umpiring is to keep the players away from the official. … The way to secure the best results from an umpire is to encourage him in his work rather that abuse him."[20]

Heeding the suspension, the Orioles played on without McGinnity. And on a trip west to Chicago, the star pitcher and McGraw, newly fitted into his leg cast, paid a humble visit to Johnson at his office. "McGinnity confessed that he violated the rules and had also been guilty of conduct hurtful to the game, but he pleaded that his offense was not so serious as to warrant his expulsions," the *Baltimore Sun* reported.[21]

After now having heard both sides of the argument, Johnson said, "I expect McGinnity to be pitching next week," the article said.

Days later, Johnson stuck to his word and reinstated McGinnity on the condition that the pitcher pay a fine to the American League office and give an apology to Connolly. McGinnity agreed and pitched the same day, tossing a shutout against Milwaukee.[22]

"That is all there is to it," Johnson said of his decision. "Circumstances, I find, were not all against the pitcher, and as he shows a disposition to rectify his wrong, I am glad to put him back in the game."[23]

The *Detroit Free Press* disagreed, and advocated for a longer suspension for McGinnity. "A man who will spit in another man's face is not fit for any society," the paper wrote. "If a ballplayer can't be a gentleman he should not be allowed to play, but should be sent back to carry the hod."[24]

A newspaper reporter caught up with Connolly days after McGinnity's suspension was overturned. He was umpiring the Orioles' latest series in Cleveland, but had yet to hear from the pitcher. "And I don't care to see him," Connolly said. He would be willing to overlook a player, in the heat of the moment, punching him in the face or hitting him with a "rib roaster," he said.

"My hand would go out to him in forgiveness in a moment," Connolly said. "But when, as in McGinnity's case, a man leaves the bench, rushes up to me and deliberately spikes me and spits in my face, as he did, twice in succession, I do not care for his apology."[25]

Sources

The author used Baseball-Reference.com in addition to sources cited in Notes.

Notes

1. "Ends in Small Riot," *Baltimore Sun*, August 22, 1901: 6.
2. "Ends in Small Riot."
3. "Ends in Small Riot."
4. "Connolly Still Angry," *Topeka State Journal*, September 6, 1901: 2.
5. *The Baltimore Sun Almanac*, 1910, 14. The *Sun* article from August 21, 1910 mentions Gittings only by his rank and surname. The Almanac lists him as Charles W. Gittings, a captain in the Northeastern district.
6. "Ends in Small Riot."
7. "Ends in Small Riot."
8. "Ends in Small Riot."
9. "Ends in Small Riot."
10. "Ends in Small Riot."
11. "Ends in Small Riot."
12. "Ends in Small Riot."
13. "Ends in Small Riot."
14. "Ends in Small Riot."
15. "One from Detroit," *Baltimore Sun,* August 20, 1901: 6; "They Could Not Hit," *Baltimore Sun*, August 21, 1901: 6.
16. "McGraw Out for the Season," *Baltimore Sun*, August 23, 1901: 6. Doctors told McGraw "he would have to have his knee incased in a plaster cast and lie in bed for three weeks," the *Sun* reported, "and that he could not play again this year."
17. "Ends in Small Riot."
18. "McGraw Out for the Season."
19. "M'Ginnity Is Driven Out," *Baltimore Sun*, August 23, 1901: 6.
20. "Discipline in Baseball," *Detroit Free Press*, August 26, 1901: 8.
21. "M'Graw and Johnson Meet," *Baltimore Sun*, August 31, 1901: 6.
22. "M'Ginnity Is Reinstated," *Baltimore Sun*, September 4, 1901: 6.
23. "M'Ginnity Is Reinstated."
24. "Timely Sporting Gossip," *Detroit Free Press*, September 8, 1901: 9.
25. "Connolly Still Angry."

Little Napoleon vs. the Czar

June 28, 1902: Baltimore Orioles 9, Boston Americans 4 (8 innings), at American League Park, Baltimore

By Chris Corrigan

On a gloomy afternoon, more than 3,000 fans settled down in American League Park.[1] The forecast for June 28, 1902, called for rain. But clashing personalities, not weather, ended the game early.

Little Napoleon

The new Orioles had been a franchise only since 1901, when they finished three games over .500 but were still 13½ games out of first place. The 1902 season was worse; they were 26-30 before this game was played. The team finished in last place.

Managing the Orioles was the pugnacious "Little Napoleon," John McGraw. As a player with the old Baltimore Orioles, McGraw was one of the best leadoff men of the era. He batted .320 for nine consecutive years, led the league in runs scored and walks, and stole 436 bases. He and the Orioles won three National League pennants in a row from 1894 through 1896. But they, and McGraw, were known more for a strategy of cheap tricks and intimidation.

The early Orioles (1882-1899) were infamous for nasty play, and McGraw was one of their nastiest players. They held onto runners by their pants loops, spiked basemen, and notoriously baited, insulted, and belittled umpires.

"Our Baltimore club had a reputation as umpire fighters," McGraw remembered. "I guess we did make life pretty miserable for some of them. ... It was our second nature to fight for the smallest point, and as a consequence, the umpires often had to take the brunt of our wrath."[2]

"The Orioles," remembered former umpire and National League President John Heydler, "were mean, vicious, ready at any time to maim a rival player or umpire if it helped their cause. The things they would say to an umpire were unbelievably vile, and they broke the spirits of some fine men."[3]

The Czar

The National League contracted from 12 to eight teams in 1900, disbanding Baltimore's franchise. Western League President Ban Johnson saw an opportunity and relocated his teams to the vacated cities. He renamed his operation the American League and declared it equal to the National League, whose players he stole, enticing them with more lucrative contracts.[4] McGraw agreed to be a player-manager for the new Baltimore club and insisted on having an ownership stake in the team. Johnson accepted the terms.[5]

Johnson's reputation for totalitarian control of the American League earned him the nickname of "Czar."[6] He detested rowdyism, promising more wholesome play to attract fans. He supported his umpires' decisions and quickly suspended players who acted out. "My determination was to pattern baseball in the new league along the lines of scholastic contests, to make ability and brains and clean, honorable play, not swinging of clenched fists, coarse oath, riots or assaults upon the umpires decide the issue."[7] Johnson's baseball was not the game McGraw played.

After Johnson directed a series of suspensions and fines against the Orioles, McGraw suspected that he was targeting Baltimore's team. "As President of the American League, [Johnson] was constantly picking on the Baltimore club," McGraw asserted. "Setting me down for frequent suspensions and frequently disciplining other players. His severity was unusual and unjust, I thought. This crippled us considerably."[8]

Tensions came to a head on June 28, 1902.

The Rundown

Tommy Connolly umpired the game, the first of a two-game series against the Boston Americans. Connolly and the Orioles had a history: In 1901, he ruled that McGraw had interfered with a runner and allowed the run to score. That day, Connolly needed a police escort to leave the field.[9]

Joe McGinnity took the hill for Baltimore, and Cy Young for Boston. McGraw was in the lineup at third base for the first time in five weeks after being spiked in the knee in Detroit.[10]

Before the fifth inning, McGinnity was in control, allowing only one run on five hits. Meanwhile, whatever residual pain may have been in McGraw's knee didn't affect him at the plate. He led off the game with a triple and scored when center fielder Joe Kelly got a base hit. In the seventh McGraw bunted for a hit, stole second, and reached third on an error. The Orioles had a three-run lead going into the sixth inning. But Cy Young limited the damage and kept Boston in the game long enough for the wheels to come off McGinnity.[11]

In the sixth, Boston manager-third baseman Jimmy Collins hit a single. Center fielder Chick Stahl followed with a double. Buck Freeman, who would lead the league in RBIs in 1902, drove them both home. After McGinnity secured two outs, Freddy Parent singled and was driven in by Lou Criger's double.

McGraw tried to stop the bleeding in the seventh by giving the ball to right-hander Jack Cronin. Cronin walked left fielder Patsy Dougherty, Collins got another hit, and both men were driven in when Stahl hit a triple. It was 8-4, Boston.

Then came the eighth inning.

With Baltimore at the plate, first baseman Dan McGann lined a base hit into center field. Next came an infield hit by Cy Seymour. Young tried to hold McGann on second base but overthrew the ball past the defender, allowing both runners to advance.

Baltimore utility catcher Roger Bresnahan followed with a grounder on the third-base side. With McGann on third, Seymour on second, and Bresnahan on his way to first, McGann broke for the plate. With no one out, if Collins opted to take the sure out at first, McGann would score a run. However, if McGann could sustain a rundown between Collins and Boston catcher Criger, Bresnahan would make it to first safely and Seymour would be able to advance on the play.

"We always took chances," McGraw later remembered. "There is always an advantage in taking those chances. It puts the other fellow in the worry about what to do."[12]

A Pair of Suspenders

Few in the audience paid attention to what the other runners were doing. While everyone watched Collins and Criger try to catch McGann, Seymour went to third.[13]

Seeing that Bresnahan had made it to first safely, McGann broke back for third and Seymour retreated for second. McGann slid safely into third. For a brief moment, the Orioles had the bases loaded with no one out.[14]

Quickly, Boston shortstop Freddy Parent called for the ball and tagged Seymour on second base, arguing to Connolly, the umpire, that Seymour had run past third but failed to retouch it when he ran back to second. Connolly agreed and called Seymour out. McGraw ran out to argue.[15]

The *Baltimore Sun* insisted that "McGraw did not talk roughly to the umpire, nor was he as strenuous as he has been on numerous occasions this year when he was not penalized."[16] The *Boston Globe*, on the other hand, insinuated that McGraw threatened to hang Connolly.

Whatever was said, Connolly ejected McGraw, but the Baltimore manager refused to go. The umpire then declared the game a forfeit to Boston.

The *Globe* insisted that it was fortunate that the police were on the scene to protect the players and Connolly from the "enraged" Baltimore fans.

Ban Johnson suspended McGraw two days later. "I am convinced Umpire Connolly was absolutely right," he stated. "He knew what he was doing and because he knew the rules, I am glad he maintained his position and humiliated Mr. McGraw."[17]

McGraw was not surprised to hear the news: "Ban is a great suspender. Why, he's almost a pair of suspenders."[18]

"Johnson is down on Baltimore and would like to see it off the map," McGraw said during the suspension. "I am sick and tired of the whole business and I don't care if I never play in the American League again."[19] McGraw left the Orioles, going to the Giants, promising on record not to tamper with the Baltimore club on his way out.[20]

Little Napoleon vs. the Czar

However, Joe Kelly and McGraw sold their ownership of the Orioles to Kelly's father-in-law, Sonny Mahon. Mahon turned around and sold those holdings to the Cincinnati Reds and New York Giants. Immediately, both clubs began transferring talent from Baltimore to their respective clubs. By July 17, Baltimore was unable to field a team against St. Louis and was forced to forfeit its second game in 15 days.[21]

The next year, Ban Johnson moved the Orioles to New York, where they would later become the Yankees. Although the Yankees eventually came to dominate the sport, for nearly two decades the Giants would be Gotham's main attraction.

Winning 10 pennants and three World Series, the Giants led New York baseball in attendance for 15 of the next 20 years.[22] Only in 1920, with the help of Babe Ruth, did the Yankees consistently surpass their crosstown rivals in popularity.

McGraw and the Giants faced the Yankees in the 1921 World Series. He welcomed the team that was once his Baltimore Orioles to the big stage by beating them five games to three.

Sources

In addition to the sources cited in the Notes, the author consulted Baseball-Reference.com.

Notes

1. "Forfeited to Boston," *Baltimore Sun*, June 29, 1902.
2. John McGraw, *My Thirty Years in Baseball* (New York: Boni and Liveright, 1923), 78.
3. Charles C. Alexander, *John McGraw* (Lincoln: University of Nebraska Press, 1995), 55.
4. Joe Santry and Cindy Thomson, "Ban Johnson," Society for American Baseball Research, sabr.org/bioproj/person/dabf79f8, accessed November 15, 2019.
5. Alexander, 77.
6. "M'Graw and Johnson: Talk of Trouble Being Fomented by American League's Enemies," *Baltimore Sun*, July 29, 1901.
7. Frank Menke, "Life of Ban Johnson," installment number 1, quoted in Eugene C. Murdock, *Ban Johnson: Czar of Baseball* (Westport, Connecticut: Greenwood Press, 1982), 39.
8. McGraw, 130.
9. "Make a Poor Start," *Baltimore Sun*, August 16, 1901.
10. "'Mugsy's Way," *Boston Globe*, June 29, 1902.
11. "Forfeited to Boston."
12. McGraw, 88.
13. "Forfeited to Boston."
14. "Forfeited to Boston."
15. "Forfeited to Boston."
16. "Forfeited to Boston."
17. "Ban Suspends Again," *Baltimore Sun*, July 1, 1902.
18. "Ban Suspends Again."
19. "Baseball Change Expected: McGraw's Tilt with Ban Johnson May Let New York Secure Him as Manager," *New York Times*, July 3, 1902.
20. "M'Graw Has Release," *Baltimore Sun*, July 9, 1902.
21. Jimmy Keenan, "Joe Kelly," Society for American Baseball Research, sabr.org/bioproj/person/17b00755, accessed November 15, 2019.
22. Keenan.

Two Teams Going in Very Different Directions

September 29, 1902: Boston Americans 9, Baltimore Orioles 5, at American League Park (Oriole Park IV)

By Bill Nowlin

Monday, September 29, was the last day of the American League's 1902 season. The National League wrapped up its season with a Sunday doubleheader in St. Louis on October 5. There was only the one game in the AL played on the 29th. The last-place Baltimore Orioles hosted the Boston Americans, who were in third place, seven games behind the champion Philadelphia Athletics. The game meant nothing for either team in terms of its place in the standings.

Both teams were led by future Hall of Famers. Catcher Wilbert Robinson had taken over from John McGraw as manager of the Orioles around the end of June.[1] This September game was Robinson's last as a player. Jimmy Collins managed the Bostons. Collins played third base and managed for the next four seasons.[2]

The game was played in an atmosphere that was "almost like a funeral," as described by a subhead in the *Baltimore Sun*.[3] The Coal Miners Glee Club was on hand to entertain the crowd, but the crowd itself numbered a scant 138, said the *Sun*. The Orioles' season had fallen apart. There had been optimism at the outset, but while "starting full of hope last April," the team's "best players were repeatedly laid off on charges of misbehavior on the ball field." The *Sun* hinted at a conspiracy theory that may have obtained: "These things may not have been intended for the obliteration or removal of the club, but they would have made a good starter if such an object had been intended. Next came injuries to players, and next a match of wits between President Johnson, of the American League, and Manager McGraw, of the Orioles. ... McGraw left and disrupted the playing strength of the nine. Patchwork was tried. It has failed."

It had been learned in late August that the AL planned to field a team in New York City, and not field one in Baltimore.[4] That home games later in the season drew small crowds was not surprising.

The Orioles had lost the season opener, in Boston, on April 19, when the Bostons scored four runs in the bottom of the ninth and won, 7-6. There had been such turnover on the Baltimore ballclub during the season that Robinson was the only player in the lineup for both the first and last games of the Orioles' season. Indeed, at the tipping point of the midseason turmoil, the Orioles had forfeited their July 17 home game to the visiting St. Louis Browns because only five players had come to American League Park for the game. The club itself therefore forfeited its franchise "by failure of the team to appear for play."[5] The league acted quickly, and the same newspaper article reported that "a new team has been gotten together with the assistance of the other clubs in the organization."[6] For instance, pitcher Lewis "Snake" Wiltse – who started the September 29 game for the Orioles – was "contributed" by the Philadelphia Athletics. Jack Katoll, the left fielder in the last game, had been contributed by the Chicago White Sox. Harry Arndt came from Detroit, and Lew Drill from Washington.

The Orioles played on July 18 with what the *St. Louis Post-Dispatch* referred to as an "improvised Baltimore aggregation."[7] Ban Johnson was on hand in Baltimore and planned to stay for a while, "directing the affairs."[8]

The September 30 *Boston Globe* was understandably not impressed with the competition. "To win from the disorganized Orioles was the easiest sort of task for Collins' men, and they did it with such complete ease that the game was totally lacking in interest."[9]

Lefty Snake Wiltse started for the Orioles. Right-hander Tully Sparks pitched for the visitors. But, said the *Globe*, "Selbach, Gilbert, and Williams were out of the game, and Wiltse knew that the team for which he was pitching had no earthly chance to win."[10] Kip

Selbach was the regular left fielder, Billy Gilbert the shortstop, and Jimmy Williams the second baseman. Pitcher Jack Katoll played left field. Another pitcher, Ike Butler, played eight field.

Still, it was a game. Boston batted first and scored twice in the top of the first inning on singles by Patsy Dougherty and Buck Freeman and an error by third baseman Jimmy Mathison. Baltimore scored once in the second. In the third inning, though, Boston scored five times. Dougherty, Freddy Parent, Chick Stahl, Buck Freeman, and pitcher Tom Hughes (who played right field in the game) each collected base hits which, combined with Orioles errors, resulted in the five runs. It was a relatively error-free game for the times; each team committed three.

The Orioles put across another run in the bottom of the fourth on base hits by Harry Arndt and Jimmy Mathison, and a sacrifice fly by Wiltse. They added two more in the sixth when Arndt walked and Mathison singled to left, Arndt reaching third base and Mathison taking second on a bad throw in by Dougherty. Then Robinson doubled to deep left field, driving them both in.

The Orioles scored another run in the bottom of the seventh when Katoll singled and Harry Howell doubled to center field. Two outs followed, but then Katoll scored on a throw that Parent dropped. It was 7-5, not at all a game that appeared quite as hopeless as both major newspapers seemed to suggest. Though the gap had closed to two runs, however, there was an evident lack of anything approaching excitement in the "crowd" – which numbered only about five times the combined number of the two ballclubs. A dispatch to the *Boston Herald* dubbed it "a listless, careless event."[11]

Boston scored twice in the top of the eighth to pad its lead, and that ended the scoring.

The Orioles had 11 base hits in the game, three of them by Robinson. Katoll, Howell, and Arndt each had a pair. For Boston, Patsy Dougherty's 5-for-5, all singles, accounted for a third of Boston's 15 hits. Stahl, Freeman, and catcher Lou Criger each had two base hits. Sparks had a two-base hit, the only one for extra bases for the Americans.

Wiltse struck out two; Sparks stuck out three. Each pitcher walked one. There were six stolen bases in the game, five of them by Boston.

Tommy Connolly was the umpire. The game lasted 1:30.

It had to be depressing to have only 138 fans in attendance. The Glee Club "chirruped" their best songs, but "their notes went up into the big, empty grandstand, mixed up with the rafters there and returned by the echo route, sound like a dirge for the departed glories of baseball in old Championtown."[12]

These were, indeed, two teams going in very different directions. One to become a world champion team the very next year, and the other to something like oblivion. Or New York City.

When it was all over, it was all over, "and the Baltimore club had ended the most disastrous season in its career. It finished, for the first time since it had learned the delights of championship, absolutely in last place."[13] The Orioles finished at 50-88, 34 games out of first place. Ominously, the hometown paper suggested that the team "may fall off the map."[14]

And so it did. The 1903 season was without major-league baseball in Baltimore. The franchise had been forfeited, and Ban Johnson had overseen the formation of a new eighth team in the American League, in New York City, known as the Highlanders and later the New York Yankees. That new team became one of some renown, though it wasn't until 1923 that it won its first World Series.[15]

It was only in 1903 that the World Series as we now know it began. It was the Boston Americans who won that World's Series (as it was called) from the Pittsburgh Pirates, becoming the first World Series champions in baseball. Boston won the American League pennant again in 1904, and John McGraw's Giants declined to play them, effectively allowing Boston to remain as world champions until the World Series became an annual event in 1905.

There was baseball played in Baltimore, of course, but the city did not have its own major-league team until more than half a century later, when the St. Louis Browns franchise relocated to Baltimore in time for the 1954 season.[16]

Sources

In addition to the sources cited in the Notes, the author relied on Baseball-Reference.com and Retrosheet.org. Thanks to David B. Stinson and John Thorn for suggestions for greatly improving this article.

Notes

1 After several serious disagreements with AL President Ban Johnson, McGraw was "suspended indefinitely" by Johnson. McGraw negotiated his unconditional release to the Baltimore club and essentially jumped back to the National League, leaving the Orioles in midseason to become the third manager of the 1902 season for the New York Giants. See some of the background in John Thorn, "The House That McGraw Built," ourgamemlblogs.com, February 29, 2012. ourgame.mlblogs.com/the-house-that-mcgraw-built-2bf6f75aa8dc. Regarding McGraw's suspension, Burt Solomon wrote: "McGraw had counted on being suspended – planned on it, in fact. Ten days earlier he had slipped away to New York at Andrew Freedman's invitation. They had met in the Tammany man's private office. When McGraw brought his lawyer in, Freedman objected to discussing private business before a stranger. Mac insisted that if Freedman's clerks could sit in the next room and listen, his lawyer could sit in, too.

"Freedman had a scheme in mind – to snatch John McGraw and Joe Kelley for the National League. Even Freedman's enemies among the National League magnates had seen the genius in the plan. It would cripple the American League. McGraw, more than anyone, had turned the Western League into the American League by giving it a strong eastern presence. Luring him back to the National League was something Freedman's colleagues would help him pay for. As a war measure, so to speak." Burt Solomon, *Where They Ain't, The Fabled Life And Untimely Death of the Original Baltimore Orioles, The Team That Gave Birth to Modern Baseball* (New York: The Free Press, 1999), 226-231.

2 His last game was August 25, 1906. At that point, with the team 35-79, Chick Stahl took over as manager. The team went 14-26 under Stahl, who committed suicide during spring training in 1907. Robinson later managed the Brooklyn Dodgers from 1914 to 1931, during which time they were sometimes known as the Robins, in his honor.

3 "Farewell Baseball," *Baltimore Sun*, September 30, 1902: 6. All quotations from the *Sun* come from this article.

4 John Thorn writes, "On August 25, Johnson announced what McGraw had already known: the AL's intention to move the Orioles to New York in 1903, with Clark Griffith as the Americans' manager." John Thorn, "The House That McGraw Built." The planned New York AL team was already being assembled at the time. See "Signs Players for New York," *Chicago Tribune*, August 27, 1902: 6.

5 "New Club Ready," *Boston Globe*, July 18, 1902: 5.

6 "New Club Ready."

7 "Burkett's Star Catch Gave Browns Victory," *St. Louis Post-Dispatch*, July 19, 1902: 3. James H. Bready wrote, "[W]ith a roar, Johnson declared Baltimore's franchise forfeited to the league. The AL's founder-president moved in a ragtag of utility men from other teams to play out the season. Wilbert Robinson was left in charge (at ballpark and bistro)." James H. Bready, *Baseball In Baltimore, The First 100 Years* (Baltimore: Johns Hopkins Press, 1998), 106-113.

8 "On a Firm Footing," *Boston Globe*, July 19, 1902: 5.

9 "Last of the Season," *Boston Globe*, September 30, 1902: 5.

10 "Last of the Season."

11 "Boston's Last Game," *Boston Herald*, September 30, 1902: 5.

12 "Farewell Baseball."

13 "Farewell Baseball."

14 "Farewell Baseball."

15 The Highlanders were not the Orioles reconstituted. Griffith was the manager. Only five players on the 1903 Highlanders had been on the 1902 Orioles – Ernie Courtney, Harry Howell, Herm McFarland, Jimmy Williams, and Snake Wiltse.

16 David B. Stinson points out that McGraw and Robinson, along with other principals at the time – Ned Hanlon and Joe Kelley all ended up back in Baltimore – at New Cathedral Cemetery. See David B. Stinson, "New Cathedral Cemetery and the Four Hall of Fame Baltimore Orioles," March 21, 2012, at davidbstinsonauthor.com/2012/03/21/new-cathedral-cemetery-and-the-four-hall-of-fame-baltimore-orioles/.

Bugle Field

By Bill Johnson

Baltimore in the early part of the twentieth century "languished in ballpark poverty."1 The city, once home to one of the finest squads in the professional game, had hosted only minor-league teams since 1902, and the existing ballparks of the time were not top-notch facilities. Many of the local ballfields were more "field" than "athletic venue," often with little more than simple wooden bleachers behind the team benches, while other sites were simply too small. As Robert Leffler wrote, "Maryland Park, for many years a favorite among African-American fans, became a junk lot. Oriole Park at 29th and Greenmount was segregated for International League games and, though possibly available to black teams on a rental basis, seated only 10,495. … Municipal Stadium – constructed of earth, cement and wood in 1922 to compete with Philadelphia for the yearly staging of the Army-Navy (football) game – accommodated 70,000 football fans; it did not have a baseball diamond."2

So in 1912, when Edward C. Lastner, an ambitious employee of the Simpson and Doeller Company, a firm that printed labels for cans, approached his boss, Harry Doeller Sr., about sponsoring an industrial-league baseball team, the latter gave Lastner $100 and an admonition that "the rest is up to you."3 In a 1954 retrospective interview, Lastner filled in some of the details of the field's origin:

"Well, we heard of a cow pasture east of Belair road just across the city line, off what is now Edison highway. And we found that it really was a cow pasture. There were ten or eleven fine Guernseys there, the property of a local dairy owned by Mrs. Carrie Snyder. But she agreed to rent us the field for $25 a year. Every night after quitting time, we'd take rakes and shovels and work to level the ground. When this was finished, we realized we'd have to have a grandstand if we wanted to get a crowd and make some money. But, of course, it would cost plenty of money to erect a grandstand and we didn't have it. We solved this problem by holding a series of raffles in Northeast Baltimore, around Gay street, with Morris chairs as prizes.

So the grandstand was built. It had a seating capacity of 520, it cost $450 – and it had a roof. Right away we began packing them in because the field was convenient to Northeast Baltimore and you could get there either by walking or riding a little jerkwater streetcar. … The second year … we still had to chase the Guernseys off the diamond before we could play. That year our biggest games were on Sunday, which meant bigger crowds because Sunday baseball was not permitted in the city. As many as 2,500 people would come out to the field. …"4

The field was named for the company's team, the Label Men, and dubbed the Label Men Oval. On that diamond, the Label Men won the Baltimore city championship four times between 1912 and 1917.5

On a modern (ca. 2019) map, the field was located on the northeast corner of the intersection of Federal Street and Edison Highway (currently 1601 Edison Highway). Back in 1918, however, it was just another ballfield on the eastern edge of the city. That year, with the work force drain imposed by the war effort in Europe and following the devastating influenza epidemic, the company sold its pasture lease to Dr. Edward J. Cook, whose ballclub, St. Andrews, used it as a home field until 1924.6

In 1924 "Papa" Joe Cambria bought the lease from Cook.7 Cambria had recently purchased the Bugle Coat and Apron Supply Company, one of the largest dry cleaners in the region, from the Bugle family.8 Cambria intended to use the former pasture to host the company baseball team, the Bugle Coat Apron Nine, and he named the field Bugle Field. In addition to baseball games, Cambria brought in high-school, college and professional football, rodeos, boxing, and even lacrosse to the venue.[9] In 1932 Cambria added lighting for night games, and extended the grandstands down the foul lines to accommodate more paid admissions. According to Cambria's biographer, Brian McKenna, he also "purchased a pair of ponies to walk the streets of Baltimore displaying advertising for the club." He also joined with George Rossiter to buy the Baltimore Black Sox of the East-West League, but the club disbanded.[10] The next season, Baltimore joined the Negro National League, but that effort failed due to competition from Ben Taylor's Baltimore Stars and an independent team that also called itself the Black Sox.

There are no official records of measurements of Bugle Field's dimensions or seating capacity, but a former sandlot player, Paul Bonomo, remembered that it was 420 feet in right field and 389 feet in left.[11] A 1932 article in the *Evening Sun* notes that Bugle offered 3,900 seats,[12] but later modifications raised the capacity to somewhere in the neighborhood of 7,000. Although there was no formally segregated seating, Bob Luke noted that "black fans preferred seats behind home plate, and whites tended to sit in the baseline bleachers. … [P]eople tended to sit among their own race."[13]

The Nashville Elite Giants were a team without a home in 1935, and in 1936 and 1937 they scheduled several games in Baltimore.[14] By 1938, after temporary auditions in both Columbus, Ohio, and Washington, D.C., the marriage with Baltimore became official. Tom Wilson's team changed its name to the Baltimore Elite Giants, and adopted Bugle as their home field. With the Elites playing most of their local schedule at Bugle Field, which was situated in a largely Negro section of Baltimore, the facility thrived. Still, it was a relatively small arena, and opportunities to bring in revenue were always en vogue with Cambria. After the 1943 season, in order to generate additional revenue, the Elite Giants challenged a team of genuine minor-league all-stars, named the International All Stars, to a seven-game series in Baltimore. The Giants won the series six games to one, and attendance thrived.[15] The team also allowed a number of sub-lessors to share the field as well, including the Maryland Amateur Baseball Association,[16] the Maryland Scholastic Athletic Association (football),[17] and the less organized sandlot Interclub League.[18]

The opening of the 1944 season was another highlight in Bugle's history. A reported crowd of about 7,000 filled the available seating as the Elite Giants welcomed Roy Campanella and Pee Wee Butts back from World War II, and from time playing in Mexico. The following evening, an even larger crowd, estimated at 8,000, overflowed the seats to watch Baltimore take on the mighty Homestead Grays.[19] That Grays team was a powerhouse, led by Josh Gibson, Buck Leonard, and Jud Wilson, and featuring immortals like Cool Papa Bell, Vic Harris, Piper Davis, and Ray Brown. This, then, was the caliber of baseball available in East Baltimore thanks to Bugle Field.

In the 1940s, Oriole Athletic Club boxing promoter Matt Reinhold managed Bugle Field. He frequently reassured the Elite Giants that they need not worry about access, that no other white club would want such a relatively small arena, but team ownership continued to seek opportunities to buy the field outright. This seeming instability had no adverse effect on the team's performance. In 1948, the year of what proved to be the final Negro World Series, the Elite Giants took on the Homestead Grays in a seven-game series.

In Game Three, after a pair of Baltimore losses, the Elite Giants found themselves staring into the figurative baseball abyss, tied with the Grays, 4-4, at 10:52 P.M. According to league rules, no inning was permitted to start after 11:15 P.M. The Elite Giants misinterpreted this to mean that any game lasting beyond 11:15 would be suspended and replayed from the start the next day. Facing a 3-0 series deficit, and seeing their pennant chances deteriorate, Baltimore played the delay gambit and simply stopped making outs in hopes of stretching the game past 11:15. "I threw the ball to right field instead of throwing to first base and let 'em run," Frazier Robinson, the Elites catcher, said. "We let 'em run all the runs they wanted to run just so we could prolong the inning."[20]

The game ended at 11:15, and Baltimore fully expected to replay the entire game on Saturday. The Negro National League president, Rev. John H. Johnson, "instead ordered the two teams to resume the game."[21] Baltimore immediately protested the ruling and refused to play the game pending a full hearing on the matter. On Sunday, September 19, the Elite Giants won their game 11-3, but ended up forfeiting Game Three. Homestead went on to win the series, and moved on to play (and win) the World Series against Birmingham.

A year later, in 1949, Bugle Field hosted the first games of the now-consolidated Negro American League championship series, the second played on September 18, 1949. The Elite Giants were prodigiously talented, with a roster that included Joe Black, Junior Gilliam, Lester Lockett, and Leon Day, and swept the four-game series. The two games against the American Giants were the final baseball games played at Bugle, as the Elite Giants took to the road for the remainder of the series against Chicago. In August 1949, the current owners, the Gallagher sisters (their financial footing derived from real-estate trading), who had purchased the team from Cambria in 1947 as his interests expanded beyond the Mid-Atlantic, sold the former pasture to the Lord Baltimore Press. "The day after the campaign was over … wreckers moved on the old wooden stadium."[22] On September 30 and October 1, 1949, the following ad, auctioning lumber from Cambria's labors, ran in the *Baltimore Sun*:

> WRECKING BALL PARK – Used 2x4 to 8x8, 10, 60 foot Creosoted poles, plus other lumber. Apply Bugle Field. See Mr. Reinhold PE 0371.[23]

The final sporting event at Bugle was a local soccer match on December 28,[24] and the ballpark's story ended with a whimper instead of a bang. Today, there is no trace of the old baseball field, and as of 2019 the property was occupied by a fabric manufacturer, Rockland Industries.

Bugle Field was not only a community gathering grounds, where amateurs could play baseball, soccer, football, and the like, but was one of several Baltimore professional baseball venues between 1924 and 1949, and it hosted some of the highest caliber of baseball of the day. The Elite Giants' rosters of the time included players like Biz Mackey and Roy Campanella, and the organization hosted a string of baseball immortals at Bugle such as Buzz Clarkson, Pat Patterson, Art Pennington, Willie Wells, Mule Suttles, Monte Irvin … the list of spectacular players who crossed the lines at Bugle Field goes on and on. Bugle was, by any measure, never the most spectacular venue in town, or on the respective league circuit, but it sat in the midst of a baseball-hungry section of Baltimore, and served both its tenants and visitors equally well throughout its relatively brief life.

Former Site of Bugle Field at Federal Street and N. Highland Avenue, January 2020.
Courtesy of David B. Stinson.

Notes

1. Robert V. Leffler, "Boom and Bust: The Elite Giants and Black Baseball in Baltimore, 1936-1951," *Maryland Historical Magazine* (Summer 1992): 171-198.
2. Leffler.
3. Bob Luke, *The Baltimore Elite Giants* (Baltimore: John Hopkins University Press, 2009), 27.
4. Edward C. Lastner, "I Remember Bugle Field and The Label Men," *Baltimore Sun*, March 29, 1953: 12.
5. Lastner.
6. Lastner, 30.
7. Brian McKenna, "Joe Cambria" SABR BioProject, sabr.org/bioproj/person/4e7d250, accessed November 13, 2019.
8. Joanna Sullivan, "Linen Firm Closing Shop," BizJournals.com, July 13, 1998. bizjournals.com/baltimore/stories/1998/07/13/story6.html. Accessed November 18, 2019.
9. Luke, 30.
10. McKenna.
11. Luke, 161.
12. "Black Sox, All-Stars Set to Open Fall Ball Series," *Baltimore Evening Sun*, September 24, 1932: 9.
13. Luke, 31.
14. Leffler, 172.
15. Luke, 85.
16. "Full Sandlot Schedule Listed for Bugle Field," *Baltimore Sun*, July 21, 1942: 14.
17. "Maryland Scholastic Association Football Schedule, 1946," *Baltimore Evening Sun*, September 12, 1946: 37.
18. "Sandlot Loop to Open 40th Season," *Baltimore Sun*, April 30, 1939: 28.
19. Leffler, 177.
20. Luke, 1.
21. Luke, 1.
22. Leffler, 181.
23. Byron Bennett, "Bugle Field – Home of the Baltimore Elite Giants," Deadball Era, https://deadballbaseball.com/2013/10/bugle-field-home-of-the-baltimore-elite-giants/ (accessed June 8, 2021).
24. Bennett.

Terrapin Park/Oriole Park (V)

By David B. Stinson

Terrapin Park, also known as Oriole Park (V), was the home of the Federal League Baltimore Terrapins in 1914 and 1915, and of the International League Orioles from 1916 to 1944.[1] It was located at the northwest corner of what is now Greenmount Avenue (formerly York Road) and 29th Street, across the street from the site of Oriole Park (II) and (IV).[2] First base paralleled East 29th Street, right field paralleled Greenmount Avenue, left field paralleled East 30th Street, and third base paralleled Vineyard Lane.[3]

Ned Hanlon, the manager of the National League Orioles from 1892 to 1898, played an important role in bringing major-league baseball back to Baltimore in 1914. After the 1899 season, Baltimore lost its National League franchise when the league contracted from 12 teams to eight. An inaugural member of the American League in 1901, the Orioles played only two seasons in Baltimore. In December 1902, after the demise of the American League Orioles,[4] Hanlon purchased American League Park for $3,000.[5] In 1903 Hanlon acquired an Eastern League franchise from Montreal and moved it to Baltimore.[6] Hanlon renamed the team the Orioles and the team moved into the former American League Park, rebranded as Oriole Park,[7] installing former National League Oriole Wilbert Robinson as manager of the team.[8]

While owner of Baltimore's Eastern League Orioles, Hanlon was also manager of the National League Brooklyn Superbas from 1899 to 1905, and the National League Cincinnati Reds in 1906 and 1907.[9] His hopes of bringing a major-league team back to Baltimore at the former American League Park never materialized and, after the 1909 season, Hanlon sold the team, and the ballpark, to Jack Dunn, a former American League and Eastern League Oriole, as well as one of Hanlon's Brooklyn Superbas' star pitchers.[10]

In 1913 the Federal League was formed as an independent league with six teams located in the Midwest.[11] In October 1913 Baltimore was offered a franchise in the Federal League for the 1914 season.[12] As observed by the *Baltimore Sun*:

> This is considered the time to step into a new major league that has a chance to become as good as any. If Baltimore lets the chance slip, it may have to resign itself to being a minor league town for the balance of its day.[13]

On October 27, 1913, Baltimore filed its Federal League Articles of Incorporation, which called for issuance of both preferred and common stock.[14] As for the location of the team's ballpark, the *Sun* reported the likelihood of building on a tract of land owned by Hanlon just across the street from Oriole Park (IV):

> Those interested in the club have an option on a fine tract for a ball park, lying just northwest of the present Oriole Park, although it has not definitely been selected. The ground belongs to Edward Hanlon, former manager of the champion Orioles.
>
> The proposed ground is that upon which was situated the old Brady mansion for a time used as a school-house. It is said that not a great amount of grading will be necessary as the elevation is such that the bleachers could be built upon it without much excavation
>
> The ground is 90 feet west of York road and on the east extends from Twenty-ninth to Thirtieth street, a distance of about 400 feet. The land runs westward to Gilmer Lane, a distance of about 600 feet. Gilmer lane runs at an angle of about 45°, making the plot irregular.

• Terrapin Park/Oriole Park (V) •

"Terrapin Park, Federal League, Baltimore Md," postcard published by The Chessler Company. Courtesy of David B. Stinson.

If the ground is selected, there will be a triangle used for automobiles. It is said that the grandstand may be placed along Gilmer lane and Twenty-ninth street and that the sun would thus never strike the patrons. The bleachers could be arranged so that the sun would strike them from the side.

Mr. Hanlon's counsel has just completed arrangements for the purchase of a small piece of land at Gilmer lane and Twenty-ninth street, which thus gives Mr. Hanlon a field considered very desirable.

Wherever the park is located, the plans are to build a better stand than Baltimore has ever had and to have a seating capacity on all stands of at least 15,000.[15]

Baltimore officially was admitted to the Federal League on November 1, 1913.[16] The team reviewed plans for the ballpark on November 7, 1913.[17] As reported in the *Baltimore Sun*:

> According to the plan as presented, the grandstand would be built near the southwest corner of the lot, curving behind the home plate. At either end pavilions are proposed and in right field a bleacher stand. If the grandstand is built with an upper deck, a total seating capacity will be about 10,000. If a single decker is built, the seats will be 3,000 to 4,000 fewer.
>
> Behind the grandstand is a space that it is proposed to make a parked place for automobiles.[18]

On November 12, 1913, Hanlon was elected a director of the Baltimore Federal League club and reportedly purchased "a considerable amount of the stock."[19] Hanlon told the *Baltimore Sun*:

> "This is not the first time that I have tried to bring big league ball back to this city and I know something of the difficulties. If we make no effort to break the present monopoly in organized baseball, Baltimore seems permanently side-tracked in a league from which no matter how many stars we might develop they would promptly be taken away to strengthen teams in cities perhaps smaller than Baltimore."[20]

As a director of the Baltimore franchise, Hanlon insisted that the team sell $10 shares of the corporation to encourage fan participation in the club itself, giving each stock owner full voting power and a first lien on the club's property, plus 7 percent dividends.[21] At the end of December 1913, the team selected Hanlon's tract of land and Hanlon completed his purchase of additional land necessary to construct the new Baltimore Federal League ballpark:

> The Feds have selected the lot just in the rear of Oriole Park, which is owned by Ned Hanlon. It was not until yesterday that the deal was put through for a small tract which was necessary to make a suitable ball ground.
>
> Hanlon yesterday purchased from James Keelty and his wife a tract beginning at the southeast corner of Gilmer lane and Thirtieth street measuring 73.8 by 293 feet. The sale was made in fee simple and the title was examined by the Title Guarantee and Trust Company.
>
> With all the necessary ground in their possession – for the directors of the local club have decided upon Hanlon's lot as the home of their team – it is probable that the work of grading and building the stands will begin in a very short time. The directors are not at all worried about having the grounds in tiptop shape for the opening of the championship season, for Hanlon has called their attention to the very short time required to transform old Union Park from a lot into a ball yard.[22]

The ballclub petitioned the First Branch City Council for an ordinance approving its plans for the ballpark at York Road on January 12, 1914.[23] The plans submitted by the team called for "a large wooden structure on steel supports in the triangle formed by the York road, Twenty-ninth street, Thirtieth street and Gilmer lane."[24] The ordnance specified additional details about the ballpark:

> The ordinance authorizes the club to build a grandstand 110 feet long, 65 feet high and 69 feet wide within the triangle. It is to extend east on Twenty-ninth street, a distance of 182 feet and 08 inches, and northeast on Gilmer lane 182 feet. There is to be a single deck stand on Twenty-ninth street, starting 20 feet east of the grandstand and extending parallel with Twenty-ninth street for a distance of 180 feet, and to be 85 feet high and 52 feet wide.
>
> Provision is also made for a single deck stand on Gilmer lane, 84 feet northeast of the grandstand, and to be 115 feet long, 38 feet high and 59 feet wide.
>
> The bleachers are to be on the York road, according to the plan filed with Building Inspector Stubbs by Architect Simonson, and they will be 145 feet long and 190 feet wide. There is to be another wooden stand for bleachers on Thirtieth Street.[25]

Construction of the new ballpark began on January 20, 1914, with a groundbreaking ceremony, featuring Baltimore Mayor James H. Preston and directors of the club.[26] Architect Otto G. Simonson submitted his plans and specifications for the ballpark on January 26, 1914, and bids for construction of the ballpark grandstand, two covered pavilions, and bleachers were set to be opened on January 31, 1914.[27] The architect's plans for the ballpark were as follows:

> In round figures the seating capacity will be about 13,000 persons, divided thus: Grandstand, 7,000: pavilion A, 2,509; pavilion B, 1,400, and the bleachers, 2,100. Pavilions A and B will be covered. Directly in the rear of the grandstand will be parking space for motor and other vehicles.
>
> The distance from home plate to the left-field fence is about 300 feet, to the right field fence about 335 feet and to the intersection of centre and left-field fences about 460 feet. Between home plate and the grandstand will be a distance of 76 feet.[28]

Joe Smith was named groundskeeper for the new ballpark, and in March 1914 he installed beneath the diamond "a network of passages in which will be put the tile for draining purposes."[29] The new team was named the Terrapins and its new home was named Terrapin Federal League Ball Park.[30] The team's uniform included a Terrapin emblem on the front of the shirt.[31] According to the *Baltimore Sun*, "[T]he words 'Terrapin Park' will be placed in large letters over the main entrance to the park and also above the other egresses."[32]

Construction of Terrapin Park neared completion by the end of March. A 12-foot fence was erected

Terrapin Park/Oriole Park (V)

"from the right-field bleachers to the extreme point in centre field, and thence to the left field pavilion."[33] The dressing rooms and showers for the Terrapins, the visiting clubs, the club secretary, and the umpires were located beneath the right section of the grandstand, "only a few steps" from the field.[34] Five flagpoles were installed inside the park, with the largest placed in center field.[35]

Although the ballpark was built mainly of wood, the *Baltimore Sun* remarked, "[I]f patrons of the game will help keep big league ball here the concrete stand will replace the wooden ones and the park will be as imposing as any in the country."[36] The grandstand and the press gates were located at the intersection of Barclay and Twenty-ninth streets.[37] A press box sat atop the grandstand.[38] The ballpark included "12 turnstiles in all, four being placed at each of the three entrances."[39] Patrons entering the right-field pavilion walked "directly up a short flight of steps," while those in the left-field pavilion walked "beneath the grandstand, and along a cement walk."[40] The ballpark included "five large exits" to "permit the crowd to disperse quickly after the game."[41]

Opening Day at Terrapin Park was April 13, 1914, with Mayor Preston declaring the afternoon a municipal holiday to "enable the officials and employees to attend the opening game of the Federal League baseball season."[42] Before the game, the city held a parade in honor of both teams, with thousands lining the parade route "east on Baltimore street from Calvert, to Holliday, to Lexington, to St. Paul street, south on St. Paul street to Baltimore, to Charles, north on Charles to North avenue east to the York road to the grounds."[43] Paid admissions to the park totaled 27,692, with 12,000 spectators standing and several thousand outside the ballpark, unable to get in.[44] "The big grandstand, the right and left field pavilions, the bleachers were taxed to their capacity," with "hundreds of chairs on the field that were pressed into service."[45] According to the *Baltimore Sun*, "[E]verybody was happy, none more so apparently than the ticket scalpers who did a thriving business," with fans paying $3 for a $1 ticket.[46] The Terrapins defeated the Buffalo Buffeds 3-2, and "Baltimore was universally first in the standings."[47] According to the *Baltimore Sun*, "[T]he tremendous crowd, the wild enthusiasm and terrific rooting rivaled the glorious days of the old Oriole championship team 17 years ago."[48] Across from Terrapin Park on Twenty-Ninth Street, the International League Orioles lost an exhibition game to the National League New York Giants, 3-2, at Oriole Park (IV) before an audience of 3,000.[49]

More than 45,000 attended all three games of the opening series at Terrapin Park.[50] As noted by the *Baltimore Sun*, "[T]hat's going some for a city which has been considered a poor baseball town in the ranks of organized ball."[51] Ticket prices were: bleacher seats, 25 cents; pavilion seats, 50 cents; grandstand seats, 75 cents; and reserved grandstand seats and box seats, $1.[52] After the first homestand, the club built a higher fence in center field "in order to give batters a better view of the ball."[53] The club also added "a screen on the grandstand to shield the right fielders from the sun."[54]

The Terrapins were in first place on May 5, 1914, and remained there for over a month before dropping to third place.[55] In September they were in a tight pennant race with Chicago, Indianapolis, Brooklyn, and Buffalo.[56] The *Sun* noted:

> That the Federal teams are so evenly matched is wonderful when it is considered that managers were forced to search all the leagues in the country for players to fill out their rosters. A walkaway for any team in the Independent circuit would have caused interest in the third major to slacken, but the

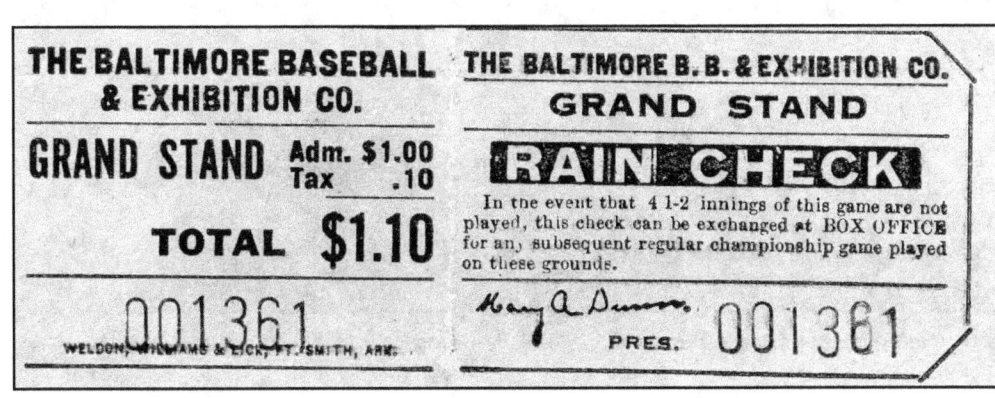

Grandstand ticket stub, Terrapin Park / Oriole Park (V), circa 1929 to 1943 - with signature of Mary Dunn who took over as team owner after the death of her husband, Jack Dunn. Courtesy of David B. Stinson.

great fight which is now being waged, with Baltimore a very strong contender, makes the first real race of the invaders very attractive.[57]

The Terrapins ended the season in third place, 4½ games behind the pennant winner, Indianapolis.[58] During the season the ballpark hosted other baseball events. In June a local school league, sponsored in part by the Sun Newspapers, played a championship series at Terrapin Park in front of 2,000 students.[59] On June 30 Terrapin Park hosted a game between members of the Baltimore City Police and the *Baltimore Sun* and *Evening Sun*, for the benefit of the Babies' Milk and Ice Fund.[60] On July 14 the Terrapins "invited the inmates of Baltimore orphanages to witness the double-header between the Diamondbacks and the Buffeds."[61] In 1915 the use of Terrapin Park was expanded to include boxing matches and movies.[62]

Hope for the Terrapins seemed strong for Baltimore as the 1915 Federal League season began. In the offseason, the Terrapins had acquired future Hall of Fame pitcher Chief Bender, who it was thought could help bring a championship to Baltimore.[63] On Opening Day an impressive crowd of 18,391 watched the Terrapins lose 7-5 to the Newark Peppers (formerly the 1914 league champion Indianapolis Hoosiers).[64] The 1915 season did not turn out as Baltimore fans had hoped and attendance fell off drastically.[65] Bender won only four games and posted 16 losses.[66] By the end of the season, Baltimore was in last place, losing more than twice as many games as they won, with a record of 47-107, and 40 games behind the pennant-winning Chicago Whales.[67]

But in the end it really did not matter, as the Federal League folded after the season. Hanlon and other Terrapin Club officials continued in US District Court an action filed earlier by the Federal League, challenging Organized Baseball's hold on the national pastime, claiming it violated the Sherman Anti-Trust Act.[68] Ultimately, in 1922, the Supreme Court dismissed the Federal League challenge, holding that baseball was not subject to the Sherman Act because baseball was a state activity and did not qualify as interstate commerce.[69]

The major-league Baltimore Terrapins lasted just two seasons. It would not be until 1954 that Baltimore again would be back in the majors, when the city got its second American League franchise, the original 1901 Milwaukee franchise, which moved to St. Louis in 1902.

The two years the Federals were in Baltimore proved most difficult for Dunn and his International League team. In 1914 Dunn signed, and then sold, Babe Ruth out of St. Mary's Industrial School for Boys to play for his International League Orioles.[70] As reported in the *Baltimore Sun*:

> The Oriole magnate signed another local player yesterday. The new Bird is George H. Ruth, a pitcher, who played with teams out the Frederick road. Ruth is six feet tall and fanned 22 men in an amateur game last season. He is regarded as a very hard hitter, so Dunn will try him out down South.[71]

Nicknamed Babe because of his youth, and as a reference early on to his being "Jack Dunn's Babe," Ruth was sold by Dunn to the Boston Red Sox, and assigned to the International League Providence Grays.[72] Dunn had received permission from the league to sell Ruth and other Orioles to help pay off the considerable debt he had incurred to run his team once the Terrapins took up residency across the street from him.[73] Before the 1915 season, unable to compete with the Federal League's hold on Baltimore baseball

Terrapin Park, Opening Day of the Federal League season April 13, 1914 – Baltimore 3, Buffalo 2.
Courtesy of the Baltimore Orioles.

Terrapin Park/Oriole Park (V)

fans, Dunn moved his International League Orioles to Richmond, Virginia.[74] After the Federal League's demise, he purchased the Jersey City International League franchise and moved it to Baltimore.[75]

In March 1916, Dunn purchased Terrapin Park, which then became the fifth Baltimore ballpark known as Oriole Park. Wrote the *Sun:*

> It is believed that Dunn agreed to pay about $30,000 for the stands, which, with the improvement made upon the grounds, cost the 600 Terrapin stockholders in the neighborhood of $90,000. Of course, Dunn got a bargain, for there never were more comfortable or more substantial wooden stands ever built than those put up for Baltimore's representative in the Baby Major.
>
> The lot, of course, was not included in the sale because that belongs to Ned Hanlon. Dunn will pay $4,000 a year rent for the lot, but has the privilege of buying it any time within the next eight years for $65,000.[76]

Hanlon sold Dunn the land on which the ballpark sat in January 1921.[77]

The Orioles played respectable ball during 1916 season, posting a record of 74-66, and placing fourth, eight games back of the league champion Buffalo Bisons.[78] The 1916 season saw the first of a dozen exhibition games that Babe Ruth would play at Oriole Park (V), with his final exhibition-game appearance there on May 1, 1930. On April 18, 1919, while with Boston, Ruth hit four home runs in an exhibition game against the Orioles, which the Red Sox won 12-3.[79] The next day he hit two more home runs, with five hit in a row (the last three at-bats of the first game and the first two at-bats of the second game).[80]

Dunn helped lead the charge to bring Sunday baseball to Baltimore. In 1918 he was arrested for violating Baltimore's blue laws, which restricted on Sundays the charging of admission to public events like baseball.[81] In 1910 Dunn built a ballpark in Baltimore County at Back River Park, to avoid the city's blue laws, and allow his Orioles to play baseball on Sundays.[82] By 1921 Dunn had won the right to stage baseball games on Sundays in Oriole Park (V).[83]

Beginning in 1919, Dunn built his Orioles into an International League powerhouse, winning over 100 games that year and the first of seven straight league championships.[84] In 1920 Dunn signed future Hall of Fame pitcher Robert Moses "Lefty" Grove. During his five seasons with the Orioles, Grove won 108 games and lost only 36.[85] Dunn sold Grove to the Philadelphia A's after the 1924 season for $100,600, the extra $600 added "to make it a sum greater than what the Yankees had paid Boston for Babe Ruth."[86] Grove would win 300 games in the major leagues.[87]

Dunn died suddenly after the 1928 season.[88] During their final seasons at Oriole Park (V), 1926 until 1943, the International League Orioles never again won the league championship.[89] The Baltimore Elite Giants played some of their games at Oriole Park (V), and by 1939 "were finally accepted as occasional Sunday afternoon tenants of Oriole Park."[90]

In 1944 the Orioles once again won the International League pennant, beginning their season at Oriole Park (V).[91] However, they did not win their league crown there. On July 4, 1944, the ballpark was destroyed by a fire, and the Orioles played their remaining games that season (and through 1953) at Baltimore Municipal Stadium, which later became Memorial Stadium.[92]

The *Baltimore Sun* reported on the destruction of the ballpark:

> Fire of undetermined origin razed the stands of famed Oriole Park, home of the Baltimore International League Club, today, causing a loss estimated by club officials at $150,000.
>
> The wooden stands burned so rapidly that within little more than an hour only charred and smoking timbers remained around the field where Jack Dunn once led his Orioles to seven straight league pennants, and where he developed such famous stars as Babe Ruth, Lefty Grove, Joe Boley, Tommy Thomas, Max Bishop and others.[93]

The site now is occupied by row houses, the Barclay Elementary School, and Peabody Heights Brewery.[94] In 2015 Peabody Heights Brewery hired the company that performed the original survey of Terrapin Park to help determine the exact, former location of home plate:

> Home plate, it turns out, stood in what is now a grass strip, midway up the east side of the 2900 block of Barclay St. The spot faces windows on the Barclay Elementary/Middle building. The pitcher's mound was not far from the south-facing wall of what is now the Peabody Heights Brewery, the former Royal Crown bottling plant.

The surveyors relied upon a well-preserved 1914 original survey of the park created by the S.J. Martenet Co., a firm that remains in business in Baltimore's Mount Vernon neighborhood. They found the coordinates to pinpoint where the base lines would have been.

"We laid out the base lines, bleachers and grandstands in 1914," said Joel Leininger, an owner of Martenet. (It's his daughter who assisted in this week's resurvey.) He told me the outlines of the park property came into discussion recently when a neighboring building was sold. When land is transferred, it is customary for it to be resurveyed. It was this resurvey of the former DuPont warehouse that sparked the current conversation about the ballpark.[95]

Beginning in 2017, the SABR Baltimore Babe Ruth Chapter has held its annual SABR Day meetings at Peabody Heights Brewery, in an area of the brewery that was once the left-field pavilion of Terrapin Park and Oriole Park (V).[96]

In March 2021, a historical marker honoring "Old Oriole Park" and Terrapin Field was placed in the Beer Garden at Peabody Heights Brewery, thanks to the efforts of Stephen Johnson, David Stinson, and the Baltimore/Babe Ruth Chapter of SABR.[97]

Notes

1 Byron Bennett, " Baltimore's Other Major League Ballfield – Terrapin Park/Oriole Park," Deadballbaseball.com, December 6, 2012, https://deadballbaseball.com/2012/12/baltimores-other-major-league-ballfield-terrapin-parkoriole-park/ (accessed June 8, 2021).

2 Byron Bennett, "The Six Different Ballparks Known as Oriole Park," DeadballBaseball.com, December 30, 2013. https://deadballbaseball.com/2013/12/the-six-different-ballparks-known-as-oriole-park/ (accessed June 8, 2021).

3 Byron Bennett, "The Six Different Ballparks Known as Oriole Park."

4 The future owners of the New York Highlanders/Yankees bought the Baltimore franchise and moved it to New York.

5 "Will Old League Buy? Receivers Appointed to Sell the Stands at New Baseball Park," *Baltimore Sun*, October 21, 1902: 6.

6 "Promise a Good Team: Hanlon to Have One in the Eastern League, Gets the Baseball Park," *Baltimore Sun*, January 30, 1903: 9.

7 In the succession of ballparks by this name, it has come to be known as Oriole Park (IV).

8 "Promise a Good Team."

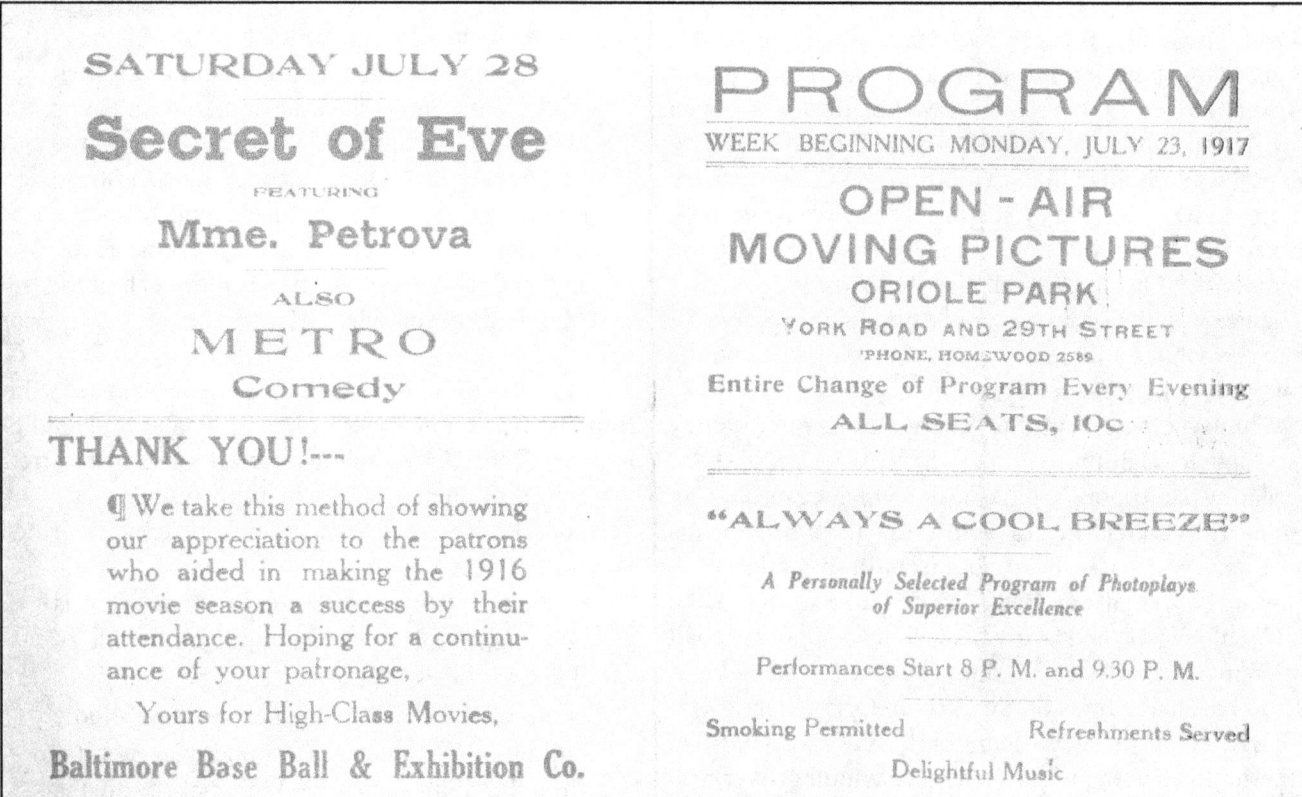

Program for Open-Air Moving Pictures at Terrapin Park / Oriole Park (V), for the week of July 23, 1917, presented by the Baltimore Base Ball & Exhibition Co. Courtesy of David B. Stinson.

• Terrapin Park/Oriole Park (V) •

9 baseball-reference.com/bullpen/Ned_Hanlon (accessed January 2, 2020).

10 James H. Bready, *Baseball in Baltimore, The First 100 Years* (Baltimore: Johns Hopkins Press University Press, 1977), 116-117; "Dunn as Team Owner: Jack Wants to Buy Local Club's Franchise, Hanlon Says He Will Sell, but the Manager Declares He Must Get 'Proper Price,'" *Baltimore Sun*, October 8, 1909: 10; "Hanlon Is Sole Owner: He Buys Up All the Stock Of Baltimore Baseball Club/Frank And Winternitz Sell, Hughey Jennings Also Lets His Bit Go and Jack Dunn May Become Real Oriole Magnate," *Baltimore Sun*, November 11, 1909: 10; "Jack Dunn Buys Orioles: Former Manager Is Sole Owner of Baltimore Baseball Club, Old Robbie Is a Director, Charles H. Knapp Is Third Director and Secretary and Treasurer -New Faces to Be Seen," *Baltimore Sun*, November 17, 1909: 10.

11 "Federal League Is Formed in The West," *Baltimore Sun*, March 9, 1913: A1.

12 "Major League Ball Offered Baltimore: Federal League, After One Season, Intends to Invade the East, This City Can Get Franchise, Independent Organization Said to Have Ample Financial Backing, and the Intention to Make Itself Second to None – Plenty of Players to Pick From," *Baltimore Sun*, October 21, 1913: 6.

13 "Major League Ball Offered Baltimore."

14 "Big League Plan Launched: Articles of Incorporation of Federal Club," *Baltimore Sun*, October 28, 1913: 16.

15 "Big League Plan Launched."

16 "Baltimore Is Admitted to Federal League," *Baltimore Sun*, November 2, 1913: S1.

17 "Ball Park Plans Scanned," *Baltimore Sun*, November 8, 1913: 7.

18 "Ball Park Plans Scanned."

19 "Hanlon With Federals: Famous Old Baseball Manager Enthusiastic for New League," Elected Director of Club, *Baltimore Sun*, November 13, 1913: 12.

20 "Hanlon With Federals."

21 "Club Stock for 'Fans' Federal League Preferred Will Be Sold at $10 a Share, Hanlon Demanded This Move," *Baltimore Sun*, November 20, 1013: 2.

22 "Hanlon Buys Ground for Feds' Ball Park, Deal Is Closed for Tract Required to Make Playing Field Sufficiently Large," *Baltimore Sun*, December 31, 1913: 5.

23 "New Ball Park Plans In, City Council Asked to Authorize Big Buildings at York Road and Twenty-Ninth Street," *Baltimore Sun*, January 13, 1914: 5.

24 "New Ball Park Plans In."

25 "New Ball Park Plans In."

26 "Russell Ford, Edgar Willet and Howard Camnitz Sign With Federal League; to Break Ground Today; Mayor Preston Will Start Work at Federal League Park, *Baltimore Sun*, January 21, 1914: 11.

27 "Park Bids Are Open, Baltimore Feds Will Award Contract Saturday for New Home, to Seat Nearly 13,000 Fans," *Baltimore Sun*, January 27, 1914: 9.

28 "Park Bids Are Open."

29 "Schoolboys to Root, Friends Will Send a Squad Of 100 to Terrapins' Opening Game, Fans Inspect New Ball Park," *Baltimore Sun*, March 16, 1914: 8.

30 "It's 'Terrapin Park,' Baltimore Federal Magnates Decide Upon Name for Their Home; All Grandstand Seats Sold," *Baltimore Sun*, March 18, 1914: 8.

31 "It's 'Terrapin Park.'"

32 "It's 'Terrapin Park.'"

33 "Work Progressing at Terrapin Park," *Baltimore Sun*, March 29, 1914: S2.

34 "Work Progressing at Terrapin Park."

35 "Work Progressing at Terrapin Park."

36 "Terrapin Park Is Ready to Welcome Baltimore Fans," *Baltimore Sun*, April 12, 1914: S2.

37 "Terrapin Park Is Ready."

38 "Terrapin Park Is Ready."

39 "Terrapin Park Is Ready."

40 "Terrapin Park Is Ready."

41 "Terrapin Park Is Ready."

42 "Municipal Holiday Today," *Baltimore Sun*, April 10, 1914: 14.

43 "28,000 See Contest; Inspiring Sight at Terrapin Park as Federal League Season Opens," *Baltimore Sun*, April 14, 1914; 1.

44 "28,000 See Contest."

45 "28,000 See Contest."

46 "28,000 See Contest."

47 Bready, 127.

48 "Baseball Features of the Day," *Baltimore Sun*, April 14, 1914: 1.

49 "Baseball Features of the Day."

50 "More Than 45,000 Fans Attend the Terrapin Games, *Baltimore Sun*, April 19, 1914: SS1.

51 "More Than 45,000 Fans Attend."

52 Classified Ad 7, Baltimore Sun, April 18, 1914: 1.

53 "Zinn Will Be Out of Game Several Days," *Baltimore Sun*, April 25, 1914: 11.

54 "Zinn Will Be Out."

55 "Brady, 127.

56 "Baseball Races Close, Federal, National and International Furnishing Thrills, Baltimore Strong Contender," *Baltimore Sun*, September 17, 1914: 5.

57 "Baseball Races Close."

58 Brady, 127.

59 "School No. 42 Victor: Defeats No. 48 in Initial Championship Ball Game; 2,000 Children See Struggle," *Baltimore Sun*, June 23, 1914: 14.

60 "Dare 'Cops' to Take It; Game of Ball with Newspaper Men to Be Red-Hot One, for Babies' Milk and Ice Fund," *Baltimore Sun*, June 18, 1914: 4.

61 C. Starr Mathews,"Orphans Will See Games at Terrapin Park Today," *Baltimore Sun*, July 14, 1914: 5.

62 "Kid Must Like the Air: Williams Won His Greatest Battles in Outdoor Rings, Scored Three Knockouts," *Baltimore Sun*, July 21, 1915: 5; "Taylor Badly Battered, New Yorker No Match for Kid Williams, King of Bantams, Knocked Down in Thirteenth," *Baltimore Sun*, July 25, 1915: I10; "Dunn Buys Terp Park, Will Take Possession of Federal League Plant April 1, Price Believed About $30,000," *Baltimore Sun*, March 4, 1916: 11.

63 "Bender Will Pitch for the Terrapins, Player Committee Decides Indian Is Needed to Bolster Up Twriling Staff, Signed Two-Year Contract," *Baltimore Sun*, December 8, 1914: 1.

64 "Terrapins Lose Opening Game, Newark Peppers Capture First Contest of Season Before 18,391," April 11, 1915: 1.

65 "Now Is The Time to Assure Ourselves of a Permanent Place on the Baseball Map – And IF It Is Not Done Now, It Will Be Never," *Baltimore Sun*, June 7, 1915: 6; "Ten-Cent Ball Today, New Prices to Go Into Effect Here at Terrapin Park, Two Games for the One Price," *Baltimore Sun*, August 13, 1915: 12.

66 Bready, 128.

67 Bready, 128.

68 "Terrapins to Keep Up Fight, Baltimore Trying to Block Baseball Settlement, Says Report, Would Continue Anti-Trust Suit," *Baltimore Sun*, December 23, 1915; 14; "Terrapins May File $900,000 Suit Today, Case Against O.B. and Federal Pacifists Will Be Fought in Philadelphia," *Baltimore Sun*, March 17, 1916: 10. "Terps Fire Opening Gun in Suit Against Organized Ball: Cost O.B. a Million to Put Out Federals, Terms of Peace Pact Out in Trial of Baltimoreans' $900,000 Suit, Terps Ignored, They Claim," *Baltimore Sun*, June 12, 1917: 8.

69 *Federal Baseball Club v. National League*, 259 U.S. 200 (1922).

70 Bready, 134.

71 Dunn Now Trying to Bolster Club," *Baltimore Sun*, February 15 1914: S3.

72 Bready, 134-135.

73 "3 More Orioles Sold, Ruth, Shore And Egan Purchased by the Boston Red Sox, They Leave the Nest Tonight," *Baltimore Sun*, July 10, 1914: 5; "None to Quit, He Says; International President Declares All His Clubs Will Stick, Approves Sales by Jack Dunn," *Baltimore Sun*, July 13, 1914: 5.

74 "Richmond Gets Orioles, Virginia League Accepts Offer to Let in International, Jack Dunn to Head Company," *Baltimore Sun*, January 13, 1915: 11.

75 Bready, 143.

76 "Dunn Buys Terp Park: Will Take Possession of Federal League Plant April 1, Price Believed About $30,000," *Baltimore Sun*, March 4, 1916: 11.

77 "Jack Dunn Lifts Option on Baseball Grounds," *Baltimore Sun*, January 3, 1924: 12.

78 baseball-reference.com/bullpen/1916_International_League_season (accessed January 4, 2020).

79 Bready, 139.

80 Bready, 139.

81 "Jack Dunn Under Fire, Charged with Violating Sunday Law at Oriole Park, Sold Admissions, Is Charged," *Baltimore Sun*, July 16, 1918: 5; "Birds Trim the Leafs, Sunday Baseball in City Inaugurated with Victory, About 9,000 Cheer Dunnmen," *Baltimore Sun*, June 17, 1918: 5.

82 "To Have Sunday Ball, Dunn Will Build Stand and Grounds Opposite Prospect Park; to Lease the Property Today," *Baltimore Sun*, March 11, 1910: 10; Bready, 118.

83 "Great Throng at Oriole Park Attests Popularity of Game: Largest Sunday Baseball Crowd Overflows Stands and Fields – Gates Are Closed Momentarily and Thousands Turn Away," *Baltimore Sun*, April 21, 1925: 8.

84 Bready, 145.

85 baseball-reference.com/register/player.fcgi?id=grove-002rob (accessed January 5, 2020).

86 Bready, 154.

87 Bready, 154.

88 Bready, 186.

89 James H. Bready, *The Home Team Our Orioles* (25th Anniversary Edition) (self-published, 1959), 44.

90 Bready, *Baseball in Baltimore*, 175; "Stars to Meet Giants in National Negro Loop at Oriole Park Today," *Baltimore Sun*, June 27, 1937: S3; "Elite Giants Play Homestead Grays Today," *Baltimore Sun*, July 25, 1937: SS7; "Elite Giants to Open Season Next Sunday," *Baltimore Sun*, May 3, 1942: S3.

91 Brady, *The Home Team*, 45.

92 Brady, *Baseball In Baltimore*, 204-208; Jesse A. Linthicum, "Sunlight on Sports," *Baltimore Sun*, July 5, 1944: 15.

93 Oriole Ball Park Destroyed by Fire: Baltimore Team Loses Uniforms and Trophies, *Baltimore Sun*, July 5, 1944: 19.

94 Byron Bennett, "Baltimore's Other Major League Ballfield – Terrapin Park/Oriole Park," DeadballBaseball.com, December 6, 2012. deadballbaseball.com/?p=1805 (accessed December 29, 2019); Bennett, "The Six Different Ballparks Known as Oriole Park."

95 Kelly Jacques, "Surveyors Find Home in a City Neighborhood: Documents Show Layout of Oriole Park, Which Burned In '44," *Baltimore Sun*, May 2, 2015: A3.

96 "Drinking Beer in The Left Field Tasting Room at Old Oriole Park," https://davidbstinsonauthor.com/2015/07/31/drinking-beer-in-the-left-field-tasting-room-at-old-oriole-park/ (accessed June 8, 2021).

97 Kelly Jacques, "Burned down and built over, 'Old' Oriole Park gets a deserved plaque," *Baltimore Sun*, April 10, 2021.

Maryland Park - The Park That Time Almost Forgot

By Steve Behnke

Prior to 1921 the Baltimore Black Sox were an independent team playing most of their home games at such places as Oriole Park (also known as Terrapin Park) and Westport Park in Baltimore. They did not have what they could call their own home field. The team was owned by two White businessmen, George Rossiter and George Spedden.[1]

By 1918 they were a team of note in the area. The *Afro-American* newspaper reported on October 4, 1918, that the Black Sox would play a championship series of seven games against the Semi-Pro All Stars beginning October 6. The Black Sox had a record of 35 wins and 5 losses. Three of the losses were by one run. The winner of this series would be presented with a silver cup and $25 in gold. The games were to be played at Westport Park. The Black Sox won the championship and were ready for bigger and better days.[2]

On February 6, 1920, the *Afro-American* published a piece that said, "The Black Sox are now building bleachers and a grandstand the baseball park at Westport. It is said the total cost will amount to $15,000 and that the local team will have the best grounds."[3] Maryland Ballpark was about to be born. It was located on a peninsula of land between Ridgely's Cove to the north and Gwynns Falls to the south. A portion of the Patapsco River was to the west. The first-base line ran adjacent to Maryland Avenue. The Black Sox' previous home field, Westport Baseball Grounds, was in close proximity. The location was important to fans who would attend games. The Westport streetcar line bordered the new facility for easy accessibility.[4]

The research of Professor Bernard McKenna of the University of Delaware has determined that the exact location of Maryland Park can be confirmed. The Maryland Port Authority commissioned aerial photographs of Baltimore in the 1920s. Professor McKenna discovered these photos in his research of the park and the Black Sox.[5] A lost ballpark had been found.

Construction commenced in February of 1920, with the park ready for play at the start of the 1921 season. The dimension can be somewhat determined by the aerial photographs. McKenna's detailed examination of the photographs clearly shows the foul lines and the pitcher's mound as well as the fences. He used right angles and the Pythagorean formula to determine the park's measurements. It was 320 feet to the left-field foul pole; 391 feet to dead center field; the power alleys in left-center and right-center fields were 387 feet; it was 361 feet to the right-field foul pole. There was also a short porch in right field 351 feet from home plate.[6]

On Friday, July 24, 1920, the Black Sox filed for incorporation with the Maryland Tax Commission through their attorney, Arthur E. Briscoe. Capital stock amount to $20,000 and was authorized at $100 per share. The incorporators were William H. Bruner, Charles F. Spedden, Dr. Frank J. Sykes, Charles H. Owens, and John P. Copper.[7] The Black Sox were on firm financial footing to go forward.

The Black Sox immediately made capital improvements to their new ballpark. They created two separate entrances, one was for the grandstand and the other for the bleachers. This would reduce customer congestion. They reseeded the outfield and leveled it. They also installed hot and cold showers for the players.[8] All of these alterations and enhancements increased the value of the park to an estimated $35,000. On February 21, 1924, owner Charlie Spedden announced that "the Sox own and operate a $35,000 plant fully paid for."[9]

On March 10, 1922 an article in the *Afro-American* reported on "[t]he initial steps to what promises to be the greatest colored baseball team in Baltimore." The Black Sox announced that the team's players would

• Baltimore Baseball •

Left: Aerial photo of Maryland Park taken by the Maryland Port Administration, circa 1927. Photo discovered by Professor Bernard McKenna, courtesy of Johns Hopkins University.

Below: Former Site of Maryland Park, currently Wheelabrator Baltimore. The distinctive smokestack of the incinerator is visible at the intersection of I-95 and I-395. Courtesy of David B. Stinson.

be under contract for $125 to $200 per month. Such a salary was to replace the percentage of revenue they had previously been paid. Improvements to the park were planned. The bleachers were covered and the grandstands were extended.[10]

Not all changes to the park were successful. On August 18, 1928, the team ran an ad in the *Afro-American* declaring, "Maryland Ballpark has been beautifully electrified."[11] Night baseball got off to a very rocky start. The first night game was scheduled for June 23, 1930. Professor McKenna wrote, "[T]he lighting was so poor that Frank Winfield, the Black Sox manager, would not let his players take the field, fearing injury."[12] Fans were refunded their money. The club tried again on August 30, with a different outcome. It was the second game of a doubleheader against the House of David. The Black Sox won the game 5-0 behind the no-hit pitching of John Wesley "Neck" Stanley.

The Black Sox played their first game at Maryland Park on Sunday, May 15, 1921. They split a doubleheader with the Rex Athletic Club. The *Afro-American* said the teams played before a "big crowd."[13]

With a new park as their home, the Black Sox were now poised for the next step in their existence. On December 16, 1922, the Eastern Colored League was formed with Edward H. Bolden as chairman. The Black Sox played well enough to finish second in 1924 and again in 1928. The league folded in 1928. However, in 1929 the teams regrouped into the American Negro League. This time the Black Sox finished in first place with 49 wins and 21 losses.[14]

Maryland Park was twice host to a Negro League World Series. It was common at this time for the Negro Leagues to hold the series away from the home fields of the participants. It was advantageous to move the series around to other parts of the country to showcase the stars of the Negro Leagues.

The first series was played in 1924. The Kansas City Monarchs defeated the Hilldale club, five games to four. Gate receipts for this series came to $52,113.90. The Black Sox took in $1,407 as the team's share for hosting the series.[15]

The second time the series came to Maryland Park was 1926. This pitted the Chicago American Giants of the Negro National League against the Atlantic City Bacharachs of the Eastern Colored League. The Chicago team won the series, five games to four. There was one game of note in this series. Claude "Red" Grier of Atlantic City hurled a no-hitter on October 3, 1926. Grier did not have a particularly illustrious career. In four years (1924-1927) he won only 31 games.[16] But this day at Maryland Park he was unstoppable. He struck out seven and walked six in leading the Bacharachs to a 10-0 win.[17] Attendance was reported to be 2,859 with gate receipts of $3,070.[18]

• Maryland Park •

This series was likely the zenith of Maryland Park. Four months after the 1926 World Series, the first blow came that eventually led to the park's demise. Charles Spedden, one of the principals of the Black Sox, was also in charge of the World Series finances for the league. Spedden failed to report $385 of recipients during the series. George Rossiter, owner of the Black Sox, released Spedden from his duties with the team. Spedden had been an original owner of the Black Sox. By this time, he had sold his shares in the club to Rossiter, and had stayed on as manager and financial director of the club until this incident.[19]

Rossiter was then in charge of the operation of the Black Sox. But the park had begun to fall into disrepair. It was reported by the *Afro-American* on March 31, 1928, that it would cost the club between $15,000 and $18,000 to get the grounds and stands into proper condition.[20] To date no improvements had been made.

In 1929 the Black Sox joined the American Negro League and went on to win the league championship. The core of the team was its "million-dollar infield," It was made up of Jud "Boojum" Wilson, Frank Warfield, Sir Richard Lundy, and Oliver "Ghost" Marcell. (The term "million dollar infield" was based on what they would have earned if they had played in the major leagues.)[21]

Rossiter was not the same owner that Spedden had been. Professor McKenna describes him as "aloof, irritable, misunderstood, or even racist."[22] On March 9, 1929 the *Afro-American* reported that Rossiter had backed out of a deal to sell the club to a group of Black businessmen. The park was owned by the B&O Railway, which leased it to the Black Sox for $2,400 a year. The Black Sox management was responsible for the park's upkeep.[23]

In 1932 Joe Cambria became the co-owner of the team with Rossiter. But Cambria's interests lay with another Baltimore ballpark, Bugle Field, which he owned. Cambria made it the home of the Black Sox, and began to dismantle Maryland Park to use the wood at Bugle Field.[24]

By 1934 no more ballgames would be played at Maryland Park It went into disrepair over time. It slowly became a junkyard. Professor McKenna indicates that remains of the park could be seen for a long time. He suggests that aerial photographs from the early 1950s show that parts of the clubhouse could still be seen, and says that it remained a junkyard until the 1970s.[25] At this time part of the land was taken to build a highway. The rest of the land is now used by the Wheelabrator Incinerator Company, which converts waste to energy. The location today is 1801 Annapolis Road.

For approximately 12 years Maryland Park was home to the Baltimore Black Sox, 1929 champions of the Eastern Colored League. It was the park where a no-hitter was pitched in the Negro World Series. Maryland Park, lost to time, has been found again.

Sources

This ballpark profile could not have been written without the diligent research done by Professor Bernard McKenna, University of Delaware.

Notes

1 nlbemuseum.com. nlbemuseum.com/history/teams/baltblacksox.html.
2 "Black Sox to Play Series of Games for Championship," *Afro-American* (Baltimore), October 4, 1918: 5.
3 "New Park for Black Sox," *Afro-American*, February 6, 1920: 7.
4 Bernard McKenna, "A Field of Their Own: The Baltimore Black Sox and Maryland Park," *Black Ball: A Negro League Journal*, Volume 7 (Jefferson, North Carolina: McFarland & Company, Publishers, 2013).
5 "Baltimore's Ballparks Found – Aerial Photos of Baltimore's Lost Ballparks," deadballbaseball.com, November 17, 2011. https://deadballbaseball.com/2013/11/baltimores-ballparks-found-aerial-photos-of-baltimores-lost-ballparks/ (accessed June 8, 2021)..
6 McKenna.
7 "Black Sox Incorporate," *Afro-American*, July 29, 1921: 2.
8 "Sox Sign Catcher and New Pitchers," *Afro-American*, February 9, 1923: 12.
9 Baseball League War Goes On," *Afro-American*, February 22, 1924: 14.
10 "Black Sox Club to Be Real Ball Team," *Afro-American*, March 10, 1922: 9.
11 *Afro-American*, August 18, 1928: 10.
12 McKenna.
13 "Baseball Scores," *Afro-American*, May 20, 1921: 2.
14 nlbemuseum.com/history/teams/baltblacksox.html.
15 "World Series Receipts Amount to $52,113.90/Black Sox Get $1,407," *Afro-American*, October 31, 1924: 5.
16 Seamheads.com. seamheads.com/NegroLgs/organization.php?-franchID=BBS.
17 "Grier Pitches No-Hit Game; Bacharachs Lead World's Series," *Afro-American*, October 9, 1926: 15.
18 "20,396 Attended World Series," *Afro-American*, October 30, 1926: 13.
19 "Spedden No Longer Black Sox Boss," *Afro-American*, February 12, 1927: 14.
20 'Talking It Over," *Afro-American*, March 31, 1928: 13.
21 blackbaseball.com/2010/12/baltimore-black-sox-of-1929/.
22 McKenna.
23 "Rossiter Won't Sell Black Sox, Local Men Say," *Afro-American*, March 9, 1929: 11.
24 "Joe Cambria," SABR BioProject, sabr.org/bioproj/person/4e7d25a0.
25 Author interview with Professor Bernard McKenna, November 20, 2019.

Red Grier's Negro World Series No-Hitter

October 3, 1926: Atlantic City Bacharach Giants 10, Chicago American Giants 0, at Maryland Park

By Jim Overmyer

Red Grier wouldn't have had the chance to pitch one of the most famous games in Negro leagues history in 1926 if he hadn't hurled so poorly the day before. Grier was the choice to start the second game of the Negro World Series for his Atlantic City Bacharach Giants, the Eastern Colored League champions, on October 2. But, as the team's hometown *Atlantic City Daily Press* put it, Red "was not up to his usual form,"[1] which was an understatement – the Chicago American Giants of the Negro National League chased him with a seven-run second inning and hung on for a 7-6 win.

The Game Two assignment from Bacharachs manager Dick Lundy befitted Grier's status as one of the team's two best starters, with a 16-8 record against ECL and other top-level teams.[2] So, since Grier hadn't had too much of a workout the day before (at least not by the standards of the average Negro league team, where two or three starters ate up a majority of innings), Lundy sent him out again on the 3rd. All tuned up, Grier cruised through nine hitless innings, striking out eight American Giants while giving up six walks. The hot-hitting Bacharachs had 14 hits as Grier, a .266 hitter that season, had three of his own, plus a walk. Atlantic City won 10-0. His masterpiece was the first no-hitter in the black World Series, and one of only two ever tossed in that Negro league showcase.

Although neither Series team was from Baltimore, a Negro World Series contest in a neutral place such as Maryland Park, the ECL Baltimore Black Sox home field, wasn't unusual. The Negro leagues' primary fan base, African Americans in urban areas of the East and Midwest, was a population with less-than-average income and limited discretionary spending. It was good for the business of Black baseball to move games around, appealing to fans outside the areas from which the Series combatants came. Only eight of the 11 games (the best-five-of-nine format also included two ties), were played in Atlantic City and Chicago. In addition to this game in Baltimore, the series also moved to Philadelphia for a pair of contests at the white major-league Phillies' Baker Bowl.

The Bacharach Giants were charter members of the ECL in 1923 and fielded middling to good teams most years. A chronic lack of first-rate pitching began to be solved in 1925 by the acquisition of Chauncey "Rats" Henderson from the nonleague Richmond Giants, and Grier, whose first name was Claude, from the Wilmington Potomacs when that ECL team folded in midseason. This helped Atlantic City to its first pennant in 1926. Henderson was considered the ace of the Bacharach staff and started the first World Series game. That brought on Grier for the second contest and, as it turned out, the famous third one.

In the top of the first inning Grier briefly looked as if he might still be shaky from the day before. He walked the leadoff hitter, right fielder Jelly Gardner. Gardner stole second as the next batter, left fielder Sandy Thompson, struck out, and commenced to third when first baseman Jim Brown grounded out. Gardner would have scored and the no-hitter would have vanished in the first had not Bacharach shortstop Lundy "raced back" to grab a popup by catcher John Hines that was falling into short left field.[3]

Red had clearly settled down – the second and third innings were six men up and six down, two on strikeouts, with nothing hit out of the infield. The only thing close to a base hit was an infield roller in the third by Chicago pitcher Webster McDonald on which first baseman Chance Cummings "made a fine play."[4] Grier walked two more in the fourth, although one of them, Thompson, tried to steal second and was thrown out by catcher Willie Jones on a strikeout/throw-out double play.

Red Grier's Negro World Series No-Hitter

Then in the fifth, the American Giants loaded the bases on two walks and an error by Cummings. But a pair of force outs at second had been interspersed, and when Thompson hit an infield grounder, Grier pounced on it and threw him out. The sixth was less dramatic. According to the *Daily Press*, second baseman Chano Garcia "made a swell stop" of a grounder for out number one. After Hines struck out, center fielder George Sweatt "looked wistfully at the third strike being called and went to the dugout."[5]

Grier was pretty much on cruise control in the seventh and eighth, with only one baserunner in each inning, on an error and a walk, neither advancing past first. Many no-hitters have at least one late-game at-bat where the gem could be spoiled but for an outstanding fielding play. This happened with one out in the top of the ninth. Lundy, Cummings, and Garcia had gotten credit for good plays earlier in the game, but the *Daily Press* reporter specifically noted that third baseman Oliver Marcelle "saved Grier of a hit" on a grounder by his counterpart, Dave Malarcher. Then Chicago shortstop Stanford Jackson hit a bouncer to Garcia, and the no-hitter was in the books.[6]

Other than having been generous with bases on balls, Grier pitched a great game, even for a no-hitter. Only three balls were hit out of the infield, including the Texas Leaguer that Lundy snared in the first inning.

Grier's gem tied the series at one win each (the opening game had been a 3-3 tie, called after nine innings because of darkness). After five games the Bacharach Giants were up two games to one, with another nine-inning tied game called off as the sun began to set in Philadelphia. On October 6 Grier was back on the mound with a luxurious (by Negro league standards) three days of rest, and he was sharp again, limiting the American Giants to six hits and three walks in a complete-game 6-4 win.

By the time eight games had been played the Bacharachs were on the verge of taking the Series, with four wins to Chicago's two. But with Grier again on the mound on Monday, October 11, the American Giants won the ninth game, 6-3. Grier threw another complete game and didn't pitch terribly – he gave up only seven hits and struck out nine – but he again walked six batters and hit one. Two of the American Giants who had gotten free passes scored, as did the hit batsman. Things only got worse for the Bacharachs, who had been limited to three runs in each of their last two games and then were shut out in the last two Series contests, giving Chicago the crown.

The 1926 Series, understandably, was the highlight of Grier's career. But his descent from that peak was swift. He wasn't able to pitch in 1927 until late in the season because of a sore arm, and his major-league career was about finished. The Bacharachs cut him loose, and he caught on in Baltimore with the Black Sox in 1928. But he seems to have gotten into only one game, a start on July 1 in which he was pulled after the first inning. The local Black paper reported that "Red Grier is still off form, probably it's the old arm, so Manager Taylor sent him to warm the bench in the second inning."[7]

James A. Riley, who interviewed scores of Negro leaguers and used their evaluations of their peers in his *Biographical Encyclopedia of the Negro Leagues*, hit on a likely underlying reason for Grier's plummet: "an unwillingness to adhere to proper training procedures. … [H]ad he taken good care of himself, he would have had a long career and he could have been one of the best left-handers of all time."[8]

Grier eventually returned to his hometown of Newton, North Carolina, where he found work as a mill worker and an estate caretaker. He died in the hospital there on March 1, 1967, of arteriosclerosis and heart congestion, just three weeks shy of his 63rd birthday.[9]

Grier's absence from the Bacharachs' rotation in 1927 was partially countered by promoting former part-time hurler Luther "Red" Farrell to be a regular starter. Farrell, a left-handed pitcher and batter, was a powerful hitter who had spent most of his time in the Negro leagues as an outfielder. But he split his appearances in 1927 between the garden and the mound, where he led the team in wins with 16 against league and other top-flight competition.[10] Farrell took Grier's place in one other way, too. When the Bacharachs repeated as ECL champions he too threw a Negro World Series no-hitter, again against Chicago, on October 8 in Atlantic City. Farrell's game wasn't as outstanding as Grier's – the American Giants scored two runs on walks and errors, and rain stopped the contest after seven innings. It was still a 3-2 World Series victory, even though, as in the year before, Atlantic City lost the Series to Chicago.

Baltimore Baseball

Notes

1 "Chicago American Giants Win First Tilt in Series," *Atlantic City Daily Press*, October 3, 1926.

2 James E. Overmyer, *Black Ball and the Boardwalk* (Jefferson, North Carolina: McFarland, 2014), 255. None of the Negro leagues kept complete and accurate player statistics, but current research has reconstructed the statistics to a remarkable extent, using historical newspaper searches for box scores. There is no completely agreed upon set of numbers available. The statistics for the Bacharach Giants cited here include most of the team's games against league and other high-level competition. For another thoroughly compiled version, see the Negro Leagues Database at Seamheads.com, which has statistics for most Negro League seasons.

3 "Grier Heaves Perfect Game to Even Series," *Atlantic City Daily Press*, October 4, 1926.

4 "Grier Heaves Perfect Game to Even Series."

5 "Grier Heaves Perfect Game to Even Series."

6 "Grier Heaves Perfect Game to Even Series."

7 "Hilldale Starts Series Here," *Baltimore Afro-American*, July 7, 1928; "Fan-Sees," *Baltimore Afro-American*, July 7, 1928.

8 James A. Riley, *Biographical Encyclopedia of the Negro Leagues* (New York: Carroll & Graf, 1994), 340.

9 World War II Draft Registration Card and Certificate of Death for Claude Grier, accessed through Ancestry.com.

10 Overmyer, 256.

Memorial Stadium ticket stubs, May 6, 1973, Baltimore Orioles versus California Angels. (See Municipal Stadium/Memorial Stadium chapter on page 85.) Courtesy of David B. Stinson.

Baltimore Black Sox Beat Lefty Grove and All-Stars Team

October 14, 1928: Baltimore Black Sox 9, All Stars 3, at Maryland Park

By Bill Nowlin

Future Hall of Famer Lefty Grove was coming off a 1928 season with Connie Mack's Philadelphia Athletics in which he was 24-8, leading the American League in victories. He had a 2.58 earned-run average and struck out a league-leading 183 batters. His 2.86 strikeouts-to-walks ratio led the major leagues. He was the starting pitcher for a team billed as Major League All-Stars, who played another in a series of three October games against the Baltimore Black Sox of the Eastern Colored League.

The Athletics had won 98 games that year, finishing just 2½ games behind the New York Yankees.

Other major leaguers of note in the game were Athletics teammate Max Bishop at second base and the Detroit Tigers' Johnny Neun at first base. rest of the "All Stars" were, John Holway writes. "fleshed out with Triple-A Baltimore Oriole players."[1] The players were only listed by last name in the box score, but looking at the Orioles roster from 1928, one guesses that Dick Porter was the center fielder and that Eddie Mooers was almost certainly the third baseman.

Randy Moore or Eddie Moore, both major leaguers, may have been the left fielder. The catcher was Calvin "Ducky" Davis, charged with five errors in the game.[2]

George Maisel played right field. He'd played in part of four big-league seasons ranging between 1913 and 1922. The year 1928, with the Orioles, was the last of the Catonsville, Maryland, native's 16 seasons in professional baseball.

His older brother Fritz Maisel, who had played his six major-league seasons with the New York Yankees, pinch-hit in the game. Fritz was the one who had organized the team billed as All-Stars.

The Baltimore Black Sox-All-Stars series was played at Maryland Park, the first on October 7 and the final one on October 21. The Black Sox featured a pair of future Hall of Famers, Biz Mackey behind the plate and Oscar Charleston playing left field and first base.[3] Rap Dixon played right field. And Luther "Red" Farrell pitched. Farrell had no-hit the Chicago American Giants the previous October 8, winning 3-2 for the Bacharachs at Atlantic City. He'd walked five in the game and seen his teammates commit a few errors, but not allowed a base hit.

The October 14 game was the second of three played on successive Sundays between the two teams.

Some 10,000 fans had watched the game on October 7 when the All-Stars came from behind in the sixth inning and prevailed, 8-5, even though Farrell had struck out 14. Pitching for the All-Stars was Eddie Rommel (177-119 as a major-league pitcher in 13 seasons for the Athletics. He later umpired in the American League for 22 years, 1938-59.) There was to have been a second game, and it started, but was called in the second inning with the Stars ahead, 6-3, "due to the crowd swarming out on the field."[4]

The October 14 game was scoreless for the first two innings. In fact, it took only three pitches for Farrell to retire all three batters in the second. In the bottom of the third, the Black Sox got to Grove. Second baseman Frank Warfield reached first on a fielding error and Rap Dixon homered over the left-field fence. It was 2-0, but the Stars tied it with a pair of their own in the top of the fourth. Porter reached on a one-out walk. Moore reached when first baseman Ben Taylor dropped the throw on a grounder. Mooers hit a Texas leaguer and both baserunners scored.

The Sox scored once in the bottom of the fourth, and then added two in the fifth and four more in the sixth. Warfield doubled. Left fielder Christopher "Crush" Holloway reached first base on a muff by Mooers. It appears that Warfield scored on a single by Dixon and that Wilson and Charleston doubled in succession. With a double in the game as well, Dixon was a triple shy of hitting for the cycle. He was also said to have "return[ed] the ball from deep right field to home plate with deadly speed and accuracy."[5]

Combining two of their six hits, the All-Stars got their third run in the top of the ninth. Holloway reportedly made a spectacular one-handed catch of a smash that might have driven in two more.

Grove struck out 10, and Farrell struck out seven. (He whiffed Grove three times.) Grove walked seven; Farrell walked three. The Black Sox outhit the All-Stars, 11-6. One of the hits for the Stars was Fritz Maisel, who pinch-hit for Grove in the top of the ninth and doubled.

This game drew well. The *New Journal and Guide* reported that "10,000 fans cheered and howled."[6]

There was an attempt at a second game again, this one 2-2 reaching into the third inning. No reason for the ending of the game was given but it was likely encroaching darkness.

The Black Sox beat the Stars, 2-1, in the rubber match of the three-game set, on October 21. Pitching for Baltimore was Laymon Yokely, with Jack Ogden of the St. Louis Browns pitching for the All-Stars. The lone run for the All-Stars was a solo home run by Jimmie Foxx leading off the second inning. The Black Sox's John Beckwith (he'd played for the Homestead Grays during the 1928 season) hit a two-run homer in the bottom of the first. The two home runs accounted for all the scoring in the game.

The game wasn't the first time Grove had faced an Eastern Colored League team. On October 2, 1926, he had pitched for Earle Mack's All-Stars in Shibe Park against Nip Winters and a squad described as "a black team composed mostly of players from the Homestead Grays and the Philadelphia Hilldales."[7] Winters gave up seven scattered singles. Grove lost, 6-1, seeing Oscar Charleston hit a fifth-inning homer into the right-field stands and Otto Briggs collect three hits off him.[8] In what was a six-game series between the teams, according to Jim Kaplan, Grove also pitched on October 7, when the All-Stars were shut out, 3-0, by Phil Cockrell. The ECL team won five of the six games.

Sources

In addition to the sources cited in the Notes, the author consulted both Baseball-Reference.com and Retrosheet.org. Thanks to Larry Lester and Jim Overmyer.

Notes

1   John Holway, *Blackball Stars* (Westport, Connecticut: Meckler Books, 1988), 289.

2   "Dixon, Charleston Shine in Victory," *Afro-American* (Baltimore, Maryland), October 20, 1928: 15.

3   Holway's book has "Carter" at first base and center field, but the *Afro-American*'s headline, text, and box score all have it as Charleston. "Dixon, Charleston Shine in Victory," *Afro-American* (Baltimore), October 20, 1928: 15. It should be noted, however, that the newspaper box score was deficient (it declared that there were six hits but showed only four; the two Holway says right fielder George Maisel got were omitted from the box score.) George Maisel was left out of the *Afro-American* box score with the result that there was no one at all shown playing right field. There is no way to reconcile the information available, so some elements of the game remain a mystery. There was no box score accompanying the brief article that ran in Norfolk, Virginia's *New Journal and Guide*, but the text does mention Charleston. See "Black Sox Rout Lefty Grove Sunday," *New Journal and Guide*, October 20, 1928: 6.

4   "Mackey's Errors Lose for Sox," *Afro-American* (Baltimore), October 13, 1928: 17.

5   "Black Sox Rout Lefty Grove Sunday."

6   "Black Sox Rout Lefty Grove Sunday."

7   Jim Kaplan, *Lefty Grove: American Original* (Cleveland: SABR, 2000), 120. The All-Stars included Heinie Manush, Emmet McCann, and that year's American League MVP, George Burns.

8   "Hilldale Nine Victor over Mack Stars," *Chester* (Pennsylvania) *Times,* October 4, 1926: 15.

Municipal Stadium/Memorial Stadium

By David B. Stinson

Memorial Stadium was located at 900 East 33rd Street in Baltimore, a mile northeast of Oriole Parks (I)-(V).[1] Memorial Stadium was the home of the American League Baltimore Orioles from 1954 to 1991, and the National Football League Baltimore Colts from 1953 through 1983.[2]

Memorial Stadium was built on the site of Municipal Stadium, also known as Venable Stadium, Baltimore Stadium, and Babe Ruth Stadium.[3] In December 1921, Mayor William F. Broenig announced plans to build a city stadium that would house, without charge, "important football games," as well as "high school games and other athletic meets, for pageants and civic meetings at a nominal charge."[4] Several locations were considered for the stadium, including the former Mount Royal Reservoir, near Druid Hill Park, and Johns Hopkins University's Homewood Field.[5]

Ultimately the city decided on Venable Park for the stadium site, and the stadium's name.[6] Ned Hanlon, manager of the 1890s National League champion Orioles, who also was involved in bringing the Eastern League Orioles to Baltimore in 1903, and the Federal League Baltimore Terrapins in 1914 and 1915, was a member of the city Park Board that selected Venable Park as the location for the stadium.[7] The construction cost for the earthen stadium with wood bleacher seats was estimated at $325,000.[8] Located on a 15-acre parcel, the stadium was designed to be "40 feet high from the surface of the athletic field to the top of the rows of seats," with an "inside width, from barrier to barrier," of 340 feet, an "inside length of 600 feet," and a seating space of "100 feet wide all around, except at the opening."[9] The stadium included "a 15-foot walkway at the top for standing room and walking about."[10]

On May 8, 1922, the same week that New York broke ground for Yankee Stadium, Baltimore broke ground on Venable Park, with Mayor Broening and Theodore Mottu, a member of the Park Board, welding the pickax and shovel.[11] At the event, J. Cookman Boyd, president of the Park, said, "[t]here has been enough talking about a stadium. We've stopped talking and are down to work."[12] The city's construction schedule was tight; it pledged to have the stadium ready in time for the December 2, 1922, annual football game between the US Army's Third Corps Area and the US Marine Corps.[13] In addition, the mayor stated:

> When completed the stadium will seat between 40,000 to 45,000 people, but the nature of the ground is such that with a minimum expenditure the land can be built up to enlarge the seating capacity. In addition, it will have an emergency capacity of about 15,000.[14]

By October 1922, the playing surface was covered with sod in preparation for the Army-Marine football game.[15] As reported by the *Baltimore Sun*:

> Work on the stadium is being pushed to the utmost. Contracts for small frame buildings to house the showers and other facilities have been let. Construction of the temporary wooden seats to accommodate 43,000 persons will be completed in a few days.[16]

The stadium was "divided into 39 sections of 1,100 seats each."[17] In October the city arranged for installation of a trolley-car line to the stadium, running along Montebello Avenue to the stadium.[18] According to the *Sun*:

> Announcement was made by Herbert B. Flowers; vice-president and general manager of the United Railways, that the car line to the Stadium would be completed by next Wednesday. Tracks were laid to Thirty-third

Fan photo of entrance to Municipal Stadium on 33rd Street, circa 1930s. Courtesy of David B. Stinson.

street yesterday, and by noon today the line will be extended 900 feet past Thirty-third street, the tentative end of the trolley.[19]

The seven-month construction project cost the city $458,000.[20] It included "modern" amenities to the stadium, including telephones, lights, and a radio station:

> The movements of the game will be gathered through a regulation army field telephone system, similar to the ones established on the battle field, and "spies" will be stationed throughout the "sectors" of Venable Stadium, who will tell what they see to the chief scorer. They will be in speaking communication with the scorer at every stage of the game.
>
> Arrangements were made yesterday for placing of telephones in boxes to be occupied by John W. Weeks, secretary of war, and Edwin Denby, secretary of the Navy. The Third Corps Area will install a radio station at the bowl and the plays of the game will be broadcasted over the country.

Stadium to Be Illuminated

The Stadium will be in a completed stage tonight and will be illuminated for the first time, J. Cookman Boyd, president of the Park Board, said.[21]

A parade was scheduled for the morning of the inaugural game.[22] Soldiers and Marines numbering 12,000 assembled at Mount Vernon Place, with the parade proceeding on Cathedral Street, Maryland Avenue, Charles Street and Thirty-Third Street to the stadium.[23] As for the stadium dedication:

> The dedicatory ceremonies will be simple – the raising of a flag on the high flagstaff, the national anthem by the massed bands, with 10,000 or more soldiers and marines standing at salute, while the 30,000 civilians bare their heads. Then the game.[24]

President Warren G. Harding listened to the game by radio:

> In the quiet Washington, in the quieter study of the White House, the President of the United States and Mrs. Harding heard it all. The boom and crackle of the Marine and Army yells came to them, the songs that rose from a choir of 5,000 voices and the story of the game told by a calm-voiced Marine sergeant who stood on the side lines, buffeted by the storm of a crowd gone pleasantly mad, and talked conversationally into a megaphone mounted on a tripod.[25]

The Marines defeated Army, 13-12 in front of a crowd of 43,034 seated, 10,000 standing on the sidelines, and 7,000 outside the stadium who could see the field.[26] The game grossed $35,000 from ticket sales alone.[27]

Municipal Stadium/Memorial Stadium

Baltimore continued adding to the stadium over the next few years, increasing the seating capacity of the stadium to 74,000.[28] The Parks Board also paid to pave streets surrounding the stadium.[29] A formal front entrance, costing an estimated $150,000, was added as well:

> Fronting on Thirty-third street and of pure Grecian style of architecture, it is to be a brick structure, faced with concrete. ...
>
> With colonnade walls on either side, the main building will resemble the front of the White House in Washington; it will contain a reception hall 20 by 30 feet, entered from an imposing lobby. On one side of the lobby there will be a modern hospital room. Opposite will be a gracefully winding staircase leading to the second floor, with an office room on the side.
>
> Other features of the first floor include a large room for the use of the players and shower baths and lavatories, entered from the main lobby.
>
> To the left of the staircase, second floor, there will be a banquet hall 30 by 54 feet, with facilities to seat 200 persons. A committee room, service room, baths and lavatories will occupy the remaining half of the second floor. The ceiling of the banquet hall will be 19 feet from the floor. On the third floor will be a loft for storage purposes.[30]

Above the entrance was a sign stating "Baltimore Stadium."[31] Although the stadium continued to be called Venable Park or Venable Stadium for a while, eventually the names Baltimore Stadium, Municipal Stadium, and Baltimore Municipal Stadium took root.

In 1924 the stadium hosted the Army-Navy football game. The celebration included a parade of Navy midshipmen and Army cadets proceeding to the stadium from Clifton Park, with "tens of thousands" lining the parade route.[32] President Calvin Coolidge attended the game, and a luncheon that preceded it.[33] The president and his party spent the first half of the game sitting on the Navy side of the stadium and the second half on the Army side.[34] Army defeated Navy 12-0 on four dropkicks.[35]

In January 1925 the Park Board approved a resolution to restrict stadium use "to such events only as are worthy of its importance."[36] The head of the Park Board stated his opposition to "any effort" to add a baseball diamond to the stadium.[37] Ned Hanlon, still a member of the Park Board, voted against the resolution.[38] By June 1926 the stadium had reached a capacity of 83,000, and already was showing its age.[39] The city began plans to replace the original 42,000 seats that had been "rotting gradually."[40] Over the years, upkeep of the wooden benches was a constant problem, with every year between 10,000 and 20,000 seats "shown to be dangerously rotten."[41] In September 1932 the cost of the stadium had "doubled to $1 million because of the constant replacement of rotting seats."[42] In October 1936 the city began installing new wooden seats, preserved with chemicals, that had a lifetime of 20 years.[43] By 1940 the city condemned 20,000 stadium seats as unsafe and ordered their replacement.[44]

The city continued to use the stadium for high-school and college football games, as well as various events, such as Easter sunrise services.[45] On September 6, 1943, the Green Bay Packers played the Washington Redskins in the first professional football game played there.[46] The Packers won, 23-21.[47] Several more professional football exhibition and charity games were played at the stadium throughout the 1940s.[48] However, the stadium stood empty more than it was used, with some critics referring to Municipal Stadium as "Lonely Acres."[49]

On July 4, 1944, Oriole Park (V), home of the International League Baltimore Orioles, was destroyed by a fire.[50] Mayor Theodore R. McKeldin arrived at the ballpark while it was still burning and offered the Orioles the use of Municipal Stadium for the remainder of the season.[51] During a 12-day period that the Orioles were on the road, Municipal Stadium was converted for baseball.[52] The Orioles played their first game there on July 16, 1944, with the Orioles defeating the Jersey City Giants in a doubleheader, 9-3 and 10-1.[53] As for the reconfigured stadium:

> The majority of the sun-baked 12,999 fans approved of the baseball layout as constructed under the direction of Orioles Business Manager Herb Armstrong, and so did right-handed hitters all over the International League. Many agreed the temporary, emergency job had been well done and that the new field offered an excellent test of baseball skills, except for the short left field (290 feet).
>
> They liked the wide-open spaces in center and right fields which gave speedsters an opportunity to show off their talent when they

drove the ball between the outfielders. There were six triples in the first two games, a sight seldom seen at Oriole Park.[54]

The Orioles' first seven days of that initial homestand attracted 63,500 fans to Municipal Stadium, with the Orioles winning nine of 10 games.[55] The three-week homestand ended with the Orioles winning 21 games and losing 6 before 167,000 fans.[56] In August 1944 Mayor McKeldin revealed plans for rebuilding Municipal Stadium, noting that Baltimore "has made an impressive demonstration that it is in fact a baseball city that merits representation in a major league."[57]

The Orioles won the International League pennant that 1944 season.[58] On October 2 members of Ned Hanlon's family (he had died in 1937) visited Municipal Stadium and presented Baltimore native and Orioles manager Tommy Thomas with a loving cup designed by Hanlon in 1919.[59] According to the *Baltimore Sun*:

> It was not a new trophy, Hanlon having offered it in competition during the old days of the Eastern Shore League, the Blue Ridge League and the Middle Atlantic League. It was returned to him about ten years ago, and when members of the Hanlon family, who have followed the Orioles closely this year, found the town baseball crazy, they decided to have the trophy engraved and presented personally to the present Oriole manager. ...
>
> The trophy is 15 inches in height and is typically baseball in design. The handles are represented by bats and it stands on a baseball base.[60]

The Orioles' arrival at Municipal Stadium marked a turning point for Municipal Stadium and professional baseball in Baltimore. On October 9, 1944, the Orioles played their first home game of the Little World Series at Municipal Stadium, losing to the Louisville Colonels, 5-4, in front of 52,833.[61] That same night, the St. Louis Cardinals and the St. Louis Browns played in the World Series in front of 31,630 spectators.[62] The Orioles closed out the final two home games of the Little World Series in Baltimore, defeating the Colonels 10-0 and 5-3, and winning the series before a total attendance for the three home games of 95,882.[63]

The baseball world took notice.[64] Sportswriter Grantland Rice noted:

> The situation today is something of a joke. While the Cardinals and Browns were playing a World Series game before a less-than capacity 31,630 spectators, Baltimore and Louisville, two so-called minor league teams, were playing to 52,833 fans in Baltimore in a Junior World Series contest. Baltimore has no big-league team and St. Louis has two. Baltimore will draw 60,000 for any Navy-Notre Dame football game. It will draw close to 40,000 for any pro-football game.
>
> Baltimore is a stronger sporting center than St. Louis, but has no big league club, while St. Louis has two. If this is to be continued suppose we drop the names majors and minor leagues. It doesn't make any sense. The time isn't very far away when you'll see a very decided change – or a big revolt against the present senseless system. This can't go on forever.[65]

In the fall of 1944, a crowd of 65,000 came to see Navy defeat Notre Dame, 32-13, at Municipal Stadium.[66] On December 2, 1944, a crowd of 80,000 watched Army beat Navy, 23-7, in a game that decided college football's national championship.[67]

In March 1945 the Orioles signed a lease with the city promising $250 rent per game.[68] In January 1946 The Orioles negotiated a new lease with the city, after threatening to move the Orioles to another city.[69] The bankrupt Miami Seahawks of the All-American Football Conference moved to Baltimore for the 1947 season and were renamed the Baltimore Colts by a fan contest.[70] On September 7, 1947, the Colts defeated the Brooklyn Dodgers 16-7, with 27,418 in attendance.[71]

The Negro American League Baltimore Elite Giants requested permission to play exhibition games in Municipal Stadium in August 1945, but were turned down by the Park Board, ostensibly because of conflicts in the stadium schedule.[72] Citing objections from the surrounding neighborhood to the noise and disruption caused by baseball games at the stadium, the Park Board "deemed it inadvisable to grant permission for the use of the Stadium to baseball clubs operated for profit other than the Baltimore Orioles."[73] Not until 1950 were the Elite Giants permitted to play games at Municipal Stadium.[74] On May 12, 1950, a crowd of more than 10,000 watched them defeat the Philadelphia Stars, 4-3, in the opening game of the Negro American League season.[75] As noted by the *Afro-American*:

Municipal Stadium/Memorial Stadium

Memorial Stadium. Courtesy of the Baltimore Orioles.

A shirt-sleeved crowd of 10,511 cash customers took advantage of the first opportunity to see an all-colored contest in Baltimore's Municipal Stadium, and were treated to as dramatic a finish as had ever been put on at Bugle Field, the locals' old home ground.[76]

In 1945 Roger H. Pippen, sports editor of the *Baltimore News-Post*, began what turned out to be a decade-long crusade to have a new stadium built, including the prospect of adding a roof over the current stadium, in hopes of bringing major-league baseball back to Baltimore.[77] The city considered building a covered stadium seating 100,000 at the Municipal Stadium site, or possibly at another site in the city.[78] Ultimately, the city decided to build a new stadium on the site of Municipal Stadium.[79] In 1947 voters approved a $2.5 million bond for construction of a new stadium. It ultimately covered only part of the cost.[80]

With the death of Babe Ruth on August 16, 1948, a controversy erupted over the naming of the proposed new stadium, with Mayor Thomas D'Alesandro and some members of the Park Board deciding to "'dedicate' the proposed new stadium to Maryland's dead in World War II and to name it the Babe Ruth Stadium,"[81] A wooden sign stating "Babe Ruth Stadium" was hung at the entrance to Municipal Stadium.[82] Public outrage grew over the Park Board's hasty selection of the stadium name, with some calling for it to be named as a memorial to Marylanders killed in World War II.[83] In October 1948 the Gold Star Mothers sought to have the structure renamed Memorial Stadium."[84] Some called for the defeat of a second stadium loan being sought on the November ballot unless the name was changed.[85] Baltimore political activist Marie Bauernschmidt argued for a "suitable tablet to adorn the facade of the building to be erected next year," honoring those who have "made the supreme sacrifice."[86]

In March 1949 Baltimore City requested bids on demolition and alterations to Baltimore Stadium.[87] On November 31 Mayor D'Alesandro approved "a veteran's committee's request that the official name of municipal stadium be changed to 'The Baltimore Memorial Stadium.'"[88] The Mayor's Stadium Commission also resolved that "a recreation area be established at the Old Oriole Baseball Park on Twenty-ninth street as a memorial to Babe Ruth, and that it be named 'The Babe Ruth Recreational Center.'"[89] The stadium was renamed "as a tribute to the city's World War II dead."[90]

In December 1949 the city accepted the low bid of $747,345 submitted by DeLuca-Davis Construction Company and Frederick D. Carrozza Company for construction of 10,310 permanent seats at Memorial Stadium.[91] The bid was part of the first phase of the stadium construction extending the seating bowl, which included 20,440 additional seats, for a total of 30,750.[92] In 1950, with the support of Mayor D'Alesandro, voters approved a second bond, paving the way for completion of the new stadium.[93]

In October 1952 the city unveiled its plans to complete the stadium's second deck, increasing seating to 62,500.[94] The city sought construction bids in February 1953, with the project scheduled for completion in April 1954.[95] The city began its stadium expansion project in April 1953.[96]

In September 1953 the Colts returned to Baltimore and Memorial Stadium, after having left the NFL following the 1950 season.[97] On September 20 the Colts played an exhibition game at Memorial Stadium against the Washington Redskins before a crowd of 22,800.[98] The following week the Colts began the regular season with a win against the Chicago Bears before a crowd of 23,715.[99] The Colts would play the next 30 years at Memorial Stadium.

The 1953 International League Orioles finished with a record of 82-72, fourth in the league, with a home attendance of 207,182.[100] The Orioles played their final home games that season at Memorial Stadium in September 1953, with games against the Rochester Red Wings during the International League semifinal playoffs.[101] They won on September 17 and 18[102] but lost their final game at Memorial Stadium and traveled to Rochester where they lost the last two games and the playoff series, four games to three.[103] That was to be the final season of the International League Baltimore Orioles.

On March 14, 1953, Mayor D'Alesandro reached an agreement with Bill Veeck, owner of the St. Louis Browns, to bring the Browns to Baltimore.[104] On September 29, 1953, the American League voted 8 to 0 to allow the Browns franchise to move to Baltimore.[105] Two earlier votes by the league had failed to approve the sale, one on September 27, 1953, by a tie vote, and the other in March 1953, by a vote of 5 to 2.[106] Attorney Clarence W. Miles of Baltimore agreed to purchase 80 percent of the Browns stock for $2,450,000, and the team was named the Baltimore Orioles.[107] Browns owner Bill Veeck agreed to remain with the team "temporarily in order to help get things rolling."[108] The earlier league votes had failed because the Browns owners sought to retain some ownership in the Baltimore franchise.[109]

The International League Orioles were bought out for $350,000, with Jack Dunn III, their owner, given a five-year contract with the American League Orioles.[110]

The Orioles inaugural Opening Day was held at Memorial Stadium on April 15, 1954. An estimated 350,000 people lined a 3.4-mile parade route from 34th Street to City Hall.[111] Connie Mack, owner-manager of the Philadelphia Athletics, and Clark Griffith, owner of the Washington Senators, took part in the parade.[112] Vice President Richard M. Nixon threw out the game's first pitch, standing next to club President Clarence Miles and Governor McKeldin.[113] The Orioles defeated the Chicago White Sox 3-1, before a crowd of 48,000, with a paid attendance of 46,354. Bob Turley started the game and ended up the winning pitcher.[114]

As for the stadium, the *New York Times* observed:

> Although considerable polishing of the rough edges on reconstructed Memorial Stadium remains to be done, the arena was ready enough for the occasion. ... It's a fine ball park and a worthy acquisition by the major leagues. ... A novel touch was the picnic-on-the-green enjoyed by standing-room customers who assembled on the terraced turf behind the six-foot wire fence that runs across center field from the wings of the permanent concrete stands.
>
> Memorial Stadium is a symmetrical park. Each foul-line measures 309 feet. From that point, however, the fourteen-foot wall angles sharply away from the plate to a depth of 447 feet in right and center-field. ... The huge center-field scoreboard, erected only last Monday, miraculously was in operation. Its works involve more than forty miles of electric wire. Erected by a local brewing company, it cost $172,000.[115]

On September 9, 1954, Mayor D'Alesandro helped lay Memorial Stadium's cornerstone near the main entrance to the stadium before a game between the Orioles and the New York Yankees.[116] A sealed box

• Municipal Stadium/Memorial Stadium •

containing an autographed baseball, a scorecard, and other memorabilia was placed behind the stone before it was moved into place.[117] A final inspection of the stadium was held on October 8, with R.E.L. Williams, the building construction engineer, and the builder, Joseph F. Hughes Company.[118]

A plaque honoring Babe Ruth, "Baltimore's Most Famous Baseball Son," was installed at the ballpark and dedicated on August 13, 1955, with Claire Merritt Hodgson Ruth, Babe Ruth's widow, and Mamie Moberly, his sister, in attendance.[119] The plaque, erected by the Old Timers Baseball Association of Maryland, recognized Ruth as the "Greatest Slugger in the history of the National Pastime. His home run prowess with the New York Yankees, never equaled, earned him the title 'Sultan of Swat.'"[120]

On Memorial Day 1956, Baltimore formally dedicated Memorial Stadium between games of an Orioles-Red Sox doubleheader.[121] A crowd of 33,791 "jammed Memorial Stadium to watch the game and see the stadium dedicated to war dead from Baltimore.[122] Mayor D'Alesandro led the dedication, assisted by James C. Anderson, president of the Park Board, and Maj. Gen. Raleigh R. Hendrix, antiaircraft commander for the 2nd Army."[123] The ceremony honored "[m]others whose children were killed in either world war and the Korean conflict."[124] A five-minute memorial program was held between games.[125] The mayor presented a brass urn to Anderson to take to France and fill it "with earth from all the American military cemeteries in Europe."[126] The mayor also presented the Gold Star Mothers delegation a floral tribute, acting as honorary escorts, Ted Williams, a veteran of World War II and the Korean War, and Chuck Diering, a World War II veteran, who "carried the flowers to the center-field flagpole as players of both teams lined the first and third-base lines."[127]

Above the front entrance to the stadium on 33rd Street was a memorial wall with the following dedication:

> As A Memorial To All Who So Valiantly Fought And Served In The World Wars With Eternal Gratitude To Those Who Made The Ultimate Supreme Sacrifice To Preserve Equality And Freedom Throughout The World.
>
> Time Will Not Dim The Glory Of Their Deeds.[128]

The last line of the dedication is a quote from General John J. Pershing, who commanded the American Expeditionary Force in World War I.[129] The urn containing earth from United States military cemeteries was encased in the memorial wall.[130]

Baltimore hosted the All-Star Game on July 8, 1958, before 48,829 spectators.[131] The city added temporary platforms in front of the stands, extending from the dugouts to the left- and right-field corners to hold 1,500 additional chairs and raise the ballpark's seating capacity from 47,778 to 49,278.[132]

In 1961 the city made the first of several structural changes to the ballpark, inserting "field-edge boxes, lowering the 8-foot wall that had distanced the fans

Fan photo of the inaugural football game at Venable Stadium (later named Municipal Stadium and Baltimore Stadium), December 2, 1922, US Marine Corps defeat the US Army's Third Corps Area, 13-12 in front of an estimated 60,000 spectators. Courtesy of David B. Stinson.

from the players, and shrinking a foul ground that had bedeviled fielders and batters alike."[133] In 1964 the city added escalators and extended the upper deck on either end of the stadium's horseshoe, increasing its capacity to 54,017.[134] The city also replaced wood benches with metal benches, and installed seats or chair backs in the upper deck.[135] Additional changes over the next 20 years included renovation of the press box and its restaurant-lounge, and "on the mezzanine, the closing of several sections to make an owner's box, a Designated Hitters box, additional broadcasting boxes and several corporation-rental sky boxes."[136] In 1985 the city added office space and fan restrooms to the exterior of the ballpark facing 33rd Street.[137]

The original center-field scoreboard was installed by the Spencer Display Corporation in 1954, with the $152,000 cost being covered by advertising dollars from the Gunther Brewing Company.[138] The scoreboard was 65 feet tall with a clock advertising Longines watches and took a crew of two to operate.[139] The city installed a $903,000 electronic scoreboard in 1970 advertising National Beer.[140] As noted by the *Baltimore Sun*, "[w]hile this is electronic age, 12,468 light bulbs, 377,135 electrical connections, 14,997 relays and 123,848 solid-state components represents a lot of potential for typographical human error."[141] In 1985, next to the main scoreboard, the city installed a Diamond Vision video scoreboard to broadcast replays.[142]

Both the Colts and the Orioles made sports history during their years at Memorial Stadium. The Colts were the NFL champions in 1958 and 1959, and won Super Bowl V in 1971.[143] The 1959 championship was won in Memorial Stadium, 31-16 over the New York Giants, before a crowd of 57,545.[144] The 1958 game, played at Yankee Stadium, is considered by many to be "the greatest game ever played."[145] *Chicago Tribune* sportswriter Cooper Rollow famously described the scene of a Colts game at Memorial Stadium as "the world's largest outdoor insane asylum."[146]

During a playoff game between the Colts and the Pittsburgh Steelers in 1976, an airplane crashed into the stadium's upper deck. "Fortunately," wrote an observer, "the game had been a rout, and spectators began leaving early in the fourth quarter. Had the score been close, the crowd would have remained and there is no way to approximate the extent of the casualties."[147] The Colts played their last home game at Memorial Stadium on December 18, 1983, a 20-10 victory over the Houston Oilers before 20,418.[148]

Mayflower moving trucks containing the team's belongings departed Memorial Stadium on March 28, 1984, for the Colts' new home in Indianapolis, and Baltimore was left without a football team for after 31 seasons.[149]

The Orioles won three World Series championships at Memorial Stadium, in 1966, 1970, and 1983. They clinched the 1966 World Series at Memorial Stadium with a 1-0 shutout of the Los Angeles Dodgers, and the 1970 World Series with a 9-3 victory over the Cincinnati Reds.[150] The Orioles lost three other World Series, in 1969, 1971, and 1979. Oriole Hall of Fame pitcher Jim Palmer holds the distinction of having played in each of the Orioles' six World Series.[151]

The Orioles played their final game at Memorial Stadium on October 6, 1991, a 7-1 loss to the Detroit Tigers in front of a sellout crowd of 50,700.[152] That game helped the 1991 Orioles set the team's single-season attendance record for the ballpark at 2,552,753.[153] During a pregame ceremony, Brooks Robinson and Johnny Unitas threw "out the 'last' first balls."[154] Mike Flanagan was on the mound for the final pitch, and after the game many famed Orioles returned to the field one last time while the public-address system played James Horner's *Field of Dreams* soundtrack. A *Sun* sportswriter noted that "Frank Robinson made the last run from third base to the plate before it was uprooted and transported to the new stadium. The All-Time Orioles Team was introduced one by one, beginning with Brooks Robinson at third base, then Frank, then Boog Powell and Jim Palmer and a parade of former players that numbered 78 in all."[155]

The Orioles moved to Camden Yards after the 1991 season, and the Eastern League Bowie Baysox played their inaugural season at Memorial Stadium in 1993.[156] The Baltimore Stallions of the Canadian Football League played their home games there in 1994 and 1995, winning the league championship their second season in Baltimore.[157] The NFL Baltimore Ravens played two seasons at Memorial Stadium, 1996 and 1997.[158]

Demolition of the ballpark began in February 2001.[159] Opposition by preservationists momentarily held off destruction of the stadium's front façade and memorial plaque while the city debated whether a portion of the structure was worth saving.[160] Their efforts were unsuccessful and the remaining portion of Memorial Stadium met the wrecking ball.[161]

The former site of Memorial Stadium as of 2020 was a youth baseball and football field, as well as

• Municipal Stadium/Memorial Stadium •

a YMCA and a retirement center.[162] The YMCA gymnasium includes portions of Memorial Stadium's Ring of Honor hanging above the basketball court.[163] Part of the original memorial wall ("Time Will Not Dim The Glory Of Their Deeds") along with the urn that once was in Memorial Stadium, now reside in a plaza in Camden Yards between Oriole Park (VI) and M&T Bank Stadium.[164] The two foul poles installed at Camden Yards were once used at Memorial Stadium and the plaque honoring Babe Ruth that was dedicated at Memorial Stadium in 1955 now is located at Camden Yards on Eutaw Street.[165]

Notes

1 Byron Bennett, "The Six Different Ballparks Known As Oriole Park," deadballbaseball.com, December 30, 2013, https://deadballbaseball.com/2013/12/the-six-different-ballparks-known-as-oriole-park/ (accessed June 8, 2021).

2 Byron Bennett, "Memorial Stadium – Time Will Not Dim the Glory of Their Deeds," deadballbaseball.com, February 12, 2012, https://deadballbaseball.com/2012/02/memorial-stadium-time-will-not-dim-the-glory-of-their-deeds/ (accessed June 8, 2021). The Colts left in March 1984.

3 Bennett, "Memorial Stadium – Time Will Not Dim the Glory of Their Deeds."

4 "City-Owned Stadium, Is Demand of Mayor," *Baltimore Sun*, December 22, 1921: 15.

5 "City-Owned Stadium."

6 "Venable Park Is Chosen for Huge Stadium," *Baltimore Sun*, April 14, 1922: 24; "Applicants Rush for Stadium Jobs," *Baltimore Sun*, April 16, 1922: 4.

7 "Hanlon Now on Park Board," *Baltimore Sun*," October 3, 1916: 9; "Officials Hustling on Army-Navy Game," *Baltimore Sun*, April 18, 1922: 24.

8 "Venable Park."

9 "Venable Park."

10 "Venable Park."

11 "Ground Is Broken for New Stadium," *Baltimore Sun*, May 9, 1922: 3; John Steadman, "The Seven-Month Miracle, Baltimore's Original Stadium," in *The House of Magic, 1922-1991, 70 Years of Thrills and Excitement on 33rd Street* (Baltimore: Baltimore Orioles, 1991), 76.

12 "Ground Is Broken."

13 "Ground Is Broken."

14 "Ground Is Broken."

15 "Work on Stadium Pushed to Utmost," *Baltimore Sun*, October 7, 1922: 7.

16 "Work on Stadium."

17 "Officials Inspect Venable Stadium," *Baltimore Sun*, October 14, 1922: 3.

18 "To Push Stadium Car Line," *Baltimore Sun*, October 26, 1922: 26.

19 Army Declares War on Ticket Scalpers, Intelligence Department Keeping Watch on Army-Marine Game Admissions, Profiteering Is Reported, Car Line to Stadium Will Be Completed Before Day of Contest," *Baltimore Sun*, November 22, 1922: 20.

20 Steadman, "The Seven-Month Miracle," 79.

21 Phones to Be Used in Following Game," *Baltimore Sun*, November 30, 1922: 5.

22 "Invites Educators to Army Day Event," *Baltimore Sun*, October 19, 1922: 3.

23 "40,000 to See Army-Marine Classic Today," *Baltimore Sun*, December 3, 1922: 20.

24 "40,000 to See."

25 "Baltimore Devotes Day to Football Contest Dedicating Stadium," *Baltimore Sun*, December 3, 1922: 1.

26 "70,000 in Stadium for Game, Is Estimate of J. Cookman Boyd," *Baltimore Sun*, December 3, 1922: 3.

27 "70,000 in Stadium for Game."

28 "New Seating Plan for Stadium Ready," *Baltimore Sun*, December 11, 1923: 7; 30,000 Additional Seats at Stadium Under Way," *Baltimore Sun*, July 30, 1924: 22.

29 "City to Pave Three Streets at Stadium," *Baltimore Sun*, May 14, 1924: 3.

30 "Baltimore Stadium as Planned by Park Board," *Baltimore Sun*, February 11, 1923: ES24.

31 Charles DeLuca, "Old Baltimore Stadium," *Baltimore Sun*, April 22, 1991: 6A.

32 "Parade Gives Throngs Thrill Before Game," *Baltimore Sun*, November 30, 1924: 1.

33 "City to Be Host to President Before Game," *Baltimore Sun*, November 22, 1924: 22.

34 Chief Executive of United States Merely Glimpsed by Stadium Crowd," *Baltimore Sun*, November 30, 1924: 5.

35 Henry Hyde, "Army Downs Navy, 12-0," *Baltimore Sun*, November 30, 1924: 1.

36 "Use of Stadium Limited by Vote Of Park Board," *Baltimore Sun*, January 7, 1925: 24.

37 "Use of Stadium."

38 "Use of Stadium."

39 "New Seats at Stadium Will Be Made oif Wood," *Baltimore Sun*, June 29, 1926: 6.

40 "New Seats at Stadium."

41 "Highlights of Stadium's History," *Baltimore Sun*, November 18, 1979: C4.

42 "Highlights of Stadium's History."

43 Stanton Tiernan, "Preserved Seats for the Stadium," *Baltimore Sun*, October 18, 1936: M9.

44 "20,000 Stadium Seats Condemned as Unsafe by Buildings Bureau," *Baltimore Sun*, September 14, 1940: 24.

45 "Stadium Sets Up All-Time Attendance Record in 1942," *Baltimore Sun*, January 15, 1943: 4; "Easter Sunrise Service at Baltimore Stadium, *Baltimore Sun*, April 6, 1941: M11.

46 "Highlights of Stadium's History"; Craig E. Taylor, "Redskins Play Here Sunday," *Baltimore Sun*, August 29, 1943: SP3.

47 "Highlights of Stadium's History."

48 Craig E. Taylor, "Stadium Gets Two Pro Tilts," *Baltimore Sun*, May 19, 1944: 14; Craig E. Taylor, "Redskins Get 2 Grid Dates," *Baltimore Sun*, January 6, 1945: 10; Craig E. Taylor, "Pro Football Teams Signed," *Baltimore Sun*, April 13, 1946: 14.

49 John Steadman, "Goings on in Lonely Acres," in *The House of Magic, 1922-1991, 70 Years of Thrills And Excitement on 33rd Street*, 80.

50 James H. Bready, *Baseball in Baltimore: The First Hundred Years* (Baltimore: Johns Hopkins, 1998), 204-208; Jesse A. Linthicum, "Sunlight on Sports," *Baltimore Sun*, July 5, 1944: 15; "Oriole Ball Park Destroyed by Fire," *Baltimore Sun*, July 5, 1944: 19.

51 Frank Lynch, "Out of the Ashes," in *The House of Magic, 1922-*

Baltimore Baseball

Fans visit stadium in May 2000 courtesy of the Maryland Stadium Authority.

After the Orioles departed in 1991, the Eastern League Bowie Baysox called Memorial Stadium home in 1993. The NFL Ravens played their first two seasons at Memorial Stadium in 1996 and 1997. After the Ravens departed, Baltimore City spent several years debating what to do with the stadium and the land that surrounds it. The Maryland Stadium Authority gave Baltimore sports fans one last chance to visit the stadium and its playing field on May 21, 2000. That following February 2001, the City began demolition of the stadium structure. A valiant fight over what to do with the 10-story memorial wall dedicated to the memory of those "who so valiantly fought and served in the World Wars" delayed completion of the task until the Spring of 2002.

Above: Fan photo of Memorial Stadium, circa 1954, the year major-league baseball returned to Baltimore. Scaffolding is visible on the right side of the photo.

Left: Memorial Stadium as it appeared from Eastern High School across 33rd Street in May 2001.

All photos courtesy of David B. Stinson.

Municipal Stadium/Memorial Stadium

1991, 70 Years of Thrills And Excitement on 33rd Street, 65; "Orioles Plan Stadium Use for Present," *Baltimore Sun*, July 5, 1944: 22.

52 Lynch, 66.

53 Lynch, 66.

54 Lynch, 66-67.

55 Lynch, 68.

56 Lynch, 68.

57 "Huge Baltimore Athletic Stadium Backed by Mayor," *Washington Post*, August 31, 1944: 8.

58 Bready, *Baseball In Baltimore*, 206-209.

59 Jesse A. Linthicum, "Sunlight on Sports," *Baltimore Sun*, October 3, 1944: 14.

60 Linthicum.

61 Lynch, 69.

62 Lynch, 69.

63 Lynch, 69.

64 "Oriole Fans Jam Stadium in 'Big World Series' Style," *Baltimore Sun*, October 10, 1944: 1.

65 Lynch, 70.

66 "65,000 See Navy Eleven Crush Notre Dame," *Baltimore Sun*, November 5, 1944: 1.

67 Steadman, "Goings on in Lonely Acres," 80-81.

68 "Highlights of Stadium's History."

69 "Orioles Agree to New Terms for Stadium," *Baltimore Sun*, January 25, 1946: 24.

70 "Highlights of Stadium's History."

71 "Colts Turn Back Brooklyn By 16-7," *Baltimore Sun*, September 8, 1947: 29.

72 "Ruling Due Soon on Stadium Games," *Baltimore Sun*, August 8, 1945: 24.

73 "Team Barred Stadium Use," *Baltimore Sun*, August 9, 1945: 22.

74 "10,000 Watch Elites Open NAL Season," *Afro-American*, May 13, 1950: 18. For reasons unknown, ProQuest Historical Newspapers has this filed under the *Baltimore Sun*.

75 "10,000 Watch Elites."

76 "10,000 Watch Elites."

77 Steadman, "The Great Ballpark Controversy," in *The House of Magic, 1922-1991, 70 Years of Thrills and Excitement on 33rd Street*, 71-72.

78 "Stadium Site in Druid Hill Is Proposed," *Baltimore Sun*, October 20, 1946: 32.

79 Steadman, "The Great Ballpark Controversy," 71.

80 Steadman, "The Great Ballpark Controversy," 72; "Now It's June, Stadium Plans Again? Ask Cynics," *Baltimore Sun*, June 6, 1948: 28; "Stadium Unit's Possible Costs Undetermined," *Baltimore Sun*, October 30, 1948: 24.

81 Linthicum, "Sunlight On Sports," *Baltimore Sun*, August 18, 1948: S17; "Babe Ruth's Name Given To Stadium," *Baltimore Sun*, August 21, 1948: 20.

82 "Mayor Backs Stadium Plea, Approves Move to Change Its Name to 'Memorial' Bowl," *Baltimore Sun*, December 1, 1949: 26.

83 "Stadium Issue to Be Argued, Mothers Called to Meeting on Naming of Memorial," *Baltimore Sun*, October 5, 1948: 11.

84 "Stadium Issue to Be Argued"; "P.T.A. Poll Today on Stadium Name," *Baltimore Sun*, November 30, 1049: 30.

85 "Mrs. B. Opposes Stadium Loan, Wants Bowl Made Solely a Memorial to War Dead," *Baltimore Sun*, October 26, 1948: 8.

86 "Mrs. B. Opposes Stadium Loan"; "Marie Bauernschmidt's Family," June 3, 2014, mariesfamily.wordpress.com/ (accessed January 10, 2020).

87 "Proposals: City of Baltimore Department of Public Works," *Baltimore Sun*, March 12, 1949: 21.

88 "Mayor Backs Stadium Plea."

89 "Mayor Backs Stadium Plea."

90 "Stadium Renamed Memorial Bowl, Park Board Takes Action at Meeting With Veterans," *Baltimore Sun*, December 7, 1949: 32.

91 "10,310 Stadium Seats Assured, Low Bid of $747,345 Submitted for Bowl Job," *Baltimore Sun*, December 15, 1949: 15.

92 "Stadium Job Is Awarded, 10,310 Additional Seats Due to Be Finished by Spring," *Baltimore Sun*, December 22, 1949: 11.

93 Steadman, "The Great Ballpark Controversy," 72-73.

94 "Highlights of Stadium's History."

95 "Bids Sought for Stadium Upper Deck," *Baltimore Sun*, February 19, 1953: 34.

96 "Local Stadium Expansion Starts," *Baltimore Sun*, April 7, 1953: 13.

97 "Time Will Not Dim the Glory of Their Deeds, Memorial Stadium: A Commemorative Issue," *Baltimore Sun*, September 29, 1991: T4.

98 "Colts' Slightly Damp Debut Brings Out 22,800 for Game," *Baltimore Sun*, September 21, 1953: 28.

99 "And Joy, 23,715 Cheer Colts in Victory," *Baltimore Sun*, September 28, 1953: 32.

100 Bready, *Baseball in Baltimore*, 221-222.

101 "Kerns and Caballero Homer as Birds Beat Wings 5-3" *Baltimore Sun*, September 18, 1953: 21.

102 "Kerns And Caballero; Birds Rally for Two Runs in Eighth Inning to Edge Rochester," *Baltimore Sun*, September 19, 1953: 12.

103 "Standing in 3 Leagues, International League Semi-Final Playoffs," *Baltimore Sun*, September 20, 1953; Walter Taylor, "Orioles," *Baltimore Sun*, September 22, 1953: 13; "International League," *Baltimore Sun*, September 22, 1953: 13; "International League," *Baltimore Sun*, September 23, 1953: 21.

104 Linthicum, "Baltimore's Return to Big Leagues Is All but Signed," *Baltimore Sun*, March 15, 1953: 1.

105 "Big League Ball Back in City as Browns Deal Is Approved," *Baltimore Sun*, September 30, 1953.

106 James H. Bready, *The Home Team Our Orioles* (25th Anniversary Edition), (self-published, 1959), 49.

107 "Big League Ball Back in City."

108 "Big League Ball Back in City."

109 "Big League Ball Back in City"; Bready, *Home Team Our Orioles*, 49.

110 Bready, *Home Team Our Orioles*, 49.

111 "Gala Parade to Welcome Orioles Here," *Baltimore Sun*, February 21, 1954: 38; Jim Bready, "The First Opening Day," *The House of Magic, 1922-1991*, 6.

112 Bready, "The First Opening Day," 8.

113 Bready, "The First Opening Day," 5.

114 Bready, "The First Opening Day," 8-9; "Turley Triumphs Over Chicago, 3-1," *Baltimore Sun*, April 16, 1954: 25.

115 Joseph M. Sheehan, "Baltimore Hails Return to Majors," *New York Times*, April 16, 1954: 25.

116 "Stadium Project Ceremonies Held," *Baltimore Sun*, September 10, 1954: 20.

117 "Stadium Project Ceremonies Held."

118 "Stadium Work Draws Praise on Final Tour of Inspection," *Baltimore Sun*, October 9, 1954: 11.

119 Lou Hatter, "Burk Passes for Two Scores as Eagles Whip Colts," *Baltimore Sun*, August 14, 1955: 1D.

120 Hatter, "Burk Passes."

121 "Parades, Memorial Stadium Dedication Schedule Today."

122 "Rites at Stadium Viewed by 33,791, Mayor Dedicates Bowl to Baltimore War Dead," *Baltimore Sun*, May 31, 1956: 32.

123 "Parades, Memorial Stadium Dedication Schedule Today."

124 "Parades, Memorial Stadium Dedication Schedule Today."

125 "Parades, Memorial Stadium Dedication Schedule Today."

126 "Parades, Memorial Stadium Dedication Schedule Today."

127 "Parades, Memorial Stadium Dedication Schedule Today."

128 Bennett, "Memorial Stadium – Time Will Not Dim the Glory of Their Deeds."

129 Bennett, Memorial Stadium – Time Will Not Dim the Glory of Their Deeds."

130 Bennett, "Memorial Stadium – Time Will Not Dim the Glory of Their Deeds."

131 Lou Hatter, "American Leaguers Triumph, 4-3," *Baltimore Sun*, July 9, 1958: 1.

132 Bob Maisel, "Interest Up on All-Stars, Baltimore to Become World Diamond Capital Tuesday," *Baltimore Sun*, July 5, 1958: S13; Bob Maisel, American Stars Rated 13-10 Over Nationals, *Baltimore Sun*, July 6, 1958: 1D.

133 Jim Bready, "Taming the Monster," *The House of Magic*, 23.

134 Bready, "Taming the Monster," 23-24, 27; "Board Urges 2 Escalators for Stadium," *Baltimore Sun*, February 20, 1963:44.

135 Bready, "Taming the Monster," 24.

136 Bready, "Taming the Monster," 24.

137 Bready, "Taming the Monster," 23.

138 "Meeting Called on Scoreboards," *Baltimore Sun*, March 19, 1954: 36; "Approval Given for Scoreboard," *Baltimore Sun*, October 24, 1953: 4.

139 Bready, "Taming the Monster," 24-25; Jim Elliot, "Frank Robinson Defends League," *Baltimore Sun*, October 1, 1966: B1.

140 Lou Hatter, "New Scoreboard Enjoys Preview," *Baltimore Sun*, August 22, 1970: B1.

141 Hatter, "New Scoreboard Enjoys Preview."

142 Sandy Banisky, "Diamond Vision Screen Goes by Board at Memorial Stadium," *Baltimore Sun*, June 18, 1992: 5D.

143 sportsteamhistory.com/baltimore-colts (accessed January 24, 2020).

144 John Steadman, "You Can Still Hear the Echo," *The House of Magic*, 49.

145 Childs Walker, "Greatest Came from NFL's Best," *Baltimore Sun*, December 14, 2008: D1.

146 Steadman, "You Can Still Hear the Echo," 46.

147 Steadman, "You Can Still Hear the Echo," 62.

148 Vito Stellino, "3 Interceptions, Dickey Pace Win," *Baltimore Sun*, December 19, 1983: D1.

149 Steadman, "You Can Still Hear the Echo," 62-63.

150 baseball-almanac.com/ws/yr1966ws.shtml (accessed January 12, 2020); baseball-almanac.com/ws/yr1970ws.shtml (accessed January 12, 2020).

151 baseball-almanac.com/players/playerpost.php?p=palmeji01&ps=ws (accessed January 12, 2020).

152 Peter Schmuck, "Wave It Bye-Bye, Flanagan Provides Last Bit of Magic," *Baltimore Sun*, October 7, 1991: 1D.

153 Schmuck; Kent Baker, "Turnstiles Spinning at a Record Pace, Attendance Record Only 33,155 Away," *Baltimore Sun*, October 6, 1991: 3D.

154 Bob Brown, "So Long, Farewell, Goodbye," *The House of Magic*, 113.

155 Schmuck.

156 Chris Kaltenbach, "Twenty-Five Years Ago, Memorial Stadium Enjoyed the Start of One Last Fling With Professional Baseball," *Baltimore Sun* (Online), March 27, 2018, baltimoresun.com/features/retro-baltimore/bs-fe-retro-baysox-20180325-story.html (accessed January 8, 2020).

157 Ryan Baillargeon, "After 20 years, a Grey Cup Celebration at Last," *Baltimore Sun*, July 27, 2015: D.1.

158 Bennett, "Memorial Stadium – Time Will Not Dim the Glory of Glory of Their Deeds".

159 Carl Schoettler, "Timeless Tribute as Memorial Stadium's Demolition Looms," *Baltimore Sun*, November 11, 2000: 1E; Byron Bennett, "A Drive Around Baltimore's Memorial Stadium," deadballbaseball.com, February 3, 2015, https://deadballbaseball.com/2015/02/memorial-statium-drive-around-baltimore/ (accessed June 8, 2021).

160 Jamie Stiehm, "Demolition Advised for Dedicatory Wall at Memorial Stadium," *Baltimore Sun*, October 26, 2001: 3B.

161 Bennett, "Memorial Stadium – Time Will Not Dim the Glory of Their Deeds"; Bennett, "A Drive Around Baltimore's Memorial Stadium."

162 Bennett, "Memorial Stadium – Time Will Not Dim the Glory of Their Deeds."

163 Bennett, "Memorial Stadium – Time Will Not Dim the Glory of Their Deeds."

164 Bennett, "Memorial Stadium – Time Will Not Dim the Glory of Their Deeds."

165 "The Goddess 'Gentlemen's Club' – The Bar That Ruth Bought," davidbstinsonauthor.com, June 20, 2013, davidbstinsonauthor.com/2013/06/20/the-goddess-gentlemans-club-the-bar-that-ruth-bought/ (accessed January 11, 2020).

Good Luck Birds: The Orioles Return to Baltimore After 52 Years

April 15, 1954: Baltimore Orioles 3, Chicago White Sox 1, at Memorial Stadium

By Bob LeMoine

The streets of Baltimore were jam-packed with an estimated 350,000 baseball fans who warmly welcomed (at least in name) their Orioles home. "A wonderful, wonderful parade!" exclaimed one fan, Blanche McGraw.[1] She was the widow of John McGraw, the longtime New York Giants manager whom old-timers would tell you was first a star on the diamond with the original Orioles of the 1890s. Baltimore cherished its rich baseball heritage, which included native son Babe Ruth, but had suffered a huge void for over half a century. The old Orioles left Baltimore for New York after the 1902 season and later became known as the Yankees. Except for the brief Federal League era, Baltimore became a minor-league town. However, the St. Louis Browns, usually the doormat of the American League, were given new life and moved east to become the new Orioles in 1954.

As the parade wound down, rain began to fall, complicating the traffic situation. But who cared? "To Baltimore baseball fans," wrote Patrick Skene Catling of the *Baltimore Sun*, "it was the parade of the century."[2] With streets being closed for the parade, some fans parked three-quarters of a mile away and walked in the rain.[3] It was a "bleak and blustery afternoon," according to Lou Hatter of the *Baltimore Sun*, who nevertheless added that it was a "never-to-be forgotten day in the sports history of Baltimore."[4]

Vice President Richard Nixon had no trouble arriving to throw out the ceremonial first pitch. "This is a great day for baseball and a great day for Baltimore," he said.[5] Memorial Stadium, home to the International League Orioles, had received a $6.5 million upgrade, yet was still lacking in amenities at game time. Both the team and the ballpark were works in progress. "There was still some wooden scaffolding covering uncompleted brick facing around the outside of the park," wrote Herb Heft in *The Sporting News*. "Only six of the nine runways connecting upper stands with the lower were in operation, and some of the approaches to the turnstiles were still unpaved. However, every seat was in place, the grass was a lush green, the infield smooth, and the baseball-hungry fans of Baltimore, impatient for deliverance from the minor leagues after more than half a century, were all too happy to forgive any slight inconvenience."[6]

The Orioles hoped for a fresh start and distance between themselves and the disheartening history of the Browns. A charter member of the American League in 1901 (actually spending their first year in Milwaukee), the Browns had only 12 winning seasons in their history and one pennant, during the World War II years when replacement players donned major-league uniforms. St. Louis could boast of two major-league franchises for half a century, but the Cardinals always outshone the Browns, and fans in Baltimore dreamed of the day when they could just have a team again. Baltimore supported their Triple-A minor-league Orioles yet longed to see major-league stars again. While the Braves, Athletics, Dodgers, and Giants moved west during the 1950s, taking their team names and identities with them, the 54-100 Browns moved east, and the Orioles were born.

The Orioles had split their first two games in Detroit. Bob Turley was given this historic home opener for the Orioles. The 23-year-old right-hander had finished 2-6 with a 3.28 ERA in 10 appearances with the Browns at the end of his rookie season of 1953. Turley later won both a Cy Young Award and World Series MVP, but those honors did not come while he was wearing an Orioles uniform. Turley was opposed by the 37-year-old veteran Virgil Trucks. Trucks was a household name throughout baseball, having won 20 games in 1953, a season split between the Chicago White Sox and the Browns. This was the eighth time in 11 seasons that Trucks reached double-digit wins, and his strikeout totals frequently ranked in the top 10 of American League pitchers. Throwing a shutout was always a possibility: He threw 33 of them in his career.

The White Sox had been in contention for the AL pennant in the early part of 1953, but despite an 89-65 record were 11½ games behind the Yankees. The White Sox of the 1950s had strong teams but were always looking up at the Yankees until they finally got to the World Series in 1959. The White Sox had lost their first two games of this season to the visiting Indians.

Eddie Rommel umpired at home plate while Larry Napp (first base), Red Flaherty (second), and Johnny Stevens (third) worked the bases.

Turley surrendered a leadoff single to Chico Carrasquel and walked Bob Boyd. With two out, Ferris Fain lofted a foul pop to left. Sam Mele chased it down and made the catch, leaping into the Opening Day red, white, and blue bunting. Both teams were scoreless after one inning. The White Sox put runners on again in the second with singles by Sherm Lollar and Johnny Groth. Turley came back to shut the door by striking out Trucks and Carrasquel.

The first run in the history of Memorial Stadium happened in the third when Orioles catcher Clint Courtney launched a home run to right. "The grinning, bespectacled 'toy bulldog,'" Lou Hatter of the *Baltimore Sun* said of Courtney, "circled the bases with Baltimore's first American League home run in 52 seasons."[7] The Orioles went on to load the bases on a single and two walks. Mele hit a screaming grounder to short, where Minnie Miñoso leaped to his left, made the stop, and threw to second for the force out, preventing further damage.

Vern Stephens had a power surge as well and lined a home run to left into "the eager grasp of the cheering bleacherites near the 'Good Luck Birds' sign

After hitting "Baltimore's first American League home run in 52 seasons," Clint Courtney approaches home plate at Memorial Stadium on Opening Day 1954. Courtesy of the Baltimore Orioles.

Good Luck Birds: The Orioles Return to Baltimore After 52 Years

on a supplementary scoreboard – near the 380-foot marker," wrote Hatter.[8] The infant Orioles had a 2-0 lead after four innings.

The lead held until the top of the seventh. With two out, Carrasquel reached on an infield single and scampered to third on Nellie Fox's single to right. Bob Boyd singled to center to score Carrasquel, but Miñoso struck out to end the inning. The White Sox had cut the lead to 2-1.

The Orioles had an immediate answer in their half of the seventh. Baltimore native Bobby Young doubled just inside the left-field line, driving Trucks to the showers. In from the bullpen came the lefty Billy Pierce, as Chicago manager Paul Richards was strategizing with three left-handed-batting Orioles due up. Pierce was a regular feature in the Chicago rotation. He won 18 the year before and started the All-Star Game for the American League. He also usually pitched a few innings of relief every year. The first lefty was Eddie Waitkus, who laid down a perfect bunt single along the third-base line, where the hustling Young ended up. Orioles manager Jimmy Dykes countered Richards' lefty-on-lefty strategy by sending up right-hander Don Lenhardt to hit for center fielder Gil Coan. Richards then came out to get Pierce and bring in right-hander Fritz Dorish. Lenhardt turned away from an inside pitch but inadvertently got the bat on the ball and tapped to second, where Fox threw out Young, who was caught in a rundown. Vic Wertz singled sharply to right and the Orioles scored the run anyway. Mele grounded into a double play to end the inning, but the Orioles led, 3-1.

Chuck Diering jogged in to play center field for the Orioles to start the top of the eighth. He closed the inning by catching a fly ball off the bat of Jim Rivera as the White Sox went down 1-2-3. The Orioles were also blanked in their half of the inning.

The White Sox started the ninth with two veteran left-handers being sent up to pinch-hit against Turley. Willard Marshall, batting for Groth, grounded out to short. Bud Stewart batted for the pitcher Dorish and lined to first, where a leaping catch by Waitkus "brought the house down."[9] Carrasquel and Fox both walked, putting the tying run on first in what the *Sun's* Hatter called a "spine-tingling ninth."[10] Boyd grounded back to Turley, however, and the pitcher tossed him out to put the finishing touches on a historic day in Baltimore. "Delirium prevailed," Hatter wrote.[11]

The Orioles played 3,005 more games at Memorial Stadium and won 1,686 more times before moving into the new Oriole Park at Camden Yards in 1992. The 46,354 fans there on April 15, 1954, witnessed the beginning of a new era in Baltimore baseball history. It was an event that was a half-century in the making.

Sources

Besides the sources mentioned in the Notes, the author relied on Retrosheet.org and Baseball-reference.com for information on the game.

Notes

1. Patrick Skene Catling, "The Parade," *Baltimore Sun*, April 16, 1954: 1.
2. Catling.
3. Charles G. Whiteford, "Plane-Directed Traffic Plan Reduces Jams to Minimum," *Baltimore Sun*, April 16, 1954: 1.
4. Lou Hatter, "The Game," *Baltimore Sun*, April 16, 1954: 16.
5. John Van Camp, "Sun Is Happy Omen for Oriole Partisans," *Baltimore Sun*, April 16, 1954: 1.
6. Herb Heft, "Baltimore Flips Lid – 500,000 at Parade, 46,354 See Game," *The Sporting News*, April 21, 1954: 13.
7. Hatter.
8. Hatter.
9. Hatter.
10. Hatter.
11. Hatter.

Orioles Beat Red Sox in 17 Innings; Game Sets Records for Time and Players

June 23, 1954: Baltimore Orioles 8, Boston Red Sox 7 (17 innings), at Memorial Stadium

By Bob Fleishman

The Baltimore Orioles returned to the American League in 1954 after the St. Louis Browns franchise was sold and moved after their last-place 1953 season.

The Orioles weren't that much better than the hapless Browns, but managed to escape another cellar finish by the franchise, beating out the Philadelphia Athletics by three games.

On June 23, 1954, an epic battle between the Orioles and the Boston Red Sox took place before a crowd of 24,843 at Memorial Stadium on Interfaith Night.[1]

Baltimore had a record of 22-42 on that date, and were on pace for a second straight year of 100 losses for the franchise. Boston was also having its problems. The Red Sox were 22-38, just two games ahead of the Orioles.

The previous night's contest went into extra innings, with the Beantowners edging the Orioles 3-1 in 11 innings, defeating their ace, Bob Turley, who went the distance. That game lasted 3 hours and 35 minutes.

But that was nothing compared to what was to occur this night.

The starters for the game were Joe Coleman for Baltimore and Frank Sullivan for Boston.

The Orioles struck quickly. Cal Abrams worked Sullivan for a leadoff walk in the first. Dick Kryhoski followed with a single to right field, sending Abrams to third, from where he scored on a hit by Chuck Diering. Cleanup hitter Vern Stephens then lined a fourth straight hit to load the bases.

Boston manager Lou Boudreau replaced Sullivan with left-hander Leo Kiely. Orioles skipper Jimmy Dykes countered by pinch-hitting right-handed batter Sam Mele for Gil Coan – in the first inning!

Mele hit a groundball to shortstop Milt Bolling who started a double play that allowed Kryhoski to score. Diering attempted to score from second base and was thrown out at the plate for a triple play.

Baltimore added to its lead in the second inning in a more conventional way when catcher Clint Courtney singled to right and, with one out, light-hitting Billy Hunter did the same. Pitcher Coleman reached base on a force out, with Courtney advancing to third.

With Abrams batting, Coleman took off for second and made it without a throw by surprised Red Sox catcher Sammy White.[2] Abrams then singled to center, scoring Courtney with the Orioles' third run. Coleman stopped at third.

The score remained 3-0 until the top of the fifth, when Boston scored twice. Ted Lepcio singled to lead off the inning and scored from first on a double by Bolling. Coleman then walked Billy Consolo. Pitcher Kiely bunted; Coleman fielded the ball and forced Bolling at third. After Jim Piersall fanned, Karl Olson, subbing for the injured Ted Williams, lined a double to left, scoring Consolo, to cut the Orioles margin to one run. Coleman escaped further damage by inducing Harry Agganis to pop to second.

Baltimore extended its lead in the bottom of the sixth. Hal Brown, who had relieved Kiely in the fifth inning, walked leadoff batter Courtney.[3] Bobby Young forced Courtney at second for the first out, but Hunter doubled to left and after Coleman struck out, scored on a single by Abrams, making the score 4-2.

A highlight of the game came in the top of the seventh inning.

Boston threatened to break the game open in a dramatic manner. With one out, Consolo singled to left. With two down, Coleman gave up an infield hit to short by Piersall and walked Olson to load the bases.

Out of the Red Sox dugout strode a familiar figure, swinging two bats, preparing to pinch-hit for Agganis.

• Orioles Beat Red Sox in 17 Innings •

It was Ted Williams! The crowd rose to their feet and cheered him for over a minute.

Williams had been out of the lineup for more than two weeks with an injury, but here he was in a clutch situation with the bases loaded. Coleman, however, was up to the challenge, and got Williams to pop up to second baseman Young to end the threat, leaving Baltimore with its two-run lead.

Neither team scored in the seventh, but the Red Sox narrowed the lead to one run in the top of the eighth when White led off with a home run to left field off Coleman. With one out, Coleman walked Lepcio. Lou Kretlow came in from the bullpen and fanned Bolling, but walked Consolo and pinch-hitter Grady Hatton to load the bases. Mike Blyzka relieved Kretlow and struck out Piersall to end the threat.

The Orioles appeared to put the game away in the eighth by scoring three runs. Hunter started it off by reaching first on an error by Bolling. Another miscue by pitcher Sid Hudson on a bunt by Blyzka put two men on with none out. Abrams, who reached base six straight times in the game, came through again with a single to score Hunter.

Kryhoski then followed with a 425-foot triple to deep center field to score two more runs, giving the Orioles what seemed to be an insurmountable 7-3 lead heading into the ninth inning.

The Red Sox came back with a vengeance. Olson led off the ninth with an infield hit off Blyzka. Billy Goodman laced a pinch-hit single to left and Mickey Owen worked a walk to load the bases. With two outs, Don Lenhardt batted for Bolling and drove a double into the left-field corner, clearing the bases and bringing Boston to within a run of Baltimore.[4]

That was all for Blyzka as Howie Fox came in to relieve. Fox gave up another pinch-hit by Floyd Baker, plating pinch-runner Tex Clevenger with the tying run, capping the four-run rally. All three of manager Boudreau's pinch-hitters had come through with the big hits to even the score.

The Orioles went down in order in their half of the ninth, and the game went into extra innings. No one in the ballpark thought there would be another "seventh-inning stretch," but it did occur. Boston got runners on in the next four innings, but Fox held them scoreless for $6\frac{1}{3}$ frames. Ellis Kinder and Bill Henry pitched four innings without giving up a run for the Red Sox.

Finally, in the bottom of the 17th, with Henry on the mound, Orioles pinch-hitter Jim Brideweser led off with a single to right field. Hunter bunted and the ball got by both Henry and second baseman Floyd Baker into right field. Hunter hustled into second with a bunt double and the Orioles had men on second and third with no one out.

Ray Murray pinch-hit for reliever Marlin Stuart and was intentionally walked to load the bases. Henry got Abrams on a foul popup to third for the first out. Kryhoski then hit a groundball to Baker, who slipped and fell to his knees. His throw to the plate was too late and Brideweser slid home with the winning run.[5]

Regarding Hunter's two-base bunt, Orioles third-base coach Tom Oliver said in the clubhouse, "I never saw a hitter get a double on such a play."[6]

Orioles manager Jimmy Dykes agreed that "it was the toughest way to win one I ever saw."[7]

Several American League records were established in the contest.[8]

The game lasted 4 hours and 58 minutes, an American League record, and was almost suspended because Baltimore City had a 1:00 A.M. curfew that was to take effect in just a few minutes after the winning run was scored.

Six pitchers toiled for Boston, while the Orioles used five. The Red Sox had 19 hits and left 21 men on base. The Orioles had 17 hits and stranded 17. Boston used 22 players, Baltimore, 20. Of the 36 hits by the two teams, White's home run was the only round-tripper.

The Orioles had an offday after this marathon, and then they swept the Philadelphia A's in a four-game series, two of which also went into extra innings (10 and 11 innings). The last three games of the series were walk-off victories.

From a triple play that scored a run in the first inning, to a bunt double leading to a victory in the 17th inning, this game had everything a fan could want, especially to those who survived almost five hours of baseball.

Author note

I was just 14 years old when Baltimore had major-league baseball again, and this was my first major-league night game. My father was not really a baseball fan and after the final out in the ninth inning, said, "OK, the game is over. Let's go home." I had a tough time convincing him that when the game is tied after nine innings, it is continued. Being the great dad he was, he hung on to the glorious end.

Sources

The author used the box score at Baseball-Reference.com as a primary source of game information. Thanks also to the Enoch Pratt Free Library Archives, Baltimore.

Notes

1 Representatives of the three major religions in America – Catholics, Protestants, and Jews – gathered in unity. After an hour of festivities, the Orioles and the Red Sox began the contest at 8:00 P.M. that did not end until after midnight.

2 Mickey Owen (of World Series infamy) replaced Sammy White in the eighth inning behind the plate after White had to return to Boston, where his three-year-old son suffered a broken leg when struck by a car. It was to be Owen's last season in the major leagues. *Boston Globe,* June 24, 1954: 13.

3 Hal Brown became an Oriole the next year and spent eight seasons in Baltimore.

4 Don Lenhardt, who had a big hit for the Red Sox in the ninth inning, had been purchased from the Orioles on May 12.

5 Arthur Sampson, "Orioles Beat Red Sox, 8-7, In 17th," *Boston Herald,* June 24, 1954: 25.

6 Ned Burks, "Bird Shortstop Pushes Ball Through Infield in Bottom Half of 17th," *Baltimore Sun,* June 24, 1954: 21.

7 Burks.

8 The game time of 4 hours and 58 minutes exceeded the previous AL high of 4:49 set by Cleveland and the St. Louis Browns in a 19-inning game in 1952. The 42 players employed by both teams were also a record at the time, as were the 10 pinch-hitters used by both teams. It was also believed that the total of 38 runners left on base – 21 by Boston, 17 by Baltimore – was a 17-inning record. See Hugh Trader Jr., "Four AL Records Established As Birds Win 17-Inning Fight," *Baltimore News Post,* June 24, 1954: 24.

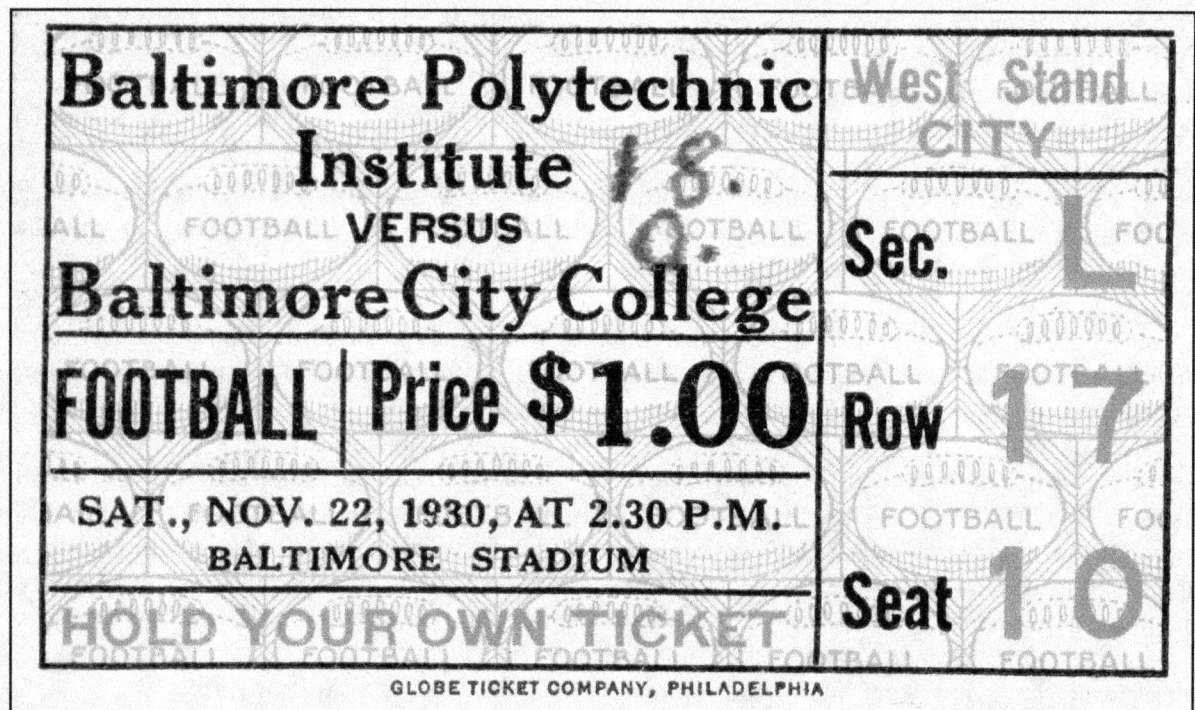

Baltimore Stadium ticket stub, November 22, 1930, Baltimore Polytechnic Institute versus Baltimore City College. (See Municipal Stadium/Memorial Stadium story on page 85.) Courtesy of David B. Stinson.

Celebrating the First Grand Slam at Memorial Stadium

July 30, 1954: Baltimore Orioles 10, New York Yankees 0, at Memorial Stadium

By Cort Vitty

Following a last-place finish by the Orioles in 1902, the city of Baltimore was left without a major-league franchise. The team packed up and relocated to New York, leaving disheartened Charm City fans rooting for a series of minor-league franchises for the next 50 years.[1]

The Boston Braves' move to Milwaukee in 1953 began a relocation trend, which lasted throughout the decade. After the St. Louis Browns' last-place finish in 1953, owner Bill Veeck considered several viable options for relocating his team, rather than habitually play second fiddle to a wealthy Cardinals organization.[2]

Meantime, Memorial Stadium, known fondly as "the old gray lady of 33rd street," received an extensive renovation in 1953, including expanded seating capacity to 47,866. The other owners blocked Veeck from moving the club to Baltimore, so he was forced to sell to a syndicate based in Baltimore, and fellow club owners subsequently voted to approve the move.[3]

When the club bade farewell to St. Louis, the contract of Browns manager Marty Marion was not renewed. In turn, the relocated franchise named baseball veteran Jimmy Dykes as the new skipper. Baltimore opened the 1954 season on April 13, splitting a two-game series with the Tigers in Detroit.

Four days later, the Orioles obtained veteran outfielder-third baseman Bob Kennedy from Cleveland, in exchange for veteran flychaser Jim Dyck. Kennedy had hit .236 in 100 games with the 1953 Indians.

Robert Daniel Kennedy was born in Chicago on August 18, 1920. In 1939 he made his major-league debut, with his hometown White Sox. He remained in the Windy City until Cleveland traded for his services in 1948, just in time for Kennedy to appear in three games with the Indians, during the 1948 World Series; he went 1-for-2 with Cleveland, which defeated the Boston Braves in the fall classic.[4]

On the pleasant evening of Friday, July 30, 1954, a crowd numbering 27,385 filed into Memorial Stadium in anticipation of the 8:00 P.M. start time. Right-hander Don Larsen was the Orioles' starting pitcher; his mound opponent was the Yankees' veteran right-hander Allie Reynolds.

Baltimore got right down to business in the bottom of the first inning, when Cal Abrams walked, took second on a single by Chuck Diering, then scored when left fielder Kennedy stroked a sharp single to right. In the third inning, Vern Stephens singled to center and moved to second on Kennedy's base on balls. Next up, Orioles catcher Clint Courtney smacked a solid triple to right field, scoring Stephens and Kennedy, giving the Orioles a 3-0 lead.

Don Larsen led off the bottom of the fourth with a groundout to second. An error by Yankees first baseman Joe Collins allowed Cal Abrams to reach base. A single to right by Eddie Waitkus moved Abrams to second. Reynolds walked Diering, putting runners on second and third. A groundout by Vern Stephens forced Abrams at home, as Waitkus moved to third and Diering to second.

With the bases still loaded, Kennedy returned to the batter's box. The 6-foot-2 outfielder powered a fastball served up by Reynolds into the left-field stands. The enthusiastic hometown crowd cheered wildly, celebrating the first grand slam at freshly renovated Memorial Stadium; Waitkus, Diering, and Stephens, scored on the decisive blow.[5]

Allowing seven runs (three earned) in four innings earned Reynolds an early shower, as reliever Marlin Stuart took the mound for New York. Despite the pitching change, Kennedy's day continued, with two outs in the bottom of the sixth. His sharp single to right scored Waitkus, giving the Orioles a solid 8-0 lead.

Left-hander Bob Wiesler relieved Stuart in the Orioles' seventh and walked the first three batters he

• Baltimore Baseball •

In the bottom of the fourth inning, Bob Kennedy hit the first grand slam at Memorial Stadium, heling beat the visiting New York Yankees, 10-0. Courtesy of the Baltimore Orioles.

faced, including Larsen. After getting Abrams to pop out to short, he walked Waitkus, too, bumping the score to 9-0 before getting the final two outs on fly balls.

The Baltimore onslaught continued into the eighth inning, as Kennedy walked and took second on Billy Hunter's groundout. Kennedy and Hunter executed a double steal, and Kennedy scored on a wild throw by Yankees catcher Yogi Berra. When the carnage finally ended, the O's had handily defeated New York, 10-0. Larsen chalked up his third victory of the season, albeit against 13 losses.

Sportswriter Lou Hatter, commenting in the *Baltimore Sun*, succinctly summed up the victory: "[L]ike a bantam bird accosting a proud, full-plumed rooster, the flock assaulted the Yanks' ace right-hander for seven tallies in the first four innings, on Bob Kennedy's single and grand slam homer and Clint Courtney's two-run triple."[6]

Adding insult to injury, the game took place on the 65th birthday of Yankees manager Casey Stengel; needless to say, the old perfessor was in no mood to celebrate.

The Orioles ended the 1954 season in seventh place, posting a 54-100 record. The Yankees clearly had an offyear following five consecutive (1949-1953) pennants. The door was open to a talented Cleveland Indians ballclub, which captured the American League pennant by winning 111 games. A formidable New York Giants team swept Cleveland in the World Series.

The rebirth of the Orioles had forced the incumbent minor-league club out of the International League and resulted in an order requesting payment of $48,749.61 to the league. The sum represented compensation for lost attendance; the figure was computed at 7 cents a person over a three-year period.[67]

The Chicago White Sox purchased Kennedy on May 30, 1955, marking his return to the city where he played from 1939 to 1948 minus time served during World War II and the Korean War. (Kennedy was a Marine Corps fighter pilot in both wars.) After a brief stop with Detroit in 1956, Kennedy ended his career with the Brooklyn Dodgers in 1957. In his final at-bat, he made the last out ever recorded by the Dodgers in Brooklyn; the club moved to Los Angeles in 1958.

Kennedy hit a lifetime .254, playing in parts of 16 major-league seasons. He went on to become a major-league coach, manager, scout, and front-office executive. Following the Chicago Cubs "College of Coaches" experiment, Kennedy was appointed to become the sole manager of the team. His oldest son, Bob, pitched in the minor leagues, while younger son Terry Kennedy became a big-league catcher. Robert Daniel Kennedy died in 2005 at the age of 84 in Mesa, Arizona.

Sources

In addition to the sources cited in the Notes, the author consulted Baseball-Reference.com.

Notes

1   James H. Bready, *Baseball in Baltimore* (Baltimore: Johns Hopkins University Press, 1998), 218.

2   Peter Golenbock, *The Spirit of St. Louis* (New York: Harper Collins, 2000), 352-353.

3   Jeffrey S. Stuart, *Twilight Teams* (Gaithersburg, Maryland: Sark Publishing, 2000), 88-89. Warren Corbett explains how the owners acted with alacrity once Veeck took himself out of the picture. See Warren Corbett, "Bill Veeck," SABR BioProject, at sabr.org/bioproj/person/7b0b5f10.

4   Phil Cola, "Bob Kennedy," SABR BioProject, sabr.org/bioproj/person/5d16f8c3.

5   Lou Hatter, "Orioles Beat Yanks, 10-0, Behind Larson," *Baltimore Sun*, July 31, 1954.

6   Hatter.

7   "Orioles to Pay $48,749, for Loss of Baltimore Team," *New York Times*, October 19, 1953: 2.5

Brooks Robinson's Debut Game

September 17, 1955, Baltimore Orioles 3, Washington Senators 1, at Memorial Stadium

By Paul Scimonelli

It was an inauspicious game. Both the Orioles and the Washington Senators were fighting to stay out of the cellar. The Orioles finished the season 57-97 in seventh place while the ever-struggling Senators finished 53-101.

Orioles manager Paul Richards tried out rookies in quick succession during the last part of the season in an attempt to shore up a team of aging veterans and so-so journeymen. Brooks Robinson was penciled in at the last minute due to an injury to another rookie third baseman, Kal Segrist. The *Baltimore Sun* erringly referred to Brooks as "Bobby" in its game recap.[1]

Robinson remembered, "I was in York, Pennsylvania [with the York White Roses]. I got there after high school in June, played about a hundred games and I was playin' my last couple. They said I would be goin' to Baltimore. George Staller was my manager; he told me. I didn't know if I would play or not; they only had about 8 or 10 games left to play. I came to Baltimore and the first couple of games I didn't play. I was just taking batting practice and fielding groundballs. Paul Richards says to me one day, 'You're in at third.'"[2]

A reported 8,734 Baltimore faithful, and surely many Senators stalwarts, whipped the turnstiles on this sunny September day.[3] "Ancient" Ed Lopat squared off against Senators ace lefty Chuck Stobbs for the penultimate game of the O's season.

Third baseman Ed Yost would do what he did best: walk. Tom Umphlett immediately grounded into a 4-6-3 double play. Veteran Mickey Vernon, in his 15th season, singled to left, followed by Roy Sievers, who singled Vernon to second. Carlos Paula, the stunning 6-foot-3 Joe Cambria Cuban find and the first black Washington Senator, got himself hit by the pitch to load the bases. And there they all stayed as usually reliable Pete Runnels flied out weakly to the shortstop.

Stobbs had his stuff that day and got Chuck Diering, Jimmy Dyck, and Dave Philley to fly out, pop out, and ground out in quick succession to take it to the second inning.

The Senators returned the favor in their half of the second as catcher Steve Korcheck, shortstop Jose Valdivielso, and pitcher Stobbs went 1-2-3.

First baseman Gus Triandos led off the home half of the second with a groundout, followed by a solid double off the bat of rookie catcher Hal Smith. A nervous Brooks Robinson stepped into the batter's box and on an 0-and-2 pitch popped out to the catcher.

"I honestly don't remember much about that first at-bat, it's been so long," Robinson said. "I just remember I didn't get good wood on the ball, is all."

Second baseman Fred Marsh made the Kiwanis Kids[4] happy, sending Hal Smith home with a solid single to put the Orioles on the board, 1-0. Shortstop Willy Miranda sent a shot to deep center field. Fred Marsh tried to score from first, but Umphlett made up for his poor batting by gunning down Marsh with a great cutoff throw to second baseman Runnels.

The Senators whimpered in the third. Despite a good single by Umphlett, Yost, Vernon, and Sievers all made outs.

Lopat and Diering began the Orioles' third with outs. Dyck reached second on a rare throwing error by Yost at third. Philley singled home Dyck to make it 2-0, Orioles. Triandos singled Philley to third but Hal Smith flied out.

The Senators failed to take advantage of some sloppy play in the top of the fourth. After outs by Paula and Runnels, Korcheck singled to center. Jose Valdivielso reached first on a very rare Willy Miranda error at short, putting Korcheck at second. Stobbs provided Robinson with his first fielding chance by grounding out to him at third, forcing Korcheck.

Leading off the fourth, with a 3-and-1 count, Robinson sent a solid single to left field. "I felt like, 'wow, how 'bout that!' I was shocked! Felt really good to get my first hit. Just gettin' the opportunity to play. I was 18 years old. It was fantastic."

Basking in the glow of his first big-league hit, Robinson was stranded at first as Marsh, Miranda, and Lopat all flied out.

The Senators made it 2-1 in the fifth, pushing a run across the plate on Yost's double to left and fly balls by Umphlett and Vernon.

The home fifth started with outs by Diering and Dyck. Dave Philley got the kids excited with a good hit to center. Triandos singled to left fielder Roy Sievers, who scooped it up quickly and looped it to Valdivielso in shallow center, who in turn gunned it to Runnels at second for a force out of Dave Philley.

Top of the sixth, 2-1 Orioles. Carlos Paula sent a muscular single to left. Runnels and Korcheck each flied out to center, leaving Paula at first. Valdivielso hit a double to left, putting Paula at third. Hoping to add a run, manager Bucky Harris sent in long-ball threat Jim Lemon to pinch-hit for Stobbs. Lemon grounded out short to first to end the rally.

Right-hander Ted Abernathy relieved Stobbs in the bottom of the sixth and got Smith, Robinson, and Marsh in a quick order.

After surrendering a single to Yost to lead off the seventh, Lopat used all his tricks to shut down the Senators once again. Umphlett sent Yost to second with a sacrifice bunt. Vernon's grounder to second advanced Yost to third. Sievers was up next. Manager Paul Richards knew how dangerous he could be with runners on base and gave him a free pass to first base. Carlos Paula tried to do too much and sent a weak grounder to shortstop Miranda, who forced Sievers at second to end the threat.

Abernathy was hot enough to cool down the Orioles 1-2-3 in the bottom of the seventh.

The top of the eighth brought Runnels up to face Lopat one last time; Runnels grounded back to the pitcher. Korcheck somehow found one of Lopat's junk-mail specials and knocked it into center field for a double. Richards, knowing when he'd seen enough, pulled Lopat for veteran right-handed reliever George Zuverink. Harris then decided to pull righty Valdivielso for lefty Mickey McDermott, who flied out to center. Harris then pulled Abernathy, too, and pinch-hit left-handed-hitting Julio Becquer, another Cambria Cuban. Becquer hit a long fly ball into deep right field that settled into Philley's glove.

Bottom of the eighth, 2-1 Orioles, and more changes. Minor-league wanderer Bobby Kline replaced Valdivielso at short and Harris brought in Panamanian-born minor-league journeyman Vibert "Webbo" Clarke to try to stem the tide. Clarke brought a little something to the plate and got Dyck and Philley to fly out to left field. Triandos turned on one of his fastballs for a double to deep center. Looking for more speed on the basepaths, Richards had Dave Pope run for Triandos. Now in a jam, Clarke tried to pitch around Hal Smith, who waited him out for a walk.

Up to the plate stepped Brooks Robinson. Looking for something good to hit, he found a fastball to his liking and took it into left-center field for a clean single, the speedy Pope scoring from second. That put Smith on third and Marsh at the plate but Smith got himself into a rundown at third, tagged out by Korcheck.

But the damage was done. The young Mr. Robinson had found a new neighborhood, providing two solid hits, and an important RBI. Robinson related:

"I played that day and I went 2-for-4, knocked in a big run for the Orioles that beat Washington. And I remember runnin' back to the hotel. It was the Southern Hotel here in Baltimore and I called up my parents and said, 'Hey mom and dad, guess what? I just played my first game, got two hits, and drove in a big run.' I said this is my cup o' tea!"

Zuverink had little trouble with the Senators in the top of the ninth, getting Yost to fly out, surrendering a single to reserve Ernie Oravetz, and then getting Mickey Vernon to ground into a game-ending double play.

It was 2 hours and 17 minutes of pure fun for the Kiwanis Kids, 5,486 paying customers, and one young man from Little Rock, Arkansas, who went on to play 23 seasons of major-league ball, all with the Baltimore Orioles, garnering American League, All-Star, and World Series MVP trophies, 16 Gold Glove awards, and a 1983 induction into the Baseball Hall of Fame, and single-handedly redefining the third-base position for the century. For his legendary performance in the 1970 World Series he was awarded the sobriquet the Human Vacuum Cleaner.[5]

Brooks Robinson's Debut Game

Sources

In addition to the sources cited in the Notes, the author consulted Baseball-Reference.com and Kates, Maxwell. "Brooks Robinson," SABR Bioproject sabr.org/bioproj/person/55363cdb.

Notes

1 Bob Maisel, "Orioles Whip Senators, 3-1: Rookie Robinson Get 2 Hits and Drives in Run," *Baltimore Sun*, September 18, 1955: 42. The noontime sun was pushing into the mid 80s and the oh-so-balmy 60 percent humidity was just a joy to play in! In D.C., nobody put their summer clothes away until November.

2 Author interview with Brooks Robinson, September 22, 2019. Unless otherwise indicated, all quotations attributed to Robinson come from this interview.

3 Of the crowd, 3,248 were Kiwanis Kids Day youngsters, whooping it up one last time for this dog-day afternoon game. Bob Addie, "Orioles Win Again 3-1, Nats Game from Cellar," *Washington Post and Times Herald*, September 18, 1955: C-1.

4 See Note 3.

5 Doug Wilson, *Brooks: The Biography of Brooks Robinson* (New York: St. Martin's Press, 2014), 3-4.

Wilson wrote, "Years after playing his last game, Brooks Robinson remains an unquestioned icon in Baltimore. His genuine, humble demeanor, friendliness and above all, ability to remain a great role model have somehow grown in significance over the years as fans are continually disappointed by sports figures who are rude, selfish and inaccessible. Brooks Robinson exhibits the exact opposite. And no matter how much fame of adoration he achieved, he never lost the sense of who he was: just a regular guy who loved the game of baseball. As one writer was prompted to remark, 'Nobody's ever named a candy bar for Brooks. Around here we name our children after him.'"

Dick Williams Homers to Tie Game at Curfew

May 18, 1957: Chicago White Sox 4, Baltimore Orioles 4, at Memorial Stadium

By Tom Mank

On the morning of May 18, 1957, there were crowds of sports fans in downtown Baltimore. Most of them were in town for another historic sports event, not baseball – it was the day of the 81st running of the Preakness Stakes, the second leg of horse racing's Triple Crown. The race would begin at 5:30 P.M. at Baltimore's historic Pimlico Race Track. Kentucky Derby winner Iron Liege was the even-money favorite to win.[1]

To watch a baseball game that night, you would need to make the short trip to Memorial Stadium on 33rd Street, home of the Baltimore Orioles since 1954. The game would start at 7 P.M., not the customary 8 P.M. – the time moved up to allow time for the Chicago White Sox to catch a train to Boston immediately after the game.[2] Both teams agreed to a 10:20 curfew – the game would end immediately at 10:20 P.M. according the home-plate umpire's watch.[3]

The White Sox had won the Friday night game, 3-2. This was their sixth win in a row, keeping them in first place in the American League standings. For the seventh-place Orioles, it was their fifth loss in a row, following a disturbing pattern of blowing early leads against contending teams.[4]

In Chicago, this team hoped to finally reach the World Series, something it had not done since 1919. This was the time of the "Go-Go Sox" with speedsters Minnie Miñoso, Luis Aparicio, Jim Rivera, and Jim Landis. The Orioles were in some ways still the St Louis Browns, but hoping to improve with young stars like Brooks Robinson starting at third base and fan favorite Gus Triandos behind the plate – a city happy to again have a major-league baseball team to root for.

The game started mildly enough. The White Sox went down without a hit in the first inning. In the bottom of the first, George Kell singled to left field with one out and Bob Nieman walked, but both runners were stranded. Kell was an All-Star third baseman playing in his final year. (He hit over .300 12 times and won the AL batting title in 1949.) He had agreed to play one last year and mentor the young Brooks Robinson.

"When the Orioles broke camp, Brooks was listed as the starting third baseman with Kell slated for duty at first," a Robinson biographer wrote. "Brooks' elation at being in the starting lineup was short-lived, however. Two weeks into the 1957 season, hustling down the line after hitting a groundball to short, he saw the first baseman come off the bag to field a bad throw and swerved to avoid the sweep tag. As he did, his knee collapsed. He was carried to the clubhouse on a stretcher. Robinson was out for two months before the season really started."[5]

The White Sox walked twice but lacked a hit in the second inning. The Orioles loaded the bases with none out in their half, but did not score.

Chicago starting pitcher Jack Harshman singled to right field with one out in the third inning, but did not score. In the Orioles' third, there was controversy. After Gus Triandos flied out to center and Bob Nieman struck out, Tito Francona singled to right field. While on first base, "Earl Battey, the White Sox catcher, pegged poorly endeavoring to pick Francona off first base," said a game account. "When [Walt] Dropo, the rival first sacker, wheeled to pursue the errant throw into right field, he collided with Francona. There developed a torrid shoving match, with the Oriole runner forced to retreat to his original perch. Following a heated debate spearheaded by manager Paul Richards, Larry Napp, the umpire in chief, settled an apparent disagreement between two of his contemporaries. Napp's decision, obstruction of Francona's progress by Dropo, awarded Francona second base. This evoked wails of dissent from the White Sox."[6] Eventually a protest was filed. Dick Williams flied out to left to end the inning.

The fourth inning ended for the White Sox with Miñoso caught trying to steal third base on a strikeout.

• Dick Williams Homers •

Rescuing the Orioles from defeat in a night game planned in advance to end at 10:20 PM, first baseman Dick Williams hit a solo home run in the bottom of the ninth to create a 4-4 tie. Courtesy of the Baltimore Orioles.

The Orioles did not score in their half of the fourth.

The White Sox stranded a walk in the fifth inning. In the bottom of the inning, the Orioles wasted leadoff singles by Kell and Triandos without scoring.

After the White Sox went 1-2-3 in the sixth, the Orioles broke through. Kell gave the home crowd something to cheer about when he doubled to center to score Jim Brideweser (single) and Billy Gardner (walk). Gus Triandos and Bob Nieman followed with singles to score Kell.

Then the White Sox countered in the seventh inning. After a leadoff single by Larry Doby, pinch-hitters Jim Rivera, Sherm Lollar, and Dave Philley all singled to score two runs. After striking out pinch-hitter Sammy Esposito, Connie Johnson walked pinch-hitter Ron Northey to load the bases. Nellie Fox's sacrifice fly tied the game and Miñoso followed with a single to left to give the White Sox the lead. White Sox manager Al Lopez had used five pinch-hitters and two pinch-runners in the inning, not only giving his team the lead, but also wasting precious time, with the 10:20 curfew was approaching soon.[7]

The Orioles were retired 1-2-3 in the seventh as were the White Sox in the top of the eighth. In the bottom of the inning the Orioles' Bob Boyd drew a pinch-hit leadoff walk and Triandos delivered a one-out single. After Bob Nieman was retired on a popup, Richards summoned left-handed reliever Paul LaPalme to face left-handed-hitting Tito Francona. LaPalme was off to a great start in 1957 and had pitched two innings to get the save in the previous night's win.[8] He struck out Francona to hold the lead.

The ninth inning was the crazy one. The White Sox were retired quickly in the top of the inning. With the curfew fast approaching, the Orioles' Dick Williams ran to home plate. LaPalme's first pitch was a ball. Williams fouled off the second pitch. The clock in center field said 10:19, but it was the umpire's watch behind home plate that mattered.

As Al Lopez remembered 38 years later: "(LaPalme) had to make a pitch. ... He couldn't just stand there. The umpire would have called him on it. LaPalme's instructions were not to give Williams anything good to hit. But he had that knuckler, sometimes it didn't break at all. LaPalme's first knuckleball was high, and Williams took it. He lined the next one foul down the left-field line. Napp looked at his watch but said nothing"[9]

On the third pitch, Williams hit a home run to left field. As soon as he touched home plate, the umpire called the game a 4-4 tie.[10]

"The third pitch was another knuckler, up some, but I swung and hit it out of the park," Williams said.[11]

Two days later, the sports scribes were still talking about the game.

"Al Lopez, who is usually alert to what's going on, was caught fast asleep Saturday night. ... Sixty seconds of stalling could have brought the game to an end. LaPalme could have walked Williams or the bench could have called time for a conference with the pitcher," commented a *Baltimore Sun* columnist.[12]

Another wrote: "The question was: Why did LaPalme give Williams a ball to hit? Why didn't he walk him, throw the ball into the screen, re-tie his shoes, do anything to stall until the umpire Larry Napp signaled that it was 10:20?"[13]

"Kell said it was the screwiest thing he had ever seen, the fact they even pitched to me," Williams said.

"It wasn't like I was a home run threat – it was my first one of the year. One or two pitches away from me and it would have been over."[14]

"Lopez went bananas over the thing," Triandos said. "The poor guy (LaPalme) was raked over the coals after that."[15]

"After the game, Bob Maisel, who covered the game for the *Sun*, walked into the White Sox clubhouse to find Lopez still seething. 'Al was in shock,' Maisel said. 'His mouth was hanging open. He couldn't believe it. I saw him at the Hall of Fame a few years ago and needled him about it. Lopez said, 'I'm still in shock.'"[16]

Brooks Robinson said, "The curfew game was one of the weirdest ever."[17]

One might think that this would be Dick Williams's most thrilling moment in baseball, but of course he was the manager of the Boston Red Sox in 1967 during their "Impossible Dream" season, and was later elected to the Hall of Fame.

Bold Ruler beat Iron Liege by two lengths in the Preakness – not the only unexpected ending in Baltimore that day.

Sources

In addition to the sources mentioned in the Notes, the author also relied on baseball-reference.com and retrosheet.org.

Notes

1. William Boniface, "Seven Slated to Start for Triple Crown's Second Jewel," *Baltimore Sun*, May 18, 1957.
2. Lou Hatter, "Blow in 9th Nips Curfew," *Baltimore Sun*, May 19, 1957: 2D.
3. Irving Vaughan, "South Siders Seconds Shy from 7 In Row," *Chicago Tribune*, May 19, 1957: 2, 1.
4. Bob Maisel, "Minoso Hits Double for Two in 8th," *Baltimore Sun*, May 18, 1957: 13.
5. Doug Wilson, *Brooks: The Biography of Brooks Robinson* (New York: St. Martin's Press, 2014), 69-70.
6. Hatter.
7. Vaughan.
8. Maisel.
9. Doug Brown, "Near Suspension and Utter Disbelief," *Baltimore Sun*, June 8, 1995.
10. Hatter.
11. Brown.
12. Jesse A. Linthicum, "Sunlight on Sports – Al Lopez Caught Napping." *Baltimore Sun*, May 20, 1957: 14.
13. Brown.
14. Linthicum.
15. Linthicum.
16. Linthicum.
17. Linthicum.

Billy O'Dell Pitches Three Scoreless Innings in American League All-Star Game Victory

July 8, 1958: American League 4, National League 3, at Memorial Stadium

By Gary Sarnoff

Orioles pitcher Billy O'Dell was surprised when he was greeted by a host of reporters after the American League's 4-3 win in the 1958 All-Star Game. Two days earlier, he believed he had no chance of getting into the game, and now he was the All-Star Game's MVP. "I had good stuff all right," O'Dell told the reporters.[1] "I'll tell you something about O'Dell," said Orioles catcher Gus Triandos. "On a day or night when Billy is right, he's as good as any batter he faces."[2] On this day O'Dell needed just 27 pitches to retire nine consecutive batters in the last three innings.

The 25th All-Star Game, on July 8, 1958, was the first played in Baltimore. "The weather was hot and humid, but every seat was taken long before game time in picturesque Memorial Stadium, for this was a big day in the history of baseball in Baltimore and the folks weren't going to miss a minute of it," wrote *New York Times* sportswriter John Drebinger.[3] The game featured another All-Star Game first: The players selected the starters instead of the fans. "It was a good system," Ted Williams said of the new system, "although I believe it would be good to let the fans back in on the voting." Most believed that Williams and Yogi Berra would've been in the American League's starting lineup had the fans voted. "Yes, maybe," said Williams. "But Bob Cerv deserved it. He's having a great year."[4]

This game wouldn't go down as a thrilling midsummer classic. "The most forgettable of all times," said a National Leaguer. "It was one of the dullest," penned a sportswriter.[5] The two teams combined for 13 singles and no extra-base hits.

Willie Mays, the game's first batter, stepped in to face American League starting pitcher Bob Turley. The leadoff spot was unusual for Mays, and it baffled him. "What do I do up there?" he asked before the game. "The leadoff man is supposed to draw walks, Willie," Stan Musial said with a smile. "That's right, Willie," said National League manager Fred Haney. "That's no fun," Mays said with alarm. Then he beamed happily when he realized he was being teased.[6]

Mays drilled the game's first pitch for a bullseye, a shot that hit third base and bounced into left field for a hit. After an out, Musial advanced Mays to third on a single to right field. A long fly out by Hank Aaron was deep enough to allow Mays to score the game's first run. A hit batsman, a walk, and a wild pitch followed to give the National League a 2-0 lead.

The American League scored an unearned run in its first inning against National League starting pitcher Warren Spahn. Nellie Fox led off with a grounder that shortstop Ernie Banks fielded but threw high for an error. Mickey Mantle followed with a single to put runners on the corners. Fox scored when the next batter, Jackie Jensen, grounded into a double play. The National League made it 3-1 with a tally in the top of the second. Mays, who reached base on a fielder's choice, attempted to steal. Triandos threw to shortstop Luis Aparicio, covering second. The catcher's low throw skipped past Aparicio and rolled into the outfield to allow Mays to advance to third. "It wasn't a bad throw at all," Triandos said after the game, "but with Mays sliding, Aparicio couldn't get his glove on the ball."[7] Bob Skinner singled between short and third to score Mays, and that was all for Turley. American League manager Casey Stengel summoned Ray Narleski from the bullpen. "I didn't have much, that's for sure," Turley said after the game. "I guess it just wasn't my day."[8]

The American League cut the lead to one with a run in the bottom of the second. Triandos singled, Aparicio forced him at second, Narleski smacked a sharp single to center, and Fox produced an RBI single.

In the bottom of the fifth, with the score still 3-2, National League, 40-year-old Mickey Vernon, pinch-hitting for Narleski, hit Bob Friend's first offering for a single. Nellie Fox, the only player to get more than one hit in the game, also singled, and Mantle walked on four pitches to load the bases. Jensen followed with a short-hopper to Friend's left. A force at home was in sight, but Friend was unable to come up with the ball. Second baseman Bill Mazeroski got to the ball and threw out Jensen at first base, but a run scored on the play to tie the game.

Early Wynn came on to pitch for the American League in the top of the sixth and retired the side in order. Frank Malzone began the bottom of the inning with a single. Gus Triandos was due up, but Stengel elected to go with a pinch-hitter, which did not appease the hometown crowd. The spectators grew angrier when Yogi Berra, a Yankee, was the pinch-batter. "Did that bother you?" a writer asked Stengel after the game. "No, I knew I was going to get it when I sent up Berra for their catcher (Triandos)," he replied. "I knew I was going to get it, too," Berra said with a laugh. "They boo us all over the league, but I believe they do a better job of it here than anywhere else."[9] Triandos agreed with the manager's decision. "We were tied and Casey was out to win a ballgame, not a popularity contest. The booing was unfair to Casey and embarrassing to me."[10]

After Berra popped out, Ted Williams batted for Aparicio and grounded to the left side of the infield. Third baseman Frank Thomas stepped to his left, gloved the ball, and then dropped it as he tried to extract it from his mitt.

Now with runners on first and second with only one out and the pitcher due up, Stengel called on his "Mr. Versatility,"[11] Gil McDougald, another Yankee, to pinch-hit, and as expected, the crowd gave another Bronx cheer. The move paid off, however, as McDougald delivered an RBI single to give the American League a 4-3 lead.

The stage was now set for O'Dell, and his presence on the mound in the top of the seventh baffled the scribes in the press box. Why would Stengel elect to go with O'Dell, who had yielded 10 runs on 22 hits in his last two starts, instead of the hottest pitcher in the league? Billy Pierce had allowed just one earned run in his last 42⅔ innings and appeared in four previous All-Star Games. Unbeknown to the sportswriters, Pierce's pitching arm had stiffened during the last few innings of his 8-1 win over the Tigers the previous Saturday.

"Casey told me to let him know if the arm felt all right after I threw in the bullpen," Pierce explained after the game. "The stiffness was still there."[12] O'Dell retired the National League in order in the top of the seventh. In the bottom of the inning, Turk Farrell came on for the National League and was impressive. After issuing a walk to start the inning, he retired the next three batters, two by strikeout. "He's really fast," National League catcher Del Crandall said of the 22-year-old Farrell. "I haven't seen anyone faster."[13]

O'Dell believed that the top of the eighth would be his biggest challenge, because Musial, Aaron, and Banks were due up. "Musial was the man I feared the most," said O'Dell. "I got him out on a slider." Then, after retiring Aaron on a groundout, O'Dell offered Banks nothing but sliders. "I tried him on fastballs in Arizona this spring, and a couple of them disappeared out into the desert," the pitcher said. Sticking with sliders, O'Dell got three past Banks.[14]

Farrell struck out Malzone and Williams to retire the American League in the bottom of the eighth. Then, to the delight of a capacity crowd of 48,829, O'Dell retired the National League in order in the top of the ninth for a 4-3 American League win.

Sources

In addition to the sources cited in the Notes, the author consulted Retrosheet.org.

Notes

1   Bob Maisel, "O'Dell Best, Stengel Says," *Baltimore Sun*, July 9, 1958: Part 1, 1.

2   Louis Effrat, "O'Dell of Orioles Is the Brightest of All-Stars at Baltimore," *New York Times*, July 9, 1958: 31.

3   John Drebinger, "Wynn Gets Credit for 4-3 Triumph," *New York Times*, July 9, 1958: 30.

4   Maisel, Part 1, 16.

5   Edward Prell, "Wynn Winning Hurler in Dull All-Star Game," *Baltimore Sun*, July 9, 1959: Part 3, 1.

6   Arthur Daley, "Sports of the Times," *New York Times*, July 9, 1958: 30.

7   Maisel, Part 1, 16.

8   Maisel, Part 1, 16.

9   Maisel, Part 1, 1.

10   Effrat.

11   Lou Hatter, "McDougald's Hit Wins Game; Oriole Pitcher has 3 Perfect Innings," *Baltimore Sun*, July 9, 1958: Part 1, 1.

12   Edward Prell, "Casey Stengel Jeered by Oriole crowd; Pierce Ailing," *Baltimore Sun*, July 9, 1958: Part 3, 1.

13   Roscoe McGowen, "Haney Supports Players' Choices," *New York Times*, July 9, 1958: 30.

14   Maisel, Part 1, 1.

Orioles Knuckleballer Hoyt Wilhelm No-hits Yankees

September 20, 1958: Baltimore Orioles 1, New York Yankees 0, at Memorial Stadium

By Mike Huber

The game only took one hour and 48 minutes. Before a last-day-of-summer crowd of 10,941, Baltimore's Hoyt Wilhelm joined the record books by pitching a no-hit game against the New York Yankees. He started the game against Don Larsen, who had pitched a perfect game in the 1956 World Series.[1] Even with the few fans in the stands, braving a steady rain, millions more may have witnessed this piece of history, as it was the nationally televised "Game of the Week."[2]

Wilhelm, a relief pitcher for most of his career, was making only his third start for the Orioles and the ninth of his career, in his seventh season in the majors. He had pitched for the New York Giants and the Cleveland Indians, and he was claimed on waivers by the Orioles from the Indians on August 23, 1958. Many thought his career was washed up.[3] Larsen had last pitched on August 10, but he missed six weeks with an inflamed right elbow.

With seven games left to play in the regular season, New York had already clinched the American League pennant. Baltimore, entering the contest with a 68-77-1 record, had defeated the Yankees on September 19, but they knew that they would have to endure another losing season.[4]

Both pitchers were in command. Wilhelm retired the first seven batters he faced, before walking Bobby Richardson in the third. Larsen appeared sharp, especially early on, "mixing a good curve and changeup with his speed."[5] With one out in the first, Bob Boyd reached on a drag bunt single. That was the only hit Larsen would allow. From about the third inning on, intermittent showers kept the grass wet. By the fifth inning, the rain was steady. The Yankees tried to bunt for a hit on three different times, but each time the ball rolled foul. It must not have affected Wilhelm, as he struck out eight and only walked two.

By the sixth inning, the rain began to fall a bit harder, so the umpires requested that the lights be turned on at Memorial Stadium. At the end of the sixth, the game was still scoreless, and both teams had one combined hit. New York manager Casey Stengel kept Larsen in the dugout in after the Yankees batted in the seventh, and Bobby Shantz came on in relief. Leading off for the Orioles, Gus Triandos swung at a 2-and-1 offering from Shantz and launched a solo home run over the centerfield fence, above the 410-foot sign, giving the Orioles a 1-0 lead and the only run Wilhelm would need. Triandos' home run was his 30th of the season, tying the American League season mark, set by New York's Yogi Berra in 1952 (and duplicated by Berra in 1956).[6]

In the eighth, New York had its best chance to break up the no-no. Leadoff batter Norm Siebern "hit a tantalizing high bouncer which was perfectly placed in the hole between first and second."[7] Billy Gardner, Baltimore's second baseman, raced to his left, scooped up the ball, and flipped it to first baseman Boyd for the bang-bang out.

Baltimore came to bat and created a mini rally. Wilhelm led off by grounding out to the second baseman. Dick Williams stroked a double to left. Boyd then struck out, and Jim Busby, who had entered the game as a defensive replacement in the seventh, singled in a ball he dribbled back to the pitcher. Baltimore had runners at the corners, but Brooks Robinson flied out to left to end the inning.

In the Yankees' ninth, Richardson flied out to center. Enos Slaughter pinch-hit for Shantz and hit a liner to right, but Willie Tasby ran it down for out number two. Hank Bauer, New York's last hope, attempted to bunt the first offering by Wilhelm, but it rolled foul. This "drew a loud round of boos from the fans."[8] He swung through the second pitch for strike two. This brought on cheers. With pitch number three, Bauer popped out to Gardner at second, and the Orioles players mobbed Wilhelm near the mound. He had just pitched a no-hitter.

Larsen had pitched superbly, allowing only the bunt single to Boyd in the first frame. He had walked two and struck out two. Wilhelm also only walked two batters, as he kept "his exceptionally hard-to-handle knuckleball under remarkable control."[9] He used 99 pitches, with "about 90 per cent of them knucklers,"[10] according to

The Baltimore Sun. Although this was only his third win of the season, against 10 losses, Wilhelm's "performance simply was something out of this world,"[11] as it was the first no-hitter by a Baltimore major league pitcher in 60 years. Jim Hughes of the National League's Baltimore Orioles had pitched a no-hitter against the Boston Beaneaters on April 22, 1898. Coincidentally, that was the exact same day that Ted Breitenstein of the Cincinnati Reds hurled a no-hit game against the Pittsburgh Pirates. Additionally, Wilhelm's feat came exactly two months after Detroit's Jim Bunning no-hit the Red Sox on July 20, 1958, by a score of 3-0.

This was also the first no-hitter to be pitched against the Yankees since Virgil Trucks stopped the New York bats on August 25, 1952, at Yankee Stadium. Forty-five years would go by before another team, the Houston Astros, used six pitchers to no-hit New York (June 11, 2003, in an interleague game).

In an interview after the game, Wilhelm praised his catcher, not for homering, but for being his battery mate. He stated, "I thought Gus caught a great game for me."[12] When pressed about the no-hitter, Wilhelm replied, "I really didn't get to thinking much about it until Gus hit that homer. After all, you've got to have a run. Up until then, I'm only thinking about winning a game, and I haven't gotten many runs this year."[13]

Even the New Yorkers were impressed. Mickey Mantle, one of Wilhelm's strikeout victims, commented, "I thought his fast ball was lousy and so was his curve,"[14] grinning good-naturedly. Yankees skipper Stengel chimed in with, "I give that feller full credit. He earned it."[15] And the Bombers' Berra, who caught three no-hitters in his career, including Larsen's perfect game, told reporters, "It's a guessing game when you're hitting against him. You know it's coming but you don't know where. I don't think he does, either."[16]

By the way, this game was played on Wilhelm's ninth wedding anniversary. The night before the historic game, he telephoned his wife Peggy at their home in Huntersville, NC. According to *The Baltimore Sun*, he said to her, "I neglected to send you a card. What do you want for our anniversary tomorrow?" She responded, "Honey, send me something real good. Let's win one."[17] A no-hitter definitely qualifies as "something real good." On top of that, he was given a $150 watch for being voted as "the outstanding player of the game"[18] by the Game of the Week crew.

Sources

In addition to the sources mentioned in the notes, the author consulted baseball-reference.com, mlb.com and retrosheet.org.

Hoyt Wilhelm humbled the first-place New York Yankees, striking out eight, walking two, and throwing a no-hitter won by the thinnest of margins, 1-0, thanks to a home run by his catcher Gus Triandos, depicted here wearing #11. Courtesy of the Baltimore Orioles.

Notes

1 Larsen was the only pitcher to have pitched a no-hitter in the post-season (a perfect game on October 8, 1956, against the Brooklyn Dodgers) until Philadelphia Phillies star Roy Halladay no-hit the Cincinnati Reds on October 6, 2010, in the first game of the National League Division Series (Halladay's post-season debut).

2 Wilhelm Pitches No-Hitter, Downs Yanks, 1-0," *The Philadelphia Inquirer*, September 21, 1958: 87.

3 With renewed confidence from the Orioles (three All Star selections in the next four seasons), Wilhelm turned his career around and retired with the most appearances by a pitcher in history (1,070), which has since been bested by five other pitchers. Jesse Orosco currently holds the record with 1,252 appearances, all but four games as a reliever. Hoyt Wilhelm was elected to the Hall of Fame in 1985.

4 The Orioles put together a seven-game win streak, but then they lost their last two games, finishing at 74-79-1. Although the Birds did have a .500 season in 1957, their last winning season was in 1945, as the St. Louis Browns.

5 Bob Maisel, "Wilhelm Hurls No-Hitter As Birds Beat Yanks, 1-0," *The Baltimore Sun*, September 21, 1958: 62-63.

6 Triandos finished the 1958 season with 30 homers. As of the beginning of the 2017 season, the AL record for home runs in a season by a catcher is 35, held by Ivan Rodriguez (Texas Rangers, 1999). The Major League record is 42, set by Javy Lopez (Atlanta Braves, 2003).

7 Maisel.

8 Maisel.

9 *The Philadelphia Inquirer*.

10 Maisel.

11 John Drebinger, "Wilhelm's No-Hitter Trips Yanks for Orioles, 1-0," *New York Times*, September 21, 1958: S1.

12 Lou Hatter, "Hoyt's Wife Gets Big Gift," *The Baltimore Sun*, September 21, 1958: 62.

13 Hatter.

14 Maisel.

15 Maisel.

16 Maisel.

17 Hatter.

18 Maisel.

Time Runs Out for O's and Chisox in 18-Inning Marathon

August 6, 1959: Baltimore Orioles 1, Chicago White Sox 1, at Memorial Stadium

By Richard Cuicchi

The Baltimore Orioles and Chicago White Sox had a tendency to play extra-inning games against each other in 1959. The one on August 6 took the prize for longest but it ended, frustratingly, without a winner. The two teams battled for an Orioles-record 18 innings, but at the end of the night the exhausting game was all for naught. The game, which remained tied 1-1 after 18 innings, was called because of a midnight curfew, and it was replayed later in the season.

The two teams had battled in two 10-inning and two 17-inning games earlier in the season. The White Sox had taken three of those games, including the two marathons.

The White Sox, managed by Al Lopez, had flirted with first place the entire season, as they battled the Cleveland Indians. The White Sox were never more than 4½ games behind the league leader. During a 12-day stretch in the first half of June, they either held first place or were tied with Cleveland. There was a similar stretch of 11 games in the second half of July. Chicago finally took possession of the lead on July 28, and did not relinquish it for the balance of the season. Coming into the game on August 6, Paul Richards' Baltimore squad was in third place, 10 games behind the White Sox.

The grueling 4-hour 8-minute game on August 6 remarkably used only four pitchers.[1] Billy Pierce was the workhorse for the White Sox, going 16 innings before yielding to Turk Lown. Orioles starter Billy O'Dell threw eight innings, followed by 36-year-old Hoyt Wilhelm, who finished the game. O'Dell was very familiar with the White Sox lineup, since it was his sixth start of the season against them, including two against Pierce. Each pitcher had recorded a winning decision.

The game was played before 8,707 fans at Baltimore's Memorial Stadium.

The White Sox scored first, in the top of the third inning, when John Romano tripled with two out, scoring Al Smith from first. Romano's hit bounced off the padding atop the seven-foot wire fence in left-center. Orioles left fielder Gene Woodling could have possibly made a play on the hit; he was able to run to the fence in time, but since there was no warning track at that spot on the field, he did not position himself to jump and attempt the catch.[2]

For the next four innings, each team had only one chance to hit with a runner in scoring position, but failed to push across a run.

In the bottom of the eighth, Richards went to his bench in an attempt to manufacture a run, and it worked. Chico Carrasquel pinch-hit for Willy Miranda and led off with a single. Running for Carrasquel, Albie Pearson took second on a sacrifice bunt by Bob Boyd, who pinch-hit for O'Dell. After pinch-hitter Bob Nieman was intentionally walked, Willie Tasby singled to score Pearson for Baltimore's only run of the game.

Wilhelm entered the game in the top of the ninth. Normally a starter in 1959, the knuckleballer had just won a complete game against the Indians four days before. He had a scare in the 11th inning, when Romano reached third as a result of a walk, a sacrifice, and a passed ball. But Wilhelm struck out Billy Goodman to get out of the inning.

Pierce was magnificent after the run-scoring eighth: He retired 12 in a row until Joe Ginsberg singled with two outs in the 12th. He survived two threats in the last two innings of his outing. Left fielder Smith threw out Wilhelm at the plate in the 15th when he tried to score from second base on the Orioles' third single of the inning. Pierce gave up a two-out double to Walt Dropo in the 16th, but again got out of the inning without allowing a run.

Wilhelm was even better: He had an eight-inning no-hitter in relief going into the top of the 17th inning, but he wound up giving a two-out single to Goodman. Lown relieved Pierce in the bottom of frame and retired the side in order.

With the game approaching the city's 11:59 P.M. curfew, both teams had been informed that no inning would start after 11:55. Thus, when the 17th inning ended at 11:52, everyone knew the next frame would be the last.[3]

The White Sox made a last-ditch effort to end the marathon in the final inning and nearly succeeded at the expense of the exhausted Orioles team. Wilhelm gave up his second hit, to Sammy Esposito, who hit a slow roller over the mound. Shortstop Billy Klaus's throw to first base skipped past Dropo, but a heads-up play by catcher Ginsberg, backing up the throw to first, kept Esposito from taking second. However, Esposito then advanced on a passed ball by a tired Ginsberg, who had caught the entire game. After an intentional walk to Nellie Fox, another passed ball advanced the White Sox runners to second and third. But Wilhelm retired Smith on second baseman Billy Gardner's catch of a fly ball far down the right-field line to end the threat.[4]

Baltimore was unable to take advantage of its last chance to win the game. Lown retired the side, allowing only one baserunner. The game finished 13 minutes after midnight.[5]

Pierce scattered 11 hits and three walks (including two intentionally), while striking out seven. Lown, one of the White Sox' main stoppers along with Gerry Staley, closed out the game. He struck out two and yielded one hit. Lown had pitched six innings in relief in the 17-inning game on July 25 and was credited with the win.

O'Dell completed eight innings, yielding five hits and four walks, while Wilhelm gave up three walks and two hits. Wilhelm jokingly told O'Dell after the game, "I'm not relieving you any more, O'Dell. You got all the runs."[6]

The White Sox offense was severely constrained by the first three hitters in the lineup (Luis Aparicio, Fox, and Smith) managing to get only two walks in 24 plate appearances. Romano was the only White Sox player with more than one hit. The Orioles' 12 hits included two each by Brooks Robinson, Tasby, Dropo, and Ginsberg.

The game was the longest in both leagues in 1959. It was the longest (in innings) for the Orioles franchise since it moved to Baltimore in 1954. When the franchise existed in St. Louis, the Browns played a 19-inning game in 1921.

Wilhelm was not unfamiliar with the reliever role. He broke in as a relief specialist as a 29-year-old rookie with the New York Giants in 1952. In fact, the 1959 season was the only one of his 21-year major-league career in which he was used primarily as a starter. The right-hander wound up leading the American League in ERA (2.19). He was still making appearances out of the bullpen at age 49 and became the first full-time reliever to be elected to the Baseball Hall of Fame.

The deadlocked game was replayed on September 11 as part of a twilight-night doubleheader. The Orioles shut out the White Sox twice. There was a bit of déjà vu in

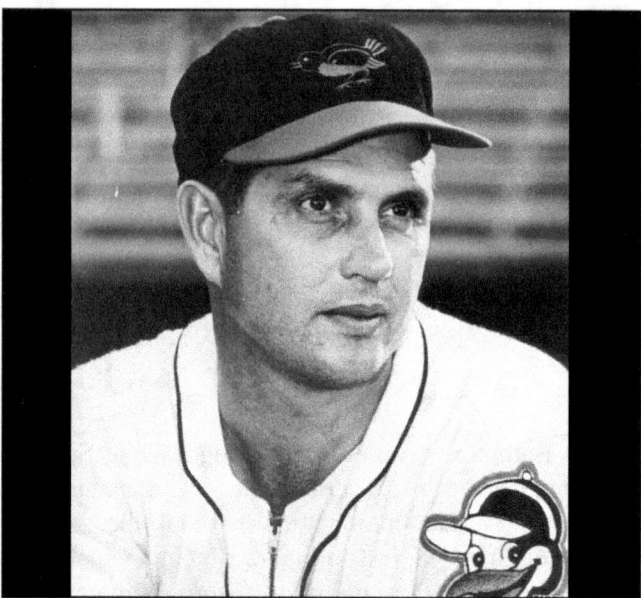

Working 10 innings of relief – the 9th through the 18th innings – Hoyt Wilhelm helped battle the visiting White Sox to a 1-1 18-inning tie game at Memorial Stadium. Courtesy of the Baltimore Orioles.

the second game of the twin bill, which lasted 16 innings with a 1-0 score. It was the teams' sixth extra-inning contest against each other in 1959.

Baltimore fell to sixth place by the end of the season, 20 games behind the White Sox.

The White Sox retained their first-place lead throughout the rest of the season. After finishing in second place behind the New York Yankees in 1957 and 1958, they claimed their first American League pennant since 1919, the year they were involved in the infamous Black Sox Scandal in the World Series.

Known as the "Go Go Sox" for a scrappy style of play that included the most stolen bases and the fewest home runs in the American League, they lost the 1959 World Series to the Los Angeles Dodgers in six games. In the only two seasons of the 1950s in which the Yankees did not win the American League pennant, Lopez took teams to the World Series, including the '54 Indians.

Sources
In addition to the sources cited in the Notes, the author consulted Baseball-Reference.com and Retrosheet.org.

Notes
1   Bob Maisel. "Birds Tie ChiSox, 1-1; Curfew Ends Game After 18," *Baltimore Sun*, August 7, 1959: 20.

2   Maisel: 19.

3   Edward Prell, "18 Innings to a Tie! – Sox, 1; Orioles 1,"*Chicago Tribune*, August 7, 1959: 4,1.

4   Maisel: 20.

5   Prell.

6   Maisel: 20.

Jerry Walker's Masterpiece

September 11, 1959: Baltimore Orioles 1, Chicago White Sox 0 (16 innings, game two of a doubleheader), at Memorial Stadium

By Dave Moniz

For 20-year-old Jerry Walker, only two years removed from high school in Ada, Oklahoma, it was a fairytale ending to his third season with the Baltimore Orioles.

Starting against the league-leading Chicago White Sox on September 11, 1959, Walker threw 16 shutout innings in the second game of a doubleheader at Memorial Stadium. in Baltimore. His gem followed a first-game 3-0 three-hit shutout by teammate Jack Fisher, who two years later would be remembered as the pitcher who surrendered home run number 60 to the New York Yankees' Roger Maris in his historic chase of Babe Ruth's single-season home run record. Billy Pierce worked the full game for the White Sox.

Walker was a member of the Orioles' "Kiddie Korps" of talented young starting pitchers, and earlier in the summer had started the second All-Star Game of 1959 in Los Angeles for the American League.[1]

On "Westinghouse Night" on September 11, Walker faced a scrappy White Sox team built around speed and pitching. Filling out Chicago's lineup that night were their star middle infielders, shortstop Luis Aparicio and second baseman Nellie Fox; veteran slugger and first baseman Ted Kluszewski; and center fielder Jim Landis. The "Go-Go" White Sox went on to win 94 games in the regular season and finished with the best record in baseball before losing to the Los Angeles Dodgers in the World Series.

Sixty years removed from his best season as a professional, Walker remembered the September 11 game in vivid detail. He was 80 at the time of an interview in 2019 and only recently retired from front-office work with the Cincinnati Reds. The game against the White Sox was his 11th and final win of the 1959 season for an Orioles team that was beginning to build the foundation that would become a mid-1960s powerhouse. He recalled throwing 178 pitches that night, a mix of fastballs, sliders, and changeups. He allowed six hits, all singles, and was seldom in trouble though he recalled being extremely fatigued when the game ended just a few minutes short of the midnight curfew in Baltimore.

"I remember I did not do much the next day," he said in the interview.[2]

The White Sox and Orioles played 25 innings of baseball that day and the light-hitting White Sox rarely threatened. In the second game, Aparicio and Kluszewski combined for four of their team's six hits, all singles. The 31-year-old Fox, who had been selected to 10 All-Star squads and finished the season hitting .306 with a .380 OBP, was 1-for-6.[3]

It looked as if Chicago might end its doubleheader scoring drought in the first inning of game two. Fox and Kluszewski both rapped singles off Walker but Landis, safe on a fielder's choice, was stranded at third when catcher John Romano flied to center to end the inning. That was the only time in the game that a White Sox runner advanced as far as third base.

Walker again shut down a White Sox scoring chance in the fifth. After right fielder Jim McAnany singled, pitcher Barry Latman walked with one out. But Walker got Fox to fly out and Aparicio to line out. Their next best scoring chance came in the ninth, when Kluszewski singled to right to lead off the inning. But according to Lou Hatter's game account in the *Baltimore Sun*, a great play by Baltimore shortstop Billy Klaus on a slow roller by left fielder Al Smith ended the threat.[4]

After the ninth, Walker didn't permit even one White Sox runner past first and his catcher, Gus Triandos, in Hatter's period game story verbiage, "twice cut down would-be base bandits with unerring pegs."[5]

The Orioles outhit the White Sox eight to six and left 12 runners on base. But their offense was only modestly better. In the first inning, they stranded runners at second and third with no outs when White Sox starter Latman induced a foul out to first, a fly ball to shallow center, and a groundout to third by Brooks

Robinson. Walker tried to do his part at the plate, banging out two singles. But from the first inning through the seventh, Latman set down 21 Oriole batters in a row.

The Orioles blew chances to end the game in the eighth and the 10th. In the eighth, right fielder Al Pilarcik popped out to third with runners at first and third. In the 10th, second baseman Billy Gardner and Walker both singled with one out but Gardner was left at second after 39-year-old White Sox reliever Gerry Staley, brought in for Latman by White Sox manager Al Lopez, struck out pinch-hitter Bob Nieman and got Pilarcik to ground to first.

With two outs in the top of the 16th, Aparicio tried to get into scoring position by stealing second base but was thrown out.

The game ended in the bottom of the 16th. Pilarcik singled to center and was sacrificed to second by Barry Shetrone. After an intentional walk to Gene Woodling, Pilarcik took third on a groundout to second. He scored on a single to left off Staley by Robinson, the Orioles' 22-year-old third baseman and Walker's roommate. Walker remembered that his roommate had not yet developed keen offensive skills but his future greatness as a defensive player was evident in his uncommonly quick hands and feet.[6]

Walker said his own team's offensive futility that night allowed him to pitch as long as he did. He said his manager, Paul Richards, told him starting in the ninth inning that if he came to bat with a runner on base, Richards would pinch-hit for him.

"I felt fine," Walker recalled. "I only had two runners after the ninth and one was thrown out stealing."[7] The two hitters he feared most, Fox and Aparicio, were a combined 3-for-13.

Walker's 16-inning shutout, however impressive, was not a major-league record. Four pitchers, including the Washington Senators' Walter Johnson and New York Giants great Carl Hubbell, threw 18-inning shutouts. Walker nonetheless touched greatness that night, nearly matching one of the signature achievements of two Hall of Fame pitchers.

For Walker, the game was a high-water mark in a meteoric career. Beset by arm injuries, he left Baltimore after the 1960 season and pitched another four years for the Kansas City Athletics and Cleveland Indians, finishing his career with a 37-44 record and an earned-run average of 4.36. Had he stayed in Baltimore, and remained healthy, he would have been 27 years old during the team's World Series-winning season in 1966. The 1959 season turned out to be Walker's best:

Right-hander Jerry Walker only struck out four, but he pitched all 16 innings of a 1-0 game in the second game of a doubleheader against the White Sox, capping a day when O's pitchers threw 25 innings of scoreless ball. Courtesy of the Baltimore Orioles.

He finished with a 2.92 ERA and allowed only 160 hits in 182 innings.

Walker's 16-inning shutout is almost inconceivable today as even nine-inning complete games are rare for starting pitchers. During his breakout season, Walker tossed seven complete games, including his marathon effort. In contrast, during the 2019 season, no major-league team had more than six nine-inning complete games and the American and National League averages for complete games was 1.5 per team.

Sources

In addition to the sources cited in the Notes, the author consulted Baseballalmanac.com, the *Baltimore Sun*, and Baseball-Reference.com.

Notes

1 The game in Los Angeles was the first time the major leagues played a second All-Star Game, a prime motivation being to generate more revenue for the players' pension fund. Two All-Star Games were played each season from 1959 to 1962.

2 Author interview with Jerry Walker, July 3, 2019.

3 By the end of his career, Fox had been named to 15 All-Star squads.

4 Lou Hatter, "Orioles Defeat Chisox, 3-0 and 1-0 in 16 Innings, *Baltimore Sun*, September 12, 1959: Sports pages 13, 16.

5 Lou Hatter.

6 Walker interview.

7 Walker interview.

Umpire's "Time" Call Nullifies Ted Kluszewski's Apparent 3-Run Home Run

August 28, 1960: Baltimore Orioles 3, Chicago White Sox 1, at Memorial Stadium

By Bob Brown

In late August of the seventh season since the St. Louis Browns' move to Baltimore, the Orioles were in the midst of a full-fledged pennant race for the first time since the relocation. Well on their way to their first winning season in Baltimore, they were within striking distance of the first-place New York Yankees when the Chicago White Sox visited Baltimore for the first of a two-game series at Memorial Stadium. With both teams within 2½ games of the top spot, the series was expected to have significant pennant implications.

On a sunny Sunday afternoon, the pitching matchup for the first game of the series showcased 21-year-old Milt Pappas taking the mound for the Orioles against the 42-year-old future Hall of Famer Early Wynn, who made his major-league debut with the Washington Senators four months after baby Milt came into the world. Lineups featured Brooks Robinson, Minnie Miñoso, Jim Gentile, Ted Kluszewski, Ron Hansen, and Luis Aparicio. However, headlines the following day cited third-base umpire Ed Hurley as more influential on the outcome than any of the stars.

After routine three-up/three-down first innings for both teams, the Orioles struck first with two runs in the bottom of the second. After a leadoff walk to Jim Gentile and Gus Triandos's strikeout, Gene Stephens singled to right, and Ron Hansen plated Gentile with a single to center. Marv Breeding lofted a sacrifice fly to left, scoring Stephens, before Minnie Miñoso's relay doubled up Hansen at second to end the inning.

Quiet third and fourth innings featured both pitchers cruising, until the Orioles struck again in the fifth. After Breeding singled and Gene Woodling was given an intentional walk, Brooks Robinson singled to center to score Breeding and give the Orioles a 3-0 lead.

After two more quiet innings, Pappas had yielded no runs on two hits through seven innings while showing no sign of fatigue. At this point, the game certainly displayed no evidence that it would be cited 60 years later in a compendium of memorable Orioles games, but that would change in the top of the eighth.

With two outs in that half inning, Aparicio and Nellie Fox singled, putting runners at the corners. Roy Sievers singled to right, scoring Aparicio and moving Fox to second. With two on, Kluszewski pinch-hit for Miñoso, representing the potential go-ahead run. Kluszewski lined Pappas's second pitch into the right-field bleachers to give the White Sox an apparent 4-3 lead.

As the *Baltimore Sun* reported, "But down at third base came help from a most unlikely source. Hurley was making like a helicopter, supported nobly by Brooks Robinson, signaling 'no play' while Kluszewski circled the bases." Hurley explained to manager Al Lopez that he had called time before the pitch to address the fact that two White Sox players – outfielder Floyd Robinson and first baseman Earl Torgeson, both of whom had just made the first two outs of the eighth as pinch-hitters, were warming up behind first base in foul territory, preparing to take the field in the bottom of the inning. Hurley had called time to instruct the two players to move to the designated bullpen area farther down right field, and Kluszewski was ordered back to the batter's box.[1] After an anticlimactic flyout to end the inning, the score remained 3-1 in favor of the Orioles. The Orioles went quietly in their half of the eighth, but not before White Sox second baseman Nellie Fox was ejected for arguing the nullification. The White Sox announced that they were playing the game under protest.

With one out in the top of the ninth, the White Sox loaded the bases, and Orioles manager Paul Richards summoned knuckleballer Hoyt Wilhelm to shut the door on a potential rally. Wilhelm struck out Torgeson and got Aparicio to fly to center field to end the game. With the win, coupled with a Yankees doubleheader split with the Detroit Tigers, the Orioles moved to within two games of first place, while the White Sox dropped to third place, three games back.

Not surprisingly, the White Sox were irate, and club President Bill Veeck filed a formal protest with American League President Joe Cronin. Veeck declared that Hurley's ruling was a ridiculous decision. "I doubt that Hurley or any umpire in Hurley's position on the field has the right to stop play at the time that Hurley did." Lopez fumed, "He's always sticking his nose into something that doesn't concern him. He's way over there on third base. (First-base umpire John) Flaherty told 'em to move down to the bullpen, but he didn't call time. Neither did the guy at the plate (John Stevens)."[2]

Veeck based the protest on three rules that all essentially stated that an umpire cannot call time while a play is in progress – Veeck and Lopez contended that the pitch from Pappas was already in progress when time was called, and therefore not valid. Cronin dismissed the protest with a terse telegram, stating: "By reason of Organized Baseball's rules 3.12 and 9.04 (b-2), your protest of the Chicago Baltimore game on August 28, 1960 is disallowed. Best wishes, Joe Cronin." Rule 3.12 reads "When the umpire suspends play, he shall call time. ... Between the call of 'time' and the call of 'play,' the ball is dead." Rule 9.04(b-2) reads "a field umpire's ... duties shall be to take concurrent jurisdiction with the umpire-in-chief in calling 'time,' balks. ..." Veeck appealed Cronin's decision to Commissioner Ford Frick, but the appeal was disallowed based on the constitution of the league, which grants full authority to the league president.[3]

Hurley admitted he regretted calling time. "I wanted to dig a hole right in the ground and go down in it when that ball sailed right out of the park, but there's nothing I could do about it. I probably feel worse about it than the White Sox do. But I called 'time' and there was no way I could take that back." He added, "Sure, if I had it to do over again, I would wait. But you can't call those things back. Suppose Klu had popped up. That wouldn't have counted." Earlier in the season, Hurley recalled, a similar situation happened at Memorial Stadium, when a Yankee popped out after time was called. He made sure to point out that Orioles manager Paul Richards did not say a word about the nullified out.[4]

The win ignited a seven-game Orioles winning streak – one week later they were in first place, with a two-game lead over the Yankees. However, the next two weeks were not kind to the Orioles: They saw their hopes for Baltimore's first American league pennant evaporate as they lost 10 out of their next 14 games, leaving them four games behind the Yankees. Meanwhile, during the same stretch, the WhiteSox were 12-10 and found themselves even with the Orioles. Neither team could overcome the Yankees' 15-game winning streak to end the season. New York won the pennant by 8 and 10 games over the Orioles and White Sox respectively, thereby rendering the late-August controversy essentially moot.

Hurley umpired through the 1965 season, when he was forced to retire with two other umpires (Joe Paparella and Bill McKinley) by the American League, which had lowered the mandatory retirement age from 60 to 55. Hurley had turned 55 in September of 1965.[5]

In December Kluszewski was selected by the Los Angeles Angels in the major-league expansion draft. He retired after one season with the Angels. Five years later, in December 1965, Pappas ended his solid career in Baltimore and was part (along with Jack Baldschun and Dick Simpson) of one of the most lopsided trades in baseball history – the trade that brought Frank Robinson to Baltimore.

Sources

In addition to the sources cited in the Notes, the author consulted Baseball-Reference.com and Retrosheet.org.

Notes

1 Ed Brandt, "Kluszewski Homer with 2 on Voided," *Baltimore Sun*, August 29, 1960: 13.

2 "Ump Cancels Klu's Homer, Sox Lose," *Chicago Tribune*, August 29, 1960: 51.

3 Edgar Munzel, "Ump Regrets Time Out Call," *The Sporting News*, September 7, 1960: 5.

4 Munzel.

5 Russell Schneider, "Bitter Hurley Plans to Fight 'Retirement' as A.L. Umpire," *The Sporting News*, February 12, 1966: 6.

19-Year-Old McNally Makes Quick Work of A's in Impressive Debut

September 26, 1962: Baltimore 3, Kansas City 0 (first game of doubleheader), at Memorial Stadium

By Richard Cuicchi

When Dave McNally started the 1962 season with Class-A Elmira, he never expected to be pitching in Baltimore's Memorial Stadium at the end of the season. His major-league debut against Kansas City on September 26 resulted in a sterling performance that impressed the Orioles enough to earn him a permanent major-league job for the next season. The left-hander's two-hit shutout was a big factor in the game, which was played in 1 hour and 32 minutes, the quickest game in Orioles history.[1]

McNally was only two seasons removed from pitching in American Legion baseball, when he had an 18-1 record and his team finished second in the 1960 national championship finals to the New Orleans-based team that featured Rusty Staub. McNally's high school, Billings (Montana) Central Catholic, did not field a baseball team.[2]

Not yet 18 years old, McNally signed with the Orioles for an $80,000 bonus in September 1960. He was a promising amateur player who had a rude awakening in professional baseball. The Orioles overestimated his readiness when they started him off at the Double-A level in 1961; after only four starts, he was quickly demoted and spent the rest of the season in Class B, where he finished with a combined record of 8-13, 4.42 ERA, and 1.604 WHIP.

Baseball Digest had the following scouting report on McNally going into spring training in 1962: "Displays good speed and balance. Curve ball fair, but should get better with control."[3] He was much improved at Class-A Elmira: He threw 13 complete games and finished with a 3.08 ERA while averaging a strikeout per inning. But his control was still an issue, since he also led the Eastern League in walks and wild pitches.[4]

McNally was one of a number of Orioles prospects, including Pete Ward, Bob Saverine, John Miller, and Andy Etchebarren, who were brought up for a look in September 1962. Orioles manager Billy Hitchcock, thinking forward to his roster for the next season, decided to give them all a chance to play. The Orioles were in seventh place and had nothing to lose in giving McNally a start in late September. The Orioles had recent history of taking a chance on young pitchers. Previous upstarts Steve Barber, Milt Pappas, Jack Fisher, and Chuck Estrada were now manning the starting rotation anchored by 35-year-old Robin Roberts.[5]

With both teams finishing in the lower half of the American League, it was understandable that only 2,840 fans attended the game at Memorial Stadium. They sat through a constant drizzling rain in the first game of a twilight-night doubleheader in the last homestand of the season and were rewarded with one of the best Orioles pitching performances of the season.[6]

Bill Fischer, a 31-year-old right-hander, got the starting assignment for the A's. His major-league career had been spotted since his rookie season in 1956. His last six decisions were losses, although he had not issued a walk in his previous 11 appearances. Fischer would later become a scout, pitching coach, pitching coordinator, and special adviser spanning 50 years.

Etchebarren, 19 years old, was McNally's batterymate. He was already familiar with McNally; he had been the lefty's catcher at Elmira. Etchebarren, a prized $85,000 bonus signee, was making his major-league debut as well.

The Orioles got on the scoreboard first in the bottom of the second inning. Jim Gentile led off with a single and went to third on Ward's double. After Boog Powell popped out to the catcher, Saverine's groundout to second scored Gentile. Etchebarren singled in his first major-league at-bat to score Ward.

McNally gave up his first hit in the top of the third when Bobby Del Greco doubled, and he yielded a

Dave McNally threw a two-hit shutout in his major-league debut, beating the Kansas City Athletics, 3-0. Courtesy of the Baltimore Orioles.

single the next inning to Ed Charles. These were the A's only two hits, as McNally retired the next 17 batters after Charles.

Fischer gave up only six hits in seven innings before being lifted for John Wyatt in the top of the eighth. Jerry Adair added the Orioles' final run on his 10th home run of the season. The final score was 3-0.

Baltimore's hitting was led by Adair's and Brooks Robinson's two hits apiece, out of a total of eight for the team.

Fischer extended his streak of consecutive innings without issuing a walk to 79, which was the most in major-league history.[7] However, he took his 11th loss of the season. Each team sent only 31 batters to the plate, contributing to the relatively quick game.

In the second game of the doubleheader, the Athletics rebounded, winning 6-2, with Orlando Pena pitching a complete game.

McNally credited Orioles pitching coach Harry Brecheen with helping him get through some early struggles with his control. He said, "My curve and my slider were breaking low during the first five innings and Harry noticed I was dropping my arm too much to the side."[8]

Earl Weaver, who had managed McNally and Etchebarren at Elmira, was in Baltimore for Orioles organizational meetings when the two prospects made their major-league debuts. He said, "I thought (McNally) pitched a real smart game. Not like a lot of rookies who just try to blow the ball past batters." He added, "One thing I've always thought was in his favor – when he didn't have his real good fastball, he could get his breaking stuff over." Regarding Etchebarren's debut, Weaver said, "I thought Etchebarren did a good job catching him, too. He didn't drop a ball all night. Got a big hit, too. Remember, this is a kid who played just 19 games of professional baseball before this season."[9]

Weaver felt both players needed more minor-league seasoning in 1963, but didn't rule out that both could make contributions to the big-league club.[10]

Brecheen was also impressed by McNally's performance and believed he could earn a shot with Baltimore the next season. He said, "When a 19-year-old wins 15 games in his second year as a pro and then shuts out a team that hits the ball hard like Kansas City, you've got to like his chances. He's got all the pitches. All he needs is work."[11]

Despite having an established rotation from the previous year, McNally did wind up getting his shot with the Orioles in 1963. But he experienced growing pains and struggled at times during his 20 starts. He

19-Year-Old McNally Makes Quick Work of A's in Impressive Debut

finished with a 7-8 record and a 4.58 ERA. By 1965 he got a better handle on his control, posting his best record to date, 11-6 with a 2.85 ERA. He was a big part of the Orioles capturing their first-ever World Series in 1966. He led the team in innings pitched, compiling a 13-6 record and 3.17 ERA.

McNally later won 20 or more games in four consecutive seasons, helping the Orioles become one of the better teams in the American League. He was runner-up for the Cy Young Award in 1970 when the Orioles won their second World Series in five seasons. He finished fourth in the voting in two other seasons.

McNally was reunited with Weaver when his former minor-league skipper replaced Orioles manager Hank Bauer in midseason 1968. Etchebarren proceeded to a 12-year career with the Orioles. Weaver turned out to be the most successful manager in Orioles history and was elected to the National Baseball Hall of Fame in 1996.

In addition to his on-the-field success, McNally is remembered along with Andy Messersmith for winning the battle against the major leagues' reserve clause, thus creating the free-agency era beginning with the 1976 season. McNally never realized the fruits of victory: He wound up retiring after the 1975 season. Messersmith signed a five-year, $1.5 million contract with the Atlanta Braves.[12]

McNally was elected to the Baltimore Orioles Hall of Fame in 1978.

Sources

In addition to the sources cited in the Notes, the author consulted Baseball-Reference.com and Retrosheet.org.

Notes

1   Jim Elliott. "Rookie, 19, Sparkles in Debut," *Baltimore Sun*, September 27, 1962: 31.

2   Mark Armour, "Dave McNally," SABR BioProject. sabr.org/bioproj/person/11d59b62.

3   "Scouting Reports on 1962 Major League Rookies," *Baseball Digest*, March 1962 (Vol. 21, No. 2): 77.

4   "Scouting Reports on 1963 Major League Rookies," *Baseball Digest*, March 1963 (Vol. 22, No. 2): 112.

5   Barber was 22 years old and Estrada was 20 in their 1960 rookie season. Pappas was 18 in his 1957 rookie season. Fisher was 20 in his 1959 rookie season.

6   Elliott.

7   Lou Hatter, "Walks Rare by Fischer," *Baltimore Sun*, September 27, 1962: 31.

8   Lou Hatter, "Praises Fall on McNally," *Baltimore Sun*, September 27, 1962: 31.

9   "Praises Fall on McNally."

10 "Praises Fall on McNally."

11 "Praises Fall on McNally."

12 David Pietruza, Matthew Silverman, and Michael Gershman (eds), *Baseball: The Biographical Encyclopedia* (Total Sports Illustrated: New York, 2000): 764.

Wally Bunker Throws One-Hitter

May 5, 1964: Baltimore Orioles 2, Washington Senators 1, at Memorial Stadium

By Joseph Wancho

The Baltimore Orioles were beginning their 11th season since relocating from St. Louis before the 1954 season. Because the Orioles inherited the Browns players, maturing into a competitive club after so many down years in St. Louis had been a slow process. This was not going to be an overnight success story. Not by any means.

The Orioles finished in the second division of the American League from 1954 to 1959 but a surprising second-place finish in 1960 and third place in 1961 indicated that the tide was changing in the Charm City.

The Orioles ended the 1963 season in fourth place with a 86-76 record in the AL. Brooks Robinson was already winning Gold Gloves at third base and a young Boog Powell was providing the power. The pitching corps was led by veterans Milt Pappas, Steve Barber, and an aging Robin Roberts. Orioles fans were also getting their first look at a 20-year-old southpaw named Dave McNally.

Another young pitcher the Orioles were keeping their eye on was Wally Bunker. The right-hander had posted a 16-2 record his last two years at Capuchino High School in San Bruno, California. Major-league scouts flocked to San Bruno, 10 miles south of San Francisco.

Bunker signed with Baltimore after his father negotiated a $75,000 bonus deal. Bunker reported to Stockton of the Class-A California League and posted a 10-1 record with a 2.55 ERA for the Ports. His fine season earned him a ticket to Baltimore, or Detroit in this case, where he started the Orioles' final game of the 1963 season at Tiger Stadium. Bunker had a rough debut, surrendering six runs in four innings as Detroit prevailed, 7-3.

Hank Bauer succeeded Billy Hitchcock as manager in 1964. The Orioles brass had an important decision to make. Since Bunker was a "bonus baby," he was required to remain on Baltimore's big-league roster for two years. If the Orioles wanted to send him to the minors, they risked another team picking him up.

Bunker made his first 1964 start against Washington on May 5. The Orioles were 8-7 so far; they had just dropped two of three games to Cleveland.

The Senators sent sending Jim Hannan to the hill. He was also making his first start of the season after appearing in five games as a reliever.

Before the game, the Orioles players, coaches, and some front office personnel visited various hospitals in the Baltimore area. Three days before, on May 2, a child had been killed and 46 injured in an incident with an upper-deck moving stairway at Memorial Stadium. Children were stomped on and crushed as the moving stairway heaped them into piles at the upper-deck platform and on the west-side moving stairway steps. A portable gate, allowing only about one child at a time to pass, stopped children from going to the upper deck.[1]

Many of the children were released after hospital treatment. One girl, Annette Costantini, 14, was pronounced dead on arrival at St. Joseph Hospital. The Orioles contingent broke into three groups to visit the children who were still being treated.[2]

As the game progressed, the 19-year-old Bunker was showing no signs that he was the least bit overwhelmed or intimidated by the big-league hitters. He retired the first seven Senators he faced before walking John Kennedy in the third inning. After Bunker struck out Hannan for the second out, Kennedy was erased for the third out when he was caught stealing, catcher John Orsino to shortstop Luis Aparicio.

In the top of the fourth inning, the Senators' Ed Brinkman led off with a walk. Don Blasingame lined out to short. Chuck Hinton bounced a single through the infield and into center field. Bunker walked Jim

Wally Bunker Throws One-Hitter

King to load the bases. Moose Skowron stepped into the batter's box and rapped a grounder toward Robinson at third. Robinson threw to second to get the force on King, but Skowron beat the relay. Brinkman scored and the Senators led 1-0. "That's the kind of call you like to have a reprieve on," said first-base umpire Cal Drummond. "I started to call Skowron out, then I decided he had beaten (Jerry) Adair's throw and it wasn't a double play. It was very close but Skowron was safe."[3]

Baltimore couldn't get anything going against Hannan. Aparicio led off the bottom of the fourth inning with a double to center field. But he tried to steal third and was gunned down by Washington catcher Ken Retzer.

Hannan retired nine consecutive Orioles until Robinson singled to left with one down in the seventh. Norm Siebern followed with his second home run of the year. The baseball just cleared the right-field foul pole. The shot put the O's in front, 2-1. "It was a slider," said Siebern. "I knew it was going far enough as soon as I hit it. The only question was whether it would stay fair. It did – by 20 or 30 feet."[4]

With Baltimore in front, Bunker bore down and retired the next six Senators, giving the Orioles a 2-1 win. He set down 16 in a row after the Senators scored their lone run in the fourth inning. He threw 99 pitches, mostly fastballs and sinkers. "This was my greatest game, no doubt about it," said Bunker. "I threw a no-hitter when I was in the sixth grade and nothing better than a one-hitter in high school."[5]

"Those 99 pitches seemed like 199," said Bauer. "Those close games, oh my. That ninth inning is the longest and that last batter is the longest. I was worried about the game, not any one-hitter. We're only leading 2-1. I got Stu (Miller) warming up in the eighth and ninth and (Wes) Stock was out there in the fourth when they filled those bases."[6]

The Orioles finished the 1964 season in third place with a 97-65 record. Baltimore trailed first- place New York by only two games, and second-place Chicago by one. They had a winning record against all of their AL rivals except for an 8-10 record against Cleveland.

Bunker's record in 1964 was 19-5 with a 2.69 ERA. He led the Orioles starting pitchers in both categories.

Two years later, the Orioles won the AL pennant and swept the Dodgers in the World Series. It was the first world championship in franchise history, St. Louis or Baltimore. Bunker was the starting pitcher in Game Three. He pitched a six-hitter as the Orioles won, 1-0.

Sources

In addition to the sources cited in the Notes, the author consulted Baseball-Reference.com and Retrosheet.org.

Notes

1 "14-Year Old Girl Killed, 46 Children Injured in Moving Stairway Accident at Stadium Here," *Baltimore Sun*, May 3, 1964: 1.

2 Jim Elliott, "Orioles Cheer Up Children Hurt in Stadium Accident," *Baltimore Sun*, May 6, 1964: 30.

3 Lou Hatter, "Bonus Boy Excels in 1964 Debut," *Baltimore Sun*, May 6, 1964: 30.

4 Hatter, "Bonus Boy."

5 Hatter, "Bonus Boy."

6 Hatter, "Bonus Boy."

Rookie Orioles Pitcher Jim Palmer Hits First Career Homer and Earns First Career Win

May 16, 1965: Baltimore Orioles 7, New York Yankees 5, at Memorial Stadium

By Mike Huber

The Baltimore Orioles "carried the big sticks, blasting four homers for a 7-5 win"[1] over the New York Yankees in a mid-May contest at Baltimore's Memorial Stadium. A modest crowd of 25,740 fans turned out for the Sunday afternoon game. Baltimore's rookie hurler Jim Palmer, making just the seventh appearance of his career, earned the victory and helped his own cause by hitting his first big-league home run.

The last-place New York Yankees (12-16), finishing a 14-game road trip, had taken the first two games of the four-game series against Baltimore (15-13). For game three of the series, right-hander Jim Bouton took the mound for New York, making his eighth start. His record stood at 3-3, with a 4.47 earned run average. Baltimore sent southpaw Dave McNally to oppose him. McNally was 1-1, with a 3.24 ERA, and he had pitched at least eight innings in each of his three previous starts.

Bouton's control was suspect from the start. In the top of the first, after retiring Paul Blair and Luis Aparicio, Bouton grooved a pitch to Curt Blefary, who deposited the pitch into the bleachers for his eighth home run of the season. Bouton then walked the bases loaded, issuing free passes to Boog Powell, Norm Siebern and John Orsino. Bob Johnson flied out to center to end the rally. In the second, Bouton gave up a single to Davey Johnson and walked Blair after a McNally sacrifice bunt, before getting out of the inning.

Meanwhile, McNally had cruised through the first two frames, giving up a lone single in the second to Joe Pepitone. Unfortunately, in the third, McNally was "wild and hittable."[2] New York sent seven men to the plate. McNally retired Doc Edwards on a routine grounder to third, but then the next five batters reached (two walks and three singles, with RBIs by Bobby Richardson, Tom Tresh and Mickey Mantle), plating four runs, and "McNally went out of sight."[3] Orioles manager Hank Bauer brought in the rookie Palmer to replace his starter. To this point in the season, Palmer had been used as a mop-up reliever. Inserted into a game trying to prevent a blowout, Palmer called on the pitcher's best friend, getting Hector Lopez to ground into a 4-6-3 double play to end the inning.

In their accounts of the game, the newspapers stressed that Palmer had earned a $50,000 signing bonus as a pitcher for the Orioles. In doing so, he had rejected offers from other clubs to play the outfield. "I decided to take the better offer and pitch."[4] It turned out to be the right decision for the future Hall of Famer.

In the bottom half of the third, the Orioles struck again. With two outs, Siebern hit a solo homer (his third of the season), making the score 4-2, still in New York's favor. An inning later, Bouton was tagged for the third homer of the game. This time, it was Palmer. Bob Johnson had grounded out and then Davey Johnson reached on an error by shortstop Phil Linz. Palmer settled into the batter's box with one out. "I looked for the bunt sign, but didn't see it, so I thought I'd better swing away."[5] Palmer did swing and the result was that he hit his first career home run. He added, "I figure if I missed the sign, they'd tell me later."[6] The two-run shot knotted the score at 4-4. Palmer found out after the game that the bunt sign had not been flashed.

The score remained tied until the sixth. Palmer retired Lopez and Pepitone but then walked Clete Boyer. With Edwards batting, Palmer uncorked a wild pitch, advancing Boyer to second. Edwards drew a walk. With two on and two out, Yankees manager Johnny Keane inserted Tony Kubek to pinch-hit for Steve Hamilton (who had replaced Bouton on the mound to start the bottom of the fifth). Kubek hit a grounder to third baseman Bob Johnson's left. Instead of attempting to catch the ball, Johnson ran to his right for the bag. The ball rolled into the outfield and Boyer

• Rookie Orioles Pitcher Jim Palmer Hits First Career Homer and Earns First Career Win •

Rookie right-handed pitcher Jim Palmer retired 11 of 15 batters faced. Courtesy of the Baltimore Orioles.

scored the go-ahead run. Linz grounded out for out number three, but the Yankees had grabbed the lead.

Russ Snyder pinch-hit for Palmer in the bottom of the sixth, ending the rookie pitcher's day (unfortunately, Snyder struck out). However, Blair drew a walk and Aparicio followed with a two-run round-tripper which gave the Birds the lead for good, ensuring Palmer would earn the victory.

Don Larsen pitched the seventh for the Birds, keeping the score at 6-5, but then Bauer brought in Stu Miller to start the eighth. Miller, described in the papers as "the ancient bubble-thrower" and "the old slowballer,"[7] allowed one hit. The 37-year-old right-hander, who had pitched for the Yankees in 1957, shut down his former team, blanking them in two innings of work. In his last six appearances (covering 14 1/3 innings), Miller was unscored upon, allowing just two hits and three walks, while striking out 18.

In the bottom of the eighth, Baltimore added an insurance run. With one out, Blair singled and promptly stole second. An out later, Blefary doubled to left, driving home Blair. The final score was 7-5. Blefary, a Baltimore rookie who grew up in Brooklyn, New York, rooting for the Yankees, went 2-for-5 with two runs batted in in the game. Further, he was 7-for-17 (.412) in five games against the New Yorkers, with three home runs, two doubles and eight runs batted in. In his rookie season, Blefary batted .362 (17-for-47, more than 100 points above his season's .260 batting average) and slugged .894 with six home runs and 13 runs batted in against the New York Yankees.

The Baltimore victory was not without miscues. Skipper Bauer said, "We played lousy and still won."[8] Late-inning defensive replacement Jackie Brandt made his second error in three games, playing right field. Davey Johnson was picked off base for the second time in three games. The third mistake occurred when Bob Johnson failed to try fielding Kubek's single in the sixth, which put New York ahead 5-4.

The loss brought the Yankees' road trip record to 5-8.[9] Bouton served up three home runs in his 4-inning start and in 50 1/3 innings of work so far in the season had "allowed nine gophers"[10] and owned a 4.65 ERA. One bright spot for New York was the batting of Pepitone, whose two singles might have been wasted in this game. However, in seven games, he had 13 hits in 26 at-bats against the Orioles, with only 12 hits against the rest of the league. The Yankees collected eight hits in the game, but they were all singles. The Orioles put up 10 hits, but only three were singles. The rest were three doubles and four home runs.

Palmer truly earned the victory, both offensively and defensively. His homer tied the game and his pitching stopped the New York squad from blowing the game wide open. In his 19-season career, Palmer managed to hit only two other home runs,[11] but his first was memorable, as it came in the game where he earned his first big league victory on the mound.

Sources

In addition to the sources mentioned in the Notes, the author consulted baseball-reference.com, sabr.org, and retrosheet.org.

Notes

1 Joe Trimble, "Aparicio's Homer, Birds' 4th, Ends Yankees' 'Streak', 7-5," *Daily News* (New York, NY), May 17, 1965: 370.

2 Trimble.

3 Trimble.

4 "Blefary And Palmer Harness Their Long-Time Idols," *Daily Times* (Salisbury, Maryland), May 17, 1965: 10.

5 "Blefary And Palmer Harness Their Long-Time Idols."

6 "Blefary And Palmer Harness Their Long-Time Idols."

7 Trimble.

8 "Blefary And Palmer Harness Their Long-Time Idols."

9 Baltimore bested New York the next day, 9-2, dropping the road trip mark to 5-9 and their overall record to 12-17.

10 Trimble.

11 Due to the institution of the designated hitter rule in the American League, which took effect in 1973, Palmer's last at-bat in a regular season game took place in 1972. In seven seasons, he had 489 at-bats, hitting three home runs.

Frank Robinson's Home Run Out of the Ballpark

May 8, 1966: Baltimore Orioles 8, Cleveland Indians 3 (second game of doubleheader), at Memorial Stadium

By Mark R. Millikin

Pennant fever for Baltimore Oriole fans was unusually high as the 1966 season began because the newest Oriole, Frank Robinson, had excelled for the Cincinnati Reds the previous 10 seasons. His teammates admired his leadership qualities, hitting, and overall play during spring training, beginning on March 7, and many fans considered Robinson to be the same caliber player as Hank Aaron, Willie Mays, and Mickey Mantle.

The Orioles started fast out of the gate in 1966, in large part due to the hot bats of the "Robinson Boys" (Brooks and Frank). Hank Bauer's second-place club entered a four-game series with the league-leading Cleveland Indians (14 wins, one loss) on May 6 at Memorial Stadium with a 12-3 record. The series shaped up as a classic battle between Cleveland's stellar starting rotation of Sam McDowell, Sonny Siebert, Luis Tiant, John O'Donoghue, and Gary Bell versus the Orioles' hitters and home-run sluggers.

After the teams split the first two games of the series, the Orioles needed to win both games of a doubleheader on Sunday, May 8, to tie the Indians for first place. A Mother's Day crowd of 49,516 (37,658 paid) watched Baltimore win the first game, 8-2, behind Jim Palmer's pitching and home runs by Boog Powell, Frank Robinson, and Curt Blefary.

The second game figured to be especially tough for the Orioles hitters because Indians starter Luis Tiant was coming off three straight shutouts for Cleveland to start the season. Orioles pitcher Wally Bunker retired the Indians quietly in the top of the first inning. Then Frank thrilled Oriole fans again with his slugging.[1] He stepped to the plate with one out and Luis Aparicio on second base and walloped a low and inside fastball by Tiant down the left-field line toward the bleachers. Third-base umpire Cal Drummond signaled that it was fair as it soared over the fence and completely out of the ballpark beyond the back of the bleachers.

Unlike today, exit velocity was not a measurement we could make 50 years ago, but observers agreed that it got out of the ballpark in a hurry. Spectators on the first-base side had a clear view of Robinson's home-run wallop, but some on the third-base side were left in momentary suspense about whether the homer left the ballpark because they did not have a clear sightline of the ball as it approached the back of the left-field bleachers. Baltimore baseball historian James Bready recalled, "We were sitting under the overhang on the third-base line and couldn't see much of the flight of Frank's homer."[2] Another fan, Dr. Michael Fine, recalled: "We were sitting on the third-base side, lower level down the left-field line. The ball took off like a rocket. We turned to watch it, but I think the upper deck overhang partly blocked our view. We had a transistor radio, so we pretty much knew right away [from the announcers] that it went out of the park."[3]

Eddie Watt recalled that Orioles relief pitcher Dick Hall said to his teammates in the bullpen, "My goodness, that ball went completely out of the stadium."[4] Bob Maisel, sports editor of the *Morning Sun,* told the author: "When Frank hit his home run, we (Maisel and sportswriter Lou Hatter) followed the ball from the press box [behind home plate] as it went over the fence and then we looked at each other and said, 'Where the hell did it go?' And then we realized it had gone out of the stadium."[5]

At the beginning of the second inning as the Orioles took the field, public-address announcer Bill Lefevre announced, "Frank Robinson's home run was the first ball *ever* hit completely out of Memorial Stadium." Robinson tipped his cap several times during a standing ovation that lasted almost a full minute. "I was a little embarrassed," he said. Later he recalled that he had a lump in his throat. "It really hit the soft spot," he said.[6]

As Mike Sparaco (age 15) and Bill Wheatley (14) crossed the parking lot beyond the left-field bleachers, they heard the crowd roar and then saw the fans from the top of the bleachers pointing out to them where the ball landed. Soon after, the boys found the ball beneath a parked car. A man offered them $50 for it, but Bill and Mike refused, saying "they didn't think it was right to accept money for the ball."[7] Orioles officials at the site estimated that the ball landed 451 feet on the fly and then came to a rest 540 feet from home plate underneath the parked car. The club allowed the boys to watch the rest of the game from the mezzanine and in exchange for Robinson's home-run ball gave them each a ball signed by the Orioles players and season passes for the remaining home games. They had their picture taken with Frank Robinson holding the ball. Sparaco delivered papers for the *News American* the next day and saw his picture on the front page over and over, again.

After Robinson's out-of-the-ballpark home run, Blefary doubled Powell home, extending the Orioles' lead over the Indians to 3-0. The Indians scored a run in the top of the second inning on Pedro Gonzalez's sacrifice fly before the Orioles countered with run-scoring singles by Davey Johnson and Vic Roznovsky in the bottom of the third for a 5-1 lead. Indians catcher Duke Sims singled home Leon Wagner and Fred Whitfield in the top of the fourth, and after one more Cleveland batter, manager Bauer replaced starter Bunker with rookie left-hander Frank Bertaina. In the bottom of the seventh after Frank Robinson's triple, Brooks Robinson drove him home with a double and then Powell homered with Brooks on base to give Baltimore an 8-3 lead that would be the game's final score. Bertaina pitched the final 5⅓ innings for the win. The Orioles' win in the second game of the doubleheader tied them with the Indians for first place with identical 15-4 records.

The Orioles Advocates held a brief pregame ceremony on May 19 at Memorial Stadium when they commemorated Robinson's out-of-the-park home run.[8] The Advocates hung a small flag (about three by five feet with black letters spelling the word "HERE" on an Oriole orange background) from a pole on the back wall of the left-field bleachers marking the spot where the May 8 home run left the ballpark. The Orioles kept several versions of the flag there for 25 years until Memorial Stadium's last Orioles game in October 1991.

By the beginning of July, the Orioles' 50-win and 25-loss start gave them a four-game lead over the Tigers and a 5½-game lead over the Indians. Except for some brief periods in August and September when team injuries mounted, Baltimore kept comfortable leads over the second- and third-place teams on the way to clinching the AL pennant on September 22.

Frank Robinson's consistency in hitting led him to win the AL Triple Crown with 49 home runs, 122 runs batted in, and a .316 batting average. His overall confidence and team leadership gave his teammates a sense that they could win the AL pennant and it continued in their four-game sweep of the Los Angeles Dodgers in the 1966 World Series.

On Mother's Day 1966, Frank Robinson hit a home run that completely left Memorial Stadium. Courtesy of the Baltimore Orioles.

Orioles reliever Moe Drabowsky told John Eisenberg years later: "Sometimes you can point to one incident in a season as a big one. To me, when Frank hit that ball out of the stadium off Tiant, it galvanized the whole team. It was like, 'We're going to be tough to beat this year.'"[9]

Postscript

During the Orioles' last season at Memorial Stadium, 1991, I saw Red Sox rookie Mo Vaughn wallop a long home run over our heads in the right-field bleachers aimed at the same area as Robinson's home run in the left-field bleachers in 1966. As the ball approached us, I thought, "I hope this ball doesn't go out of the stadium, but I think it might." Sure enough, Vaughn's home-run ball (his first as a major leaguer), landed about three rows from the back of the bleachers, barely staying within Memorial Stadium. Robinson's home run remained the only fair ball ever hit completely out of Memorial Stadium when the Orioles finished their playing days there in October 1991.[10]

Notes

1 Douglas Brown, "Orioles Tie for Lead by Wrecking Indians," *Evening Sun* (Baltimore), May 9, 1966.

2 James Bready, telephone interview with the author, February 2003.

3 Dr. Michael Fine, telephone interview with the author, February 2003.

4 Eddie Watt, telephone interview with the author, February 20, 2003.

5 Bob Maisel, telephone interview with the author, October 9, 2003.

6 Douglas Brown, "Fans' Long Tribute Is Embarrassing," *Evening Sun*, May 9, 1966; Doug Brown, "F. Robinson Powers First Drive Out of Oriole Park," *The Sporting News*, May 21, 1966: 27.

7 "Here's a Switch: Boys Refuse $50 for Baseball," *News American* (Baltimore), May 9, 1966.

8 Jim Walker, "Robinson's HR Spot Due Marker, Rite," *Evening Sun*, May 18, 1966.

9 John Eisenberg, *From 33rd Street to Camden Yards: An Oral History of the Baltimore Orioles* (New York: Contemporary Books, 2001), 164.

10 Joe Castiglione with Douglas B. Lyons, *Broadcast Rites and Sites: I Saw It on the Radio with the Boston Red Sox* (Lanham, Maryland: Taylor Trade Publishing, 2004), 108. Joe Castiglione's memory of Mo Vaughn's home-run ball landing three rows from the back of the bleachers is the same as the author's.

Wally Bunker Shuts Out Dodgers in Game Three of 1966 World Series

October 8, 1966: Baltimore Orioles 1, Los Angeles Dodgers 0, at Memorial Stadium

By Austin Gisriel

It was anybody's game heading into the bottom of the fifth on the sunny Saturday afternoon of October 8, 1966 in Baltimore's Memorial Stadium. The Dodgers' southpaw, Claude Osteen, had surrendered only two hits through the first four innings, and if Los Angeles could find a way to win this game, they might yet recover from a two games to none deficit. This was especially true since the Dodgers would have future Hall of Famers Don Drysdale and Sandy Koufax pitching in Games Four and Five. After all, the Dodgers had lost the first two games of the World Series to the Minnesota Twins the previous year and still managed to take the Series in seven.

Standing in the Dodgers' way, however, was 21-year-old Wally Bunker, who thus far had matched Osteen zero-for-zero. Bunker was only two years removed from his stellar rookie season in 1964 in which he went 19-5 and was named *The Sporting News* American League Rookie Pitcher of the Year. That September, however, in his next to last start of the season at Cleveland, he hurt his shoulder and was never the same pitcher again.[1] His record fell to 10-8 in 1965 and 10-6 in 1966. Beset with other injuries as well, Bunker was nursing a sore right elbow this day and had hot packs and oil applied to his arm. It "was pure red and blistered from all the stuff they were putting on between innings," recalled the right-hander.[2] Nevertheless, Bunker had allowed only three hits and a walk himself to this point.

With two outs in the bottom of the fifth, 22 year-old Paul Blair stepped to the plate. The right-handed hitting Blair had shared center field duties during the season with the left-handed hitting Russ Snyder and was the youngest non-pitcher in the Series. He launched the first pitch he saw from Osteen, an inside fastball, 430 feet into the left-field bleachers.[3] Blair sped around the base paths and the Orioles would have the only run they would need.

"As soon as I hit it, I knew it was gone. Everyone said I should have taken my time and gotten to trot around the bases, but I never trotted. I just liked to hit my home runs and get back to the dugout," said Blair.[4]

Blair had hit only five home runs during the regular season.

Maury Wills led off the Los Angeles half of the sixth with a single, and advanced to second on a groundball off the bat of Wes Parker. Willie Davis then hit a deep fly to center fielder Blair, advancing Wills to third, but Ron Fairly was retired on a comebacker and the Dodgers rally died.

Lou Johnson singled in the seventh, his second hit of the day, and Tommy Davis, pinch-hitting for Osteen singled to lead off the eighth. Both were stranded and Bunker retired the side in order in the ninth. The 1-0 victory was Bunker's first shutout of the season and required only 91 pitches, all fastballs and sinkers.[5] The official time of game was a tidy one hour and 55 minutes.

The Orioles never got another hit after Blair's home run and no Bird ever reached second base at any point, except, of course, for Blair. The Dodgers doubled the Orioles hit total with six, but a Wes Parker ground-rule double to right-center in the fourth represented Los Angeles' only extra base-hit.

Steve Barber, a 20 game-winner for the Orioles in 1963, and who would have no doubt started a Series game but for his own arm troubles, said later, "The game Bunker pitched was to that point, the best pitched game I'd ever seen. I went down to the clubhouse after the game and said, 'Great job, but you're not that _____ good and you know it!'"[6]

The Orioles used the same formula the next day, only this time it was a Frank Robinson home run and a Dave McNally shut out that propelled them to another 1-0 victory, a Series sweep, and the first championship in modern day Baltimore baseball history.

Wally Bunker Shuts Out Dodgers in Game Three of 1966 World Series

Claude Osteen, who pitched a great game in a losing effort, would pitch for nine more seasons, winning 20 games for the Dodgers in 1969 and 1972. He would never appear in another post-season game.

Paul Blair won the first of eight Gold Gloves the following season and become a two-time All-Star. The regular center fielder for Baltimore's World Series teams of 1969-1971, he appeared in two more Series with the Yankees in 1977 and 1978 as a reserve outfielder.

Wally Bunker continued to be plagued by his bad shoulder and other arm miseries and logged only 159 innings and five victories for the Orioles over the next two seasons. Chosen by the Kansas City Royals as the 25th pick in the 1969 expansion draft, Bunker threw the first pitch in Royals' history and went 12-11 in their inaugural season. He retired from professional baseball after throwing 36 innings for Double-A Omaha in 1972 at the age of 27.

Author's note

I was 9 years old when my parents took me to see this game. For $8 a ticket, we sat in the upper deck. In the fifth inning I yelled, "C'mon, Paul! You can do it!" and he did. At that point, I became the favorite good luck charm of every old guy basking in the sun and in the glory that day. I'm sure that those "old guys" were younger than I am now. The sense that somehow, I had contributed to the win is the strongest memory I have of that game.

Sources

The only additional source used in addition to the ones below was baseball-reference.com.

Notes

1   Mike Klingaman, "Catching Up With . . . former Oriole Wally Bunker," *Baltimore Sun,* July 21, 2009. Accessed on November 2, 2015 at http://weblogs.baltimoresun.com/sports/thetoydepartment/2009/07/catching....

2   John Eisenberg, *From 33rd Street to Camden Yards: An Oral History of the Baltimore Orioles.* (Chicago: Contemporary Books, 2001), 178.

3   Gordon Beard, *Birds on the Wing: The story of the Baltimore Orioles*, with an introduction by Hank Bauer (New York: Doubleday & Company, 1967), 112.

4   Louis Berney, *Tales From the Orioles Dugout* (New York: Sports Publishing, LLC, 2004), 68-70.

5   Beard, 112.

6   Eisenberg, 179.

McNally Fires Orioles' Third Consecutive Shutout as Baltimore Sweeps Los Angeles

October 9, 1966: Baltimore Orioles 1, Los Angeles Dodgers 0, at Memorial Stadium

By Frederick C. Bush

The Los Angeles Dodgers entered Game One of the 1966 World Series against the Baltimore Orioles on October 5 as 8-to-5 favorites.[1] They had swept the New York Yankees in 1963 and had defeated the Minnesota Twins in seven games the previous season, so it was understandable that the oddsmakers predicted a third title in four years.

However, as they entered Game Four on October 9, the Dodgers had not scored in the past 24 innings of play and were facing the prospect of being on the wrong side of a quick and ignominious sweep. Frank Robinson, Baltimore's Triple Crown-winning outfielder, had hoped that the Dodgers would emerge as the National League champs because, he said, "We always feel we're good for three or four runs, and against the Dodgers, that could be enough."[2] After Game Four, *Los Angeles Examiner* columnist Mel Durslag would comment drily, "Enough, he [Robinson] obviously meant, for a whole Series."[3]

Dave McNally, who had allowed the Dodgers' only two runs of the Series, took the mound determined to atone for his 2⅓-inning stint in Game One. He had tough acts to follow as Moe Drabowsky, his Game One reliever, had hurled 6⅔ scoreless innings that were followed by Jim Palmer's 6-0 blanking of LA in Game Two and Wally Bunker's 1-0 whitewashing in Game Three. McNally came out inspired and threw the Orioles' third consecutive shutout, a 1-0 game that "was virtually a carbon copy of the October 8 triumph."[4] In Game Three, Paul Blair had hit the winning home run in support of Bunker; in this game it was Frank Robinson whose solo blast provided the winning margin. After McNally's gem, the Baltimore pitching staff had a new World Series record of 33 consecutive scoreless innings that surpassed the old mark of 28 set by the New York Giants against the Philadelphia Athletics in 1905.

A partisan crowd of 54,458 fans filled Memorial Stadium in hopes of witnessing history in the making in the form of Baltimore's first major-league championship since 1897.[5] Orioles fans were so confident that before the start of the game, a group of them displayed a sign that read, "Support the Dodgers – Give Blood."[6] Although the placard was directed at the Dodgers' hitters, starting pitcher Don Drysdale, who had been tagged for four runs in Game One, also had appeared as though he could use a transfusion. On this day, however, he pitched more like his usual self, with the exception of one mistake thrown to Robinson. In the 1-0 duel, which was played in a crisp 1 hour and 45 minutes, true action was limited to only a handful of plays, a theme that was in keeping with a World Series in which the winning team batted .200 and the losers a record-low .142.

In the bottom of the second inning, Drysdale allowed a leadoff single to Brooks Robinson and issued a one-out walk to Curt Blefary, but he escaped trouble when Davey Johnson grounded into a double play. McNally, for his part, allowed only a walk and a single through the first four innings. In the bottom of the fourth, Frank Robinson woke both teams and the fans out of their slumbers when he belted one of Drysdale's pitches into the left-field stands for what would be the lone run of the game. Drysdale later said, "It was a fastball up high. I knew the moment he hit the ball, it would take a guy with a ticket to catch it."[7] Although Drysdale's attitude was not as blasé as it may appear in print, columnist Jim Murray gave the Dodgers' star hurler no quarter when he wrote, "Don Drysdale, who used to knock Frank Robinson down regularly when he was in the National League, apparently didn't recognize him. For the second time in the Series, he put a ball over the plate that he might better have put over his head. Robinson put it over the wall."[8]

• McNally Fires Orioles' Third Consecutive Shutout as Baltimore Sweeps Los Angeles •

Home run ball hit by Frank Robinson in Game Four of the 1966 World Series. Courtesy of the Babe Ruth Museum.

After Brooks Robinson grounded out, Boog Powell sent another Drysdale pitch over the wall, but Dodgers center fielder Willie Davis – the goat of Game Two when he had committed three errors in a single inning – made what one reporter called "the top defensive play of the series" when he "actually pulled the ball back from homer territory with a mighty leap and a one-handed stab."[9]

In the top of the fifth, Dodgers second baseman Jim Lefebvre led off with a line-drive single to left. Wes Parker came to bat and hit a ball that looked as though it could go through the hole on the left side for a hit, but third baseman Brooks Robinson – displaying the defensive acumen that would garner him the nickname "Human Vacuum Cleaner" – deftly scooped it up and started a 5-4-3 double play.

From that point forward, things were relatively quiet again until Lefebvre led off the top of the eighth inning with a long fly ball to center. Orioles center fielder Blair showed why manager Hank Bauer had just sent him into the game as a defensive replacement as he "leaped at the fence near dead-center for a two-handed catch of Lefebvre's bid for a game-tying homer."[10] After Drysdale set the Orioles down in order in the bottom of the eighth, it was up to McNally to complete the shutout and the Series sweep.

McNally started the ninth in style by striking out Dick Stuart, who was pinch-hitting for John Kennedy, but then he ran into danger. Al Ferrara, pinch-hitting for Drysdale, singled to center and Maury Wills worked a walk to put the tying run in scoring position. Davis came up and hit a hard liner right to Frank Robinson in right field, and the Dodgers were down to their last out in the person of Lou Johnson. After flailing at McNally's first two offerings, Johnson lofted a routine fly ball to Blair that put the Dodgers out of their misery and set off celebrations throughout Charm City.

Although most of the attention centered on the performance turned in by Baltimore's pitching staff, Frank Robinson garnered the Series' MVP award on the strength of his .286 batting line that included two homers and a Series-leading three RBIs. The low-key Robinson, who was in the middle of a Hall of Fame career, was happy enough on this occasion to say, "I think it was the best season I ever had by far."[11]

As for the Dodgers, it was the worst World Series ever played by any team. In addition to the record-setting 33 scoreless innings and .142 team batting average, they also set all-time Series lows for fewest runs (2), fewest RBIs (2), and fewest hits (17).[12] Interestingly, the previous records for fewest runs (4) and fewest hits (22) had belonged to the 1963 New Yankees, leading Dodgers manager Walter Alston to observe, "Now I know how the Yankees felt when we beat them four straight in '63."[13]

When Alston was asked if the Dodgers needed to trade for power hitters in the offseason, he downplayed such a need and defended his team, saying: "We've known we've lacked power for two years. We're not going to rush out and make a lot of trades because we lost four straight in the Series. We're not known as a power club, but this team doesn't have much to be ashamed of. They won two straight pennants."[14]

Wills echoed his manager when he confessed about the Dodgers, "We never scared anybody in our league, anyway. Most of the clubs in the National League didn't have much respect for us. You'd hear players calling us minor leaguers and saying things like, 'Watching the Dodger offense is like watching a silent movie.'"[15] After the Series, not only did NL opponents disparage the Dodgers, but the LA press piled on, stating, "[T]hey still propose to go to Japan the middle of this month. As we understand it, it will be a five-week trip, unless, of course, they blow it in four."[16]

While the Dodgers were having their epitaph written in Los Angeles, the Orioles were being feted in their hometown. The *Baltimore Sun* aptly summed up baseball's newest champions:

In L.A., the only question was not whether the Dodgers would win, but how many games it would take them.

That's all changed now. Not once in this entire series did the Birds trail, nor did they commit a single error. Both Palmer and Bunker surpassed Waite Hoyt as the youngest men ever to pitch World Series shutouts. The record belongs to Palmer now, because he's 20 and Bunker 21…

But, as it was all year, this was no one, or two man job. For a young team, playing in its first World Series, this one performed faultlessly.[17]

It was the beginning of a golden age for Baltimore baseball: The team would compete in three consecutive World Series from 1969 to 1971 and capture a second championship in 1970.

Notes

1 Jim Elliot, "Orioles Complete Series Sweep as McNally Blanks Dodgers, 1-0/F. Robinson Clouts Home Run in Fourth," *Baltimore Sun*, October 10, 1966: 26.

2 Mel Durslag, "Pity Too Good for Dodgers," *Baseball Digest*, December-January 1967: 30.

3 Durslag.

4 "Orioles End Dodger Reign with Third Shutout in Row," *The Sporting News*, October 22, 1966: 12.

5 The first incarnation of the Baltimore Orioles belonged to the National League. Between 1894 and 1897, the team competed for the Temple Cup championship every year, losing the first two and winning the latter two; their final championship was a five-game series victory over the Boston Beaneaters in 1897. In 1899 the National League contracted from 12 teams to eight with the Baltimore franchise being one of the four that was eliminated. Baltimore briefly had major-league baseball again in 1901-1902 when the reorganized Orioles joined the upstart American League; however, this team, which became the New York Yankees, won no championships. After that, Baltimore was a minor-league city until the hapless St. Louis Browns moved to town and became the current incarnation of the Orioles.

6 Alan Goldstein, "L.A. Hears 'Taps' Before Finish," *Baltimore Sun*, October 10, 1966: 25.

7 "Fourth Game," *The Sporting News*, October 22, 1966: 13.

8 Jim Murray, "The Dodger Story: A Classic Case of Ineptitude," *Los Angeles Times*, October 10, 1966: 45.

9 Elliot.

10 Elliot.

11 "Robby Sees Series Homers as His 'Greatest Thrills,'" *The Sporting News*, October 22, 1966: 12.

12 "Dodgers Rewrite World Series Record Book with Inept Hitting/ L.A. Lumber Fires Blanks," *Baltimore Sun*, October 10, 1966: 29.

13 W. Lawrence Null, "Walt Alston Not Planning to Jump Off Any Bridges," *Baltimore Sun*, October 10, 1966: 29. It should be noted that the 1963 Yankees actually shared the record for fewest hits with the 1914 Philadelphia Athletics.

14 Null.

15 Charles Maher, "Dodgers Take Final Series Defeat Calmly," *Los Angeles Times*, October 10, 1966: 49.

16 Charles Maher, "Aftermath: Ecstasy, Indifference/L.A. Takes It Calmly," *Los Angeles Times*, October 10, 1966: 45.

17 Bob Maisel, "The Morning After," *Baltimore Sun*, October 10, 1966: 25.

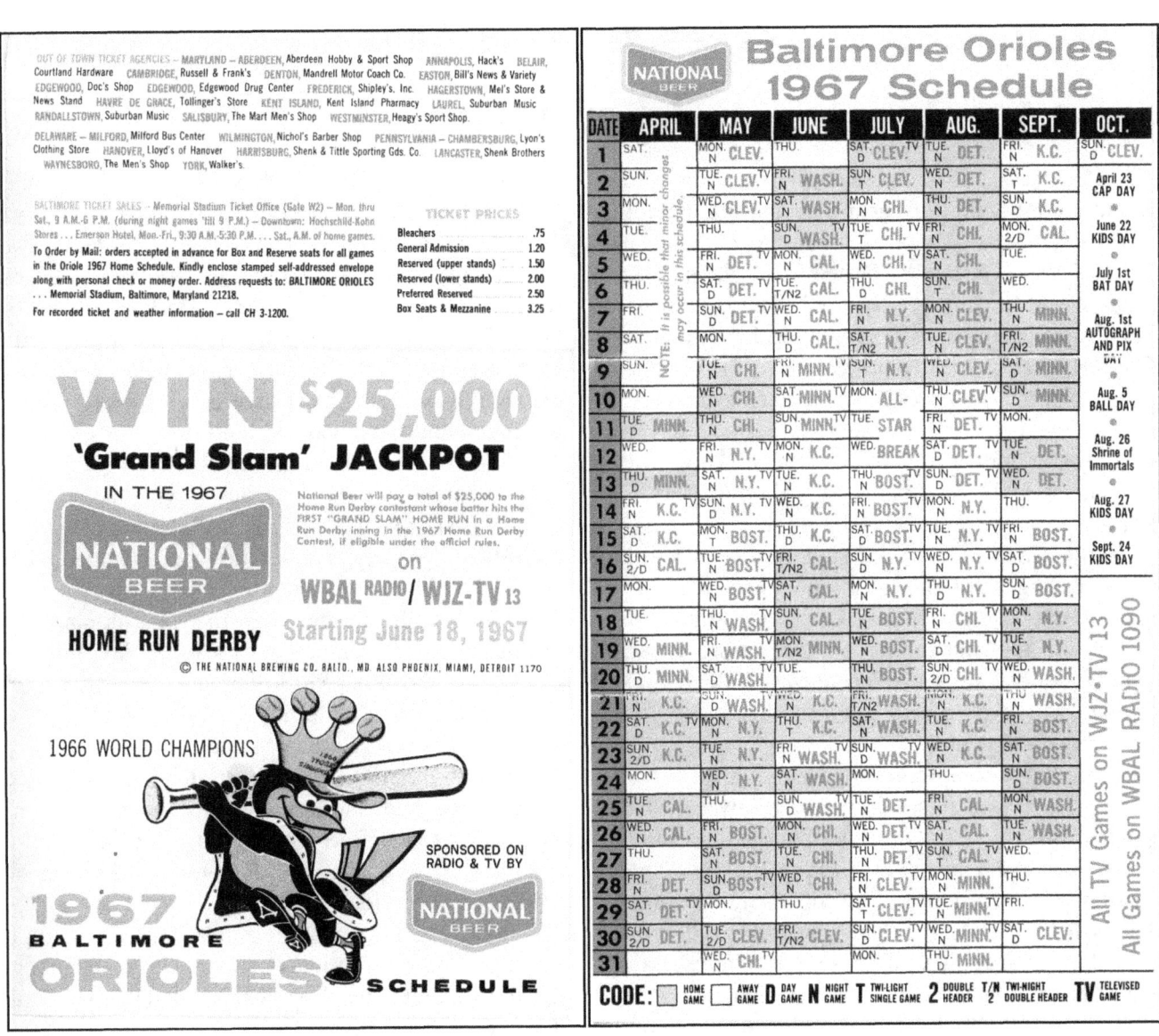

The World Champion Baltimore Orioles 1967 pocket schedule. Courtesy David B. Stinson.

Steve Barber and Stu Miller Combine for No-hitter in a Loss

April 30, 1967: Detroit Tigers 2, Baltimore Orioles 1, at Memorial Stadium

By Jimmy Keenan

In late April of 1967, the Detroit Tigers traveled to Baltimore to play four games against the defending world champion Orioles at Memorial Stadium. The Orioles' Dave McNally bested the Tigers' Denny McLain in the first contest, 5-3. Detroit's Mickey Lolich evened the score the following day by defeating Wally Bunker, 4-2. On April 30, 1967, the two teams wrapped up the series with a Sunday afternoon doubleheader. Orioles manager Hank Bauer gave the starting assignment to southpaw Steve Barber in the opener, while Tigers skipper Mayo Smith went with right-hander Earl Wilson.

Barber, making his third start of the season, had been battling tendonitis in his pitching elbow since late in the 1966 season. The Birds lefty retired the side in the first inning without giving up a hit, allowing only a walk to Tigers center fielder Mickey Stanley. This would be a common theme for Barber throughout the game.

Wilson, who entered the game with a 12-5 lifetime record against Baltimore, allowed just two singles, one to Andy Etchebarren and the other to Frank Robinson, in the first seven innings. On the Orioles' side, Barber was even better, holding the Tigers hitless through eight frames. The downside was Detroit had a man on base every inning except the fifth via a walk, error or hit batsman.

The Birds finally got to Wilson in the bottom of the eighth. Curt Blefary started off with a base on balls. A sacrifice bunt from Woodie Held moved Blefary over to second. Wilson then intentionally walked Charlie Lau, who pinch-hit for Etchebarren to get to Barber. The Orioles pitcher worked Wilson for a free pass to load the bases. Luis Aparicio followed with a sacrifice fly to Tigers right fielder Al Kaline, Blefary scoring on the play. Kaline's throw from the outfield got by catcher Bill Freehan allowing Lau and Barber to advance a base. With runners on second and third, Baltimore's Russ Snyder flew out to first baseman Norm Cash to end the inning.

Barber, with his no-hitter still intact, was continuing to have difficulty throwing strikes, walking Cash and Ray Oyler to start off the ninth. Dick Tracewski was sent in to run for Cash while Jake Wood replaced Oyler on the bases. The next batter, Wilson, helped his own cause by executing a sacrifice bunt that advanced both runners.

Willie Horton, pinch-hitting for Dick McAuliffe, popped up to catcher Larry Haney, who had replaced Etchebarren, for the first out. With the count 1-2 on Mickey Stanley, Barber threw a changeup that bounced in the dirt past Haney. Tracewski came home from third on the errant toss with Wood moving over to third. Barber eventually walked Stanley, his 10th free pass of the afternoon, which drew manager Hank Bauer out of the Oriole dugout. When Bauer got to the mound he told Barber, "I tried to get it for you," referring to the no-hitter. A frustrated Barber replied, "If you can't get the ball over the plate you don't deserve to win."[1] Barber received a rousing ovation from the 26,884 fans at Memorial Stadium as he walked off the field.

With the score tied at one apiece, Bauer brought in Stu Miller from the Orioles bullpen. The first batter he faced, Don Wert, smacked a ground ball up the middle that shortstop Luis Aparicio ranged far to his left and caught on the run. Aparicio then gave a backhanded toss to second baseman Mark Belanger, who had just entered the game as a defensive replacement, for the force out. The normally sure-handed Belanger's bare hand got in the way of the throw causing the ball to drop out of his glove. The error allowed Wood to score the Tigers' second run of the game. The next hitter, Al Kaline, hit a sharp grounder that caromed off third baseman Brooks Robinson's glove. The ball took a fortuitous bounce into the waiting hands of Aparicio,

• Steve Barber and Stu Miller Combine for No-hitter in a Loss •

Steve Barber (depicted here) threw 8 2/3 innings and Stu Miller closed out a no-hitter against the Detroit Tigers but lost the game, 2-1. Courtesy of the Baltimore Orioles.

who threw to Belanger covering second for final out of the inning.

Fred Gladding came in to pitch the ninth for Detroit. He retired Frank Robinson and Brooks Robinson on fly balls before striking out Mike Epstein to preserve the 2-1 Tigers win.

There seems to be at least one outstanding defensive gem in every no-hitter and in this game it was Barber who made the play. The Birds pitcher pounced off the mound and threw out Jim Northrup at first base after taking a hard shot off his leg from the Detroit left fielder in the second inning.

Detroit's Norm Cash spoke to the press about Barber after the game, "All his pitches were really moving. He was hard to hit. None of his pitches were down the middle."[2]

Speaking to reporters about coming out of the game without giving up a hit Barber remarked, "If I hadn't been pitching a no-hitter I would have been out long before that. I was out of gas in the fifth inning. I'm not upset about losing the no-hitter. I'm more concerned about losing the game. No-hitters are not worth anything in the books unless you win."[3]

Orioles right fielder Frank Robinson joked with Barber who was icing his sore elbow in the training room, "Next time give up a hit in the first inning, will you Steve? You make me feel like an old 31 standing out there through that."[4]

Barber came close to pitching a no-hitter earlier in the season. In his first start of the year on April 16 he held the California Angels hitless for eight innings, allowing only three walks, until Jim Fregosi doubled with one out in the ninth. Summing up his pitching performance against the Tigers, Barber told Doug Brown of *The Sporting News*, "I was aiming at the middle all day, but I couldn't hit it. I had no idea where I was throwing. I haven't been so wild since I was a rookie in 1960. I can't understand it. But I'm going to find out. I don't think Hank [Orioles manager Hank Bauer] could stand this all season."[5]

Author's note

Barber and Stu Miller's collaborative no-hit effort was the second time in baseball history that multiple pitchers had combined to lose a no-hitter. On May 26, 1956, the Reds' Johnny Klippstein, Hershell Freeman, and Joe Black combined to hold the Milwaukee Braves hitless for nine innings. Black gave up a double with two outs in the 10th before serving up the game-winner in the 11th inning, losing 2-1. Prior to 1967, the other major-league pitcher to lose a no-hitter in a nine-inning game was the Astros' Ken Johnson who lost to the Cincinnati Reds 1-0 on April 23, 1964.

Notes
1 Murray Chass, "Ninth Inning Walks Give Tigers 2-1 Triumph," *The Day* (New London, Connecticut), May 1 1967: 27.
2 Chass.
3 Chass.
4 Doug Brown, "Steve Drops 2-1 Verdict to Bengals," *The Sporting News* May 13, 1967: 7.
5 Brown.

5 Hours and 18 Minutes Later

June 4, 1967: Baltimore Orioles 7, Washington Senators 5 (19 innings), at Memorial Stadium

By Gary Sarnoff

On June 4, 1967, on a Sunday afternoon at Baltimore's Memorial Stadium, the Washington Senators and the Baltimore Orioles battled for 5 hours and 18 minutes before the Orioles scored two runs in the bottom of the 19th for a 7-5 victory. "Not only was it the longest game the Orioles ever played," penned Bob Maisel of the *Baltimore Sun*, "It was one of the strangest."[1]

The defending World Series champion Orioles entered the contest in third place in the American League, with a 22-20 record and four games out of first place, mostly due to a 1-9 record against two of the league's top contenders, the Tigers and the White Sox. "We'll start beating them," assured Orioles third baseman Brooks Robinson. "Just wait and see."[2] The Senators arrived in ninth place and needed a win to avoid a Baltimore series sweep. They came to town with a four-game winning streak and a new edition, Mike Epstein, who was projected for stardom. Epstein, obtained from the Orioles six days before, was ready to play, but Washington manager Gil Hodges made it clear that he was not going to play his promising rookie until the next series.

In the Orioles clubhouse before the game, scheduled starting pitcher Steve Barber crumbled a large sheet of scratch paper into a ball and took aim at a large trash can less than three feet away. He went into a windup, made the pitch and completely missed his target. "Haw! Haw! Haw!" laughed a sportswriter. Barber, who had mysteriously developed an inability to find the strike zone this season, cracked a smile. "Looks like another great day, doesn't it?" he said as he shook his head.[3] His game didn't start off well when his first three pitches were balls. He eventually completed the walk, but then settled down to retire the next six batters.

Orioles left fielder Curt Blefary got a two-out broken-bat single in the Orioles' first, but the inning quickly ended when the next batter, Frank Robinson, fouled out against Washington's starting pitcher, Phil Ortega. With one out in the bottom of the second, Brooks Robinson singled, and the next batter, Vic Roznovsky, making his first start since joining the Orioles four days earlier from Triple-A Rochester, hit Ortega's first offering into right field for a hit. Second baseman Davey Johnson followed with a drive off the left-field wall to score both baserunners.

The score became 3-0 when Barber helped his own cause by delivering an RBI single. An out and another hit put runners on first and second with two outs, and then Ortega uncorked a wild pitch to allow the runners to advance. Senators catcher Paul Casanova quickly recovered the errant pitch but threw wildly to third base, allowing the runner to score the inning's fourth run. Another hit and walk loaded the bases and paved the way for Ortega's departure. Relief pitcher Dick Lines ended the inning by inducing Boog Powell to pop out.

Barber's four-run cushion vanished in the next half inning when the Senators batted around in a five-run rally. Barber began the inning by walking the first three batters. After hearing it from the hometown patrons and receiving a visit from Orioles pitching coach Harry Brecheen, he was tagged by Ken McMullen for a hit past shortstop Luis Aparicio, scoring two runs, and when Blefary overran the ball, the Senators had runners on second and third with nobody out. Center fielder Hank Allen plated another run on a groundout and Frank Howard snapped a 0-for-17 slump with an RBI single to tie the game, 4-4. That was all for Barber, who departed to a salvo of boos.

Wally Bunker came in from the bullpen and responded by retiring the first batter, but was then victimized by a passed ball and an RBI single by Casanova to give Washington the lead, 5-4.

• 5 Hours and 18 Minutes Later •

In the bottom of the fifth, the Orioles got two singles to put two on with two outs. Manager Hank Bauer sent Andy Etchebarren up to bat for Roznovsky, but Etchebarren grounded out to end the threat. Hodges played his hand in the top of the seventh when, after Frank Howard walked with one out, he had Fred Valentine run for Howard. Cap Peterson, the Senators' leading hitter, came through with a long drive to left field. The ball landed for a hit, and with a fast runner like Valentine on the basepaths, the Senators seemed certain to add another run, but after taking a high bounce, the ball disappeared over the fence for a ground-rule double. "Valentine could've scored easily had the ball stayed in play," insisted Washington sportswriter George Minot Jr.[4] With runners on second and third and only one out, Washington had an opportunity to extend its lead, but nobody delivered in the clutch. Casanova was called out on strikes, and after the next batter, Dick Nen, was intentionally passed, Eddie Brinkman grounded one toward the gap on the left side of the infield. Orioles shortstop Aparicio scooted to his right, stabbed the ball, leaped high into the air, "spun a la Angelo Bertelli and fired to (Orioles second baseman) Johnson for a big force play" to end the inning.[5]

In the bottom of the seventh, Orioles outfielder Russ Snyder lined one to left field. Fred Valentine, who stayed in the game after running for Howard, made what appeared to be a diving catch, but when he lifted his glove hand to show the umpire he had made the catch, the ball fell from his mitt and hit the ground, resulting in a double for Snyder. The next batter, Blefary, singled to score Snyder and tie the game, 5-5. Frank Robinson popped out for the first out of the inning. Then Powell singled to put runners at first and third. Hodges called reliever Dave Baldwin from the bullpen and he got the job done by retiring Brooks Robinson on an inning-ending double play.

As the game moved through the eighth and ninth and into extra innings, the Senators produced baserunners but couldn't score, while the Orioles couldn't put a single runner on base. After the seventh inning, the next 16 Baltimore batters went down. With one out in the bottom of the 13th, Orioles center fielder Paul Blair drew a walk to snap the streak. With a speedster in Blair on base, the Orioles tried a hit-and-run. The strategy backfired when Brooks Robinson swung and missed for strike three and Blair was cut down at second. In the bottom of the 14th, Andy Etchebarren bounced one off Senators pitcher Joe Coleman for the first Orioles hit since the seventh inning. Davey Johnson's sacrifice put Etchebarren in scoring position, but Coleman, the fifth Washington pitcher of the day, retired the next two batters.

In the top of the 18th, Hodges surprised the sportswriters when he sent Bernie Allen to the plate in a left-handed pinch-hitting situation. The scribes were expecting to see Mike Epstein. "If Hodges expects to start Mike against the Yanks tomorrow night at Yankee Stadium, he must have been capable of pinch-hitting?" questioned Bob Maisel.[6] "I would have used Mike had anyone else been pitching," Hodges explained after the game. The Washington manager said he believed Epstein wasn't ready to bat against Stu Miller, a crafty 15-year veteran who had whiffed five batters since entering this game in the 15th inning.[7]

Both teams went down in order in the 18th inning. Stu Miller struck out another batter, giving him six for the day and the Orioles a franchise record of 21

Andy Etchebarren pinch-hit in the fifth inning, then stayed and caught a game he finally won – in the bottom of the 19th inning – with a long home run into the left-field bleachers. Courtesy of the Baltimore Orioles.

for the game. In the bottom of the inning, Bob Priddy, with an 0-2 season record and the third highest ERA on the Senators staff, was on the mound. "I believe I am all straightened out," Priddy said in the dugout before the game, "but apparently, there was something he overlooked," wrote Merrell Whittlesey of the *Washington Star*.[8]

Brooks Robinson led off the bottom of the 19th with a single. Bauer played for the winning run by ordering Etchebarren to bunt. He popped his first attempt into the air. First baseman Dick Nen, charging toward the plate on the play, dived and got his glove on the ball, but couldn't corral it for the putout. Another bunt attempt rolled foul. Now with two strikes, Etchebarren swung away and connected "with a clout that was never in doubt the moment it left the bat."[9] Whittlesey described the drive as "a mammoth shot" that traveled 375 feet before landing in the left-field bleachers. As Etchebarren circled the bases, the remnants of a crowd of 12,612 stood and cheered. After 318 minutes of baseball, the Orioles had finally won.

Sources

In addition to the sources cited in the Notes, the author consulted Baseball-Reference.com.

Notes

1 Bob Maisel, "Morning After," *Baltimore Sun*, June 5, 1967: C1.
2 Maisel.
3 Maisel.
4 George Minot Jr., "10th Inning Homer Beats Senators, 7-5," *Washington Post*, June 5, 1967: B1.
5 Jim Elliot, "Birds Beat Senators, 7-5, in 19th," *Baltimore Sun*, June 5, 1967: C4.
6 Maisel.
7 Merrell Whittlesey, "Gil Turns to New Men for Boost Tonight," *Washington Star*, June 5, 1967: A18.
8 Whittlesey.
9 Whittlesey.

Hard Slide Ends Weis's Season, Knocks Out Frank Robinson

June 27, 1967: Chicago White Sox 5, Baltimore Orioles 0, at Memorial Stadium

By Laura H. Peebles

The visiting White Sox (40-26) were leading the American League by 4½ games over Detroit. The Orioles at 32-35 were tied for seventh, 8½ games back.

The Orioles sent Steve Barber (4-7, 4.04 ERA), the wild left-hander, to the mound. In his 13 games so far in 1967, he had allowed 38 hits ... and 58 walks.[1] This outing started well enough: two strikeouts and a groundout, and he was back in the dugout.

Joe Horlen (8-1, 2.14 ERA) took the mound for the White Sox. He, too, had made 13 starts but his 71 hits allowed well exceeded his 18 walks. Paul Blair greeted him with a double to right. Mark Belanger sacrificed Blair to third but he was stuck there when Frank Robinson and Boog Powell both grounded out.

All Barber allowed in the second was a one-out double to Ron Hansen. Tommy McCraw struck out, then Pete Ward was out on a foul pop, leaving Hansen at second. Horlen induced three more groundouts in the bottom of the frame.

Duane Josephson opened the top of the third with a single to left field. Horlen bunted him to second. However, the White Sox were unable to capitalize on the runner in scoring position: Al Weis grounded to third and Dick Kenworthy flied out to center. In the bottom of the frame, Horlen struck out the opposing pitcher and then induced two more groundouts for a 1-2-3 inning.

The top of the fourth was another quick frame. Ken Berry reached when Frank Robinson in right dropped the ball after catching it. That was Robinson's first error in 99 games, dating back to the previous August 25.[2] Berry was erased when Tommie Agee grounded into a 5-4-3 double play. Hansen grounded out to end the inning with the score still a pristine 0-0.

The memorable events of the game occurred in the bottom of the fourth. Frank Robinson singled to left. Brooks Robinson grounded toward third base. Frank ran hard toward second: Trying to avoid a double play, he slid hard into second baseman Weis as he forwarded the ball to first. Despite wearing his batting helmet,[3] Frank hit Weis's knee hard enough to knock himself out and knock Weis off the base. Weis had managed to throw the ball to first before falling but not in time to beat Brooks. As their teammates congregated around the injured Weis and the unconscious Frank, right fielder Berry called for the ball from first baseman McCraw and tagged out Frank since he was lying on the field not in contact with the base – and no one had called time. Umpire Nestor Chylak had ruled that Weis came off the bag too soon, so Frank was not out on the original throw from the third baseman. The slide at least had been effective to avoid the double play since Brooks reached first safely. This play resulted in an unusual line in the play-by-play: Groundout: 3b-2b-1b-rf/Force out at 2B.

Weis eventually managed to get up and limp off the field. He required surgery to repair ligaments in his knee and was out for the season.[4] He was replaced at second by Jimmy Stewart.

A stretcher was brought out for Frank Robinson but he came to and managed to leave the field with assistance.[5] When he came to he wanted to go back into the game, but his answers to the standard questions indicated that he was definitely suffering from a concussion. When asked where he was, he responded UCLA; when asked what day it was, he responded "A good day to play baseball." He was taken to the hospital for observation.[6] Russ Snyder took his place in right field. He was out for a month, and the concussion had long-term consequences for him resulting in double vision.

Returning to the game action: Boog Powell singled to advance Brooks to second. Curt Blefary then reached when Stewart bobbled the ball to load the bases. The Orioles could not take advantage, though, as Luis Aparicio grounded into a 6-4-3 double play.

The White Sox broke through in the top of the fifth inning. Barber, who had been solid so far, reverted to his wild side. First he walked McCraw, who then stole second. Although he struck out Ward, he threw a wild pitch to Josephson, allowing McCraw to advance to third. Josephson reached safely, although the play was scored as a fielder's choice so he was not credited with a hit. The Orioles did not get an out: Second baseman Belanger's throw to the plate was not in time. Another wild pitch, this time to Horlen, allowed Josephson to advance to second. Josephson scampered to third on Horlen's fly out to right, then scored on Stewart's two-out single. Barber would have been out of the inning on Kenworthy's attempted hit-and-run, but Stewart scored from first when Blefary first fumbled the ball, then threw to second not noticing that Stewart had a green light from third-base coach Grover Resinger.[7] The first baseman dropped a potential foul pop for another error but that one proved harmless as Berry flied out to the shortstop to finally end the inning. The score was three runs for the White Sox, two errors and two wild pitches for the Orioles.

All the Orioles could muster in the bottom of the fifth was a single by Vic Roznovsky. The sixth inning passed almost as quickly: The White Sox managed only a walk and a stolen base against the new pitcher Jim Hardin, and the Orioles were out 1-2-3.

Josephson opened the top of the seventh with a single, but was caught stealing second. A strikeout and a fly out completed the half-inning. Horlen continued his effective outing in the bottom of the frame with another 1-2-3 effort.

The White Sox padded their lead in the top of the eighth. Kenworthy singled and was replaced by Don Buford as a pinch-runner. Buford was up to the task: He stole second, then scored on Berry's single. That was all for the White Sox, though: Hardin buckled down and induced two strikeouts and a groundout to hold the score at 4-0, White Sox.

It looked as if the Orioles might get something going in the bottom of the eighth when Davey Johnson drew a walk. But Blair and pinch-hitter Andy Etchebarren both flied out, leaving the inning to Snyder. He singled to center, allowing Johnson to take third. But he was left there when Brooks Robinson flied out.

Eddie Fisher took over the pitching for the Orioles in the top of the ninth. He started by allowing back-to-back singles to Ward and Josephson. Horlen earned his first RBI of the year with his sacrifice fly.[8] A groundout and a fly out ended the White Sox' scoring opportunities with the score 5-0 in their favor. The Orioles went quietly in the bottom of the ninth, although Aparicio reached on an error.

The loss of Frank Robinson's team-leading bat midway through the game may have contributed to the Orioles' lack of run production, although the White Sox also boasted that they had "a book on Frank" that allowed them to neutralize him.[9]

The Orioles crept up to sixth in the AL by the end of the season, finishing 15½ games back of Boston. The White Sox held a share of the league lead as late as September 6 but ultimately finished fourth, three games back, after a five-game losing streak in the last week of the season.

Sources

In addition to the sources mentioned in the Notes, the author consulted baseball-reference.com, retrosheet.org, and sabr.org.

Notes

1   Barber only made one more start with the Orioles. On July 4 he was traded to the New York Yankees for players to be named later, Ray "Buddy" Barker, and $20,000 cash. There had been some friction between him and the Orioles. Bill Tanton, "Last Kiddie Korpsman, Barber, Leaves Birds," *Baltimore Sun*, July 5, 1967: C6. His statistics did not improve with the Yankees.

2   Frank Robinson was charged with only one other error in 1967.

3   Bill Tanton, "Stanky, Sox, Lose Weis, Can Win Without Him," *Baltimore Sun*, June 28, 1967: C8.

4   Phil Jackman, "Chisox 'Book' on F. Robby Compounds Oriole Troubles," *Baltimore Sun*, June 28, 1967: C8.

5   Jim Elliot, "Birds Bow to ChiSox by 5-to-0," *Baltimore Sun*, June 28, 1967: C1.

6   Jackman.

7   Elliot.

8   It wasn't his last RBI, though: He finished 1967 with five RBIs and a .169 BA, not bad for an AL pitcher. In 1967 he made his only All-Star appearance, and he finished second in the AL Cy Young Award voting (although that was obviously for his 19-7 record and league-leading 2.06 ERA and 0.953 WHIP, not his batting).

9   Jackman.

Tom Phoebus Throws Orioles' Third No-Hitter

April 27, 1968: Baltimore Orioles 6, Boston Red Sox 0, at Memorial Stadium

By Jimmy Keenan

Hometown boy makes good. This time-honored cliché certainly applies to Orioles pitcher Tom Phoebus, who was born and raised in Remington, a predominantly Italian neighborhood in the northwestern section of Baltimore. After receiving a $6,500 signing bonus from the Baltimore Orioles in 1960, Phoebus established himself as one of the future stars in the Birds' fertile farm system. On August 15, 1966, while pitching for the Rochester Red Wings, he threw a no-hitter against the Buffalo Bisons. A few weeks later, he was called up to the Orioles.

The 5-feet-8, 185-pound right-hander tossed shutouts in his first two major-league starts, only the seventh pitcher since 1900 to accomplish this feat. Then in 1967 Phoebus had an outstanding year, going 14-9 with a solid 3.33 earned run average. To top off his excellent season, he was named "The American League Rookie Pitcher of the Year" by *The Sporting News*.

Phoebus was the O's winning pitcher on opening day in 1968, defeating Oakland 3-1. On April 27, the Orioles were scheduled to play the second of a four-game series against the defending American League champion Boston Red Sox at Memorial Stadium in Baltimore. Pheobus, now 2-1, was listed as the starter but his status was up in the air after he had to leave the ballpark in the middle of the game the night before due to sickness. The next morning, Phoebus spoke with manager Hank Bauer on the phone in regard to his availability to pitch that day. Shaking off the effects of a severe cold and sore throat, Phoebus told Bauer he was ready to go.

Saturday, April 27, was a cool and overcast day with the temperature hovering around 60 degrees. Intermittent rain showers throughout the morning and early afternoon led to an hour and 23 minute delay before home plate umpire Frank Umont finally called "play ball." There were 3,147 paid customers in the stands along with an additional 11,568 children and their parents who were part of the "Safety Patrol Day" crowd.

The 26-year old Phoebus, who hadn't pitched in a week, ran into trouble in the top of the first inning. With one out, he walked Red Sox third baseman Joe Foy, who took second on a wild pitch to batter Carl Yastrzemski. Foy then tried to steal third but was cut down by catcher Curt Blefary on what Lou Hatter of the *Baltimore Sun* described as "A flawless peg to [Brooks] Robinson."[1] Blefary was filling in for first-string catcher Andy Etchebarren, who was struck on the hand by Red Sox pitcher Lee Stange the night before. Blefary, the 1965 American League Rookie of the Year, was listed in the Orioles media guide as an outfielder/first baseman. This was only the fourth time he appeared as a catcher in a major-league game.

From that point on, Phoebus found his groove, although a bit of controversy arose in the Boston half of the third inning. With two out, Red Sox second baseman Mike Andrews hit a high chopper back up the middle that tipped off the top of Phoebus' glove. Oriole shortstop Mark Belanger charged in and gathered up the ball on the run just behind the mound. Making an off-balance toss, Belanger's throw landed in first baseman Boog Powell's mitt just before Andrews crossed the bag, first-base umpire Bill Valentine signaling out on the play. Andrews along with Red Sox manager Dick Williams and first-base coach Bobby Doerr argued vehemently with Valentine over the call. Andrews was so upset he slammed his batting helmet on the ground, the carom narrowly missing Valentine. This led to Andrews' ejection as the embattled arbiter felt that the Red Sox second baseman had intentionally tried to hit him with his helmet.

For the remainder of the game Phoebus had the hard-hitting Boston lineup at his mercy. The Red Sox next chance for a hit came in the seventh inning but another fine play by Belanger on a Joe Lahoud check swing grounder kept Phoebus' no-hitter intact.

With one out in the top of the eighth, Boston shortstop Rico Petrocelli drilled Phoebus' first offering towards the hole between short and third. Brooks Robinson, manning the hot corner, instinctively dove out to his left, fully extended, and snared the scorching liner just inches above the ground. In regard to his remarkable play that saved the no-hitter, Robinson told Doug Brown of *The Sporting News*, "Petrocelli got out in front of the ball and it curved back toward me. Otherwise, I never would have had it."[2]

Robinson's grab was considered to be the defensive gem of the game by Phoebus, who retired the next four batters, including Joe Foy, who struck out to end the game. Phoebus threw 110 pitches, fanned nine, and walked three. It was the third no-hitter thrown by an Oriole pitcher since Baltimore rejoined the American League in 1954.

The Birds scored four times in the third and once in the fifth off Red Sox starter Gary Waslewski. Garry Roggenburk relieved Waslewski in the sixth. He finished out the game, allowing one more Baltimore run in the eighth inning.

Brooks Robinson broke the game open in the third inning with a bases-loaded double down the right-field line that plated three runs. Oriole second baseman Davey Johnson compiled three hits on the afternoon including a double and two RBIs. Helping his own cause, Phoebus garnered two singles and he drove in a run.

Blefary spoke to sportswriter Jim Elliot of the *Baltimore Sun* after the game. "There is no doubt that this is my biggest thrill in baseball, primarily because I never caught the guy before. Tom was simply fantastic-unbelievable. He made it easy-threw everything for a strike-fastball, curve and slider. He had great stuff-great stuff. After the fourth inning, he popped the ball where he wanted to."[3]

Pitching coach George Bamberger was equally thrilled with Phoebus' performance, telling Elliot "Most major league pitchers have one exceptional pitch. He has three, a real good fastball, a real good slider and a real good overhand curve."[4]

On the Boston side there were still lingering hard feelings over the Andrews play at first. However, manager Dick Williams, who had longstanding ties with the Baltimore organization, didn't want to take anything away from Phoebus. When asked about the

Tom Phoebus no-hit the Boston Red Sox, 6-0. He walked three and struck out nine. Courtesy of the Baltimore Orioles.

play by a reporter after the game, Williams remarked, "No comment. You go write about that no-hitter. We were overmatched. Give him credit. He should get an awful lot of ink. And give Brooksie credit for his catch and Blefary caught a helluva game. That was a helluva throw he made to get Foy trying to steal third in the first. Foy got a big jump too. It was a big play and Blefary barely got him."[5]

Red Sox first-base coach Bobby Doerr was equally impressed with Phoebus, saying, "He was getting his curveball over exceptionally well. The way he was throwing his fast ball, you couldn't lay for that breaking stuff. There are five or six guys in our lineup who are hitting well and he stopped them all. Only one ball was hit well all day and that was Petrocelli's."[6]

The hero of the day, Phoebus, told the *Baltimore Sun,* "This is a great thrill – my greatest. I'll tell you especially to get it against Boston. The Red Sox are the champs and they are a great hitting team so it would have to be a double thrill to beat them. I felt a little pressure in the ninth and decided I would just try to get the ball over. With that defense behind me, it was the only thing to do."[7]

The following afternoon, Phoebus was presented with *The Sporting News* Rookie Pitcher of the Year Award (for 1967) at Memorial Stadium. According to *The Sporting News*, Oriole personnel director Harry Dalton tore up Phoebus' contract the next day and wrote out a new one. The *Baltimore Sun* noted that he received a well-deserved $1,000 bonus for tossing the no-hitter.

Author's note

The author watched this game on TV at his home in Baltimore with his grandfather, former Oriole Jimmy Lyston.

Sources

In addition to the sources cited in the Notes, the author consulted Baseball-reference.com, *Tuscaloosa News,* and the following:

Klingaman, Mike. "Catching Up With Former Oriole Tom Phoebus," *Baltimore Sun*, April 28, 2009.

Steadman, John. "Oriole Parade Marches On For Phoebus," *Baltimore Sun* 1991.

Joe Posedenti, interview with author, March 27, 2014. Mr. Posedenti was a longtime resident of Remington in Baltimore city.

George Henderson, intview with author, April 1, 2014. Mr. Henderson was a coach and recruiter for the Leones baseball team. He was also the Orioles scout who signed Phoebus in 1960.

Notes

[1] Lou Hatter, "Tom Phoebus In No-Hitter," *Baltimore Sun,* April 28, 1968: A1.

[2] Doug Brown, "Phoebus Aches but Bosox Suffer More," *The Sporting News*, May 11, 1968: 5.

[3] Jim Elliot, "No-Hit Catcher Gets Top Thrill," *Baltimore Sun,* April 28, 1968: A1.

[4] Jim Elliot, "No-Hitter By Phoebus Has Catcher Up in the Air," *Baltimore Sun,* April 28,1968: A2.

[5] Jim Elliot, "Phoebus Credits Defense For His Greatest Thrill," *Baltimore Sun,* April 28, 1968: A2.

[6] Elliot, "No-Hitter By Phoebus Has Catcher Up in the Air."

[7] Elliot, "No-Hitter By Phoebus Has Catcher Up in the Air."

Orioles Blast White Sox, Setting Team Hits, Total Bases, and Runs Records

July 27, 1969: Baltimore Orioles 17, Chicago White Sox 0, at Memorial Stadium

By Mike Huber

Frank Robinson's solo home run in the first inning was all the offense Baltimore needed, but the Orioles scored a total of 17 runs on as many hits in the first five frames to secure a blowout victory over the Chicago White Sox on July 27, 1969. According to the *Baltimore Sun*, "The merry-go-round was the greatest in Memorial Stadium history."[1] Baltimore's Jim Hardin pitched a two-hitter and helped his own cause at the plate with a three-run home run.

A crowd of more than 25,000[2] showed up to witness the historic shellacking, as the two teams concluded a four-game series. The American League East Division first-place Orioles were seeking a sweep. Chicago had lost five in a row and 14 of its last 19 games, and the White Sox were firmly planted in fifth place in the West Division.

Right-hander Hardin toed the pitching rubber for the home team. The 25-year-old was in his third season in the majors. He had struggled a bit this season and split time as a starter and reliever. (This was his 13th start and 19th overall appearance.) For the visitors, Billy Wynne took to the mound. The Chicago right-hander was six days older than Hardin but was pitching in only his first full major-league season. Wynne entered the game with a 3-1 record and 3.50 earned-run average. Both starters had started their major-league careers as free agents signed by the New York Mets.

Chicago had two baserunners in the top of first, after Bobby Knoop led off with a single to right and advanced to second when Gail Hopkins reached on a one-out error by second baseman Davey Johnson (his fourth of the season). But Hardin worked his way out of the jam by retiring Pete Ward and Carlos May.

Wynne lasted only 1⅓ innings. Don Buford singled to start the O's in the bottom of the first, but was erased trying to steal second. After Paul Blair flied out, Frank Robinson crushed a home run to give Baltimore a 1-0 lead. Boog Powell drew a walk and scored when the next batter, Brooks Robinson, tripled to right field.

An inning later, Baltimore exploded for five runs. Johnson and Mark Belanger started the frame with back-to-back singles. After Hardin struck out, Buford hit an RBI single to left, driving in Johnson. This brought Chicago manager Don Gutteridge to the mound for a pitching change. Wynne gave way to Jerry Nyman. Blair greeted him with a run-producing single and then Frank Robinson launched his second home run of the game, with Buford and Blair scoring ahead of him. Powell singled to right, and Nyman's night was done. Veteran right-hander Gary Bell was called from the White Sox bullpen, and he retired Brooks Robinson and Elrod Hendricks to end the inning. The Birds had batted around.

In the third inning, Knoop singled to center with one out for the White Sox. Former Oriole Luis Aparicio then hit a grounder to Johnson, who collided with Knoop in making the force out at second. Knoop, who "in an effort to prevent a relay throw to first base for a double play, went in low and put a by-block on Johnson,"[3] sustained a bloody nose and bruised face and did not return to the game, replaced by journeyman Woodie Held.

The Orioles scored a run in the bottom of the third. Johnson walked, Belanger singled, and Hardin advanced them with a sacrifice. Bell retired Buford on a grounder to second baseman Held, but Johnson crossed the plate on the play for run number eight.

In the fourth inning with one out, a frustrated "21-year-old Carlos May flung his bat at Umpire Russ Goetz … and was banished from the contest," after Goetz called him out on a strike three (looking) from Hardin. May exchanged words, walked toward the Chicago dugout and then flung his bat at the umpire. After Goetz "thumbed May out of the game and the youngster took [another] step toward the dugout, [he] turned and threw his batting helmet."[4] Gutteridge ran

Orioles Blast White Sox, Setting Team Hits, Total Bases, and Runs Records

onto the field to restrain May. Bill Melton then struck out, to bring the Orioles to bat again. Walt Williams trotted out to right field to replace May.

And again the Baltimore batters batted around. Frank Robinson reached on a walk and jogged around the bases when Powell launched a home run. Brooks Robinson walked. Bell retired Hendricks and Johnson, and Belanger stroked his third straight single, bringing Hardin to the plate. With two outs, the pitcher swung away, and he shot Bell's offering out of the park for a three-run homer. Hardin's wallop was only his sixth hit of the season, but it was his second home run (both of the season and for his career). After the game, he told reporters, "I got me a great big Boog Powell model bat – 36 ounces and 36 inches long. If you swing it the same place every time, sooner or later the ball is gonna hit that bat."[5] Buford flied out to end the inning, but the Baltimore nine had added five more tallies to the scoreboard.

As the two teams played the fifth inning, heavy clouds were gathering in the west, bringing a threat of rain, but they stayed clear of the ballpark and the game became official when the inning ended. But not before Baltimore struck again. Blair tripled and scored on Frank Robinson's groundout. Powell doubled to left (Chico Salmon came on as a pinch-runner). After Brooks Robinson struck out, Hendricks walked and Johnson hit a two-run double to left. He scored when Belanger singled through the right side. Hardin then grounded out to third for the final out.

The Orioles had gone through their lineup four times in five innings. With the score 17-0, Chicago "suffered the indignity of seeing Manager Earl Weaver of Baltimore remove his three stars – Brooks and Frank Robinson and Boog Powell – after only five innings of work."[6]

The final four innings elapsed without incident. Hardin retired every Chicago hitter he faced. Baltimore had three more hits but couldn't get a runner past third base. Despite the three big innings by Baltimore, the time of the game was only 2 hours and 33 minutes and the final score remained 17-0.

Frank Robinson delivered two homers and drove in five runs. Buford, Blair, Powell, and Johnson each had three hits. Belanger went 4-for-5, raising his average to .287. It was the second four-hit game for the season for "the Blade." The first also occurred against Chicago, in the second game of a June 15 doubleheader. Baltimore won that game, too, 13-2.

The blowout win moved the Birds to 12½ games ahead of the Detroit Tigers in the East and raised their record to 69-31. Chicago dropped its eighth straight game to the Orioles.

The tally of 17 runs was a new record for Baltimore, surpassing the old mark of 14 (which they accomplished three previous times, including against the New York Yankees on May 4 of this season). The Orioles also set all-time records for most hits in a game (tied at 20) and most total bases in a game (39). They stroked nine extra-base hits, including four homers and two triples. The 17 runs were their largest margin of victory in franchise history and were the most runs ever scored at Memorial Stadium.

Hardin improved his record to 5-4 with the complete-game victory. It was his first shutout and third complete game of the 1969 campaign. Both hits he allowed were singles by Knoop, and after Knoop batted in the third, Hardin set down every Chicago batter in order (20 in a row). Hardin lowered his earned-run average from 3.87 to 3.49. Even more impressively, Hardin's career record against the Sox rose to 6-1; he had allowed only 16 runs in 69⅔ innings pitched against Chicago.

Meanwhile, the White Sox kept skidding. George Langford of the *Chicago Tribune* wrote, "That dark cloud that has been hovering over the White Sox all season opened up today and it poured."[7] Following the Orioles' 17-run storm, Gutteridge remarked, "That makes 16 of the last 20 that we've lost. We're the most welcome club in baseball. Everybody wants us to stay."[8] In the Orioles' clubhouse, skipper Weaver was grinning. "Four in a row, seventeen tonight. That makes me feel a lot better than when we left Boston oh and three, last Sunday."[9]

Sources

In addition to the sources mentioned in the Notes, the author consulted baseball-reference.com and retrosheet.org.

Notes

1 Jim Elliott, "Birds Blast ChiSox, Hit 4 Home Runs," *Baltimore Sun*, July 28, 1969: 21.

2 According to Elliott, the attendance was 25,395, with 17,864 paid.

3 George Langford, "Sox Crushed, 17-0; Cubs Beaten, 6-2," *Chicago Tribune*, July 28, 1969: 63, 66.

4 Langford.

5 Lou Hatter, "Junior Miss Clean-Up Threat," *Baltimore Sun*, July 28, 1969: 25.

6 Langford.

7 Langford.

8 Hatter.

9 Hatter.

Jim Palmer No-Hits the Athletics

August 13, 1969: Baltimore Orioles 8, Oakland Athletics 0, at Memorial Stadium

By Jimmy Keenan

Jim Palmer gained national acclaim early in his major-league career by hurling a four-hit shutout against the Los Angeles Dodgers in Game Two of the 1966 World Series. He was the youngest pitcher (age 20) to toss a complete game shutout in the history of postseason play. The Orioles went on to sweep the heavily favored Dodgers in the series.

A 15-game winner in 1966, Palmer battled shoulder and back problems for the next two seasons, spending most of that time on the disabled list or in the minor leagues. The Orioles placed him on waivers in September of 1968 but none of the 24 major-league teams were willing to risk the $25,000 claiming fee on the oft-injured pitcher. In October both Kansas City and Seattle passed on the future Hall of Famer in the American League expansion draft.

In the fall of 1968, Palmer, known for his high leg kick and fluid effortless pitching motion, played for the Orioles' Clearwater team in the Florida Instructional League. From there he joined up with Frank Robinson's Santurce Crabbers in the Puerto Rican winter league, posting a 6-1 record. Speaking about regaining the confidence of the Oriole front office, Palmer told United Press International, "As far as I know my arm is fine now. But I have to show them that. I know it's a challenge every time I go out there. Why? Because I know what everybody is thinking. They're thinking this guy is finished."[1]

Healthy for the first time in two years, Palmer started off the 1969 campaign with a stellar 9-2 record. However, he was sidelined in late June with a torn muscle in his lower back. After a 41-day stint on the disabled list, he returned on August 9, pitching six strong innings in a 5-1 victory over the Minnesota Twins.

Palmer made his next start on the evening of August 13, 1969, against the Oakland Athletics at Memorial Stadium in Baltimore in front of 16,826 fans. Right-hander Chuck Dobson was in the box for the visiting Athletics. At this point in the season the Orioles were running away with the American League East, 14 1/2 games in front of the second-place Detroit Tigers. Oakland was contending in their division as well, trailing the American League West-leading Minnesota Twins by only one game.

Palmer handled the A's without incident in the first, allowing only a walk to slugger Reggie Jackson, before retiring the side. In the bottom half of the inning, leadoff man Don Buford got the Birds' offense rolling with a triple to left-center field. Buford, normally the Orioles left fielder, was playing second base in place of Davey Johnson, who was out with a pulled back muscle. Buford scored the first run of the game when the next batter, Paul Blair, lofted a sacrifice fly to left field. This tally would prove to be the game winner.

Palmer found his groove early and the Athletics were unable to muster a single hit against the 6'3" 195-pound right-hander for the rest of the game. The closest they came was when his mound opponent, Dobson, led off the third inning by blooping a fly ball into no-man's land behind the shortstop and second base bag. Paul Blair, playing his usual shallow center field, ran in to make the grab but the ball glanced off his glove and fell to the ground. The official scorer gave Blair an error on the play, which kept Palmer's eventual no-hitter intact. Starting off the sixth inning Orioles shortstop Bobby Floyd, filling in for Mark Belanger, who was out with a lacerated toe, misplayed a short-hop grounder by his Athletics counterpart, Bert Campaneris, but Campy was left stranded on the bases. These were the only two Baltimore errors of the game.

There is usually at least one outstanding defensive play in every no-hitter; in this game there were two.

Jim Palmer No-Hits the Athletics

Oriole right fielder Frank Robinson ran back and to his left to haul in a long fly ball off the bat of Athletics first baseman Danny Cater to end the sixth inning. In the eighth, Orioles third baseman Brooks Robinson got in the act, making a nice pick on a hard hit ground ball by pinch-hitter Bob Johnson, and easily throwing out the former Oriole at first base.

In the ninth, things got a little dicey when Palmer walked Jackson, who was leading the major leagues with 42 home runs, on four straight pitches. It was Jackson's third free pass of the game. Athletics third baseman Sal Bando followed with a line drive to center that Blair gathered in for the first out of the inning. The next batter, Danny Cater hit what looked like a sure double play ball to Bobby Floyd who fought off a nasty in-between hop to get the force on Jackson at second. Palmer then had difficulty locating the strike zone, walking Dick Green and Tommie Reynolds to load the bases. Former Oriole catcher Larry Haney was up next. After working the count to 1-2, Haney hit a grounder to Floyd. The Orioles shortstop had to take a step back in order to glove the high bouncer before tossing the ball to Buford for the last out of the game. Palmer, who earned his eighth straight victory, struck out eight while issuing six walks. He threw 142 pitches on the night, 123 fastballs, one changeup and the rest curves.

When asked in a post game interview about walking Reggie Jackson three times, Palmer replied, "I wouldn't say I pitched around him. I respect Jackson and his power and tried to pitch him away. I just didn't make good pitches. I'd like to see him break Babe Ruth's record but not at my expense."[2]

The Orioles amassed eight runs and ten hits off four A's pitchers — Dobson, Vida Blue, George Lauzerique, and finally Jim Roland. Buford led the Birds attack with a three-bagger, two singles, a walk, and a stolen base plus two RBIs. Brooks Robinson chipped in with a three-run homer off Lauzerique in the bottom of the seventh inning. The ball landed in the extreme corner of the upper deck in left field, just behind the foul pole. It was Robinson's 20th round-tripper of the season and number 193 of his career, moving him past Cleveland's Al Rosen (192) on the all-time list.

Palmer helped his own cause with two hits, a single and a double, plus he drew a walk and drove in a run. He scored once but was thrown out at home in the fourth inning by left fielder Reynolds while attempting to score from second base on a Buford base hit. Palmer slid hard into A's catcher Dave Duncan before tumbling into Dobson, who was backing up the throw behind home plate. Palmer bruised his heel on Duncan's shin guards but was able to finish out the game.

Earlier in the 1969 season, Oriole pitchers Dave McNally and Mike Cuellar came close to pitching no-hitters against Minnesota. On May 15, the Twins Cesar Tovar singled off McNally with one out in the ninth inning. On August 10, Tovar did it again when he spoiled Cuellar's no-hit bid with a base knock leading off the ninth. Three days later, Palmer, with his no-hitter on the line, had a little good-natured fun with McNally and Cuellar. In the bottom of the eighth inning he walked in front of the two Oriole aces in the Birds' dugout, putting his hands up to his throat, mimicking the choke sign. Palmer told *Baltimore Sun* sportswriter Lou Hatter after the game, "I didn't take it seriously though until the ninth inning. Then, you realize there are only three outs to go. It was really a matter of luck. They (the Athletics) were always hitting the ball at somebody."[3]

Orioles catcher Elrod Hendricks, who was behind the plate for the historic contest, told the *Baltimore Sun*, "He [Palmer] was quick but he didn't seem to have good stuff in the first inning. After that he picked up momentum."[4]

After the game Palmer spoke to the *Associated Press* about overcoming his past injuries. "When you have arm trouble you constantly think about your future. But I never thought I was finished. My most serious doubts were last August when I suffered nerve damage in my back and the question was whether the nerve would regenerate."[5]

This wasn't Palmer's first brush with no-hit ball in the professional ranks. He threw a no-hitter on June 19, 1964, in his first year as a pro with Cal Ripken Sr.'s Aberdeen Pheasants in the Class A Northern League, besting the Duluth-Superior Dukes 8-0. Palmer tossed his second no-hitter on December 22, 1968, defeating the Mayaguez Indians 4-0, in the Puerto Rican winter league.

Palmer, though pleased with his performance against the A's, still considered the Orioles triumph in the 1966 fall classic to be his greatest thrill on the diamond, telling the *Baltimore Sun,* "Anybody can pitch a no-hitter. But winning a World Series that's a team thing. You don't get in a World Series that often. It's the culmination of everything."[6]

Sources

In addition to the sources cited in the Notes, the author also consulted Baseball-Reference.com and the following:

Armour, Mark. "Jim Palmer," SABR Biography Project.

Bock, Hal. "Jim Palmer Hurls First AL No-Hitter of 1969 Against Oakland; McClain Wins 18th," *Gettysburg Times*, August 14, 1969: 25.

Brown, Doug, "Palmer's No-No Was Bad Word Only For A's," *The Sporting News*, August 30, 1969: 5.

Elliot, Jim, "16,826 See Mound Gem At Stadium," *Baltimore Sun*, August 14, 1969: C-1

"Orioles Palmer Fashions No-Hitter," *Ocala* (Florida) *Star-Banner*, August 14, 1969: 3B.

"Palmer Wouldn't Talk But He Did Try A Joke," *St. Petersburg Times*, August 14, 1969: 2C.

Van Hyning, Thomas, *The Santurce Crabbers: Sixty Seasons of Puerto Rican Winter League Baseball* (Jefferson, North Carolina: McFarland, 2008).

Notes

1. "Palmer's No-Hitter Climaxes Comeback," *News and Courier* (Charleston, South Carolina), August 14, 1969: D1-2.
2. Lou Hatter, "Palmer's Choke Is Comic Relief," *Baltimore Sun*, August 14, 1969: C-1, C4.
3. Hatter.
4. Hatter.
5. "Beat Koufax in the Series Palmer Tries Comeback," *Sarasota Journal*, March 12, 1969: 23.
6. Hatter.

Orioles Win First-Ever ALCS Game

October 4, 1969: Baltimore Orioles 4, Minnesota Twins 3 (12 innings), at Memorial Stadium
Game One, American League Championship Series

By Jimmy Keenan

On October 4, 1969, nearly 40,000 fans filed into Memorial Stadium in Baltimore for the first-ever American League Championship Series. Beginning in 1969 the American and National Leagues were separated into two divisions, East and West. At the end of the season, each division winner would square off in a best-of-five series to decide who went to the World Series.

The Baltimore Orioles (109-53) had taken over first place in the newly formed American League East on April 16, 1969. The high-flying Birds stayed in the top spot for the remainder of the season, running away with the division by 19 games. The Minnesota Twins (97-65), under new manager Billy Martin, finished nine games in front of the second-place Oakland A's in the American League West.

O's manager Earl Weaver started lefty Mike Cuellar (23-11) in Game One while Twins skipper Billy Martin countered with right-hander Jim Perry (20-6). Both pitchers led their teams in wins with Cuellar being named co-winner of the American League Cy Young Award with Tigers pitcher Denny McLain.

Cuellar and Perry each allowed one hit while tossing goose eggs in the first three frames. After the Twins failed to score in the top of the fourth, the Orioles' Frank Robinson broke the ice with a scorching line drive off the left-field foul pole for a solo home run. The Twins evened the score in the fifth after Tony Oliva lashed a double to right and went to third on Frank Robinson's error. Oliva then scored on Bob Allison's sacrifice line drive to left.

The Orioles regained the lead in the bottom of the fifth thanks to light-hitting shortstop Mark Belanger's two-out solo home run that bounced off the auxiliary scoreboard in left field. Belanger, who hit a career-high .287 in 1969, connected on a 2-0 pitch for his first round-tripper since going deep against the Tigers' Denny McLain on April 23. When asked about Belanger's blast after the game, Twins manager Martin told Jim Elliot of the *Baltimore Sun*, "If we walk Belanger it doesn't hurt us with two out and the pitcher up." When asked by another reporter what he'd do to a pitcher who grooved one to the number eight hitter in that situation Martin joked, "We usually shoot them."[1]

Minnesota jumped ahead in the top of the seventh. Cuellar walked Harmon Killebrew and then hung a curveball that Tony Oliva belted over the right-center field fence for a two-run homer.

In the top of the ninth, southpaw Pete Richert relieved Cuellar, with the Orioles still trailing, 3-2. Richert issued two walks, one intentional, before working his way out of trouble. Twins pitcher Jim Perry took the mound to start off the bottom of the ninth. Perry had already given up two homers in the game, despite having been stingy with the long ball all season, allowing one home run for every 14 innings pitched.

The Baltimore faithful didn't have to wait long for something to cheer about as Boog Powell led off with a towering 400-foot blast that soared high over the fence in right-center field. With the game now tied, Martin called on his bullpen ace, lefty Ron Perranoski (9-10, 31 saves) to stop the Birds' rally.

The next batter, Brooks Robinson, greeted Perranoski with a single that Twins left fielder Ted Uhlaender, who had just entered the game as a defensive replacement, misplayed into a double. Curt Motton, pinch-hitting for Elrod Hendricks, lifted a shallow fly ball down the foul line behind first base that second baseman Rod Carew dropped for an error. Robinson, holding the bag at second, was unable to advance. After Davey Johnson popped out, Belanger hit a groundball that forced Motton at second, Robinson moving to third on the play.

With two outs and runners on the corners, Orioles manager Earl Weaver sent Merv Rettenmund in to pinch-hit for Richert. Hoping to catch Minnesota off-guard, Weaver called for a double steal to send home the winning run. Unfortunately for the Birds, Perranoski read the play perfectly, tossing the ball to catcher George Mitterwald, who threw to Killebrew at third for the tag out on Robinson. Weaver had pulled off the same play successfully earlier in the season against Oakland's Vida Blue. Speaking about the ill-fated steal attempt, Brooks Robinson told the press, "Perranoski was just too smart for us. He just threw to the plate."[2]

Right-hander Eddie Watt relieved Richert in the 10th while Perranoski stayed in the game for the Twins. Neither team scored in the next two innings although Baltimore threatened in their half of the 11th, leaving two men stranded on the bases.

Birds manager Weaver brought in southpaw Marcelino Lopez to start the 12th inning. After a walk to Killebrew and an Oliva fly out, Ted Uhlaender singled. Lopez then uncorked a wild pitch in the dirt that allowed both runners to advance. With first base open Weaver ordered Lopez to intentionally walk Rich Reese and brought in from the bullpen Dick Hall, a 39-year-old pitcher who had been an infielder/outfielder early in his big-league career.

The next hitter, Leo Cardenas, attempted a safety squeeze with one strike, but he fouled Hall's offering back to the screen. Cardenas struck out on the next pitch. John Roseboro, pinch-hitting for Mitterwald, flew out to end the inning. "Cardenas committed himself a split second too soon," Hall said after the game about the unsuccessful bunt attempt. "He turned just before I was about to release the ball, and then I threw the ball up around his eyes."[3]

Belanger led off the bottom of the 12th with a hard ground ball that glanced off third baseman Harmon Killebrew's glove into left field, the official scorer ruling it a hit. It was a tough chance for Killebrew, who was playing third instead of his usual first-base position. Martin made the switch in order to get hot-hitting Rich Reese's bat in the Twins' lineup against the lefty Cuellar.

The next batter, Andy Etchebarren, laid down a sacrifice bunt that moved Belanger over to second. Don Buford grounded out to shortstop Frank Quilici, Belanger taking third on the play. Up next was Orioles center fielder Paul Blair, who was 0-for-4 with a walk for the game and mired in a 4-for-44 slump. Blair took Perranoski's first offering for a ball and then took a mighty hack at the second pitch from the Twins reliever, fanning the air. On the next pitch, Blair surprised nearly everyone in the ballpark by dropping a bunt down the third-base line. The ball rolled about 30 feet and stopped in front of a charging Perranoski and Roseboro. Belanger, attuned to Blair's impromptu move, got a great jump from third and raced home with the winning run before Roseboro got a handle on the ball. When asked about the play in a post-game interview Belanger told the press, "Any time Blair or Don Buford are at bat, I'm alert for that play."[4]

Orioles third-base coach Billy Hunter was also thinking bunt, telling Belanger when he got to third, "Be alive, Paul's liable to lay it down."[5]

A jubilant Blair speaking to the media in the Orioles clubhouse said, "I decided to do it in the on-deck circle. I figured I would try to drive him in first by swinging away. I haven't been hitting much and I went to the plate thinking about a bunt. I wanted to take one swing, though, with Mark on third. I figured Perranoski would throw me an off-speed pitch at that point, and that is the best kind to bunt. I think it was a screwball."[6]

Perranoski observed, "We couldn't do anything with it — it was a perfect bunt. With his speed and a man on third, our only hope is if he bunts it foul or we can make a play on it. If Blair thinks that was an off-speed pitch he is wrong. Maybe it looked off-speed because I was running out of gas."[7]

Twins manager Billy Martin talked with reporters in the visitors clubhouse, saying, "The bunt was perfect, it was a good play — nothing at all wrong with it even if it didn't work — great bunt, and if you don't think we anticipated it look at our scouting reports. We are aware Blair's capable of doing it."[8]

Lost in the excitement was Brooks Robinson's four-hit day along with Mike Cuellar's three-hit pitching effort. Orioles catcher Elrod Hendricks spoke glowingly after the game about Cuellar's solid performance: "Mike was pitching great ball. He made only three bad pitches all day. He got away with one of them, but Oliva hurt him with the other two. One was a high screwgie that didn't do anything and the other was a hanging curve."[9]

Billy Martin summed up the tough loss, telling a sportswriter, "There's no way to beat a perfect bunt."[10]

Orioles Win First-Ever ALCS Game

Sources

In addition to the sources cited in the Notes, the author also consulted the *1970 Orioles Media Guide* and the following newspapers: *Eugene* (Oregon) *Register, Florence* (Alabama) *Times Daily, Michigan Daily-News, Milwaukee Journal, Rome News-Tribune,* and *The Sporting News*.

Author's note

The author Jimmy Keenan attended this game with his grandfather, former Oriole Jimmy Lyston.

Notes

1 Jim Elliot, "Weak West Puts Up Fight," *Baltimore Sun*, October 5, 1969: A1.

2 "Big Payoff For Orioles—Blair's Bunt Was His Own Idea," *Daytona Beach Morning Journal* October 5, 1969: 1C, 2C, 3C.

3 "Big Payoff For Orioles—Blair's Bunt Was His Own Idea,"

4 "Big Payoff For Orioles—Blair's Bunt Was His Own Idea,"

5 Jim Elliot, "Slump Prompted Bunt By Blair," *Baltimore Sun*, October 5, 1969: A1, A14.

6 "Big Payoff For Orioles—Blair's Bunt Was His Own Idea."

7 Elliot, "Slump Prompted Bunt By Blair."

8 Elliot, "Slump Prompted Bunt By Blair."

9 Bob Maisel, "Morning After," *Baltimore Sun*, October 5, 1969: A1, A14.

10 "Bunt Beats Twins in 12th 4-3," *Reading Eagle*, October 5, 1969: 59, 68.

Dave McNally Tosses 11-Inning Masterpiece in ALCS

October 5, 1969: Baltimore Orioles 1, Minnesota Twins 0 (11 innings), at Memorial Stadium

By Brian M. Frank

The Minnesota Twins couldn't have been happy to be facing Orioles left-hander Dave McNally in Game Two of the 1969 ALCS after losing Game One of the first-ever American League Championship Series. McNally faced the Twins three times during the 1969 season, including a game in Minnesota in May when he carried a no-hitter into the ninth inning. In that game, César Tovar lined a ball into center field with one out in the final frame for Minnesota's only hit. After the game, McNally declared: "It was as good as I've ever pitched."[1]

McNally, who was 20-7 with a 3.22 ERA during the regular season, faced Baltimore native Dave Boswell, who was 20-12 with a 3.23 ERA for the Twins. Earl Weaver's squad was looking to take a commanding two-games-to-none lead in the best-of-five series, after winning the first game 4-3 on a squeeze bunt by Paul Blair in the 12th inning.

The second inning began promisingly for the Orioles: consecutive singles by Boog Powell, Brooks Robinson, and Davey Johnson loaded the bases with nobody out. But Boswell escaped the inning without any damage by getting Mark Belanger and Andy Etchebarren to pop out and striking out McNally.

In the third inning the Orioles had another mini-rally, but were once again unable to bring a run home against Boswell. Frank Robinson doubled with two down and moved to third on a wild pitch. A walk to Powell put runners at the corners, but Boswell got Brooks Robinson on a popout to retire the side.

Meanwhile, McNally was once again dominating the Twins. After giving up a single to Tony Oliva in the fourth inning, he threw hitless ball for the next eight innings. With Boswell equally effective, the game was scoreless through eight frames.

Earl Weaver showed his confidence in McNally when he allowed him to bat in the ninth inning with two on and two out. McNally, who batted just .085 during the season, almost rewarded his manager by sending a ball to deep left field, but it was caught by Bob Allison, and the game went into extra innings.

Twins catcher George Mitterwald led off the top of the 10th inning against McNally and put a scare into the Baltimore crowd by ripping a ball deep into the upper deck in left field, but it was "foul by about two feet."[2] Mitterwald later said, "When I hit it, I knew it was out. It was 20 feet fair when it started, but it had too much overspin."[3] McNally also thought the ball was fair when it left Mitterwald's bat: "From the angle it left the bat, when he first hit it, I thought it was headed over our bullpen – high and plenty fair. I saw the fans looking, but I couldn't believe it was foul. What a relief."[4]

McNally went on to strike out Mitterwald, and then got Leo Cardenas swinging and Boswell looking. Despite his effectiveness, McNally later revealed that he suffered from cramps in his left forearm during the 10th and 11th innings. "It was worse in the 10th inning than the 11th," he said. "Three or four times in the 10th, I'd get the cramp after I threw a breaking pitch. It would draw up my fingers. You might have seen me tap my hand against my leg. That seemed to relieve it. Once it did it on my fastball, and that really worried me."[5]

McNally entered the 11th inning having allowed only three hits and retired 19 of the last 20 batters to face him. However, in the 11th, "both his fast ball and curve temporarily strayed from the strike zone."[6] Harmon Killebrew walked with two down. McNally then walked Tony Oliva on four pitches and threw three straight balls to Allison, making it nine consecutive balls, and bringing Earl Weaver "to the edge of the dugout steps."[7] Perhaps just one more ball from exiting the game, McNally threw a called strike, followed by three straight pitches that Allison fouled off, the final one caught by left fielder Don Buford to end the inning. McNally didn't blame his wildness on his arm cramping or on tiring. He said, "This is the first time I ever pitched 11 innings, I believe. But I didn't feel tired, I just couldn't find the plate in the 11th inning."[8]

Dave McNally Tosses 11-Inning Masterpiece in ALCS

Boswell walked Powell to lead off the bottom of the 11th. Brooks Robinson sacrificed him to second and Boswell intentionally walked Davey Johnson. Belanger fouled off a ball that looked to be out of play, but Killebrew "reached over the rail near the Oriole dugout" for the second out.[9] With left-handed-hitting Elrod Hendricks due up, Twins manager Billy Martin pulled Boswell after 10⅔ innings, in favor of left-handed closer Ron Perranoski, who had saved 31 games during the regular season. Weaver then made the obvious move and sent up right-handed-hitting Curt Motton, a .303 hitter during the regular season, to bat for Hendricks. Martin explained his decision to remove Boswell: "Boswell was tremendous. Both pitchers were. We simply made the move. It was a tough decision. But Motton's a high-ball hitter and we had a low-ball pitcher coming in. Besides, now they're down to one catcher and that may be trouble."[10] Boswell himself commented, "Sure I would have liked to have stayed in. I would have pitched until my arm fell off. But he's the boss, and I'm not going to second-guess him."[11]

As Boswell walked off the mound, the crowd showed its appreciation for the Baltimore native by giving him a standing ovation. "It made me feel downright proud of my hometown, when they stood up like that and cheered," Boswell said.[12]

Motton greeted Perranoski by lining a 1-and-1 pitch toward right field. Second baseman Rod Carew made a leaping attempt for the ball, and later explained: "I thought it was coming straight to me. Then when it was about 10 or 15 feet away it started to rise. I figured maybe if I jump high enough I can knock it down in front of me and keep Powell from scoring. But it was higher than I could leap. It did go off the fingers."[13] After Carew's glove nicked the ball and slowed it down a bit, a charging Tony Oliva picked it up and fired it toward the plate as Powell raced home with the potential winning run. The throw was a tad up the third-base line, causing catcher George Mitterwald to move up the line to try to make a play. The ball skipped off the top of Mitterwald's glove as Powell shoved him and crossed the plate with the winning run. Powell said that if Mitterwald had caught the ball, "I was going to try to run right over him. Had that happened the ground might still be shaking from the collision."[14] Earl Weaver laughed after the game about his decision to not use a pinch-runner for the lumbering Powell, saying, "If he had been thrown out at the plate, I probably would have been kicking myself."[15]

Both starting pitchers were magnificent. Boswell managed to escape tight jams all day. Baltimore had runners on base in eight of the 11 innings. Boswell in 10⅔ innings allowed a lone run on seven hits and seven walks. "My best game? They're never your best game when you lose," Boswell said. "I would have pitched until my arm fell off. I never want to quit when I'm out there. No matter what the situation. You're tired but you never quit."[16]

But this day belonged to McNally. Orioles catcher Andy Etchebarren said it was the best he'd ever seen the lefty: "He was perfect. … He did it all, got the slider, the curve, the fastball, everything right where he wanted it. That's the best fastball he's ever had."[17] McNally allowed just three singles, nine after the fourth. He walked five and struck out 11 in his 11 innings of work. McNally compared his playoff performance to the one-hitter he threw earlier in the season against the Twins: "I had the same kind of stuff this time as I did back in May." He continued, "That one-hitter was a big thrill. It would have been a bigger thrill if it had been a no-hitter. This time, though, so much more was at stake."[18] Of this game, he said, "That's the best ever."[19]

Sources

In addition to the sources cited in the Notes, the author consulted Baseball-Reference.com and Retrosheet.org.

Notes

1 Phil Jackman, "Mac Settles Debt; Misses Bid for No-hitter," *Baltimore Evening Sun*, May 16, 1969: D1.

2 Dave Mona, "Twins Fall 1-0; Birds Lead 2-0," *Minneapolis Tribune*, October 6, 1969: 36.

3 Mike Lamey, "'Rookie' Mitterwald Acts Like Money Player," *Minneapolis Star*, October 6, 1969: 9B.

4 Lou Hatter, "McNally Calls Win 'Best Ever,'" *Baltimore Sun*, October 6, 1969: C8.

5 Bob Maisel, "The Morning After," *Baltimore Sun*, October 6, 1969: C8.

6 Mona.

7 Mona.

8 "McLucky McNally Hurls Nickname Away," *Minneapolis Tribune*, October 6, 1969: 36.

9 Jim Elliot, "Orioles Nip Twins Again 1-0, in 11th" *Baltimore Sun*, October 6, 1969: C1.

10 Seymour S. Smith, "Boswell Reveals He Would Pitch 'Until Arm Fell Off,'" *Baltimore Sun*, October 6, 1969: C8.

11 "Baltimore Pitching Cools Twins Bats," *Minneapolis Star*, October 6, 1969: 10B.

12 "Baltimore Pitching."

13 Seymour S. Smith, "Motton Hit Low Sinker," *Baltimore Sun*, October 6, 1969: C-8.

14 Maisel.

15 Bill Hengen, "Twins Tempers on Short Fuse," *Minneapolis Star*, October 6, 1969: 9B.

16 Smith.

17 Maisel.

18 Hatter.

19 Hatter.

Orioles Extend Their Winning Streak Against the Royals to 23 Games

August 2, 1970: Baltimore Orioles 10, Kansas City Royals 8, at Memorial Stadium

By Sean Church

August 2, 1970, was a nice hot, sunny Sunday afternoon in Baltimore. The city, like the rest of the country, was in the middle of a dry spell. Sweltering heat brings bad moods, but as the 1970 progressed, the Orioles fan base had little to complain about – and certainly not when they played the Kansas City Royals.

The Orioles were coming off a World Series defeat by the New York Mets, a Series in which they had been heavily favored. After winning the first game, they lost four in a row to the underdog, Tom Seaver-led Mets. Despite having one of the best records in American League history (109-53) in 1969, the Orioles left New York with a bitter taste in their mouth, something they were looking forward to shake.[1]

The Baltimore faithful saw the second-year expansion Kansas City Royals meet up against their defending AL pennant-winning Orioles. With the young Royals and the American League defending champions, this was expected to be a one-sided matchup from the start.

The first time these two teams met had been on May 9, 1969, at Memorial Stadium, when Royals pitcher Dick Drago threw a complete game to lead his team to its first-ever win over the powerful Orioles. The Royals had done well in their first month, but that win by the upstart Kansas City team turned out to be a fluke. The Orioles proceeded to win that series, and every one of their next 22 games against the Royals.

On August 1, 1970, the Orioles were in first place in the AL East by 7½ games over the second-place Detroit Tigers. They were a powerhouse squad on their way to winning their second straight pennant. They were facing the Royals, already 27½ games out of first place in the AL West. The Orioles wanted to extend what seemed like a nearly impossible winning streak against a given opponent; the Royals were looking to stop the bleeding. Bob Lemon had taken over as Royals manager, replacing Charlie Metro after the season's first 52 games.

The pitching assignments for the day had Baltimore ace Mike Cuellar face off against Jim Rooker of the Royals. From the start it was clear the Royals had their work cut out for them. After Cuellar got out of the first inning giving up only a hit to Cookie Rojas, the Orioles jumped on Rooker right away: The first five batters reached base, and Rooker was knocked out of the game before he could get a single out. The Orioles' Merv Rettemund, Paul Blair, and Frank Robinson each reached base; Brooks Robinson singled in two runs and Curt Motton tripled in two more, making it a short day for Rooker. Al Fitzmorris replaced Rooker and gave up an RBI double to Davey Johnson. He then got three straight outs, but the Orioles found themselves up 5-0 after just one inning.

In the fourth, Kansas City got on the board. After Cookie Rojas doubled to start the inning, Royals All-Star Amos Otis smacked a two-run homer high over the fence in left to cut the Orioles lead to three runs. The 1969 Rookie of the Year, Lou Piniella, knocked a single, and the Royals looked to rally for more runs, but Piniella was picked off first base thanks to lefty Cuellar's killer pickoff move. Bob Oliver struck out and Paul Schaal grounded out to Brooks Robinson at third to end what could have been a Royals rally.

In the bottom of the inning, the Orioles provided the type of play manager Earl Weaver loved.[2] Paul Blair's bloop single to center and Frank Robinson's walk provided the baserunners for Curt Motton's three-run homer to left that extended the Orioles' lead to 8-2.

Given the great success the Orioles had enjoyed over the Royals since that first lone Kansas City win and with Cuellar on the mound, one might think that

• Orioles Extend Their Winning Streak Against the Royals to 23 Games •

this game was essentially over. Cuellar had been 23-11 in 1969 and already had 14 wins in 1970. But this day, it seemed it might be different. The Royals truly wanted their losing streak to end.

In the top of the sixth inning, the Royals got back into the game, a far cry from games between these two teams in the past. They got their runs the old-fashioned way – with walks and hits. Three hits and two walks, with RBI singles by Piniella and Schaal, knocked Cuellar out of the game. He'd given up eight hits. Earl Weaver waved in Dick Hall.

As quickly as the Royals sliced the deficit to three runs, the Orioles came back for more. In the bottom of the sixth, Terry Crowley singled off first baseman Bob Oliver's glove and Brooks Robinson reached on an error by Schaal. Motton moved both runners up with a bunt to the pitcher.[3] After an intentional walk to Davey Johnson, Andy Etchebarren singled in two runs off Wally Bunker to extend the Orioles' lead to five runs again. It was 10-5, Orioles, after six.

The Royals scored a run in the top of the seventh, although Cookie Rojas's double-play grounder with runners on first and third cut short any Royals comeback.

Dick Hall seemed to be on his way to a long save, cruising his way to the ninth inning, but in the ninth, the Royals showed they were not just going to roll over. Consecutive hits by Billy Sorrell, Pat Kelly, and Rojas drove in two more runs and knocked Hall out. Into the game came Eddie Watt with Rojas on first base. But Watt got three straight force-play grounders to shortstop to get the save and extend the Orioles winning streak over the Royals to 23.

"The Royals threw a scare into the Orioles in the ninth inning of their final game of the season this afternoon, but that was all," wrote the *Kansas City Star*.[4]

Rojas and Piniella each had three hits as the Royals outhit the Orioles, 13 to 12. The 10 runs the Orioles scored in the game matched the highest run total of any of the prior 22 wins. Curt Motton, who had come into the game batting .219, had five runs batted in for Baltimore, and his sacrifice in the bottom of the sixth had helped set up the ninth and 10th runs, the two that made the difference.[5]

What some expected might be an easy victory for the Orioles turned out to be closer than anyone would have thought after the first inning. A five-run deficit is hard to come back from, especially with a team that went on to win 109 games for the second season in a row. But the Royals did not go away lightly, knowing that this crazy losing streak to one team had to end.

"We'll get them next year," said KC's Bob Lemon. What more could he say? He had said, perhaps a bit sardonically, "I thought maybe we'd score nine runs in the ninth, and then hold them."[6]

Baltimore third baseman Brooks Robinson said, "I don't think this will ever happen again. It seems impossible, even now."[7]

"It's hard to believe," said right fielder Frank Robinson, "that one big-league club can beat another 23 times in a row. You have to be very fortunate, and have breaks go your way. The Royals have played us tough."[8]

The streak did indeed end, but not until April 30, 1971, in Kansas City, when the Royals beat Baltimore, 5-4, on a walk-off single by Freddie Patek in the bottom of the ninth inning. The Royals won five of their 11 games against the Orioles in 1971 and were 6-6 in 1972.

The Orioles won the World Series in 1970, beating the Cincinnati Reds in five games. The Royals wound up at 65-97, 33 games behind the Minnesota Twins in the AL West.

Sources

In addition to the sources cited in the Notes, the author consulted Baseball-Reference.com and Retrosheet.org. Thanks to Mike Huber for supplying several newspaper accounts of the game.

Notes

1 Their 1969 winning percentage of 1969 of .673 ranks them 10th all-time.

2 Terry Pluto, *The Earl of Baltimore* (Piscataway, New Jersey: New Century Publishers, 1982), 91.

3 Jim Elliott, "Birds Hold Off Royal Rally, 10-8," *Baltimore Sun*, August 3, 1970: C-1, 2.

4 Paul O'Boynick," O's Stick Loss 23 on Royals," *Kansas City Star*, August 3, 1970: 20.

5 An appreciation of Motton ran in the next day's *Baltimore Sun*. See Lou Hatter, "Motton Consoles Self on Bench," *Baltimore Sun*, August 3, 1970: C-1, 2.

6 Mike Recht (Associated Press), "Orioles Extend Streak; Twins Defeat Detroit," *Hagerstown* (Maryland) *Daily Mail*, August 3, 1970: 21.

7 Recht.

8 Recht.

Orioles Clinch 1970 World Championship in Game Five

October 15, 1970: Baltimore Orioles 9, Cincinnati Reds 3, at Memorial Stadium

By Jimmy Keenan

The 1970 Cincinnati Reds [102-60] ran away with the National League East by 14½ games before taking three straight from the Pittsburgh Pirates in the playoffs. Their opponents in the upcoming fall classic were the Baltimore Orioles who were attempting to rebound from a demoralizing World Series loss to the New York Mets the previous season. Baltimore [108-54] was as equally impressive as Cincinnati in 1970, winning the American League by 15 games. The Orioles went on to sweep the Minnesota Twins in the playoffs for the second year in a row.

When asked about the Orioles, Reds manager Sparky Anderson told the *Associated Press*, "Our scouting report is that Baltimore is the best defensive club in baseball, has the best front line pitching in the game and is the third or fourth best offensive team."[1]

The Orioles finished the regular season with 11 straight wins. Speaking to a reporter about his team's strong finish, Orioles manager Earl Weaver replied, "Sure we've won 14 in a row [including the playoffs]. But they don't count now. It's not the winning streak I like; it's the type of people we have on the ballclub. If we had lost 14 in a row, I'd still think this team could beat Cincinnati."[2]

Game One was played at Riverfront Stadium in Cincinnati. It was the first time in the history of the fall classic that a game would be played on artificial turf. Another notable milestone occurred during this series when Emmett Ashford became the first African-American to umpire a World Series game. The Orioles came out on top in the first two tilts by the scores of 4-3 and 6-5. The series then moved to Memorial Stadium in Baltimore where the O's won Game Three 9-3. It appeared a sweep was imminent but a three-run homer by Lee May off reliever Eddie Watt in the eighth inning of Game Four propelled the visiting Reds to a 6-5 victory.

The stage was now set for Game Five at Memorial Stadium. Baltimoreans woke up on the morning of October 15 to a steady downpour that was coming down all over the city. The showers continued intermittently throughout the morning and early afternoon. A sign reading "Make the Reds Blue" hung outside of Memorial Stadium as the rain-soaked fans made their way through the turnstiles into the ballpark.

Head groundskeeper Pat Santarone and his crew were able to keep the infield covered but the rest of the field was a different story. The umpires gave the soggy outfield the once over and after considerable deliberation deemed the grounds playable. The Memorial Stadium lights were turned on a few minutes before game time in order to offset the dark storm clouds that were looming overhead. A light drizzle started coming down as the Orioles took the field in the top of the first inning, causing umbrellas to pop up all over the ballpark.

Oriole manager Earl Weaver chose lefty Mike Cuellar [24-8] as his starter while Reds manager Sparky Anderson went with southpaw Jim Merritt [20-12]. Cuellar was hoping to rebound from a poor Game Two performance where he allowed four runs in 2 1/3 innings. After leadoff hitter Bobby Tolan struck out, Pete Rose sliced a fly ball to right that skipped on the wet grass before caroming off Frank Robinson's glove. Rose, hustling all the way, slid headfirst into second for a double. After Tony Perez flew out, Johnny Bench stroked a hard shot into right center for an RBI single. Lee May and Hal McRae followed with back-to-back two-baggers that plated a pair of runs.

With the rain finally subsiding and Cuellar struggling, Earl Weaver got Tom Phoebus up in the Orioles bullpen. The Cuban-born portsider was able to keep his composure retiring the next batter, Tommy Helms, on a groundball to shortstop Mark

• Orioles Clinch 1970 World Championship in Game Five •

Belanger. After the game Weaver told the media, "If Helms had hit the ball hard for extra bases I guess Mike would've had to come out. But if he had hit another double like Pete Rose's I'd have gone with him another batter."[3]

The Orioles got on the board in the bottom of the first thanks to a two-run homer by a Frank Robinson. The Reds wouldn't score for the rest of the game as Cuellar retired 24 out of the next 27 batters. With two on and two out in the second inning, Anderson took Merritt out of the game. He was replaced by Wayne Granger who was tagged for RBI base hits by Mark Belanger and Paul Blair before retiring the side. Merritt, who been battling elbow problems, spoke to the press after the game, "I was throwing free and easy and there was no pain. I wouldn't have pitched if my arm was hurting. I was however disappointed in my control."[4]

After Granger was touched up for two more runs in the third Anderson brought in Milt Wilcox. The 20-year-old right-hander dispatched five straight batters before giving way to Tony Cloninger in the top of the fifth. Cloninger pitched the next two frames allowing one run on a Merv Rettenmund solo shot over the high wall in the right-field corner.

Ray Washburn replaced Cloninger in the seventh. Washburn tossed one scoreless frame before giving up a run in the bottom of the eighth. With two on and one out Clay Carroll came in for Washburn. Carroll allowed the Orioles' ninth run to score before finishing out the inning.

In the top of the ninth Johnny Bench led off with a line drive down the third-base line. Oriole third baseman Brooks Robinson lunged to his right back-handing the hot liner just inches above the ground in foul territory. Robinson made a number of phenomenal defensive plays like this during the series. Thanks to the national television coverage people from around the country were now getting a glimpse of what Baltimore fans had been witnessing first-hand for years. The next batter Lee May whiffed on a tantalizing curve ball from Cuellar for the second out. Anderson inserted pinch-hitter Pat Corrales for McRae. Corrales proceeded to ground out to Robinson at third, clinching the series for Baltimore.

The Oriole victory erased all the bad memories from the previous year's World Series loss to the Mets. Baltimore amassed 50 hits in five games against the Reds pitching staff, including a record ten home runs and seven doubles.

Brooks Robinson was named Most Valuable Player of the series. Aside from his amazing glove work he set a five-game fall classic record with 17 total bases, which included two home runs, two doubles and five singles. He and teammate Paul Blair tied the mark for most hits in a five-game set with nine. "I'm the happiest I've ever been" exclaimed Robinson during the Orioles clubhouse celebration. Nothing will ever the replace the first one [1966 World championship]. But it does make up for everything last year."[5]

Winning pitcher Mike Cuellar talked with reporters after the game about his first inning troubles, "I knew that the team would get me some runs. I had to stop using my screwball but I knew that Brooksie and the other guys would catch my mistakes."[6]

A dejected Pete Rose spoke to *Baltimore Sun* sportswriter Ken Nigro in the visitors' clubhouse saying, "Deep down in my heart I don't think they're 4-1 better than we are. I think when two teams are as evenly balanced as we are it has to be closer."[7]

Reds manager Sparky Anderson closed out his press conference by saying, "It's about time you gave Earl Weaver the credit he deserves. He's won 217 games in two years and now he's won the World Series. I know they say he has a great team, but I've got a great team too, and he beat us. Give him the credit."[8]

Sources

In addition to the sources cited in the Notes, the author also consulted the *1970 Orioles Media Guide,* Baseball-Reference.com, *Bend* (Oregon) *Bulletin, Gettysburg Times, Lakeland* (Florida) *Ledger, Lewiston* (Maine) *Daily Sun, Spokane* (Washington) *Spokesman Review,* and *The Sporting News.*

Author's note

The author, Jimmy Keenan, attended this game with his cousin Bill Stieren and grandfather, former Oriole Jimmy Lyston. My granddad and I had two tickets for the game purchased through the Oldtimers Baseball Association of Maryland. However we needed one more ticket for my cousin. My granddad was able to buy the third ticket at the stadium the day of the game. My cousin Bill (age 11) and myself (age 10) sat in our original seats in the Preferred Reserve section on the third-base side. In addition to being a former pro baseball player my granddad was a retired captain in the Baltimore City Police Department. He had been in command of the Traffic Division, which included all of the motorcycle and mounted police in Baltimore City, from 1960-1964. Knowing nearly every usher and policeman who was working the game, he was able to walk throughout the ballpark unimpeded. He told us later that he spent a few innings sitting with his former Oriole and barnstorming teammate Lefty Grove before moving on to chat with other friends. During the game my cousin Bill and I talked about running onto the field when the Orioles won. When the final out was recorded we decided that discretion was the better part of valor. While the hordes of jubilant Oriole fans were swarming the field my cousin and I made our way through the crowd inside the stadium to link up with our grandfather at our predetermined meeting place.

Notes

1 Associated Press, "Reds Orioles Match Set For World Series," *Rome News-Tribune* (Rome, Georgia), October 6, 1970: 6-7.

2 "Reds, Orioles Match Set for World Series."

3 Lou Hatter, "Mike Junks Screwball After First," *Baltimore Sun*, October 16, 1970: C1.

4 Seymour S. Smith, "Lack Of Control Hurts Merritt," *Baltimore Sun*, October 16, 1970: C1.

5 Mike Rathet, "Orioles Capture Series By Winning Fifth Game," *Observer-Reporter* (Washington, Pennsylvania), October 16, 1970: AI, B6.

6 Lou Hatter, "Mike Junks Screwball After First," *Baltimore Sun*, October 16, 1970: C1, C6.

7 Ken Nigro, "Red's Manager Refuses to Alibi," *Baltimore Sun*, October 15. 1970: C1, C6.

8 Bob Maisel, "Morning After," *Baltimore Sun*, October 16, 1970: C1, C6.

Frank Robinson Hammers His 500th Home Run

September 13, 1971: Detroit Tigers 10, Baltimore Orioles 5 (second game of doubleheader), at Memorial Stadium

By Joseph Wancho

The year 1971 was a good time to be a sports fan in Baltimore. The Baltimore Colts had won Super Bowl V earlier in the year, defeating Dallas 16-13. It was the Colts' third NFL championship. Earlier in the spring, the Baltimore Bullets made it to the NBA finals before getting swept by Milwaukee.

And then there were the Baltimore Orioles. The O's were on cruise control as the 1971 baseball season neared completion. The two-time pennant winners were looking for the three-peat and a third flag to join the two that fluttered in the wind above Memorial Stadium. And what the heck, why not add another world championship banner to go with the ones from 1966 and 1970?

But first things first, which meant wrapping up the American League East. On Monday, September 13, Baltimore (88-51) was hosting second-place Detroit (81-64) for a twilight-night doubleheader that opened a three-game series. For the Tigers to put a dent in the Orioles' 10-game lead, a sweep of the O's was an absolute must. Anything less and, well, it was back to the drawing board next spring in Lakeland, Florida.

And just like that, the Orioles proved to be the rudest of hosts, stomping on the Tigers 9-1 in the opener. Dave McNally had little trouble pitching a complete-game win to raise his record to 19-4. The Baltimore offense exploded as Frank Robinson smacked a three-run home run in the first inning. It was his 24th homer of the season and the 499th of his marvelous career.

Brooks Robinson added a solo shot and Davey Johnson drove in three runs to help lead the offense. The Orioles' lead ballooned to 11 games. Many in the minuscule crowd of 13,292 who turned out for the doubleheader headed for the exits after the opener. After all, it was a school night and the fans were confident that there would be October baseball.

Frank Robinson was one round-tripper away from becoming only the 11th player to reach the 500-homer milestone. Robinson was already one of the most accomplished players in baseball history. Thus far he had won the Rookie of the Year Award (1956) and a Gold Glove (1958), and was the only player to win the Most Valuable Player Award in both the National League (1961) and the American League (1966). He was named MVP of the World Series (1966) when Baltimore won its first Series title.

Earlier in 1971, Robinson had smacked a two-run home run in the All-Star Game and was named the game's MVP. Reggie Jackson gets the most notoriety in that game for the tremendous clout he hit off Dock Ellis that hit the light tower above Tiger Stadium. But it was Robby who walked away with the hardware.

Seemingly, Frank Robinson was headed to Cooperstown one day when his career ended. Smashing 500 home runs would cement his enshrinement. And the sooner to get the drama over, the better.

The nightcap of the doubleheader featured a pitching matchup of Joe Niekro (6-7 4.50 ERA) for Detroit and Pat Dobson (17-7, 2.93 ERA) for the Orioles. Right-hander Niekro was in his second year with the Tigers and was used mostly as a spot starter by Detroit manager Billy Martin. Righty Dobson, on the other hand, was an established starter for Baltimore and had won 12 straight games from June 17 to July 31.

But it was the Tigers who scored first, jumping on Dobson for three runs in the first inning. A two-run home run by Gates Brown was followed by a double to right field off the bat of Norm Cash. The Detroit first baseman scored on a single by Bill Freehan.

In the bottom of the first inning, the Orioles loaded the bases with one down. Martin had to go to his bullpen earlier than he anticipated when Niekro was removed because of a muscle strain in his rib cage under his right arm. Niekro did not pitch for the rest of the season.

Baltimore Baseball

Martin brought in lefty reliever Fred Scherman, who shut the door on the Orioles rally.

Maybe the Tigers sensed that their season was slipping away and decided to do something about it. In the third inning they equaled their three-run total from the first inning with three more. With one away, Cash and Freehan connected for back-to-back singles to right field. After Jim Northrup struck out, Mickey Stanley shot a grounder toward second base and through the legs of Davey Johnson to score Cash. Ed Brinkman singled to left to plate Freehan.

Baltimore skipper Earl Weaver summoned left-hander Grant Jackson to the mound and sent Dobson to an early shower. Scherman greeted Jackson with a single to right field, scoring Stanley, and the visitors were in front with a comfortable lead of 6-0.

The Orioles put a run on the scoreboard in the bottom of the third inning. Don Buford and Merv Rettenmund both doubled (Buford made it only to third), and a groundout by Boog Powell gave the Orioles their initial run. But RBI singles by Brinkman and Dick McAuliffe in the top of the fifth inning increased the Tigers' advantage to 8-1. Many of the remaining fans at Memorial Stadium headed for the exits.

Detroit scored two more runs in the top of the eighth, making it 10-1. In the bottom of the frame, Frank Robinson led off the inning and flied out to center field. It looked as if history would have to wait another day. Brooks Robinson stroked a two-out double to right field and scored on a single to right by Johnson.

With one down in the bottom of the ninth inning, Curt Motton doubled to left. After Rettenmund flied out, Powell stepped in and singled home Motton for the Orioles' third run. Up to the plate stepped Frank Robinson. He swatted the first pitch offered by Scherman and the ball landed just over the left-field wall, 375 feet from home plate. It was Robinson's 500th home run and the hardy souls who remained cheered him as he rounded the bases. The clock showed the time in neon lights: 11:50 P.M. The *Baltimore Sun* reported that the historic baseball was caught by Leo Resop, a senior at St. Mary's Seminary College.[1]

"It was a fastball, down and in," said Robinson. "I jammed myself, didn't hit it with the good part of my bat."[2] It was the fourth consecutive game in which Robinson had hit a home run.

The Tigers gained the split, winning the second game 10-5. Scherman (10-6) was the winner while Dobson (17-8) took the loss.

"My first reaction on hitting the ball?" said Robinson in reply to a sportswriter's question. "It was, 'Do I have enough of it?' I felt that I had the right direction and that it was just a question as to whether it was hard enough. It was the toughest homer of my career."[3]

The 10 players who had hit 500 home runs before Robinson were Babe Ruth, Jimmie Foxx, Mel Ott, Ted Williams, Willie Mays, Mickey Mantle, Eddie Mathews, Henry Aaron, Ernie Banks, and Harmon Killebrew.

The Orioles (101-57) won the AL East by 12 games over Detroit (91-71). The O's had four pitchers who won 20 or more games: Mike Cuellar (20-9), Jim Palmer (20-9), Dobson (20-8), and McNally (21-5).

Baltimore swept Oakland in the ALCS in three games. But they lost the World Series in seven games to the Pittsburgh Pirates.

Sources

In addition to the sources cited in the Notes, the author consulted Baseball-Reference.com and Retrosheet.org.

Notes

1 Jim Elliott, "Robinson Runs HR Gamut," *Baltimore Sun*, September 14, 1971: C1.
2 Elliott.
3 Elliott, C4.

Don Baylor Whacks Four Extra-Base Hits to Lead Orioles' Opening Day Rout

April 6, 1973: Baltimore Orioles 10, Milwaukee Brewers 0, at Memorial Stadium

By Malcolm Allen

The Orioles' most one-sided Opening Day victory in Baltimore came in 1973. Aging stars Brooks Robinson and Dave McNally had a lot to do with it, but the brightest star of the day was 23-year-old left fielder Don Baylor. On the day the American League ushered in the designated-hitter era, Baylor – a future outstanding DH – notched 11 total bases, still a team record for the first game of the season.

Baylor appeared on the cover of *The Sporting News* in 1972 along with Bobby Grich and Terry Crowley as the "High Flying Trio of Young Orioles." Baltimore had so much confidence in the young slugger that they'd dealt away the great Frank Robinson to make room for him. Baylor slumped deeply, however, as a sputtering Baltimore offense caused the team to slip from three straight pennants to third place. Anxious to improve, Baylor returned to the Puerto Rican winter league to learn more playing for Robinson's Santurce Crabbers. With a lighter bat and a new stance slightly farther off the plate, Baylor crushed the ball so consistently in spring training that Earl Weaver predicted, "People are going to be calling him 'Frank.'"[1]

Baylor, Grich, and Crowley all made their first Opening Day starts on April 6, 1973, to that point the earliest opener for the modern Orioles as they commenced their 20th season.[2] Only 12,000 advance tickets had been sold when the team worked out at muddy Memorial Stadium the day before the game, but the front office hoped a promising forecast after a rainy spring would attract a sizable walkup crowd to the Friday afternoon opener and get attendance over 20,000. Clear, sunny skies and a 61-degree temperature helped coax 26,543 fans into the ballpark. While that meant nearly half the seats in Memorial Stadium remained empty, only three larger crowds came there to watch the Orioles all season.

The Zim Zemarel Orchestra and US Army Marching Band entertained the early arrivals. Shortly after Maryland Governor Marvin Mandel threw out the ceremonial ball, home-plate umpire Red Flaherty hollered, "Play ball!" and all eyes turned to Dave McNally, the southpaw making his fifth and final Opening Day start for the team. The Brewers' Dave May, a former Oriole who'd appropriately spent his offseason working for a brewery in Milwaukee, led off for the visitors. The Brewers, in their fourth season and hoping to avoid 90 losses for the first time, managed only a harmless single in the opening inning.

Milwaukee manager Del Crandall wanted Bill Parsons to pitch the season opener, but his shoulder was sore. The second choice, Jerry Bell, couldn't go because his infant daughter accidentally scratched his cornea. So while Baltimore's McNally was a four-time 20-game winner, Crandall gave the ball to a guy with 19 career starts: converted reliever Jim Colborn. Colborn's claim to fame was sharing an alma mater (Whittier College) with President Richard M. Nixon, who'd been re-elected to a second term during the offseason.

Colborn retired the first two batters, but Baltimore's Boog Powell wound up in scoring position after his sinking line drive to right field was misplayed for a two-base error. "I was scared to death when I went out there to start the game," confessed Milwaukee right fielder Gorman Thomas, who was making his big-league debut. "I didn't know what to do. I didn't see the ball too good on that play. I lost it for a minute in the light standards, it was moving almost like a knuckle ball."[3]

Powell scored when Brewers shortstop Rick Auerbach made a wild throw after fielding a grounder on the next play. After Don Baylor doubled to left to keep the inning going, up stepped Baltimore's beloved Brooks Robinson, starting his 17th straight Opening Day. Robinson looked old at the plate in 1972, when he failed to homer until June and saw his season total decline from 20 to 8. For his first swings of 1973, Robinson borrowed a bat from rookie teammate Enos Cabell. When Colborn, the Brewers' player representative, delivered a waist-high fastball over the inside part of the plate, Robinson – the Orioles' player rep – clubbed it 390 feet into the left-field bleachers to make it 4-0, Orioles.

Both teams debuted their first designated hitters in the second inning, about 30 minutes after Ron Blomberg of the Yankees made history pioneering the position in Boston. Milwaukee's "Downtown" Ollie Brown, batting sixth, had ironically pitched for a season in the Midwest League, starting 21 games and hurling a no-hitter. He grounded out and finished the day hitless in three tries. Baltimore's Terry Crowley, batting eighth, popped out in his first chance, but he'd make two kinds of history before the day was over, as illustrated by his wise-cracking teammate Merv Rettenmund. "Terry has a chance to do two things on Opening Day that Joe DiMaggio never did," quipped Rettenmund. "Crowley can get a base hit as a designated hitter and also get a hit swinging from the number-eight spot."[4]

Baltimore added a run in the third after cleanup-hitting catcher Earl Williams reached on an error for the second straight time. Third baseman Don Money, starting his first of nine openers for Milwaukee, flubbed his first grounder after breaking records for his defensive prowess with the 1972 Phillies before an offseason trade. Baylor made the Brewers pay immediately, driving a triple through the wind blowing in from right field to make it 5-0, Orioles. All of the runs were unearned.

McNally looked fully recovered from the shoulder soreness that plagued him the previous year. He stranded Thomas at third after the rookie's two-out triple off the fence in the fifth. After the Brewers put runners at second and third with one out an inning later, Baltimore's Paul Blair raced in from shallow center field to snag the second out, and McNally got George "Boomer" Scott on a broken-bat, inning-ending comebacker to preserve his shutout.

By then the lead was 6-0. After Williams doubled just inside the left-field line for his first Orioles hit, Baylor – that man again – ripped his third hit of the game, over the third-base bag. No Baltimore player before him had ever doubled twice on Opening Day.

The lead increased an inning later after Crowley delivered the first Orioles hit by a designated hitter. With the bases loaded two batters later, Rettenmund singled home two more runs against reliever Bill Champion.

Champion was still on the mound in the seventh when Baylor became the first Oriole ever to record four hits on Opening Day by clubbing a 400-foot homer to left-center. (Baylor would get four more hits on Opening Day 1975 in Detroit). "I've gotten four hits in a game before. But I never got four in a major-league game before. And the four hits I got in the minors weren't all for extra bases either," Baylor said. "That is the first time I ever got four extra-base hits in a single game – anywhere."[5]

Baylor missed the cycle only because he hit the ball too hard. With two doubles, a triple, and a home run, he needed only a single. His 11 total bases as of 2020 remained an Opening Day record for Baltimore players. "I'm not even going to watch that guy hit from now on," McNally joked in the postgame locker room. "It's downright demoralizing for a pitcher to watch anybody hit the ball like that."[6]

Brooks Robinson followed by walloping another inside, belt-high fastball over the fence, marking the first time the Orioles hit back-to-back homers in a season opener (Luis Matos and Melvin Mora joined the club in 2006). Robinson also became the first Baltimore player to hit two home runs on Opening Day. The second homer also fulfilled his spring-training prediction that he'd collect the two hits he needed for 2,400 in his career in the season's first game.

McNally completed a three-hit shutout without walking a single batter. Two hours and 13 minutes after it started, the game ended with George Scott grounding into a 6-4-3 double play. "Right now I like the designated hitter rule," insisted McNally, who'd hit nine home runs of his own – plus two more in the World Series – before 1973. "I don't miss hitting. Not today."[7]

"There are other ways of winning ballgames, but that's one way I especially like," remarked Weaver.[8]

In the next morning's *Baltimore Sun*, columnist Bob Maisel summed it up this way: "There was no bad news."[9]

Sources

In addition to the sources cited in the Notes, the author consulted Baseball-Reference.com and Retrosheet.org

Notes

1 Lou Hatter, "Orioles Dust Off F. Robby Pattern for Basher Baylor," *The Sporting News*, April 28, 1973: 20.

2 The city's NBA franchise played its final home game as the Baltimore Bullets later that night, just 10 weeks after the Baltimore Colts of the NFL ended an era by trading away Johnny Unitas. Two years earlier, Baltimore simultaneously boasted the champions of the World Series and Super Bowl, plus an NBA finalist. The 1973 Orioles were under .500 in early June, while the surprising Brewers briefly surged atop the AL East. By mid-July, Don Baylor's batting average sank to .219, but he batted .366 the rest of the way to drive the resurgent Orioles back into the playoffs with the league's best regular-season record. Jim Palmer won the first of his three Cy Young Awards, and Al Bumbry earned Rookie of the Year honors, but it was an atypical ballclub for a franchise noted for pitching, defense, and three-run homers. The 1973 Orioles were the only Orioles team ever to lead the league in triples and –led by Baylor's 32 stolen bases – the only Weaver-managed club to pace the circuit in steals.

3 Tom Flaherty, "Brewers Opener an Inglorious Beginning," *Milwaukee Journal*, April 7, 1973: 13.

4 Lou Hatter "Weaver, Hunter Confident Orioles Can Regain Top Form," *Baltimore Sun*, April 6, 1973: C5.

5 Jim Elliot, "Oriole Heroes Lauded," *Baltimore Sun*, April 7, 1973: B6.

6 Lou Hatter, "Orioles Dust Off F. Robby Pattern for Basher Baylor."

7 Jim Elliot, "Oriole Heroes Lauded."

8 Jim Elliot, "Oriole Heroes Lauded."

9 Bob Maisel, "The Morning After," *Baltimore Sun*, April 7, 1973: B1.

Jim Palmer Hurls 8 1/3 Perfect Innings

June 16, 1973: Baltimore Orioles 9, Texas Rangers 1, at Memorial Stadium

By Brian M. Frank

Jim Palmer was attempting to recover from an intestinal virus as he entered his start against the Texas Rangers. He reported that he'd slept 28 of the 50 hours leading up to the game. "I felt pretty good this morning when I got up," Palmer said, "but then I felt a little dizzy about a half an hour before the game."[1] The fact that he'd been wild, walking 16 batters in his previous 22⅓ innings, combined with the fact that he was ill, didn't seem like a recipe for success.

Palmer's teammates gave him great support early on, jumping all over Rangers starter Steve Dunning in the first inning. Al Bumbry led off with a walk and stole second. Dunning retired the next two batters, but after walking Tommy Davis, he surrendered an RBI single to Earl Williams to put the Orioles up 1-0. Paul Blair's double brought home Davis and sent Williams to third. Brooks Robinson drew a walk to load the bases. The next batter, Elrod Hendricks, laced the ball toward right and Larry Biittner was unable to leg it down. Biittner "slipped on a muddy warning track" and "by the time order was restored" Hendricks was at third with a three-run triple, and Baltimore had a 5-0 lead.[2]

The Orioles tacked on a few more runs in the fourth, with three singles, two walks, and a sacrifice fly. Bobby Grich had the big hit of the inning, a two-run single, and Blair had the sacrifice fly to give Baltimore a commanding 8-0 lead.

Palmer was rolling, showing no outward signs of the ailment that had left him indisposed the last two days. Through five innings he retired the Rangers in order on 10 fly outs, two groundouts, and three strikeouts. As he continued to mow down the Rangers in order, he became aware that he might be in the midst of a historic outing. "I told (Orioles outfielder) Rich Coggins at the end of the fifth inning that I knew I had a perfect game going and that since I had gone this far, I would have to go for it," Palmer said.[3]

Palmer's perfect night looked to be in jeopardy a few times, but some nice defensive plays kept it intact. Ken Suarez almost broke through with a hit in the sixth, when he hit a smash toward first base that "handcuffed Earl Williams temporarily, but the big catcher-infielder held on and won a race to the bag."[4] In the seventh, Toby Harrah drove a ball that initially looked as if it might be over Paul Blair's head. But the speedy center fielder was able to track it down with a nice catch on the warning track.

Blair, who already had an RBI double, an infield hit, and a sacrifice fly in the game, added to the Orioles' lead in the seventh. He collected his third hit, a solo home run to left off reliever Steve Foucault, to put Baltimore up 9-0.

The Rangers hit a couple rockets off Palmer in the eighth. Rico Carty lined a shot to second baseman Bobby Grich for the first out of the inning. After Alex Johnson grounded out to Mark Belanger, Biittner hit a hard smash to left that Al Bumbry squeezed for the third out.

Palmer took the mound in the ninth attempting to throw the 10th perfect game in the history of the major leagues and the first since Catfish Hunter hurled one for Oakland in 1968. He was also trying to throw his second career no-hitter, having already accomplished the feat against the A's in 1969. Palmer faced Vic Harris, Ken Suarez, and Jim Mason in the final frame in his quest for baseball history.

Palmer struck out Harris to begin the ninth, the 25th consecutive batter he retired, as the Memorial Stadium crowd erupted. Up stepped Ken Suarez, a 5-foot-9 catcher who was hitting .320 entering the game. Before the inning, Palmer joked with Hendricks about the prospect of walking Suarez if he retired Harris. "Suarez had hit the ball hard twice," Palmer later said, "and I knew I couldn't strike him out the way he chokes up."[5] Palmer, who'd been ahead of hitters all day, threw two straight balls to start Suarez off. Hendricks later joked that "Jimmy was only kidding (about walking Suarez,) but after he threw two balls, I started to believe him."[6]

The diminutive Suarez said he went up looking for a fastball, "because I didn't think he could throw the curve for a strike – because of my size." He added, "I had decided that I wasn't going to walk – not if he threw me strikes."[7]

Palmer threw a 2-and-0 fastball that Suarez drilled up the middle. Shortstop Mark Belanger dove but was unable to corral the ball, as it went into center field for the Rangers' first hit of the game. "I never touched the ball," Belanger said, "but I wasn't that far away."[8] Belanger noted that he normally played Suarez toward the second-base bag, but when the count went to 2-and-0, he moved "about a quarter-step" toward third.[9] "With a 2-and-0 count, I thought Jimmy would just try to get the ball over and I didn't want a cheap hit in the hole."[10] Commenting on whether he would have gotten to the ball if he hadn't moved to his right, the slick-fielding shortstop said, "I don't know if I would have gotten to the ball or not, but I wasn't far from it as it was."[11]

After surrendering the first hit of the game, Palmer gave up his first walk, to Jim Mason, moving Suarez to second. The next batter, Dave Nelson, grounded a curveball up the middle for the second hit of the inning, driving home Suarez and ending the shutout. "I didn't let up," Palmer said, "but sometimes a club can catch fire for a minute or two, I guess that's what happened to them."[12] With runners at the corners, Palmer got Toby Harrah to hit into a 6-4-3 double play to end the game.

Palmer had thrown a complete game, allowing one run on two hits and a walk, while striking out six. He retired 25 batters in a row until Suarez's single broke the streak. Palmer commented on his failed effort at perfection, saying, "It would be nice, but the idea is to win, so I'm not disappointed. It was fun."[13]

Palmer was worn out from his complete-game effort after spending two days bedridden with the flu. "I'm tired now," he said, "but when you're working on a no-hitter, you're not tired." He added "I would have been sicker if I had stayed home and heard us get those nine runs without me pitching."[14]

Sources

In addition to the sources cited in the Notes, the author consulted Baseball-Reference.com and Retrosheet.org.

Jim Palmer had O's fans on the edge of their Memorial Stadium seats, throwing a perfect game for 8 1/3 innings, before finally giving up a pair of hits sandwiched around a walk, a run, and then getting a double play. Courtesy of the Baltimore Orioles.

Notes

1 Jim Elliot, "Palmer Was Going for 'Perfecto,'" *Baltimore Sun*, June 17, 1973: B2.

2 Mike Shropshire, "Palmer Perfect Enough," *Fort Worth Star-Telegram*, June 17, 1973: B1.

3 Elliot: B1.

4 Merle Heryford, "Rangers Bow, 9-1," *Dallas Morning News*, June 17, 1973, 1B.

5 Phil Hersh, "Palmer Stifled Yawns," *Baltimore Evening Sun*, June 17, 1973: C8.

6 Associated Press, "Dream Tilt Turns to Dust for Palmer," *Fort Worth Star-Telegram*, June 17, 1973: B4.

7 Elliot: B2.

8 Elliot: B2.

9 "Dream Tilt Turns to Dust for Palmer."

10 "Dream Tilt Turns to Dust for Palmer."

11 "Dream Tilt Turns to Dust for Palmer."

12 Heryford.

13 Lou Hatter, "Palmer Misses Perfecto – One Away in Ninth," *The Sporting News*, June 30, 1973: 26.

14 Elliot: B2.

Kaline Collects 3,000th Career Hit as Tigers Fall to Orioles, 5-4

September 24, 1974: Baltimore Orioles 5, Detroit Tigers 4, at Memorial Stadium

By Jody Madron

After 2,826 games ... 11,564 plate appearances ... and nearly 22 years in the major leagues, Al Kaline was heading to his hometown of Baltimore near the end of the 1974 season just one hit shy of a milestone which, at that point, had only been achieved by 11 major leaguers before him.

Kaline and his Tigers arrived in Baltimore for a two-game series with the Orioles beginning on Tuesday, September 24. It was on that night – in front of a sparse Memorial Stadium crowd of 11,492 – that Kaline would finally collect career hit number 3,000.

The 39-year-old Kaline had entered the season needing 139 hits – only 27 more than he had in all of 1972 and 1973 *combined* – to reach the milestone. As a concession to age, and perhaps to the importance of reaching the milestone, the 10-time Gold Glove Award winner had moved from his customary outfield position to the relatively new designated-hitter role for the 1974 season.

Left-hander Dave McNally was the starting pitcher for Baltimore on this evening, and Kaline was quite familiar with the four-time 20-game winner. Prior to this game – which would turn out to be the last-ever meeting between McNally and Kaline – the two had squared off in 123 plate appearances, with Kaline registering 28 hits in 110 official at-bats (.255 average), including five home runs.

As the game began, the Tigers' record stood at 71-82, and since mid-August they had been languishing in the American League Eastern Division basement, where they would ultimately finish the season.

The Orioles, on the other hand, entered play on September 24 looking to move back into first place in the division, as their 83-71 record positioned them one game behind the division-leading Yankees.

The game began with McNally setting down the Tigers in order in the top of the first inning; Kaline, batting third in the lineup on this night, grounded out to shortstop Mark Belanger to end the half inning.

The Tigers' starter on this night was 23-year-old rookie right-hander Vern Ruhle, who was making just the second start of what would become a 13-year major-league career.

Despite allowing three singles in the bottom of the first inning, Ruhle escaped without allowing a run. This was due in large part to catcher Bill Freehan throwing Rich Coggins out on a stolen-base attempt and a foul popout by third-place hitter Bobby Grich.

After a scoreless second inning, the Tigers plated a run in the top of the third when Ron LeFlore's double to the right-center-field gap drove home ninth-place hitter Ed Brinkman, who had drawn a two-out walk. Gary Sutherland then lined out to second base to end the inning, leaving Kaline in the on-deck circle still on the brink of history.

Ruhle worked around a two-out double by Paul Blair in the bottom of the third inning, and the Tigers still led 1-0 when Kaline led off against McNally in the top of the fourth.

At 8:20 P.M., McNally threw his first pitch of the inning – a fastball – and Kaline promptly sliced it down the right-field line.[1] Right fielder Rich Coggins fished the ball out of the corner and fired back into the infield, where Kaline was already standing on second base.

On WJR radio, Tigers broadcaster Paul Carey – who was in the second season of what would become a 19-year run alongside Ernie Harwell on the Detroit airwaves – described the scene this way:

> "There's a drive down to right field into the corner; it'll be in for a base hit, maybe extra bases. Al is digging for second. He's in with a stand-up double. A two-base hit for Al Kaline, hit number three thousand in his fabulous career of 22 years as a member of the Tigers. Listen to this standing ovation. ..."[2]

After Kaline's historic hit, the game was stopped for about three minutes and Kaline was congratulated by his parents who were seated in box seats behind the Tigers' dugout.

According to the *Detroit Free Press*, "The festivities following Kaline's historic hit were remarkably brief, primarily because Al wanted them that way."[3]

The ball and bat from the milestone were presented to American League President Lee MacPhail, who subsequently delivered them to the Baseball Hall of Fame in Cooperstown, New York.

"I hit a fastball that was sailing away," Kaline told the *Baltimore Sun* after the game. "The ball was really curving and I thought it would go foul at first. I almost forgot to run when I hit it. ... When I reached second, I said a little prayer of thanks to God for giving me a strong body."[4]

When action resumed, McNally showed he was not rattled by the occasion, striking out Bill Freehan, getting Reggie Sanders to ground out to third baseman Brooks Robinson, and then catching Leon Roberts looking to strand Kaline at second and end the inning.

The Tigers held onto their 1-0 lead until the bottom of the fifth when Mark Belanger ignited a two-out rally by singling to left. Rich Coggins followed with a single to center and the Orioles had men on first and second when Paul Blair hit a routine fly ball to center field that dropped at the feet of LeFlore. Both Belanger and Coggins scored on the play, while Blair ended up at second on the two-base error charged to LeFlore.

LeFlore partially atoned for his error in the top of the sixth when he led off with a double. Gary Sutherland's infield single sent LeFlore to third for Kaline, who drove a single to center – career hit number 3,001 – to score LeFlore and tie the game.

The Tigers could do no further damage in the inning, however, and the Orioles came to bat in the bottom of the sixth with the score knotted at 2-2.

Tommy Davis led off with a single to center and moved to second on a sacrifice by slugger Boog Powell, who was in the final weeks of his Orioles career.[5] Don Baylor then singled to center to score Davis with the go-ahead run and knock Ruhle from the game.

Relief ace John Hiller came on to put out the fire, however, and the sixth inning ended with the Orioles leading 3-2.

This back-and-forth game saw yet another lead change in the top of the seventh when a drive by Ed Brinkman just reached the seats in left field for a home run, scoring Aurelio Rodriguez, who had singled with one out. This gave the Tigers a 4-3 lead – their last advantage of the game – and two batters later, Gary Sutherland's single drove McNally to the showers in favor of right-hander Bob Reynolds.

Hiller and Reynolds each stopped the bleeding for their respective teams until the bottom of the eighth, when the Orioles again rallied. Don Baylor doubled to left field with one out and was doubled home by the next hitter, Brooks Robinson, tying the game at 4-4.

Hiller then uncorked a wild pitch that sent Robinson to third as the next hitter, Andy Etchebarren, stepped in. Etchebarren executed a perfect suicide-squeeze bunt, reaching safely on the play and driving home Robinson to give the Orioles a 5-4 advantage that they would carry into the ninth inning.

Reynolds then prevented any further drama for the evening, striking out Ben Oglivie, Gates Brown, and Ron LeFlore – the final two looking – to seal a 5-4 Orioles victory. Reynolds was the game's winning pitcher, upping his record to 7-5, while Hiller missed an opportunity to add to his American League record for relief wins in a season, falling to 17-12.[6]

The win – coupled with the Yankees being swept at home in a doubleheader by the Red Sox – moved the Orioles back into first place where they remained through season's end, winning their second consecutive AL East championship.

But while the Orioles celebrated a critical victory in the final days of the 1974 pennant race, Kaline and the Tigers were finally able to enjoy the future Hall of Famer's career milestone and relax a bit now that the chase for 3,000 was finally over.

After the game, Kaline told WJR Radio:

"I'm happy it's over with and it's tremendous. I'm very sorry in a way that I couldn't wait and get it in Detroit, but if I didn't get it there I'm very happy to get it here (in Baltimore) because I had a lot of relatives. My mom and dad were here and my sister and my wife's relatives were here and I'm very happy that it's over with. I'm very relieved that it's all over and I'm just sorry in a way that we didn't win because I think that would have just capped it off perfectly if we could have held on and won the game."

In the eight games that followed this one, the Tigers won just once, with Kaline going 6-for-25 to close out his career, collecting his final hit – number 3,007 – on Tuesday, October 1, in a 7-6 loss to the Orioles at Tiger Stadium.

The Orioles went 7-0 after the September 24 battle with Detroit to finish the 1974 season on a nine-game winning streak, claiming the division by two games over the second-place Yankees. Baltimore lost in the American League Championship Series to the eventual World Series champion Oakland Athletics by three games to one.

• Kaline Collects 3,000th Career Hit as Tigers Fall to Orioles, 5-4 •

Sources

In addition to the sources cited in the Notes, the author relied on Baseball-Reference.com and the WJR-AM play-by-play recording, available online at youtube.com/watch?v=Qx0eo4M5Y-g.

Notes

1 Jim Hawkins, "Kaline Enters 3,000-Hit Club on the Double," *The Sporting News*, October 12, 1974: 13.

2 Paul Carey, WJR-AM broadcast, September 24, 1974.

3 Jim Hawkins, "Hall of Fame Next for Al," *Detroit Free Press*, September 25, 1974: D-1.

4 Ken Nigro, "Brooks Partially Eclipses Kaline's Milestone Hit," *Baltimore Sun*, September 25, 1974: C-7.

5 After the season the Orioles traded Powell to Cleveland.

6 Hiller finished the season 17-14. His 31 decisions came in 59 game appearances, none of which was a start.

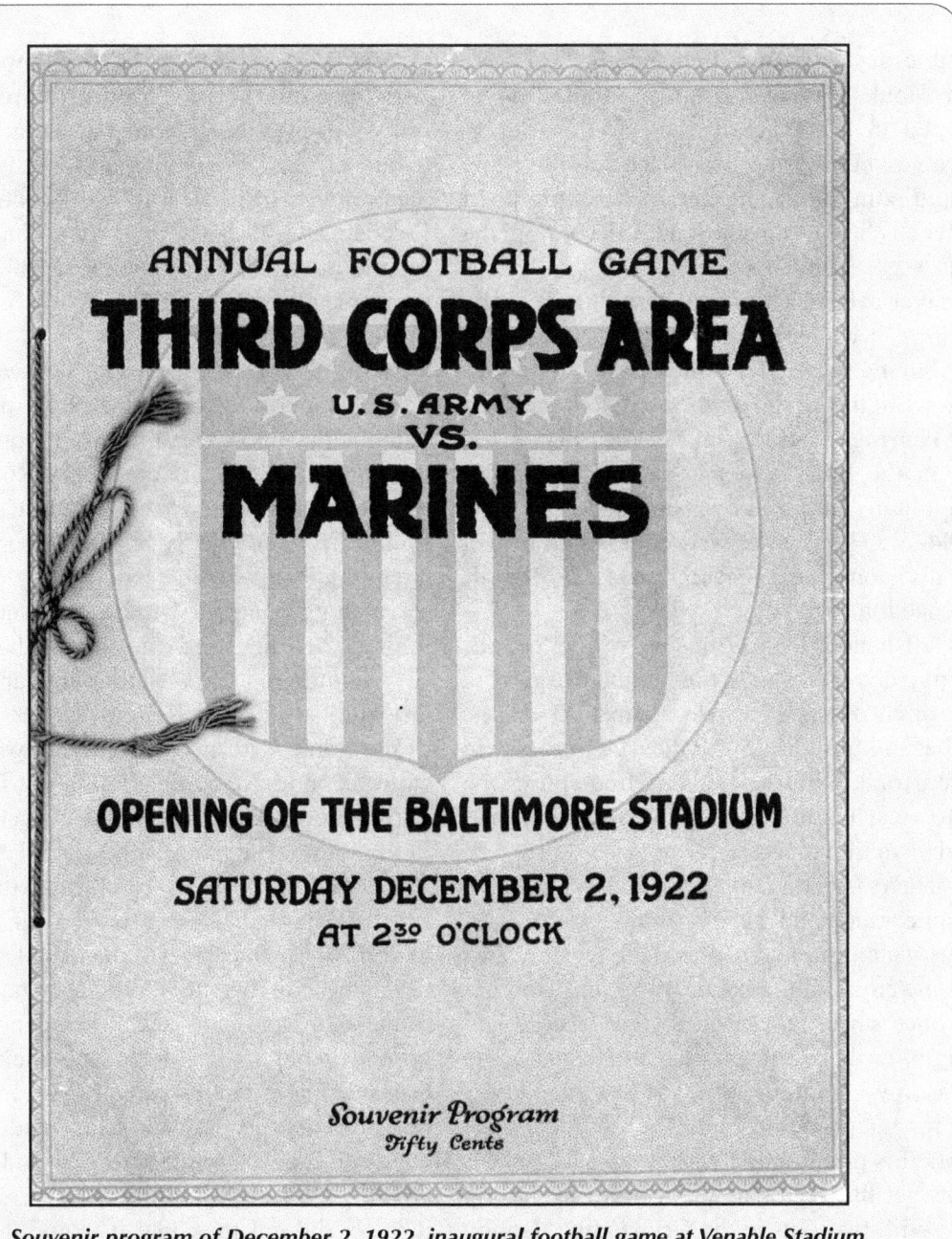

Souvenir program of December 2, 1922, inaugural football game at Venable Stadium between U.S. Marine Corps and U.S. Army's Third Corps Area. (See Municipal Stadium/Memorial Stadium story on page 85.) Courtesy of David B. Stinson.

Orioles Rally in Ninth
Lolich Reaches Wrong Side of 20; Stays in First Place

September 25, 1974: Baltimore Orioles 5, Detroit Tigers 4, at Memorial Stadium

By Luis A. Blandon Jr.

On Wednesday evening, September 25, 1974, Ralph Houk was managing an aging Tigers squad trapped in last place in the AL East at 71-83, 12½ games behind the first-place Orioles. The season's high point had come the previous night. Al Kaline reached "his promised land," becoming the 12th player to get 3,000 hits.[1]

Earl Weaver's 1974 Orioles played "Moneyball" decades before it became trendy.[2] The Orioles were on a tear, having won 21 of their last 27 games, coinciding with the disintegration of a large Red Sox lead. The night before, the Orioles had taken first place in the East by defeating the Tigers 5-4 and taking a half-game lead over the Yankees with a record of 84-71. The Orioles were in position to win their fifth division championship since the playoff era commenced in 1969.

Orioles left-hander Ross Grimsley, winner of four of his last five decisions, took the mound against the Tigers in search of his 19th win against 13 losses. Grimsley became an Oriole for the 1974 season in an offseason trade with the Reds. A free spirit, "he preferred to wear his black hair long and curly, and he didn't always like to shave."[3]

At 33, Tigers starting pitcher Mickey Lolich's physical appearance hid an enormous talent. "All the fat guys watch me and say to their wives, 'See, there's a fat guy doing okay. Bring me another beer,'" he once said. Lolich had a 16-19 record and was closing in on 300 innings pitched. He had come into the season with a figure of 20 as a goal and "[F]ortunately for his peace of mind, (he) didn't realize how accurate his premonition was."[4]

Grimsley set the Tigers down in order in the top of the first. With two outs in the Orioles first, Bobby Grich walked and stole second. Lolich stanched the rally with Tommy Davis grounding out to Aurelio Rodriquez at third. The Tigers jumped on Grimsley with three runs in the second. Bill Freehan started the rally with a walk. With one out, Leon Roberts singled to Enos Cabell in right, advancing Freehan to third. Dan Meyer tripled in the left-center gap, scoring Freehan and Roberts and "doubling his RBI total for the month."[5] Rodriguez's sacrifice fly to Cabell drove in Meyer. Eddie Brinkman grounded out to end the half inning.

With a 3-0 lead, Houk believed Lolich had enough support to win. But Lolich struggled with his command, walking leadoff hitter Don Baylor. Baylor used his speed to score on Brooks Robinson's double to left. Lolich retired Bob Oliver, Cabell, and Andy Etchebarren on two fly balls and a grounder to third, stranding Robinson at second.

Pitching controlled the action for the next three innings. In the third the Tigers had a rally with two singles by Gary Sutherland and Freehan, but Grimsley struck out Reggie Sanders. In the bottom of the frame with two outs, Grich walked again and stole second base again. Lolich got Davis to ground out again to Rodriguez. Each side went down in order in the fourth. Each managed a single in the fifth.

Leading off the Tigers' sixth, Kaline and Freehan singled. Kaline scored on Sanders' single to left. With the Tigers ahead 4-1, Weaver pulled Grimsley for Wayne Garland, who came in with runners on first and second and no outs. Roberts grounded out to Robinson, advancing the runners. Garland intentionally walked Meyer, setting up the resulting double play by Grich and Mark Belanger on Rodriguez's groundball. Garland dominated the next three innings, holding the Tigers scoreless, "but it really did not look like it would do any good, the way Lolich kept pitching out of trouble."[6]

The resilient Orioles cut the deficit to 4-2 in the

• Orioles Rally in Ninth •

sixth. Lolich could not get Grich out, walking him for the third consecutive time. Davis cued a single to right. With Grich on second, Lolich retired the next two batters on fly balls to short and left. But Oliver, a late-season acquisition from the California Angels, drove Grich home with a single to Ron LeFlore in center.

The seventh and eighth innings were uneventful. Gene Lamont took over Tigers catching duties in the seventh inning as Freehan fell ill.[7] Davis and Baylor singled off a tiring Lolich in the eighth but were left stranded on base.

In the top of the ninth, Meyer grounded out to Garland. Rodriguez and Ed Brinkman flied out to center and left. With a 4-2 lead, Lolich took the mound. Cabell flied out to defensive substitution Mickey Stanley in left as "many in the small turnout of 10,552 began heading home, convinced the Orioles' tenuous hold on first place had evaporated."[8]

Etchebarren smacked a grounder through Rodriguez's legs that was called a single. Rich Coggins ran for Etchebarren. Pinch-hitting for Belanger, Curt Motton "looked at what appeared to be strike three to everyone in the ballpark except for Joseph Brinkman, the home plate umpire."[9] Motton walked, with Al Bumbry pinch-running. Paul Blair drove a single to left, scoring Coggins. Lolich faced his nemesis, Grich, who walloped a 400-foot drive to deep center field with a look of homer and a win for the Orioles. But from a life as a troubled Detroit youth and in Michigan prisons, LeFlore was referred as "a former professional armed robber."[10] Leflore "raced back to the fence and plucked [Grich's] drive just as it was sailing over the barrier."[11] Bumbry and Blair tagged to third and second.

With first base open, Houk chose to pitch to Davis. Davis was experiencing a career renaissance with the advent of the designated hitter in 1973. The role "was a job perfectly suited for Davis, a latter-day Wee Willie Keeler, the master of "hit 'em where they ain't."[12] Davis hit Lolich's first pitch "off the end of his bat and the soft liner squibbed out to centerfield, agonizingly out of the reach of everyone."[13] The ball "floated over second like a dying quail and then took a tricky hop away from the frustrated [Sutherland] who desperately tried to retrieve it in an effort to cut off the winning run."[14] From center field, LeFlore desperately raced toward the ball. Bumbry and Blair scored as "the ball bounced only about 10 feet beyond the infield dirt and rolled ever so slowly toward the outfield."[15] As Blair scored the winning run, "Etchebarren led the exuberant charge out of the Oriole dugout."[16] Weaver ran toward the mound to congratulate Davis.[17]

Davis's hit kept the Orioles in first place. As a hitter, "Davis can do more tricks with his hands than Minnesota Fats with a cue stick," quipped a Baltimore sportswriter.[18] Houk was incredulous: "What the hell, the ball was not hit that good."[19] Weaver was in awe: "The guy is a magician with the bat, no question about it."[20] Davis exclaimed, "[T]he last time I was that excited was when I was playing basketball in high school."[21]

The Tigers were unimpressed as "[Y]ou would have thought the Birds had just clinched a pennant or something the way they reacted."[22] Houk vented, "[T]hat SOB behind the plate beat us. Lolich had Motton struck out, there's no question about it. It's the worst exhibition of umpiring I've seen in a long time."[23] It was a "manifestation of home-stadium bias."[24] Questioned over his decision to pitch to Davis, Houk "disdained the idea of walking Davis intentionally" because "Baylor's been hot too."[25] Handed his 20th loss, Lolich asserted that he struck out Motton, with umpire Brinkman's performance "the worst uninspired game. ... He missed pitches that were unbelievable. I guess the pennant race got the best of him."[26] Robinson noted: "It's a screwy game. A guy jumps over the fence and catches a three-run homer, and you think maybe it's all over there. But the way things have been happening, you know."[27]

The Orioles won the AL East (91-71) but lost to the eventual champion Oakland Athletics in the playoffs. The Tigers ended 72-90 in last place, 19 games behind the Orioles. Lolich ended the season 16-21. For the fourth consecutive season, he went over 300 innings pitched. Garland was used sporadically in 20 games with six starts, going 5-5 with a 2.97 ERA. Davis won the Outstanding Designated Hitter Award,[28] finishing with a .289 average and 181 hits, leading the Orioles with 84 RBIs.

As the Orioles and Tigers played that day, in Los Angeles Dr. Frank Jobe operated for three hours on a Dodgers pitcher with an experimental graft reconstruction of the ulnar collateral ligament to repair what was considered a career-ending injury to the pitcher's throwing elbow.[29] The next day, Tommy John began the 18-month rehabilitation back to the majors.

Sources

In addition to the sources cited in the Notes, the author consulted baseball-reference.com, retrosheet.org, and mlb.com.

Notes

1 Associated Press, " Al Kaline: Prince of Detroit Reaches His Promised Land," *St. Petersburg Times*, September 25, 1974: 4-C; exhibits.baseballhalloffame.org/3000_hit_club/kaline_al.htm, accessed September 13, 2019.

2 The Orioles teams during the Weaver era annually ranked among the best in walks and on-base percentage.

3 Bruce Markusen, "Cooperstown Confidential: Ross Grimsley and the Swingin' '70s," hardballtimes.com, May 21, 2010, tht.fangraphs.com/cooperstown-confidential-ross-grimsley-and-the-swingin-70s/, accessed September 26, 2019.

4 Jim Hawkins, "Tigers' Mick Loses No. 20," *Detroit Free Press*," September 26, 1974: 1D.

5 Jim Hawkins, "The Mick Loses His 20th, 5-4," *Detroit Free Press*, September 26, 1974: 10D.

6 Ken Nigro, "Orioles Score 3 in 9th to Nip Tigers, Hold Lead," *Baltimore Sun*, September 26, 1974: C5.

7 Associated Press, "Orioles Remain on Top by ½ Game," *Hartford Courant*, September 26, 1974: 8.

8 Nigro.

9 Mike Roberts, "Orioles Foil Robbery," *Washington-Star News*, September 26, 1974: D1.

10 Roberts.

11 Nigro.

12 Alan Goldstein, "Davis's 'Magic' Bat Produces 'Lucky' Winning Hit," *Baltimore Sun*, September 26, 1974: C8.

13 Nigro.

14 Goldstein: C5.

15 Nigro.

16 Hawkins, "Tigers' Mick Loses No. 20."

17 Hawkins, "Tigers' Mick Loses No. 20."

18 Goldstein: C5.

19 Nigro.

20 Goldstein: C8.

21 George Minot Jr., "Davis Hit Preserves Half-Game Margin: Davis Taps Lolich, Orioles Keep Lead," *Washington Post*, September 26, 1974: E1.

22 Hawkins, "Tigers' Mick Loses No. 20."

23 Nigro.

24 Roberts.

25 Nigro.

26 Goldstein: C8.

27 Roberts.

28 The award was renamed for Edgar Martínez in September 2004.

29 Chris Landers, "Just Who Is Tommy John, and Why Does Everyone Talk About His Surgery All the Time?" Cut 4 by MLB.com, February 27, 2019, mlb.com/cut4/why-is-it-called-tommy-john-surgery. Accessed September 26, 2019.

Brooks Robinson's Last Career Home Run

April 19, 1977: Baltimore Orioles 6, Cleveland Indians 5 (10 innings), at Memorial Stadium

By Bill Haelig

Entering the 1977 season, expectations were low for the Baltimore Orioles. After they won 88 games the season before and finished second behind the pennant-winning Yankees, many experts were picking the Orioles to finish in the lower half of the American League East. The lowered expectations were primarily due to major-league baseball's first year of free agency and the Orioles' subsequent loss of key players Reggie Jackson, Bobby Grich, and 20-game winner Wayne Garland.

On the evening of Tuesday, April 19, 1977, the Cleveland Indians entered Memorial Stadium for the middle game of a three-game series with both clubs having 4-4 records.

The starting pitcher for the Orioles was Mike Flanagan, making his first start of the year, while the Indians countered with Dennis Eckersley, who was making his third start of the young season.

The game was scoreless until the top of the third inning, when Indians catcher Ray Fosse led off with his first home run of the season. The Orioles tied the game in the bottom of the inning when right fielder Ken Singleton singled to center field, driving in second baseman Billy Smith, who had doubled.

The Orioles broke the tie in the fourth, scoring an unearned run off Eckersley. With one out, first baseman Lee May doubled. Center fielder Larry Harlow reached base on a fielding error by Indians second baseman Duane Kuiper, moving May to third. May then scored on catcher Rick Dempsey's sacrifice fly to right.

Kuiper atoned for his fielding miscue the next inning when he executed a successful suicide squeeze bunt to bring in Fosse, who had led off the inning with a single and moved to third on a hit to center field by shortstop Frank Duffy.

Due to strong pitching efforts by both Flanagan and Eckersley (and the Indians' Dave LaRoche, who pitched the ninth), the game remained tied at 2-2 after regulation play.

The Orioles brought in left-hander Tippy Martinez, in his first appearance of the season, to pitch the top of the 10th inning. He encountered problems immediately when the first batter he faced, right fielder Charlie Spikes, doubled. After Fosse struck out, light-hitting Frank Duffy tripled to right, scoring Spikes to give Cleveland the lead. Martinez's trouble continued when he walked center fielder Rick Manning and then faced pinch-hitter Larvell Blanks, who lined a ball off Martinez's ankle for an infield hit, allowing Duffy to score.

Manager Earl Weaver replaced Martinez with right-handed Dyar Miller, who got himself in his own trouble by walking pinch-hitter Jim Norris to load the bases. Veteran DH Rico Carty, who had been held hitless up to this point, struck an RBI single to right that scored Manning and extended the Indians' lead to 5-2. Miller struck out the next two batters, left fielder Buddy Bell and first baseman Andre Thornton, to escape further damage.

Going into the bottom of the 10th, the Indians stayed with LaRoche in hopes of shutting down the Orioles and earning him his third win of the still-young season.

LaRoche had set the Orioles down in order in the ninth (two by strikeouts), but ran into problems in the 10th. Ken Singleton led off with a base hit to center, and LaRoche walked third baseman Doug DeCinces. LaRoche struck out rookie DH Eddie Murray, earning himself temporary relief. That relief was indeed temporary as Lee May singled to left field, scoring Singleton from second and bringing the Orioles to within a run of a tie.

Orioles rookie Harlow was the next scheduled hitter, but Weaver instead sent up Brooks Robinson as a pinch-hitter. Robinson was 39 years old and in his 23rd season with the Orioles (working as a player-coach.) It was only his third plate appearance of the season.

Indians manager (and former Orioles teammate) Frank Robinson went out for a mound visit with LaRoche to see if he wanted to pitch to Brooks. It was decided that the left-handed LaRoche would pitch to the right-handed-hitting Robinson.

After the game Robinson said, "Frank probably looked up and said, 'Here comes old Brooksie. It's a tailor-made double play.'"[1]

In front of a crowd that was by then somewhat less than the announced 4,826, Brooks strode up to the plate. Bill Tanton of Baltimore's *Evening Sun* reported, "As Brooks dug in to face reliever Dave LaRoche, a chant went up in the grandstand near third base: 'Let's Go, Brooks, Let's Go, Brooks.'"[2]

Robinson worked the count to 3-and-2 and after fouling off several offerings from LaRoche, he made solid contact with a belt-high fastball and connected for a home run that landed about seven rows deep in the left-field bleachers. The Orioles dugout merrily emptied to greet a grinning Robinson as he approached home plate after providing the Orioles and their fans with an exciting 6-5 walk-off victory.[3]

"This was my biggest thrill in a long time," Robinson said after the game. "It's a day-to-day thing for me. I was lucky to get a contract this year."[4]

"An emotional moment?" laughed Earl Weaver. "It's gotta be. I'm only sorry I've been around here for the last 10 years. He's been doing things like that for the last 20."[5]

Ironically, both pitchers of record (LaRoche & Miller) were dealt to the California Angels within two months of this game. Indians manager Frank Robinson was fired by the Indians in mid-June and the Orioles – despite their losses in free agency – surprised a lot of people by winning 97 games in 1977, finishing just 2 1/2 games behind the eventual World Series champion New York Yankees.

As for Brooks Robinson, he only had 49 more plate appearances after the April 19 game, with only six hits, before retiring as a player and becoming a full-time coach on August 21 to make room for Rick Dempsey, who was coming off the disabled list.[6]

Brooks Robinson homered for the first time late in the 1956 season off Washington Senators pitcher Evelio Hernandez. The home run he hit on April 19, 1977, was his 268th and last (and possibly most improbable) of his illustrious Hall of Fame career.

Perhaps the entire game of April 19 (and Robinson's career) could be summed up by someone mentioning to him during the postgame locker-room celebration that he looked "like a kid out there tonight" and with the future Hall of Famer responding, "I feel like a kid every time I put this uniform on."[7]

Brooks Robinson pinch-hit in the bottom of the 10th and homered to win a 6-5 game over the Indians. It was his 268th – and last – career home run. Courtesy of the Baltimore Orioles.

Sources

In addition to the sources cited in the Notes, the author utilized Baseball-Reference.com for box scores and player, team, and season pages as well as the game's pitching chart kept by the Orioles' Scott McGregor.

Notes

1 Associated Press, "Brooksie Shines in Rare Chance," *Lawrence (Kansas) Journal World,* April 20, 1977: 9.

2 Bill Tanton, "Brooks Provides an All Time Thrill," *Baltimore Evening Sun,* April 20, 1977: C1.

3 The game-winning home run can be seen at youtube.com/watch?v=QWpMNiQn6ZI.

4 "Brooksie Shines in Rare Chance."

5 Michael Janofsky, "Brooks: 'The Kid Can Still Play,'" *Baltimore Evening Sun,* April 20, 1977: C1.

6 *Baltimore Orioles 1978 Information Guide,* 85.

7 Tanton.

Orioles Magic Is Born

June 22, 1979: Baltimore Orioles 6, Detroit Tigers 5, at Memorial Stadium

By Austin Gisriel

The Orioles entered the bottom of the ninth down 5-3 to the Detroit Tigers, but Ken Singleton's one-out home run off reliever Dave Tobik put a buzz into the Memorial Stadium crowd of 35,456 who began to hope for another comeback win. In their last home game, on June 10, the Orioles scored three runs in the bottom of the ninth for a 5-4 victory over Texas, building momentum for a road trip that saw them go 7-1, including winning the final six games in a row. Anticipation of a seventh consecutive victory grew when Eddie Murray followed Singleton's home run with a single to right field. He represented the potential tying run, but Gary Roenicke popped out to second, and Doug DeCinces became the last hope for the Birds.

A familiar chant from superfan Wild Bill Hagy's roost in Section 34 of the upper deck mingled with anxious cheering: *"Come on DeCinces: Over the fences"!*[1]

The Orioles third baseman took a high curve for ball one.

The count ran to 1-and-1 when DeCinces took a "big rip" at a fastball and fouled it straight back.[2]

The "Charge!" call rang out over the public-address speakers, and a full-throated "Charge!" answered back. Baltimore announcer Bill O'Donnell then described the birth of Oriole Magic:

"Here's a fly ball to deep left field! It's way back. ... It's gone! Home run! Home run! Home run! The Orioles win it![3]

O'Donnell could barely be heard over the crowd, and his partner in the booth that night, longtime Baltimore sports broadcaster Charlie Eckman, became even more excited than O'Donnell.

It might get out of here! Get out of here! This place is going crazy![4]

And indeed they were. DeCinces was mobbed at home plate by the entire Orioles team and several members of the grounds crew.[5] The fans refused to leave even after DeCinces and the victorious Orioles had disappeared into the clubhouse, but his teammates pushed him back onto the field for a curtain call. Orioles Magic had been born. DeCinces described it best:

"That night, that game, that home run, it triggered something. It was the game that triggered things. The emotion just multiplied from there. It was such an event, and the chemistry was there already. The radio broadcast had a lot to do with it. I heard the tape later. The announcers, Bill O'Donnell and Charley Eckman, were going wild. Their excitement really came through."[6]

Such games never look promising early on, of course. Orioles starter Mike Flanagan gave up a run in the first and three in the second, aided by three errors, including a catcher's interference call on Rick Dempsey. Flanagan, who was exhibiting none of the form that would win him the Cy Young Award after the season, yielded a home run to Lance Parrish in the third, and when John Wockenfuss singled two batters later, skipper Earl Weaver lifted southpaw Flanagan in favor of Sammy Stewart. Baltimore, which had matched Detroit's first-inning run, scored two more in the third off Tigers rookie Pat Underwood. With Lee May on second and DeCinces on third, Underwood was pulled in favor of Kip Young, who retired Rich Dauer on a fly ball. Young proceeded to throw five shutout innings, striking out four of the final five batters he faced, including DeCinces in the seventh. This was the best outing of Young's season, and one of the best of his brief career, 1978-79.

Meanwhile, Sammy Stewart cruised into the seventh inning, then issued a two-out walk to Ron LeFlore, which was followed by Alan Trammel's single. Tippy Martinez came on in relief, and retired Steve Kemp on a fly ball to left to squelch the budding rally. The score remained 5-3 heading into the bottom of the ninth when Tigers manager Sparky Anderson opted for Tobik.

Then the Magic began.

If there was any doubt that Orioles Magic was now a real power, the Orioles used it again the next day in a Saturday doubleheader. They scored three runs in the bottom of the ninth in game one on Eddie Murray's homer for an 8-6 win, then plated two in the seventh and one in the eighth of game two for a 6-5 victory. Terry Crowley's pinch-hit single off none other than Dave Tobik sealed the nightcap, although it was starter Jack Billingham who took the loss.

The Orioles played .793 baseball in June, going 23-6, and never looked back before the magic ran out in the World Series against the Pirates.

Several events had taken place which set the stage for DeCinces' theatrics that June night. The Orioles had switched their radio flagship station from WBAL to WFBR, a smaller station, but one that attracted a younger, more energetic audience; the same kind of fans who were beginning to fill Section 34 and view Wild Bill Hagy as a folk hero. Furthermore, the Baltimore Colts football team, long the city's favorite sports team, was in decline, and the Orioles were at the beginning of their second period of glory, culminating in the World Series championship in 1983 with largely the same team.

One key player missing from the '83 champions, however, was Doug DeCinces. He was traded to the California Angels in 1982 to make room for rookie Cal Ripken. When Earl Weaver moved Ripken to short later that season, a glaring hole was created at third; a hole not adequately filled until Ripken moved back to the position 15 seasons later, in 1997.

DeCinces not only endured an unceremonious exit from Baltimore, he had a tough beginning to his career as well. Traded to make room for Cal Ripken, he was also the guy who replaced Brooks Robinson. Nevertheless, DeCinces, whose 15-year career ended in 1987, would be the key player in one of the greatest moments in Orioles history.

Sources

In addition to the sources mentioned in the Notes, the author also relied on Baseball-Reference.com.

Notes

1   Skip Dorer with Wayne Kaiser, *In the O Zone* (Baltimore: Arbutus PBA, Inc., 1980), 10.

2   Bill O'Donnell's play by play on WFBR via YouTube: youtube.com/watch?v=IKp8ZKWQSx8.

3   O'Donnell's play by play on WFBR.

4   O'Donnell's play by play on WFBR.

5   Baltimore Orioles Baseball, "Orioles Magic: 1979 Baltimore Orioles Baseball: Orioles Magic is Born," published April 10, 2012. youtube.com/watch?v=khPbyMj1teA.

6   John Eisenberg, *From 33rd Street To Camden Yards: An Oral History of the Baltimore Orioles* (Chicago: Contemporary Books, 2001), 336.

Third baseman Doug DeCinces hit a two-run homer in the bottom of the ninth to catapult the Orioles to a 6-5 win over the Tigers. Courtesy of the Baltimore Orioles.

Tippy Martinez Retires 23 Consecutive Batters in Relief

July 23, 1979: Baltimore Orioles 7, Oakland Athletics 4, at Memorial Stadium

By Brian M. Frank

Tippy Martinez hadn't pitched in 13 days as the Orioles headed into the second game of a two-game series with Oakland. Before the game the lefty reliever went up to Memorial Stadium's legendary public-address announcer Rex Barney and told him, "Next time I come in to pitch, you'd better explain to the fans who I am. I haven't pitched in so long I think they might have forgotten me."[1] With the remarkable performance he was about to have, he didn't need to worry about Orioles fans remembering who he was.

The Orioles had the best record in baseball with a 63-32 record. They sent Mike Flanagan to the mound to face Oakland's Matt Keough. Flanagan was having a characteristically solid season with a 13-6 record and a 3.60 ERA. By contrast, both the A's and Keough were struggling. Oakland had lost seven out of eight games and 23 of its last 27, to sink to a major-league-worst 26-72 record. Keough was having a disastrous season. After making the All-Star team in his rookie campaign of 1978, he'd taken a loss in 22 out of 24 decisions, including 15 in a row. He started the 1979 season with a dreadful 0-11 record and a 5.85 ERA.

Because of the threat of thunderstorms, only 13,132 spectators were on hand, but the Baltimore faithful who did attend saw the Orioles jump out to an early lead. Eddie Murray singled home Al Bumbry for the first run of the game, and John Lowenstein's sacrifice fly put Baltimore on top 2-0 in the first inning.

The A's battled back in the second. Jim Essian doubled to lead off the inning. Flanagan struck out Tony Armas, but Dave Revering singled to put runners at the corners. That's when the A's bats exploded. Consecutive doubles by Mike Edwards, Rob Picciolo, and Rickey Henderson gave Oakland a 4-2 lead and knocked Flanagan out of the game.

Orioles manager Earl Weaver called on Tippy Martinez for the first time in 13 days. After the game Martinez said, "I have been keeping in shape by throwing in the bullpen. In fact, I think that I've warmed up 170 times this year. Still, when the team is winning but you're not in there, you feel like things are drifting apart. You're not part of what is happening."[2] Martinez had trouble finding his control after such a long layoff. He walked Dave Chalk on four pitches, and then went 2-and-0 on the next batter, Mike Heath. But Martinez got Heath to line out to left field, then retired Jeff Newman on a grounder back to the mound to escape any further damage.

From that point on, Martinez was locked in. He held the A's at bay, retiring them in order in the third, fourth, and fifth innings, before Baltimore was able to cut into Oakland's lead. In the fifth inning, Bumbry walked with one out, moved to second on a wild pitch, and raced home on Ken Singleton's hit to left, to cut the A's lead to just a run at 4-3.

Martinez continued to be lights-out. "I just went out there and figured I had to pitch a shutout and hope that we would come back," he said. That's my job, keeping them from getting any more runs."[3] When he struck out Newman to end the eighth, he'd retired 20 consecutive batters since he walked Chalk in the second inning. After eight innings, the game was the longest relief outing of Martinez's major-league career, with 6⅔ innings in the books.[4] Previously, his longest relief effort had been 6⅓ shutout innings three months earlier against the A's. He also dominated in that extended outing, allowing just two hits and two walks.

Keough entered the eighth inning with a one-run lead, but immediately put the tying run on by walking Singleton to lead off the inning. The next batter, Eddie Murray, singled to right, moving Singleton to second. That was it for Keough, who was replaced by lefty Dave Hamilton. Hamilton faced only one batter, John Lowenstein. Lowenstein laid down a successful sacrifice bunt with two strikes to advance both runners. Dave Heaverlo came out of the A's bullpen and intentionally walked Doug DeCinces to load the bases. The strategy looked as if it might be successful when Gary Roenicke fouled out to first baseman Dave Revering on Heaverlo's first pitch to him for the second out of the inning.

Earl Weaver sent Pat Kelly up to pinch-hit for Rich Dauer with two down and the bases full of Orioles. Kelly had been Baltimore's best pinch-hitter all season, going 8-for-15 (.533) with 2 home runs and 11 RBIs. Kelly worked the count to 3-and-1, before Heaverlo delivered a fastball that Kelly jumped on and sent sailing toward right-center field. Tony Armas raced back and it initially looked as though he might be able to make a play. But the ball continued to carry and sailed over the fence for a grand slam. "When I hit it, I knew I had hit it good, but I didn't know if it was going out," Kelly said.[5] "I hit it to the deepest part of the park, but, thank God, it cleared the fence."[6] Kelly's dramatic homer gave Baltimore a 7-4 lead.

Pitching with a lead for the first time in the game, Martinez retired Essian on a groundball back to the mound, struck out Armas, and got Revering to pop out to third to finish the game and seal the Orioles' win.

Martinez threw 90 pitches in the longest relief outing of his career. He struck out four and induced 11 groundouts. After walking the first batter he faced in the second inning, he set down the A's in order until the end of the game, retiring 23 consecutive batters. "I've never been that good," he stated succinctly.[7] The lefty had come through at a time when the Orioles desperately needed a good relief outing with key pitchers Jim Palmer and Tim Stoddard on the disabled list. "I know Tippy is there when I need him," Weaver said. "It's not my fault our starters have pitched complete games five of the last seven times out."[8] It was the Orioles' fifth consecutive win and increased their lead in the American League East to 4½ games over Boston.

The ecstatic Baltimore crowd demanded curtain calls from both Orioles heroes, Kelly and Martinez. Earlier, Martinez had joked that PA announcer Rex Barney would have to remind the fans who he was because he hadn't pitched in so long. After the game, the fans chanted, "Tip-py! Tip-py! Tip-py!" as Martinez went to the top step of the Orioles dugout, doffed his cap, and waved back to the adoring crowd. It was clear the fans needed no reminder.[9]

Sources

In addition to the sources cited in the Notes, the author consulted Baseball-Reference.com and Retrosheet.org.

Notes

1   Bill Tanton, "Curtain Calls Continue," *Baltimore Evening Sun*, July 24, 1979: C-4.

2   Terry Pluto, "Birds' Kelly, Tippy Produce Still Another Set of Miracles," *Baltimore Evening Sun*, July 24, 1979: C-4.

3   James H. Jackson, "Orioles Stun A's on Kelly's Slam," *Baltimore Sun*, July 24, 1979: C-5.

4   Martinez had one outing longer than this earlier in his career, but it was a start. He went 7⅓ innings for the New York Yankees against the California Angels on August 24, 1975.

5   Jackson.

6   Jackson.

7   Tom Weir, "Dirty Dozen for Keough," *Oakland Tribune*, July 24, 1979: D4.

8   Pluto.

9   Tanton.

With one out on the second inning, Tippy Martinez relieved starter Mike Flanagan and threw 7 2/3 innings of no-hit ball. The four runs Baltimore scored in the bottom of the eighth gave them the winning margin, 7-4. Courtesy of the Baltimore Orioles.

Baltimore Sweeps Doubleheader to Extend Earl Weaver's Final Pennant Race

October 1, 1982: Baltimore Orioles 8, Milwaukee Brewers 3; Baltimore Orioles 7, Milwaukee Brewers 1 (doubleheader), at Memorial Stadium

By Rich Ottone

It was a story that could only happen in baseball. On the morning of October 1, 1982, the Baltimore Orioles arrived home from Detroit trailing the Milwaukee Brewers by three games. For Baltimore's beloved manager Earl Weaver, who had announced in March that he would retire after the season, his final mission at the helm was clear. Win each game of the weekend series with the Brewers and he would lead the Orioles to their seventh division title in his 14 seasons. Lose any of the four games and the Brewers would win their first-ever division title. Long before the season, the major-league schedulers had seen fit to assure that these teams would square off at Memorial Stadium starting with a Friday night doubleheader.

Both teams started the season slowly. Weaver's impending retirement did not seem to inspire his team and the aging Orioles lost 10 of their first 12 games. On Memorial Day they were in fifth place with a 23-24 record. Milwaukee, managed by Buck Rodgers, was a half-game behind at 22-24. Preseason expectations for the Brewers had been high and owner Bud Selig lost patience; on June 2 he replaced Rodgers with the team's popular hitting coach, Harvey Kuenn.

Weaver and Kuenn couldn't be any more different. Weaver started his playing career in the St. Louis Cardinals organization and was never able to make the big-league club. "The only thing I'd ever wanted in my life was to be a major-league ballplayer, but I had to admit to myself that I wasn't good enough, it broke my heart," he once said.[1] As a manager Weaver was famous for his quick temper and was ejected 97 times during his career.[2] He kept his distance from his players because "you're the person who decides all the worst things in their lives."[3] Weaver was ahead of his time, favoring a combination of pitching and three-run homers. He once stated that 'your most precious possessions on offense are your 27 outs.'"[4]

Kuenn, on the other hand, had a successful big-league career, finishing with a career batting average of .303. After his playing career ended, Kuenn suffered from several health issues that ultimately led to the amputation of his leg in 1980.[5] As a hitting coach for the Brewers, the laid-back Kuenn developed good relationships with Selig and many of the players.

Immediately after the hiring, Kuenn told his players to just go out and have fun.[6] Led by the stellar play of MVP Robin Yount, Paul Molitor, and Cecil Cooper as well as the solid pitching of Cy Young Award winner Pete Vuckovich and closer Rollie Fingers, the team responded to the new manager's style by going 71-40 before the final weekend series. They finished the season with 216 homers and earned the moniker Harvey's Wallbangers.

The struggling Orioles also needed a spark and Weaver made two decisions that seemed to bolster his team. He moved rookie slugger Cal Ripken from third base to become the starting shortstop. He also inserted 20-year-old Storm Davis into the team's pitching rotation. Those moves, coupled with the consistent excellence of Eddie Murray and a rejuvenated Jim Palmer, proved to be a successful formula in 1982. Like the Brewers, the Orioles rallied by going 68-43 before the final weekend series.

While pursuing the Brewers, the Orioles found time to honor their beloved manager. On September 19, before 41,127 appreciative fans, the team retired Weaver's number 4 in a pregame ceremony before taking on the Indians. Fittingly, the Orioles won the game when Rich Dauer hit a walk-off two-run homer in the bottom of the ninth inning. It was Dauer who had coined the phrase "Let's win for the Duck" as a team rallying cry in reference to his manager's lame-duck status.[7]

Despite the excitement created by that game and their hot September, it seemed as if Weaver's final pennant drive would fall short as the team could get no closer than a game out of first place.

Nonetheless, prior to the first game of the series, it seemed as if Baltimore was bursting at the seams. A raucous crowd of 51,883 poured into Memorial Stadium on that Friday afternoon. John Fairhall of the *Baltimore Evening Sun* likened it to a World Series atmosphere.[8] Two young men carried a banner on which was scrawled "Sweep Four!" around the ballpark. It wasn't long before the rest of the fans were screaming the message.[9] Orioles superfan Wild Bill Hagy stood on top of the home-team dugout folding his arms into a semblance of each letter imploring the crowd to spell out Orioles.[10]

The Orioles responded to the enthusiasm by chasing an ineffective Vuckovich after 4⅓ innings before winning the first game, 8-3. Trailing 1-0 in the second inning, the Orioles scored three times when, with one out, Jim Dwyer singled, Ripken walked, and Joe Nolan singled, scoring Dwyer. Dauer followed with a hit-and-run groundball. Yount fielded it but his throw to Jim Gantner was too late to force Nolan. Gantner's relay throw to first was wild, allowing Ripken and Nolan to score.[11] The Orioles extended the lead in the third on Ken Singleton's 14th homer. In the fourth Nolan tripled and scored on Dauer's double to make it 5-1. The Brewers showed some life in the sixth when Ted Simmons and Ben Oglivie hit back-to-back homers, cutting the gap to 5-3. But Orioles starter Dennis Martinez settled down and in the bottom of the frame Terry Crowley's pinch-hit single brought two runs home to push the lead back to four runs. Weaver handed the ball to Tippy Martinez in the seventh and he retired eight of the next nine batters to close out the win.

Davis started the second game by retiring Molitor, Yount, and Cooper in order. The Brewers sent Mike Caldwell to the mound. With one out in the first, Dauer reached on his fourth hit of the evening. One out later, Caldwell served a high fastball over the plate to Murray. The future Hall of Famer deposited the ball in the left-field seats for his 32nd homer, giving the Orioles a 2-0 lead. With the crowd whipped into a frenzy, Benny Ayala reached on an infield single and scored on Gary Roenicke's double, increasing the lead to 3-0.

Davis ran into trouble in the second when he issued three consecutive two-out walks to load the bases. At one point during this stretch, Davis tossed 11 consecutive balls.[12] After the third walk, Weaver and team trainer Ralph Salvon paid him a visit.[13] "I looked out and saw Mike Boddicker warming up and Earl has a thing late in the season of taking a guy out earlier," Davis said later. "But Earl just came out and said, 'Relax and throw the fastball. You've got a good fast ball tonight.'"[14] Davis took Weaver's advice to heart, striking out Gantner to end the inning.

In the bottom of the inning, the Orioles continued to feast on Caldwell's pitching when ex-Brewer Lenn Sakata homered to increase the lead to 4-0. It was Sakata's 14th career homer and his fifth against his former team. Later in the locker room, Molitor said, "When they got those four runs the crowd got in the game and we were in trouble."[15]

The Brewers got on the board in the seventh when Moore led off the inning with a double and came home on Gantner's one-out single to left. The Orioles again responded in the bottom of the inning. John Shelby hit his first career homer and two batters later Ripken established a new team standard for rookies[16] by hitting his 28th, increasing the lead to 7-1. Kuenn lifted Caldwell in the eighth but the damage was done. After a late-season hot streak in which he won 10 of 11 starts while holding opponents to a .215 average and a 0.93 WHIP in his last two starts, the Orioles got to him for 25 hits and five homers.

The score was still 7-1 when Davis allowed a one-out ninth-inning single to Charlie Moore. Weaver once again visited the mound. With the club's second-largest regular-season crowd ever[17] imploring him to let the young starter finish the game, Weaver returned to the dugout. Davis then retired Bob Skube and Gantner to finish the first complete game of his career and cut the Brewers' lead to one game.

Inside a jubilant locker room Ripken sounded a cautiously optimistic note: "They still have the upper hand. They just have to win one game. But the mood on the club now is not to let them win."[18] The *Wisconsin State Journal*'s Bill Brophy wrote, "It was so quiet in the Milwaukee Brewers clubhouse here late Friday night that you could almost hear a division lead vanish."[19] The always optimistic Kuenn said, "I'll tell my club the same thing I've said, play, relax, and have a good time. Why not? We're still one game up. It will not carry over into tomorrow."[20]

Weaver managed the Orioles to an 11-3 win the next day, but the Brewers won the final game of the set, 10-2, on Sunday afternoon, and thus won the division by one game.

Baltimore Sweeps Doubleheader to Extend Earl Weaver's Final Pennant Race

Sources

In addition to the sources cited in the Notes, the author consulted Baseball-Reference.com for the box score and play-by-play.

Notes

1 Warren Corbett, "Earl Weaver," SABR BioProject, sabr.org/bioproj/person/0cfc37e3.

2 Jay Hurd, "Earl Weaver: Strategy, Innovation, and Ninety-Four Meltdowns," *Baseball Research Journal,* Summer 2010, sabr.org/research/earl-weaver-strategy-innovation-and-ninety-four-meltdowns.

3 Corbett.

4 Corbett.

5 Dale Voiss, "Harvey Kuenn" SABRBio Project, sabr.org/bioproj/person/a79cd3a2.

6 Voiss.

7 Kent Baker, "41,127 See Orioles Retire an Awed Earl Weaver's No. 4," *Baltimore Sun*, September 20, 1982.

8 John Fairhall, "51,883 Foot Stampers Cry – SWEEP FOUR!" *Baltimore Evening Sun*, October 2, 1982.

9 Fairhall.

10 Patrick McGuire, "Gutsy Play Keeps Birds in the Race," *Baltimore Sun*, October 2, 1982.

11 Bill Brophy, "Gulp! Orioles Closing Fast," *Wisconsin State Journal* (Madison), October 2, 1982.

12 Kent Baker, "Birds Romp 8-3 and 7-1," *Baltimore Sun*, October 2, 1982.

13 Baker, "Birds Romp."

14 Bill Free, "Dauer Dazzles with His Defense," *Baltimore Sun*, October 2, 1982.

15 Brophy.

16 Jim Henneman, "Title Hopes Still Alive," *Baltimore Evening Sun*, October 2, 1982.

17 Baker, "Birds Romp."

18 Baker, "Birds Romp."

19 Brophy.

20 Baker, "Birds Romp."

Nearing the end of the 15th of his 17 seasons as skipper of the Orioles, Earl Weaver helped bring Baltimore to within one game of qualifying for postseason play. Courtesy of the Baltimore Orioles.

Brooks Robinson Celebration Night

August 5, 1983: Baltimore Orioles 5, Chicago White Sox 4, at Memorial Stadium

By Austin Gisriel

Orioles fans were positively giddy during the first week of August in 1983. A then-record crowd of 12,000 people journeyed to Cooperstown to see Brooks Robinson inducted into the Hall of Fame on July 31 and now, on the evening of Friday, August 5, some 39,544 had come to Baltimore's Memorial Stadium for "Brooks Robinson Hall of Fame Celebration Night." Not only was their hero in the Hall of Fame, but the current bunch of Birds were in first place in the American League East and taking on the AL West-leading Chicago White Sox. As game time drew near, however, it started to rain; not so hard as to make many run for cover but hard enough to wash the mustard off a foot-long hot dog before you could finish it.

Oriole fans were not going to leave, however, not with one more chance to cheer Brooks. Finally, after about 90 minutes, the rain stopped and the festivities got under way. The Human Vacuum Cleaner was chauffeured around the warning track in a 1955 Thunderbird, commemorating Brooks' first season in Baltimore. In his speech to the soggy thousands, Brooks stated that he had taken "a lot of ribbing from some of the players because they said this is my third or fourth retirement party. But I assure you, this will be the last one."[1] For that statement, he was good-naturedly booed, but No. 5 brought tears to the eyes of more than a few when he concluded by saying, "I only wish I had 20 more years to give you."[2]

It was not until approximately 10:00 p.m. that the game actually began. The White Sox jumped on starter Mike Boddicker for two runs in the first when with two down, Harold Baines' homer was followed by a Greg Luzinski single and a Greg Walker triple. The Orioles put two on with none out in their half of the first against starter Randy Martz, but were unable to score. Indeed, the Orioles stranded runners in each of the first four innings. Meanwhile, Boddicker settled down and retired 10 in a row from the second through the fifth, then yielded another run in the sixth. The Orioles answered with two runs in their half of the sixth on singles by Rick Dempsey and Jim Dwyer. Boddicker, in his rookie season, retired the Sox in order in both the seventh and eighth innings, then yielded a lead-off homer to Luzinski in the ninth.

Down 4-2, Al Bumbry started the Baltimore ninth with a single off Salome Barojas, who had relieved Martz during the Oriole uprising in the sixth. Sox manager Tony La Russa replaced Barojas with Dennis Lamp, who promptly induced a double-play grounder off the bat of Dan Ford. It was now past 1:00 a.m. and hopes for an Oriole victory on Brooks Robinson's Hall of Fame Celebration Night were as wet as the outfield grass. Still, the crowd had hung in there this long and when Cal Ripken and Eddie Murray singled, a noticeable stir moved through the damp air. John Lowenstein then singled home Ripken and when Ken Singleton singled home Murray, Memorial Stadium rocked. Dick Tidrow relieved Lamp and took the sign as Rich Dauer stood in. Dauer, who would finish the season with a .235 batting average, fought off a pitch and floated the ball into right field for the game-winning single. Five straight singles—the Orioles' 14 hits on the night were all singles—with two out had produced a 5-4 Baltimore victory.

Cheering wildly, the fans refused to leave until after Dauer had taken a bare-chested curtain call, giving it his best Tarzan pose.

"It was a fastball inside," he recounted after the game, "and you probably noticed that I didn't exactly get around on it. I wasn't trying to pull it. I was trying to go up the middle, I guess. It fell in, and that's all that counts."[3]

The Orioles increased their East lead to two games with the victory as Detroit was losing to New York, 12-3. The Birds, however, wouldn't win again for a week, losing seven in a row before defeating the

Brooks Robinson Celebration Night

White Sox in Chicago, 5-2, the following Saturday. An eight-game win streak later in the month, however, one that began with another wild, come-from-behind victory over the Toronto Blue Jays that saw Tippy Martinez pick off three Toronto runners in one inning, propelled them to the American League East crown. The Orioles defeated the White Sox for the American League pennant, and Mike Boddicker was named the Division Series Most Valuable Player.

The fireworks that had been scheduled for after the game as part of the ceremony were postponed until the following evening. None of the fans cared, however. Dauer's floater was a fitting grand finale on a night that they had come to cheer Brooks Robinson once more.

Author's note

I attended this game with my wife, Martha, and several friends. We had attended Brooks' induction ceremony in Cooperstown, and we had come out to cheer my boyhood hero one more time. As we waited for the ceremonies to begin, we stayed in our seats, declaring that "This isn't so bad." After about half an hour, we decided that it was that bad, but since we were already wet, it didn't matter. I don't think we ever dried out until we got home, but that didn't matter either because we went home happy.

Notes

1 Jim Henneman, "Brooksie Gives 'Last' Adieu Amid Good-Natured Boos," *Evening Sun*, (Baltimore), August 6, 1983: 10.

2 Henneman, "Brooksie Gives 'Last' Adieu Amid Good-Natured Boos."

3 Jim Henneman, "Dauer Unlikely Hero As Orioles Go Singles Route," *Evening Sun*, August 6, 1983: 7.

Tippy Martinez Picks Off Three Blue Jays in One Inning

August 24, 1983: Baltimore Orioles 7, Toronto Blue Jays 4 (10 innings), at Memorial Stadium

By Austin Gisriel

The 25,882 fans who ventured to Memorial Stadium in Baltimore on the evening of August 24, 1983, saw an exciting, extra-inning win by the home team in the midst of a tight pennant race. As a bonus, they also witnessed baseball's version of *The Twilight Zone*.

The Orioles came into that Wednesday night game against the Blue Jays in second place, but just half a game behind Milwaukee. The Tigers and Blue Jays were only 1½ games out, while the Yankees trailed by a mere 3½ games. Only Boston (11 GB) and Cleveland (19½ GB) were out of the American League East race.

It was a typical hot summer night in Baltimore, and the game began in a typical fashion. A Garth Iorg sacrifice fly off Oriole southpaw Scott McGregor in the top of the third was matched by an Al Bumbry sacrifice fly in the bottom of the inning off Jim Clancy. A Todd Cruz error in the fifth gave the Blue Jays an unearned run and another sacrifice fly, this one off the bat of Buck Martinez in the eighth, put Toronto on top 3-1 heading to the bottom of the ninth. At this point the game began to morph into a bizarre sequence of improbable events that only baseball can provide.

John Shelby laid down a bunt single with one out, but Gary Roenicke, pinch-hitting for Rich Dauer, struck out looking. Lenn Sakata, who had entered the game in the eighth at second when Dauer moved from second to third, drew a walk. With left-handed hitting catcher Joe Nolan due up, Toronto manager Bobby Cox brought in lefty Dave Geisel. Oriole skipper Joe Altobelli countered with the last player left on his bench, the right-handed hitting Benny Ayala, who promptly singled to score Shelby. Al Bumbry followed with a single to score Sakata, and the game was tied. Joey McLaughlin then relieved for the Jays and struck out Dan Ford to send the game into extra innings.

Extra innings presented a problem, however. Todd Cruz and Rich Dauer, the starting third baseman and second baseman respectively, were out of the game.

Catcher Joe Nolan, for whom Ayala had pinch-hit, had himself pinch-hit for starting catcher Rick Dempsey in the seventh, and Altobelli was now without either of his backstops. With little choice in the matter, outfielder Gary Roenicke went to third for his first ever appearance at the hot corner, John Lowenstein went to second base where he hadn't played since 1975, and Lenn Sakata, who had gone to second when Dauer replaced Cruz at third, went behind the plate. As it turned out, it seemed not to matter who was where when Cliff Johnson crushed reliever Tim Stoddard's first pitch over the center field fence for his 20th homer of the season. Stoddard then gave up a single to Barry Bonnell, and Tippy Martinez was brought on to face Dave Collins, who was pinch-hitting for Jesse Barfield.

Everyone in Memorial Stadium knew that the Blue Jays would try to run, and indeed the switch-hitting Collins stepped into the left-handed batter's box against the left-handed Martinez in order to give Bonnell an even better chance of stealing. Martinez had only a fair move to first, but Bonnell took such a huge lead that he was easily picked off, although the out was officially recorded as a caught stealing since Bonnell continued to second, stopped and was tagged out by first baseman Eddie Murray.

Martinez walked the speedy Collins, who was as anxious to run as had been Bonnell. He was just as quickly picked off. Willie Upshaw then hit a bouncer behind second that Lowenstein fielded, but on which he could make no throw. Upshaw had barely taken his lead when Martinez picked *him* off first.

The fans were cheering wildly, but the Orioles were still down a run. The craziness, however, had just begun. Cal Ripken, who would be the Most Valuable Player that year, led off with his 18th homer—on his 23rd birthday—to tie the score off McLaughlin, who then walked Eddie Murray. Second baseman

Tippy Martinez Picks Off Three

Lowenstein grounded to first, moving Murray to second and Bobby Cox ordered an intentional pass to John Shelby, then brought in Randy Moffitt to face Roenicke. Third baseman Roenicke struck out, bringing catcher Lenn Sakata to the plate. As befitting the night, Sakata launched a three-run, game-winning home run for a 7-4 Baltimore victory.

"Our strategy," said Sakata after the game, "was to keep throwing to first until the lights went out."[1] An unlikely hero in a season filled with unlikely heroes for the Orioles, Sakata had been booed only the night before when he made two errors at second base.[2]

The victory proved to be the beginning of an eight-game winning streak that propelled the Orioles to the division crown and ultimately the World Championship. Milwaukee maintained its half-game lead over the Orioles with a 1-0, 14-inning victory over California that night, but Tippy Martinez was again the victor on Thursday evening against Toronto when Baltimore scored two in the bottom of the tenth to win 2-1. Mike Boddicker's 9-0, three-hit shutout on Friday over the Minnesota Twins moved the Birds a half game in front of Milwaukee, establishing a lead they would never relinquish as they won the division by six games.

Despite regular catcher Rick Dempsey's postgame remark that Sakata "looked good. I think he oughta start tomorrow,"[3] the utility infielder appeared in only one other game during the win-streak, pinch-running for Rich Dauer in the top of the ninth in the Orioles' 12-4 victory over the Kansas City Royals on August 30.

This game marked Lenn Sakata's only appearance in the major leagues as a catcher and that explains how Tippy Martinez became the only pitcher in big league history to pick off three runners in a single inning. Those pickoffs explain how Martinez retired none of the batters he faced yet got credit for one inning pitched and the win. Sakata's second of three homers on the season explains how a Cal Ripken extra-inning, game-tying home run, on his birthday no less, didn't make Jim Henneman's *Evening Sun* game story until the *fourteenth* paragraph.

Perhaps the Orioles 1984 *Media Guide* said it best: "No one who was there or who listened to that game on the radio will ever forget it."[4]

Author's note

We never forgot it. Lying in bed listening through the ear-piece of a transistor radio, my wife already asleep, I was on a wild emotional ride as the Orioles tied it in the ninth only to fall behind immediately in the 10th. After Martinez' second pick-off, however, I awakened my wife. "You gotta hear this! Tippy's about to pick off his third runner in a row!" Sometimes Fate makes plain what It will do, and after Cal's home run, it was clear that someway, somehow, Lenn Sakata was going to win that game. It took a long time to fall back to sleep.

Sources

In addition to the sources cited in the Notes, the author consulted Baseball-Reference.com and Retrosheet.org.

Notes

1 Jim Henneman, "Sakata's Third Man Theme is a Win Song," *Evening Sun* (Baltimore), August 25, 1983: E1.

2 Bill Swaggerty, for example, pitched six innings in his first big-league appearance, helping to end the Birds' second seven-game losing streak of the season. John Stefero, who amassed all of 14 plate appearances that year, had consecutive walk-off singles against Milwaukee on September 18 and 19.

3 Kevin Cowherd, "Sakata Squats, Then Swats," *Evening Sun*, August 25, 1983: E7.

4 "Game Highlights," *1984 Orioles Media Guide*, 44.

Fred Lynn Hits Walk-Off Home Runs in Back-to-Back Games

May 10, 1985: Baltimore Orioles 6, Minnesota Twins 5
May 11, 1985: Baltimore Orioles 4, Minnesota Twins 2
Both games at Memorial Stadium

By Rich Ottone

Anyone who has stepped up to the plate in a baseball or softball game has dreamed about hitting a game-winning home run in the bottom of the ninth inning. On one magical weekend in 1985 it was more than a dream for Orioles center fielder Fred Lynn. On May 10 and 11 at Memorial Stadium his home runs in the bottom of the ninth inning propelled his team to twin victories.

Orioles general manager Hank Peters was probably particularly satisfied by Lynn's accomplishments that weekend. After winning the World Series the season before, the Orioles finished the 1984 season in fifth place in the American League East. Peters decided to aggressively approach the free-agent market. Adding to Peters' sense of urgency was the fact that the Orioles competed in what was widely considered the best division in baseball. In 1984 five teams had won more games than the Western Division winner, Kansas City.

After signing outfielder Lee Lacy and reliever Don Aase, Peters focused his attention on Lynn. The California Angels outfielder had an impressive résumé. A former batting champion and four-time Gold Glove winner, nine years earlier he was the first player to win the both the Rookie of the Year and MVP honors in the same season.[1] On December 11 he joined Cal Ripken and Eddie Murray as the first players to sign a contract with Baltimore that would pay them over a million dollars per season. For Lynn the decision was easy: "They had the best offer on the table."[2]

Peters' moves seemed to light a fire under the team and when they took the field for the series opener the Orioles sat atop the division. Manager Joe Altobelli tapped Dennis Martinez as his starting pitcher while Twins manager Billy Gardner countered with John Butcher. Martinez didn't make it out of the third inning, allowing seven hits and four runs before being pulled by Altobelli in favor of Sammy Stewart. Butcher wasn't much better (119 pitches, 10 hits, and 3 walks),[3] pitching out of several jams before being pulled with one out in the sixth inning. Gardner, looking to preserve a 4-3 lead, replaced him with Rick Lysander.

Stewart kept the Twins in check until the seventh inning, when Tom Brunansky hit a one-out home run, pushing the Twins lead to 5-3, their third two-run lead of the game. As they had earlier in the contest, in the bottom of the inning the Orioles battled back. With one out Lynn doubled and rookie Larry Sheets sent a Lysander pitch towering past the Twins bullpen in right field,[4] tying the game at 5-5.

Lysander started the eighth inning with a leadoff walk to Rick Dempsey prompting Gardner to summon Pete Filson from the bullpen. Filson fielded Gary Roenicke's bunt and forced Dempsey at second for the first out. Gardner then turned to his closer, Ron Davis. After retiring Fritz Connally on a groundout, Davis struck out Ripken to end the inning.

After Aase set the Twins down in order in the ninth, Davis began the bottom of the inning by striking out Murray. Lynn followed and Davis threw him a curveball. Later, Lynn said, "I was looking for a fastball and he happened to get one of those curveballs on the inner half of the plate and I got it on the good part of my bat."[5] Lynn pulled the pitch into the right-field stands for his 200th career home run, giving the Orioles a 6-5 win. It earned him a curtain call by the frenzied fans in Memorial Stadium, "the first one I've ever gotten in my career."[6]

After the game Davis said, "You saw the pitch and what he did. Don't ask me about it. Ask him."[7] Lynn summed it up simply saying, "We all have dreams, but never in my dreams did I hit one like that."[8]

The following evening featured a picnic cooler giveaway and 49,092 spectators, the second largest crowd of the season, returned to Memorial Stadium. Beachballs were seen bounding among the festive fans.[9]

Fred Lynn Hits Walk-Off Home Runs

The game was a tight pitchers' duel. In the second inning Orioles starter Mike Boddicker issued a one-out walk to Mike Stenhouse and Roy Smalley moved Stenhouse to second on a single to right field. Gary Gaetti followed with a single to left, bringing Stenhouse home with the game's first run. Gaetti and Smalley were left stranded when Boddicker struck out Tim Teufel on three pitches[10] and induced Mark Salas to pop out to second baseman Rich Dauer to end the inning.

The Orioles tied it in the fourth when Jim Dwyer reached on a bunt single. Wayne Gross walked, moving Dwyer to second. Twins starter Ken Schrom got Ripken on a called third strike. Murray followed by bouncing a checked-swing grounder past a diving Smalley, bringing Dwyer home. Lynn followed and Twins first baseman Kent Hrbek made a diving stop of his one-hop grounder and forced Murray at second base while Gross took third. With a chance to give his team the lead, Sheets ended the inning by grounding out to Schrom.

The score remained tied until the eighth, when Brunansky homered to left field to give the Twins a 2-1 lead. In the top of the ninth, the Twins once again had runners on first and second with one out but Kirby Puckett, who entered the series with a league-leading .350 average,[11] grounded into an inning-ending double play, making him 0-for-9 in the series. It was indicative of the Twins' play: They wasted several opportunities to break both games open, mustering just three hits in 20 at-bats with runners in scoring position.

In the bottom of the ninth it seemed as if no one in Memorial Stadium was ready to pack up their coolers and beachballs and head home. After all, Ripken, Murray, and Lynn – the team's three millionaires – were due up. Even though Schrom had allowed five hits in what had been his best start of the year, it was Davis who took the mound to start the bottom of the inning.

"I took Schrom out because he said his elbow was bothering him," Gardner said after the game. "He said I'll go out (to pitch) if you want me to. I wasn't going to take him out of the game the way he was pitching. I said Schrommy, your elbow is bothering you? I'll get Davis. What am I supposed to do? I'm going to send him out there if his elbow is bothering him?"[12]

Ripken started things by looping Davis's first pitch to center.[13] Murray then sent his next offering through the hole between first and second for a single.[14] With the left-handed-batting Lynn due up, Gardner called upon 24-year-old rookie southpaw Curt Wardle.

Wardle's first offering was a fastball. Lynn swung and made contact, sending a fly ball to left-center field. "I saw (Wardle) shake off the sign and I was just hoping he would throw a fastball," Lynn said. "And he did. My concentration has been very good the last few days and the ball's been carrying as well as I've seen it carry here. The wind was blowing straight out so you really didn't have to hit it real well to get it out."[15] The ball barely cleared the fence, giving the Orioles a 4-2 win.

"When he hit it, I thought I had a chance," Twins left fielder Mickey Hatcher said after the game. "But what happened? We only throw three pitches that inning. It wasn't far over the fence. We (Hatcher and Puckett) got to the fence about a step away from having a chance. He split us perfectly. But that's the way it's been going."[16]

After the game a devastated Wardle said, "To tell the truth, when he hit the ball I ran behind home plate. ... I thought there was going to be a play at the plate, and I was going to back it up. Shows how much

It was deja-vu of a sort when Fred Lynn hit a walkoff home run to win the May 10 game and then hit a walkoff home run to win the May 11 game. It was a solo homer on the 10th and a three-run homer on the 11th. Courtesy of the Baltimore Orioles.

I know. I just can't do a thing right. My whole big-league career has been one big screwup so far."[17] Later in the season Wardle was part of the trade that landed Bert Blyleven from the Indians. After 1985 he was out of the major leagues for good.

Even though Lynn had been a thorn in the Twins' side for years (he entered the series with a .336 average and 23 home runs against them), an incredulous Smalley was slow to leave the field after the game. "The fact that we lost for the second time in a row in the ninth inning to the same guy, that's kind of beyond belief," he said.[18]

The good feelings didn't last long. Peters' preseason moves did result in an improved offense as the Orioles led the league in home runs with a team-record 214 and finished second in runs scored. The pitching staff, however, struggled throughout the season and they fell from second to seventh in team ERA while yielding 97 more runs than they had in 1984. Legendary former manager Earl Weaver replaced Altobelli on June 12 but the team could only muster a fourth-place finish while winning 83 games.

Author's note

I attended the game on May 10. I brought a date, and while I remember her name, where we sat (upper deck between home plate and third base), and her fascination with Kirby Puckett's "bubble butt," I also remember that Lynn's night ended up a lot better than that date.

Sources

In addition to the sources cited in the Notes, the author relied on Baseball-Reference.com.

Notes

1. Lynn won both awards with the Boston Red Sox in 1975.
2. Richard Justice, "Orioles Sign Lynn for 5 Years and $6.8 Million," *Baltimore Sun*, December 12, 1984.
3. Kent Baker, "Lynn Powers Orioles Past Twins, 6-5," *Baltimore Sun*, May 11, 1985.
4. Howard Sinker, "Twins Lose on Lynn Homer Off R.D.," *Minneapolis Star-Tribune*, May 11, 1985.
5. Sinker, "Twins Lose."
6. Baker, "Lynn Powers Orioles."
7. Baker, "Lynn Powers Orioles."
8. Kent Baker, "Lynn Strikes on HR in 9th, 4-2." *Baltimore Sun*, May 12, 1985.
9. Baker, "Lynn Strikes."
10. Howard Sinker, "Lynn Homers in 9th Again to Trip Twins," *Minneapolis Star-Tribune* May 12, 1985.
11. Sid Hartman "Year Later Puckett Hits His Way to Top," *Minneapolis Star-Tribune*, May 11, 1985.
12. Sinker "Lynn Homers."
13. Baker, "Lynn Strikes."
14. Baker, "Lynn Strikes."
15. Baker, "Lynn Strikes."
16. Sinker, "Lynn Homers."
17. Sinker., "Lynn Homers."
18. Sinker, "Lynn Homers."

Orioles "Slam" Rangers with Nine-Run Fourth Inning but Still Lose Game

August 6, 1986: Texas Rangers 13, Baltimore Orioles 11, at Memorial Stadium

By Frederick C. Bush

It's not often that a team hits two grand slams in one game, but when the Baltimore Orioles turned that very feat in one inning against the Texas Rangers at Memorial Stadium on August 6, 1986, the hometown fans surely thought that the game had turned in favor of their team. After Texas second baseman Toby Harrah's grand slam in the second had given the Rangers a 5-0 lead, the Orioles scored nine runs in the fourth, when Larry Sheets and Jim Dwyer connected for Baltimore, and eventually totaled 11 runs in the game on only seven hits. Baltimore's flurry of runs was due to both the largesse of the Rangers' pitching staff, which issued 10 walks, and a key error by Texas third baseman Steve Buechele. With Baltimore leading 11-6 going into the eighth inning, Orioles manager Earl Weaver looked forward to a victory as well, but the Rangers stormed back for a 13-11 triumph, prompting Weaver to caution, "I had the feeling it was over, that's a bad feeling to get in baseball. You should never feel that way."[1]

Both squads were in the race for their respective division titles entering the game, with the Rangers trailing the California Angels by 2½ games in the AL West and the Orioles also just 2½ games in back of the Boston Red Sox in the AL East. The Rangers sent inconsistent rookie Bobby Witt, who would end up leading the American League with 143 walks, to the mound against Orioles starter Ken Dixon. Though both hurlers worked around a walk in the first inning, neither would pitch more than a third of the game.

Dixon's troubles started in the top of the second when Gary Ward led off with a single and Larry Parrish followed with another hit. Dixon lost sight of the strike zone and walked Don Slaught and Buechele, the latter of which forced in Ward with the Rangers' first tally of the day. Up to the plate stepped Harrah, who had been batting below .200 for much of the season. In spite of his struggles, Texas manager Bobby Valentine had decided a couple of weeks earlier to give the 37-year-old Harrah regular playing time. According to Valentine, he had called Harrah into his office. "I wanted to know if he had quit on the season," Valentine said. "I wanted to know if he'd already tallied up the final stats on his career. He told me that he hadn't. He told me he wanted to slap high fives and be part of the fun and that's all I had to hear."[2]

Harrah certainly enjoyed himself on this evening as he launched one of Dixon's offerings over the fence for the first grand slam of the game. By the end of the night, Harrah would have a 5-for-5 batting line with three runs scored and four RBIs, falling a triple shy of hitting for the cycle while raising his season batting average 20 points to .218.

Harrah's homer sent Dixon to the showers as Weaver trotted Odell Jones out to the hill in relief. Jones got out of the inning without allowing the Rangers to add to their 5-0 lead, though Texas did get to him for a run in the top of the third when Pete Incaviglia led off with a double and Ward followed with an RBI hit. Texas threatened to score again in the top of the fourth, but Jones escaped unscathed thanks to the only blight on Harrah's day. Harrah led off with a single and went to second on Oddibe McDowell's hit, but he was thrown out at home by right fielder Lee Lacy as he tried to score on Scott Fletcher's flyball out.

Witt had managed to overcome the four walks he had issued over the first three innings, but he finally paid the price for his wildness in the bottom of the fourth. He walked the first three batters – Cal Ripken Jr., Dwyer, and Jim Traber – to load the bases. Sheets then socked Baltimore's first grand slam of the day to bring the Orioles within two runs of the Rangers. After Tom O'Malley singled, Valentine put Witt out of his misery and sent Jeff Russell in to quell the uprising.

Russell, however, fared no better than his predecessor as he, too, had trouble throwing strikes. After walking Rick Dempsey, he induced popouts by Juan Bonilla and Lacy to Harrah at second base, but then he walked Fred Lynn and loaded the bases once more. Ripken reached base when Buechele booted his grounder at third, allowing O'Malley to score and keeping the bases full. Dwyer, who had been red-hot entering the game, took advantage of the situation by clearing the bags with Baltimore's second slam, giving the home team a 9-6 lead. Dwyer now had 15 RBIs in his last nine games and eight homers in 116 at-bats, which was one more than he had hit in 233 at-bats the previous year.[3] In the aftermath of the game, all Dwyer had to say was, "First grand slam ... took me 12 years to do it."[4] The total of three grand slams in one game set a major-league record.

At this point, Mike Mason took over for Russell and retired Traber for the final out of the inning. Both teams took a break from scoring as Jones struck out the side in the top of the fifth and Mason retired the Orioles in order in the bottom of the inning.

Jones's day came to an end after he allowed consecutive singles by Buechele and Harrah to open the top of the sixth. Brad Havens took over and retired two hitters before loading the bases with a walk to Pete O'Brien. Rich Bordi, Baltimore's third pitcher of the inning, struck out Incaviglia to end the Rangers' threat. Mason did not fare as well in the bottom of the frame as he issued a leadoff walk to Bonilla that Lacy followed with a home run to increase the Orioles' lead to 11-6. Mason finished the inning without further trouble and Mitch Williams pitched a scoreless seventh for the Rangers before the Texas team's comeback began.

Buechele, whose error had set up Dwyer's grand slam, led off the top of the eighth with a home run off Bordi that sparked the Rangers' offense back into action. Harrah and McDowell singled and, after Fletcher struck out, O'Brien mashed a three-run round-tripper that brought Texas to within one run of Baltimore. Buechele joked afterward, "I was the official starter for both sides tonight. I got them going and I got us going."[5] Indeed, the Rangers were not finished yet. Incaviglia and Ward got hits before Weaver finally removed Bordi in favor of Nate Snell. Parrish greeted Snell with a two-RBI double that gave Texas a 12-11 advantage before Snell got out of the inning courtesy of an unusual 2-5 double play on Slaught's fly ball.

Bordi had taken his shellacking due to a taxed Baltimore bullpen that was missing injured relief ace Don Aase. Bordi understood the situation, saying, "I knew it had to be me, no one had to tell me. I knew I had to finish up. ... I felt just as good in the last inning as I did in the first [when he retired the side in order]. But everything I threw up there got hit hard."[6]

Dale Mohorcic pitched the final two innings for Texas to earn his fourth save while Williams earned his eighth win of the season. The Rangers added their final run in the top of the ninth when Harrah hit a one-out double and scored on Fletcher's single to make the final score 13-11. Weaver tried to console his team, himself, and Orioles fans by commenting, "It's just like a 1-0 loss, look in the paper: one more loss."[7]

The Rangers, of course, had a different perspective on the game. Valentine enthused, "If that's not the greatest Rangers victory ever, it's tied for first."[8] The entire Texas squad was especially happy for Buechele's

Larry Sheets hit the first of two Orioles fourth-inning grand slams, but the Rangers still prevailed, 13-11. Courtesy of the Baltimore Orioles.

Orioles "Slam" Rangers with Nine-Run Fourth Inning but Still Lose Game

role in the comeback, with O'Brien stating, "If anyone wanted to win this game, it was Boo (Buechele). We knew their bullpen was a little short and if we kept swinging the bat, we could get back in it."9

The devastating loss was the first in what became a five-game Baltimore losing streak that started a tailspin from which the team never recovered. The Orioles posted a 10-19 record in August before losing 24 of their final 32 games in September and October to finish at 73-89, 22½ games behind first-place Boston.

Sources

Baseball-reference.com was consulted for the game box score and individual player statistics.

Notes

1 United Press International, "Rangers Outscore Orioles in Slugfest," *Marietta* (Georgia) *Journal*, August 7, 1986: 20.

2 Paul Hagen, "Valentine's Talk Inspires Harrah," *Fort Worth Star-Telegram*, August 7, 1986: 77.

3 Tim Kurkjian, "Orioles Hit 2 Grand Slams – Lose, 13-11," *Baltimore Sun*, August 7, 1986: 44. The article cited here states that Dwyer had 15 RBIs in his past seven games; however, baseball-reference.com's statistical breakdown for Dwyer's 1986 season shows that it actually took him nine games – between July 24 and August 6 – to accrue the 15 RBIs in question. See baseball-reference.com/players/gl.fcgi?id=dwyerji01&t=b&year=1986#1002-1010-sum:batting_gamelogs.

4 Kurkjian.

5 Kent Baker, "Never-Say-Die Rangers Fight Back with New Spirit," *Baltimore Sun*, August 7, 1986: 44.

6 Kurkjian.

7 Kurkjian.

8 Jim Reeves, "It Ain't Over Till Rangers Win, 13-11," *Fort Worth Star-Telegram*, August 7, 1986: 69

9 Reeves: 77.

Juan Nieves Throws No-Hitter Against Orioles

April 15, 1987: Milwaukee Brewers 7, Baltimore Orioles 0, at Memorial Stadium

By John J. Burbridge Jr.

The beginning of the 1987 season had been a fun ride for the Milwaukee Brewers. After they beat the Baltimore Orioles on the nights of April 13 and 14, their record was 8-0. This was a Milwaukee team that had finished in sixth place in the American League East Division in 1986. It appeared that 1987 might bring a happier result for the team.

The Orioles had also struggled in 1986, finishing last in the American League East with 89 losses, but had also gotten off to a good start in 1987, winning five of their first six games. However, after losing the first two games of the Milwaukee series, they now had three losses.

For the final game of the series, Juan Nieves was the starting pitcher for the Brewers and Mike Flanagan took the hill for Baltimore. Nieves had won his first start of the season against the Texas Rangers but was a bit lucky in that he gave up six runs and eight hits in 5⅓ innings. Flanagan had been hit hard by the Cleveland Indians in his first start but the Orioles prevailed, winning 12-11 in 10 innings.

This game featured some of baseball's biggest stars. Paul Molitor and Robin Yount were in the starting lineup for the Brewers. The Orioles featured Cal Ripken Jr. and Eddie Murray. All four would eventually be enshrined in the Baseball Hall of Fame. Other notable players in the starting lineup were Cecil Cooper for the Brewers and Fred Lynn and Ray Knight for the Orioles. Knight had signed with the Orioles in the offseason after playing with the World Series champion New York Mets in 1986. Knight was the MVP of the but was unable to agree on a contract with the Mets and signed a two-year deal with the Orioles.[1]

The weather for this April 15 night contest was not ideal. The forecast was for a chilly evening with the possibility of rain. A cold front that was headed to the region could make the night even more uncomfortable.

The chill didn't seem to bother either pitcher as they retired the opposition in order in the first inning. In the top of the second, Flanagan walked Greg Brock with two outs but retired Jim Paciorek on a fly to right field. In the bottom of the inning Murray led off with a liner to left field but Paciorek made a diving catch.[2] After another out, Nieves walked Knight but Lee Lacy flied out, ending the inning.

Neither team scored in the third inning. With one out in the top of the fourth Dale Sveum hit a home run, giving Milwaukee a 1-0 lead. Ripken opened the bottom of the inning with a line drive that Molitor speared at third. Murray then popped up to the catcher and Lynn flied out to center field. In the bottom of the fifth, Molitor made another outstanding play on Floyd Rayford's line drive. Neither team scored in the sixth inning. Nieves had still not allowed a hit.

In the top of the seventh, Flanagan encountered some difficulty. Paciorek led off with a double. Bill Schroeder beat out a bunt, moving Paciorek to third. Jim Gantner flied out to left field, but Molitor doubled to left field, scoring Paciorek. When left fielder Ken Gerhart misplayed Molitor's hit, Schroeder also scored, giving the Brewers a 3-0 lead. Dave Schmidt replaced Flanagan and got out of the inning with no further scoring.

In the bottom of the seventh, Nieves appeared to be a bit rattled as he walked leadoff batter Murray on four pitches.[3] Lynn then hit a sharp grounder up the middle that Nieves appeared to deflect. The ball was handled by shortstop Sveum, who turned it into a 6-4-3 double play. Knight's popout ended the inning. After the game, Nieves said of the seventh inning, "I was so pumped up. I was trying to throw the ball through the catcher and the backstop. It wasn't just Eddie Murray. They have lot of big bats in their lineup."[4]

Juan Nieves Throws No-Hitter

In the Brewers' eighth, Cecil Cooper's leadoff single followed by Sveum's double put runners at second and third. Brock then homered, making the score 6-0. Schmidt then retired the Brewers. In the bottom of the inning, Nieves set down the Orioles in order, striking out John Shelby and Rayford for the last two outs. In the top of ninth, Glenn Braggs hit a home run. The Brewers led 7-0.

As the game entered the bottom of the ninth, the Orioles remained hitless. To preserve his no-hitter, Nieves had to face Gerhart, Rick Burleson, and Ripken. Gerhart led off by grounding out to Molitor. Burleson hit a soft liner to Molitor for the second out, bringing up Ripken. After two balls, Bill Schroeder, the Brewers catcher, decided to put Ripken on base. "I didn't want this to slip away. I didn't want the kid to lose a no-hitter on a 2-and-0 pitch," he said.[5]

The dangerous Eddie Murray was now at bat. Murray drilled a fly ball to deep right-center field. Yount, the center fielder, ran approximately 15 yards, dived to his left, and caught the ball, preserving the no-hitter.[6] Yount commented about the catch, "I didn't have time to think. I wasn't going to do anything but catch it. You don't think about it, you just react. I'm just happy we accomplished a no-hitter."[7] Tom Trebelhorn, the Brewers manager, said of the catch: "When it came off the bat, it started to hang a little bit and I thought Robin would't have any problem with it. Then it started to die and I thought, 'Oh gee, there goes the kid's no-hitter.' It was just a remarkable game."[8] Cal Ripken Sr., the Orioles manager, said, "I didn't think Eddie's ball was going to drop when I saw Robin break for it. The guy's a pretty good center fielder and when he gets a jump like that he's going to catch it."[9]

Nieves said he had a "mediocre fastball and my slider was awful."[10] As to whether he knew he was pitching a no-hitter, he commented, "I didn't really think about the no-hitter until the last out, when all of my teammates started tackling me."[11] Nieves also said, "I think I'm going to drink a couple big bottles of champagne, then I think it will all hit me."[12]

In pitching the no-hitter, Nieves struck out seven batters and walked five. He threw 128 pitches, Nieves' no-hitter has been the only one by the Brewers through the 2019 season.[13] It was also the first no-hitter pitched against the Orioles in Memorial Stadium since they came to town in 1954.[14]

The no-hitter was the high-water mark for Nieves. He finished the season with a record of 14 wins and 8 losses but with an ERA of 4.88. In 1988 he suffered a career-ending shoulder injury and never again pitched in the major leagues. He returned to the major leagues in 2007 as the bullpen coach for the Chicago White Sox. While with the White Sox, he was mentored by their esteemed pitching coach, Don Cooper. In 2013 he was hired as the pitching coach for the Boston Red Sox and was with them when they won the World Series that year. He was fired after the 2015 season and was the Miami Marlins pitching coach from 2016 through 2018.

The Brewers improved substantially in 1987, winning 91 games and finishing third in the American League East, seven games behind the division-leading Detroit Tigers. The Orioles once again struggled, losing a very disappointing 95 games.

Memorial Stadium was demolished after the 1991 season as the Orioles moved to Oriole Park at Camden Yards. However, the memories of Nieves' no-hitter and Yount's thrilling catch to end the contest on a very cold night in April 1987 still endure. To quote Tim Kurkjian, "The 11,407 who saw it can tell their kids they witnessed probably the greatest finish to a no-hitter in baseball history."[15]

Sources

In addition to the sources mentioned in the Notes, the author consulted Baseball-Reference.com.

Notes

1 Ralph Carhart, "Ray Knight," SABR BioProject, sabr.org/bioproj/person/8ec64433.

2 Richard Justice, "Nieves No-Hitter Stops Orioles, 7-0," *Washington Post*, April 16, 1987: B1.

3 Justice.

4 Justice.

5 Rory Costello, "Juan Nieves," SABR BioProject, sabr.org/bioproj/person/937353ab.

6 "Brewers' Nieves Hurls No-Hitter," *New York Times*, April 16, 1987: B11.

7 "Brewers' Nieves Hurls No-Hitter."

8 "Brewers' Nieves Hurls No-Hitter."

9 "Brewers' Nieves Hurls No-Hitter."

10 "Brewers' Nieves Hurls No-Hitter."

11 "Brewers' Nieves Hurls No-Hitter."

12 Tim Kurkjian, "Brewers' Nieves No-Hits Orioles 7-0," *Baltimore Sun*, April 16, 1987: 1D.

13 nonohitters.com/milwaukee-brewers-no-hitters/.

14 nonohitters.com/memorial-stadium-no-hitters/.

15 Kurkjian.

Orioles Soar to Victory on Mike Young's Two Extra-Inning Home Runs

May 28, 1987: Baltimore Orioles 8, California Angels 7, at Memorial Stadium

By Gary Belleville

In the 30-year period from 1957 to 1986, the Baltimore Orioles compiled the best record in the major leagues, collecting three World Series championships, six American League pennants, and eight division titles along the way. And then suddenly, after winning the 1983 World Series, the team went into a rapid decline, winning progressively fewer games in each of the next five seasons. They suffered their first last-place finish in 1986. The 1987 Orioles were even worse. Eddie Murray and Cal Ripken Jr. were the only holdovers from the starting nine of the championship team of four years earlier, and their roster was littered with lumbering sluggers who were past their prime.

Baltimore's once proud pitching staff had also fallen on hard times, posting a 5.01 ERA in 1987, worse than any big-league team other than the woeful Cleveland Indians. Their starting pitching, normally the O's strength, was now the weakest in the American League. The lefty duo of 33-year-old Scott McGregor and 35-year-old Mike Flanagan were pale imitations of their 1983 selves. In four short years, their combined record with the Orioles slipped from 30-11 with a 3.22 ERA to 5-13 and a bloated 5.75 earned-run average in 1987.

Fortunately for the Orioles, their veteran sluggers were able to carry the team through the first seven weeks of the 1987 season, and the team entered its May 28 game against the California Angels on a five-game winning streak, which moved it into third place with a surprising 25-20 record. Baltimore sent its ace, Mike Boddicker (4-1, 2.28 ERA), to the hill looking for a sweep of the two-game series. The Angels countered with 23-year-old right-hander Willie Fraser, who had an impressive 2.51 ERA in his 10 appearances, five of which were starts. Fraser was hoping to snap the five-game losing streak that had dropped California into fifth place in the Western Division with a 21-24 record.

The two teams combined to club five home runs in the first four innings, with the Orioles jumping out to a 5-1 lead. The rookie Fraser served up four of the homers. Larry Sheets went deep in each of his first two at-bats, launching a two-run shot in the second inning and a solo blast in the fourth. The other Baltimore round-trippers were solo home runs by Ripken and 36-year-old Rick Burleson.[1] The lone California run came on a solo home run by Ruppert Jones in the top of the third.

The Angels cut the deficit to 5-2 when they added a run in the top of the fifth on an RBI single by their young first baseman, Wally Joyner. In the bottom of that inning, they brought in 24-year-old lefty Chuck Finley to replace Fraser, triggering Baltimore manager Cal Ripken Sr. to use Mike Young as a pinch-hitter for the left-handed DH Jim Dwyer.[2] Young struck out, but the substitution would pay significant dividends later in the game.

The 27-year-old switch-hitter had returned from thumb surgery two weeks earlier and, with the Orioles bats booming, he was still battling for regular playing time. Young had finished fifth in the 1984 Rookie of the Year voting and posted what turned out to be a career year in 1985, batting .273 with 28 home runs and 81 RBIs. He struggled in 1986 and was sent to the minors in late July. He returned a month later and hit .288 for the remainder of the year. The late-season performance was enough to persuade the Orioles to pencil him in as their full-time DH for 1987, although those plans were shelved when Young injured his thumb in the second exhibition game of the spring.

The Angels continued to whittle away at the lead in the top of the sixth inning. Dick Schofield chased Boddicker from the game with an RBI double, and

• Orioles Soar to Victory on Mike Young's Two Extra-Inning Home Runs •

Mark McLemore singled off lefty Jack O'Connor to plate Schofield and make the score 5-4. It remained that way until Joyner led off the top of the ninth inning with a game-tying solo home run off Ken Dixon.

After the Orioles were held scoreless in the bottom of the ninth, California pinch-hitter Mark Ryal opened the 10th inning with a double off Dixon. One out later, center fielder Gary Pettis drove Ryal home with a single to give the Angels their first lead of the game.

Young, now 4-for-22 in the season with no extra-base hits, led off the bottom of the 10th inning against DeWayne Buice. The rookie right-handed reliever had a devastating forkball, and he was quickly becoming one of the most effective hurlers in the Angels bullpen. Batting from the left side, Young connected on a Buice fastball for a solo home run that tied the game at 6-6.[3]

The score remained tied into the top of the 12th when the Angels put runners on first and third with one out on singles by Darrell Miller and Schofield. Pettis followed with a grounder to the second baseman, Burleson, who threw to first for the second out. Schofield, after initially retreating toward first base, was caught in a rundown and eventually made it safely into second by evading Murray's tag. While the Orioles were in the process of botching the rundown, Miller scampered home to give California a 7-6 lead.

Buice tempted fate by issuing a leadoff walk to Lee Lacy in the bottom of the 12th. As was the custom of the day, the home team played for the tie when trailing in extra innings, and so Ripken Sr. ordered the next batter, Young, to put down a sacrifice bunt despite having homered off Buice two innings earlier. Young bunted the first two pitches foul before swinging away and fouling off pitch number three. The next pitch from Buice was a forkball that Young, once dubbed "Mighty Mike Young" by his former manager Earl Weaver, hammered over the Angels bullpen in right-center field for a two-run, walk-off home run.[4]

"I got to give him credit on that second one," Buice admitted afterwards. "It was a good pitch, low and away. I didn't make a mistake. He hit my best stuff."[5] Young accepted responsibility for his two failed sacrifice attempts in his postgame comments. "My job was to get the bunt down," he said. "I didn't do it."[6] To the surprise of few, Ripken Sr. said that Young wouldn't be fined for his inability to lay down a bunt in a key situation.[7]

Baltimore's six home runs in the game were the most ever hit by the team at Memorial Stadium.[8] The eight round-trippers slugged by the two clubs also set a single-game record for the most combined home runs at the ballpark.[9] Young's second homer gave the Orioles the major-league record for the most home runs (56) in one month, surpassing the 55 hit by the New York Giants in July of 1947 and the Minnesota Twins in May of 1964. The O's hit two more that May to extend the record to 58.[10]

Young became only the fifth major leaguer to hit two extra-inning homers in a game and the first since Ralph Garr of the Atlanta Braves turned the trick against the Mets on May 17, 1971.[11] Young also posted an exceptionally high Win Probability Added (WPA), a measure of an individual player's impact on the outcome of a game.[12] His WPA of 1.087 (or 108.7 percent) turned out to be the third highest WPA posted in any big-league game in the 1980s.[13]

The walk-off win moved the Orioles six games over .500, although that turned out to be their high-water mark for the 1987 season. With Flanagan on the DL with an elbow injury, the pitching collapsed, and the team lost 30 of its next 35 games to drop out of the race. The beleaguered pitching staff was lit up for a combined 6.25 ERA in those 35 games. Baltimore finished with a dismal 67-95 mark, the team's worst winning percentage (.414) since 1955. To make matters worse, the Orioles' farm system had become barren, and so owner Edward Bennett Williams fired both GM Hank Peters and farm director Tom Giordano in the offseason.

The team finally hit rock bottom in 1988, dropping its first 21 games of the season on the way to setting a team record for futility with a record of 54-107.[14] The Orioles' playoff drought lasted until 1996 when the team made the first of two back-to-back appearances in the American League Championship Series.[15]

Sources

In addition to the sources cited in the Notes, the author consulted Baseball-Reference.com and Retrosheet.org.

Notes

1 It turned out to be the final home run of Rick Burleson's 13-year career. When he was released on July 11, 1987 Burleson was hitting .209 with 2 homers and 14 RBIs in 206 at-bats.

2 Although Chuck Finley made his major-league debut in relief on May 29, 1986, he was still being used in a mop-up role for much of the 1987 season. Finley was converted to a starting pitcher when John Candelaria was traded away in September of 1987, which created an opening in the Angels rotation.

3   United Press International, "Mike Young Atoned for His Inability to Bunt by...," May 29, 1987, upi.com/Archives/1987/05/29/Mike-Young-atoned-for-his-inability-to-bunt-by/4970549259200/, accessed September 29, 2019.

4   Thomas Boswell, "Young Stands Taller Now, at the Plate, with Orioles," *Washington Post*, washingtonpost.com/archive/sports/1984/08/27/young-stands-taller-now-at-the-plate-with-orioles/96152f1d-48f9-4a9e-8086-93f8a484a35b/?utm_term=.655d95545774, accessed September 29, 2019. United Press International, "Mike Young atoned for his inability to bunt by..."

5   Mike Penner, "Orioles Hit 6 Homers, Top Angels," *Los Angeles Times*, May 29, 1987, latimes.com/archives/la-xpm-1987-05-29-sp-1908-story.html, accessed September 29, 2019.

6   Penner.

7   Associated Press, "Orioles' Young Can't Bunt So He Lofts a Homer Instead," *Vancouver Sun*, May 29, 1987: H5.

8   The Cleveland Indians also hit six home runs in a game at Memorial Stadium (June 10, 1959). In the 38 years that the Orioles played in Memorial Stadium (1954-1991), no team ever hit more than six home runs in a game there. As of the end of the 2019 season, the single-game team record for home runs in Baltimore was eight, set by the Orioles against the Phillies on June 16, 2015 and equaled by the Minnesota Twins on April 20, 2019, at Oriole Park at Camden Yards.

9   The record of eight home runs by both teams in a single game at Memorial Stadium was never broken. As of the end of the 2019 season, the record for most combined home runs in a game at Oriole Park at Camden Yards was 11. It was set on July 1, 1994 by the Orioles and Angels and matched on April 20, 2019 by the Orioles and Twins.

10 The major-league record for most home runs in a month (58) was equaled a dozen years later by the Seattle Mariners in May of 1999. Baltimore and Seattle shared the record until the Yankees shattered the mark by blasting 74 home runs in August of 2019.

11 As of the end of the 2019 season, only nine players had hit two extra-inning home runs in the same game. Aside from Mike Young and Ralph Garr, the others were Vern Stephens (St. Louis Browns, September 29, 1943), Willie Kirkland (Cleveland Indians, June 14, 1963), Art Shamsky (Cincinnati Reds, August 12, 1966), John Mayberry Jr. (Philadelphia Phillies, June 4, 2013), Matt Adams (St. Louis Cardinals, September 4, 2013), Curtis Granderson (New York Mets, September 17, 2016), and Chris Davis (Baltimore Orioles, May 16, 2017).

12 Win Expectancy (WE) or Win Probability (WP) is the percentage chance of a team winning a game at a specific point of that game. It is calculated by comparing the current state of the game to similar situations in historical major-league games. Win Probability Added (WPA) captures the change in Win Expectancy from a plate appearance or baserunning event (i.e. stolen base, caught stealing/pickoff, or balk) and credits or debits the player accordingly. For instance, if a player hit a home run to increase his team's Win Expectancy from 25 to 65 percent then that player would be assessed a WPA of 0.40. WPA is an excellent way of measuring a player's impact on the outcome of a game.

13 Mel Hall of the Cleveland Indians recorded a 1.206 WPA on June 27, 1984 against the Minnesota Twins. Hall's big hits were the two-out double in the bottom of the eight inning that tied the score 3-3 (42% WPA) and his two-out, three-run home run in the bottom of the 10th inning that turned a 4-3 deficit into a 6-4 win (80% WPA). The only other single-game WPA mark in the 1980s greater than Mike Young's 1.087 was a 1.134 WPA registered by Will Clark of the San Francisco Giants on June 22, 1988 versus the San Diego Padres. Clark's clutch hits were a one-out RBI single in the bottom of the first inning to tie the game 1-1 (10% WPA), a one-out, three-run home run in the fifth inning to cut the Padres' lead to 5-4 (22% WPA), and a two-out, three-RBI double with two outs in the bottom of the ninth inning to turn a 7-5 deficit into an 8-7 win (84% WPA).

14 The 1988 Baltimore Orioles held the team record for the lowest winning percentage until 2018, when the team went 47-115 (.290). As of the end of the 2019 season, the 1939 St. Louis Browns (43-111, .279) still held the franchise record for the lowest winning percentage.

15 The Orioles fell short in the ALCS both years. They lost in 1996 to the Yankees (four games to one) and in 1997 to the Indians (four games to two).

There's No Place like Home; There's No Place like Home; There's No Place Like Home!

May 2, 1988: Baltimore Orioles 9, Texas Rangers 4, at Memorial Stadium

By Alan Cohen

The team once known as the St. Louis Browns had escaped to Baltimore in 1954. Their 35th season in Baltimore began on an awful note. To begin the season, they had lost 21 consecutive games (the Brownies never did that), and coming into the game on May 2, they had lost 23 of 24. They were returning home from a road trip during which they went 1-11.

It was a painful time. Billy Ripken had been beaned in the only win, on April 29, and missed the last two games of the road trip. But he was back in the lineup on May 2. And there was a bit of the absurd. On the last day of the trip, Fred Lynn thought he had a three-run homer only to find out that the runners had held up. When he got to second base, teammate Larry Sheets had possession of the base. Lynn was called out.[1]

Orioles management pulled out all the stops to assure a big crowd on May 2, including reducing ticket prices to two bucks. At noon, there was a pep rally at the city's Inner Harbor where Mayor Kurt Schmoke proclaimed the day to be "We Love Our Orioles in Baltimore Day." On "Fantastic Fan Night," the city, which had in recent years lost the NFL Colts and NBA Bullets, was encouraged to support its only remaining big-league sports franchise. The result was 50,402 fans in the stands at old Memorial Stadium for the first of a two-game set with the Texas Rangers. The fans, most of whom were wearing the team colors of orange and black, were treated to a wonderful evening of entertainment and a 9-4 win by the home team – and they went home wearing lapel patches with the slogan "I'm sticking with the Orioles."[2]

Those in attendance were also told, before the game by Maryland Governor William Donald Schaeffer, that agreement had been reached to build a new ballpark in Baltimore and have it ready for the 1992 season. Orioles owner Edward Bennett Williams had signed a 15-year lease with a five-year option on the new ballpark.

During the 21-game losing streak, local radio personality Bob Rivers had taken to the airwaves for 258 consecutive hours, vowing to stay on the air until the Orioles finally won a game, which they did on April 29. On Fantastic Fan Night, he was presented with a team jersey and threw out the ceremonial first pitch.[3]

Before the game, the crowd was treated to a video display of the Orioles of yesteryear including Earl Weaver's machinations, and the hitting and fielding excellence of Frank and Brooks Robinson. And, oh yes, the attendance was stimulated by a giveaway promotion, as if the low ticket prices weren't enough of an incentive. Some of the Orioles highlights had been provided by pitcher Scott McGregor in the 1983 World Series.

"I still feel good, but I wasn't able to get people out. I gave it everything I had, and the results weren't there."
– Scott McGregor[4]

"I had directions to the ballpark, and I needed them. I had never been here before."
– Orioles pitcher Jay Tibbs[5]

Things had taken a downturn, not only for the Orioles, but also for McGregor. On the day of the May 2, 1988, contest McGregor, who had been scheduled to start, was informed by team vice president Roland Hemond that he was being released. Jay Tibbs started in his place. Tibbs had woken up that morning in Toledo, Ohio, as a member of the Rochester Red Wings. He wasted no time in getting to Baltimore.

Frank Robinson was in the building having taken over as Orioles manager during the 21-game losing streak when Cal Ripken Sr. was fired. At the time of Ripken's dismissal, the team was 0-6.

• Baltimore Baseball •

As the game began, there was a feeling of "here we go again," as the Rangers' Oddibe McDowell walked and went to second on an infield hit by Cecil Espy. But Tibbs managed to pitch his way out of the inning.

Morganna the exotic dancer made an appearance. During her prime, she would dash onto the field and place a kiss on an unsuspecting ballplayer before being whisked away. This time, with the cooperation of Baltimore officials, she ran at a slower place when Cal Ripken Jr. was batting in the bottom of the first inning. She trotted in from right field, kissed Ripken on the cheek, and left the field. In the aftermath of the interruption, Texas pitcher Jose Guzman committed a balk. Billy Ripken, who was on first base at the time via a walk, advanced to second. Guzman then struck out Cal Ripken, who was still suffering the aftershocks of the kiss, and Eddie Murray to get out of the inning.

They game was scoreless for the first two innings and the Rangers were dispatched without a run in the top of the third.

Guzman was victimized by the Orioles in the third inning. After Billy Ripken grounded out to start the inning, Cal hit a solo homer. An inning later the wheels fell off and Guzman, who entered the game with a 1.41 ERA, surrendered five runs. Keith Hughes, who had three consecutive hits in the game, opened the inning for the Orioles with a single. A double by Terry Kennedy put runners on second and third. Hughes scored on a one-out single by rookie Pete Stanicek and Kennedy scored on a single by Billy Ripken. Then things got sloppy. A wild pitch by Guzman sent Stanicek scampering home with the third run of the inning and moved Billy Ripken to second base. Third baseman Steve Buechele was unable to corral a groundball by Cal Ripken. Murray, responding to the "Ed-Die, Ed-Die!" chant screamed out from the stands, singled home Billy Ripken, who had advanced to third on the prior play. Cal Ripken scored from third on a balk by Guzman – his third balk of the game.

The cheering was led by Notre Dame of Maryland student Ray Lopez, attired in a leprechaun outfit. He was about the only one not dressed in orange and black. His outfit included green velvet knickers, a green vest, and a green jacket, and he strutted atop the Orioles' dugout along the first-base line.[6]

The Rangers scored their first run in the top of the fifth inning. Curtis Wilkerson tripled with one out and scored on a wild pitch by Tibbs.

Guzman, despite the Orioles' fourth-inning outburst, was still in the game when Baltimore came to bat in the sixth inning. With one out, Billy Ripken walked, and brother Cal doubled. Murray walked and Guzman was removed from the game. Jose Cecena came into the game for the Rangers and the first batter, Sheets, hit a grounder to shortstop. Scott Fletcher, hoping for an inning-ending double play, threw to second, forcing Murray, but Sheets beat the relay to first base and Billy Ripken scored. Cecena then was overcome by wildness, walking Lynn to fill the bases and issuing another pair of walks. Jeff Russell relieved Cecena and stopped the bleeding. By then, the Orioles had a 9-1 lead, and had batted around twice within a three-inning span.

Tibbs tired in the ninth inning and issued a two-out, three-run homer to Ruben Sierra after walking Mike Stanley and yielding a double to Fletcher. Doug Sisk came on in relief and got the last out of the game.

After the game, Billy Ripken said, "It was like Opening Day all over again, except we won. Maybe we can pretend that this was Opening Day and forget all those losses."[7]

An optimistic Hemond, in his first year as GM of the Orioles, added, "Now I can understand why players have always been so proud to be Orioles and why so many (players) move to Baltimore to live."[8]

Baltimore could not overcome its terrible start in 1988 and wound up the season losing 107 games, the most since moving to Baltimore. It was rock bottom for a team that from 1960 through 1985 had finished above .500 in 24 of 26 seasons and won three World Series championships.

The Orioles would not repeat the disaster of 1988 for another three decades. In 2018 they lost 115 games. As of 2020 they had not been to the World Series since winning it in 1983.

Murray, who had been with the Orioles since 1977, was traded to the Los Angeles Dodgers in the offseason. With Baltimore from 1977 through 1988, Murray hit 333 homers and delivered 2,021 hits. During the 1996 season, he was traded back to Baltimore (by Cleveland) and added 59 hits, 10 of which were homers. He was Rookie of the Year in 1977 and was named to seven All-Star teams. He was inducted into the Hall of Fame in 2003.

Sources

In addition to Baseball-Reference.com and the sources shown in the notes, the author used:

Baker, Kent. "Released by Orioles, McGregor Retires with Heart on his Sleeve," *Baltimore Sun*,

May 3, 1988: D1, D4.

Campbell, Steve. "Devotion: Sense of Loyalty Prompts Robinson to Manage Orioles," *Fort Worth Star-Telegram*, May 3, 1988: 3-3.

Chisholm, Elise T. "Fans Don't Have to Be Losers Just Because a Team Is Losing," *Baltimore Sun*, May 3, 1988: E3.

Hawkins, John. "Orioles Turn Fantastic, Breeze Before 50,402," *Washington Times*, May 3, 1988: D1, D3.

Heller, Dick. "Sadly, O's Had to Cut McGregor," *Washington Times*, May 3, 1988: D1, D3.

Kurkjian, Tim. "Orioles Provide Reason to Cheer: Win No. 2, 9-4," *Baltimore Sun*, May 3, 1988: D1, D4.

Littwin, Mike. "On a Wonderful Night, Orioles' Fans Show They Still Believe in Magic," *Baltimore Sun*, May 3, 1988: D1, D4.

Moran, Malcolm. "Fans Rally for Orioles, and Vice Versa," *New York Times*, May 3, 1988: D32.

Reimer, Susan. "New Lease Lifts Crowd of 50,402," *Baltimore Sun*, May 3, 1988: D1, D4.

Siegel, Morris. "Orioles, Morganna Cheer Up Faithful," *Washington Times*, May 3, 1988: D3.

Notes

1 Steve Jacobson, "In Love with Their Losers," *Newsday*, May 3, 1988: 139.

2 Jon Roe, "Ice-Cold Orioles Get Warm Welcome Home," *Star Tribune* (Minneapolis), May 3, 1988: 1C.

3 Tim Liotta (Associated Press), "Orioles Not Short on Fans, Just Victories," *Clarksdale* (Mississippi) *Press Register*, May 3, 1988: 6.

4 Ben Walker (Associated Press), "Orioles Release Veteran Pitcher," *Sunbury* (Pennsylvania) *Daily Item*, May 3, 1988: 15.

5 Les Bowen, "In Baltimore, It Was a Day of Rare Sights," *Philadelphia Daily News*, May 3, 1988: 78.

6 Veronica Jennings and Paul Valentine, "Orioles Fans' Faith Rewarded with a Win," *Washington Post*, May 3, 1988: A1.

7 Tim Kurkjian, "Orioles Win Second Game, 9-4," *Baltimore Sun*, May 3, 1988: D4.

8 Thomas Boswell, "Fans Forgive the Present in Celebration of the Future," *Washington Post*, May 3, 1988: E5.

New-Look Orioles Begin 1989 Season on Winning Note

April 3, 1989: Baltimore Orioles 5, Boston Red Sox 4 (11 innings), at Memorial Stadium

By Jody Madron

Much as the 1989 season would prove to be a refreshing change from the dreariness of the 54-107 season that preceded it, the afternoon skies in Baltimore on April 3, 1989, surprised forecasters and fans with pleasant sunshine and warm temperatures.

The 1989 Opening Day game between the Orioles and Red Sox at Memorial Stadium arrived with a wide variety of storylines, including these:

• The Orioles feeling the pressure that would come on the heels of their record-setting 0-21 start to the 1988 season. After enduring a full year as a national punchline, the Orioles were anxious to silence the talk of another potential season-opening losing streak.

• The soap-opera-like saga of Red Sox third baseman Wade Boggs, whose spring training was marked by a scandal involving his former mistress, Margo Adams. In February 1989, Adams provided sordid details of their relationship and revealed less-than-flattering things Boggs had allegedly said privately about many of his teammates, all of which provided plenty of fodder for fans and media alike.

• A visit from the President of the United States, George H.W. Bush, who brought a large group of dignitaries, including Egyptian President Hosni Mubarak.

• And *Boston Globe* writer Dan Shaughnessy's public prediction of an Opening Day no-hitter for Red Sox starting pitcher Roger Clemens several weeks earlier, which made the rounds of spring training and provided bulletin-board material for the Orioles in advance of the game.

Yet in spite of all those storylines, when the day had concluded it was a simple fly ball in extra innings – along with Cal Ripken's three-run home run in the seventh – that the 52,161 in attendance were talking about.

After a first pitch from President Bush, fans greeted Boggs with taunts related to his embarrassing scandal as the Boston leadoff hitter stepped in to face Orioles starting pitcher Dave Schmidt to begin the game. Schmidt retired Boggs on a groundball back to the mound and set down the side on just seven pitches.

When Roger Clemens took the mound for the bottom of the first inning on this day, he brought with him a 78-34 record through five seasons – and a pair of Cy Young Awards (1986 and 1987).

This matchup – of a 26-year-old pitcher at the very top of his game and a hapless Baltimore lineup that had traded away future Hall of Famer Eddie Murray the previous offseason – was a big part of what led the *Globe's* Shaughnessy to offer up his prediction of a no-hitter prior to this game.

"Can Roger Clemens pitch an Opening Day no-hitter as Bob Feller did 49 years ago in Chicago?" Shaughnessy wrote. "It seems that all the planets are in line. The Orioles stink. Clemens is 6-2 lifetime against Baltimore with a 2.69 ERA. The weather should favor a fastball pitcher."[1]

If Clemens was bothered by the hype surrounding the prediction of a no-hitter, he didn't show it, as he retired the Orioles in order in the bottom of the first.

In a scoreless game in the top of the third inning, Boston first baseman Nick Esasky drove a pitch from Schmidt to the wall in right-center field. Rookie right fielder Steve Finley raced for it, extended his arm and made the grab just before slamming into the wall at full speed.

The sensational catch brought the crowd to its feet, but it also would eventually knock Finley from the game. Finley was replaced by Joe Orsulak in the top of the fourth, and it was later revealed that Finley suffered a sprained right shoulder that would keep him out of the lineup for nearly three weeks.

Finley's catch helped Schmidt avoid allowing his first hit. In fact, through the first 2½ innings, neither Schmidt nor Clemens allowed a base runner in a fast-paced start to the game.

New-Look Orioles Begin 1989 Season on Winning Note

But in the bottom of the third inning Craig Worthington lined a single to left field, giving the game its first baserunner and ending all discussion about a Clemens no-hitter, though Worthington was caught stealing on the very next pitch and the game remained scoreless.

In the bottom of the fourth, Brady Anderson led off with a walk and, after Phil Bradley struck out, stole second base with Orsulak at the plate. Orsulak then lined a single into center field that scored Anderson with the game's first run.

The score remained 1-0 Baltimore when the Red Sox finally got to Dave Schmidt in the sixth. Boggs led off the inning with a double and was doubled home by Dwight Evans. Mike Greenwell followed Evans's double with a two-run home run to right-center, giving the Red Sox a 3-1 lead.

Anderson led off the Orioles' sixth with a double to right and Bradley followed with a walk. After a groundout by Orsulak advanced the runners, no one would have questioned Clemens if he had pitched around the Orioles' best hitter, Ripken, who was due up next.

But Clemens instead chose to pitch to Ripken, and on the seventh pitch of the at-bat, Ripken lined a chest-high Clemens fastball over the left-field wall for a three-run home run, giving the Orioles a 4-3 lead and sending Memorial Stadium into a frenzy.

After the game, Red Sox manager Joe Morgan explained, "Ripken's the potential leading run. You don't want to just put him on base." Clemens added, "I wanted to pitch him high. I just made a pitch that ran back across the plate. If I had to do it all over again, I'd do the same thing. Come right at him."[2]

The 4-3 lead proved to be short-lived, as the Red Sox quickly tied the game in the top of the seventh when Jody Reed singled home Esasky, who had doubled to lead off the inning. Left-hander Kevin Hickey – making his first big-league appearance in six years – replaced Schmidt and retired Boggs before yielding to Brian Holton.

Holton got Barrett to end the inning with a groundout and preserve the tie. The game remained tied at 4-4 into the bottom of the 11th inning, when Boston reliever Bob Stanley walked Mickey Tettleton with one out to put the potential winning run on base. Randy Milligan then lined a single into right field that sent Tettleton to third base and knocked Stanley from the game.

Right-hander Mike Smithson entered for the Red Sox and Boston manager Morgan opted for a five-man infield, moving left fielder Greenwell just to the left of second base in an attempt to prevent a groundball from getting through and scoring the winning run.

But the strategy didn't work, as Craig Worthington's shallow fly ball into left field eluded a diving attempt by center fielder Ellis Burks, allowing Tettleton to scamper home with the game-winning run.

After the game the focus in the Boston clubhouse was on the failed strategy, with Smithson saying that had the five-man infield not been employed, "we'd still be playing."[3] And manager Morgan conceded, "I'd have to say that backfired. Normally, the center fielder gets to that ball. Tettleton never would have scored. This is only the second time it's ever backfired on me. I would not have done it if I had had a second thought."[4]

From the Orioles' perspective, the home run by Ripken and Worthington's game-winning hit received plenty of postgame attention, but manager Frank Robinson insisted that another player was actually the key to the victory.

"Out of all the things that contributed to this win, if I had to pick out one thing, it would be Holton's pitching. He held us in the game. Gave us the chance to win."[5] Holton, indeed, was the game's winning pitcher, allowing just three hits – and no runs – over $4\frac{1}{3}$ innings.

The dramatic victory proved to be the beginning of an unlikely turnaround season in 1989 that saw the Orioles occupy first place in the AL East from May 23 through August 31 before they were overtaken by the Toronto Blue Jays. The team's 87-75 record left them in second place and represented an improvement of 33 wins over the previous season.

The Red Sox would not repeat as AL East champions in 1989, finishing in third place with a final record of 83-79.

Three decades later, the 1989 "Why Not?" season endures as one of the favorites of Orioles fans. And the Opening Day game stands out as one of the year's highlights.

Sources

In addition to the sources cited in the Notes, the author used Baseball-Reference.com for research assistance.

Notes

1 Dan Shaughnessy, "Masterpiece?" *Boston Globe*, April 3, 1989: 35.

2 Leigh Montville, "This Time, Ripken Trumped the Ace," *Boston Globe*, April 4, 1989: 79.

3 Steve Fainaru, "Orioles Sink Sox in 11th, 5-4; Clemens, Strategy Fall Short," *Boston Globe*, April 4, 1989: 79.

4 Tim Kurkjian, "0-21? Not This Year, as Orioles Win, 5-4," *Baltimore Sun*, April 4, 1989: 1B.

5 John Eisenberg, "Orioles Were Perfect in the Important Ways," *Baltimore Sun*, April 4, 1989: 1B.

"Untouchable" Wilson Alvarez Pitches A No-Hitter in Second Major-League Start

August 11, 1991: Chicago White Sox 7, Baltimore Orioles 0, at Memorial Stadium

By Leonte Landino

The Wilson Álvarez no-hitter journey began in the Maracaibo Little Leagues. The boy from Parroquia Santa Lucía became known for constantly achieving seamless performances.

As a kid, Álvarez threw 11 no-hitters.[1] His 12th provided the foundation for a career in the major leagues.

The Texas Rangers called the 19-year-old Álvarez up in 1989 for an emergency start against the Toronto Blue Jays. Expectations were huge for the lefty, but after facing only five batters and allowing three hits and three runs, including two home runs, he was returned to the minors after the game and was eventually traded to the Chicago White Sox.

The White Sox provided a fresh start. Álvarez spent 1990 and half of 1991 in the minors. He married his wife, Daihanna, in 1990 and later that year, on August 11, their first child died five days after he was born of a pulmonary infection.

On August 11, 1991, the White Sox gave Álvarez a second chance.

"I couldn't believe I was getting back and pitching on the same day when we lost our baby," Álvarez said. "I had a million things on my mind, I was nervous because I was afraid that I was not going to be able to make an out like in 1989. I didn't know what to think or do because of the chance to pitch back on this level. When we arrived on the bus to the ballpark I realized I had left my bag with all my clothes and equipment at the lobby of the hotel. The team sent a person to get my stuff where my wife was waiting. When the bag arrived I got dressed and ran to the bullpen with the belt in my hand to prepare for the game and only was able to warm up for half an hour."[2]

The White Sox players were getting dressed in the clubhouse. Ozzie Guillén, a fellow Venezuelan, remembers that veteran pitcher Charlie Hough said: "Something special is going to happen at this ballpark today."[3]

A crowd of more than 40,000 filled Baltimore's Memorial Stadium that Sunday. The Orioles were in sixth place but they had a collection of power hitters in their lineup, led by Cal Ripken.

Back home in Venezuela, Venevisión, the country's largest national television network, planned to broadcast the game on its traditional *Game of the Week* so the whole country could follow White Sox shortstop Guillén, a national idol. But the night before, Álvarez's sudden callup spread across the country by word of mouth. By 1:00 P.M., Venezuela had stopped to watch Álvarez.

White Sox bats began the game doing their part. Robin Ventura singled and Frank Thomas hit a home run off Orioles starter Dave Johnson. Álvarez came to the mound with a 2-0 lead.

The first pitch to Orioles center fielder Mike Devereaux was a strike. Five pitches later, Álvarez had his first major-league out, a strikeout. Second baseman Juan Bell struck out on five pitches. And it took five more to strike out Cal Ripken. Three up, three down.

Álvarez finally had the chance to breathe at the major-league level. "After that first inning I got trust in myself. I knew I belonged at that level. I said to myself that this was the level where I wanted to be and there was no turning back."

The second inning started with a walk to Dwight Evans but Álvarez quickly got out of trouble when Randy Milligan grounded into a double play. David Seguí grounded out to end the second. In the third Chris Hoiles and Leo Gomez were retired by consecutive fly balls and Bob Melvin struck out swinging. The fourth and fifth innings saw six straight outs by popups and lineouts.

In the Chicago second, Ozzie Guillén led off with a double and the White Sox scored two more runs for a 4-0 lead. They scored three more in the top of the sixth.

In the bottom of the sixth with one out, Álvarez walked Leo Gomez but retired Melvin and Deveraux on a pop fly and strikeout.

In the dugout, nobody was talking to Álvarez. He thought it was because he was the new guy in the

"Untouchable" Wilson Alvarez Pitches A No-Hitter in Second Major-League Start

clubhouse. He was lonely in the dugout. His mind was not on the game, but on the loss of his child. He was not savoring the moment but only pitching as if he were a robot in spikes. He was in a mechanical mode, amazed about where he was, after all he had to go through, after all the years learning the game and working his way from Maracaibo, which seemed to be a far and distant land.

In Venezuela everybody remembers that afternoon. People called one another to confirm that everyone was watching the game, in case anybody was missing it or had stepped out. The whisper was universal … "Wilson is pitching a no-hitter."

In the seventh inning with one out, Cal Ripken hit a slow grounder that sank almost in front of the plate. Catcher Ron Karkovice picked up the ball, but threw wild to first; Ripken took second on the error. Evans was out on a pop fly, but Milligan walked. With two runners on base David Seguí popped to right field for the third out.

In the eighth inning Hoiles, leading off, hit a ball between right field and center that looked unreachable, but center fielder Lance Johnson appeared out of nowhere and made a magnificent sliding catch that saved the gem. When Johnson lifted his glove, Wilson saw the scoreboard for the first time during the afternoon.

"I saw the board and I said to myself, 'Wow … they don't have any hits.' I didn't realize I was pitching this good or this far in the game. That's when my heart started pumping and I got nervous."[4]

He was able to get two more outs in the eighth inning. Johnson caught the third out and pointed out the scoreboard with zero hits after the play.

The Orioles were losing, 7-0, but when Álvarez came out in the ninth the 40,000 fans at Memorial Stadium were cheering for the rookie. It was a surreal afternoon. The vibe was felt back in Venezuela. Álvarez was doing what no Venezuelan had ever done.

Deveraux flied out for the first out and Juan Bell fanned. With two outs, Cal Ripken was up, the most feared hitter on the team. Karkovice called semi-intentional walks for him and veteran Dwight Evans, so Álvarez could face Randy Milligan. Álvarez was visibly nervous at this point. To those watching, Álvarez looked different than he had the first six innings. He was sweating, kind of lost, looking at the sky at all times. Ozzie Guillén approached the mound and said, "Kid, don't think about anything that is happening here, just keep pitching the way you have been pitching and don't worry about anything."[5]

Pitching to Milligan, Álvarez threw a strike. Then Milligan fouled one off, then fouled off another, then took a ball. The count was 1-and-2. Álvarez threw a curveball in the dirt and Milligan swung and missed. It was done.

"No-Hit-No-Run!" screamed Gonzalo López Silvero, the Venevisión announcer. He kept screaming it, again and again.

Álvarez was astonished, always looking at the sky. "You took my son and gave me this instead," he said.[6] Meanwhile Karkovice was hugging him and the White Sox were jumping around him as if they had just won the World Series.

Two years earlier, Álvarez was unable to get anybody out. This day he got everybody. In the meantime, he lost a child and became one of the idols of his country. This achievement took him to another level. He was the first one. The best in Venezuelan baseball history.

Álvarez followed Bobo Holloman as the second in history to get a no-hitter in his first or second major-league start.[7] From then, in every one of his starts he had that feeling that he could do it again. He became better known as "El Intocable" (The Untouchable).

Wilson Álvarez's no-hitter opened the doors of big-league baseball for him. He played six more years with the White Sox, becoming an ace of the rotation, helping the White Sox in the 1993 postseason and winning Game Three of the ALCS against his nemesis, the Blue Jays. In 1997 was traded to the San Francisco Giants and in 1998 signed as a free agent with the Tampa Bay Devil Rays, becoming the first starter for the new franchise. He finished his career with the Los Angeles Dodgers in 2005, becoming the first Venezuelan pitcher with over 100 wins in the majors.[8]

This article was originally published in SABR's book No-Hitters *(2017), edited by Bill Nowlin.*

Notes

1 *Revista IND.* (Caracas, Venezuela), August 1984.

2 All quotations by Wilson Álvarez are from interviews with the author unless otherwise attributed.

3 Personal conversation with Ozzie Guillén about Álvarez's no-hitter, March 2017.

4 Baseball Zone – Tripleplay Sports Productions. Maracaibo, Venezuela, March 2001.

5 Conversation with Ozzie Guillén.

6 *A La Carga!* – Official Magazine of Aguilas del Zulia (Maracaibo: Tripleplay Sports Productions), 1997-2002.

7 "Rookie No-Hitters," MLB.com, mlb.mlb.com/mlb/history/rare_feats/index.jsp?feature=rookie_no_hitter.

8 "Wilson Álvarez," baseball-reference.com/players/a/alvarwi01.shtml.

Orioles Play Their Final Game at Memorial Stadium

October 6, 1991: Detroit Tigers 7, Baltimore Orioles 1, at Memorial Stadium

By Thomas J. Brown Jr.

A season was drawing to a close. In Baltimore, an era was also drawing to a close as the Orioles prepared to play their final game at Memorial Stadium. It was the only home the Orioles had known since they moved to Baltimore in 1954.

For many fans, it was bittersweet to see the ballpark, which had been the site of six American League pennants and three World Series titles, close its doors. John Eisenberg of the *Baltimore Sun* wrote about "the moments or rituals that made you feel franchised at Memorial Stadium, as if the place suddenly were your own."[1]

Memorial Stadium was packed for the game although the Orioles were finishing a dismal season. They had a 67-94 record heading into the final day of the campaign. Their opponent, the Detroit Tigers, tried to stay in contention most of the season but finished tied for second place behind the Toronto Blue Jays.

Bob Milacki got the starting nod for the Orioles. He led the pitching staff with 10 wins. Milacki had pitched nine solid innings in his last outing but didn't earn the win when the Orioles lost to the Yankees in 11 innings. "I thought I was going to be nervous going into the game, but I wasn't," the 28-year-old right-hander said after the game about pitching the last game in a ballpark that held good memories for so many fans and players.[2]

The Tigers wasted no time scoring as they sent eight batters to the plate in the first. Milt Cuyler led off with a single and landed on third when Lou Whitaker reached on an error by first baseman Glenn Davis. Lloyd Moseby followed with a single to bring Cuyler home. After Cecil Fielder fouled out, three more Tigers singled to plate three more runs. By the time Travis Fryman grounded into a double play, the Orioles were already in a deep hole.

The Orioles gave the fans some hope when Mike Devereaux tripled to lead off the bottom of the first inning and scored on Joe Orsulak's fielder's-choice grounder. It turned out to be the only run the Orioles would score all afternoon.

Milacki held the Tigers scoreless in the second and retired the first two batters in the third. But then he walked Tony Phillips and surrendered two singles to send Phillips across the plate with the fifth Tigers run. Orioles manager Johnny Oates replaced Milacki with Todd Frohwirth. Milacki said he felt fine warming up but "it was just one of those days when it didn't happen. I just pitched bad. Basically, I gave up a few early hits and it snowballed on me. I wish that I could have ended things better."[3]

Meanwhile Frank Tanana, the Tigers starter, shut down the Orioles after the first inning. Tanana entered the game with a 12-12 record. After giving up the run in the first, he didn't allow another hit until the fifth. "After Mike's hit, I was pretty much in control," Tanana said afterward.[4]

The Orioles got back-to-back singles in the fifth but were unable to capitalize on them. Tanana got the next three batters out on six pitches and none of the balls left the infield. Glenn Davis's leadoff single in the seventh was the last hit by an Oriole at Memorial Stadium.

It was the second time in the season that Tanana won in the opening or closing of a ballpark. He beat the White Sox in the first game at Chicago's new Comiskey Park on April 18. Tanana pitched a complete game that day and did the same against the Orioles. He had also spoiled the stadium opener for the Seattle Mariners in 1977. Of the Orioles game he commented, "When you get 14 hits and seven runs like that, you should win."[5]

In the eighth inning, the fans began calling for Mike Flanagan to come out of the bullpen. Flanagan started his career with the Orioles in 1975. He had been a starter when they lost to the Pirates in the 1979 World Series and when they won the 1983 World Series.

Flanagan had pitched for Toronto for the past four seasons. He had returned to the club this season and was one of the stalwarts in the Orioles bullpen. He

• Orioles Play Their Final Game at Memorial Stadium •

The ball Mike Flanagan threw for the last pitch thrown by an Oriole at Memorial Stadium, October 6, 1991. Courtesy of the Babe Ruth Museum.

made 63 appearances before this game and entered it with a 2.40 ERA.

But Greg Olson took the mound in the top of the ninth. He got Phillips out on a weak grounder to first. After the play, Olson called his manager to the mound. "I wanted to get in the game and face a hitter. That was all I wanted. Then I wanted to get him out here. Flanny is the fan's favorite. Everything that has gone on here means so much to him," said Olson.[6]

As Flanagan finished his warmup pitches, the scoreboard announced that he had agreed to come back for the 1992 season. The crowd cheered on the fact that he "was ringing out the old and would be back to ring in the new."[7] Flanagan faced two batters and struck out both as the crowd roared approval.

"All weekend I've looked around, and there's no part of the park that I can look at and not see things people had done over the years. Out there today, I thought of all the players who never got to come back for one last ovation," Flanagan told reporters after the game.[8]

In the bottom of the ninth, Devereaux struck out swinging but reached first on a passed ball. Joe Orsulak flied out to center field. The last chance to create some magic fell to Cal Ripken Jr. When he hit into a double play, it probably didn't matter to many of the fans.

They had spent the season watching Ripken play perhaps the best season of his life. Ripken would soon win his second MVP award. He shared his disappointment at making the final out when he said: "I kind of went outside of myself and tried to do more than I could. In the back of my mind, I wanted to hit a home run, and that's the worst thing that you can do."[9]

After the final out, the celebration finally began. The Orioles introduced the stars who had made so many memories at the ballpark. First the all-time Orioles team was introduced. Brooks Robinson took his old position at third base followed by Frank Robinson and Boog Powell. After Jim Palmer took his place on the mound, a parade of other Orioles took the field. All told, 78 players lined up around the infield as the crowd stood cheering.

"I just can't put it into words, but I just got that feeling. That's the Oriole team, the winning spirit, the fans," said Orioles first baseman Randy Milligan.[10]

As the ceremony drew to a close, Frank Robinson made the last run from third base to home plate. Then the plate was removed by the grounds crew and placed in a stretch limousine. It was sent across town to Camden Yards under police escort. Minutes later, the crowd watched on the scoreboard as it was put in place at the new ballpark, an important connection between the old and the new for Orioles fans.

Author's note

The author attended this game with his sister. He remembers that it was a chilly day in Baltimore but that didn't prevent him from having a chill go up his back as he watched all the former Orioles take the field after the game while every fan stood in appreciation of their hometown heroes.

Sources

In addition to the sources cited in the Notes, the author used the Baseball-Reference.com and Retrosheet.org websites for box-score, player, team, and season pages, pitching and batting game logs, and other material pertinent to this account.

Notes

1   John Eisenberg, "Private Moments Are the Ones We'll Miss the Most," *Baltimore Sun*, October 5, 1991: 23.

2   Kent Baker, "Post Game Events Ease Pain of Milacki's Bad Day," *Baltimore Sun*, October 7, 1991: 34.

3   Baker.

4   Gene Grum, "Tigers Finish Tied for 2nd With 7-1 Victory Over O's," *Detroit Free Press*, October 7, 1991: 34.

5   Grum.

6   Peter Schmuck, "Flanagan Provides Last Bit of Magic," *Baltimore Sun*, October 7, 1991: 34.

7   Schmuck.

8   Schmuck.

9   Schmuck.

10 Schmuck.

Oriole Park at Camden Yards

By Curt Smith

Baseball only decrees 90 feet between bases and 60 feet 6 inches from home plate to the mound. Elsewhere, look backward, angel. "Thanks to Alexander Cartwright," said former Commissioner Bowie Kuhn, "the outfield distance, fence height, and space between the seats and lines vary. Parks could do as they liked."[1] Some have been liked better.

In 1908 vaudevillian Jack Norworth wrote the lyrics to "Take Me Out to the Ball Game." Baseball's first steel and concrete park, Shibe Park, opened the next year in Philadelphia. By 1923, Forbes Field, Comiskey Park, Fenway Park, League Park, Griffith Stadium, the Polo Grounds, Crosley Field, Navin Field, Ebbets Field, Wrigley Field, Braves Field, Sportsman's Park, and Yankee Stadium – 14 in all – rose from the grid of urban streets.[2] Each fit on finite turf, which often made for odd, even aberrant angles. Most parks had "steel, rather than concrete trusses, an arched brick façade, a sunroof over the gentle slope of the upper deck, an asymmetrical playing field, and natural grass turf," observed *The Ballpark That Forever Changed Baseball*, writing about Oriole Park at Camden Yards.[3]

In Flatbush, Ebbets resembled a pinball machine. In Pittsburgh, Forbes's vast outfield acreage grew heavy with base hits. In Cincinnati, Crosley seemed more at one with post-World War II Little League. "Across the country entire cities revolved around them," said Larry King, growing up in Brooklyn USA.[4] For a half-century such Xanadus of personality sired a oneness with the spirit the past, and an infinite feeling for baseball's essence. In person, by radio, or on television, America inhaled the wakes and triumphs of a thousand afternoons – through the 1950s, the "classic park" the place where much of the Republic lived.

Foolishly, baseball spent the next quarter-century ditching such jewels for multisport lookalikes, trying vainly to fuse its DNA (triangular) with football's (rectangular). The Braves invaded sterile Atlanta-Fulton County Stadium. St. Louis dealt cozy Busch Stadium for a same-name oval. The Reds and Phillies left for Riverfront and Veterans Stadium, respectively. Baseball braved Kingdome, Three Rivers Stadium, and Olympic Stadium[5] – The Big O, as in *zero*. Some even felt Fenway passé! As clones multiplied, others cried: Give *us* a cookie-cutter. Out: intimacy and individuality. In: vast foul turf and seats in another county. Worst, they precluded building the baseball-*only* park that had and would again stir baseball *interest*.

If "baseball-only" was the solution, almost no one acted to enact it. Then, in 1983 a small group of architects founded the Kansas City firm Helmuth, Obata, and Kassabaum, which in time became HOK Sport. "The idea was laughed at," said chief architect Joseph Spear, who had designed that city's much-lauded Kauffman (née Royals) Stadium, "that a company could thrive by designing only sports."[6] Few laughed when HOK's 19,500-seat Triple-A Pilot Field opened in 1988 to critical acclaim in downtown Buffalo. By then, HOK had begun to design Baltimore's Oriole Park in Camden Yards, which opened in 1992 having cost $110 million, seating 48,041 (later reduced to 46,550 and then 45,971),[7] and becoming the dream that changed *everything* –awakening cities *sans* baseball-only plots to grasp what they might have.

If, as Shakespeare wrote, "What's past is prologue," success was facilitated before Camden's first pitch. For one thing, the one-time railroad center is 12 minutes west by foot from Baltimore's Inner Harbor and only two blocks from the birthplace of the man who entered our vernacular in a long-ball way, choosing to never leave. George Herman "Babe" Ruth was born in Baltimore in 1895. Between 1906 and 1912, his father operated Ruth's Cafe on the ground floor of the family residence located at Conway Street & Little Paca, now beneath center field at the

Oriole Park at Camden Yards

Yard.[8] What remains is the legend of the Everyman/Superman. In 1969, professional baseball turning 100, "The baseball writers and broadcasters voted Babe Ruth "the Greatest Player Ever,' George Vecsey wrote – "a title so Twentyish, so circus-posterish, that it was Ruthian in its sweep. The man even had an adjective in his honor."[9] The Babe became "the first national superstar," said George Will, "the man who gave us that category."[10]

Another reason to prophesy Oriole Park's success, if not phenomenon, was that a ballpark must acquire a persona: be old yet new, high-tech yet antique, bridge, not disengage, the years. The Yard became local, of Baltimore, yet universal, of Classic sites – "like Nixon goes to China,"[11] said 1969-84 Commissioner Bowie Kuhn – for baseball, the dividing line in form and content between what came before and what exists today. Helping were: under contract to HOK, the urban design firm of RTKL, landscape architecture firm Wallace, Roberts and Todd, and engineering firms Bliss and Nyitray; Rummel, Klepper and Kahl; and Kidde Consultants, Inc. –a and, under contract to the Orioles, the interior design firm Forte Design and graphic design firm David Ashton and Associates.[12] A third reason for success was where it happened, for few cities have had a greater baseball heritage, minor and major league, or known better the need for a field to provide prosperity and panache than Baltimore. To sum up a century before Camden Yards:

In 1892, the American Association Orioles joined the National League, winning the 1894-95-96 pennants and the final two 1896-97 of the four Temple Cup title series with a famed quartet – Hughie Jennings, Wee Willie Keeler, John McGraw, and Wilbert Robinson.[13] In 1901 the Birds joined the American League as the charter O's, then became the New York Highlanders (later, Yankees). The Orioles trekked to the International League for the next half-century. In 1944 Oriole Park on 29th Street and Greenmount Avenue burned down.[14] As the Birds began a two-week road trip, football's Municipal (later, a.k.a. Baltimore, Venable, Babe Ruth, then Memorial after World War II) readied for baseball, wooing 52,000 that fall for a Junior World Series game. The Birds' aviary rebuilt for hopefully a big-league team, Memorial Stadium, at Ellerslie Avenue, Edmore Road, and East 33rd and 36th Streets, 10-12 minutes by car from downtown.

Above Memorial's entrance was a eulogy to veterans noting, "Time Will Not Dim the Glory of Their Deeds."[15] Plain, large, and horseshoed, it anchored a residential neighborhood on Baltimore's north side – said longtime *News-American* columnist John Steadman, "from the outside resembling a large school."[16] Military personnel like those lauded by the stadium played pickup games in World War II, Babe Ruth often throwing out the first ball. Too old to serve, Ruth raised money for service groups and for events like a Baseball Writers' Association of America fundraiser for the Finnish Relief Fund. "To the average GI training to go abroad," said broadcaster Mel Allen, charged with driving Babe to events, "it was like talking to God."[17]

Babe died in 1948. In 1953 Baltimore got a franchise, the Colts, in the National Football League. If not a changing of the guard, baseball's International League seemed now old-hat. Said Steadman: "We wanted the bigs."[18]

After Anheuser-Busch Brewery bought the St. Louis Cardinals in 1953, Browns owner Bill Veeck, unable to get an AL OK for Baltimore, sold the franchise to a syndicate, which moved it there.[19] The next April, Baltimore tried to expiate its 52-year big-league void in a "gigantic parade," said the O's first major-league Voice, 1954-59's Ernie Harwell. "A stirring welcome to Baltimore."[20] The 1953 Browns had drawn 297,238. Memorial lured 46,354 to its 1954 opener and 1,060,910 for the year. (Capacity was 47,708, baseball's sole roofless upper tier wrapping home plate beyond each line.) Foul poles stood 309 feet away. (An 11-foot 6-inch wall reached each 446-foot alley.) The first year a 10-foot hedge linked left- to right-center field. (Center was 445). "The hedge was beautiful," said Harwell. "Sadly, for hitters it rarely entered the area of play."[21]

For a time, until dimensions shrank, power alleys, like foul terrain, were cyanide to offense – thus, fan involvement. Then, in 1960, the Birds found an antidote, coming out of nowhere to nearly take the pennant, its Memorial record 1,187,849 attendance third in the last eight-team league.[22] In 1964, the O's again almost winning, third baseman Brooks Robinson was voted MVP. In December the Birds acquired Frank Robinson from Cincinnati. On May 8, 1966, he hit the first fair ball out of Memorial Stadium. "Every game," added Chuck Thompson, from 1955 to and beyond 2000 retirement the most beloved-ever Voice of the Orioles and Colts, "you saw this flag marked HERE beyond the left-field seats."[23]

F. Robby's 49 homers, 122 RBIs, and .316 average won the Triple Crown: the first ALer since Mickey

• **Baltimore Baseball** •

Mantle in '56. Boog Powell added 34 taters. Shortstop Luis Aparicio, second baseman Davey Johnson, and center fielder Paul Blair helped forge the league's fewest errors. The O's drew a new record 1,203,366 and swept LA in Baltimore's first World Series, blanking it a record 33 straight innings.[24] It was harder to warm to the park. "Looks more like football bowl than ball park," *Sports Illustrated* wrote of Memorial Stadium. Entering, a visitor saw ramps, left- and right-field bleachers, and three tiers in a semicircle – also, "the only seats with backs [were] in the lower deck"; "for sun, the east side of [the] stadium"; or for a "five-mile view" of the city, the upper deck, framing Baltimore.[25]

The 1969-71 Birds won each pennant: in the Series, losing to the Mets, beating Cincinnati, and bowing to Roberto Clemente, respectively. In 1970 they drew only 27,608 for League Championship Series Game Three. Attendance flagged this decade, too. Then, "in one summer," Steadman said of 1979, "Baltimore became a baseball town,"[26] having always meant the Colts. In 1979 new radio flagship WFBR began marketing "Orioles Magic," promo and song heard in a bar, at a stoplight, on the beach. Meanwhile, 40 miles away, Washington, deserted by baseball in 1971, adopted the Orioles. "The Gas crisis kept people at home, with baseball inexpensive," said Baltimore announcer Tom Davis. "Most of all, the team had a new hero every night,"[27] winning one game after another on a key hit, fine catch, and pitching based on fidelity to fundamentals and work – what longtime O's player, scout, coach, and manager Cal Ripken baptized the "Oriole Way."[28]

Memorial became "Birdland" or "The House at 33rd Street." Bill Hagy, a taxi driver in Section 34, twisted his body to spell ORIOLES atop the dugout. In August 1979, DC legal icon Edward Bennett Williams bought the Birds, fueling worry that they might move. The barrister said it would depend on attendance, which, ending angst, soared to 1,681,009 from 1,051,724 in 1978.[29] The O's won the AL East, took the ALCS, and extended the Series to Game Seven, attendance far from the 1971 Classic, with 15,003 *fewer* seats sold for Games Six-Seven than One-Two.[30] After 1979 virtually no one was ever heard again to speak of the Orioles moving. In 1982 they lost a last-day pennant upon Earl Weaver's retirement. Afterward, 51,642 roared for the bantam skipper. The next April, 50,000 jammed boats, filled blocks, and chanted O-R-I-O-L-E-S at an Opening Day rally at Inner Harbor. In retrospect, the moment's intensity presaged Camden Yards.

That spring former Red Sox radio Voice Jon Miller arrived from Boston. "People ask, 'How do Oriole fans compare to the Red Sox?'" he told the rally. "I think you should ask, 'How do Boston fans compare to the Orioles?'"[31] The throng roared. Jon arrived to a sense of caring for the O's that the radio-TV talent of Harwell, Thompson, Bill O'Donnell, and cable Home Team Sports' Mel Proctor had or would abet. In the 1980s TV cameras panned Memorial Stadium on "Seat Cushion Night" as another Voice who followed his own drummer, HTS's John Lowenstein, ad-lib sailed his cushion onto the field. Hundreds more followed, halting play till each cushion was removed."[32] Such interest rose in 1984 after the Colts left without warning in the dead of night for Indianapolis. Stunned, the State of Maryland's agency, the Maryland Stadium Authority, vowed to keep the Orioles. "The Colts had owned the town," said *Washington Post* writer Richard Justice. "Now baseball was all it had."[33]

At best, Memorial had paled like yellowy B movies. With football gone, the City of Baltimore accorded the Birds new respect. A new park would be owned and operated by the MSA. "The message from the Chesapeake Bay was clear from the outset," said HOK's Joe Spear. "What the Orioles and the Authority had in common in doing was to set a new standard."[34] Memorial was too old, its infrastructure too fragile, to consider renovation. Some wanted a new baseball-football plot. The Orioles adamantly refused. "We saw that the franchises that were the most successful, that were truly great, all had baseball-only facilities," mused their president, Larry Lucchino.[35] Camden Yards flew largely from his vision. Lucchino had been born and grew up in Pittsburgh. "I loved Forbes Field," he said. "I'd seen the damage done when they left it for Three Rivers."[36]

Perhaps no city suffered more than Pittsburgh by leaving a classic park for a sameness of dimension, dreary sightline, and stands where you needed a radio or television simply to follow play. In 1960 Lucchino, 15, had left school vainly hoping to watch on his family's TV the end of thrilling World Series Game Seven. Instead, at 3:36 P.M. Bill Mazeroski hit a home run to beat the Yankees, 10-9, at Forbes. "I threw my radio toward the sky," Larry said, racing home "on air."[37] A second baseman on Pittsburgh's city high school title team, Lucchino felt kinship with Maz. The Pittsburgh All-City League basketball player,

• Oriole Park at Camden Yards •

Princeton University and Yale Law School graduate, member of founder Williams's DC law firm, Williams and Connolly, became a partner in 1978 and Orioles VP/general counsel on Williams's acquiring them in 1979.[38] Always he felt identity with his hometown's 1909-70 heirloom.

At Forbes, you could almost reach out and touch the 1960s Clemente, Maz, or Stargell. By contrast, moving to Three Rivers in 1970 the Bucs found faux grass, a huge upper deck, and football's body snatching baseball's soul. The Pirates almost left by the mid-'80s, no longer fitting in the city's emotional luggage. Lucchino, now 40, knew "the damage" that had been done – and from his childhood that only by going back to its future could baseball save itself. By then, he had become Williams's pick to chart Memorial's successor. From this choice rose Oriole Park at Camden Yards – father to two dozen retro, or "new old," classic ballparks. Williams, dying of cancer, was a Red Sox fan wanting a site to rival Fenway. Brilliant architect and O's VP Janet Marie Smith helped form the park's core and flair. Each shared Lucchino's vision that they could, in Thomas Paine's words, "Begin the [here, baseball] world over again."[39]

HOK Sport shared that vision, though its initial plan for the Yard resembled bland New Comiskey Park, opening in 1991 to lukewarm review. Like Williams, his ballpark point man hated it. "We said we don't *want* that kind of facility," Lucchino said, keeping design control in-house. "We want something distinctive … more like a traditional old ballpark"[40] – but where? He, Williams, and then-Mayor, later Governor, William Donald Schaefer wanted downtown to aid commerce. HOK looked at more than two dozen baseball-only sites in and around Baltimore. "The public was asked for input," said Spear. "Ultimately, we thought if the park was downtown, people would make a day of it."[41] HOK was particularly helpful sealing the Yard's *place,* the response to Pilot Field confirming its and the Birds' view. Buffalo's minor-league park fit grandly into downtown's grid of alleys. "Instead of building generically," said Bisons owner Bob Rich. "they begin with a city's landscape and architecture."[42]

After years of debate over form, locale, and even name, the O's and the Stadium Authority announced what George Will called among the three most important developments of the postwar era, with free agency and integration.[43] It came, to quote a saying best described as a Chinese curse, "in interesting times."[44] The Yard teetered on conception as its future occupant seemed comatose on the field. In 1986 Baltimore had made the AL East cellar. Next September 14, it yielded a bigs' single-game record 10 homers to Toronto. The 1988 Orioles began the season 0-21, only the 1904 Senators and 1920 Tigers even losing their first 13 sets. "Some clubs are lucky to find one storyline," said Joe Angel, 1988 his first year as an O's announcer. "Our team had a bunch."[45] Amid the streak, the Birds briefly came home, tested the water, and decided to market the first game back from a more extended trip as "Fantastic Fans Night," hailing "great stars of the past Jim Palmer, Boog Powell, and Brooks and Frank [Robinson]," said Angel, "and their Series title as recently as 1983."[46]

The night of May 2, a crowd of 50,402 that sold out Memorial to hail the 1-23 Orioles was electrified as Governor Schaefer announced that Williams and the Stadium Authority had agreed on a 15-year lease for a new ballpark to be built at Camden Yards in time for the 1992 season.[47] The park would be on an 85-acre parcel parallel to turn-of-the-century trolley tracks, near the historic Camden Railroad Station of the old Baltimore & Ohio, and two blocks from the Sultan of Swat's birthplace, a short fly ball from Inner Harbor.[48] The 1988 team lost 107 games, but a year later finished 87-75, losing the AL East the final weekend in Toronto. "*More* storylines," Joe Angel mused. "After a while, you run out of ink."[49] On June 28, 1989, the Orioles broke ground on the park and the plot was razed. Eventually, the Yard evoked other ballparks that had been part of a city. Writer Michael Gershman recalled being taken at age 6 by his parents to Ebbets Field to celebrate his mother's birthday. "I remember walking through the marble rotunda at the entrance, and how every sound echoed," he observed. "To me, it was like Grand Central Station. And then I saw it – the grass on the field. It was like seeing Oz."[50]

On August 13, 1988, Williams died of cancer, Lucchino having become O's president a year earlier and later owner. Incessantly he pressed HOK for *personality,* his ally NL President A. Bartlett Giamatti, turning commissioner in 1989. In each post, Bart asked, "Why can't we have modern amenities *and* idiosyncrasies? Give me sharper quirks and odder angles," recalling his first game, at 10, with dad at Fenway Park.[51] Then Giamatti died in September 1989. "When this park's complete, every team will want one," he had said. "If you build it [right], they will come."[52] Two decades later renamed HOK Sports Venue Event changed its name again to "Populous" after a managers' buyout by HOK Group and became a global international and architectural design practice. Its bona fides were nonpareil. From 1992 to 2012, HOK/Populous designed 14 new major-league parks, and renovated four current ballparks. Reviews delighted cities like Pittsburgh, Houston, and San Francisco, and merely pleased others like Cleveland and Detroit. Its Hope Diamond was the Yard, whose theme and outlook could be seen in every client, each hoping to be the Original.[53]

In retrospect, crucial to the ballpark's magic was that it took essentially 33 months from the time razing began of structures on Oriole Park's lot until the first Opening Day on April 6, 1992.[54] "Looking back," said Janet Marie Smith, "we had an extra year to plan, because we had an extra year to demolish the plot, and that made all the difference in the world. We never would have had the confidence or the time to study those old ballparks" – Fenway, Wrigley, Forbes, Ebbets – "and incorporate their features."[55] On February 6, 1990, construction began after eight months of demolition at the site. Meanwhile, debate continued regularly and vocally for two years about the new park's name until – on October 3, 1991, the eve of Memorial Stadium's last weekend – a compromise was announced that pleased each side Oriole Park at Camden Yards.[56] Cal Ripken Jr.'s river ran through 34 homers, 114 RBIs, and league-high 368 total bases. It ended on a magical October 6, after Cal hit into a game, season, and stadium-closing double play.

Home plate was removed and ferried by a chauffeured limousine to the O's new park.

Since 1955 Chuck Thompson had lyrically voiced the Birds. His most poignant moment – "almost unbelievably moving," he said, years later – now began. First, the field was cleared. "Next, the background music began from *Field of Dreams* over the PA system. Then Brooks [Robinson] emerged from the dugout to take his position at third base – followed by Frank [Robinson] in the outfield, followed by Jim Palmer," winning a Birds-record 268 games, "on the mound," then Boog Powell at first base: former players saying farewell. "This is how the team said goodbye to Memorial Stadium – asking all former Orioles to return. The crowd didn't know, hadn't expected this. When it happened, they were stunned."[57]

More than 75 players ran to their position, each wearing the age's uniform and their number –"scattered around the field – no introduction, just music, and that music kept rolling," Chuck said.[58] He used binoculars to eye players like Brooks and Boog – "and they were, like me, drained. It was hard to keep from breaking down completely." Improbably, there was no cheering – "none," the crowd too emotionally rent to speak. "Instead, thunderous applause, and enough tears for a river."[59] Later, walking to his car, Chuck Thompson saw a sea of red-eyed love. The phrase "'There's no crying in baseball,'" from film's *A League of Their Own*, that day daubed art, not life.[60]

On April 6, 1992, the world of baseball architecture turned upside down, the O's new home opening on downtown Baltimore's western edge. Announcer Tom Davis noted how Camden made prior stadiums archaic. "In a pre-Opening-Day tour," he said, "I understood for the first time the inferiority of circular stadia."[61] Like Saul on the Damascus Road, suddenly all things had been made clear. The first ball was tossed by President George H.W. Bush, who loved the game, captained his team at Yale, and inevitably bounced the pitch on one hop, as he did this day, blaming it on his 42-pound steel vest mandated by the Secret Service. Later, out of office, Bush ditched a vest but still bounced the ball. "Baseball's a game of habit," Bush said, *it* being *his*.[62] A crowd of 44,568 attended. Other firsts: Pitcher: Rick Sutcliffe. Batter: Kenny Lofton. Hit: Paul Sorrento. Orioles' hit: Glenn Davis. Run: Sam Horn, on Chris Hoiles's double. RBI: Hoiles. Score: Birds, 2-0. Time: 2:02.[63] That August a crowd filled the Yard in August for an O's game and to film a scene for the movie *Dave*, released in 1993, actor Kevin Kline tossing a first ball.

"Field of Dreams Comes True in Baltimore," the *New York Times* wrote of Baltimore – *Time* called it "one of the 10 best designs of 1992."[64] Many felt: Here was a perfect park. In sites like Oakland, seats half-circled each foul line. Camden's nuzzled them. Wall height uniformity smothered multisport stadiums. The Yard segued from 7 feet tall (left and center field) to 25 (in-play right-field board), left-field bleachers intersecting the wall. "About a dozen times a year," said Lucchino, "fielders reached into the stands and grabbed a homer."[65] At most ballparks, fences then gently curved. The Yard began at 333 feet from the plate (left field), receded to 364 (left-center), leapt to 410 (deepest left-center) and center (400), sharply angled to right-center (373), and dropped off a shelf (318, right).[66] Instead of phony turf, the right stuff gleamed. Foul ground was scarce, Camden felt a homer palace. In truth, fair balance crowned the game.

• Oriole Park at Camden Yards •

Opening Day for Oriole Park at Camden Yards. Courtesy of the Baltimore Orioles.

In 1781 French general Comte de Rochambeau and thousands of French troops camped here, then known as Ridgely's Delight,[67] en route to Yorktown. Throngs camped during 1992. The Orioles sold out eight of their first 23 home dates, then began a streak of 59 dates through season's end. Averaging 44,047, Baltimore tallied 3,567,819 paid to shatter 1991's prior record 2,552,753. The effect, however, was more than numerical, almost mystical. Outlanders to the city would walk blocks around the Yard to stare from a myriad of angles. Passing the Yard on I-95, drivers would slow or move to the shoulder – and stopping, simply gaze, like pilgrims to Lourdes. More than 30,000 parking spaces were available in secure garages and open lots within walking distance. Baltimore Metro put a visitor at the nearby Camden Station building. Some sailed to Inner Harbor Marina, three blocks away. All entered the ballpark through wrought-iron gates and arched portals, typical of Janet Marie Smith's devotion to detail. To many, the O's had taken the best of the old ballparks and stirred them into one.

An arched red-brick façade mimed old Comiskey Park. Left field was triple-tiered like Yankee Stadium. The center-field scoreboard and ivied backdrop leapt from Ernie Banks. The right-field scoreboard evoked Carl Furillo playing caroms at Ebbets Field. "The board is emblematic of the park," said Chuck Thompson. "Camden's is traditional,"[68] linking ads, blurbs, and out-of-town scores. A standing-room area topped it, where often hundreds crowded. Behind right field, the longest building on the East Coast, the 1,016-foot-long and 51-foot-wide brick B&O Railroad Warehouse, built between 1898 and 1905, enfolded the park.[69] "Some wanted to tear it down," said Will, also an O's board member. "Instead they refurbished it," housing sports bars, eateries, and team offices. "It became part of the park, made it seem intimate."[70] Between the park and Warehouse, a 60-foot promenade extended Eutaw Street, becoming a potpourri of shops and people and making "Eutaw a carnival," said Tom Davis, airing there his regular pregame TV show.[71] Boog Powell, whose smash hit "Boog's Bar-B-Q" became a Camden staple, often joined Davis, guesting. Visitors nearby read plaques dedicated to members of the Orioles Hall of Fame and 5-inch baseball-shaped plates embedded into the pavement to designate where blasts first hit the Eutaw Street surface.[72] Meanwhile, smoke kept wafting from Boog's, its proprietor among the many O's alumni to work for or with the team.

Central to the Yard's allure was that going back or forward, its design etched baseball's core. Back: Each aisle seat bore a replica of the logo of the famed 1890s Orioles of Willie Keeler and John McGraw. An upper-deck sunroof ringed the plate from left field to the right-field corner. Inadvertently, a bronze statue unveiled in 1995 at the park's northern Eutaw Street entrance by artist Susan Luery recalls how even in death Babe could own the room, errantly showing a *left*-handed pitcher Ruth as a 1914 pitcher for the IL Orioles, "clutching on his hip a *right*-handed fielding glove."[73] In 1992 the Yard put Memorial's right-field foul pole atop the tall wall in right field. In 2001 it installed the old joint's left-field pole, as well.[74] Forward: Hard-of-hearing could dial a "hearing assistance channel" from their seat. In left-center field, double-tiered pens let you see every reliever warming up. A grounds crew shed lay in front of the bleachers. "What a great ground rule. Balls hitting the roof and bouncing back onto the field were a homer," said Jon Miller, who from his booth heard and saw an aria of other notes.[75]

Longtime public-address Voice and 1943 and 1946-50 Brooklyn pitcher Rex Barney moved from Memorial Stadium, his "Thank yoouuu!" a ritual after any announcement. A double-faced clock, seen from outside and inside the park, topped the right-center-field board. A fine view of Baltimore could be had from any seat until major completion of a Hilton Baltimore Hotel in 2008, wrote *Sun* writer Peter Schmuck, "blocked out the best part of the ... skyline."[76] Yet few there will forget the initial feeling of bricks and mortar of another kind bringing grace to a city where the game *belonged*. "It's like Ebbets or Wrigley Field," said John Steadman. "The community *became* the team."[77] Added Fox TV's Kenny Albert: "Opening, Camden Yards wanted to be Fenway or Ebbets. Since then, new parks want to be Camden Yards."[78] Visit Pittsburgh, PNC Park designed by the Forbes II Task Force. Forty miles from the Yard, Nationals Park mentally used it to inspire. Relive how finally, after so many charmless copy-cats, Charm City made baseball realize what it had.

For the Orioles and baseball, Camden Yards' bewitchment began right off the bat, long before season one ended September 28 before sellout number 67. The '92ers won 22 more games than in 1991. O's pitcher Mike Mussina was first in league win percentage (.783); second in shutouts (four); third, ERA (2.54); and fourth, victories (18-5). On April 22, 1993, the home sellout skein ended at 65 games, 22,317 scattered for an evening makeup with the White Sox.[79] In July the All-Star Game returned to Baltimore for the first time since 1958 to cap a weeklong and first-of-its-kind "Upper Deck All-Star FanFest," the city revolved around the sport. Finally, someone, Seattle's Ken Griffey Jr., struck the Warehouse in the All-Star Game Home Run Derby: 439 feet from the plate.[80] Three greats threw out a first pitch – Brooks Robinson, Baltimore native Al Kaline, and the Baltimore Elite Giants' Leon Day.[81] Vice President Al Gore attended, a lifelong fan. The Phillies' John Kruk comically flailed at Seattle's Randy Johnson and the crowd booed AL skipper Cito Gaston for not using Mussina after warming him up. Americans win: 9-3.

That week, Ripken Jr. broke Banks's record for most home runs hit by a shortstop (278). Its import un-noted till offseason, the Orioles installed an orange left-field seat to mark the site. The '93ers slid to 85-77, Chris Hoiles their sole AL top-five player: .416 on-base, .585 slugging, and 1.001 OPS. Attendance hit 3,644,965. Turning the page, in October, trial lawyer Peter Angelos and other investors bought the club from Eli Jacobs for a record $173 million. Lucchino left the Orioles to oversee the design and construction of another jewel, San Diego's Petco Park, then as Red Sox president led a group rebuilding Fenway Park. On August 12, 1994, a player strike began that lasted until April 2, 1995 – canceling the World Series for the first time since 1904, aborting each season, and undoing each's record, Baltimore ending 63-49, averaging a franchise record 46,097,[82] Mussina again sparkling at 16-5 and Lee Smith saving 33 games.

The 232-day strike dimmed baseball interest overall, even in Baltimore. One man brought it back. By September 5, 1995, the Orioles were headed for third place in the AL East. Few noticed – nor Hoiles dinging in the second inning, Jeff Manto, Mark Smith, and Brady Anderson going deep back-to-back-to-back later in the frame, or each power surge tying a club mark: O's, 8-0.[83] What counted was Ripken tying Lou Gehrig's 2,130 consecutive games played. Next night, Wednesday the 6th, ESPN TV visited. Shedding the strike, baseball needed help from such history as Cal's 2,131st straight game. Usually network ball-and-striker Jon Miller would call the match, but the Voice also of the O's declined, calling it a national "game" but a Baltimore "thing."[84] While Jon opted for Birds radio, Chris Berman did ESPN, Miller wearing a tuxedo to host ceremonies on the field.

Leaving the White House to share Cal's summit was Bill Clinton, Bush's successor as president, who found their office, like baseball, a marathon. (Gore joined him, the first time America's top two office-holders attended a professional sports event together.[85]) Clinton, who grew up in Arkansas hearing the Cardinals' Harry Caray over KMOX Radio, was to join Jon on Orioles wireless in the fourth inning. An inning earlier Miller had run to the restroom "just to make sure I was set."[86] The plan exploded when the Secret Service, also assigned security for Al Gore, blocked him trying to leave the restroom for the booth.

"I'm the broadcaster," Jon said. "I'm going to interview the president next inning." The agent said, "I don't think so," making clear he was not a straight man for a Miller ad. "This huge night," Jon mused, "me and the president and the booth might as well be in Boise." Thankfully, another Secret Service agent, an Orioles fan, then appeared. "Hey, let him through!" he said. "He's going to be interviewing the president." Passing agent number one, Miller tried not to rub it in.

Fourth inning: Clinton goes on the air, the count on Cal goes to 3-and-0, and Jon makes a funny. "This night of all nights," he said.[87] "He [Angels pitcher Shawn Boskie] can't be walking Cal, not in this game. Maybe you could send a presidential order down there ordering him to throw Cal a strike." Clinton paused. "I know one thing," the president said. "Cal wants to hit this pitch, but if it's not a strike he'll take the walk for the good of the team because that's the kind of guy he is." Jon: "That's very true. On the other hand, if he [Boskie] grooves one, even on three and oh ..."

"Oh, well," said Clinton, "then Cal'll hit it a long way." At that moment Cal swings – and *boom*! Home run! Jon starts describing it, but Clinton, with his own microphone, began yelling, "Go! Go! Yes! Ah-ha!" The president is clapping his hands, shouting into the mic, and helping to call the homer! What does Miller do? What *could* he do? He couldn't grab Clinton's mic away – so Jon became background noise, his voice almost disembodied.

"The bad news was that it kinda put me off, because this was a major moment in baseball history," Miller continued, tongue in cheek, "but the good news mattered more. He was the president of the United States. The First Fan. He's reflecting the excitement of the night better than any broadcaster could." Plus, Jon thought, "I could now put on my résumé, 'Worked with President Bill Clinton, a very close friend.'"

At the end of the top half of the fifth inning, the game now official, applause rocked the warehouse. Cal repeatedly tipped his cap, Rafael Palmeiro and Bobby Bonilla finally pulled him from the dugout, and Ripken circled the park, high-fiving and handshaking. Many forget the tenor of the age. Clinton fueled eight years of peace and prosperity, but polarization and impeachment left an electorate divided. Ripken became the perfect player in an imperfect time. Clinton and Miller fit like missing pieces in completing a historic night: each then a grand communicator. Depending on the occasion, each could be huckster, reporter, or cornball self. Clinton's Ripken riff drew wide applause, a precursor of his 1996 reelection, pleasing Jon, an admirer of the 42nd president and, as we know, "a very close friend." Next year the president returned to Camden, liking its feel as a "new old" park, to toss a ball a second time.

The O's ended 1995 by blanking Detroit, 6-0, 12-0, and 4-0, to tie the big-league mark of five shutouts in a row set by the 1974 Birds and the 1962-63 Cardinals. Despite the strike, Camden's 3,098,475 gate topped the league the first of four straight times. On October 8 Pope John Paul II celebrated Mass before more than 50,000, the fifth of seven big-league parks to host a papal Mass.[88] The Orioles were not a religion, though they could reward your faith. Earl Weaver hadn't managed in a decade, but his legacy of pitching, defense, and the three-run homer lingered. In May 1996 Hoiles hit a two-out, bases-full, ninth-inning blast to beat Seattle, 14-13 – the bigs' 20th sudden-death grand slam. In July the club hailed Weaver a week later making Cooperstown, unveiling a dugout plaque with his number 4. Eddie Murray, having returned in a midseason trade with Cleveland, later smashed his 500th homer, Birdland happy to again bellow "Ed-die! Ed-die!" An orange right-field seat now signifies the spot.[89]

The '96ers finished four games behind New York in the East, lured 3,646,950, and bombed a big-league-high 257 taters, including a league second-best 50 by Anderson; 39, Palmeiro; 26, Ripken; and 22, Alomar. In the last week Alomar spit at umpire John Hirschbeck, the men in blue vowing to KO postseason if the infielder wasn't suspended. He wasn't, they didn't, and on October 1, 1996, the wild card beat Cleveland in the Division Series, 10-4.[90] After Alomar homered in the final set, O's winning, 4-3, they split LCS Games One and Two in the Bronx. Baltimore then headed home, the series bereft of any home-field edge, New York sweeping,

5-2, 8-4, and 6-4.[91] The 1996 postseason was the Birds' first since 1983. Next year they encored: to that point only the fifth big-league team to lead their division or league wire-to-wire.

With a lot to cheer, many did: to wit, 1997's record 3,711,132. On April 26, Roberto Alomar became the first to go deep thrice, vs. Boston. On May 30 Mike Mussina had a perfect game end with one out in the ninth, blanking Cleveland on one hit, 3-0.[92] Four days later, the O's, rallying, beat the Yankees in 10 innings, 7-5.[93] On August 12, a day after Rex Barney died, Baltimore beat Oakland, 8-0, in a game without a PA announcer. The press-box seat was empty the rest of the year, fill-in PA voices working from the video control room. In his memory a plaque was installed in Rex's old seat with his name, famous "Thank yoouuu!" and old Brooklyn Dodgers uniform number 26.[94] Before October, Randy Myers had a league-best 45 saves. Mussina, a regular-season 15-8, beat Randy Johnson a second time to win the Division Series, 3-1. The O's then dropped the ALCS in six sets despite outhitting Cleveland, .248-.193. You gorged on such Yard favorites as quesadillas and Chesapeake Bay crab cakes – and increasingly, a dozen imported beers when the late '90s introduced a cause to drink – the first of 14 straight years of sub-.500 O's.

The farm system began to dry up. Signings didn't work. The NFL returned to Baltimore as the Ravens in 1996, the same year radio's Jon Miller was not renewed because, as owner Angelos said, "Jon didn't bleed enough black-and-orange" – his leaving, said talk-show host Nestor Aparicio, "an earth-shattering news story in Baltimore."[95] O's success became where you could find it. In 1998 Eric Davis began a club-high 30-game hit streak. In the season's last home game, Ripken, after moving to third base in 1996, ended his streak at 2,632 straight, Ryan Minor subbing. In 1999 Baltimore became the first big-league team to host a Cuban club on US soil. On September 28, 2000, 11 O's either got a hit or scored a run, nine players having an RBI, bombing Toronto, 23-1, for a team record. Next year, they returned to some changes at the Yard: some apparent, some not.

The field had been built to be 16 feet below street level, contain an advanced irrigation and drainage system below grass turf, and cut rainouts by curbing the length of a rain delay. It worked, making the field ready for play within a half-hour after rain ended by automatically removing as many as 75,000 gallons of water in an hour. After the 2000 season, the infield and outfield were rebuilt, replacing the dirt, sand rootzone mix, sod, and drainage. Drainage improved by using an inlaid piping system topped by a fabric mesh and gravel to protect pipes and the playing surface. Later the warning track and sod were replaced, the latter by a darker sand-based blend of Kentucky bluegrass, giving Camden a more vibrant green color.[96] In 2001 players back from offseason found that to rejigger the surface and drainage, the plate had been put seven feet nearer the backstop to lengthen the outfield. This *didn't* work, the batter's-eye wall angle dimming and, refuting forecast, patron sightline not improving: In 2001 original distances returned with only slight alterations.[97]

None of this seemed to affect Cal Jr., whose calendar seemed to stand still, number 8 batting .340 in 1999 with hit 3,000 in 2000. Through good or ill, the Red Sox and Yanks remained the Birds' primo draws. On April 4, 2001, Boston's Hideo Nomo threw a 3-0 no-hitter. That August 11-12, the O's lured 96,785 vs. the Red Sox – Oriole Park's largest two-game series. (Boston also holds the three-game [146,786] and four-game [195,722] record, set in 2007 and 2005 respectively.)[98] On October 6, a decade after leaving Memorial, Ripken Jr. retired, entering Cooperstown in 2007. A dugout plaque was installed for late dad Cal Sr., a scout, coach, manager, and mentor to players and staff for 36 years.[99] His son's 2002 absence was noted, the gate falling more than 400,000 to 2,682,439, under 3 million for the first full season at the Yard. (As usual, most called it Camden Yards, not Oriole Park.) The Oriole Way seemed a way off.

Memorial Day 2003, a monument at the south end of the warehouse on Eutaw Street was dedicated – a lighted 11-foot-tall black granite wall honoring Maryland residents killed in the nation's wars. It contained Memorial Stadium's original lettering, "Time Will Not Dim The Glory Of Their Deeds." Also included: An urn from the old park with soil from all foreign US military cemeteries and a plaque on the Birds' 1954-91 home.[100] 2004: The concrete padded wall backstop yielded to brick. 2005: Baseball returned to DC, the renamed Nationals starting to split the area market. A Red Sox-O's set wooed a still-largest home crowd, 49,828. Recently the nearby Babe Ruth Museum had opened "Sports Legends at Camden Yards" at Camden Station. Its 22,0000-square-foot tour hailed Maryland's major- and minor-league O's, Negro Leagues, Colts and Ravens, college sports – and, of course, Babe. Q: How many times did Ruth hit for the cycle in his career? A: Never. Aubrey Huff became the first Bird to do so at the Yard.[101]

In 2007 Melvin Mora's two-out bases-full bunt single, scoring Tike Redman to beat the Yanks, was redolent of Paul Blair's to win the 1969 ALCS Game One. Next season Baltimore fell to fifth, its first of four years there drawing under 2 million. In August Camden lured its "50 millionth fan" more quickly than any other ballpark and the "100 millionth fan" saw a game there or at Memorial. Each got $50,000 and $100,000, respectively, and season tickets for five years.[102] A year later a newly gilded club level and suites showed Series and ALCS trophies and Gold Glove, MVP, and Cy Young awards[103] -- and a series of orange circles with the numbers inside retired by the team was unveiled on the facing of the left-field upper deck. L to R: Frank Robinson (his number 20 retired in 1972), Brooks Robinson (5, 1977), Earl Weaver (4, 1982), Jim Palmer (22, 1985), Eddie Murray (33, 1998), and Cal Ripken Jr. (8, 2001) – plus a Dodgers blue 42 for Jackie Robinson.[104]

In August 2010 Buck Showalter replaced Juan Samuel as 32-73 O's skipper and won 34 of the season's last 57 games, "turning the worst team in the majors into the AL East's best," wrote Paul Salotaroff.[105] Next September 28, the Orioles, behind with two out and none on in the ninth, shocked the Red Sox, 4-3, to give Tampa Bay, not Boston, a last-day wild card. The 2012 Birds at least temporarily invoked the old Guy Lombardo standard "Seems Like Old Times" to finish second. In his second game, Manny Machado hit two home runs and scored four runs – the first big to get a triple and two homers in his first two sets. On September 26, Baltimore hit seven homers vs. Toronto. All year, 4-foot-tall bronze sculptures were unveiled beyond left-center field of the six Birds with numbers retired by the club, each from 600 to 1,000 pounds, selected and created by sculptor Antonio Tobias "Toby" Mendez of Frederick, Maryland, watching the team play since the 1970s.[106]

That October 5, the Orioles beat Texas in their first wild-card game for a first postseason W since 1997. Three days later, Wei-Yin Chen edged the Yanks, 3-2, in Game Two of the 2012 Division Series, New York prevailing. Chen finished 12-11. Designated hitter Chris Davis bashed 33 home runs, center fielder Adam Jones added 32, and catcher Matt Wieters hit 23. A period reminiscent of past emphasis on fundamentals continued a year later. Jim Johnson became the only pitcher beside Eric Gagne with back-to-back years of 50 saves[107] -- and Baltimore set a big-league record for fewest errors (54), highest fielding percentage (.991), and most errorless games (119).[108] Moved to first base, Davis lashed 53 homers, 138 RBIs, and a .286 average. His outlier was making contact: 199 K's.

In "Long Time Gone," Crosby, Stills, & Nash sang, "It's been a long time comin'." The O's surely felt that winning the 2014 East title, their first in 17 years. Baltimore drew a team-best since 2005's 2,464,473, hit 211 homers, third straight year over 200, but stole just 44 bases, lowest since 1961. Nelson Cruz wed 40 home runs and 108 RBIs. Jones averaged an everyday-player-high .281. Davis batted only .196 with 173 K's in 450 at-bats, 26 homers including the O's' first walk-off pinch-homer in 26 years. Under Showalter, Chen was 16-6, Chris Tillman 13-6, and Bud Norris 15-8. On August 3, Zack Britton's scoreless ninth inning earned his 23rd of 37 saves that season – and set a team high of 35⅓ straight scoreless frames at home.[109]

Five days later the Birds turned 60 by bashing St. Louis, 12-2, with 22 Orioles Hall of Famers, the most gathered at one site, lighting a gala laser show. On September 16 Baltimore clinched its first title at home since 1979. A 12-3 battering of Detroit in the Division Series debut set a postseason team record for runs (eight) in an inning (eighth). Next day, a four-run eighth-inning rally gave the Birds a 7-6 dramaturgy and 2-0 series lead; noise at the Yard deafened. In Game Three, Britton saved Norris's 2-1 decision over David Price: O's sweep. The Birds advanced to the LCS, where they themselves were swept. Kansas City won twice at Camden, 8-6 in 10 innings and 6-4, then interred Baltimore, 2-1, in each game out west.

The AL East Birds, in baseball's best division, were a regular-season seven games better than the weak Central's Royals. Few expected the LCS outcome. Few also thought civic unrest in Baltimore would close the Yard – until it did to ensure public safety for an April 29, 2015, game with Chicago.[110] The home team led off with six runs, Davis and later Machado dinging: O's 8-2, in the first big-league set with a zero crowd. That season the Birds hit a team-record eight homers vs. the Phillies and Gerardo Parra became the 1,000th

Oriole to wear big-league garb.[111] The '15 O's clung to .500, vaulted to second next year, and in 2017 hailed the quarter-century's birth of the park that changed baseball by lauding the 1992 team. Baltimore placed last in 2017-19, hitting a Yards record low 1,307,807 in 2019. Even so, the park's cachet is secure.

It is hard for the historically astute to visit Oriole Park at Camden Yards and not recall Winston Churchill's "[w]e shape our buildings and afterwards our buildings shape us"[112] – the Yards perhaps more than any ballfield since the original Yankee Stadium, shaping the game within. Abraham Lincoln played town ball as president on the White House Ellipse. According to Camden Yards' history, *The Ballpark That Forever Changed Baseball,* Lincoln passed through Camden Station on several occasions, including the railroad journey that took him from Springfield, Illinois to Washington to be inaugurated as president in 1861.

Before Lincoln left the Great Western Railroad Station, he looked at the huge crowd gathered to say goodbye and realized that he knew most as friends and neighbors. Then he spoke poignantly to them in what is known today as the Farewell Address. "To this place, and the kindness of these people, I owe everything," he said. "I now leave, not knowing when, or whether ever, I may return, with a task before me greater than that which rested upon Washington." Lincoln continued, briefly, then concluded, "I bid you an affectionate farewell."[113]

Lincoln left for civil war, death, and history, his funeral car stopping at Camden Station on its 1865 return for his burial in Springfield. Tomorrow is enriched by recalling the timeless ear of yesteryear. Just as Lincoln ennobled America, so Camden Yards, less monumentally but still sublimely, richens baseball.

Sources

Selected games in text were chosen by 2017 fan ballot among the "25 most memorable games in Oriole Park at Camden Yards history." In addition to the sources cited in the Notes, most especially the Society for American Baseball Research, the author consulted Baseball-Reference.com and Retrosheet.org websites' box scores, player, season, and team pages, batting, and pitching logs, and other material relevant to this history. FanGraphs.com provided statistical information. In addition to the sources cited in the Notes, the author also consulted:

Books

Loverro, Thom. *Home of the Game: The Story of Camden Yards* (Dallas: Taylor, 1999).

Koppett, Leonard. *Koppet's Concise History of Major League Baseball* (Philadelphia: Temple University, 2015).

Lowry, Philip J. *Green Cathedrals: The Ultimate Celebration of Major and Negro League Ballparks* (New York: Walker and Company, 2006).

O'Connell, Kevin, and Josh Pahigian. *The Ultimate Baseball Road Trip: A Fan's Guide to Major League Stadiums* (Guilford, Connecticut: Lyons Press, 2012).

Smith, Curt. *Storied Stadiums: Baseball's History of Its Ballparks* (New York: Carroll & Graf, 2005).

Seymour, Harold, and Dorothy Seymour Mills. *Baseball: The People's Game* (New York: Oxford University Press, 1990).

Thompson, Chuck, with Gordon Beard. *Ain't the Beer Cold!* (South Bend, Indiana: Diamond, 1996).

Newspapers

The *Baltimore Sun* has been a primary source of information about Oriole Park at Camden Yards. Other key sources include Associated Press, *Baseball Digest*, the *New York Times*, *SportsBusiness Daily*, *The Sporting News*, and *USA Today*.

Interviews by author

Kenny Albert, September 2008.
Mel Allen, February 1972.
Joe Angel, April 2004.
George H.W. Bush, June 2015.
Tom Davis, June 1998.
Ernie Harwell, May 1983, September 1988, and November 2004.
A. Bartlett Giamatti, December 1988.
Richard Justice, November 1998.
Larry King, June 1992.
Bowie Kuhn, February 1983.
Larry Lucchino, June 1993, December 2010, and March 2011.
Jon Miller, April 1993, November 1995, and December 2007.
Bob Rich, October 2011.
Joseph Spear, January 1988.
John Steadman, February 1985.
Chuck Thompson, June 1986, April 1993, and April 1994.
George Will, April 1989.

• Oriole Park at Camden Yards •

Notes

1. Bowie Kuhn interview, February 1983.
2. Ron Smith, *The Ballpark Book: A Journey Through the Fields of Baseball Magic* (St. Louis: The Sporting News, 2000), 11-14
3. "The Ballpark That Forever Changed Baseball," mlb.com. mlb.com/orioles/ballpark/information/history.
4. Larry King interview, June 1992.
5. Ron Smith, *The Ballpark Book*, 18-19.
6. Joseph Spear interview, January 1988.
7. mlb.com/orioles/ballpark/information/history ("History").
8. mlb.com/orioles/ballpark/information/history ("History").
9. George Vecsey, "Babe Ruth," in Gerald Astor, *The Baseball Hall of Fame 50th Anniversary Book* (New York: Prentice Hall, 1988), 141.
10. George Will interview, April 1989.
11. Kuhn interview.
12. mlb.com/orioles/ballpark/information/history ("History").
13. John Thorn, ed., *Total Baseball 2001* (New York: Total Sports Publishing, 2001), 274, 275, 276, 277.
14. baltimoresun.com/news/bs-xpm-1994-07-01-1994182219-story.html.
15. mlb.com/orioles/ballpark/information/history/milestones.
16. John Steadman interview, February 1985.
17. Mel Allen interview, February 1972.
18. Steadman interview.
19. sabr.org/bioproj/person/7b0b5f10.
20. Ernie Harwell interview, May 1983.
21. Harwell May 1983 interview.
22. baseball-reference.com/teams/BAL/attend.shtml.
23. Chuck Thompson interview, June 1986.
24. nytimes.com/1966/10/10/archives/orioles-triumph-over-dodgers-10-to-sweep-series-frank-robinsons.html.
25. "Analysis of This Year's Orioles," *Sports Illustrated*, April 15, 1957: 57.
26. Steadman interview.
27. Tom Davis interview, June 1998.
28. sabr.org/bioproj/person/4f1fdc5f.
29. baseball-reference.com/teams/BAL/attend.shtml.
30. *Total Baseball 2001*, 353.
31. Jon Miller interview, April 1993.
32. informationcradle.com/mel-proctor/.
33. Richard Justice interview, November 1998.
34. Spear interview.
35. Larry Lucchino interview, June 1993.
36. Lucchino 1993 interview.
37. Lucchino 1993 interview.
38. bentley.edu/news/larry-lucchino-president/ceo-boston-red-sox-delivers-commencement-address-93rd-annual-bentley.
39. azquotes.com/quote/223472.
40. Larry Lucchino, 2001 interview.
41. Spear interview.
42. Bob Rich interview, October 2011.
43. baltimoresun.com/sports/orioles/bs-sp-orioles-camden-yards-0401-20120330-story.html.
44. quoteinvestigator.com/2015/12/18/live/.
45. Joe Angel interview, 2004.
46. Angel interview.
47. mlb.com/orioles/ballpark/information/history/milestones.
48. mlb.com/orioles/ballpark/information/history ("History" and "Sports Legends").
49. Angel interview.
50. nytimes.com/1993/10/03/nyregion/placing-ballparks-in-the-sweep-of-history.html.
51. A. Bartlett Giamatti interview, December 1988.
52. Giamatti interview.
53. populous.com/portfolio.
54. mlb.com/orioles/ballpark/information/history ("History").
55. mlb.com/orioles/ballpark/information/history/milestones. Janet Marie Smith's quote and relevant information on it can be found under the year 2012: "Orioles Celebrate the 20th Anniversary of Oriole Park at Camden Yards."
56. mlb.com/orioles/ballpark/information/history/milestones.
57. Chuck Thompson interview, April 1994.
58. Thompson 1994 interview.
59. Thompson 1994 interview.
60. shmoop.com/quotes/theres-no-crying-in-baseball.html.
61. Davis interview.
62. George H.W. Bush interview, June 2015
63. mlb.com/orioles/ballpark/information/history" ("Firsts").
64. nytimes.com/1992/03/05/garden/design-notebook-field-of-dreams-comes-true-in-baltimore.html.
65. Larry Lucchino interview, December 2010.
66. mlb.com/orioles/ballpark/information/history ("Dimensions").
67. waymarking.com/waymarks/wm11WJV_On_to_Yorktown_Baltimore_MD.
68. Chuck Thompson interview, April 1993.
69. mlb.com/orioles/ballpark/information/history ("Warehouse").
70. Will interview.
71. Davis interview.
72. Bob Brown, senior editor, *1993 Orioles Yearbook: An All-Star Season* (Glen Burnie, Maryland: French Bray, 1993), 17.
73. Jon Morgan, "The wrong glove on the right man," *Baltimore Sun*, June 12, 1995.
74. mlb.com/orioles/ballpark/information/history ("Foul Poles").
75. Jon Miller interview, April 1993.
76. Peter Schmuck, "The First Word," *Baltimore Sun*, July 17, 2008: 3Z.
77. Steadman interview.
78. Kenny Albert interview, September 2008.
79. baseball-reference.com/boxes/BAL/BAL199304220.shtml.
80. mlb.com/orioles/ballpark/information/history/milestones.
81. Rick Vaughn, ed., *1993 All-Star Edition Orioles program* (Baltimore: Stephenson, 1993), 58.
82. baseball-reference.com/teams/BAL/attend.shtml.
83. mlb.com/orioles/ballpark/information/history/milestones.
84. Jon Miller interview, November 1995.
85. mlb.com/orioles/ballpark/information/history/milestones.
86. Miller 1995 interview.
87. Miller 1995 interview. Dialogue and play-by-play of next four paragraphs attributed to him, ending with "very close friend."

• Baltimore Baseball •

88 mlb.com/orioles/ballpark/information/history/milestones.

89 mlb.com/orioles/ballpark/greatest-games (Game 14).

90 *Total Baseball 2001*, 434.

91 *Total Baseball 2001*, 436.

92 mlb.com/orioles/ballpark/greatest-games (Game 16).

93 mlb.com/orioles/ballpark/greatest-games (Game 25).

94 mlb.com/orioles/ballpark/information/history/milestones.

95 wnst.net/top-story/crabs-n-beer/the-peter-principles-ch-5-king-peter-silences-jon-miller-and-anyone-else-who-doesn't-bleed-orioles-orange/.

96 mlb.com/orioles/ballpark/information/history ("Playing field").

97 mlb.com/orioles/ballpark/information/history ("Alterations").

98 mlb.com/orioles/ballpark/information/history/milestones.

99 mlb.com/orioles/ballpark/information/history ("Improvements").

100 mlb.com/orioles/ballpark/information/history/milestones.

101 mlb.com/orioles/ballpark/information/history/milestones.

102 mlb.com/orioles/ballpark/information/history/milestones.

103 mlb.com/orioles/ballpark/information/history ("Improvements").

104 mlb.com/orioles/ballpark/information/history/milestones.

105 web.archive.org/web/20120902004300/http://archive.mensjournal.com/is-this-man-too-smart-for-baseball/print/.

106 sportscollectorsdigest.com/news/yard-birds-stand-tall.

107 mlb.com/orioles/ballpark/information/history/milestones.

108 www.mlb.com/documents/7/9/0/77355790/Notes0529_trjai1mk.pdf.

109 mlb.com/orioles/ballpark/information/history/milestones.

110 mlb.com/orioles/ballpark/information/history/milestones.

111 mlb.com/orioles/ballpark/information/history/milestones.

112 parliament.uk/about/living-heritage/building/palace/architecture/palacestructure/churchill/.

113 "Farewell Address at Springfield, Illinois," February 11, 1861, reprinted in *Collected Works of Abraham Lincoln*, (New Brunswick, New Jersey: Rutgers University Press, 1953, 1990), v. 4, 190.

Blanche McGraw, wife of John McGraw, at American League Park, circa 1902. (See American League Park story on page 43.) Courtesy of David B. Stinson.

Orioles Play Their First Game in Oriole Park at Camden Yards

April 6, 1992: Baltimore Orioles 2, Cleveland Indians 0 at Oriole Park at Camden Yards

By Thomas J. Brown Jr.

A new baseball season was beginning in Baltimore. It brought lots of promise as the Orioles opened their new ballpark at Camden Yards. The ballpark was located in the heart of downtown with the historic B&O warehouse beyond right field and the Baltimore skyline behind that.

It provided a link between the old and new for the city and fans of the Orioles. Mark Kram of the *Philadelphia Daily News* wrote about the Orioles' new home: "On this blessed spot where Baltimore-born Babe Ruth tended bar for his father, where the past and the present are so artfully linked, the imagination is indeed apt to soar."[1]

A crowd of 44,568 poured into the ballpark to watch the Orioles take on the Cleveland Indians. One of them was President George H.W. Bush, who threw out the first pitch. People in the stands hoped that the new ballpark would help to bring back the glory days of Baltimore baseball.

The Orioles finished the previous season with a 67-95 record, sixth in the American League East Division. The Indians were the one team in their division with a worse record. After finishing in the AL East cellar with a 57-105 record, the Indians, like the Orioles, were looking to turn things around in 1992.

Rick Sutcliffe took the mound for the Orioles. The 35-year-old right-hander had signed with the Orioles in the offseason. Baltimore manager Johnny Oates said, "I've seen him pitch in a lot of big games."[2] Oates had pressed the front office to get Sutcliffe because he felt that the young Orioles pitching staff needed the leadership the veteran pitcher could provide.

Sutcliffe was also looking to prove something. He was coming off two years of shoulder problems and there were questions about whether he could be a key part of the starting rotation.

Sutcliffe showed immediately that his arm was still solid. He also exhibited no signs of the food poisoning that had stricken him and seven other Orioles after an exhibition game two days earlier.

Sutcliffe breezed through the first inning, retiring the Indians on 12 pitches. He continued to send the Indians back to the dugout efficiently as the game continued. Paul Sorrento singled in the second and it turned out that he would be the only Cleveland scoring threat all afternoon.

It looked as though the Indians might strike first when Sandy Alomar came to bat with two outs in the second and hit one that looked like a certain double. But Mike Devereaux ran it down and made a challenging over-the-shoulder catch for the third out. Sutcliffe praised his teammate later, saying, "That play [Devereaux] made. I thought the ball was out of here. That was the kind of catch I've seen clips of Willie Mays making."[3]

Cleveland manager Mike Hargrove started Charles Nagy. Although Nagy had finished the previous season with a 10-15 record, he improved his ERA by almost two runs, 5.91 to 4.13 in 1991. His start was briefly jeopardized earlier in the day when Nagy was denied entrance to the ballpark after walking over from his hotel and asking for the ballplayers' entrance.

Nagy also started out strong. Although he surrendered a pair of singles in the second, the Indians defense prevented the Orioles from scoring. He matched Sutcliffe through the first four innings, giving up just three hits and allowing only one Orioles batter to hit the ball out of the infield.

After Sutcliffe got out of his half of the fifth, the Orioles finally got the best of Nagy. With one out he walked Sam Horn and gave up a single to Leo Gomez. Catcher Chris Hoiles then hit the second pitch from Nagy to deep left-center. It bounced on the warning track and went over the wall for a ground-rule double. Horn crossed the plate and the Orioles had their first run. With runners on second and third, Billy Ripken dropped a perfect suicide squeeze bunt down the third-base line. Gomez scored and Sutcliffe had a two-run lead to work with.

"Everybody in the dugout had the feeling that they were going to squeeze," said Nagy after the game. "I

In the first game played at Camden Yards, Rick Sutcliffe shut out the Cleveland Indians, 2-0. Courtesy of the Baltimore Orioles.

tried to throw the pitch up and in to Ripken, but I just didn't get it up and in enough and he got the bat on the ball."[4]

It turned out to be all that Sutcliffe needed. The Indians managed just two more hits against him, a second single by Sorrento in the seventh and a bunt single by Kenny Lofton in the eighth. Cleveland failed to capitalize on either hit.

Sutcliffe got the Indians out in order in the ninth to earn a complete-game victory. He wasted no time and threw just 110 pitches to finish the game in a little over two hours. It equaled the shortest Orioles home opener, played in 1954. Orioles fans were also treated to the first complete game on Opening Day in 20 years. Dave McNally had last accomplished the feat when he beat the Milwaukee Brewers in 1973.[5]

Hoiles praised Sutcliffe's pitching performance, saying, "He knew what he wanted to do. He's got so many different pitches to get a guy out with. He'll show you so many different looks. He knows how to start and finish a hitter and that's what he did all day long. When he needed a big out, he got it."[6]

Nagy didn't let the two runs slow him down. He continued to pitch well and the Orioles mustered only one more hit off him the rest of the afternoon. Hargrove said, "I thought that Nagy was as good as Sutcliffe today. It was a well-pitched game on both sides, but they got the big hit when they needed it. That was the difference."[7]

Hoiles presented the game ball to Sutcliffe as he walked off the field. Sutcliffe gave the ball to Oates, saying, "I wouldn't be here if not for [him]. I can't say enough about the guy. It's his first managing job. It's the first game in this stadium. He put his neck on the line for me. I was just happy for the opportunity."[8]

The Orioles celebrated the win and, with it, hopes for brighter days ahead in their new home. It helped them to forget their embarrassing loss in the final Opening Day at Memorial Stadium the previous season. The win also helped them to push aside their embarrassing loss "when they were crushed by the Detroit Tigers in the emotion-packed season finale"[9] at their old home six months earlier.

Although the team and fans left feeling optimistic about the season, Sutcliffe tried to put it in perspective when he said, "This is going to be one of the great moments for myself and everybody but I haven't proven anything yet. This is just one game. We're 1-0 and we're right where we want to be. But I have to put together a great year – not just a great game."[10]

Author's note

The author attended this game with his sister after witnessing the closing of Memorial Stadium the previous fall. Spring was arriving in Baltimore and the sun was shining as everyone arrived at the Orioles' new home. He fondly remembers the excitement of the fans as they crowded into Camden Yards with hopes that the new ballpark would begin a new era in Baltimore's baseball history.

Sources

In addition to the sources cited in the Notes, the author used the Baseball-Reference.com and Retrosheet.org websites for box-score, player, team, and season pages, pitching and batting game logs, and other material pertinent to this game account.

Notes

1 Mark Kram, "For Old Times Sake Check It Out," *Philadelphia Daily News*, April 6, 1992: 112.

2 Peter Schmuck, "Sutcliffe Makes Grand Opening That Much More So With 2-0 Win," *Baltimore Sun*, April 7, 1992: 35.

3 Schmuck.

4 Sheldon Ocker, "Indians Opener Is for the Birds," *Akron Beacon Journal*, April 7, 1992: D4.

5 Schmuck.

6 Schmuck.

7 Ocker.

8 Schmuck.

9 Schmuck.

10 Schmuck.

Seven Suspended, Five Injured in Worst Brawl in Orioles, Mariners History

June 6, 1993: Baltimore Orioles 5, Seattle Mariners 2, at Camden Yards

By Gary Belleville

Baseball brawls are usually limited to some vigorous pushing and shoving. Punches may be thrown, but few connect. The donnybrook on June 6, 1993, between the Orioles and Mariners, however, was the exception to the rule, with the scene at Camden Yards more reminiscent of an NHL hockey brawl. The dust-up delayed the ballgame for 20 minutes, and when all was said and done, Chris Bosio had broken his collarbone for the second time in less than six weeks, and two of Baltimore's star players had suffered significant injuries.

Bosio took to the hill that day attempting to salvage the series finale for the fifth-place Mariners. The 30-year-old right-hander had inked a four-year, $15 million free-agent contract the previous December, and the signing paid quick dividends for Seattle.[1] Bosio's first win in a Mariners uniform came on April 22 when he fired the second no-hitter in franchise history.[2] His next start was less auspicious: He broke his collarbone in a collision with Cleveland's Jeff Treadway, forcing him to miss over four weeks of action.[3] The start against Baltimore was his second since returning from the disabled list, and he entered the game with a 2-2 record and a 2.59 ERA.

Mike Mussina (7-2, 2.89 ERA) got the start for the sixth-place Orioles. Mussina, 24, one of the best young pitchers in the game, had finished fourth in voting for the American League Cy Young Award the previous season on the strength of an 18-5 record and a sparkling 2.54 ERA.

The two hurlers kept the game scoreless until the bottom of the fourth inning. Mark McLemore led off with an infield single, stole second, and moved to third on a groundball by Cal Ripken Jr. Bosio, still struggling to regain his control after his clavicle injury, uncorked a wild pitch to bring McLemore home with the game's first run. After a walk to Harold Baines, Mike Devereaux hit a two-run homer down the left-field line to put Baltimore up 3-0.

Seattle's regular catcher, 32-year-old Dave Valle, had started the previous 12 games, and so Bill Haselman was inserted into this game's lineup to give Valle some well-deserved rest. Haselman took advantage of the opportunity with one out in top of the fifth inning by driving a 3-and-1 pitch from Mussina over the left-center-field wall to cut the Baltimore lead to 3-1.

In the bottom of the fifth, Bosio raised some eyebrows in the Baltimore dugout by throwing a breaking ball behind McLemore. A few of the Orioles felt that the pitch was in retaliation for Devereaux's home run an inning earlier. The plate umpire, Durwood Merrill, saw things differently, and no warnings were issued.[4] McLemore eventually struck out, and then after Ripken singled, Baines hit a two-run homer to extend the Orioles' lead to 5-1.

Bosio upset the Orioles a second time by throwing a breaking ball behind the back of Harold Reynolds, the first batter in the bottom of the sixth inning. The Baltimore second baseman took exception to the pitch and yelled something in Bosio's direction. Several Orioles believed that the pitch was in response to Baines's home run, yet once again, no warnings were issued by Merrill.[5]

Haselman, who homered in his previous at-bat, came to the plate with two outs and the bases empty in the next half-inning. The first pitch from Mussina was a fastball that struck Haselman directly on the shoulder, and the enraged Seattle catcher immediately charged the mound, with the Orioles backstop, Jeff Tackett, in hot pursuit. Mussina dropped his glove and wrestled with Haselman until the onrushing Tackett tackled Haselman from behind, which knocked Mussina to the ground and caused the two burly catchers to land on top of him. Baltimore's rookie first baseman, Paul Carey, arrived on the scene a split-second later, throwing a punch in Haselman's direction. Both benches emptied and a huge dogpile quickly formed on the mound, as everyone in the bullpens sprinted toward the infield.

The scene descended into chaos with roughly 60 participants engaged in numerous scuffles around the infield. Baltimore's bullpen coach, 52-year-old Elrod Hendricks, even squared off briefly against 25-year-old Tino Martinez. At one point, McLemore wrestled Bosio to the ground and had him in a headlock. Jay Buhner and Seattle bench coach Lee Elia were attempting to extricate Bosio when several combatants fell on top of them. "I heard a 'pop' and a scream from Boz," Elia recounted in a postgame interview.[6] The Mariners pitcher had fractured his collarbone again, nine days after returning from the DL.

Just as things seemed to be calming down, the fighting resumed, and more punches were thrown. Order was finally restored five minutes after Haselman got plunked, and the umpiring crew huddled to determine whom to eject. They agreed that seven players would be tossed: Haselman, Bosio, Norm Charlton, and Mackey Sasser from the Mariners, and Alan Mills, David Segui, and Rick Sutcliffe from the Orioles. Many others could easily have been ejected. "We thought they were the most combative," reasoned Merrill. "Those were the guys who were prolonging it."[7]

Upon learning that Mussina wasn't one of the players ejected, Seattle manager Lou Piniella became incensed, insisting that the Orioles pitcher was responsible for initiating the brawl. Predictably, Piniella was tossed for aggressively arguing the point, causing him to angrily spike his cap to the ground and repeatedly kick dirt on home plate. It was his first ejection in a Mariners uniform, although it certainly wouldn't be his last, as the fiery manager went on to be tossed a total of 28 times in his 10-year stint with the team.

The Mariners were certain that Mussina hit Haselman intentionally. "I felt Mussina would try to hit me. ... But when they throw that high, you're going to go," Haselman said. "But he was throwing strikes all day and putting the ball where he wanted it."[8] "I can't blame my player for going to the mound," Piniella proclaimed. "Mussina told one of our players he was instructed to hit him."[9]

Baltimore manager Johnny Oates did not deny that his pitcher was ordered to plunk Haselman. Asked about it directly, Oates barked, "I'm not talking about that. End of conversation."[10] Hendricks was a bit more forthcoming. "(Bosio) was throwing at us," he said. "It's ugly, but when your players are being thrown at, you have to retaliate."[11]

There were no further incidents once play resumed. In the top of the eighth, Edgar Martínez's sacrifice fly made the score 5-2, and then Gregg Olson pitched a scoreless ninth inning to give the Orioles a sweep of the three-game series.

AL President Bobby Brown suspended all seven of the ejected players, giving the starting pitchers five games, the relievers four games, and the position players three games each. All seven players were fined $1,000 apiece, while Piniella was dinged $450.

Bosio wasn't the only player injured in the melee. Tackett suffered a black eye, and he needed a couple of stitches to close a gash on his right cheek.[12] Baltimore reliever Mark Williamson also ended up with a swollen and bloody nose after being slammed face-first into the ground.[13]

Mussina appeared to escape unscathed, though some began to ask questions after he uncharacteristically surrendered 23 earned runs in his next four starts. Initially, he denied that he was injured in the fight. However, in late July he was placed on the disabled list, and he finally admitted in August that he had aggravated pre-existing shoulder and back injuries in the brawl.[14] Mussina made six more starts that season before he was shut down in mid-September. The shoulder injury continued to plague him for almost two more years.[15]

One other injury went unreported after the game – one with the potential to change baseball history. During the brawl, Ripken slipped on the grass and felt a pop in his right knee, although with the adrenaline still pumping, he was able to finish the game.[16] He iced the knee afterward, thinking that he had nothing more than a minor sprain. The next morning, he rolled out of bed, only to find that he couldn't put any weight on the leg. With a game that evening, Ripken's streak of 1,790 consecutive games played, 340 shy of Lou Gehrig's record, was in serious jeopardy.

An MRI revealed that he had a sprained medial collateral ligament.[17] Ripken underwent treatment on the knee, and as the other Orioles arrived, word started trickling out of the training room that his streak could be over. Players whispered to one another to avoid tipping off the media. After several hours of treatment, Ripken's knee started to feel better. Although he was told that playing that night could result in further damage to the knee, he chose to have the trainer wrap it and take his chances. He played the entire game without incident, and the streak continued. Just over two years later, baseball had a new "Iron Man."

Seven Suspended, Five Injured in Worst Brawl in Orioles, Mariners History

Sources

In addition to the sources cited in the Notes, the author consulted Baseball-Reference.com and Retrosheet.org. Video of the brawl is available on YouTube at youtube.com/watch?v=eYTQE8wUuvw.

Notes

1 Chris Bosio's contract with the Mariners also included a $250,000 signing bonus.

2 Randy Johnson threw the first no-hitter in Mariners history on June 2, 1990. Bosio's no-hitter, against the Red Sox, was the first thrown by a Mariners right-hander.

3 Associated Press, "Seattle Victory Is Costly as Pitcher Breaks Bone," *Deseret News* (Salt Lake City), April 28, 1993. deseretnews.com/article/287842/SEATTLE-VICTORY-IS-COSTLY-AS-PITCHER-BREAKS-BONE.html, accessed July 10, 2019.

4 Jim Henneman, "O's Go Distance to KO Mariners," *Baltimore Sun*, June 7, 1993. baltimoresun.com/news/bs-xpm-1993-06-07-1993158093-story.html, accessed July 10, 2019.

5 Mark Maske, "Orioles, Mariners Brawl for 20 Minutes," *Washington Post*, June 7, 1993. washingtonpost.com/archive/sports/1993/06/07/orioles-mariners-brawl-for-20-minutes/4e87b5e4-6635-46f1-a0ca-794eb8beb317/?utm_term=.6bfcc061568e, accessed July 10, 2019.

6 Journal Wire Services, "Bosio Is Hurt Again," *Milwaukee Journal*, June 7, 1993: C-3.

7 Peter Schmuck, "O's, Mariners Turn Camden Yards Into Brawlpark," *Baltimore Sun*, June 7, 1993. baltimoresun.com/news/bs-xpm-1993-06-07-1993158005-story.html, accessed July 10, 2019.

8 Maske.

9 Henneman.

10 Maske.

11 John Eisenberg, "No Room for Macho in the Win Column," *Baltimore Sun*, June 7, 1993. baltimoresun.com/news/bs-xpm-1993-06-07-1993158092-story.html, accessed July 10, 2019.

12 Maske.

13 Peter Schmuck, "O's, Mariners Turn Camden Yards Into Brawlpark."

14 Peter Schmuck, "Baltimore Orioles," *The Sporting News*, August 23, 1993: 24.

15 Ken Rosenthal, "Stardom Hasn't Changed Mussina," *Los Angeles Times*, April 30, 1996. latimes.com/archives/la-xpm-1996-04-30-sp-64334-story.html, accessed July 10, 2019.

16 John Eisenberg, *The Streak: Lou Gehrig, Cal Ripken Jr., and Baseball's Most Historic Record* (New York: Houghton Mifflin Harcourt, 2017), 174.

17 Eisenberg, 175.

Remembering This Midsummer Classic: A Prodigious Blast and the Boo Birds

July 13, 1993: American League 9, National League 3, at Oriole Park at Camden Yards

By Steven C. Weiner

As much as the All-Star Game is a celebration of baseball's history and a recognition of its current and future stars, it is also a celebration of place, and Oriole Park at Camden Yards played its role perfectly in 1993. The ballpark opened in 1992 as a reminder of classic ballparks of an earlier era, such as Ebbets Field, Shibe Park, and Wrigley Field. Just beyond the right-field fence sits the B&O Warehouse, built in 1899 and standing as the longest building on the East Coast (1,016 feet).[1] The warehouse, transformed into shops, restaurants, and the offices of the Orioles, became the iconic symbol of baseball in downtown Baltimore.

The Home Run Derby was dominated by a pair of 23-year-old sluggers, Juan González and Ken Griffey Jr., as the American League easily won the team competition, 21-12. González won the individual title in a playoff and slugged the longest home run of the competition, 473 feet.[2] But it was Griffey who will long be remembered as the first player to hit the warehouse on the fly, 465 feet away.[3] "Before the event, he said his only chance to hit the warehouse would be if he were standing on second base and using a fungo bat."[4] Not true. SABR biographer Emily Hawks put it simply, "Ken Griffey Jr. possessed the sweetest swing there ever was."[5] The images of a backward-facing Mariners cap, a glistening earring, and a prodigious blast are assured of being lasting memories for many baseball fans. With that one swing, Griffey made the B&O Warehouse a co-star of the show! A baseball-shaped plaque marks the spot, simply stating: Seattle Mariners, Ken Griffey Jr., All Star Home Run Derby, July 12, 1993, 465'.

Starting pitching honors for this All-Star Game went to a pair of lefties, the Phillies' Terry Mulholland (9-6, 2.72 ERA) for the National League and the Angels' Mark Langston (9-3, 2.82 ERA) for the American League. For Mulholland, this was his first and only All-Star Game selection. In 1991 and 1992, he won 16 and 13 games, respectively, and led the National League with 12 complete games in 1992. First named an All-Star in 1987 as a Seattle Mariner, Langston was named to his third successive All-Star squad as a California Angels hurler.

It was the National League that got off to the quick start against Langston. With one out in the first inning, Gary Sheffield's home run followed Barry Bonds' double to right field for a 2-0 lead. Solo home runs by American Leaguers Kirby Puckett in the second inning and Roberto Alomar in the third inning knotted the score at 2-2.

The American League took the lead for good in the bottom of the fifth inning, facing Giants hurler John Burkett (13-3, 3.28 ERA) who was well on his way to a major-league-leading 22 wins in 1993.[6] Iván Rodriguez greeted Burkett with a double to left and advanced to third on a groundout. Successive singles by pinch-hitter Albert Belle and Griffey, sandwiched around an error, plated two runs. Burkett struck out Joe Carter but hit Cecil Fielder. When Kirby Puckett doubled to left, scoring Griffey, the American League led 5-2 and Burkett's night was finished in favor of Steve Avery, who retired Cal Ripken on a groundout.[7]

The National League did score one run in the top of the sixth inning to narrow the deficit to two runs. Bonds doubled to right, advanced to third on Gary Sheffield's single to left, and scored on Barry Larkin's sacrifice fly. However, their offensive response over the final three innings was limited to two hits.

Meanwhile, the American League added to its margin in the sixth inning, sealing the fate of the National League, all with two outs and aided by some shoddy play. With Avery still on the mound, Carlos Baerga reached base on shortstop Jeff Blauser's error and advanced to second on a walk to Albert Belle. A double by Devon White, scoring Baerga, ended Avery's

• Remembering This Midsummer Classic: A Prodigious Blast and the Boo Birds •

night in favor of John Smoltz. Smoltz proceeded to wild-pitch Belle home before walking Juan González. Smoltz also wild-pitched White home before retiring Cecil Fielder on a flyball to left to end the inning. Three unearned runs and an 8-3 lead for the American League. They added one more rather meaningless run in the seventh inning against the Giants' first-time All-Star hurler Rod Beck. Greg Vaughn opened with a single to left. With two outs, Terry Steinbach doubled to right-center, scoring Vaughn and completing the scoring for the night in the American League's convincing 9-3 win.

The most compelling story of the night was not the "game between the white lines" but rather the wrath of the hometown fans that was heaped upon Toronto Blue Jays manager Cito Gaston from the outset of the pregame introductions. Gaston certainly did not endear himself to Orioles fans with his managerial choices for the American League team.

Fans had voted three Toronto Blue Jays to the American League starting lineup – John Olerud, Roberto Alomar, and Joe Carter. Gaston added pitchers Pat Hentgen and Duane Ward, along with Paul Molitor and Devon White, meaning that 25 percent of the AL squad represented the Blue Jays. Baltimore shortstop Cal Ripken was voted by baseball fans to start for the American League, but Mike Mussina was the only other player named to represent the Orioles. Mussina was a 10-game winner, but had been rather ineffective since mid-June.

Several other Orioles with All-Star credentials were ignored, including catcher Chris Hoiles, batting .300 at the break, and reliever Gregg Olson, 23 saves and a 1.24 ERA at the break. "The top half of the AL lineup looked as if it had been lifted out of the SkyDome: Four of the game's first five AL batters were Blue Jays."[8]

So what happened to Mussina? Gaston said he intended to use one of his closers in the ninth inning.[9] Pat Hentgen recalled the conversation Gaston had with him and Mussina. "You guys are young. You're going to come back to another All-Star Game," Hentgen recalled 25 years later. "I am not going to pitch either one of you today. I am going to hold you guys off and see if we go extra innings."[10]

When Gaston brought in Blue Jays closer Duane Ward to pitch the ninth, Mussina had already decided he needed some work so he started warming up on his own in the bullpen. The hometown crowd knew only one thing and they chanted, "We want Mike." The booing aimed at Gaston continued well after the third out by Ward ended the game.[11]

There was no lack of reaction to what happened on this night at Camden Yards. Most didn't mince words. Frank Robinson, Orioles assistant general manager, said, "I'm disappointed in the fan reaction. I don't think it's right."[12] Some saw anger when they awoke the next morning to the day's blunt headline in the sports section of the *Toronto Star* – "Jays Power American Attack, Abuse of Gaston, Jays, Pathetic Performance by Baltimore Boobirds."[13]

Some tried to be diplomatic in their own way. The usually reserved Cal Ripken got excited: "I wanted to get into it, yell and scream, come on, bring Mussina in for the last out."[14] Later, *The Sporting News* gave its "Low Lights" award to Gaston for roster selection in addition to the failure to put Mike Mussina into the game.[15]

SABR biographer Ryan Brecker noted that Gaston and Mussina later made up so perhaps it is best that the last word is left for Gaston's actions one year later.[16] Gaston managed the American League in the 1994 All-Star Game in Pittsburgh. He selected Mussina and Hentgen for his pitching staff. Indeed, Mussina came in to pitch the fifth inning for the American League, retiring the side after a leadoff single by Dante Bichette, Gaston brought Hentgen in to pitch the seventh inning. He kept his word!

Author's note

Whatever happened to the baseball that hit the B&O warehouse? It sits at the Babe Ruth Birthplace and Museum, only blocks from where it came to rest when a 17-year-old high-school senior, Mark Pallack, found himself at the bottom of a pile with a baseball in hand.[17] Pallack later served on the board of directors of the museum.

Yes, the game itself did provide a lighter moment despite *The Sporting News* editor John Rawlings' observation that "anecdotal evidence conveys basebrawl is at an all-time high."[18] Laughter broke out in the National League dugout after Randy Johnson's first-pitch fastball to John Kruk in the top of the third inning sailed directly over Kruk's head. What was he thinking on the next pitch – a huge, tantalizing curveball? Never at a loss for words, Kruk responded, "I was thinking about hitting righthanded, that's what. If he was going to hit me, he was going to have to hit a moving target. ... My life was at stake."[19] Kruk meekly struck out.

Sources

The author accessed Baseball-Reference.com for box scores/play-by-play information and other data, as well as Retrosheet.org. A video of the CBS television broadcast of the game is available for interested readers and researchers.[20]

Notes

1 Josh Leventhal, *Take Me Out to the Ballpark* (New York: Black Dog & Leventhal Publishers, 2000), 39.

2 Milton Kent, "Longest Day for Griffey Gonzalez/Jr. Hits Warehouse; Juan Goes 473 Feet," *Baltimore Sun*, July 13, 1993.

3 "1993 Home Run Derby: Griffey Crushes Home Run Off Warehouse," YouTube.com, accessed July 22, 2019, youtube.com/watch?v=_iwebCJ_pJ8.

4 Kent.

5 Emily Hawks, "Ken Griffey Jr.," SABR Baseball Biography Project, sabr.org/bioproj/person/3e8e7034.

6 Burkett, Tom Glavine (Atlanta Braves) and Jack McDowell (Chicago White Sox) all won 22 games in 1993.

7 Kirby Puckett's RBI double in the fifth inning to go along with his solo home run in the second inning earned him the game's most valuable player award.

8 Mark Hyman, "Gaston and His Blue Jays Left Booed but Unbowed," *Baltimore Sun*, July 14, 1993: 7D.

9 Ken Rosenthal, "Cito Takes Care of His Kids Right to the End," *Baltimore Sun*, July 14, 1993: 1D.

10 David Singh, "Hentgen Recalls Front-Row Seat to '93 Gaston-Mussina All-Star Spat," Sportsnet.ca, July 17, 2018, accessed August 3, 2019, sportsnet.ca/baseball/mlb/hentgen-recalls-front-row-seat-93-gaston-mussina-star-spat/.

11 Peter Schmuck, "Manager Booed over Mussina," *Baltimore Sun*, July 14, 1993: 1D.

12 Hyman.

13 Dave Perkins, "Jays Power American Attack, Abuse of Gaston, Jays Pathetic Performance by Baltimore Boobirds," *Toronto Star*, July 14, 1993: E1. Boo bird is defined as "a fan given to jeers, boos, and catcalls when the home team falters." Paul Dickson, *The Dickson Baseball Dictionary*, 3rd Edition (New York: WW Norton & Company, 2009), 126.

14 Rosenthal.

15 "Openers," *The Sporting News*, July 26, 1993: 5.

16 Ryan Brecker, "Mike Mussina," SABR Baseball Biography Project, sabr.org/bioproj/person/d79f7a98.

17 Jayson Jenks, "Warehouse Shot in 1993 Home Run Derby Helped Fuel Ken Griffey Jr.'s Legend," *Seattle Times*, July 22, 2016, accessed July 28, 2019, seattletimes.com/sports/mariners/warehouse-shot-in-1993-home-run-derby-helped-fuel-ken-griffey-jr-s-legend/.

18 John Rawlings, "No Use Battling a Problem That Doesn't Exist," *The Sporting News*, July 26, 1993: 13. Basebrawl is defined as "a fight among baseball players, triggered by an event such as a batter charging the mound after being hit by a pitched ball." *Dickson Baseball Dictionary*, 77.

19 Rawlings.

20 "1993 MLB All-Star Game," YouTube.com, accessed July 19, 2019, youtube.com/watch?v=n-Nyz6CuOEk.

"Unbreakable" Record Passes: Gentleman to Gentleman

September 6, 1995: Baltimore Orioles 4, California Angels 2, at Oriole Park at Camden Yards

By Ralph Peluso

The outcome of this game was of little importance to the fans of two cities separated by less than 200 miles. The New York Yankees' record was mediocre, a pedestrian 60-61, only slightly better than that of the 56-65 Baltimore Orioles. Fans, players, and media focused on one thing. Fifty-six years earlier, Lou Gehrig, the Iron Horse, had removed himself from the lineup after playing 2,130 consecutive games. It was arguably a record that could speak more about perseverance than pure baseball skill. Now, in a game in which numbers are heralded, the baseball world watched as a new number readied to take its place on the altar of adoration. The night before, iron man Cal Ripken Jr. met Mr. Gehrig at 2,130; this evening, Ripken moved on.[1]

Robert Janes, a Vietnam veteran, strolled into Camden Yards from Eutaw Street. He gazed at the numbers across the red brick warehouse. "When this game is official, they'll change that last digit to a one. Ripken and Baltimore can call this hallowed record ours!" The not-so-veiled joy in swiping another record from the New York franchise evident, he laughed, "Nah, Gehrig was a class act."[2]

The pregame atmosphere was different. The usual competitive edge and enmity was absent. Lou Gehrig played the game and conducted his life with great dignity and professionalism. Even at the moment he understood his outlook was grim, Gehrig let the baseball world know he was thankful and fortunate for the life he had.[3] Ripken possessed similar qualities: integrity, character and humility. The mantle of longevity set to pass from one gentleman to another.

When the record you're about to break spans 14 years, it's not easy to put your finger on the moment the pressure eases. For Ripken, that occurred the night of the game. He was healthy, his name penciled onto the lineup card. In the surreal atmosphere, he was able to enjoy the moment, accepting the disruption of his pregame ritual. Hundreds of well-wishers greeted him. He handled a lengthy interview under the stands gracefully. Luminaries, including President Clinton and Vice President Gore, offered their congratulations and in return each received an autographed ball and a warm-up jacket. The warm outpouring of congratulations from world-class athletes overwhelmed Ripken. Gifts nearly filled the clubhouse. The most touching moments for Ripken, perhaps, came when Baltimore Colts legend Johnny Unitas and the man who surpassed Babe Ruth's career home-run record, Hank Aaron, presented him with their jerseys.[4]

His record-breaking moment required Ripken to just show up, play, and let the game become official. Pressure built in the final few days before the record-setter. *Just don't get hurt.* As Ripken and his Baltimore teammates took the field, nervous energy evaporated. All that was left was for the teams to complete five innings of play, unless Baltimore led after the top of the fifth.

With two outs in the top of the first, Tim Salmon homered, giving the Angels the lead. Rafael Palmeiro matched him with a homer to right field in the bottom of the frame. In the bottom of the fourth, the game still tied, Bobby Bonilla led off. With a 1-and-1 count his sweet swing sent Shawn Boskie's pitch sailing to deep center. This disrupted TV commentator Chris Berman's wordy comparison of Gehrig and Ripken as homegrown heroes playing for the teams they loved: "Edmonds turns back back back back back gone." The ballpark erupted. The Orioles took the lead and fans understood the significance. Once the cheering stopped, Ripken stepped to the plate. Boskie's first three pitches were narrowly off the strike zone. The ever-disciplined Ripken laid off. Thousands of lights flashed with each pitch. Cal readied for the next offering. Boskie served up a fastball letter-high and slightly inside. Ripken turned on it quickly, ripping the ball into the left-field stands. "Ripped to left, oh my goodness he has done it again," Berman exclaimed.

• Baltimore Baseball •

Ticket to Cal Ripken Jr.'s consecutive game #2,131. Courtesy of the Babe Ruth Museum.

"Did anyone expect Cal to limp into this streak, this record-breaking night?" Berman noted that Ripken had homered in three straight games. Icing on the cake. The Orioles lead extended to 3-1.[5] Just three outs in the top of the fifth and the game was official. As long as the Angels did not score two or more runs.

Mike Mussina took the hill. Rex Hudler hit a soft popup near the left-field line, an easy out. Jorge Fabregas, the Angels catcher who two days earlier created consternation among Orioles fans with his hard slide into Ripken. (Cal shrugged the incident off as no big deal.) He respected players who play hard. On a full count, Fabregas hit a soft three-hopper to second, an easy out. Only Damion Easley stood in the way of history. Manny Alexander drifted back into short right and squeezed the soft fly into his glove, igniting the unprecedented midgame on-field celebration that erupted. Relief for the Orioles nation, friends, and family.

The record-breaking effort that began on May 30, 1982, continued.[6] Dramatically, "2,131" was unveiled, black and orange balloons released. Fans screamed joyously. Players clapped. Ripken, after handshakes with teammates and modest waves with his hat to the crowd, jogged to his family for hugs and kisses, after handing his hat to his wife and the "shirt off his back" to daughter Rachel.[7] He disappeared into the Orioles dugout. Fans kept on cheering. Reappearing after a few minutes in a fresh jersey, he took a seat on the bench ready to play. The fans kept on cheering. Finally, at the insistence of teammates he sheepishly walked back onto the field, waved with both hands, and patted his heart twice. Then he returned to the bench.

The fans continued to clap and cheer. In unison they chanted repeatedly, "We want CAL!" Once again Cal took the field, waved modestly, touched his heart, and returned. Boskie stood on the mound but did not move to begin his warm-ups. Ripken smiled as Bobby Bonilla and Rafael Palmeiro pushed him out onto the field. He hesitated, then slowly strolled down the right-field line. As he circled the field, he shook the hands of hundreds of fans. Arms extended to touch him. Like Gehrig in his farewell speech, Ripken connected with everyone. He thanked all: groundskeepers, ballboys, coaches, and policemen. Reaching the Angels dugout, he greeted everyone. Hall of Famer Rod Carew, the team's hitting instructor, hugged him, as did ex-teammate Rene Gonzales. Twenty minutes had elapsed. Ripken saw the clubhouse attendant Butch Barnett in tears. They hugged.[8]

Some athletes may have wanted to cherish the moment and remove themselves from the game. Not Cal Ripken: He played on. Perhaps he knew the man with steely blue eyes, who set the tone for his family looking down proudly at his son, Cal Ripken Sr. and his wife, Viv, expected nothing different.[9]

The game continued. With two out in the bottom of the fifth, Ripken came to bat with the bases loaded. Another storybook ending was not to be. He hit a soft liner that appeared to have a chance to drop, but second baseman Hudler made a one-handed over-the-head grab, ending the threat. The final four innings proved anticlimactic.

Joe DiMaggio, among others, offered a postgame tribute. Generally referred to as the greatest living player of all time when introduced, tonight DiMaggio was introduced simply as the Yankee Clipper. A hush fell over the park as DiMaggio stepped to the microphone to say, "Wherever my former teammate, Lou Gehrig, is today, I'm sure he's tipping his cap to you, Cal."[10]

Ripken delivered a "heart-tugging speech," thanking those who played an important part in his life as well as the fans. "Tonight, I stand here,

• "Unbreakable" Record Passes: Gentleman to Gentleman •

overwhelmed, as my name is linked with the great and courageous Lou Gehrig," Ripken said. "This year has been unbelievable. I've been cheered in ballparks all over the country. People not only showed me their kindness, but more importantly, they demonstrated their love of the game of baseball. I give my thanks to baseball fans everywhere."[11]

On April 26, 1920, when Everett Scott passed George Pinkney at 578 consecutive games, the game was played in front of fewer than 5,000 fans.[12] There was no postgame accolade. On August 17, 1933, Gehrig passed Scott at 1,308, in a game with sparse attendance at Sportsman's Park in St. Louis. Edgar G. Brands, publisher of *The Sporting News,* handed the Iron Horse a commemorative trophy in a modest postgame recognition.[13]

On September 20, 1998, Ripken walked into Ray Miller's office and announced to his manager that he "wanted out of the lineup," ending his consecutive-game streak at 2,632. Ryan Minor and Babe Dahlgren, the Ripken and Gehrig replacements respectively, are inexorably linked for all time as a footnote to these great accomplishments.[14]

Lou Gehrig's Yankee Stadium monument inscription reads, "an amazing player whose record of 2,130 consecutive games played should stand for all time." Most likely for Cal Ripken, 2,632 will.

Sources

In addition to the sources cited in the Notes, the author consulted Baseball-Reference.com.

Notes

1 Claire Smith, "After 2,130 Games, Mr. Ripken Meets Mr. Gehrig," *New York Times,* September 6, 1995: A1.

2 Interview with Robert Janes, September 11, 2019.

3 "Gehrig Farewell Speech," *Sports Illustrated,* July 4, 2009.

4 Vic Ziegel, "Cal Steps into the Record Book with Style as He Breaks Lou Gehrig's 'Iron Man' Record in 1995," *New York Daily News,* September 7, 1995. nydailynews.com/sports/historic-rip-cal-steps-history-books-style-article-1.2017702.

5 Chris Berman and Buck Martinez, *ESPN Baseball Game of the Week*, September 6, 1995. "Ripken's 2,131 Celebration with Original Broadcast. Uploaded onto YouTube May 17, 2016 VHS Classics, https://www.youtube.com/watch?v=djCqNPPBkB4

6 Jim Reineking, "To Celebrate the 35th Anniversary of the Start of Cal Ripken's Streak Here are Some Fun Facts," *USA Today*, May 30, 2017. https://www.usatoday.com/story/sports/mlb/2017/05/30/cal-ripken-consecutive-games-streak-fascinating-facts/102281920/

7 Scott Zucker, "Ripken Breaks Gehrig Record," UPI News, September 6, 1995. https://www.upi.com/Archives/1995/09/06/Ripken-breaks-Gehrig-record/6449810360000/

8 Buster Olney and staff reporter, "2,130: With the Streak Second to None, Cal Trots into Record Books," *Baltimore Sun*, September 7, 1995. https://www.baltimoresun.com/sports/orioles/bal-2-131-with-streak-second-to-none-cal-ripken-jr-trots-into-record-books-20150830-story.html

9 Buster Olney and staff reporter.

10 Richard Justice, "Ripken Reaches Magic Number," *Washington Post*, September 6, 1995: B1.

11 "Cal speaks after 2,131st game," September 6, 1995. Uploaded to You Tube November 5, 2014 MLB Videos. https://www.youtube.com/watch?v=dEAOQc7hWIA

12 Billy Evans, "Everett Scott Plays in 1000th Game Today," *Miami News*, May 2, 1923.

13 James P. Dawson, "Gehrig Sets Mark as Yankees Lose," *New York Times*, August 18, 1933: 11.

14 Roch Kubatko, "Calling His Own Number Ripken Ends Streak," *Baltimore Sun*, September 27, 2001.

Cal Ripken Jr. plays in his 2,131st consecutive game. Courtesy of the Baltimore Orioles.

Hoiles Hits a Walk-off Grand Slam

May 17, 1996: Baltimore Orioles 14, Seattle Mariners 13, at Oriole Park at Camden Yards

By Matt Clever

When manager Lou Piniella's Mariners opened a weekend series in Baltimore on Friday night, May 17, 1996, it presented a matchup of two ballclubs on the rise. Seattle came in with a record of 21-18, after reaching the postseason for the first time in franchise history the year before. Led by the sweet swings of Ken Griffey Jr., Edgar Martinez, and Alex Rodriguez, they had scored a whopping 5.92 runs per game to this point in 1996 (despite being no-hit by Dwight Gooden three days earlier in New York).

The Orioles had not been to the playoffs since 1983. But they had spent big money after the 1995 season, bringing in free agents including second baseman Roberto Alomar to join their beloved shortstop Cal Ripken Jr., and they entered this contest just 1½ games behind the New York Yankees in the AL East. Like Seattle, the Orioles featured a powerful offense and a below-average pitching staff.

Rookie right-hander Jimmy Haynes allowed only an infield single by Griffey in a scoreless first inning. His counterpart, fellow rookie Bob Wolcott, was not as sharp in the bottom half of the frame. Center fielder Brady Anderson ripped a leadoff double, then scored on a home run off the bat of Luis Polonia and it was 2-0, Baltimore. The Orioles loaded the bases with one out, but Wolcott escaped further damage by getting Ripken to ground into a force out at the plate, then retiring catcher Chris Hoiles on a fly out.

The Orioles added two more in the second, when a leadoff walk to Jeffrey Hammonds and a one-out single by Polonia set the stage for Rafael Palmeiro's two-out, two-RBI double off the top of the wall in right-center.[1] But the Mariners got those two runs right back in the top of the third on a hit by Darren Bragg, a ringing double by Griffey, and a line-drive single by Martinez. Then it was Haynes's turn to strand the bases loaded, when he got second baseman Joey Cora on a groundball handled by Alomar.

Baltimore knocked Wolcott out of the game in the third. After a single by Ripken and a one-out double by Hammonds, veteran southpaw Joe Klink came on and struck out Anderson. When right-handed-hitting Mike Devereaux pinch-hit for Polonia, the Mariners brought in right-hander Bob Wells, who issued back-to-back walks to force the fifth Orioles run home, then gave up a two-run single to Palmeiro to make it 7-2.

Haynes held that lead through the fourth and fifth innings, retiring the Mariners' Cora with the bases loaded again on his final pitch. He left the mound confident that he was about to earn his fourth major-league win. Unfortunately for Haynes, Arthur Rhodes, who took over in the top of the sixth, surrendered two runs on three hits and a walk before Roger McDowell was summoned to relieve him. A throwing error by Alomar allowed Rodriguez to score to make it a 7-5 game, and then third baseman B.J. Surhoff's throwing error on a single by Dan Wilson made it 7-6. McDowell got Cora to fly out to end the inning. It was the third straight at-bat in which Cora made the third out with multiple runners aboard.

Cora was involved in another ignominious play in the bottom of the sixth, on a ball hit by Surhoff. As Buster Olney described it for the *Baltimore Sun*: "Surhoff was running to first base … when Cora's off-balance throw drilled him in the left ear. Surhoff, staggered by the throw, stepped awkwardly and turned his ankle inward."[2] Surhoff was credited with a single, but had to leave the game.

In the seventh, McDowell gave up hits to Rodriguez and Griffey, but he struck out Martinez to preserve the 7-6 lead. The sellout crowd of 47,529 at Camden Yards was jubilant as they stood for the seventh-inning stretch. They were even more so when a few minutes later Palmeiro stroked a two-run homer off Scott Davison – Palmeiro's fifth hit of the game, to go along with six RBIs. Orioles 9, Mariners 6.

But the Mariners' offense would not go down quietly. Three straight hits off McDowell to open the

• Hoiles Hits a Walk-off Grand Slam •

eighth cut the lead to 9-7, with runners on first and third. Cora hit a soft groundball that McDowell fielded and flipped home in time for Hoiles to put the tag on Seattle's Paul Sorrento for the first out of the inning. Jesse Orosco emerged from the bullpen to get the second out.[3] Alan Mills entered the game to face pinch-hitter Brian Hunter, and walked him to load the bases for Rodriguez.

Rodriguez was blossoming in 1996, at the age of 20, on his way to his first All-Star Game appearance and his only AL batting title. And on this comfortable May evening in Baltimore, with the bases loaded and two out in the top of the eighth, he blasted a grand slam to give Seattle the lead, 11-9. The hometown fans were stunned to silence.

Ripken, who was extending his record by playing in his 2,192nd consecutive game, reawakened the crowd with an eighth-inning solo homer off Mike Jackson to bring the O's back within a run, 11-10.

There was presumably no doubt in Piniella's mind about which of his relievers he would entrust to finish off this victory. Norm Charlton had helped Piniella win the World Series with the Reds in 1990. Over the next five seasons, the mullet-topped left-hander got traded, and released. He underwent Tommy John surgery[4] and then was hit in the face by a line drive shortly after returning.[5] But he had been dominant for the Mariners down the stretch in '95, a key contributor to their AL West championship. When Piniella handed him the ball with two out in the bottom of the eighth on May 17, Charlton was the undisputed anchor at the back end of the bullpen, with a 1.69 ERA and a team-high five saves so far in 1996. He walked Anderson, but retired Mike Devereaux for the third out.

Despite having so epically coughed up the lead in the eighth, Mills took the mound again to pitch the ninth inning for Baltimore. Some fans headed for the exits after the Mariners' Jay Buhner drilled a two-run homer to extend the score to 13-10. Those who remained would be rewarded in the bottom of the ninth.

Alomar drew a leadoff walk. Charlton struck out Palmeiro – the only time he was retired all night. But Bobby Bonilla delivered a hard-hit double into left, sending Alomar to third and bringing the tying run to the plate. The next man up was light-hitting utility infielder Jeff Huson, who had replaced the injured Surhoff. Manager Davey Johnson scanned his bench in search of a pinch-hitter who could knock one out of the park. But having already called upon Devereaux, the best option Johnson had was Bill Ripken, who fouled out, bringing up his elder brother representing Baltimore's last hope. Cal worked a walk (Charlton's second of the inning and third of the game) to keep the Orioles alive and load the bases for Hoiles.

Chris Hoiles was never an All-Star. He never hit 30 home runs in any season. Never won a Gold Glove. But he certainly had a flair for the dramatic during his 10-year career, spent entirely with the Orioles. His first big-league home run had been a walk-off shot at old Memorial Stadium in 1990. The following year he had hit a game-tying grand slam in the ninth inning of a game at Kansas City. In '95 his ninth-inning homer won a game at Chicago. And on May 17, 1996, he stepped to the plate against Charlton with three on, two out, and his team down by three in the bottom of the ninth. And, fittingly, he worked the count full, giving all three runners a head start. And then Hoiles lifted a hanging forkball just beyond the outstretched glove of a leaping Brian Hunter, into the first row of seats near the 364-foot marker on the left-field fence, for that most dramatic hit conceivable – a walk-off grand slam.

"Those who are still here at Camden Yards are just berserk! You've never seen a scene like this!" exclaimed broadcaster Jon Miller as Hoiles' teammates gathered around home plate to pummel him in celebration when he arrived.[6]

This improbable 14-13 win stands out as one of the most memorable highlights of the Orioles' 1996 season, when they brought playoff baseball to Camden Yards for the first time.

Sources

In addition to sources cited in the notes, the author consulted Baseball-Reference.com and Retrosheet.org.

Notes

1 Peter Schmuck, "O's, Hoiles Out-Slam Seattle, 14-13/2-out Shot in 9th Answers Mariners' Grand Rally in 8th; Teams Combine for 41 Hits; Orioles Had Blown 7-2 Lead; Palmeiro has 6 RBIs, Ripken 4 Hits," *Baltimore Sun*, May 18, 1996. baltimoresun.com/news/bs-xpm-1996-05-18-1996139044-story.html.

2 Buster Olney, "Surhoff, Huson Put on 15-day DL, Strange Mystery Plays Sideline O's Infielders," *Baltimore Sun*, May 19, 1996. baltimoresun.com/news/bs-xpm-1996-05-19-1996140079-story.html.

3 This was Orosco's 834th career appearance on the way to the major-league record of 1,252.

4 Jerry Briggs, "Tenacious Charlton Developed a 'Nasty' Reputation," *San Antonio Express-News*, January 27, 2013. mysanantonio.com/news/local_news/article/Tenacious-Charlton-developed-a-nasty-reputation-4226660.php.

5 Don Bostrom, "Nasty Boy Charlton Bounces Back After Pitcher's Nightmare," *Allentown* (Pennsylvania) *Morning Call*, May 29, 1995. mcall.com/news/mc-xpm-1995-05-29-3033109-story.html.

6 MLB, "SEA@BAL: Jon Miller Calls Hoiles' Walk-off Grand Slam," *YouTube*, July 11, 2017, youtube.com/watch?v=rD_y6BAF07w

Eddie Murray Clouts 500th Career Home Run During Rainy Evening

September 6, 1996: Detroit Tigers 5, Baltimore Orioles 4 (12 innings), at Oriole Park at Camden Yards

By Gordon Gattie

Excitement filled the Baltimore air in early September as the Orioles fought for a playoff spot. They had last played postseason baseball in 1983, when they defeated the Philadelphia Phillies in the World Series. During the ensuing 12 seasons, the Orioles finished above .500 six times but consistently missed the playoffs. After an August in which they shaved six games off the AL East-leading New York Yankees' lead, the Orioles tussled with the Chicago White Sox, Seattle Mariners, and Boston Red Sox for the lone wild-card slot. Entering September, the Orioles were tied with Chicago for the spot.[1]

Baltimore was an offensive powerhouse, breaking their season record of 214 home runs with still a month remaining in the season. Brady Anderson exceeded the 40-homer plateau, Rafael Palmeiro passed number 30, and five additional Orioles topped 20. During the summer, Baltimore added more power by acquiring veteran Eddie Murray. Murray started his career with Baltimore, playing first base from 1977 to 1988. After stints with the Los Angeles Dodgers, New York Mets, and Cleveland Indians, he returned to Baltimore on July 21, 1996, when Cleveland traded him to the Orioles for Kent Mercker and cash. Baltimore shortstop Cal Ripken Jr. praised Murray's return: "To me, he's a positive on the field and in the clubhouse. … To me, he carries himself very professionally and does his job."[2] The trade was unpopular among Cleveland players, with Kenny Lofton echoing accolades: "Eddie Murray means so much to this team. Everyone here was looking forward to seeing him hit his 500th homer, and see him do it in Cleveland. I guess Baltimore's going to get that thrill now."[3]

Murray slumped during late August, hitting career homer number 498 on August 16 at Oakland, then getting only eight hits and zero homers in 42 at-bats over the next two weeks. He insisted he wasn't pressing to reach the notable milestone: "I haven't really been trying to hit homers. I might've had pitches to hit, and I missed them. … When you're trying to hit them, you don't."[4] Murray hit round-tripper number 499 on August 30 at Seattle. Baltimore had four more road matchups before a seven-game homestand.

Exactly one year after Ripken broke Lou Gehrig's consecutive-games streak in Baltimore, the Orioles opened a four-game series against the 50-90 Detroit Tigers. The Tigers struggled all season, posting 9-18 April and 4-23 May records to firmly plant themselves in the AL East cellar. The offense was led by outfielder Bobby Higginson and the pitching staff by Omar Olivares. Heading into their Baltimore series, Detroit's leadership focused on the positives, with team President John McHale commenting, "The team looks a lot better than it did in June."[5]

Baltimore manager Davey Johnson chose David Wells for the hill. The veteran was spending his first season with the Orioles; on December 26, 1995, Baltimore had sent Curtis Goodwin and minor-leaguer Trovin Waldez to Cincinnati in exchange for Wells.[6] Halfway through his career, Wells fired a mid-90s fastball complemented with a big curve or changeup when needed, though he was prone to allowing homers.[7]

Detroit manager Buddy Bell selected Felipe Lira to face Baltimore. The youngster was pitching in his second major-league season, and was 6-12 with a 5.35 ERA over 175 innings. He joined Detroit's rotation halfway through his rookie season and became their most reliable starter during a challenging 1996 season. Lira's effectiveness relied more on movement and changing pitch speeds than outright velocity. His hard-cutting fastball ran away from left-handed hitters, though he occasionally struggled with his command.[8] Entering this contest, Lira had lost his last five decisions.

Eddie Murray Clouts 500th Career

The game was scheduled for a 7:35 P.M. start, but a 2-hour and 20-minute rain delay caused by Hurricane Fran meant the game didn't begin until just before 10 P.M. Wells was ready for the matchup; he struck out Detroit leadoff hitter Kimera Bartee and Mark Lewis looking, then struck out Travis Fryman swinging. In the bottom half, Lira retired Baltimore in order.

The Tigers collected the game's first hit when Ruben Sierra delivered a second-inning infield single; after Tony Clark struck out, the inning ended on a 5-4-3 double play. The Orioles scored first when Palmeiro homered on a 2-and-0 offering in their half of the inning. Murray, who was lifetime 0-for-7 against Lira, made his first appearance with two outs and walked on five pitches. B.J. Surhoff singled as Baltimore threatened to build upon its lead, but Chris Hoiles grounded into a fielder's choice as Lira escaped the jam.

In the third inning, Phil Nevin evened the score when his blast reached the left-field seats. Wells experienced trouble when Phil Hiatt and Brad Ausmus singled and Bartee's sacrifice moved them into scoring position. Hiatt scored on Lewis's groundout. Fryman struck out, but now Detroit led 2-1. In the bottom half, Anderson was hit and took third on Todd Zeile's double to left. Alomar flied out to deep center; Anderson scored and Zeile moved to third. Neither Palmeiro nor Bonilla hit the ball out of the infield as the game remained tied 2-2.

Sierra started the fourth inning by hitting a single to right field. He advanced to second when Melvin Nieves grounded out, then scored on Nevin's single to left as the Tigers inched ahead, 3-2. In the bottom half, Murray appeared for the second time and grounded out on a spectacular play by Tigers shortstop Fryman.[9] After the initial flurry of long balls in the early innings, the teams each managed one baserunner midway through the seventh inning.

Ripken started the bottom of the seventh with an infield groundout. Approaching midnight and with about 25,000 still present, Murray stood in the batter's box for his third appearance. On the first pitch, Murray launched Lira's split-fingered fastball into the right-field bleachers for career home run number 500. Murray joined an exclusive club with that clout, as only Hank Aaron, Willie Mays, and Murray were 500-homer, 3,000-hit club members. Murray received an 8½-minute ovation and multiple curtain calls as the crowd celebrated his achievement. Baltimore's front office was prepared for the occasion with streamers, video clips, and scoreboard graphics; however, Murray's teammates were completely taken off guard when the moment actually happened and rushed to greet their slugger at home plate.[10] The quiet superstar clearly appreciated the celebration, shaking hands with several fans and friends, commenting afterward, "It was nice to see everybody get fired about it."[11] Once the fanfare settled down, a groundout, walk, and strikeout ended the inning with a 3-3 score after seven innings.

Leadoff hitter Higginson, pinch-hitting for Bartee, immediately quieted the enthusiastic crowd by depositing a pitch by Alan Mills into the bleachers as Detroit regained the lead. Mills retired the next three batters and the Orioles needed a rally. Baltimore responded with two singles surrounding a strikeout, bringing Bobby Bonilla up with one out and runners on the corners. Bonilla's sacrifice fly scored Zeile and the game was tied, 4-4. Ripken ended the threat by flying out.

Orioles closer Randy Myers relieved Mills for the ninth inning and allowed no runs. Murray faced José Lima to start the bottom half as the crowd cheered for a dramatic ending. Murray lined out, Surhoff struck out, Hoiles singled (then was replaced by pinch-runner Manny Alexander), and Anderson walked as Baltimore threatened again with runners on first and second. Zeile hit into a fielder's choice, and the game headed into extra innings.

In the 10th inning, both teams placed a runner at first who advanced no further. During the next frame, each team went three up and three down as the clock moved past 1 A.M. In the 12th inning, Detroit pressured Orioles reliever Terry Mathews with two consecutive one-out walks. Mathews rallied to strike out Ausmus on five pitches. Higginson foiled Baltimore again by driving in Nevin on a center-field single. Curtis Pride was caught stealing home in a daring attempt as the Tigers attempted to pad their lead. In the bottom half, John Cummings, pitching his third inning, retired Anderson and Zeile, and then walked Alomar. Palmeiro popped out to second on Cummings's first pitch, and Detroit emerged with a 5-4 victory.

The Orioles finished 88-74, second in the AL East and as the wild-card winner. They defeated the Indians in the AL Division Series before losing to the Yankees in the Championship Series. Murray completed the 1996 season with Baltimore, hitting .260 with 22 homers and 79 RBIs, and finished his career the following season, splitting time between the Anaheim

Angels and the LA Dodgers. Over his 21-year career, the switch-hitting Murray played in 3,026 games and delivered 3,255 hits, including 504 homers, and 1,917 RBIs. Murray was praised for his consistency; he often appears on "Best of the 1980s" lists at first base.[12] He appeared defensively at first base 2,413 times, the most in baseball history. Murray was elected to the National Baseball Hall of Fame in 2003, receiving 85.3 percent of the votes, in his first year of eligibility.[13]

Sources

Besides the sources cited in the Notes, the author consulted Baseball-Almanac.com, Baseball-Reference.com, Retrosheet.org, and the following:

2019 Baltimore Orioles media guide

James, Bill, and Rob Neyer. *The Neyer/James Guide to Pitchers: An Historical Compendium of Pitching, Pitchers, and Pitches* (New York: Fireside Books, 2004).

Thorn, John, and Pete Palmer, et al. *Total Baseball: The Official Encyclopedia of Major League Baseball* (New York: Viking Press, 2004).

Notes

1 Buster Olney, "O's, Johnson Go Distance, 7-6," *Baltimore Sun,* September 1, 1996: 1D.

2 Buster Olney, "O's Bring Home Murray, 10-6 Win," *Baltimore Sun,* July 22, 1996: 1C.

3 Olney, "O's Bring Home Murray, 10-6 Win."

4 Buster Olney, "Home Nice, but Murray Wants 500th," *Baltimore Sun,* September 1, 1996: 6D.

5 John Lowe, "McHale Echoes Team's More Positive Vibrations," *Detroit Free Press,* September 6, 1996: 7C.

6 Peter Schmuck, "Orioles Round Out Rotation With Wells," *Baltimore Sun,* December 27, 1995: 1C.

7 "David Wells" in Josh Dewan and Don Zminda, eds., *The Scouting Notebook 1996* (Skokie, Illinois: Stats, Inc. Publishing, 1995), 425.

8 "Felipe Lira," in Dewan and Zminda.

9 John Lowe, "Murray Hits 500th Deep Into Night," *Detroit Free Press,* September 7, 1996: 7B.

10 Jason LaCanfora, "500th is Spontaneous Joy to O's," *Baltimore Sun,* September 7, 1996: 7D.

11 Peter Schmuck, "Murray Hits No. 500," *Baltimore Sun,* September 7, 1996: 1.

12 James, Bill. *The New Bill James Historical Abstract* (New York: The Free Press, 2001), 302.

13 Laura Vecsey, "Hitting the Hall," *Baltimore Sun,* January 9, 2003: C1.

Mike Mussina Retires 25 Straight While Firing Brilliant One-Hitter

May 30, 1997: Baltimore Orioles 3, Cleveland Indians 0, at Oriole Park at Camden Yards

By Gordon Gattie

The Baltimore Orioles were flying high as June 1997 approached. The 34-15 Orioles carried the AL's best record, and a 7½-game lead over the New York Yankees in the AL East Division, into a two-game weekend showdown against the AL Central-leading Cleveland Indians. Baltimore opened the 1997 season with a four-game winning streak and maintained the division lead since Opening Day. The Orioles were building upon the previous season's success, when they finished second in the AL East and defeated Cleveland in the Division Series before losing to New York in five games in the Championship Series.

Baltimore boasted a powerful offense, hitting a record 257 home runs in 1996,[1] led by Brady Anderson (50), Rafael Palmeiro (39), and Bobby Bonilla (28). Their starting infield all hit at least 20 homers apiece and four Orioles topped 100 RBIs. After the season, the club shifted its focus from offense to pitching and defense,[2] adding veteran pitcher Jimmy Key, slick-fielding shortstop Mike Bordick, and key bullpen components, while losing Bonilla, Eddie Murray, and Todd Zeile to free agency.[3] Embattled second-year manager Davey Johnson, who had the best record among active major-league managers entering the season, was excited about Baltimore's changes and its playoff prospects. Although his reputation as a controversial figure preceded his arrival in Baltimore, Palmeiro noted his clubhouse demeanor: "I saw him as arrogant. But when I got a chance to play for him, I saw he has a lot of respect for players. I'd call him a players' manager."[4]

The 27-22 Cleveland Indians, managed by Mike Hargrove, led the Milwaukee Brewers by 3½ games in the AL Central Division. The Indians had dominated the division for the past two seasons but wanted to atone for their disappointing ALDS loss in 1996. The ballclub had solid offense, bullpen depth, infield defense, and bench strength, though the starting rotation wasn't deep.[5] The offense was led by future Hall of Famer Jim Thome, but table-setter Kenny Lofton and slugger Albert Belle departed during the offseason.

Mike Mussina, Baltimore's ace and that evening's starting pitcher was among the top five pitchers in Cy Young Award votes for three consecutive years. A Gold Glove winner and three-time All-Star, he established career highs with 243⅓ innings and a team-record 204 strikeouts during 1996.[6] The veteran developed a varied pitching repertoire, throwing a two-seam fastball, four-seam fastball, knuckle curve, cut fastball, overhand curve, changeup, and slider.[7] Mussina entered the matchup with a 6-1 record and 4.26 ERA over 63⅓ innings. He won three of his previous four starts, including a victory at Cleveland six days earlier when he struck out a season-high nine in seven innings. Mussina frequently struggled against Cleveland; the win was only his third against the Indians in nine decisions. After his victory, he commented, "The last two times I pitched here, the playoff game and this game, were probably the best two games I've thrown against Cleveland in a while, especially in this ballpark [Jacobs Field]."[8]

Charles Nagy started for Cleveland. The Indians ace and 1996 All-Star compiled a 6-2 record and 3.82 ERA in 77⅔ innings. His last appearance was against the Orioles in Cleveland, the night after Mussina's win. He had allowed three runs in seven innings. Three times Baltimore had rallied to tie the score but never pushed ahead.[9] Nagy relied on a sinker, slurve, splitter, and changeup to disrupt hitters' timing.[10]

A sellout crowd of 47,759 watched Mussina waste no time attacking Cleveland's vaunted lineup, which entered the game leading the majors with 77 home runs and a third-best .290 batting average.[11] Mussina struck out leadoff hitter Marquis Grissom, induced a Julio Franco groundout, and struck out Thome looking.

Nagy immediately encountered trouble. Leadoff hitter Anderson doubled down the right-field line. Roberto Alomar beat out a bunt and Anderson went to third. Palmeiro hit a looping single into right field, scoring Anderson with the game's first run. Cal Ripken Jr. grounded out on a high chopper for the first out, but both runners moved into scoring position. Jeff Newman, managing for Hargrove who was attending his daughter's high-school graduation,[12] issued a rare first-inning intentional walk to B.J. Surhoff, opting to face Pete Incaviglia. Surhoff was hitting .387 in 31 at-bats against Nagy, while Incaviglia was 2-for-7.[13] The decision worked: Nagy struck out Incaviglia and Tony Tarasco to escape the inning.

Mussina quickly retired the Indians on three groundouts in the second inning. Nagy retired the Orioles on two groundouts and a strikeout. In the third inning, Mussina set down Cleveland on two strikeouts and a fly out by ninth-place hitter Omar Vizquel, who was the first Indians batter to reach the outfield.

Roberto Alomar started the home half of the third with a single to second baseman Tony Fernandez and went to second of Fernandez's wild throw. Palmeiro's groundout sent Alomar to third, and Alomar scored on Ripken's fielder's choice. Surhoff followed with a fly out and Incaviglia struck out again as Baltimore moved ahead 2-0 after three innings.

The Indians struggled against Mussina; in both the fourth and fifth innings, they mustered two groundouts and a strikeout. Nagy matched Mussina's effectiveness, though not his dominance, as the Orioles managed one hit in the fourth inning and loaded the bases in the fifth on two walks and a hit batsman. They failed to score in either inning. Mussina appeared increasingly overpowering in the sixth inning, retiring the Indians on a pop fly and two strikeouts. While walking toward the dugout after striking out Vizquel to end the inning, he received a semi-standing ovation as the crowd sensed a special game unfolding.

Chris Hoiles led off the Baltimore sixth with a single to shortstop and went to second on Vizquel's wild throw. Bordick grounded out to first and Hoiles reached third. Anderson singled into center, scoring Hoiles for a 3-0 lead. Anderson eventually took third on a stolen base and groundout, but was stranded on a popout.

In the seventh Grissom became only the second Indian to reach the outfield on a batted ball when he flied out to right field. Mussina continued piling up groundouts, as both Franco and Thome grounded out to second. Baltimore's ace walked off to an increasingly louder ovation as the fans rose for the seventh-inning stretch. Baltimore threatened again in the bottom half when Surhoff's single and Tarasco fielder's choice put two Orioles on base with one out. But Nagy stifled the threat, getting a fly out and a groundout.

Mussina retired the Indians on a popout and three fly outs during the eighth inning. Through eight innings he had remained perfect, retiring all 24 Indians hitters. Paul Assenmacher relieved Nagy in the bottom of the inning. Nagy had allowed three runs (one earned) in seven innings. Anderson grounded out, then Roberto Alomar singled to center, his third hit in the game. He was caught stealing in a "strike 'em out, throw 'em out" double play.

Fans rose to their feet as the ninth inning began: Mussina was pitching a perfect game so far. Fernandez, leading off, worked the count to 3-and-1, then grounded out to second. The next batter was Sandy Alomar Jr., Roberto's brother. Mussina was two outs from becoming the first Oriole to pitch a perfect game. On a 1-and-1 pitch, Mussina threw a fastball slightly up in the strike zone on the inside part of the plate; Cleveland's catcher laced a single into right field, ending Mussina's bid to hurl a perfect game and become the first Orioles pitcher to throw a no-hitter since 1969.[14] After Alomar singled, the crowd gave Mussina a rousing ovation. Mussina completed the shutout by striking out the next two batters, pinch-hitter Brian Giles and Grissom.

Baltimore's ace pitched a masterpiece though he didn't think he had pitched better than in previous starts. Mussina commented, "The whole game I was really amazed I was still in that situation. I haven't been in that situation in 12 or 15 years. It was kind of strange, but every time I went out there, they made three outs in a row."[15] Cleveland's hitters complimented their mound opponent; Sandy Alomar Jr. said, "He pitched an outstanding game. He had everything going – fastball, curveball, changeup. He was perfect."[16]

Mussina threw 115 pitches in the game during his brilliant performance; 77 were strikes. He struck out 10 hitters and induced 11 groundouts and six outs on fly balls or popups. His second career one-hitter increased Baltimore's lead over New York to 8½ games. A few weeks later he became a four-time All-Star. He completed 1997 with a 15-8 record and a 3.20 ERA in 224⅔ innings. Baltimore's ace finished sixth in AL Cy Young Award voting, won his second Gold Glove, and was fourth in the league with a career-high 218 strikeouts.

Sources

Besides the sources cited in the Notes, the author consulted Baseball-Almanac.com, Baseball-Reference.com, Retrosheet.org, and the following:

"Charles Nagy," in Dewan, John, and Don Zminda, eds., *The Scouting Notebook 1996* (Skokie, Illinois: Stats Inc. Publishing, 1995), 130.

James, Bill. *The New Bill James Historical Abstract* (New York: The Free Press, 2001).

McCarver, Tim, and Danny Peary. *Tim McCarver's Baseball for Brain Surgeons and Other Fans* (New York: Villard Books, 1998).

"Mike Mussina," in Dewan, John, and Don Zminda, eds. *The Scouting Notebook 1996* (Skokie, Illinois: Stats, Inc. Publishing, 1995), 37.

Thorn, John, and Pete Palmer, et al. *Total Baseball: The Official Encyclopedia of Major League Baseball* (New York: Viking Press, 2004).

Notes

1 As of 2020 the Minnesota Twins held the record, with 309 home runs in 2019.

2 Jason LaCanfora, "Decision Time Is Looming For O's," *Baltimore Sun,* November 8, 1996: 49.

3 Peter Schmuck, "Offensively Speaking, Here's a New Dimension," *The Sporting News,* March 31, 1997: 73.

4 Mike Littwin, "Lightning Rod?" *Baltimore Sun,* April 1, 1997: 39.

5 Steve Herrick, "If the Team Has Health, It Will Have Everything," *The Sporting News,* March 31, 1997: 76.

6 *1997 Baltimore Orioles Information and Record Book* (Baltimore: Baltimore Orioles, LP, 1997), 121.

7 Bill James and Rob Neyer, *The Neyer/James Guide to Pitchers: An Historical Compendium of Pitching, Pitchers, and Pitches* (New York: Fireside Books, 2004), 219.

8 Roch Kubatko, "Mussina Slips Cleveland's Punch," *Baltimore Sun,* May 25, 1997: 39.

9 Joe Strauss, "O's Have Wild Time Losing to Indians," *Baltimore Sun,* May 26, 1997: 29.

10 James and Neyer, 320.

11 Kubatko, "Baffled Indians 'Tip Hat' to Ace," *Baltimore Sun,* May 31, 1997: 38.

12 Kubatko, "Baffled Indians": 31.

13 Schmuck, "1-Hit Mussina Almost Perfect," *Baltimore Sun,* May 31, 1997: 37.

14 Schmuck, "1-Hit Mussina."

15 Ken Rosenthal, "Place Earned in Fans' Hearts, if Not History," *Baltimore Sun,* May 31, 1997: 37.

16 Kubatko, "Baffled Indians": 31.

The Quiet Night at Camden Yards

August 12, 1997: Baltimore Orioles 8, Oakland Athletics 0, at Oriole Park at Camden Yards

By Peter Coolbaugh

The regular season was starting to wind down. The Orioles had just returned from a nine-game road trip out west and were looking to add to their AL East lead as the Oakland A's came to town. But for the crowd of 46,925 on that warm August night, something was very different.

Longtime Orioles public address announcer Rex Barney was found dead that morning. He was 72 years old. The former Brooklyn Dodgers pitcher had been the Orioles PA announcer full-time since 1974. Despite health issues in later years that occasionally caused him to miss games, Barney's voice and personality were a fixture in Baltimore for decades.

A native of Omaha, Barney was signed by Brooklyn at the age of 18. Enlisting in the Army in 1943, Barney served in Europe, where he won two Purple Hearts and a Bronze Star. He eventually returned to the Dodgers, going 35-31 over his career. Known as a hard thrower, he suffered from control problems throughout pitching his career, which ended in 1950. He did throw a no-hitter against the Giants at the Polo Grounds on September 9, 1948.

"I'll go through the rest of my life knowing I didn't become as good as I should have been," he told a *Baltimore Sun* writer in 1989. "I had so much potential, and I just didn't live up to it."[1]

Barney worked his way up the radio ladder in different cities after his career ended. He came to Baltimore in 1965 and had a sports talk show on the radio until he became the full-time announcer for the Orioles at Memorial Stadium. His trademark phrases "thannnnk yoooooouu" and "give that fan a contract" (after catching a foul ball) were legendary.

Before the Athletics game got underway, Orioles broadcaster Chuck Thompson spoke to the capacity crowd and a tribute to Rex was played on the scoreboard. In his spot that night, a replacement microphone, a scorebook, and a Brooklyn Dodgers hat occupied his space. The crowd applauded when his empty chair was shown after the fifth inning and numerous fans held back tears as a plaque was unveiled in the press box. Barney's regular microphone was donated to the Babe Ruth Museum for safekeeping as it was a part of Orioles history. The entire game was played without a public address announcer. To know who was up next or if there were any defensive substitutions, you had to pay attention to the scoreboard.

The Orioles jumped out to a 4-0 lead in the bottom of the first. A three-run homer by Rafael Palmeiro was a highlight.

Scott Erickson dominated for Baltimore. He gave up just three hits, struck out eight, walked one. The shutout was his 14th win of the season.

The Orioles added to their lead in the second, fifth, and sixth innings. As a team they were 11-for-32 in the game, led by Palmeiro, who had been in a slump, but went 3-for-4. Center fielder Brady Anderson extended his hitting streak to 11 games.

Although the entire game was a tribute to Rex Barney, it was not without some other drama. In the sixth inning, with Baltimore up 7-0, Orioles second baseman Jeff Reboulet stole second. Managers Davey Johnson and Art Howe apparently traded some shots from the dugout over the necessity of the steal. When Reboulet came up to bat in the eighth, A's reliever Dane Johnson threw behind him, causing both benches and bullpens to empty twice. Reboulet was ejected for fighting and Oakland catcher Brent Mayne was ejected for arguing brushback.

Said Johnson after the game, "I don't like for anybody dictating to me when I've got to quit trying to score. That gets me hot." Johnson later added, "I mean, I am in a pennant race."[2]

With the Orioles 73rd win, they increased their AL

The Quiet Night at Camden Yards

East lead to 5½ games. The Orioles had won 15 of 19 games on their way to a 98-win season and a division title. They made it to the ALCS after their wire-to-wire regular season and fell to the Cleveland Indians. The team drew more than 3.7 million fans during the season, a franchise record, and then began a steady decline. The Orioles would not get over .500 again until 2012 when they won the wild card and fell to the Yankees in a five-game series.

Beyond the score and the fight, the game is remembered for the quiet, a tribute to a beloved voice that was no more. The newspapers the next day carried several articles reflecting on the life and the impact of Barney.

Hall of Fame pitcher Jim Palmer, an Orioles broadcaster said, "Baseball loses a great friend. He was always there for me, so easy to talk to, like having my own shrink, so gentle, compassionate and kind. I feel robbed."[3]

Fans felt the loss too; many had grown up with Barney's voice since the 1970s. The Orioles used fill-in announcers for the remainder of the regular season and postseason until a permanent hire was made in 1998. But for many in the stands and on the field, the signature voice could never be replaced.

Said former Orioles pitcher Mike Flanagan, "His voice was a like a security blanket. Being announced by Rex always gave me a quiet confidence, almost like the voice of a baseball god. He made you feel everything would be all right."[4]

After 1997 it would be 15 years before Orioles fans would feel all right again.

The author was present that evening, viewing the game from his seats in Section 312 down the right-field line. It was his third-ever game at Oriole Park at Camden Yards.

Rex Barney. Courtesy of the Baltimore Orioles.

Sources

In addition to the sources cited in the Notes, the author also consulted Baseball-Reference.com, MLB.com, and Retrosheet.org.

Notes

1 "Rex Barney, Voice of Orioles, Dies at 72; Ex-Dodgers Pitcher Served as Stadium Announcer Since 1974," *Baltimore Sun*, August 13, 1997: 1.

2 Erickson 3-Hits A's in 8-0 Romp," *Baltimore Sun*, August 13, 1997: 5D.

3 "Rex Barney, Voice of Orioles, Dies at 72."

4 "Rex Barney, Voice of Orioles, Dies at 72."

Jeff Reboulet Delivers LDS to Baltimore

October 5, 1997: Baltimore Orioles 3, Seattle Mariners 1, at Oriole Park at Camden Yards

By Joseph Wancho

The Baltimore Orioles returned to the postseason for the second straight season in 1997. They did it in style, winning the American League East championship by two games over the New York Yankees.

There was some bitterness from the season before when Baltimore met the Yankees in the LCS. In Game One, at Yankee Stadium, the Orioles were clinging to a 4-3 lead heading into the bottom of the eighth inning. With one out, Derek Jeter lifted a fly ball to right field. Tony Tarasco, who had just come into the game, went back to the wall to make the catch. But a fan reached over the wall attempting to catch the ball. The fan made contact with the ball, which caromed into the stands. Right-field umpire Richie Garcia ruled the play a home run, when clearly, at least from the Orioles' perspective, the ball should have either been caught for an out or the batter called out for fan interference. Orioles skipper Davey Johnson argued the call, or no-call in this instance, and was ejected by Garcia. The Yankees went on to win, 5-4, in 11 innings.

Although the Orioles came back to win Game Two, the Yankees swept the Orioles in the next three games at Camden Yards. The Orioles felt that a 2-0 lead going home would have made a huge difference in the series. And to lose Game One by such a blatant no-call, the Orioles felt, would gnaw at the club and its fans the whole offseason.

But the 1997 season was a new chapter and the Orioles beat the Yankees eight out 12 times. The Yankees secured the wild-card berth and it looked as though the Orioles might get another shot at their longtime nemesis in the postseason.

But the Orioles would need to get past the Seattle Mariners in the Division Series to get another shot at the Yankees. New York was pitted against AL Central champion Cleveland in the other Division Series.

Beating Seattle was going to be a tough hurdle to overcome. The Mariners beat out Los Angeles by six games in the AL West. They were a hitting machine, featuring six players with 20 or more home runs. They were led by Ken Griffey Jr. (56 home runs, 147 RBIs, and a .304 batting average). He was later named the league's MVP by the baseball writers, and the major leagues' MVP by *The Sporting News*.

Game One of the LDS at the Kingdome was a matchup of future Hall of Famers. Randy Johnson (20-4, 2.28 ERA, 291 strikeouts) took the hill for Seattle, facing Baltimore's Mike Mussina (15-8, 3.20 ERA, 218 strikeouts). Mussina went seven strong innings, giving up two earned runs and whiffing nine, while Johnson went five innings and surrendered five earned runs. The Orioles broke the game open when they scored four runs in the fifth and sixth innings, and coasted to a 9-3 victory.

The 9-3 score also prevailed in Game Two. Scott Erickson started for Baltimore and went 6⅔ innings. His counterpart for Seattle, Jamie Moyer, was not as fortunate and went 4⅔ innings. Each pitcher gave up three earned runs, and the outcome was left in the hands, and arms, of the bullpens. Brady Anderson's two-run home run in the seventh and a four-run eighth by the Orioles broke the game wide open for Baltimore.

The series shifted to Camden Yards for Games Three, Four, and Five. In a battle of left-handers, Seattle's Jeff Fassero outdueled the Orioles' Jimmy Key, and the Mariners put a hold on their winter holiday with a 4-2 win. Solo home runs by Jay Buhner and Paul Sorrento provided the margin of victory for Seattle.

Game Four was a rematch of the starters for Game One. The 48,766 in attendance badly wanted a win, but it was a tall order indeed. Johnson wasn't given the moniker the Big Unit for no reason. The 6-foot-10 left-hander was as good as they come. Would the Orioles be able to beat him a second time in a short series? The Baltimore fans were licking their chops

• Jeff Reboulet Delivers LDS to Baltimore •

in anticipation of a rematch with the Yankees. "Fate will have us play the Yankees," said Orioles fan Paul Quattrochi. "Last year we got ripped off."[1]

The Mariners failed to score in the top of the first inning, and up to bat came the Orioles, Johnson whiffed Anderson to start the frame. Jeff Reboulet stepped into the batter's box. He was starting at second base in place of Roberto Alomar. The switch-hitting Alomar was nursing a strained shoulder, making it difficult to swing right-handed against Johnson.

As the afternoon sun cast shadows around home plate, Reboulet just looked for a pitch to hit. He found one and sent the baseball over the left-field wall for a home run and a 1-0 lead. "I just kind of looked for a good pitch to hit," said Reboulet, "just trying to get a strike and put the bat on the ball and take a good swing. I don't even know if it was in or out or where it was. I was just trying to react to it."[2]

While Reboulet's homer brought some fireworks, the Orioles were not finished. Geronimo Berroa followed with a double to right field. Johnson fanned Eric Davis, but Cal Ripken Jr. singled to right field to score Berroa and the Orioles led 2-0 after one inning.

The Mariners sliced the Orioles' lead in half when Edgar Martinez homered off Mussina to begin the second inning.

Jeff Reboulet kicked off the scoring with a solo home run in the bottom of the first inning. The O's went on to win, 3-1, for a Game Four win that gave Baltimore the American League Division Series. Courtesy of the Baltimore Orioles.

The two hurlers then took over the game, mowing down the opposing lineup. Johnson was especially effective. He shook off the first inning and responded with seven strike outs in the first four innings. He made it nine when he whiffed the first two batters in the bottom of the fifth, but Berroa extended the O's lead to 3-1 with a home run to right field. "I don't know how I hit that fastball," said Berroa. "At that time of day, there are a lot of shadows and you can't even see the ball. I got lucky."[3]

Mussina set down the Mariners in order in the sixth and seventh innings, then Davey Johnson turned matters over to the bullpen. Armando Benitez worked a scoreless eighth inning. Randy Myers, who led the AL in saves with 45 during the regular season, did what he got paid to do. Seattle went down 1-2-3.

The final score was Baltimore 3, Seattle 1. The Orioles were going back to the ALCS. Mussina went seven innings, giving up two hits, striking out seven, and walking three. "Mike is such a great pitcher, I knew he'd give me a quality start," said manager Johnson. "Mike rose to the occasion. He just pitched a great game. I've never seen him pitch bad in a big game."[4]

His counterpart was no slouch. Randy Johnson pitched eight innings, striking out 13. "I'd like to congratulate Baltimore for a great year," said Seattle manager Lou Piniella. "The Orioles have been the dominant team in the league all year, and that was reflected in this series."[5]

But the celebration by the Orioles was short-lived. They did not get another shot at the Yankees, as the Indians defeated New York in five games. Cleveland also got the best of the Orioles, beating them in six games to win the AL pennant, their second in three years.

Sources

In addition to the sources cited in the Notes, the author consulted Baseball-Reference.com and Retrosheet.org.

Notes

1 Kate Shatzkin, "Orioles Fans Craving Rematch with Yankees," *Baltimore Sun*, October 6, 1997: 5D.

2 Roch Kubatko, "By Any Unit of Measurement, Reboulet Gives Johnson Fits," *Baltimore Sun*, October 6, 1997: 3D.

3 Kent Baker, "Berroa Stock Soars Against R. Johnson," *Baltimore Sun*, October 6, 1997: 5D.

4 Peter Schmuck, "O's Win; AL Series Next," *Baltimore Sun*, October 6, 1997: 6A.

5 Schmuck.

Cal Ripken's Consecutive Game Streak Comes to an End

September 20, 1998: New York Yankees 5, Baltimore Orioles 4 at Oriole Park at Camden Yards

By Thomas J. Brown Jr.

A standing-room crowd of 48,013 showed up at Camden Yards for Baltimore's final home game of the 1998 season. When the gates opened, the scoreboard showed a lineup that was familiar to them. It included Cal Ripken, batting sixth and playing third base, the position he had occupied for the past three years.

But unbeknownst to fans, the scoreboard was not accurate. Ripken had walked into manager Ray Miller's office 30 minutes before the teams were to take the field and told him, "It's time." The decision was one that only Ripken could make, so 16 years after Earl Weaver started him, he decided to let go and end one of the most impressive records in baseball history.

Ripken said after the game that he and his wife had talked and decided that he should end the streak in front of a home crowd. "It was important for us to do it here," Ripken told reporters. "Right here in Baltimore, right here in Camden Yards. And make it a celebration."[1]

Ripken had broken Lou Gehrig's consecutive-game record of 2,130 on September 6, 1995. The Orioles beat the California Angels, 4-2, that night in front of a home crowd. As soon as the final out was made in the top of the fifth, marking it as an official game, orange and white balloons were released into the night air.

Ripken was pushed back on the field by his teammates, who told him, "[W]e're not getting this thing going again until you take a lap. They physically grabbed me, threw me out there. And during the first part of that lap, I said 'OK, I'll just do it really quick.'"[2]

Once the record was broken, there were questions about whether Ripken should continue the streak. Some members of the Baltimore organization said he should end it to get some rest and allow other players to get additional playing time.

Ripken always deferred to his managers, saying it was their decision. But his managers always disagreed, leaving the decision to Ripken. Davey Johnson, the Orioles manager in 1995-1996, said that "only Cal or God can end the streak."[3]

Ripken did not seem affected by the streak. Some had argued that his defensive range had diminished. Yet Ripken had made only eight errors this season, leading American League third basemen. Others said he wasn't hitting the way he had in the past. But Ripken adjusted his swing constantly. He batted .279 in the 50 games before this last game against the Yankees, leading Miller to move him up in the batting order.[4]

Miller picked Ryan Minor to start in place of Ripken. Minor had been called up from the Class-A Bowie Baysox 11 days earlier. Minor made his debut on September 13 when he got a pinch-hit single batting for Harold Baines. When Miller told him about the start, his first reaction was, "Does [Cal] know?"[5] When he saw Ripken in the dugout a short time later, Minor told him, "Thanks for the opportunity." Ripken's response was: "Go get 'em."[6]

Many in the crowd didn't notice the last-minute change in the lineup. New York Yankees manager Joe Torre said later, "I just had a sense that something was happening because Cal wasn't doing his usual pregame throwing. He was sitting over there, waiting like a possum for something to happen."[7]

Doug Johns, who had mostly come out of the bullpen for Baltimore during the season, was given the start. Chuck Knoblauch led off for the Yankees and grounded out to shortstop.

At this point the entire Yankees team stepped out of the dugout and tipped their caps to Ripken as fans rose to their feet to give him a standing ovation. "We wanted to do something for him," Yankees catcher Joe Girardi said. "What he has done is absolutely amazing, and we owed it to him."[8]

After his second curtain call, Ripken motioned to Johns to pitch. Derek Jeter singled and went to third

• Cal Ripken's Consecutive Game Streak Comes to an End •

when Chili Davis doubled to center field. Johns got out of the jam by striking out Jorge Posada for the third out.

Johns wasn't so fortunate in the second. Chad Curtis walked with one out. He landed on third when Mike Lowell singled to right field. Curtis scored one batter later when Luis Sojo hit a line-drive single through a hole in the left side of the infield. Although Johns walked Jeter to load the bases with two outs, he got Bernie Williams to fly out to center field, limiting the Yankees to one run.

Johns pitched well through the next two innings. But the Yankees crossed the plate again in the fifth inning. After Williams and Posada singled, Tim Raines doubled to left, scoring Williams. Miller replaced Johns with Pete Smith who got the next two batters out.

Meanwhile, Orlando Hernandez, the Yankees starter, kept the Orioles off the bases, allowing three hits through the first four innings. Baltimore got on the scoreboard in the fifth when Lenny Webster hit a leadoff double and scored on Roberto Alomar's single to center field.

Chris Fussell came out of the bullpen for the Orioles in the sixth and pitched two scoreless innings before the Yankees got the better of him in the top of the eighth. Lowell and Knoblauch singled to put runners on the corners. Jeter hit the third pitch from Fussell down the right-field line. His two-out triple brought both runners home and gave the Yankees a 4-1 lead.

The Orioles closed the gap to one run in the bottom of the eighth when B.J. Surhoff hit a two-run homer over the center-field wall. But the Yankees added another run in the top of the ninth. Chili Davis singled and pinch-runner Homer Bush scored on Shane Spencer's double.

The Yankees led by two runs with the Orioles down to their final three outs. Mariano Rivera was brought in to save the game for New York. Mike Bordick flied out to center field on Rivera's first pitch to him. Alomar then doubled. Rivera got Brady Anderson to pop out to the second baseman.

Eric Davis singled with two strikes on him to score Alomar. The Orioles needed one more run to tie the game. But Rafael Palmeiro grounded out to first to end the game and give the Yankees a 5-4 victory.

But the Yankees victory was forgotten amid the celebration of Ripken's streak. After playing 2,632 games, Ripken finally took a break. He played through injury and the birth of his son, and saw the streak threatened by the players strike. Through it all, there was Ripken, the consummate professional, ready to play and help his team win.

"So that's what a day off feels like," Ripken joked after the game. "Now that I know what it feels like to take a day off, I don't want to watch many games. I tried to do what others do. But I was antsy. I was fidgety."[9] He said he would return to the lineup the next night when the Orioles took the field in Toronto.

Former Orioles pitcher Jim Palmer noted that Ripken's feat was amazing "because it was not only a physical accomplishment, but a mental one in that he had to be prepared every one of those games. It sets up different parameters than other players. Other players take a day off when they are in a slump. Cal doesn't."[10]

Jeter, who was in the batter's box in the first inning when Ripken was celebrated by the crowd, said, "I have a great deal of respect for him and what he's accomplished. That's a record that's not ever going to be broken. I mean, I'm tired right now and I haven't played in that many games."[11]

Perhaps Orioles coach Elrod Hendricks said it best when he said, "It's great to see Cal do it with class, the same way he has handled everything else in his career."[12]

Sources

In addition to the sources cited in the Notes, I used the Baseball-Reference.com and Retrosheet.org websites for box-score, player, team, and season pages, pitching and batting game logs, and other material pertinent to this game account.

Notes

1 Buster Olney, "After 2,632 Games in a Row, Orioles' Ripken Sits One Out," *New York Times*, September 21, 1998: 1.

2 Alex Coffey, "Cal Ripken Breaks Lou Gehrig's Record," BaseballHall.org, baseballhall.org/discover/inside-pitch/cal-ripken-breaks-lou-gehrigs-consecutive-games-record.

3 Jack O'Connell, "Ripken's Streak Ends at 2,632 Games," *Hartford Courant*, September 21, 1998.

4 Joe Strauss, "How Ripken May End the Run," *Baltimore Sun*, September 20, 1998: 8E.

5 Roch Kubatko, "Minor's Future Arrives Early," *Baltimore Sun*, September 21, 1998: 31.

6 Kubatko.

7 Joe Strauss, "Iron Man Ends It After 16 Years," *Baltimore Sun*, September 21, 1998: 33.

8 Richard Justice, "It's Over: Ripken Sits Out After 2,632 Games," *Washington Post*, September 21, 1998: A1.

9 Justice.

10 Strauss, "Iron Man."

11 Bill Free, "Colleagues Can Only Tip Caps to Ripken," *Baltimore Sun*, September 21, 1998: 33.

12 Free.

"They should have a mercy rule"
Orioles Score Record 23 Runs in Blowout of Blue Jays

September 28, 2000: Baltimore Orioles 23, Toronto Blue Jays 1, at Oriole Park at Camden Yards

By Mike Huber

With four games left in the 2000 season, the only role available to the Baltimore Orioles was that of spoiler. The Toronto Blue Jays were trying to make the playoffs, and the Orioles stood in their way. With four games left to play, Toronto (83-75) was 4½ games behind the American League East Division-leading New York Yankees (87-70). The Boston Red Sox (83-75) were a game ahead of Toronto.

After winning the division crown in 1997, the Orioles (70-88) found themselves once again destined to finish the season in fourth place.[1] Despite this, an announced crowd of 32,203 fans showed up at Oriole Park at Camden Yards to cheer their home team on. In fact, the Birds had already drawn over 3 million fans for the year, a mark good for fourth-best in all of baseball.

Right-hander Pat Rapp was tagged to start for Baltimore, seeking his ninth win in his final start of the season. His last win came on September 13 in Texas, which coincidentally was the last time the Orioles had scored more than two runs in an inning. Rapp had won only three of his previous 19 starts, and his earned-run average was a disappointing 6.09. Toronto countered with Chris Carpenter. The 6-foot-6-inch right-hander was making his first start since September 16, when he was struck in the face by a liner from Chicago's José Valentin. His ERA was 6.17 entering the game. Blue Jays manager Jim Fregosi was hoping to get a few good innings from Carpenter.

Rapp was perfect through the first three innings. Carpenter was not, struggling from the first batter. On a 2-and-1 count, Carpenter allowed a leadoff home run to Brady Anderson, his 200th career home run and seventh leadoff homer of the season (and the 43rd leadoff home run of Anderson's career). With one out, Delino DeShields walked and scored when Chris Richard doubled. Cal Ripken singled, driving in Richard, and the Orioles never looked back.

Baltimore scored three more runs in the second. Brook Fordyce led off with a single. Anderson walked after Gene Kingsale was retired. Jerry Hairston reached on an error after hitting a grounder to second baseman Craig Grebeck, which allowed Fordyce to score the Orioles' fourth run. DeShields singled, plating Anderson and sending Hairston to third. Blue Jays third baseman Tony Batista couldn't handle the throw, and Hairston scampered home, giving the O's two unearned runs on the play. After two innings, Baltimore led 6-0.

Shannon Stewart singled to start the Toronto fourth and made it as far as third base but was stranded when Carlos Delgado struck out. In the Orioles fourth, Fregosi brought right-hander Roy Halladay in to pitch. (Remember, Toronto was trying to get into the playoffs.) This was only Halladay's second full season in the majors, and he split time as a starter and reliever. Fregosi's strategy didn't work: 13 Baltimore hitters stepped into the batter's box. Anderson walked and Hairston reached on an error by Grebeck for the second time in the game. An out later, Albert Belle hit an RBI single past the shortstop (Anderson scored), and then Richard forced Belle at second (with Hairston taking third). With Ripken at the plate, Halladay had a chance to escape the inning with only one run allowed, because he had Hairston picked off at third. In the ensuing play, however, Blue Jays catcher Alberto Castillo made an error and Hairston scored.

As the Orioles were given new life in the inning, Ripken, Melvin Mora, Fordyce, and Kingsale all singled. That was it for Halladay. He had faced nine batters and recorded only two outs. Southpaw Lance Painter trotted in from the bullpen and gave up a two-run double on his first pitch to Anderson. Hairston singled and DeShields homered, driving in three more runs. Belle flied out and the inning finally ended. When the bottom of the fourth was over, Baltimore had scored 10 runs in the inning and led 16-0. The 10

"They should have a mercy rule"

runs tied a club record for the most runs in an inning.[2] And every one of them was unearned.[3]

Rapp gave up one hit to start the fifth, a home run to Darrin Fletcher. This was the lone run for Toronto in the game and only the second (and last) hit allowed by Rapp and Orioles pitching. With the game virtually out of reach, both sides started making substitutions. Vernon Wells and Chad Mottola came in as defensive replacements for Toronto. The Orioles hit parade made an encore performance. With one down, Ripken singled to left. Pinch-hitter Jesse Garcia (batting for Mora) walked. Mark Lewis entered as a pinch-runner for Ripken. Fordyce singled to load the bases. Kingsale singled in Lewis, keeping the sacks loaded. Anderson's sacrifice fly to center brought in Garcia. Four more consecutive singles by Hairston, DeShields (which chased Painter – John Frascatore became the fourth Blue Jays hurler), Belle, and Richard led to three more runs, for a total of five in the frame, as 11 Birds took their swings.

Rapp was cruising, facing the minimum in the sixth and allowing only a walk to Delgado in the seventh. Frascatore grooved a one-strike pitch to Fordyce in the sixth, which left the ballpark in a hurry. Fordyce's solo home run made the score 22-1, which tied the Baltimore franchise record for runs scored, set on June 13, 1999, in Atlanta. In the bottom of the eighth, the Orioles broke the record. Ryan Minor, a defensive replacement for Richard, walked and advanced to second on Lewis's single. An out later, a passed ball sent both runners to the next base. Fernando Lunar (who came in to catch in the top of the inning) rolled a grounder to short, deep enough to bring in Minor with run number 23. Lunar had been acquired in a trade with Atlanta on July 31,[4] and this was his only run batted in for the Orioles in 2000.

The only positive point for the Blue Jays was Fletcher's round-tripper, which gave Toronto seven players with at least 20 home runs, tying the major-league record (set by the Orioles in 1996). It also prevented Rapp from pitching a shutout.

The Orioles batted around twice in the contest. Roch Kubatko of the *Baltimore Sun* described the historic game: "It was quite an explosion for a lineup that's displayed pop-gun power since a series of waiver deadline trades."[5] DeShields was the offensive hero with his 3-for-4 performance (plus a walk) with two runs scored and five batted in. Of the 23 hits by the Birds, 18 were singles. Eleven Baltimore batters had hits, and nine different Orioles players drove in runs. Fordyce went 4-for-5. Ripken was 3-for-4. Anderson finished the game with a 2-for-2 performance, with two walks, four runs scored, and four runs batted in. He, Hairston, DeShields, and Belle each had four plate appearances before the fourth inning was finished. After the game, Anderson told reporters, "Obviously, it's unusual to score that many runs, no matter what kind of offense you have or what team you're playing. Most every ball we hit hard fell, and we probably had four or five bloopers fall, too."[6]

Toronto pitchers gave up 23 hits and 23 runs, but only 10 of them were earned.[7] The loss officially eliminated the Blue Jays from the American League East race. Manager Fregosi lamented, "They should have a mercy rule."[8] His counterpart, Baltimore skipper Mike Hargrove, said, "That was fun. It was nice to do that to somebody else for a change."[9] He may have been referring to the fact that Baltimore had allowed 10 or more runs 29 times in 2000, with a high of 19 runs given up to the New York Yankees on July 25.

Baltimore won the last four games of the season, blowing out Toronto in this contest and then sweeping a three-game series from the Yankees. They outscored their opponent 52-7 in those four games, hanging losses on Toronto's Carpenter and the Yankees' Andy Pettitte, David Cone, and Orlando Hernandez.

Sources

In addition to the sources mentioned in the notes, the author consulted baseball-reference.com and retrosheet.org. The author thanks Carl Riechers for his suggestions and input.

Notes

1 Baltimore finished in fourth place in the AL East in nine of 10 seasons, from 1998 through 2007, with the only exception being 2004, when they finished in third place.

2 The Orioles scored 10 runs in an inning three times in 2000. The first time was on April 7, against the Detroit Tigers. This game was the second time, and the third time occurred the very next day, on September 29, against the New York Yankees.

3 According to the Associated Press ("O's Put Beating on Jays," *Montreal Gazette*, September 29, 2000: 27), only seven of the fourth-inning runs were unearned. The home run by DeShields and the two runners aboard were charged as earned runs to the pitcher, but unearned runs to the team. According to Retrosheet, provisions of Section 10.18 (i) of the scoring rules were applied, which deals with earned and unearned runs. For more information on Section 10, see baseball-almanac.com/rule10.shtml.

4 Lunar was traded by the Braves with Trent Hubbard and Luis Rivera to Baltimore for Gabe Molina and B.J. Surhoff.

5 Roch Kubatko, "O's Do Number on Jays, 23-1," *Baltimore Sun*, September 29, 2000: 55.

6 Kubatko.

7 According to Retrosheet, provisions of Section 10.18 (i) of the scoring rules were applied.

8 Kubatko.

9 Kubatko.

Nomo Joins Elite Company With No-Hitters in Both Leagues

April 4, 2001: Boston Red Sox 3, Baltimore Orioles 0, at Orioles Park at Camden Yards

By Bill Staples Jr.

In his first start with the Boston Red Sox, Hideo Nomo pitched a no-hitter, defeating the Baltimore Orioles, 3-0, at Camden Yards. In doing so, he joined Cy Young, Jim Bunning, and Nolan Ryan as the only pitchers in major-league history to throw no-hitters in both the American and National Leagues.[1] (Randy Johnson joined the group with his perfect game in 2004.[2]) Of the five members in this elite club, Nomo is the only one not enshrined in Cooperstown. *(See Table 1.)*

After pitching six full seasons in the major leagues, Nomo signed a one-year, $4.5 million contract with Boston in December 2001.[3] "I'm going with the Red Sox because they have a strong chance to go to the World Series," Nomo said.[4] Individual awards and accomplishments are nice, but his ultimate goal had always been to win the World Series.[5]

In his first two seasons with the Los Angeles Dodgers, Nomo recorded a 29-17 record (.630 winning percentage). However, in his final three seasons he was 16-19 (.457). His struggles were due primarily to a lack of command caused by injuries. The Dodgers traded Nomo in midseason 1998 to the New York Mets. Afterward, he had one-year stints with Milwaukee and Detroit, where he finished with a combined 20-20 record.[6]

The Boston pitching staff included past and future All-Stars Pedro Martinez, Tim Wakefield, David Cone, Bret Saberhagen, and Derek Lowe.[7] The signing of the 32-year-old righty not only gave the Red Sox another weapon in their arsenal, it also gave them the distinction of becoming the first major-league team with two Japanese-born pitchers on their roster. For Japanese teammate Tomo Ohka, it was a dream come true. He was 14 years old when Nomo earned MVP honors as a rookie in the Japanese Pacific League in 1990. Nomo was Ohka's childhood hero. He admired Nomo for his accomplishments on the mound and for his role as a pioneer for other Japanese players entering the major leagues.

Despite a rocky 2001 spring training, where he had an 0-3 record and a double-digit ERA, injuries to Cone and Saberhagen allowed Nomo to secure the number-two spot in the rotation behind Martinez.[8]

The Red Sox opened the season with three games against the Orioles in Baltimore. Boston manager Jimy Williams told the press, "You never know when you're going to see a special game. You really don't. That's why I like baseball."[9] The Orioles won walk-off 2-1 victories in the first and third games of the series. But the middle game of the season-opening series belonged to Boston, courtesy of Nomo.

Nomo's first no-hitter, in Denver in 1996, was in a game whose start was delayed by rain. His start in Baltimore was also delayed, for 45 minutes, because of a power outage that hit in the bottom of the first inning.[10] Entering the game the Baltimore lineup was 8-for-51 (.157) against Nomo. David Segui, 5-for-13 (.387) with two home runs, was the only Orioles hitter with any success against him.

Also working in Nomo's favor that night was the presence of home-plate umpire Eric Cooper. During the offseason the major leagues had decided to expand the strike zone vertically, and at times Cooper appeared to be struggling with his interpretation of the new rules. A few questionable called third strikes might have created doubt in the heads of Orioles hitters, perhaps forcing them to chase pitches normally outside their comfort zone.[11]

In traditional Nomo fashion, he started off slow on the mound and gained strength as the game progressed. In the first inning, three of four Orioles hitters made solid contact. The number-three hitter, Nomo's old Dodgers teammate Delino DeShields, reached base on a walk.

In the second inning, Melvin Mora blasted a fly ball to the center-field warning track that found Carl Everett's glove. Cal Ripken reached first on an error by third baseman Shea Hillenbrand and advanced to second on a Nomo splitter that was too hot for catcher

• Nomo Joins Elite Company •

Jason Varitek to handle. (It was ruled a wild pitch.) Baltimore's rally ended when Brook Fordyce became the first of Nomo's 11 strikeout victims.

Nomo's no-hit bid was threatened again by Brady Anderson's warning-track fly to right field in the third inning, a hot fielder's-choice grounder to second by Segui in the fourth, and a laser hit by Ripken to right field for an out in the fifth.

In the sixth inning Nomo started to dominate. The righty had great command of his fastball, forkball, and splitter, and gave the Orioles nothing to hit down the middle of the plate. By peppering the corners and changing speeds, Nomo struck out eight batters from the sixth through the eighth. Baltimore outfielder Jerry Hairston was fooled all night, striking out three times. All but two Orioles (Ripken and Chris Richard) struck out at least once.

In the bottom of the ninth inning, the only thing standing between Nomo and his second no-hitter were Anderson, Mike Bordick, and DeShields. "As I was going into the ninth inning, I was not nervous," Nomo said after the game.[12] Perhaps that was because he knew the stats were in his favor. Up to this point the last three Orioles batters were a combined 2-for-31 (.065) against Nomo.

Anderson (0-11 vs. Nomo) grounded back to Nomo. Knowing that Bordick (1-8) was a notorious fastball hitter, Nomo pitched away from the right-handed hitter. On a 2-and-1 count, Bordick slapped an outside pitch toward no-man's land behind second base in shallow center field. Second baseman Mike Lansing, a late-inning defensive replacement, chased the ball down and snagged it out of the air. The play saved the no-hitter and generated a semi-emotional glove slap from the stoic Nomo. For the final out, DeShields (1-12) hit a shallow fly to left field, where Troy O'Leary tucked it away easily.

While this was Nomo's second no-hitter, the achievement represented many firsts. The crowd of 35,602 applauded Nomo for giving them the first no-hitter at Camden Yards (and, as of 2016, the only one).

His feat also marked the earliest calendar date (April 4) on which a no-hitter had been pitched. Bob Feller threw a no-hitter on Opening Day in 1940, but that occurred on April 16.

For Varitek, Nomo's no-hitter was the first of four he would catch during his career. It was the 15th by a Red Sox pitcher.

After the game, Nomo said, "Today was my first time throwing for the Boston Red Sox, and I am obviously very happy with my performance."[13]

Nomo finished the season with a 13-10 record, leading the American League in strikeouts (220) and strikeouts per nine innings pitched (10.00). He also led the league in walks (96, one more than Cleveland's C.C. Sabathia).

Nomo pitched two one-hit games for Boston in 2001. He carried a no-hitter into the seventh inning against the Minnesota Twins, eventually winning 2-0 and allowing one hit and five walks, while striking out eight. Nomo vowed to pitching coach Joe Kerrigan that he would walk fewer hitters, and made good on his promise with a one-hit shutout against the Toronto Blue Jays in which he struck out 14 and walked none.[14]

Sources

In addition to the sources cited in the Notes, the author relied on Baseball-Reference.com, baseball-almanac.com, and video of the game, at MLB Classics, "9/4/01: Nomo's Second No-No," youtube.com/watch?v=qfwNcsSPzCY, accessed November 27, 2016.* See also BaseballPilgrimages.com, "No-Hitters Thrown in Current Major League Ballparks," baseballpilgrimages.com/ballparks/no-hitters.html, accessed November 28, 2016.

*YouTube has listed the wrong date for the game, but the link still works as of February 2017.

Notes

1 Murray Chass, "Baseball; Nomo Hurls a No-Hitter in His Red Sox Debut," *New York Times,* April 5, 2001.

2 FoxSports.com, "12 Years Ago, Randy Johnson Made MLB History with This Perfect Game," foxsports.com/mlb/story/arizona-diamondbacks-atlanta-braves-randy-johnson-perfect-game-12-years-ago-051816, accessed November 28, 2016.

3 David Heuschkel, "Nomo Ready to Leave Sox," *Hartford Courant,* December 6, 2001.

4 Sean McAdam, "Red Sox Acquire Hideo Nomo," *Providence Journal,* December 15, 2000.

5 Lawrence Rocca, "Nomomania Revisted – Baseball: The International Popularity of the Dodgers' Right-Hander Is Already on the Rise," *Orange County Register* (Santa Ana, California), February 19, 1996.

6 Baseball-Reference.com, "Hideo Nomo," baseball-reference.com/players/n/nomohi01.shtml, accessed November 28, 2016.

7 Baseball-Reference.com, "2001 Boston Red Sox Roster," baseball-reference.com/teams/BOS/2001.shtml, accessed November 28, 2016.

8 Video: MLB Classics. "9/4/01: Nomo's Second No-No," youtube.com/watch?v=qfwNcsSPzCY, accessed November 28, 2016.

9 Phil O'Neill, "Japanese Blitz Will Sack Nomo / No-Hitter Will Attract Extra Media," *Worcester* (Massachusetts) *Telegram & Gazette,* April 6, 2001.

10 O'Neill.

11 Joe Capozzi, "Discomfort Zone," *Palm Beach Post,* March 1, 2001.

12 "Second No-No for Nomo, This One Against O's," *New York Daily News,* April 5, 2001.

13 "Second No-No for Nomo, This One Against O's."

14 David Kamerman, "Hideo Nomo Spins 1-Hit Gem for Red Sox," *Boston Globe,* May 26, 2001.

• Baltimore Baseball •

Table 1: Pitchers With No-Hitters in Both the American and National Leagues

Pitcher	First League No-Hitter	Second League No-Hitter	No-Hitters Career Total	HOF Induction Year
Cy Young	Cleveland Spiders (NL) Saturday, September 18, 1897 Cleveland Spiders 6, Cincinnati Reds 0; League Park (Cleveland)	Boston Americans (AL) Thursday, May 5, 1904 Boston Americans 3, Philadelphia Athletics 0; Huntington Avenue Grounds (Boston)	3	1937
Jim Bunning	Detroit Tigers (AL) Sunday, July 20, 1958 Detroit Tigers 3, Boston Red Sox 0; Fenway Park	Philadelphia Phillies (NL) Sunday, June 21, 1964 Philadelphia Phillies 6, New York Mets 0; Shea Stadium	2	1996
Nolan Ryan	California Angels (AL) Tuesday, May 15, 1973 California Angels 3, Kansas City Royals 0; Royals Stadium	Houston Astros (NL) Saturday, Sept. 26, 1981 Houston Astros 5, Los Angeles Dodgers 0; Astrodome	7	1999
Hideo Nomo	Los Angeles Dodgers (NL) Tuesday, Sept. 17, 1996 Los Angeles Dodgers 9, Colorado Rockies 0; Coors Field	Boston Red Sox (AL) Wednesday, April 4, 2001 Boston Red Sox 3, Baltimore Orioles 0; Orioles Park at Camden Yards	2	2014*
Randy Johnson	Seattle Mariners (AL) Saturday, June 2, 1990 Seattle Mariners 2, Detroit Tigers 0; Kingdome	Arizona Diamondbacks (NL) Tuesday, May 18, 2004 Arizona Diamondbacks 2, Atlanta Braves 0; Turner Field	2	2015

Inducted into the Japanese Baseball Hall of Fame in 2014.

Goodbye, Number 8

October 6, 2001: Boston Red Sox 5, Baltimore Orioles 1, at Oriole Park at Camden Yards

By Peter Coolbaugh

The moment had been coming for a while. No one wanted it to arrive, but when it did, it became much more about the man who had done so much for the game, than the game itself.

It became official back in June, when Cal Ripken Jr. announced he would retire from professional baseball at the end of the season. Along with Padres legend Tony Gwynn, who made a similar announcement, the rest of 2001 was a farewell tour for both men whose names were inexplicably tied to their respective franchises.

Ripken was named as a starter for the 2001 All-Star Game in Seattle, with Cal famously being moved back to shortstop for an inning by Alex Rodriguez and Joe Torre for one last glance from his longtime position. He also later homered and was awarded his second All-Star Game MVP (first one was 1991), capping his 19 All-Star appearances. Tony Gwynn was added as a nonplayer to the NL squad.

The lovefest for Ripken never ended. Both at home and on the road, people came out in droves to say goodbye to the famous Iron Man, often credited with helping baseball improve its image after the dreaded players strike of 1994. The breaking of the Iron Horse – Lou Gehrig's record of 2,131 consecutive games in 1995 was seen as a milestone accomplishment not just for Ripken, but for healing the rift between fans and baseball after the strike.

Cal had been with the Orioles in the majors since his cup of coffee in 1981. He played third base early in his career until Earl Weaver moved the 6-foot-4 Ripken over to shortstop, where he would revolutionize the position. Cal had already been a part of the Orioles family long before he was drafted out of high school, as his father, Cal Sr., had been in the Orioles organization as a player, scout, and coach for decades.

With the Orioles having no hope to make the postseason in 2001, originally Cal's final game as a player was supposed to be at Yankee Stadium. The terrorist attacks on the United States on September 11 caused Major League Baseball to cancel games for a week, and then schedules had to be redone for the missed games. Somehow fittingly, Cal's final game would be home at Oriole Park.

Before the game there were 45 minutes of tributes and farewells on the field. The Orioles made a large donation to Cal's future Aberdeen, Maryland, youth complex, and gave him a large hand-drawn portrait of his late father, who died in 1999. There was also a plaque dedicated to Cal Sr. in the Orioles dugout. Several politicians and dignitaries spoke, and Cal's number 8 was retired, joining Frank Robinson (20), Brooks Robinson (5), Earl Weaver (4), Jim Palmer (22), and Eddie Murray (33) on the immortal list. In fact, the starting lineup from Ripken's first start in August 1981 took the field along with Earl Weaver. Eddie Murray at first, Rick Dempsey at catcher, and Ken Singleton in right field. Shortstop was left open for the late Mark Belanger. Said Commissioner Bud Selig that evening, "Cal Ripken … has become the symbol for the American work ethic, the symbol for the American working man."[1]

After Cal's mother, Vi, threw out the first pitch, the game got underway with the pitching matchup between David Cone and Rick Bauer. The Orioles struck first, scoring in the bottom of the first on a sacrifice fly by Jeff Conine. Tim Raines Jr. came into score for the only run the Orioles would put up in the game.

Opposing players even marveled how Ripken could have been so good for so long. Said Boston starter David Cone, "He's such a class act. Cal should be the model for all professional athletes. He stays in incredible shape – you'd have to be to play all those games – and he's such a consistent performer, which you'd have to be to post up those numbers for 21 years. He's never had a season in which his numbers were glaringly different. And even at the end, he was still the toughest out for me in the lineup."[2]

Boston scored on a two-run homer by Dante Bichette in the second, and Jose Offerman hit another two-run shot in the fifth. Bauer lasted seven innings, giving up seven hits and four earned runs. Cone went eight innings, earning his ninth win of the year. Boston added another run in the top of the ninth on Joe Oliver's double. Boston finished the night with 12 hits while Baltimore managed only four.

The man of the evening, Ripken, was 0-for-3, finishing his final season with a career-low .239 average. Cal managed to line out to left, pop up to short, and in his final at-bat it was a fly out to center field. A few moments of drama happened in the top of the ninth. Cal waited on deck while Brady Anderson batted and worked a 3-and-2 count. Chants of "We Want Cal" echoed all over the ballpark from the 48,807 fans in attendance. Cal's career ended in the on-deck circle as Ugueth Urbina mowed down Anderson with a fastball. And just like that, a career was in the books.

Cal was driven around the ballpark after the game in a Corvette. Afterward, the stadium lights went dark and the man himself came to the podium to speak. It took several attempts after fighting back emotion that the Iron Man was able to speak. "One question I've repeatedly been asked these last few weeks is how do I want to be remembered," he said. "My answer has been simple: to be remembered at all is pretty special."[3]

The career long devotion of fans to Cal was apparent from every angle. The flashbulbs, the tears, and the numerous ovations easily displayed why Ripken meant so much to Charm City and its working-class roots. Fans easily admit that the city and the Iron Man were clearly a perfect fit.

The accolades did not end with this night for sure. It was a mere six years later that Cal received the ultimate honor and was inducted into the National Baseball Hall of Fame in Cooperstown. And like the Orioles players before him, he too was a first ballot inductee. To this day, the Ripken name carries so much respect and reverence in and around Baltimore.

His longtime teammate and friend Jeff Conine summed up his career almost perfectly by saying, "He's a competitor on one hand and an icon on the other. He does it as well, if not better than anyone I've ever seen."[4]

Sources

In addition to the sources cited in the Note, the author consulted Retrosheet.org, Baseball-Reference.com, and the National Baseball Hall of Fame.

Notes

1. "Baseball Bids Goodbye to No. 8," *Baltimore Sun*, October 7, 2001: 8D.
2. "A Final Salute as Ripken Bows Out," *New York Times*, October 7, 2001: 8.
3. "Ripken: Tonight Closes a Chapter of a Dream," *Baltimore Sun*, October 7, 2001: 12D.
4. "Baseball Bids Goodbye to No. 8": 9D.

On October 6, 2001, Cap Ripken Jr., shown here 20 years earlier in 1981, played game #3,001 in an Orioles uniform.
Courtesy of the Baltimore Orioles.

Orioles Lose 15-1 to Cleveland on Tuesday, Turn Tables and Score 18 on Wednesday

April 19, 2006: Baltimore Orioles 18, Cleveland Indians 9, at Oriole Park at Camden Yards

By Mike Lynch

Early in the 2006 season, the Baltimore Orioles were no strangers to blowouts, having beaten the Tampa Bay Devil Rays 16-6 in their second game of the season on April 5 before losing 14-8 to the Boston Red Sox on April 7. They ran off a string of one-run victories against the Devil Rays and Los Angeles Angels of Anaheim from April 13-15 to run their record to 7-5, then lost to the Angels on April 16 by a count of 9-3 before rebounding with a 4-2 win to take three of four in the series. At 8-6 and a second-place showing after four games of a seven-game homestand, the Orioles were hoping to enjoy their first winning season since 1997.

They hosted the Cleveland Indians for a three-game set that began with Cleveland trouncing the Orioles 15-1 on April 18 behind a 20-hit attack led by Grady Sizemore, Victor Martinez, Ben Broussard, and Casey Blake, all of whom had three hits. The second game of the series was shaping up to be another Cleveland win when the Indians jumped out to a 7-3 lead after 4½ innings, but Baltimore bounced back in midgame and capped things off with a late surge.

Right-hander Jake Westbrook took the mound for the Indians on April 19; righty Rodrigo Lopez got the nod for the Orioles. Westbrook, a 28-year-old Georgia native, was in his sixth season with Cleveland after a cup of coffee with the New York Yankees in 2000. He was off to a solid start, going 2-1 with a 3.66 ERA in his first three games, but had struggled in his last start, allowing three home runs to the Detroit Tigers in a 5-1 loss.

Lopez, a 30-year-old from Mexico, was in his fifth season with Baltimore after a brief stint with the San Diego Padres in 2000 and was off to a terrible start, going 1-1 with a 5.66 ERA in three outings. Like Westbrook, Lopez had suffered a similar fate in his previous start when he surrendered three homers to the Angels in a 6-5 Baltimore victory. Neither would redeem himself on this evening.

Cleveland scored first when Jhonny Peralta belted a shot over the right-field scoreboard with two outs and nobody on in the top of the first to give the Indians a 1-0 lead. Baltimore countered with a run in the bottom of the frame thanks to Brian Roberts' leadoff single, his steal of second, and Miguel Tejada's single to left that knotted the contest at 1-1. Neither team scored in the second, although the Indians had Lopez on the ropes again with consecutive hits by Broussard and Ronnie Belliard that put runners at first and second with no outs. Todd Hollandsworth struck out and Aaron Boone lined into a double play to end the threat. Westbrook set the Orioles down in order in his half of the inning.

Cleveland took a 4-1 lead in the top of the third when Sizemore doubled to right and came home when Lopez slipped during his delivery to Peralta and tossed a wild pitch, sending Sizemore to third. When catcher Ramon Hernandez tried to throw him out, the ball got past third baseman Melvin Mora and rolled into left field, allowing Sizemore to break the tie. Peralta walked and Martinez launched a 400-foot homer into the right-center-field bleachers to give the Indians a three-run lead.

Corey Patterson led off the bottom of the third with a bunt single and Roberts was awarded first on catcher's interference. Jeff Conine plated Patterson and sent Roberts to second with a single to center, then Roberts stole third and scored on Mora's line single up the middle. Tejada grounded into a double play and Jay Gibbons grounded to second to end the inning. Lopez and Westbrook faced four batters each in the fourth, but none scored. The former would face only four more batters before coming out in favor of veteran left-hander John Halama.

Sizemore walked to lead off the top of the fifth and went to third when Jason Michaels bunted to first for a hit and first baseman Kevin Millar committed a throwing error. Peralta fanned, but Travis Hafner blistered a double to deep left to score Sizemore and Michaels, and went to third on the throw to the plate. Halama replaced Lopez and the southpaw struck out Martinez for the second out of the inning before surrendering a run-scoring single to Belliard. He fanned Hollandsworth to stop the bleeding, but Cleveland's lead ballooned to four.

That proved to be the highlight of Cleveland's evening. Conine, Mora, and Tejada rapped out consecutive one-out singles in the bottom of the fifth to cut the deficit to three. Gibbons flied to left, but the Orioles' rally continued. Hernandez singled to right and scored Mora, and Javy Lopez ripped a two-bagger to left that plated Tejada and forced Indians manager Eric Wedge to make a decision. Rather than go with Matt Miller, who had been warming in the bullpen, Wedge chose to stick with Westbrook and Millar made him pay with a shot to center that cleared the glove of a diving Sizemore and bounced over the fence for a double that gave Baltimore an 8-7 lead.

Wedge called for Miller, but Patterson, acquired from the Chicago Cubs during the offseason, deposited Miller's second pitch into the right-field bleachers for his first homer as an Oriole. Miller walked Roberts before finally ending the inning with Conine's groundout. Baltimore had a 10-7 lead that it would never relinquish and Orioles skipper Sam Perlozzo lauded his squad. "They really showed me some character tonight," he told reporters. "I know when they came into the dugout and it was 7-3, they were still chirping about coming back."[1] They weren't through, but Cleveland wasn't giving up.

Boone blasted a homer off Halama to lead off the top of the sixth and when Halama allowed a one-out single to Michaels, Perlozzo replaced him with 26-year-old rookie Sendy Rleal, who easily got out of the inning. The Orioles extended their lead to 13-8 when Mora doubled to left, knocking Miller from the game in favor of Rafael Betancourt who allowed a single to Tejada and a three-run homer to Gibbons. Lanky righty Jason Davis took over for Betancourt and retired the next three Orioles to send the game to the seventh.

Rleal handily retired the side and Danny Graves, Cleveland's fifth pitcher of the game, returned the favor and set Baltimore down in order in the bottom of the inning. Eddy Rodriguez replaced Rleal in the top of the eighth and surrendered Cleveland's ninth and final run when Hollandsworth poked a double to right, went to third on a sacrifice fly, and scored on Sizemore's fly to left. The Orioles exacted revenge for the previous game's beating by pouring five more runs over the plate in the bottom of the inning with help from shoddy fielding by the Indians. "If a lopsided loss to the Cleveland Indians didn't raise the Baltimore Orioles' ire, it certainly awakened their bats," wrote the *Los Angeles Times*.[2]

Graves coaxed Mora to ground to Peralta, who booted the ball for an error, then Hollandsworth misplayed Tejada's fly ball into a miscue that allowed Mora to score and sent Tejada to second. Gibbons who sent Tejada to third with an infield single, and pinch-runner Nick Markakis, Tejada, and Hernandez trotted home on Hernandez's second homer of the season. Lopez whiffed for the first out, Millar singled to left, and was erased at second on Patterson's fielder's choice before singles by Roberts and Conine scored Patterson to give Baltimore an 18-9 lead.

Scott Sauerbeck relieved Graves and got Mora to fly to right for the final out. Chris Gomez replaced Millar at first base, Markakis went to right field, and Ramon Vazquez pinch-hit for Peralta to lead off the ninth. Vazquez lined to first to begin the frame, Hafner struck out looking, and pinch-hitter Kelly Shoppach singled to center. But Rodriguez fanned Broussard to close out the 18-9 victory.

"You can get waxed like we did last night and come back and put a performance together like we did tonight," Conine said after the game. "It's a good thing, and it does a lot for your confidence."[3]

Sources

In addition to the sources cited in the Notes, the author also accessed Retrosheet.org, Baseball-Reference.com, and SABR.org.

Notes

1 "Orioles Double Up on Indians, 18-9," *Los Angeles Times*, April 20, 2006: D5.

2 "Orioles Double Up on Indians, 18-9."

3 "Orioles Double Up on Indians, 18-9." The 18 runs were the most by the Orioles since they scored a team-record 23 against the Toronto Blue Jays on September 28, 2000. The confidence the O's might have gained from their win that ran their record to 9-7 didn't last long and they finished the season with a 70-92 record, below .500 for the ninth straight season.

Aubrey Huff's Milestone Cycle Not Enough to Help Orioles Beat Angels

June 29, 2007: Anaheim Angels 9, Baltimore Orioles 7, at Camden Yards

By Mike Huber

Using the minimum four at-bats needed, Aubrey Huff hit for the cycle on June 29, 2007, becoming the first Baltimore Orioles player to do so in a Baltimore ballpark. Along the way, he collected his 1,000th career hit. Despite Huff's personal milestone performance, his club squandered a lead late in the game and the Orioles fell to the Anaheim Angels, 9-7, in front of a wild crowd of 36,689 at Camden Yards.

Before Huff had even entered the batter's box, his Birds were down, 5-0, to Anaheim. Steve Trachsel, Baltimore's starting pitcher, struggled on this Friday evening. Both Huff and Trachsel were in their first seasons with Baltimore, each having signed as free agents.[1] Trachsel's counterpart for Anaheim, Kelvim Escobar, fared slightly better, lasting 4⅓ innings.

The Angels had pounced in the top of the first, as Chone Figgins started the attack with a ground-rule double on the second pitch of the game. Orlando Cabrera singled him home, and the Angels had a quick lead. In the top of the second, Howie Kendrick hit a leadoff single to center. Kendrys Morales followed with a single to left. Kendrick raced to third, but Morales was cut down trying to stretch the hit into a double. Trachsel then uncorked a wild pitch, and Kendrick scored. After Mike Napoli flied out, Trachsel served up consecutive singles to Robb Quinlan, Figgins, and Cabrera, the latter plating Quinlan. Vladimir Guerrero then doubled to center, and the lead had grown to 5-0. Trachsel's night was over as Orioles skipper Dave Trembley made the slow walk to the mound. Rob Bell came on in relief.

In his first at-bat, in the bottom of the second inning, Huff sent a 2-and-1 offering from Escobar to right-center field, and the ball careened off the scoreboard back into the middle of the outfield, allowing Huff to reach third base. It was his second triple of the season and only the 12th in his eight big-league seasons.[2] "Obviously, as a 235-pound fat guy, to get a triple out of the way, that's something that's in the back of my mind the whole game," said Huff.[3] Teammate Kevin Millar told him, "You've got to get that cycle for all the fat guys out there."[4] Melvin Mora followed with an RBI single, a weak grounder between third and short, and Baltimore had a run on the scoreboard.

In the fourth inning, Huff sent another Escobar offering to right-center field, this time for a double. Mora followed with a deep home run down the left-field line. In the fifth, with a run in and runners at the corners, Huff launched a homer over the right-field fence for his third hit of the day. The three-run shot gave the Orioles a 7-5 lead. When Mora kept the rally going by doubling to left, Escobar was finished for the day. Chris Bootcheck was called from the bullpen.

Scott Williamson became the Orioles' hurler to start the seventh. After retiring Figgins on a groundout, Williamson served up a home run to Cabrera, a shot deep into the left-field stands. A batter later, Jamie Walker was called to the mound for pitching duties, and after yielding a single to Gary Mathews, he was able to get the final out of the inning with Baltimore still ahead, 7-6.

In the bottom of the seventh, Huff approached the batter's box to a standing ovation from the crowd. The Camden Yards fans sensed that something special would happen. Huff even mentioned it after the game, saying, "Before I even went up to the plate, the crowd was going pretty crazy. I didn't even think anybody really noticed."[5] With the count 1-and-1, Huff drilled a ball down the third-base line, a sure double, but it landed inches foul. Huff said later that he wouldn't have stopped at first, even to complete the cycle. "In that situation, I'm going two [bases]. I feel like you cheat the game if you stop at first. I wouldn't even count that as a cycle."[6] The foul ball made it a nonissue. Huff swung at the next pitch and deposited a single in front of center fielder Matthews. He had joined the club of batters who have hit for the cycle and told reporters, "For me, this is probably one of the most special days of my baseball career. The triple was my 1,000th hit, the double was my 200th double and we're lucky enough to get the homer back from a fan. So I got all of the four balls. It'll be a pretty good memento."[7]

After the single, manager Trembly, who routinely pulled Huff in the late innings for defensive purposes, replaced him with pinch-runner Brandon Fahey. Huff came back onto the field for a curtain call, tipping his helmet to the roaring fans. He later said, "This is a great tradition for baseball. … To be able to do that and be the only guy to do that [in Baltimore], that means a bit more."[8]

But Huff's memorable evening did not lead to a Baltimore victory. In the top of the eighth inning, Chad Bradford, the fifth Orioles pitcher of the game, quickly retired Kendrick and Morales with groundballs, but then walked Napoli. Erick Aybar hit for Quinlan and Bradford plunked him with a 1-and-2 pitch. Figgins, Anaheim's hottest hitter, singled to right and Napoli scored the tying run, saddling Bradford with a blown save.

In the ninth, closer Chris Ray came in for the O's, and he hit Guerrero to start the inning. Matthews forced Guerrero at second and Casey Kotchman flied out to left. On a 1-and-0 count, Kendrick smashed a home run beyond the fence in deep left-center field. His 420-foot game-winning blast spoiled Huff's night. After the game, Kendrick said, "Honestly, I was trying to get something over the plate, put a good swing on it and get a hit. It just happened to be a home run. It's a crazy game. I could go back out a thousand times and not have that happen."[9] Angels closer Francisco Rodriguez pitched the bottom of the ninth, retiring Nick Markakis, Ramon Hernandez, and Fahey on fly balls to center, right, and left respectively, for his 23rd save of the season.

Aubrey Huff tripled his first time up kicking off hitting for the cycle against the Angels. He drove in three runs and scored three runs, but the Angels won, 9-7. Courtesy of the Baltimore Orioles.

Through 89 games in the season, the Orioles had lost 10 times when leading after the seventh inning.[10] The team fell to 34-45, 15½ games out of first place. Trachsel's ERA jumped from 3.39 to 4.95 in the month of June. In this contest he gave up nine hits to 12 batters. He escaped with only five earned runs, as the Baltimore defense erased two Angels runners in rundowns. Baltimore did get Trachsel off the hook by scoring seven runs, but then the bullpen faltered. Bell tossed 4⅓ scoreless innings, and Williamson, Walker, Bradford, and Ray allowed only four hits in their three innings of work but walked one and hit two batters. Anaheim capitalized, scoring four times. Had the bullpen been able to hold the lead, Bell would have won his first game in more than two years.

• Aubrey Huff's Milestone Cycle Not Enough to Help Orioles Beat Angels •

Figgins went 4-for-5 for the Angels with three singles and a double, a run batted in, a stolen base, and two runs scored. According to the *Los Angeles Times*, Figgins posted the second highest monthly batting average in Angels history with a .458 clip in June (Bengie Molina had batted .461 in May 2000).[11] In 25 games, Figgins was 51-for-111 and raised his average from .133 at the end of May to .322. His teammate Cabrera also had a productive game with three hits and three runs batted in. After this win, the Angels were comfortably in first place in the AL West, with a record of 50-30.

Huff raised his average 10 points in this game, to .272. With his home run in the fourth inning, Mora had a 3-for-4 game, falling short of the cycle by a triple. Mora and Huff had driven in six of Baltimore's seven runs. Huff became the third Oriole to hit for the cycle, joining Brooks Robinson (July 15, 1960) and Cal Ripken Jr. (May 6, 1984), but Huff was the first Baltimore player to accomplish the rare feat in front of his home crowd.

Sources

In addition to the sources mentioned in the Notes, the author consulted Baseball-Reference.com, mlb.com, and Retrosheet.org. The author sincerely thanks Meg Gers and the Enoch Pratt Free Library for assistance in obtaining sources from the *Baltimore Sun*.

Notes

1. Trachsel was traded to the Chicago Cubs on August 31, 2007. He re-signed with Baltimore for the 2008 season but was released on June 13, 2008. Huff spent 2½ seasons with Baltimore before being traded to the Detroit Tigers on August 17, 2009.
2. Huff played five more seasons and finished his career with 24 triples.
3. Geremy Bass, "Huff Third Player to Hit for Cycle in 2007," http://m.mlb.com/news/article/2056927//, June 30, 2007.
4. Mike DiGiovanna, "Huff Hits for the Cycle, but Angels Win," *Los Angeles Times*, June 30, 2007: 51.
5. Roch Kubatko, "O's Not Able to Ride Cycle, Lose in Ninth," *Baltimore Sun*, June 30, 2007: 5C.
6. Bass.
7. Bass.
8. Bass.
9. DiGiovanna.
10. Kubatko.
11. Bass.

Rangers Set Major-League Mark With 30-3 Victory

August 22, 2007: Texas Rangers 30, Baltimore Orioles 3, at Oriole Park at Camden Yards

By Thomas E. Schott

It began as a game of no import whatever, the first of a doubleheader, between a pair of teams playing out the string in the dog days of late summer. The Texas Rangers, 54-70, were 18 games out in the AL West, on their way to a last-place finish in their division, and the Baltimore Orioles almost the exact equivalent — 16½ games back at 58-65 and headed for second-to-last in the AL East. Nor was the cast of players all that luminous.

The brightest star on the field was the O's shortstop, former MVP and four-time All-Star, Miguel Tejada. The Rangers also had a four-time All-Star, shortstop Michael Young, and some whispers of future World Series teams in Ian Kinsler and Nellie Cruz. But the pitching that evening was eminently forgettable. Lefty Kason Gabbard, the Texas starter, had recently been acquired in a swap with the Boston Red Sox. This was his fifth start for the Rangers, and he would be out of baseball by the middle of 2008. The Orioles starter, 26-year-old right-hander Daniel Cabrera, although the staff's workhorse, was on his way to a seasonal 5.55 ERA and to leading the league in losses and walks.

Given the cast and teams, who could have suspected that the game would wind up in the record books? Texas scored more runs than any other team in modern baseball history, 30 of them, to Baltimore's 3. No major-league team had scored 30 runs since Chicago set the all-time record against Louisville, winning 36-7 on June 29, 1897. In the 20th century two teams had scored 29 runs, the Boston Red Sox (1950) and the Chicago White Sox (1954). (The most the Rangers had ever tallied was 26, also against Baltimore on April 19, 1996.) The 27-run beatdown was also the largest margin of victory in the modern era.

As Ranger Marlon Byrd observed, the game was "something freaky."[1] Freaky on so many levels. First off, the Orioles had actually led 3-0 going into the fourth inning. They would score no more, but at that point it appeared that Texas, which had managed to score only 28 runs in its previous nine games and only two runs on seven hits in its last two, would be up to its usual standards. And then the storm began. The Rangers scored five runs, the big blow a three-run homer by the nine-hole hitter Ramon Vazquez, to take the lead in the fourth. After a quiet fifth, rookie catcher Jarrod Saltalamacchia opened the Texas sixth with a blast into the stands in deep left-center. That shot ushered in the first of three Orioles relievers, Brian Burres, who would not survive the inning. The Rangers would proceed to score eight more runs, four on Marlon Byrd's grand slam. The O's second relief pitcher, Rob Bell, surrendered the last run of the inning.

With the score 14-3 in his favor, manager Ron Washington decided to give veteran Michael Young's sore back a break and installed utility guy Travis Metcalf at third. Metcalf had just been called up from Triple-A Oklahoma City that day. After the game an ecstatic Washington said, "When the faucet is on, you want it to stay on. You never want to cut it off."[2] Little did he realize how much his scrub infielder would keep the water gushing. Washington also decided to pull his starter after six innings' work. And so it was that Wes Littleton, a right-hander, pitched the final three innings for Texas and had the unprecedented distinction of earning a save, his first of the season, by protecting an eventual 27-run lead.

After the changes the Rangers had yet two more monstrous innings to go, and incredibly, they would surpass the 14 runs they already had. In the eighth they scored 10 runs with Metcalf slugging the game's second grand slam, Saltalamacchia adding a three-run dinger, and three more runs scoring on base hits. The rampaging Texans tacked on another half-dozen runs in their half of the ninth on a bases-loaded double by DH Jason Botts, a run-scoring single by David Murphy – his fifth hit of the game – and Vazquez's second three-run homer of the game.

Among the more "freaky" aspects of the contest, consider that Texas not only scored more runs than they made outs, but they scored those 30 runs in only four innings, an occurrence that could happen only about 1.5 percent of the time or less with a team scoring that many runs, as math wizard Michael Lugo figured out. The bottom two hitters in the Texas lineup, Saltalamacchia, whose batting average went up 83 points during the game, and Vazquez drove in seven runs apiece. Together they accounted for nine runs and eight hits, half of them home runs. Texas had four hitters who had drove in four or more runs during the game (Metcalf and Byrd the other two), something that had never happened in the American League before, or since, and only three times in the National League. The Rangers also had nine players scoring two or more runs, tying a major-league record that has been accomplished several times in both leagues. Texas's 29 hits were the most since the Milwaukee Brewers pounded out 31 in a 22-2 rout of Toronto on August 28, 1992. Their 57 at-bats tied the American League record for a nine-inning game, set in that same Milwaukee-Toronto contest.

Since the game was the first of a doubleheader, and the Rangers took the second game as well, by a score of 9-7, they set an American League record for most runs scored in a single day, 39 — three more than the previous record-holder Detroit had in a twin bill against the St. Louis Browns on August 14, 1937.

Ironically, the Orioles manager Dave Trembley had earlier that day been named the team's manager for 2008. Asked how such a crushing loss should be handled, he replied, "You have a real short memory. You let it go."[3] That's pretty much what he had to say … but baseball fans have long memories, and the record books won't be letting this game go for a long while.

Sources

In addition to the sources cited in the Notes, the author also consulted Baseball-Reference.com, scores.espn.go.com/mlb/recap?gameId=270822201, and two additional articles:

Lugo, Michael, "Texas 30, Baltimore 3." godplaysdice.blogspot.com/2007/08/texas-30-baltimore-3.html

Wood, Allan, "August 22, 2007 – Texas 30, Baltimore 3 (Not A Typo)" joyofsox.blogspot.com/2007/08/texas-30-baltimore-3-not-typo.html

Notes

1 David Ginsberg, "Thirty. That's Something," *Washington Post*, August 22, 2007.

2 Ginsberg.

3 Evan Grant, *Dallas Morning News*, August 23, 2007.

One Sugarcoated Game

June 30, 2009: Baltimore Orioles 11, Boston Red Sox 10, at Oriole Park at Camden Yards

By Thomas E. Schott

There's no way of sugarcoating it: The 2009 Baltimore Orioles were a terrible baseball team. They finished last in their division, 39 games behind the eventual World Series champion New York Yankees, with the worst record in the American League, losing 98 games. An average-hitting team—with below-average power—when it came to pitching, the Orioles set the standard for wretched.[1]

But for one glorious night game, which began in the sunshine on the last day of June, the woeful 34-42 Orioles looked like world-beaters against the powerful, division-leading Boston Red Sox. The 10-run rally in a nine-inning game the Orioles staged that evening remains the team record, but it wasn't the largest in the game's history. Three teams have come back from 11 runs behind to win in regulation. Nonetheless, in a game that lasted almost 3½ hours, including a 70-minute rain delay, the Orioles' rally remains an achievement, especially given the odds of it ever happening.[2]

The Boston visitors, actually cheered by "most of" the 31,969 attendees, virtually owned the Orioles, having beaten them in eight straight games (and 12 of 13), and boasted former, future, and present-day All-Stars, up and down: steady Dustin Pedroia at second, third baseman Kevin Youkilis, power-hitting DH David "Big Papi" Ortiz, outfielders Jacoby Ellsbury and Jason Bay, catcher Jason Varitek, plus All-Star pitchers in starter John Smoltz and closer Jonathan Papelbon, and a bullpen with a couple more standouts. Baltimore countered with little to boast of. Arguably the team's best player, center fielder Adam Jones, left the game with a shoulder injury after two innings and was replaced by youngster Félix Pié. Solid performers like first baseman Luke Scott had a 117 lifetime OPS+, and Nick Markakis in right was in his fourth year of a productive 14-year career through 2019. Rookies Nolan Reimold in left and catcher Mark Wieters rounded out a motley collection of veterans and a pitching staff of average journeymen.[3]

The contrast between the starting pitchers for this game couldn't have been starker. Boston's 42-year-old Cy Young Award winner and future Hall of Famer Smoltz was in the final year of his distinguished career. Baltimore started 29-year-old southpaw Rich Hill, who in his undistinguished previous four years with the Chicago Cubs had gone 18-17 with a 4.37 ERA and 1.268 WHIP.[4]

The ensuing game divides neatly into three parts: the first four innings, all Boston, a short two-inning intermission, and the final three frames, the Orioles' comeback to win. The Red Sox wasted no time scoring. The leadoff guy, shortstop Julio Lugo, singled sharply to left, and after Pedroia popped out, Lugo stole second. Youkilis parked a ball to deep left-center: three hitters, two runs. The Sox put another two guys on—a screaming double to center by Big Papi and a walk to Varitek, but neither scored. The Orioles went three up, three down with two strikeouts. Boston stepped up the pressure in the second. After a bunt groundout, Hill walked first-sacker Jeff Bailey and surrendered another single to Lugo. Pedroia now stroked a line-drive double to the left-center wall, scoring two more runs. The Orioles got a runner on in their half of the inning (Scott walked), but the other three hitters went out.

The Red Sox went quietly in the third, strikeout, groundout, fly out, as if preparing for their next-inning onslaught. Meanwhile, the Orioles managed to score a run on a ground single by shortstop Robert Andino, a career utility infielder, and a line-drive triple to right center by Pié. They were trailing by three when the roof caved in in the top of the fourth.

One Sugarcoated Game

Ellsbury opened with a deep line-drive homer over the fence in center-right. Then with two on (Bailey via a single and Pedroia via a throwing error from third), Youkilis doubled down the left-field line, scoring Bailey. After intentionally walking Jason Bay to load the bases, Hill allowed Ortiz to bash a single to left, filling the bases again. Pedroia scored and the other runners moved up.

This ended Hill's ugly night; righty Matt Albers came in from the pen to quench the flames and plunked the first hitter he faced, forcing in Youkilis from third. After catching the next hitter looking at a third strike, Albers gave up a line-drive single to Ellsbury, his second hit and RBI of the inning. Mercifully, with the sacks still jammed, he got Bailey to ground out. Now with an eight-run lead, Smoltz made quick work of the bottom of the inning: he gave up a one-out single to Reimold, who was erased on a double-play ball by the next batter.[5]

Then came the rain, delaying the game for over an hour. When play resumed in the top of the fifth, Albers gave up an infield single to Youkilis (his third hit of the game), but nothing otherwise. Boston's new hurler—Smoltz was obviously done after the long delay—right-hander Justin Masterton, got three straight Orioles out, two on whiffs. In the top of the sixth, both teams went three up and three down. As the game entered its final three innings, the Red Sox, leading 9-1, were driving down Easy Street. Mark Hendrickson took over pitching for the Orioles. The Red Sox added another run in the top of the seventh: With one out Bailey tripled to center and Pedroia singled him home a batter later.[6]

From this point on, the game underwent an utter transformation. The home team, trailing 10-1, could not err, and the visitors' pitching simply cratered. As one disgusted Boston writer put it: "[T]he Orioles stripped and sold the Red Sox bullpen for parts."[7] First baseman Aubrey Huff singled to open the Orioles' half of the seventh. Reimold singled on the ground to right. DH Scott hit a line-drive double to center-right, scoring Huff. At this point Baltimore sent Óscar Salazar in to hit for Melvin Mora, and he cracked the second pitch he saw deep down the left-field line for a three-run homer. Inexplicably, Masterson stayed in for the next hitter, Wieters, who grounded a single to center. Manny Delcarmen replaced Masterson on the mound. He lasted three batters, getting two groundouts before Pié stroked a single to center, scoring Andino and sending Delcarmen to the showers. Boston's fourth pitcher, Hideki Okajima, finally extricated the Red Sox from their hellish inning. Boston 10, Baltimore 6.

The Red Sox took the field with a comfortable four-run lead in the bottom of the eighth with Okajima still on the mound. He surrendered hits to every batter he faced in the inning: the first four. Line-drive single by Reimold, long fly-ball double to right by Scott, Salazar's squibber in front of the plate, and a line-drive single to left by Wieters, scoring Reimold. Unsurprisingly, Boston decided to switch pitchers, and the home team sent a pinch-hitter to the plate. The new reliever Takashi Saito, a highly effective closer himself, wasn't comfortable in his role as a late-inning set-up man for Boston's All-Star closer Papelbon. Ty Wigginton stood in to hit for Andino and lofted a long fly to deep right that scored Scott. Second baseman Brian Roberts, hitless in four at-bats (indeed, suffering an 0-for-18 skid) followed that with a grass-cutting single to left, scoring Salazar and moving Wieters to second, where pinch-runner Jeremy Guthrie replaced him. Now ahead by only a single run, Boston manager Terry Francona brought Papelbon to the mound. Why not? He was a perfect 20-for-20 in save opportunities against Baltimore. Indeed, he promptly struck out Pié. Markakis, who at that point was 0-for-7 with four strikeouts against Papelbon, jumped on the first pitch and sent a rope to deep left-center for a double that scored both Guthrie and Roberts. The lowly O's had captured the lead from nine runs back![8]

Papelbon got out of the inning with no further damage. Boston made things scary for George Sherrill, the O's closer (and those fans who had hung around through the rain and previous horrors) in the ninth. Bailey led off with his third hit. Sherrill bore down to retire Lugo and Pedroia. But then on a 1-and-2 pitch, with the crowd ready to split the sky in celebration, he hit Youkilis with a pitch, putting the tying and go-ahead runs on base. But Sherrill fanned Jason Bay on four pitches to seal the historic victory. "[A]bsolutely tremendous," Orioles manager Dave Trembley exulted. "When you talk about playing all 27 outs, that's tonight." Smoltz, who had left the game thinking the Red Sox victory was practically in the bag, was amazed. "It's just one of those games . . . you can't believe what you just saw." Papelbon put it more tersely: "We pretty much imploded."[9]

Lest anyone think that this stirring victory ignited the Orioles, don't. They blew a four-run lead in the ninth inning the following evening. Counting the Boston series, the Orioles went on to lose 18 of their remaining 27 series, winning only six and splitting three.[10]

Sources

In addition to the sources cited in the Notes, my thanks to SABR members Gregory Wolf and Bill Nowlin who provided me with research assistance. I also used the statistical data and play-by-play information available at baseball-reference.com and retrosheet.com in preparing this article.

Notes

1 As a team, Baltimore allowed more runs per game (5.41), hits, runs, and home runs, and had the worst ERA (5.15) and WHIP (1.525) in 2009 than any other major-league team. Not to mention the highest number of losses and fewest opponent strikeouts in the AL.

2 David Ginsberg, "Orioles Cap 9-Run Comeback Over Bosox," *Porterville Recorder* (Porterville, California), July 1, 2009; Stacey Long, "June 30, 2009: A Night to Remember," *Orioles Buzz*, June 29, 2011, masnsports.com/orioles-buzz/2011/06/june-30-2009-a-night-to-remember.html, accessed December 29, 2019. Data on the best comebacks for both regulation and extra-inning games is at baseball-reference.com/friv/comeback-wins.shtml, accessed December 29, 2019. In the greatest comeback in a major-league game, the Cleveland Indians erased and surpassed a 12-run Seattle lead in an extra-inning game on August 5, 2001. Chris Jaffe, "10-Year Anniversary of Baseball's Greatest Comeback," *Hardball Times*, August 5, 2011, tht.fangraphs.com/tht-live/10-year-anniversary-of-baseballs-greatest-comeback/, accessed December 29, 2019. Three teams have come back from 11 runs down in a regulation nine-inning game: Philadelphia vs. Cleveland (1925), St. Louis Cardinals vs. New York Giants (1952), and Houston vs. Cardinals (1994).

3 Bill Wagner, "Stirring Surge Shakes Up Sox," *The Capital* (Annapolis, MD), July 1, 2009: A9, A11. Basically a career minor leaguer who occasionally dipped into the Big Show, Félix Pié, who broke into the game at 17, spent parts of six seasons in the big leagues over 12-plus years in Organized Baseball. He slashed .246/.295/.369 in the majors and had a -1.6 WAR and -14 RAR.

4 Hill was with the Orioles for only this season, achieving a 3-3 record in 13 starts with a 7.80 ERA and 1.873 WHIP. Amazingly, he hung on in the big leagues for 10 more years, approximately half the time as a starter and half as bullpen guy.

5 Matt Albers has through 2019 enjoyed a 14-year career solely as a relief specialist with eight different teams in both leagues; Baltimore was his second big-league club.

6 Stacey Long, see note 2.

7 Adam Kilgore, "Stunning Moment in the Rain," *Boston Globe*, July 1, 2009: C6.

8 Associated Press, *Herald* (Jasper, Indiana), July 1, 2009. Interestingly, this second of Papelbon's blown saves of the season came on the night after he tied Bob Stanley's record for career saves with the Red Sox.

9 Kilgore; Amalie Benjamin, "Old Bawl Game," *Boston Globe*, July 1, 2009: C1.

10 Dan Connolly, "Back to Reality for O's," *Baltimore Sun*, July 2, 2009..

Pie Cycles and Tillman Gets First Career Win for Orioles

August 14, 2009: Baltimore Orioles 16, Anaheim Angels 6, at Camden Yards

By Mike Huber

On August 9, 2009, Felix Pie became just the second Baltimore Orioles player to hit for the cycle in a Baltimore ballpark. In the game, Baltimore batters smashed a record nine doubles as part of a 19-hit attack and defeated the Anaheim Angels, 16-6. Orioles rookie Chris Tillman picked up his first career win before a Friday night Camden Yards crowd of 25,836.

The Orioles-Angels matchup also pitted two Izturis brothers against each other. Maicer played second base for the West Division-leading Angels[1] and Cesar played shortstop for Baltimore, which was deep in last place in the AL East.

This was Tillman's fourth career start, and he was facing Anaheim's ace, Jered Weaver, who entered the game with a 12-3 record. Weaver had won nine of his last 14 and had struck out a career high 11 in each of his two previous starts, against Minnesota and Texas. As for Tillman, in his three previous starts, all no-decisions against Kansas City, Detroit, and Toronto), the right-hander had pitched a total of 17⅓ innings and allowed 10 earned runs.

In the first inning Tillman had trouble finding the plate. He walked leadoff batter Chone Figgins, who was thrown out stealing with Maicer Izturis at bat. Then Tillman walked Izturis. Bobby Abreu struck out, but Vladimir Guerrero singled and Izturis scored on a fielding error by Pie. Juan Rivera doubled to center, plating Guerrero. Tillman was off to a quick 2-0 deficit.

The Orioles came back with a vengeance in the bottom of the inning. Brian Roberts led off with a double deep down the right-field line. Adam Jones walked. With one out, Aubrey Huff doubled into the left-center-field gap as Roberts and Jones scored. Nolan Reimold walked, and with two outs Melvin Mora singled to center, scoring Huff. Pie then stroked a line drive into the right-field corner for the third double of the inning, and Baltimore led, 4-2. Cesar Izturis singled, giving Baltimore two more runs. Roberts singled before Jones forced Roberts at second base for the third out. Eleven Orioles had batted and the team scored six times.

In the third, Pie hit a solo home run well beyond the right-field wall, and it was 7-2. After his rough start in the top of the first, Tillman settled down and faced the minimum in the second and third innings. In the Angels' fourth, Abreu led off with a home run to deep center. Rivera hit a one-out double to center and advanced to third on a single by Kendrys Morales, but was thrown out at the plate when Erick Aybar grounded to Cesar Izturis at short, who fired home.

The Orioles responded in their half of the fourth. Jones singled and advanced on a wild pitch. An out later, Huff was intentionally walked, then Reimold also drew a walk, sending Weaver to the showers. Angels manager Mike Scioscia brought in Matt Palmer to face the switch-hitting Matt Wieters, and Wieters sent a fly ball to left, bringing in Jones. Mora walked, but Pie struck out to end the rally. Baltimore added a run in the fifth on back-to-back doubles by Izturis and Roberts.

Tillman appeared to run out of gas in the seventh. With two outs, Mike Napoli singled and O's skipper Dave Trembley pulled Tillman for Matt Albers. Albers yielded a double to Gary Matthews and a single to Figgins. Suddenly, it was a ballgame again with the score 9-5 in favor of Baltimore.

Shane Loux had retired the Orioles in order in the sixth after relieving Palmer, but in the seventh he faced 10 Orioles batters. Pie started the hit parade with a soft single to short. Izturis tripled, Roberts, Jones, and Nick Markakis all doubled and Huff was hit by a pitch before an out was recorded. With two outs and runners at first and second, Pie strode to the plate for the second time in the inning and he shot a ball into the gap in deep right-center, motoring around to third base. The fans gave Pie a standing ovation. Only then did Scioscia lift Loux for Jose Arredondo. Baltimore led by 11 runs, 16-5. Anaheim added two doubles in the eighth for one more run, and the final score was 16-6.

With the triple, Pie had completed the rare feat of hitting for the cycle. According to Baltimore's third-base coach, Juan Samuel, Pie didn't know what he had done. Samuel had to explain to him why the crowd was cheering. "He was like, 'I don't know.' So I said, 'Well, you've got a double, you've got a triple now, you've had a home run and a single. You hit for the cycle. And he said, 'Really?'"[2] This caused the 24-year-old Pie to get excited, pump his fists, and yell to his dugout, which earned him a "staredown from Angels manager Scioscia."[3] Pie apologized to the Angels after the game.

Baltimore hitting coach Terry Crowley said, "You can't begrudge a young kid his emotion when he hits for the cycle. I don't think Scioscia realized that it was the fourth hit of a cycle." He added, "That kid has worked every day. Every day, without missing any time, he just comes in and works. And he went a long span without getting to play because other guys were playing good. It's to his credit. We know he's got some ability, and tonight was a game he'll never forget."[4]

The Orioles tied a franchise record for most doubles in a game, nine. Twelve of their 19 hits were for extra bases (also a record). The Angels added five doubles of their own in a losing cause, with Rivera hitting three in his 3-for-4 performance. The record (as of 2016) for the most doubles by one team in a modern-era game is 12, set by the Boston Red Sox against the Detroit Tigers, on July 29, 1990, and equaled by the Cleveland Indians against the Minnesota Twins on July 13, 1996.[5]

Cesar Izturis nearly matched Pie, missing the cycle by a home run. Orioles skipper Trembley chimed in on Izturis's 3-for-5 game, saying, "He told me he was going to have a big series. It's his turn to turn the tables on his brother. That was fun tonight. Gosh, that was fun."[6] Maicer Izturis was 0-for-4 with a walk and a run scored.

In gaining his first career victory, Tillman matched his season high of 6⅔ innings pitched and allowed four runs (three earned).[7] He said, "It's every kid's dream to pitch in the big leagues, and to finally be here and to get the win—especially with Felix doing what he did tonight—that's awesome."[8] The 21-year-old struck out three and walked two. Weaver, on the other hand, allowed "more earned runs than he had in 21 of 23 games this season."[9] The 3⅓-inning start was his worst of the season. He threw 38 pitches in the first inning.

Pie's cycle was one of the few bright spots in Baltimore's 2009 season. Baltimore slipped into last place in the American League East Division in May and stayed there. Until this win, they had been 7-19 since the All-Star break. A 13-game losing streak to end the month of September took them to 41½ games behind division winner New York. Pie had often been used as a late-inning defensive replacement. However, after August 24, he started every game. Pie's batting average jumped 20 points to .254 after the cycle. He finished the season at .266. He told reporters that this game was "unbelievable," adding, "I'll never forget this game. When I got to the dugout, they hugged me. Good feeling."[10]

Pie became the fourth Oriole to hit for the cycle, joining Brooks Robinson (July 15, 1960), Cal Ripken Jr. (May 6, 1984), and Aubrey Huff (June 29, 2007). Pie's accomplishment came just four days after Colorado Rockies shortstop Troy Tulowitzki hit for the cycle and 12 days after Yankees outfielder Melky Cabrera did it.[11]

Sources

In addition to the sources mentioned in the Notes, the author consulted Baseball-Reference.com, MLB.com, and Retrosheet.org. The author sincerely thanks Meg Gers of the Enoch Pratt Free Library for assistance in obtaining sources from the *Baltimore Sun*.

Notes

1 Despite this loss, the Angels continued to roll, capturing the West Division crown, but they eventually lost in the playoffs to the Yankees.

2 Spencer Fordin, "Pie Hits Triple to Complete Cycle for O's," MLB.com, August 14, 2009. http://mlb.com/news/article/6428288/

3 Fordin.

4 Fordin.

5 On July 3, 1883, the National League's Chicago White Stockings hit 14 doubles against the Buffalo Bisons (Chicago won, 31-7). The St. Louis Cardinals stroked 13 doubles against the Chicago Cubs on July 12, 1931 (the Cubs added another 10 doubles to the game, as the Cardinals outslugged the Cubs in the second game of a doubleheader at Sportsman's Park, 17-13). Of the 37 hits in the game, 23 were doubles. There were no triples and only one home run. http://Baseball-Almanac.com/rb_2b2.shtml.

6 Fordin.

7 Tillman finished his first season in the major leagues with a record of 2-5 and a 5.40 ERA. He allowed 77 hits in 65 innings, striking out 39 and walking 24.

8 Dan Connolly, "Orioles Cycle Past Angels," *Baltimore Sun*, August 15, 2009: 3.

9 Mike DiGiovanna, "Weaver Rattled by Orioles," *Los Angeles Times*, August 15, 2009: 20.

10 Fordin.

11 Eight major leaguers hit for the cycle in 2009; Pie's was the seventh.

Orioles Play Spoiler, Strike Midnight on Red Sox Season

September 28, 2011: Baltimore Orioles 4, Boston Red Sox 3, at Oriole Park at Camden Yards

By Timothy Kearns

In 2010 manager Buck Showalter's arrival seemed to provide a spark for the moribund Baltimore Orioles, who mustered a .596 winning percentage under Showalter after beginning the season with a brutal 32-73 record.

The 2011 Orioles had failed to continue that success, however. After starting the season 6-1, they fell off immediately with an eight-game skid. By September 1, they were already eliminated from the playoffs.

The Boston Red Sox were seemingly the Orioles' antithesis. The Red Sox started the season 0-6, but by September 3 their record was 84-54 – a half-game behind the division-leading Yankees but still nine games ahead of the nearest wild-card "contender," the 75-63 Tampa Bay Rays.

In a stretch that was sure to please fans of Monte Carlo simulations and probabilistic scenarios, the Red Sox were a stunning 6-20 in September, including a 1-6 record against the Rays. The Red Sox entered the season finale at Oriole Park at Camden Yards with their nine-game lead over the Rays eradicated. The teams were now tied for the wild card. But the Sox controlled their own fate. If they won, their season could not end without at least one more game.

To seek that win, Boston sent Jon Lester to the mound on three days' rest for only the second time in his career.[1] Lester had struggled in September, posting an ERA of 6.97 over his last four starts, but had dominated the Orioles in his career, entering the game 14-0 in 17 starts against Baltimore.[2]

The Orioles countered with Alfredo Simon, a pitcher whose role on the Orioles had been imperiled in the offseason by his implication as a suspect in a shooting in the Dominican Republic.[3]

The teams traded zeroes in the first two innings, each side putting a runner on in their respective halves of the first and second.

To begin the third, Simon walked the Red Sox' number-nine hitter, third baseman Mike Aviles. Jacoby Ellsbury lined a single to left field, putting runners on first and second. The next batter, Dustin Pedroia, sharply grounded a single to center on the first pitch to him, driving in Aviles.

With two on and still no one out, the Red Sox were well-positioned to pad their advantage. Instead, slugger David Ortiz grounded into a double play. After an intentional walk to Adrian Gonzalez, the Orioles struck out catcher Ryan Lavarnway to limit the damage to one run.

In the bottom half, Lester walked leadoff batter Chris Davis on eight pitches before retiring the next two Orioles. With two outs, J.J. Hardy drove Lester's first-pitch cutter deep into the left-field stands to put the Orioles in front, 2-1.

Simon and the Orioles cost themselves the lead with miscues in the fourth.

With one out, Marco Scutaro doubled. He advanced to third on a fielder's choice. Simon was then called for a balk, sending Scutaro home. The score even, Aviles drove a sharp grounder under the arm of third baseman Davis before being caught stealing to end the inning.

After Lester held the Orioles scoreless, Pedroia pushed the Red Sox ahead again by driving a home run five rows into the left-field seats, making the score 3-2, Red Sox. Ortiz singled to knock Simon out of the contest. Reliever Troy Patton closed out the fifth and then worked a scoreless sixth for the Orioles.

Lester showed signs of tiring in the sixth, walking the first two batters of the inning. He was saved by a double play started by Scutaro, who ranged to his right to glove Vladimir Guerrero's grounder, then flipped the ball to Pedroia with his glove hand. Pedroia's relay narrowly beat Guerrero. Lester then walked Matt Wieters before striking out Adam Jones swinging.

The Red Sox squandered further opportunities in the seventh before the game was interrupted by a rain delay. When the top of the seventh ended, Boston was nine outs away from a trip to the wild-card game. Boston led 3-2. The Rays trailed the Yankees 7-0 in the eighth inning.

By the time the game resumed, however, Boston's fortunes had changed. They still led, but their game was now seemingly a must-win. The Rays and Yankees were now tied at 7 runs apiece thanks to a pinch-hit home run by .108-hitting Dan Johnson with two outs in the ninth inning. With Lester out of the game after the rain delay, the Red Sox bullpen was left to protect the narrowest of leads.

Alfredo Aceves entered the game for the Red Sox and hit two Orioles batters with pitches, but ultimately stranded both runners. Orioles reliever Pedro Strop blanked the Red Sox in the eighth. The latter then turned the ball over to hard thrower Daniel Bard.

Bard faced only three batters to escape the eighth inning with a 3-2 lead, with the highlight being future Hall of Famer Guerrero's final major-league at-bat. With one out, Guerrero drove a 0-and-1 pitch to deep center field, but Ellsbury handled it just shy of the warning track.

Despite entering the top of the ninth with a deficit, the Orioles called for Jim Johnson, who had largely seized the closer role in September with seven saves, to pitch. After first-base umpire Scott Barry called Ellsbury out on a weak grounder to the first-base side, home-plate umpire John Hirschbeck reversed the call, determining that Mark Reynolds had failed to control the throw from catcher Wieters. Ellsbury then stole second and moved to third on a single from Pedroia. Ortiz chopped a weak grounder a few feet in front of home plate, allowing the Orioles to retire Pedroia at second without Ellsbury scoring. After Adrian Gonzalez was given his third intentional walk of the game, Lavarnway bounced to short for a double play, quashing another Red Sox threat.

The Red Sox turned to closer Jonathan Papelbon, who had blown only two saves in 33 opportunities. Adam Jones swung over the top of a 2-and-2 two-seam fastball to lead off the inning. This brought up Reynolds, who swung under a 1-and-2 fastball, extending his all-time American League record to 196 strikeouts,[4] and the Red Sox were one out away.

Chris Davis drove Papelbon's next pitch to right field, barely beating the throw into second base. With the tying run in scoring position, the Orioles pinch-ran for Davis with rookie Kyle Hudson.

Papelbon fell behind Nolan Reimold 2-and-0, but elicited two swinging strikes to even the count and put the Red Sox one strike away from the postseason. Instead, Reimold drove the ball just to the right of center field, with the ball bouncing into the railing off the Eutaw Street bleachers for a game-tying double.

This brought Robert Andino to the plate. Andino, who had doubled home Mark Reynolds to induce Papelbon's second blown save of the season just eight days earlier,[5] took a ball outside and then watched a strike go past to even the count at 1-and-1.

Andino hit a soft liner to left, where it met a sliding Carl Crawford's glove and then the turf, as Crawford trapped the ball. Reimold, running on contact, beat Crawford's offline throw to the plate and secured a win for the Orioles.

The Orioles "celebrated like they won the World Series"[6] and Boston's hopes now depended solely upon the success of their archrival Yankees, whose game remained tied 7-7 in the top of the 12th.

Three minutes later, at 12:05 A.M., the Rays' Evan Longoria ended the Red Sox season for good by lining a home run off Yankees reliever Scott Proctor, with the line drive scooting over Tropicana Field's short left-field fence. A thrilling night in baseball history had come to a wildly improbable end.

The Orioles' unlikely comeback helped substantially alter baseball's landscape, even though the Rays were dispatched in the ALDS by the ultimate pennant-winning Texas Rangers. After Boston's elimination, manager Terry Francona was

• Orioles Play Spoiler, Strike Midnight on Red Sox Season •

fired despite winning two World Series with the Red Sox. General manager Theo Epstein left shortly thereafter for the Chicago Cubs,[7] and controversies surrounding consumption of fried chicken and beer in the clubhouse swirled over the Red Sox pitching staff.[8] The 2012 Orioles delivered on the promise of another inspiring September, making an unlikely run to the postseason on the back of incredible success in close games.[9]

The Orioles' success is celebrated in a photo display in a place few fans would expect to commemorate great moments in Orioles history: Tropicana Field, home of the Tampa Bay Rays.

Sources

In addition to the articles cited in the Notes, the author consulted Baseball-Reference.com and the MASN Broadcast of Boston Red Sox vs. Baltimore Orioles, September 28, 2011, available at youtube.com/watch?v=Qq6DNcxJn8U

Notes

1. "Red Sox, Rays: Down to One Game," *Hartford Courant*, September 28, 2011.
2. Peter Abraham, "What Can Be Expected from Jon Lester Tonight?" *Boston Globe,* September 28, 2011, boston.com/sports/extra-bases/2011/09/28/what_can_be_exp.
3. Dan Connolly, "Orioles Reliever Alfredo Simon Is Main Suspect in Fatal Shooting," *Baltimore Sun*, January 2, 2011.
4. Reynolds at the time had the ignominious ownership of the all-time single-season records for strikeouts by a batter in a season in both the National League (223 in 2009 with Arizona) and American League (196 in 2011 with Baltimore). His AL record was surpassed by Adam Dunn in the 2012 season.
5. "Papelbon, Red Sox Falter," *Portland* (Maine) *Press Herald*, September 20, 2011.
6. Peter Schmuck, "Spoiler Alert: O's Bounce BoSox Out of Postseason," *Baltimore Sun*, September 29, 2011.
7. Chad Finn, "Theo Epstein: It Truly Feels Great to Join Cubs," *Boston Globe*, October 25, 2011.
8. Bob Hohler, "Inside the Collapse," *Boston Globe*, October 12, 2011.
9. The 2012 Orioles finished the season with a record of 93-69, but with records of 29-9 in one-run games and 63-35 in games decided by three runs or fewer. Jon Meoli, "One-Run Games Are Rare for Orioles This Year, But Record in Close Games Carrying Them Again," *Baltimore Sun*, September 16, 2016.

Orioles Lead Off Game with Three Consecutive Home Runs

May 10, 2012: Baltimore Orioles 6, Texas Rangers 5 (first game of two), at Oriole Park at Camden Yards

By Bob Brown

It was a crazy week for Orioles fans in mid-May of 2012. The Sunday series finale in Boston on May 6 had them trying to complete a three-game sweep in Fenway Park after a three-game series win at Yankee Stadium. The Orioles had not won consecutive series in New York and Boston in 20 years.[1] Although that feat was already accomplished heading into the Sunday afternoon game, the visitors wanted nothing more than to sweep the Red Sox in a season that was starting to provide reason for optimism among Orioles fans, who had not seen the playoffs in 14 seasons. In a wild 17-inning affair, the Orioles got their series sweep, with designated hitter Chris Davis pitching the last two innings and recording the win after Adam Jones homered off former Oriole Darnell McDonald, a Boston outfielder who entered the game as a pinch-runner in the eighth inning before taking the mound in the top of the 17th.

After the Red Sox series, the Orioles were atop the AL East by a half-game over Tampa Bay, with the heavy-hitting Texas Rangers coming to town for a four-game series. After Texas won the opener on Monday by the lopsided score of 14-3, the second game of the series belonged to Josh Hamilton. The Rangers slugger homered four times in the game, only the 16th time the feat had been accomplished in the major leagues, in a 10-3 Rangers blowout of the Orioles.[2] A rainout on Wednesday forced a day/night doubleheader on Thursday.

The Orioles were in survival mode. Since the end of the Red Sox Series on Sunday, they had made 12 roster moves because of injuries. In addition, the bullpen was logging overtime – with the Red Sox opener lasting 13 innings and Sunday's 17-inning marathon, and the combined scores of 24-6 in the first two Rangers games.[3] The first game of the twin bill had Wei-Yin Chen taking the mound for the Orioles, facing Colby Lewis of the Rangers. The Orioles would need some offensive fireworks of their own, which didn't take long to generate.

After a quiet top of the first inning, Orioles leadoff hitter Ryan Flaherty led off the bottom of the first with his first major-league home run, to right field, off Lewis's second pitch. J.J. Hardy followed with a home run to left, and, not to be outdone, Nick Markakis went deep to right to give the home team a 3-0 lead. For just the fourth time in major-league history and the first time ever in the American League, a team led off its half of the first inning with three consecutive home runs. However, Lewis immediately settled down in a big way, retiring the next 18 batters he faced.

The Rangers got one run back in the fourth, on Michael Young's double and Yorvit Torrealba's single to make the score 3-1. In the bottom of the seventh, Adam Jones led off the inning with a home run to put the Orioles up by three. After a walk to Matt Wieters, Wilson Betemit homered, increasing the lead to a seemingly comfortable 6-1. At this point, Lewis's day was feast or famine – three consecutive home runs, followed by 18 consecutive outs, followed by a solo home run, a walk, and a two-run shot. Lewis would finish out the inning before being lifted in the eighth. His line: six runs, five hits (all home runs), and 12 strikeouts. "I can't justify that game," Lewis said. "It seemed like one of those days where you have really good stuff, and then you miss your spot or something, and it's not just a hit, it's a homer. You can't really look at it any other way. It was just kind of a weird game."[4]

The Rangers tallied another run in the eighth, on two-out singles by Elvis Andrus and Hamilton. The Orioles seemed to escape unscathed, but an error by third baseman Betemit allowed Andrus to score, making it 6-2. In the top of the ninth, Nelson Cruz led off with a single and Torrealba doubled to chase reliever Luis Ayala. The Orioles brought in closer Jim Johnson, and one out later pinch-hitter David Murphy

• Orioles Lead Off Game with Three Consecutive Home Runs •

homered to bring the Rangers to within one. Johnson recorded the final two outs and the save, with Ian Kinsler grounding out to third, followed by an Andrus strikeout to end the game.

In the nightcap, the Rangers earned a doubleheader split and a three-games-to-one series win with a 7-3 victory. Hamilton, not finished with his abuse of Camden Yards and Orioles pitching, slugged a two-run home run in the first, his major-league-leading 15th of the year in just his 29th game of the season. He finished 2012 with 43 homers, one shy of Miguel Cabrera's league-leading 44.

As of 2020 the Orioles' history-making first inning remained the only time an American League team accomplished the feat of the first three batters homering. The six occurrences are summarized in the table below.

Other interesting facts:

• The team accomplishing the feat won five of the six games; the lone loss is the Padres in 1987.

• Two players have been part of a three-home-run barrage twice: Hardy with the Brewers in 2007 and the Orioles in 2012, and Peralta with the Diamondbacks in 2017 and 2019.

• Of the six occurrences, the home team accomplished it four times, the road team (i.e., in the first three at-bats of the game) twice.

• Only once was the victimized pitcher a Cy Young Award winner that year – Scherzer in 2017.

The Orioles, led by Buck Showalter in his second full season as manager, finished 2012 at 93-69, which was good enough to play in the postseason's first one-game wild-card match, against … the Rangers. Despite their 2-5 record against the Rangers, having been outscored in the regular season 56-24, the Orioles defeated the Rangers 5-1, earning the right to play the top-seeded New York Yankees in the ALDS. It was the Orioles' first trip to the postseason since 1997, and they took the Yankees to the brink before eventually falling in the series, three games to two.

Sources

In addition to the sources cited in the Notes, the author consulted Baseball-Reference.com and Retrosheet.org.

Notes

1 Kevin Cowherd, "After Surreal Win, It Seems These Orioles Won't Go Away," *Baltimore Sun*, May 7, 2012: 21.

2 As of 2020 the four-home-run feat has been matched twice more – by Scooter Gennett of the Cincinnati Reds on June 6, 2017, against the St. Louis Cardinals, and by J.D. Martinez for the Arizona Diamondbacks against the Los Angeles Dodgers, on September 4, 2017.

3 Eduardo A. Encina, "O's Start with a Bang, Split," *Baltimore Sun*, May 11, 2012: D1.

4 David Ginsburg (Associated Press), "Hamilton Hits MLB-Leading 15th Home Run, Helps Rangers to Split," *The Monitor* (McAllen, Texas), May 11, 2012: C3.

First Three Batters Hitting Consecutive Home Runs

Date	Teams (League)	Players	Pitcher	Score
April 13, 1987	San Diego vs San Francisco (NL)	Marvell Wynne, Tony Gwynn, John Kruk	Roger Mason	Giants 13, Padres 6
May 28, 2003	Atlanta vs. Cincinnati (NL)	Rafael Furcal, Mark DeRosa, Gary Sheffield	Jeff Austin	Braves 15, Reds 3
September 9, 2007	Milwaukee at Cincinnati (NL)	Rickie Weeks, J.J. Hardy, Ryan Braun	Phil Dumatrait	Brewers 10, Reds 5
May 10, 2012	Orioles vs. Texas (AL)	Ryan Flaherty, J.J. Hardy, Nick Markakis	Colby Lewis	Orioles 6, Rangers 5
July 21, 2017	Arizona vs. Washington (NL)	David Peralta, A.J. Pollock, Jake Lamb	Max Scherzer	Diamondbacks 6, Nationals 5
June 10, 2019	Arizona at Philadelphia (NL	Jarrod Dyson, Ketel Marte, David Peralta	Jerad Eickhoff	Diamondbacks 13, Phillies 8

Young's Pinch Hit Gives Baltimore Playoff Boost vs. Detroit

October 3, 2014: Baltimore Orioles 7, Detroit Tigers 6, at Camden Yards

By Robert Kimball

Want an example of a roaring crowd? Look no further than the afternoon of October 3, 2014, when the Baltimore Orioles rallied past the Detroit Tigers, 7-6. It was a day on which former Tiger Delmon Young continued his postseason magic to help the Orioles, who were back in the playoffs after a one-year hiatus that followed a five-game Division Series loss to the New York Yankees in 2012.

The Tigers also were itching to break through, having dropped the American League pennant playoff to the Boston Red Sox the previous October, the 2012 World Series to the San Francisco Giants, and the 2011 ALCS to the Texas Rangers.

Game Two of the 2014 Tigers-Orioles Division Series was scheduled for Camden Yards less than 24 hours after the Orioles set a club postseason scoring record in a 12-3 victory.[1] Baltimore beat Tigers starter and reigning Cy Young Award winner Max Scherzer, with a boost from an eight-run eighth inning.

The second game started just past noon and the Orioles faithful were in full throat that Friday hoping Taiwanese left-hander Wei-Yin Chen could best Detroit's Justin Verlander, who in 2011 had won the Cy Young and MVP Awards.

Chen kept the Tigers scoreless for the first three innings while the Orioles reached Verlander in the third when Nick Markakis's line drive hit just above the wall in right and ricocheted onto the field. Crew chief Jeff Kellogg checked with the replay crew, who upheld the umpire's call: two-run homer and a 2-0 Baltimore lead.

But Baltimore's edge evaporated half an inning later when the first five Detroit batters reached and the Tigers grabbed a 5-2 lead. Before Chen hit the showers, J.D. Martinez and Nicholas Castellanos homered back-to-back. Kevin Gausman relieved and wound up throwing 3⅔ innings of one-run baseball.

Meantime, J.J. Hardy's RBI single in the fourth cut the Detroit lead to 5-3 in favor of Verlander, who departed one batter into the sixth for Anibal Sanchez.

Gausman's runs-allowed total could have climbed higher but for stellar defense in the eighth. Victor Martinez doubled off the center-field wall to score Torii Hunter but Adam Jones fired the ball to Jonathan Schoop, whose relay to Caleb Joseph nailed Miguel Cabrera trying to score from first.[2] The play kept the score 6-3, Detroit, for eventual winner Brad Brach, who got the final two outs. The play at the plate was also a key to the last half of the eighth.

The Tigers looked to preserve the lead and tie the series behind their relievers. First up was Joba Chamberlain, who tipped his cap to the lively Baltimore crowd as he entered from the center-field bullpen.[3]

Chamberlain's nod to the fans might have been his top moment of the day. With one out, he hit Jones with a pitch and surrendered consecutive singles to Nelson Cruz and Steve Pearce that scored one run and left a mess for Joakim Soria. Hardy then walked to load the bases and bring up Delmon Young, who, despite being a right-handed batter against a right-handed pitcher, was Baltimore manager Buck Showalter's choice to pinch-hit for lefty-swinging Ryan Flaherty. Asked why he used Young in that spot, Showalter said, "He's a professional hitter. … You can hang your hat on a professional hitter."[4]

Showalter probably also knew that Young was 10-for-20 as a pinch-batter in his first season with the Orioles, his fifth team in a 10-year career. And it probably was no surprise that Young wasted no time as he owned a .425 first-pitch batting average in 2014.[5]

"He's a fastball hitter, he swings at the first pitch," said Soria, the losing pitcher. "I threw a slider, and he was on it."[6]

With the Baltimore fans in full deafening-sounding mode, Young's line drive skipped to the left-field wall, where J.D. Martinez fielded the carom. Cruz, Pearce, and Hardy scored – and the noise from the crowd of 48,058 could be heard from Western Maryland to the lower Chesapeake Bay.

After Brian Anderson told the national cable audience on TBS that "the legend of Delmon Young

• Young's Pinch Hit Gives Baltimore Playoff Boost vs. Detroit •

in the postseason continues," color man and former big leaguer Joe Simpson noted that Martinez made a telling bobble that helped Hardy beat the relay from Ian Kinsler. "It took him two grabs to pick it up and that was the difference at home plate," Simpson said.[7]

Meantime an amazed Caleb Joseph watched from the on-deck circle. "It's still the loudest roar I think I've ever heard in my life," he told MLB.com a few years later. "It felt like the stadium was moving because so many people were excited about what was going on."[8]

As the fans buzzed, Young maintained a level outlook. "I'm always comfortable in the batter's box," he told the press after the game. "It doesn't matter whether I haven't had a hit in a while or I'm 10-for-10."[9]

Zack Britton retired the Tigers 1-2-3 in the ninth for the save, sending the series to Detroit, where the Orioles polished off the sweep with a 2-1 victory two days later. Cruz, who finished the series with six hits and five RBIs, cracked a two-run homer off David Price to make the difference.

Young's rousing hit and the series victory over Detroit were high points for the Orioles, who were swept by the Kansas City Royals in the ALCS, missed the playoffs in 2015 and then dropped a controversial AL wild-card game in Toronto the next year. Showalter will forever take heat in Birdland for not using Britton against the Blue Jays, who won 5-2 in 11 innings. The Orioles then slid into oblivion with sub-.500 years that included 100-loss seasons in 2018 and '19.

Meantime, the Tigers endured losing for the next five years after the postseason loss to the Orioles, finishing 2019 at a baseball-worst 47-114.

Young went 0-for-3 with two strikeouts for the Orioles against Detroit in the series finale at Comerica Park before getting one hit and one RBI in two games of the ALCS loss to the Royals. That completed a run of six consecutive playoff years for Young, whose October résumé included becoming the first player with four game-winning RBI in one postseason series when he helped the Tigers sweep the Yankees for the 2012 AL flag.[10]

Young's strong postseasons never translated to his private life. He was baseball's number-1 overall draft choice in 2003 of the then Tampa Bay Devil Rays, but never quite clicked in a decade-long career. He served a 50-game suspension from the minor leagues for flinging a bat that hit an umpire in 2006, sat out for seven days after he harassed people on a New York City street in 2012, and was arrested and charged with battery in Miami in 2016.[11]

The Orioles kept Young in 2015 but he lasted just 52 games before his release on July 9. Although just 29, he never played in the major leagues again. Less than a year earlier, his playoff lightning bolt made Camden Yards the perfect example of where to find a roaring crowd.

Sources
In addition to the sources cited in the Notes, the author relied on Baseball-Reference.com and Retrosheet.org for box scores and series summaries.

Notes
1 Bryan Kilpatrick, "Nelson Cruz Leads Baltimore's Offensive Onslaught in 12-3 Rout," SB Nation, October 2, 2014.

2 Dave Sheinin, "Three-Run Double by Delmon Young Gives Orioles a 7-6 Win and 2-0 Lead Over Tigers in ALDS," *Washington Post*, October 3, 2014.

3 Sheinin.

4 Sheinin.

5 Eduardo A. Encina, "Young Plays Role of Postseason Hero Again," *Baltimore Sun*, October 3, 2014.

6 Encina.

7 TBS Tigers-Orioles broadcast, YouTube.com from G4MarchMadnessHD, October 3, 2014.

8 Brittany Ghiroli, "Delmon Young an Unlikely O's Postseason Hero," mlb.com, September 23, 2018.

9 Encina.

10 Associated Press from STATS LLC, "Tigers Delmon Young Wins ALCS MVP Award," October 18, 2012.

11 Associated Press via espn.com, "MLB player Delmon Young Charged with Attacking Attendant," February 8, 2016.

Delmon Young's bases-clearing double gave the Orioles a 7-6 lead, and a win in Game Two of the 2014 ALDS.
Courtesy of the Baltimore Orioles.

Orioles and White Sox Play for Normalcy in Empty Stadium

April 29, 2015: Baltimore Orioles 8, Chicago White Sox 2, at Camden Yards

By Mike Huber

In the aftermath of a terrible city-wide tragedy, the Baltimore Orioles tried to help baseball return to normalcy with a game at Camden Yards – in front of no one. Protests and riots in Baltimore created a situation of uncertainty. Security concerns resulting after unrest surrounded the death of Freddie Gray led to overtaxed law enforcement resources, so Major League Baseball sent out the following press release: "After conferring with local officials, it was determined that Wednesday afternoon's game [between the Orioles and White Sox] should be played without fan admittance in order to minimize safety concerns."[1] Maryland's Governor Larry Hogan had declared a state of emergency and had activated the National Guard "in an attempt to restore order."[2] The previous two games had already been postponed amid ongoing riots across Baltimore; they would be made up in a later doubleheader. The start time of the game was also changed, from 7:05 PM to 2:05 PM, since a city-wide curfew of 10:00 PM had been mandated by city officials. The game was closed to the public. This was not indicative of Baltimore's reputation as Charm City or The Land of Pleasant Living, and, as Orioles slugger Chris Davis remarked, "This isn't the way you want to make history."[3]

The decision by Major League Baseball meant that there was no one to root, root, root for the home team. Even though no fans were allowed in the stadium, the press box filled three-and-a-half hours before the scheduled first pitch.[4] There were two scouts behind home plate and a few photographers strewn throughout the ballpark, but "the 45,971 seats and three decks at Camden Yards were an empty expanse of green."[5] One tradition that has occurred at Orioles games for decades is the familiar shouting during the national anthem (at the moment of "O say, does that start-spangled banner yet wave"). About three dozen fans stood outside the stadium, trying to peek through the iron fence, and they shouted, "Ohhh" at the right moment.[6] No ushers were present. No beer vendors. No peanuts or hot dogs. Even the National Anthem, normally sung in person, was pre-recorded.

The contest marked the first time "in the history of the four major American professional sports leagues that a game was played to an intentionally empty stadium."[7] There was a precedent for postponing games due to civil unrest. The start of the 1968 season was postponed due to Martin Luther King Jr.'s funeral. The Los Angeles Dodgers postponed four games due to the Rodney King verdict announcement in 1992.[8] The 2001 season was delayed after the terrorist attacks at the World Trade Center and Pentagon. The Boston Red Sox postponed a game on April 19, 2013, in an effort to support law enforcement efforts to apprehend the Boston Marathon bomber.[9] However, all of those postponed games had fans in attendance.

The official attendance for the match between the Orioles and White Sox was zero. The previous low mark in attendance at Baltimore also involved the White Sox. It was a make-up game played on August 17, 1972, at Memorial Stadium, before a meager crowd of 655 fans, even though Baltimore was in first place at the time. This game also broke the previous major-league low attendance record of six. That's right; six fans officially attended a game on September 28, 1882, between the Troy Trojans and the Worcester Ruby Legs. The Ruby Legs folded at the end of their 18-66 season.[10]

Ubaldo Jimenez started for the Birds. He retired the White Sox in order in the first, striking out Adam Eaton and Jose Abreu. No one cheered. In the bottom of the first, Chicago pitcher Jeff Samardzija got into trouble immediately. He walked Alejandro De Aza.

• Orioles and White Sox Play for Normalcy in Empty Stadium •

There were no fans to scramble for the ball Chris Davis hit for a home run in the 2015 game at Oriole Park. Courtesy of the Babe Ruth Museum.

Jimmy Paredes reached on an error by Abreu at first, and Delmon Young singled to center, loading the bases. Adam Jones sent a ball to right field, deep enough for De Aza to score on the sacrifice fly. Davis then crushed a three-run home run to deep right field. No fans scrambled after the souvenir. Only a lone television cameraman stood anywhere close to the ball.[11] Davis said, "I'll take any home run I can get at any time I can get it, but it's definitely more fun when there are fans in the stands."[12] Manny Machado kept the inning going with a double to center. Everth Cabrera traded places with Machado with an RBI double to left. Caleb Joseph singled, driving in Cabrera. An out later, De Aza singled, and then Paredes grounded out to end the inning. Baltimore had sent 11 men to the plate and had scored six runs (five earned). De Aza had reached base twice in the opening inning.

Baltimore added a run in the third, when Machado singled, Cabrera doubled, and Joseph singled for his second RBI of the game. Jimenez was dominating until the fifth inning, but then he ran into some trouble. Adam LaRoche walked, Avisail Garcia was safe on an infield single, and Alexei Ramirez reached on a two-base throwing error by Machado, allowing LaRoche to score. Geovany Soto grounded out to the shortstop, but Garcia scored on the play. Chicago had scored two unearned runs.

Machado atoned for his fielding miscue by homering in the bottom of the fifth, and the score was 8-2, where it would stay. Samardzija was tagged for eight runs in only five innings. He picked up his second loss of the season. Jimenez won for the second time, scattering three hits with a walk in seven innings, and he struck out six Sox.

Offensively for the Orioles, Davis had the big blow in the first inning, his fifth homer of the young season. Machado was 3-for-4 with three runs scored. Cabrera and Joseph each had two hits. Baltimore had an 11-hit attack and only left four men on base.

Davis tried to make the best of this bizarre set of circumstances. One of his first-base routines was to toss a ball to fans as he came off the field. In this game, he sent the balls to imaginary fans. "I threw three or four into the lower seats and then I gave some love to the fans in the upper deck," Davis mused after the game.[13]

Several of the players spoke about the eeriness in the ballpark. White Sox manager Robin Ventura told reporters, "It was just a surreal environment. I don't think we really want to play another like this…. I don't think (the Orioles) do either."[14] Baltimore closer Zack Britton remarked that "it was tougher to stay focused on the game than I thought it would be. The noise just echoed off the [B&O] warehouse…. It makes you appreciate the fans who come out and support you."[15] Britton added, "It felt like we were playing in a ghost town."[16] Joseph stated that "Between innings was the most awkward part of the game. You're used to the Kiss-Cam and all the other between-innings entertainment."[17] John Denver's "Thank God I'm a Country Boy" played as usual during the seventh-inning stretch, but there were no fans to sing along. Orioles manager Buck Showalter said "the bullpen phone could be heard ringing more than 400 feet from the dugout."[18]

Jay Jaffe, writing for *Sports Illustrated*, argued that, "In the grand scheme of things, the procession of the baseball season is a comparatively minor matter relative to the safety of the general public. Just the same, being able to play games as scheduled is a sign of normalcy and order. Here's hoping both return to Baltimore as soon as possible."[19] Showalter tried to sum up the day with, "We've made quite a statement as a city, some good and some bad. Now, let's get on with taking the statements we've made and create a positive."[20] Orioles centerfielder Jones added, "We need this game to be played, but we need this city to be healed first. That's what is important to me, that the city is healed because this is an ongoing issue. I just hope the community of Baltimore stays strong, the children of Baltimore stay strong and get some guidance and heed the message of city leaders."[21]

Sources

In addition to the sources mentioned in the notes, the author consulted baseball-reference.com and retrosheet.org.

Editor's note

For posterity, the 2020 season was affected by the COVID-19 global pandemic. MLB regular season games were played to empty stadiums. At the start of the 2021 season, the Orioles welcomed back 11,000 fans to Camden Yards, which was 25% capacity. Mid-March attendance was capped at 50% and starting June 1, 2021 all capacity restrictions were removed for fan attendance.

Notes

1 K. M. McFarland, "That Was the Strangest MLB Game Ever," found online at www.wired.com/2015/04/baltimore-ghost-baseball-game/.

2 Jay Jaffe, "Orioles-White Sox game closed to fans will be odd, historic for MLB," found online at www.si.com/mlb/2015/04/28/orioles-white-sox-camden-yards-closed-fans-baseball-history.

3 Jeré Longman, "Orioles Play in Eerily Empty Stadium, Sirens in Distance," found online at www.nytimes.com/2015/04/30/sports/baseball/orioles-play-in-eerily-empty-stadium-sirens-in-distance.html?_r=0.

4 "Orioles Beat White Sox 8-2 in Empty-Stadium Game at Camden Yards," found online at abc7chicago.com/sports/orioles-beat-white-sox-8-2-in-empty-stadium-game/686869/.

5 Longman.

6 Longman.

7 McFarland.

8 McFarland.

9 Jaffe.

10 Jaffe.

11 Longman.

12 Dan Connolly, "Orioles start fast in empty park, emerge from surreal day with 8-2 win over White Sox," found online at www.baltimoresun.com/sports/bal-baltimore-orioles-score-six-in-first-roll-to-82-win-over-chicago-white-sox-at-empty-camden-yards-20150429-story.html.

13 "Fanless Orioles game an unusual experience for ballplayers," found online at www.espn.com/espn/print?id=12789040.

14 Collen Kane, "White Sox lose to Orioles 8-2 in 'strangeness' of empty ballpark," found online at www.chicagotribune.com/sports/baseball/whitesox/ct-gameday-white-sox-orioles--spt-0430-20150429-story.html.

15 www.espn.com.

16 www.espn.com.

17 www.espn.com.

18 Longman.

19 Jaffe.

20 Connolly.

21 Kane.

Orioles Clout Franchise-Best Eight Homers in 19-3 Rout of Phillies

June 16, 2015: Baltimore Orioles 19, Philadelphia Phillies 3, at Oriole Park at Camden Yards

By Mike Lynch

The June 16, 2015, contest between the Baltimore Orioles and Philadelphia Phillies at Oriole Park at Camden Yards pitted two teams at opposite ends of the spectrum. A Baltimore 4-0 win over Philadelphia on June 15 nudged the Orioles over .500 and though they sat in fourth place at 32-31, the defending American League East champs were only three games out of first. At 22-43, the Phillies were the worst team in all of baseball and were already 13 games behind the National League East's front-running Mets. Philadelphia's offense was so anemic that the team scored only 197 runs in its first 65 games, almost 100 fewer than the league-leading Arizona Diamondbacks.

Philadelphia's pitching wasn't much better and its team ERA was about to take a massive hit.[1] Few epitomized the Phillies' struggles more than journeyman right-hander Jerome Williams, a 33-year-old former first-round pick who was selected 39th overall by the San Francisco Giants in the 1999 Amateur Draft. Williams debuted for the Giants in 2003 at only 21, but couldn't live up to his draft status and bounced around baseball, playing for six major-league teams before landing with the Phillies in 2014. Despite impressing in nine starts to close out the season, Williams had struggled through his first 13 starts of 2015 and was 3-6 with a 5.71 ERA going into the June 16 tilt.

The Orioles countered with 27-year-old righty Chris Tillman, who was drafted by the Seattle Mariners in the second round of the 2006 Amateur Draft. He spent two years in the Mariners organization before being traded to Baltimore in 2008 for pitcher Erik Bedard and was among the top minor-league prospects prior to his 2009 debut.[2] After three years of struggles in his early 20s, Tillman fashioned a three-year run from 2012 to 2014 that saw him go 38-16 with a 3.42 ERA in 82 starts. But 2015 wasn't treating him as well and he went into his start against the Phillies at 4-7 with a 5.68 ERA.

The Phillies started on a positive note when leadoff man César Hernandez walked and stole second to put a runner in scoring position less than 10 pitches into the game, but Tillman struck out Odubel Herrera, got Maikel Franco to pop out, and retired Ryan Howard on a line drive to right field. Manny Machado got the Orioles' party started in the bottom of the first when he blasted Williams's second pitch into the left-field seats to give the Orioles a 1-0 lead. Travis Snider walked and Jimmy Paredes flied out to deep left-center for the first out. Chris Davis walked and Chris Parmelee singled to load the bases for shortstop J.J. Hardy, who knocked in Snider with a single to center to increase the lead to 2-0.

Ryan Flaherty lined to right for a hit that plated Davis and Parmelee and sent Hardy to second. Caleb Joseph flied to right for the second out, but Baltimore got some help from Williams, who uncorked two wild pitches with David Lough at the plate, the second of which ricocheted toward the Phillies dugout, allowed both Hardy and Flaherty to score, and staked the Orioles to a 6-0 lead. Williams strained his left hamstring while covering the plate and his outing ended after only eight batters. Right-handed reliever Dustin McGowan was called in from the bullpen and he struck out Lough to end the inning. In the span of 26 pitches, Williams's ERA climbed from 5.71 to 6.43. McGowan would suffer an even worse fate.

Tillman needed only 15 pitches to dispatch Chase Utley, Domonic Brown, and Cody Asche in the top of the second, and the Orioles extended their lead to 9-0 in the bottom of the inning when Machado, Paredes, and Parmelee belted solo homers between outs by Snider, Davis, and Hardy. Tillman surrendered a one-out single to Freddy Galvis in the top of the third, but Hernandez rapped into a 4-6-3 double play that brought Baltimore to the plate for its third turn at bat. McGowan walked Flaherty, Joseph reached first on third baseman Franco's error, and Lough belted a three-run homer to deep right field to bump the score to 12-0.

The Phillies scored in the top of the fourth when Herrera doubled to lead off the inning and Howard drew a one-out walk to put runners at first and second. Utley's fly to deep center field advanced Herrera to third and he scored on Brown's single to put Philadelphia on the board. Tillman threw a wild pitch that sent Howard to third and Brown to second, but Asche flied to center to end the threat.

The Orioles extended their lead to 12 again when Davis led off the bottom of the fourth with a long drive to right that landed on Eutaw Street and hit the iconic Camden Yards warehouse on a bounce.[3] Parmelee and Hardy followed with consecutive singles and it looked as though the onslaught would continue, but a double-play grounder by Flaherty and Joseph's strikeout sent the game into the fifth with Baltimore up 13-1. And, with that, McGowan's evening was done. He entered the contest with a 5.40 ERA and left with a mark of 6.94 after allowing five home runs in 3⅓ innings.[4]

Tillman continued his mastery over Philadelphia and retired the side in order in the top of the fifth, then the Orioles tacked on another run against reliever Justin De Fratus when Snider's one-out two-bagger plated Machado, who had walked with one out. The Phillies made the score 14-3 in the top of the sixth when Franco followed a walk to Herrera with a two-run homer to left-center. But Baltimore kept pouring it on and scored three more in the bottom of the inning. Parmelee began the frame with a line drive into the right-field seats that gave Baltimore a 15-3 cushion and tied a team record for home runs in a game with seven.[5]

Hardy stepped to the plate and De Fratus's first pitch to him sailed far inside and almost hit the Orioles shortstop, prompting home-plate umpire Lance Barksdale to eject De Fratus with no argument from him and little pushback from Phillies skipper Ryne Sandberg.[6] Sandberg called on Venezuelan southpaw Elvis Araujo to finish the inning, but he couldn't stop the bleeding either, as Machado drove in another run with his third hit of the game and Snider doubled in Lough, giving Baltimore 17 runs in the rout. With a seemingly insurmountable lead, Orioles manager Buck Showalter replaced Tillman with Brad Brach, put Steve Pearce in Hardy's spot but at second base, and moved Flaherty from second to shortstop.

Brach allowed a two-out single to Galvis, but that was it for the Phillies in the top of the seventh. Not wanting to waste more bullpen arms, Sandberg called on outfielder Jeff Francoeur to mop up and he surprisingly retired the Orioles in order in the bottom of the inning, striking out the first batter he faced, pinch-hitter Nolan Reimold. It was the first time all night that a Phillies pitcher went three-up, three-down. It would also be the last. Showalter continued to parade reserves into the game and sent pitcher Brian Matusz to the mound in Machado's spot in the order, moved Parmelee from right field to first base, put designated hitter Jimmy Paredes at third, and sent Reimold to right.

Matusz struck out two of the four batters he faced, the only blemish being Paredes' error, and the game went into the bottom of the eighth with Francouer still on the mound. Flaherty and the Orioles made history when he led off with a home run to deep right-center field that set a new team record for homers in a game. Francouer hit Joseph with a pitch, then walked pinch-hitter Matt Wieters and Snider to load the bases with one out. Paredes drove a pitch to deep left to plate Joseph, and Francouer issued his third base on balls in the inning to load the bases again, but he got Parmelee to fly out to end the inning.

Tommy Hunter came in to finish the 19-3 victory and capped it off with a 6-4-3 twin killing off the bat of Carlos Ruiz to improve Baltimore's record to 33-31.

Sources

In addition to the sources cited in the Notes, the author accessed Retrosheet.org, Baseball-Reference.com, and SABR.org.

Notes

1 The 2015 Phillies finished 14th in the NL in ERA, runs and earned runs, and last in wins, hits, and home runs allowed.

2 Baltimore's trade with the Mariners was as lopsided as they come. In addition to Tillman, who had a decent five-year run with the Orioles from 2012 through 2016 in which he went 65-33 with a 3.81 ERA in 143 starts, the Orioles also got 22-year-old center fielder Adam Jones and veteran relief pitcher George Sherrill. Sherrill saved 51 games for Baltimore in a season and a half, but Jones was the key to the deal and went on to enjoy 11 seasons with the Orioles, making the AL All-Star team five times and winning three Gold Glove Awards. Bedard was very good for Seattle, pitching to a 3.31 ERA in parts of three seasons, but he couldn't stay healthy and made only 46 starts before being traded to Boston at the 2011 trade deadline.

3 Eduardo A. Encina, "Orioles Blast Franchise-Record Eight Homers in Win Over Phillies," *Baltimore Sun*, June 17, 2015: B1. Davis's home run was his seventh to land on Eutaw Street, the most by any player at the time, putting him one ahead of Luke Scott.

4 That was the last game McGowan would pitch in the majors in 2015. He rebounded with Miami in 2016 and had one of his better seasons, pitching to a 2.82 ERA in 55 appearances, but posted a 4.75 mark in 2017 and retired.

5 The Orioles also hit seven homers in a game on May 17, 1967, against the Red Sox; August 26, 1985, against the Angels; and September 26, 2012, against the Blue Jays. They would hit seven again on June 2, 2016, against the Red Sox.

6 Jake Kaplan, "Battered in Baltimore," *Philadelphia Inquirer*, June 17, 2015: D5. When De Fratus was ejected, he simply walked off the mound and into the Phillies' dugout. Sandberg came out to hear Barksdale's explanation, but did not argue with the ump. When De Fratus was asked after the game whether he purposely threw at Hardy, he responded, "It doesn't matter. I got tossed. That's really all I can say about that."

O's Exact Revenge on Royals with Pair of Eighth-Inning Grand Slams

September 11, 2015: Baltimore Orioles 14, Kansas City Royals 8, at Camden Yards

By Gary Belleville

There was no love lost between the Orioles and Royals in the aftermath of Kansas City's sweep of the 2014 American League Championship Series. Despite their four straight victories, the series was anything but a cakewalk for the Royals, with two of the games being decided by one run and the other two by a pair of runs, including a tense extra-inning affair in Game One. Lorenzo Cain was named series MVP, although it was the dominant Kansas City bullpen, led by Kelvin Herrera, Wade Davis, and Greg Holland, who were the difference makers.[1]

The Orioles' frustration with the Royals continued to build when the two teams met again in late August for the first time since their ALCS showdown, with Kansas City taking three of four games at Kauffman Stadium. Dating back to May 17, 2014, the Orioles had dropped nine of their last 10 games against Kansas City.[2]

The 2015 season had been a letdown for the Orioles. Baltimore's starting pitching, which was solid during its 96-win season of 2014, had become a glaring weakness. Although they had the same core group of starters, the Orioles' starting pitching fell to second-worst in the American League, with Chris Tillman, Miguel González, and Bud Norris taking big steps backward. After going a combined 38-23 with a 3.40 ERA, the trio could muster only a 22-32 record and a woeful 5.32 ERA in 2015.

Fourth-place Baltimore limped into its September 11 contest against the Royals with a 67-72 record, a whopping 12 games behind the division-leading Toronto Blue Jays. Although they were on a modest two-game winning streak, the Orioles had won only five of their last 20 games, and they sat a distant 10½ games behind the Yankees in the race for the wild-card spot. With six teams between them and New York in the overall standings, the Orioles were merely playing for pride as the season wound down.

The Royals, on the other hand, were even better than they were in 2014. After astutely signing veteran reliever Ryan Madson to a minor-league deal in the offseason, they now boasted the best bullpen in baseball, with Herrera, Madson, and Davis combining for a 1.93 ERA in 200⅓ regular-season innings pitched in 2015.[3] On August 29 Kansas City held a massive 14-game lead over the Twins in the AL Central. They lost seven of their next 10 games, dropping their record to 83-56, but the slump merely trimmed their lead to 11 games.

The Royals continued to get the better of the Orioles early on in their September 11 matchup, as the game's third batter, Cain, hit a solo home run to give the visitors an early advantage.[4] They led by either one or two runs for the first 7½ innings, and Baltimore came to the plate facing Herrera in the bottom of the eighth trailing 6-4. The Orioles' chances for a comeback looked slim, with Kansas City holding a record of 63-2 when leading after seven innings and Herrera limiting hitters to a .183 batting average up to that point of the season.[5] What followed was a wildly improbable, 38-minute half-inning in which the Orioles sent 13 men to the plate.

Jonathan Schoop opened the inning by lacing a ball that short-hopped off the center-field wall for a double. After pinch-hitter Steve Clevenger reached on an error, a struggling J.J. Hardy was caught looking for out number one. Gerardo Parra followed with an infield single that loaded the bases for left fielder Nolan Reimold.

After a solid rookie campaign in 2009, Reimold's career had been slowed by a series of injuries. The 31-year-old was designated for assignment in late August, although he accepted a demotion to Triple A, and his persistence was rewarded by being recalled on September 6. Reimold stepped into the box against Herrera and took the first two pitches for balls. He then sent a 95-mph four-seam fastball on a long, majestic arc that struck the top of the left-field foul pole for a grand slam, sending the sold-out crowd into a frenzy. The stunning grand slam, the first (and last) of Reimold's career, turned a two-run deficit into a two-run lead and chased Herrera from the game.

Left-hander Franklin Morales took to the mound and proceeded to throw gas on the fire. The first batter he faced, Manny Machado, hit a fastball into the left-center-field bleachers for his 28th home run of the season. Adam Jones then drilled a hard line drive into left field for a single. Chris Davis, who led all American League batters with 22 home runs since the All-Star break, came to the plate next. After a called strike one, Morales drilled him in the back with a 93-mph fastball, causing Davis to slam his bat into the ground, snapping it at the handle. He glared at Morales as he slowly made his way to first base. Baltimore manager Buck Showalter leapt out of the dugout to ensure that Davis stayed in the game, and once cooler heads prevailed, he approached home-plate umpire Mark Carlson to argue that Morales should be ejected for intentionally hitting Davis. Instead of ejecting Morales, the umpire chose to issue warnings to both teams. Showalter had some choice words for Carlson, which got him tossed from the game, and after vehemently expressing his displeasure, he left to a standing ovation from the enthusiastic crowd.

The ninth batter of the inning, Steve Pearce, hit a groundball up the middle that deflected off the glove of shortstop Alcides Escobar and rolled into shallow center field, allowing Jones to score and Pearce to hustle into second base with a double. Morales got the hook without retiring any of the four batters he faced.

Joba Chamberlain, released by both the Tigers and Blue Jays earlier in the season, was summoned from the bullpen, and he walked Schoop to load the bases. With the count full, Clevenger crushed a low and inside slider over the right-field wall for Baltimore's second grand slam of the inning, extending the Baltimore lead to 14-6.[6] The 10-run frame was the most runs scored by the Orioles in an inning since they plated 12 in the sixth inning of an April 11, 2002, game against the Devil Rays.[7]

Mike Moustakas drove in a pair of runs in the ninth inning to close the gap to 14-8, but that was as close as the Royals could get. The Orioles had finally gotten the better of the vaunted Kansas City bullpen.

It was only the eighth time that a major-league team had hit two grand slams in one inning, and the

Nolan Reimold kicked off a 10-run eighth inning with a grand slam. Later in inning, Manny Machado hit a solo home run and Steve Clevenger hit another grand slam.
Courtesy of the Baltimore Orioles.

first since Cliff Floyd and Carlos Beltrán of the Mets hit a pair in the sixth inning of a July 16, 2006, game at Wrigley Field.[8] Baltimore also became the first team to achieve the feat twice, as both Larry Sheets and Jim Dwyer had hit grand slams in the fourth inning on August 6, 1986, against the Texas Rangers at Memorial Stadium.

Reimold savored the grand slam and his successful return to the big leagues. "I've worked hard to get back up here," he said. "But it's good to have a good game and it felt good to go around the bases with the crowd cheering in Baltimore."[9]

The Royals, losers of eight of 11, were undeterred. "You go through stretches like this," Cain said. "We can't let it worry us. We understand we're a good ballclub."[10] Indeed they were. Kansas City went 12-10 over the remainder of the regular season and finished 12 games ahead of the Twins with a 95-67 record.

• O's Exact Revenge on Royals with Pair of Eighth-Inning Grand Slams •

After rallying to defeat the Astros in the Division Series, the Royals rolled over the Blue Jays and the Mets on the way to earning their second World Series championship in franchise history and their first in 30 years. Once again an outstanding Royals bullpen played a pivotal role in their playoff run, effectively reducing their games to six innings in length. Front offices around baseball took note, and teams began investing heavily in quality bullpen arms. This trend, boosted by the growing baseball analytics movement, revolutionized how starters and relievers were deployed for years to come.

The Orioles won 13 of their last 22 games to avoid a losing season and finish in third place with an 81-81 record. Although the 2015 season may have been a disappointment, many Orioles fans were left with fond memories of that warm September night when their team rallied over the final three innings to score a dozen runs on the best bullpen in the major leagues.[11]

Sources

In addition to the sources cited in the Notes, the author consulted Baseball-Reference.com and Retrosheet.org. Full video of the game is available on YouTube at youtube.com/watch?v=T3zg2qW2Nzk.

Notes

1   The Royals went on to lose the World Series to Madison Bumgarner and the San Francisco Giants in seven games.

2   These 10 games include the four losses against the Royals in the 2014 ALCS.

3   Greg Holland was diagnosed with a torn ulnar collateral ligament in late September of 2015 and underwent Tommy John surgery in early October. Wade Davis took over the closer role for the Royals for the remainder of the regular season and the postseason. Holland missed the entire 2016 season.

4   Lorenzo Cain added a second solo home run in the top of the sixth inning to give him the second multihomer game of his career.

5   Associated Press, "Orioles Hit Two Grand Slams to Rally Past Royals," *USA Today*, September 11, 2019. usatoday.com/story/sports/mlb/2015/09/11/orioles-use-2-grand-slams--rally-past-royals-14-8/72123156/, accessed July 22, 2019.

6   The home run was only the third round-tripper for Steve Clevenger in 375 career at-bats. He finished his career with only four home runs in 484 at-bats.

7   The 12-run outburst on April 11, 2002, set a team record for the most runs scored in an inning. It remained the record as of the end of the 2019 season.

8   Through the 2019 season no major-league team had hit two grand slams in the same inning since the Orioles did it on September 11, 2015.

9   Eduardo A. Encina, "Grand O's Party: Orioles Hit Two Grand Slams in 10-Run Eighth to Power Past K.C., 14-8," *Baltimore Sun*, September 12, 2015. baltimoresun.com/sports/orioles/bal-royal-beatdown-orioles-hit-two-grand-slams-in-10run-eighth-to-power-past-kc-148-20150911-story.html, accessed July 22, 2019.

10   "Orioles Hit Two Grand Slams to Rally Past Royals."

11   One of the 12 runs scored on the Kansas City bullpen was unearned.

Machado's Three Homers Include a Walk-Off Grand Slam

August 18, 2017: Baltimore Orioles 9, Los Angeles Angels 7, at Oriole Park at Camden Yards

By Peter Seidel

"It's always good when you get into a situation where you can put your team on top. It was a good day. Our ballclub, we kept fighting to the end. That's what we do. We fight till the last out is made, and we're not going to stop fighting."

— Manny Machado[1]

For much of the 2017 season, the bullpen had been the Angels' strong suit and a big reason why they were in the second wild-card spot. They had plenty of company, though, as there were seven teams within three games of the Angels, including this night's opponent, the Baltimore Orioles.

The Angels' strong bullpen started to crack by the end of July as they lost not one, but two games in a most improbable fashion, allowing a walk-off grand slam. On July 25 Edwin Encarnacion hit a game-winning grand slam off Bud Norris in the bottom of the 11th, giving the Cleveland Indians an 11-7 victory. Five days later, Norris gave up another walk-off grand slam, to Toronto's Steve Pearce, making the Blue Jays 11-10 victors. To add insult to injury, the Angels led 10-4 in bottom of the ninth. The two walk-off slams cost Norris his job as closer and sent the Angels bullpen into disarray, as none of them had an assigned role. The Angels were going to need their bullpen to be strong for this game; their starter, Andrew Heaney, was making his first start since returning from Tommy John surgery. At the hitter-friendly Camden Yards, asking for length from Heaney was not a realistic request.

The Angels wasted no time providing Heaney with run support. Ben Revere led off the game with a double off Orioles starter Jeremy Hellickson, the 2011 AL Rookie of the Year who had been acquired at the trade deadline from the Philadelphia Phillies. Two batters later, Albert Pujols ripped a line drive that just cleared the left-field fence, giving the Angels a 2-0 lead. Pujols' 609th career home run tied him with Sammy Sosa at eighth on the all-time list and also tied him with fellow Dominican Republic native Sosa for the most home runs by a foreign-born player. Kole Calhoun followed Pujols with a blast to center field, giving the Angels a 3-0 lead.

Leading off the top of the second, C.J. Cron blasted another shot into the left-field seats, and the Angels led 4-0. Two batters later, Kaleb Cowart crushed a Hellickson fastball into the right-field seats, and it was 5-0. At this point, Hellickson had surrendered four home runs and secured only four outs.

Former Angel Mark Trumbo got the Orioles on the board in the bottom of the second with a towering solo home run to left.

Caleb Joseph's leadoff fly ball in the third just cleared the left-field fence, nudging the Orioles a little closer at 5-2. After Tim Beckham singled to right, Manny Machado deposited a 2-and-2 offering from Heaney into the right-center-field seats, cutting the Angels lead to 5-4.

After an uneventful fourth inning, the Angels got back to teeing off Hellickson with Revere smacking another double. After working a full count, Mike Trout crushed a pitch into the left-field seats, extending the Angels' lead to 7-4. Calhoun's single chased Hellickson, who finished the night with 4⅔ innings pitched and seven runs allowed on eight hits, five of which were home runs.

Machado led off the bottom of the fifth with his second home run of the game, this time a blast to left-center field, bringing the Orioles a little closer, 7-5. Heaney retired the next three Orioles and ended his night with five innings pitched and five runs allowed on seven hits, four of which were home runs. The teams had combined for nine home runs through five innings.

• Machado's Three Homers Include a Walk-Off Grand Slam •

Manny Machado hit three home runs, the last one a walkoff grand slam. Courtesy of the Baltimore Orioles.

Heaney did strike out five Orioles. "It was good to see him out there," manager Mike Scioscia said. "Everything we're looking for is there with the exception of when he had chances to put some guys away, he wasn't able to make pitches. As he gets into his next start, he'll get better."[2] Of his first major-league start since Tommy John surgery, Heaney said, "Those guys went out and put up five runs in the blink of an eye. It's my job to make that stick. I didn't do that. I didn't really develop a feel for a breaking ball. I threw a lot of two-strike pitches in the strike zone. Really never got into a rhythm. My tempo was pretty terrible. All those things lead to bad pitches and lead to big innings. That's on me."[3]

Miguel Castro, Richard Bleier, and Darren O'Day combined for 4⅓ shutout innings of relief to keep the Orioles within striking distance. Cam Bedrosian, son of former Cy Young Award winner Steve Bedrosian, had been closing games for the Angels; he pitched a scoreless sixth inning. Blake Parker and Yusmeiro Petit each pitched a scoreless inning as well. Petit took the mound in the bottom of the ninth and gave up a single to Anthony Santander, a Rule 5 draft pick making his major-league debut. (Santander had made a great diving catch robbing Trout of an extra-base hit to end the top of the second inning.) Petit walked Seth Smith, who was pinch-hitting for Craig Gentry, to put the tying runs on base with one out. Scioscia called on 23-year-old Keynan Middleton and his 99 mph fastball to close out the game. Middleton fell behind 2-and-0 to Tim Beckham before giving up a single to right field and loading the bases for Machado, who had already homered twice. Machado crushed a 98 mph fastball that caught too much of the plate into the Orioles bullpen, where it was caught by pitcher Zack Britton. Machado's third home run of the game was a walk-off grand slam.

Machado's slam was the 10th home run of the game. "It was like a [basketball] game where everybody's dunking," Orioles manager Buck Showalter said. "What was it, 10 home runs? It was like, 'No shots tonight from the field, everybody dunk.'"[4]

To Middleton's credit, he wouldn't allow the tough ending to get the best of him. "I'll go home and get some sleep and be back tomorrow. Hopefully I'll get the same opportunity tomorrow. I'm just going out and attacking hitters, doing what I do. I'll come out tomorrow and do the exact same thing."[5]

The loss dropped the Angels into a tie with the Minnesota Twins, who had defeated the Arizona Diamondbacks 10-3. The Twins eventually clinched the second wild-card spot.

Sources

In addition to the sources cited in the Notes, the author consulted Baseball-Reference.com and YouTube.

Notes

1   Peter Schmuck, "Manny Machado Hits Three Homers, Including Walk-Off Grand Slam for 9-7 Win over Angels," *Baltimore Sun*, August 19, 2017.

2   Jeff Fletcher, "Another Walk-Off Grand Slam Sinks Angels in Loss to Orioles," *Orange County Register* (Anaheim, California), August 19, 2017.

3   Fletcher.

4   Schmuck.

5   Fletcher.

Red Sox Defeat Orioles
Behind Sale's Pitching, Benintendi's Home Run, and Bradley's Catch
May 8, 2019: Boston Red Sox 2, Baltimore Orioles 1 (12 innings), at Oriole Park at Camden Yards

By John J. Burbridge Jr.

As the Boston Red Sox journeyed to Baltimore for a three-game series beginning Monday, May 6, 2019, they were somewhat optimistic about their chances, having won six of their last seven games. They were also going to play an Orioles team that had lost 115 games in 2018.

After winning the 2018 World Series, the Red Sox started the 2019 season with a West Coast trip that proved somewhat disastrous as they went 3-8 against Seattle, Oakland, and Arizona. Once back home in Boston, they rebounded somewhat but their record was just 17-18 going into the Orioles series. The rebuilding Orioles stood at 12-22.

The Orioles were victorious in the first game, 4-1, behind left-hander John Means, while the Red Sox rebounded the following evening, winning 8-5. For the final game of the series, the ace of the Red Sox pitching staff, Chris Sale, was to pitch against Orioles pitcher Andrew Cashner. Sale had lost his first five games but did win his last start, against the Chicago White Sox. While the Orioles were struggling, Cashner had been very effective, winning four games since the beginning of the season.

The game began with Andrew Benintendi lofting a line drive toward the left-field line that Dwight Smith Jr. dropped after a long run for a two-base error. Mookie Betts then hit a long drive to right-center field that was caught by Steve Wilkerson with Benintendi taking third after the catch. The Red Sox squandered this scoring opportunity as Cashner retired J.D. Martinez on a groundball to third base and Mitch Moreland struck out swinging.

In the bottom of the first, Jonathan Villar and Joey Rickard both struck out while the third batter, Trey Mancini, grounded out to second base. In the top of the second Eduardo Nunez singled with two outs but was stranded at first. Sale retired the Orioles in order in the bottom of the inning.

The Red Sox broke through in the top of the third as Mookie Betts hit a 400-foot solo home run into the left-field seats with two outs. The Orioles got a baserunner in the bottom of the third when Wilkerson, the leadoff hitter, was hit by a pitch. Sale responded by striking out the next three Orioles.

Neither team scored in the fourth or fifth, nor did the Red Sox in the top of the sixth. As the game entered the bottom of the sixth with the Red Sox ahead, 1-0, the Orioles had yet to get a hit. After Richie Martin and Villar both made outs, Rickard singled to center field for the first Orioles hit. Mancini followed with a double to deep left-center, scoring Rickard and tying the score. This ended Sale's run of scoreless innings at 16, a streak that began in Tampa on April 28.[1] Renato Nunez then grounded out to second, stranding Mancini.

As the game entered the top of the seventh, Paul Fry replaced Cashner for the Orioles. Cashner had another quality start as he just gave up one run in six innings, striking out five batters. Fry retired the Red Sox with the only blemish a Sandy Leon single to center field with two outs. In the bottom of the seventh, Sale struck out Hanser Alberto, Dwight Smith Jr., and Wilkerson all swinging on just nine pitches, a feat known as an immaculate inning. Sale had been dominant through the first seven innings, capped by this remarkable accomplishment.

Mychal Givens replaced Fry in the top of the eighth and walked Betts With two outs Xander Bogaerts reached first base on an infield single to third base but Betts, trying to advance to third, was thrown out, ending the inning. Pedro Severino led off the bottom of the eighth with a single but was unable to score. Givens continued to pitch in the top of the ninth and retired the Red Sox but did walk Jackie Bradley Jr. with two outs.

Red Sox Defeat Orioles

Sale had thrown 108 pitches, 80 for strikes, in the first eight innings, so Red Sox manager Alex Cora decided to replace him going into the bottom of the ninth. Sale's performance was superb: He had allowed just one run on three hits and struck out 14 with no walks. After the game, Cora commented about Sale's outing, "Amazing, for everybody that was worried about velocity and all that, well, he went right and he had a good slider. He located his fastball."[2]

Matt Barnes replaced Sale and immediately got into trouble as Mancini led off with a double to deep right-center. Renato Nunez grounded out to third but Rio Ruiz got an infield single, moving Mancini to third. With runners on first and third and one out, Dwight Smith Jr. hit a grounder to Barnes and was thrown out at first while Ruiz moved to second with Mancini remaining at third. Barnes then struck out Wilkerson for the third out.

As the game went into extra innings, both teams were retired in the 10th inning and the Red Sox failed to score in the top of the 11th. Ryan Brasier was the Red Sox pitcher to start the bottom of the inning. Chris Davis pinch-hit for Rickard and struck out. Mancini then to hit a long fly ball to center field. To the players and fans, it appeared to be a game-winning home run, but Bradley, the Red Sox' center fielder, had other ideas. He ran back, dug his right foot into the barrier for leverage and reached far over the seven-foot fence to snag the ball, depriving Mancini of the home run.[3] After the catch, Mancini tipped his helmet to Bradley. At the end of the game, Bradley commented on the catch: "Just went back, tracked it, and got a good jump on it. Timed my footsteps the way I wanted to, and got up there and executed."[4] Brandon Hyde, the Orioles manager, said, "Good players and great teams make great plays in big spots, and that was an ultra-exceptional play."[5] Among the fans who stayed until the bottom of the 11th was Bradley's father. He could be seen wildly applauding his son for his catch. After Bradley's catch, Brasier struck out Renato Nunez, ending the inning.

As the game entered the top of the 12th inning, Chris Davis replaced Mancini at first with Mancini going to right field. Yefry Ramirez was the new Orioles pitcher. With two outs, Benintendi hit a 387-foot home run to right field. Betts walked, but Martinez flied out to right field, ending the inning with the Red Sox leading 2-1.

Heath Hembree was the new Red Sox pitcher in the bottom of the inning and struck out the side, ending the game.

This early-season game proved quite memorable given Sale's 14 strikeouts, his immaculate inning, and Bradley's catch depriving the Orioles of a victory. As a sign of the Orioles futility or the Red Sox pitching, the Orioles struck out 22 times without a walk.[6] Benintendi was the hitting hero for the Red Sox with his game-winning home run while Mancini with two doubles and a near-miss game-winning home run led the Orioles.

While much of the discussion after the game concerned what had transpired during the contest, another topic was addressed by Cora. The next day the Red Sox as World Series champions were scheduled to visit the White House. Several of the Red Sox players were not attending because of their dissatisfaction with President Trump. Cora, who was not attending, said, "For everybody that's talking about us, the situation, crushing us throughout the week, well, they played extra innings, they didn't give in, and you see them in the clubhouse, they're celebrating Heath because of the first save, they're celebrating Jackie, and now we go. There's a group that's going home, and there's a group going to the White House. And on Friday, we get back – back to playing baseball."[7]

The 2019 Red Sox, while winning 84 games, struggled all year to get into playoff contention. They finished 19 games behind the East Division-winning Yankees and 12 games behind Tampa Bay for the second wild card. The Orioles, in the second year of their rebuilding phase, lost 108 games. For both teams, the cry of "Wait till next year!" could be heard at season's end.

Sources

Box scores and play-by-play accounts for this game can be found on baseball-reference.com.

Notes

1 Associated Press, "Benintendi's homer in the 12th lifts Red Sox over Orioles 2-1," espn.com/mlb/recap?gameId=401075284, May 8, 2019.

2 Alex Speier, "Outfield Heroics, Sale Deliver .500," *Boston Globe*, May 9, 2019: C1.

3 "Benintendi's Homer in the 12th."

4 "Benintendi's Homer in the 12th."

5 "Benintendi's Homer in the 12th."

6 Jon Meoli. "Immaculate rejection; Sale's 9-pitch, 3-strikeout inning is biggest lowlight; for O's on long night," *Baltimore Sun*, May 9, 2019: D6.

7 Alex Speier.

Contributors

Malcolm Allen is a Baltimore-born Orioles fan who attended two Opening Days at Memorial Stadium. From 1989 to 1991, he worked there as an usher. Now he manages a warehouse for Crossfire Sound Productions in Brooklyn, New York, where he lives with his wife, Sara, and daughters, Ruth and Martina.

Steve Behnke is retired from the book publishing industry. He was in marketing and sales for 29 years with Penguin Books USA and New American Library. Upon retirement he moved to Aiken, South Carolina, from New England. He lives there with his wife and two dogs. He is originally from the Boston area and is a very loyal Red Sox fan. He is interested in all aspects of baseball with an emphasis on nineteenth century, the Deadball Era, and old ballparks.

Gary Belleville is a retired information technology professional living in Victoria, British Columbia. He has written articles for the SABR Games Project and the *Baseball Research Journal*, and has contributed to several SABR books. Before working on SABR projects, Gary was the editor and lead writer for baseball blogs devoted to local independent league and college wood-bat teams. He enjoyed a stint working for the Asheville Tourists in the South Atlantic League and served as an official scorer in the West Coast League for two seasons. Gary grew up in Ottawa and graduated from the University of Waterloo with a bachelor of mathematics (computer science) degree. He patiently awaits the return of his beloved Montreal Expos.

Luis A. Blandon Jr., a native of Washington, DC, is a producer and researcher in television, video and documentary film production and in archival, manuscript, historical, film, and image research. His creative storytelling and out-of-the-box thinking garnered numerous awards for his projects, including three regional Emmys®, regional and national Edward R. Murrow Awards, two TELLY awards and a New York Festival World Medal. The documentary films on which he has worked as a researcher and/or producer include *Jeremiah*; *Feast Your Ears: The Story of WHFS 102.3*; *Yoo-Hoo Mrs. Goldberg*; *Gold Mountain: Chinese in the Old West*, and *#GeorgeWashington*. Most recently, he was a co-producer for the documentary *The Lost Battalion*. He was previously senior researcher and manager of the story development team for two national programs, *Viewpoint with Lea Thompson* and *The Daily Apple*, both of which aired on Retirement Living Television. He has also worked as a historian for Morgan Angel & Associates, a national public-policy research firm. He is a professional affiliate with MLL Consulting LLC, conducting applied research in the National Archives, as well as in regional and local repositories throughout the nation, providing consultation and reports for Native American tribal entities, law firms, and private clients. In addition, he works for authors as a researcher on their projects, most recently serving as the principal researcher for *The League of Wives* by Heath Hardage Lee. He is also a published writer and earned a master of arts in international affairs from George Washington University.

Bob Brown, a SABR member since 2004, is a lifelong Baltimore Orioles and baseball fan who has taken full advantage of the many baseball opportunities within a two-hour drive, including three major-league teams and six minor-league teams (and two SABR chapters). In 2009 Bob was the editor of the *National Pastime* SABR publication for SABR 39 in Washington, DC, entitled *Monumental Baseball*. Bob and his wife, Arlene, live in Ellicott City, Maryland, with their dachshund, Hercules.

Contributors

John J. Burbridge Jr. is currently professor emeritus at Elon University, where he was both a dean and professor. He is also an adjunct at York College of Pennsylvania. While at Elon he introduced and taught *Baseball and Statistics*. He has authored several SABR publications and presented at SABR Conventions, NINE, and the Seymour meetings. He is a lifelong New York Giants baseball fan. The greatest Giants-Dodgers game he attended was a 1-0 Giants victory in Jersey City in 1956. Yes, the Dodgers did play in Jersey City in 1956 and 1957. John can be reached at burbridg@elon.edu

Frederick C. "Rick" Bush joined SABR in March 2014. Since that time he has written articles for numerous SABR books as well as the BioProject and Games Project websites. He has collaborated with Bill Nowlin to co-edit three SABR books about the Negro Leagues: *Bittersweet Goodbye: The Black Barons, the Grays, and the 1948 Negro League World Series; The Newark Eagles Take Flight: The Story of the 1946 Negro League Champions;* and *Pride of Smoketown: The 1935 Pittsburgh Crawfords*. While writing for the current volume, he longed for the days when a team could have four 20-game winners on its pitching staff as the 1971 Orioles did. Rick lives with his wife, Michelle, their three sons – Michael, Andrew, and Daniel – and their border collie mix, Bailey, in the greater Houston area. He is in his 16th year of teaching English at Wharton County Junior College's satellite campus in Sugar Land.

Sean Church resides in Seattle, Washington, with his dog Roxi. He does part-time sports play-by-play for his alma matter, Western Washington University, and is a full-time concierge in Bellevue, Washington. He frequently attends Mariners games and contends that when the Mariners make the playoffs, he'll go to the first game at all costs. Sean has been a SABR member for five years and plans to be one for the rest of his life. Sean's interests include early twentieth-century American League history and World Series history.

Since 1993, not a day has passed during which **Matt Clever** did not watch, read about, or dream about baseball. Growing up in eastern Pennsylvania, his heart was captured that summer by an unforgettable Phillies squad that came up just short in October. Matt is an Air Force veteran who now works as a land surveyor, and also part-time as an official scorer for the Phillies' Double-A affiliate in Reading, Pennsylvania.

Alan Cohen has been a SABR member since 2010. He serves as vice president-treasurer of the Connecticut Smoky Joe Wood Chapter and is datacaster (MiLB First Pitch stringer) for the Hartford Yard Goats, the Double-A affiliate of the Colorado Rockies. His biographies, game stories, and essays have appeared in more than 50 SABR publications. Since his first *Baseball Research Journal* article appeared in 2013, Alan has continued to expand his research into the Hearst Sandlot Classic (1946-1965), which launched the careers of 88 major-league players. He has four children and eight grandchildren and resides in Connecticut with his wife, Frances, their cats, Morty, Ava, and Zoe, and their dog, Buddy.

Peter Coolbaugh is a native of the Scranton, Pennsylvania, region and works by day as a litigation paralegal in Baltimore. On the side, he is a docent and the volunteer coordinator at the Babe Ruth Birthplace & Museum, and he has been a SABR member since 2007. Currently he serves as the inaugural vice president of the Baltimore/Babe Ruth Chapter and is part of the Orioles Designated Hitters program, a volunteer sales force that has existed since 1979. Peter proposed to his wife, Renee, at the Baseball Hall of Fame in 2012, and currently they reside in the Federal Hill neighborhood of Baltimore a mere mile from Oriole Park at Camden Yards.

Chris Corrigan is a reference librarian at the Library of Congress, a career that feeds his baseball habit by subsidizing his season-ticket package to Nationals games. His interest is in baseball history from the 1920s, specifically the 1924 season. He has been a SABR member since 2018 and is excited to make this first contribution to a SABR project.

Richard Cuicchi joined SABR in 1983 and is an active member of the Schott-Pelican Chapter. After retiring as an information technology executive, Richard authored *Family Ties: A Comprehensive Collection of Facts and Trivia about Baseball's Relatives*. He has contributed to numerous SABR BioProject and Games publications. He does freelance writing and blogging about a variety of baseball topics on his website, TheTenthInning.com. Richard lives in New Orleans with his wife, Mary.

Baltimore Baseball

Tim Deale is a SABR member and chairman of the Larry Doby Chapter of SABR. A native of Deale, Maryland, and now residing in South Carolina, he is a contributor to BioProject and a member of the Nineteenth Century Research Committee. He is a former sports talk show host in Annapolis, Maryland, which allowed him to go to spring-training camps and meet and interview many managers and players. Currently he is writing books about baseball. He enjoys researching statistics and making lists of the top players and pitchers in various categories. Tim learned about baseball at an early age listening to Baltimore Orioles games on the radio with his grandmother. He wants to help preserve baseball history and pass it on to other generations.

Bill Felber is a retired newspaper editor and the author of seven books. He has chaired the SABR Baseball Research Award Committee since 2014. His most recent book, *The Hole Truth: Determining the Greatest Players in Golf Using SABRmetrics*, was published in 2019.

Bob Fleishman is a retired dentist whose patients included many Baltimore Orioles players as well as sportswriters for the Baltimore newspapers. He has been a SABR member since 2004 and an Orioles season-ticket holder since 1967. He is currently working on a book about growing up in the post-World War II era.

Brian Frank is passionate about documenting the history of major- and minor-league baseball. He is the creator of the website The Herd Chronicles (www.herdchronicles.com), which is dedicated to preserving the history of the Buffalo Bisons. His articles can also be read on the official website of the Bisons. He was a contributor to and assistant editor of the book *The Seasons of Buffalo Baseball, 1857-2020*, and he's a frequent contributor to SABR publications. Brian and his wife, Jenny, enjoy traveling around the country in their camper to major- and minor-league ballparks and taking an annual trip to Europe. Brian was a history major at Canisius College, where he earned a bachelor of arts. He also received a juris doctor from the University at Buffalo School of Law.

Gordon J. Gattie is an engineer for the US Navy. His baseball research interests include ballparks, historical records, and statistical analysis. A SABR member since 1998, Gordon earned his Ph.D. from SUNY Buffalo, where he used baseball to investigate judgment performance in complex dynamic environments. Ever the optimist, he dreams of a Cleveland Indians-Washington Nationals World Series matchup, especially after the Nationals' 2019 World Series championship. Lisa, his wonderful wife, who roots for the Yankees, and Morrigan, their yellow Labrador, enjoy traveling across the country to visit ballparks and other baseball-related sites. Gordon has contributed to multiple SABR publications and the Games Project.

Mike Gibbons is Baltimore-born and has been a diehard Orioles fan since he attended their very first American League home opener in 1954. He served as executive director of the Babe Ruth Birthplace Foundation from 1983 to 2017 and during that tenure expanded the mission, and collection, of the organization to include Baltimore's Orioles, Ravens, and Colts, the Maryland Terrapins, and amateur baseball in Baltimore. Mike served as chairman of the International Sports Heritage Association in 2010-2011, and has served on the board of directors of the Maryland State Athletic HOF since 2013. His current responsibilities as director emeritus and historian of the Babe Ruth Birthplace Foundation include media relations, special event planning, exhibit planning, and design and collections management.

Austin Gisriel would have replaced Brooks Robinson at third base for the Baltimore Orioles, and it was only a lack of talent that kept him from doing so. "When I was eight, I saw Brooks win a game for the Orioles with a single in the bottom of the ninth, so the magic worked its spell on me early on," says Gisriel. He began writing about baseball in 1979 and his work has appeared in a variety of publications. A contributor to the SABR Biography Project as well, Gisriel is the author of *Fathers, Sons, & Holy Ghosts: Baseball as a Spiritual Experience; Boots Poffenberger: Hurler, Hero, Hell-Raiser;* and *Safe at Home: A Season in the Valley*. Austin and his wife, Martha, have two grown daughters, Rebecca and Sarah, either of whom would have been named "Brooks" had she been a boy. The Gisriels live in Stephenson, Virginia, and Austin invites you to follow his blog at: austingisriel.com.

Bill Haelig is a vice president with the Robertson Insurance Group in Bethlehem, Pennsylvania, and has

• Contributors •

been a SABR member since 1989. A lifetime fan of the Baltimore Orioles (evidenced by being a season-ticket plan holder with them despite living close to 150 miles north of Camden Yards), Bill resides in Center Valley, Pennsylvania with his wife, Cindy.

Mike Huber has been rooting for the Baltimore Orioles for more than 50 seasons, since he joined the Junior Orioles with his brothers in the late 1960s. He is in his 25th year as a SABR member and is former chair of SABR's Games Project Committee. A professor of mathematics at Muhlenberg College, Mike enjoys getting students involved in research concerning modeling and predicting rare events in baseball, such as no-hit games, hitting for the cycle, and rivalry games.

William H. "Bill" Johnson is the author of a full-length biography, *Hal Trosky: A Baseball Biography* (McFarland & Co., 2017), along with over two dozen essays for the Society for American Baseball Research's BioProject. He retired from the US Navy in 2006 after a 24-year career in naval aviation. He has presented papers at several baseball-history conferences. He graduated from the University of California (Berkeley) with a degree in rhetoric, and has subsequently earned a master of arts in military history from Norwich University and a master's in aeronautical science from Embry-Riddle Aeronautical University. He currently teaches unmanned aviation at Embry-Riddle.

Timothy Kearns, an Ohio native and devoted Indians fan, resides with his wife and cats in Washington, DC. A SABR member since 2014, Tim is a partner in a law firm where he practices primarily in plaintiffs' side antitrust and financial litigation. When not in his office (where he keeps a collection of approximately 200 bobbleheads representing at least six different sports and 10 different species), he can usually be found keeping score of Nationals games from the outfield seats at Nationals Park. His first game at Oriole Park was, at that time, the lowest-attended game in the ballpark's history – an April 2, 2008, tilt with the newly-christened Tampa Bay Rays.

Jimmy Keenan has been a SABR member since 2001. His grandfather, Jimmy Lyston, and four other family members were all professional baseball players. A frequent contributor to SABR publications, Keenan is the author of the following books: *The Lystons: A Story of One Baltimore Family & Our National Pastime; The Life, Times and Tragic Death of Pitcher Win Mercer;* and *The Lyston Brothers: A Journey Through 19th Century Baseball.* Keenan is a 2010 inductee into the Oldtimers Baseball Association of Maryland's Hall of Fame and a 2012 inductee into the Baltimore Boys of Summer Hall of Fame.

Robert Kimball lives less than 10 miles from Holy Cross College, where Ted Williams made his Massachusetts debut in an organized game when the Red Sox met the Crusaders in April of 1939. Before that Robert lived nearly 40 years in Washington mourning the loss of the Williams-managed Senators to Texas after the 1971 season and celebrating the arrival of the Expos from Montreal in 2005. In between he followed the Orioles, attending the opener of Camden Yards in 1992 and Game Seven of the '71 World Series between the Birds and Pirates. Robert spent 38 years in sports media as a producer for Curt Gowdy and writer and producer at the Associated Press and *USA TODAY*. He was also a producer at Enterprise Radio, the nation's first all-sports radio network. Recently, he contributed to SABR's *The Baseball Palace of the World: Comiskey Park.*

Leonte Landino is a Venezuelan journalist for ESPN Deportes and ESPN International who has covered baseball in the United States and Latin America since 1996. He has extensive experience in the media as a commentator, writer, and content producer and has been an adviser for many baseball organizations in Latin America in areas such as communications, digital marketing, business and market development, and content production. He has worked for Aguilas del Zulia of the Venezuelan League and the Tampa Bay Rays. Landino is the founder and chair of SABR's Luis Castro/Latin America Chapter and has done extensive research and discoveries on the life of Luis Castro, has written biographies for Luis Aparicio, Wilson Alvarez, and Manny Trillo for SABR publications. He is an active speaker on international baseball topics & trends, the impact of digital & social media, baseball content & distribution in SABR national conventions, SABR analytics conferences, and chapter activities. Landino has a master's degree in mass communications from the University of Florida and lives in Southington, Connecticut, with his wife, Mariana, and their two children, Anabella and Andres, along with the real owner of the place, their 8-pound dog, Goofy.

Baltimore Baseball

Kevin Larkin retired after 24 years as a police officer in his hometown of Great Barrington, Massachusetts. He has always been a baseball fan and has been going to minor-league and major-league games since he was five years old. He has authored two books on baseball: *Baseball in the Bay State (*a history of baseball in Massachusetts), and *Gehrig: Game by Game* (an account of all of the major-league games played by his hero, Lou Gehrig. He has also co-authored *Baseball in the Berkshires: A County's Common Bond* along with James Tom Daly, James Overmyer, and Larry Moore. The book details a history of baseball in Berkshire County, where Larkin grew up. He has authored numerous articles for SABR and also recently had published on Legends on Deck, a list of those who Larkin thinks are the top 100 Black Baseball/Negro League baseball players which became available for purchase in the summer of 2021. Researching and learning about this great game are what drives him and he loves researching, reading, and writing about the game's history. He does fact-checking and hyperlinking for SABR, as well as writing biographies and game accounts, and, according to him, is living the dream of writing and researching about the great sport of baseball.

Bob LeMoine grew up in Maine and has lived and died with the Red Sox for most of his life. He joined SABR in 2013 and has contributed to several SABR book projects. Having a love for both history and baseball, he usually contributes to most SABR book projects. Bob lives in Epping, New Hampshire, and works as a high school librarian and adjunct professor.

Len Levin, a retired newspaper editor in New England, is currently the grammarian and editor for the Rhode Island Supreme Court. He also is the copyeditor for many SABR publications, including this one.

SABR member and Massachusetts native **Mike Lynch** is the founder of Seamheads.com and the author of five books, including *Harry Frazee, Ban Johnson and the Feud That Nearly Destroyed the American League,* which was named a finalist for the 2009 Larry Ritter Award and was nominated for a Seymour Medal. His most recent work includes a three-book series called *Baseball's Untold History* and several articles that have appeared in SABR books. His collaboration with others on Negro Leagues history earned him the 2019 Tweed Webb Lifetime Achievement Award given by SABR's Negro Leagues Research Committee. He lives in the Roslindale section of Boston with Catherine and their cats, Jiggs and Pepper.

Jody Madron is a freelance copywriter and marketing consultant (MadronMarketing.com) who resides in Sykesville, Maryland, with his wife, Kristi, and his three daughters, Kacie, Kamryn, and Keegan. A SABR member since 2003, Jody is a lifelong baseball fan and has been an Orioles season-ticket holder for 30 years. Jody enjoys attending games with friends and family as often as possible and occasionally writes about the Orioles on his personal blog: TrustYourStuff.com.

Tom Mank is a lifetime Baltimore Orioles fan whose earliest baseball memories include how hoarse his father got rooting against Maris and Mantle and the other Yankees, on a Bethlehem Steel Night in the early 1960s. He received his master's degree in environmental studies at Antioch New England Graduate School in 1994 and has worked as a transportation data analyst for the past 25 years. He also toured Europe 11 times as a singer-songwriter, and has made seven recordings with his music partner/wife, cellist Sera Smolen. He has been a SABR member since 2019.

Ken Mars is a multimedia artist.

Mark R. Millikin is a member of SABR who has written two baseball books, *The Glory of the 1966 Orioles and Baltimore* and *Jimmie Foxx: The Pride of Sudlersville*. His most recent book is *The Joy and Heartache of Our 1960's Music*. He gave the keynote speech about Jimmie Foxx for the 100th-anniversary celebration of Double X in his hometown of Sudlersville, Maryland, in October 2007. He has written many articles for *Red Sox Magazine*. A native Baltimorean, Mark split time between being an Orioles fan and Red Sox fan while living in Randolph, Massachusetts, from 1957 to 1962 (ages 6 to 11) and became a more avid Orioles fan after his family returned to Baltimore in 1962. He received a bachelor of science degree in conservation and resource development from the University of Maryland (College Park) in 1973, and a master of science degree in marine biology from the College of Charleston (South Carolina) in 1983. He worked 38 years as a fishery biologist and fishery manager for NOAA's National Marine Fisheries Service. He and his wife, Debbie, live in Raleigh, North Carolina.

• Contributors •

Dave Moniz is the media adviser for the US Air Force and a former reporter for *USA TODAY*, the *Columbia State* and the *Christian Science Monitor*. He lives in Alexandria, Virginia, with his wife, Kathleen, and dog, Juno. He has been a SABR member for 10 years. He grew up as a Washington Senators fan and recounted the trauma of franchise relocation six years ago in an essay in *Bleacher Report*, "A Senators Fan and His Winding Journey Back to Baseball."

Bill Nowlin has enjoyed a few visits to Camden Yards over the years, and remembers being there the night Manny Ramirez hit his 500th career home run. He wishes he'd had the opportunity to see a game at Memorial Stadium – or to see bluegrass music in Baltimore when it was something a hotbed for artists like Buzz Busby. A lifelong Red Sox fan, he lives in Cambridge, Massachusetts, and has been active with SABR for more than 20 years.

Chad Osborne is a public-relations writer at Radford University in Virginia, and has worked in higher education for 20 years. Chad has a passion for researching and writing about baseball and inclement weather. He created The Rainout Blog in 2006 and has written several SABR Games Project articles focusing on the topic. Chad lives in Marion, Virginia, with his wife, Tina; daughter, Gracie; and son, Ty. In 2018 he took his family to Nationals Park in Washington for their first major-league baseball game. The Nationals staged a come-from-behind win over the Phillies after, fittingly for Chad, a brief rain delay.

Rich Ottone joined SABR in 2018 and is a member of the Babe Ruth Chapter. He resides in Eldersburg, Maryland, with his wife, Susan, who also happens to be a lifelong Orioles fan. They attended an Orioles game on their first date in 1991. Growing up outside of Washington, DC, Rich remembers crying with his mother while listening to the last Senators game on the radio in 1971. He became an Orioles fan but yearned for the day when a team would once again call DC home. Currently the community services supervisor for the Carroll County Bureau of Aging and Disabilities, Rich has spent most of his professional career helping adults with intellectual and physical disabilities realize fuller lives. Among other things, it meant sharing his love for baseball by arranging and accompanying the people he supported to attend Orioles, Nationals, Frederick Keys, and Bowie Baysox games. Besides baseball, Rich enjoys listening to blues music and attending live shows with his wife and son.

Jim Overmyer is a baseball history author specializing in the Negro leagues. He is the author of *Queen of the Negro Leagues: Effa Manley and the Newark Eagles; Cum Posey of the Homestead Grays: A Biography of the Negro Leagues Owner and Hall of Famer;* and *Black Ball and the Boardwalk: The Bacharach Giants of Atlantic City, 1916-1929*. He has contributed to several other publications, including *Shades of Glory*, a history of Black baseball in America. He is an editor of *Black Ball*, a scholarly journal of Black baseball history. He is a member of the Society for American Baseball Research and belongs to its Negro Leagues, Nineteenth Century, Deadball, and Business of Baseball committees. He was a member of the National Baseball Hall of Fame's 2006 special committee that voted to induct 17 people from the Negro leagues and the Black baseball period before the leagues were formed as members of the Hall. He lives in Tucson, Arizona.

Laura Peebles is a retired CPA, still writing and editing tax materials part-time for Bloomberg. She brings her writing and editing skills to SABR as an associate editor for the Games Project. Her other baseball project is writing rhyming game summaries of Washington Nationals games. She lives with her wife, two cats, and an ever-growing collection of baseballs in Arlington, Virginia.

Ralph Peluso was born in New York City and remains a loyal Yankee fan. Since becoming a member of SABR in 2009, he has been a contributing member of the Overlooked Legends committee. Ralph holds an MBA in finance from Bernard Baruch College and is now retired after 45 years in corporate finance and management consulting. His book *512*, a fictional re-imagination based on Babe Ruth, was published in 2014. He continues to work on his next release. He has had several short stories published. He began contributing to the SABR projects in 2018. Ralph trekked to the Mount Everest base camp in April 2019. His next adventure is on the drawing board. He serves as the literary editor for the Zebra Press, a monthly newspaper serving Northern Virginia, and writes the monthly book reviews. Ralph and his spouse, Janet, enjoy life in an active 55+ community near the beaches of Delaware.

Baltimore Baseball

Carl Riechers retired from United Parcel Service in 2012 after 35 years of service. With more free time, he became a SABR member that same year. Born and raised in the suburbs of St. Louis, he became a big fan of the Cardinals. He and his wife, Janet, have three children and he is the proud grandpa of two.

Benjamin Sabin is a native of San Jose, California, and has contributed as a writer to several publications for SABR. He played for the Little League Orioles when he was 11, and consequently feels closely tied to this project. He has been a proud member of SABR since 2017.

Gary A. Sarnoff has been an active SABR member since 1994. A member of the Bob Davids Chapter, he has contributed to SABR's BioProject, Games Project, and to the annual *National Pastime* publication. He is also member of the SABR Negro Leagues Research Committee and serves as the chairman of the Ron Gabriel Committee. In addition, he has authored two baseball books: *The Wrecking Crew of '33* and *The First Yankees Dynasty*. He currently resides in Alexandria, Virginia.

Thomas E. Schott, an American history Ph.D. (LSU, 1978), writer, poet, long-suffering Rangers fan, from New Orleans living in Norman, Oklahoma, is a longtime contributor to SABR publications. He has written the standard biography of Alexander H. Stephens, the Confederate vice president, as well as numerous scholarly articles and book reviews. He co-edited a multivolume series on Confederate generals in the Western and Trans-Mississippi Theaters in the Civil War.

Dr. Paul Scimonelli was a member of the music faculty and director of strings at the Landon School in Bethesda, Maryland, until his retirement in 2014. Paul received his doctorate in music education from The Catholic University of America, where he was the instructor of the CUA Jazz Ensemble. Dr. Scimonelli is currently a member of the CUA Symphony Orchestra and the part-time faculty. Dr. Scimonelli also holds a bachelor of music degree from CUA and his master of music from University of Arizona. Along with teaching, Paul is an active professional performer throughout the greater Washington/Baltimore area. He has performed with symphony orchestras from Richmond to Philadelphia. In the world of Washington theater, Paul has played for dozens of shows at the National, Ford's, Toby's, Olney, and many regional theaters. Dr. Scimonelli's first book, *Roy Sievers: The Sweetest Right-Handed Swing in 1950's Baseball*, is available at Amazon, Barnes & Noble, and McFarland books. He is working on his second book, *Joe Cambria: Saint or Scoundrel: The Baseball Life of the Washington Senators "Super Scout."*

Peter Seidel is a lifelong Yankee fan who recently moved to Texas. A member of SABR since 2012, Seidel has contributed content to about a half-dozen books as well as over a dozen articles for the SABR Games Project.

Curt Smith was raised in an age when his home town, Rochester, New York, was the Orioles' Triple-A affiliate. He has written about such O's Voices as Chuck Thompson and Jon Miller, Jon saying, "I don't care what Chuck says as long as Chuck says it." Smith's 17 books include *The Presidents and the Pastime: The History of Baseball and the White House; Voices of The Game; The Voice;* and *Pull Up a Chair: The Vin Scully Story*. He is senior lecturer of English at the University of Rochester, a GateHouse Media columnist, and past host or keynote at the Great Fenway Writers Series, Cooperstown Symposium on Baseball and American Culture, the NINE Conference, and Smithsonian Institution series. He also wrote more speeches than anyone for President George H.W. Bush, who threw out the first pitch at Camden Yards' inaugural.

Bill Staples Jr. of Chandler, Arizona, has a passion for researching and telling the untold stories of the "international pastime." A SABR member since 2006, he includes among his areas of expertise Japanese-American and Negro Leagues baseball history as a context for exploring the themes of civil rights, cross-cultural relations and globalization. He is a board member of the Nisei Baseball Research Project, vice president of the Japanese American Citizens League-AZ Chapter, and chairman of the SABR Asian Baseball Committee. He is the author of *Kenichi Zenimura, Japanese American Baseball Pioneer* (McFarland, 2011), and co-author of *Gentle Black Giants: A History of Negro Leaguers in Japan* (NBRP Press, 2019). His other works are listed on his blog, zenimura.com. Bill's Baltimore baseball connection: In 2007 he played for coaches Brooks and Frank Robinson with the Orioles in a fantasy camp. Brooks was super nice; Frank was super competitive, even in a fantasy camp.

• **Contributors** •

Bill Stetka has worked for his hometown Baltimore Orioles for the past 25 years and has been director of Orioles Alumni since 2008. He has worked in the communications industry for the past 42 years, including positions in media, public relations, and marketing. He worked in the team's public-relations department for 13 years including 8½ years as director of the department before being named to his current position. He has overseen the creation of a player alumni program to better engage former players with fans and to assist the club's sales, marketing, and community efforts; oversees the storage and display of the club's historical artifacts, documents, and photographs; and serves as the de facto club historian. While in public relations, he assisted on Cal Ripken's record-breaking "2131" game as assistant director in 1995, then coordinated media events for both Ripken's 3,000th hit in 2000 and his retirement season in 2001. He began his professional career as a sportswriter for the *Baltimore News American*, covering college and professional sports including the Orioles, and also served as an official scorer for Major League Baseball for nine years before joining the Orioles front-office staff. He saw his first Orioles game in 1961.

David B. Stinson is the administrator & photographer for the lost ballpark website deadballbaseball.com and posts blogs discussing Baltimore baseball history on his website, davidbstinsonauthor.com. He is the author of *Deadball, A Metaphysical Baseball Novel*, and co-author of *The College Baseball Primer: A Guide to College Baseball, Recruiting, Scholarships, and Summer Collegiate Wooden Bat Leagues*. David spent 10 years coaching youth baseball and is a former board member of the Cal Ripken Collegiate Baseball League (CRCBL), and former general manager of the league's Silver Spring-Takoma Thunderbolts. David assisted Jane Leavy with historical research concerning Babe Ruth in Baltimore for Ms. Leavy's book *The Big Fella: Babe Ruth and the World He Created*. He has consulted on Baltimore baseball history for Sagamore Development Company (now Weller Development Group) and its redevelopment of Port Covington in Baltimore and for the Peabody Heights Brewery in Baltimore, which sits on the former site of Terrapin Park and Oriole Park (V). He currently is assisting an effort to place a historical marker at Peabody Heights Brewery recognizing the baseball history of that site. His lifetime goal is to find a photograph of John McGraw and Wilbert Robinson's Diamond Café, Baltimore's first sports bar, which from 1897 to 1915 was located at 519 North Howard Street.

Joseph Wancho has been a SABR member since 2005. He serves as the vice chair of the Baseball Index Project and occasionally contributes to the BioProject as well as the Games Project.

Steven C. Weiner, a SABR member since 2015, is a retired chemical engineer and a lifelong baseball fan starting with the Brooklyn Dodgers of the 1950s. During his undergraduate years at Rutgers University, Steven worked in the sports information office and broadcast baseball and basketball play-by-play on WRSU radio. Steven obtained his doctoral degree in engineering and applied science from Yale University and has been a contributor to the technical literature on hydrogen and fuel cell safety. Steven currently serves as assignments editor for the SABR Games Project with essay contributions in three prior SABR books: *Moments of Joy and Heartbreak; Met-rospectives;* and *The Base Ball Palace of the World: Comiskey Park*. He volunteers as an in-classroom tutor at a local middle school. You can often find him at Nationals Park for a ballgame.

SABR BioProject Team Books

In 2002, the Society for American Baseball Research launched an effort to write and publish biographies of every player, manager, and individual who has made a contribution to baseball. Over the past decade, the BioProject Committee has produced over 6,000 biographical articles. Many have been part of efforts to create theme- or team-oriented books, spearheaded by chapters or other committees of SABR.

THE 1986 BOSTON RED SOX:
THERE WAS MORE THAN GAME SIX
One of a two-book series on the rivals that met in the 1986 World Series, the Boston Red Sox and the New York Mets, including biographies of every player, coach, broadcaster, and other important figures in the top organizations in baseball that year. .
Edited by Leslie Heaphy and Bill Nowlin
$19.95 paperback (ISBN 978-1-943816-19-4)
$9.99 ebook (ISBN 978-1-943816-18-7)
8.5"X11", 420 pages, over 200 photos

THE 1986 NEW YORK METS:
THERE WAS MORE THAN GAME SIX
The other book in the "rivalry" set from the 1986 World Series. This book re-tells the story of that year's classic World Series and this is the story of each of the players, coaches, managers, and broadcasters, their lives in baseball and the way the 1986 season fit into their lives.
Edited by Leslie Heaphy and Bill Nowlin
$19.95 paperback (ISBN 978-1-943816-13-2)
$9.99 ebook (ISBN 978-1-943816-12-5)
8.5"X11", 392 pages, over 100 photos

SCANDAL ON THE SOUTH SIDE:
THE 1919 CHICAGO WHITE SOX
The Black Sox Scandal isn't the only story worth telling about the 1919 Chicago White Sox. The team roster included three future Hall of Famers, a 20-year-old spitballer who would win 300 games in the minors, and even a batboy who later became a celebrity with the "Murderers' Row" New York Yankees. All of their stories are included in Scandal on the South Side with a timeline of the 1919 season.
Edited by Jacob Pomrenke
$19.95 paperback (ISBN 978-1-933599-95-3)
$9.99 ebook (ISBN 978-1-933599-94-6)
8.5"x11", 324 pages, 55 historic photos

WINNING ON THE NORTH SIDE
THE 1929 CHICAGO CUBS
Celebrate the 1929 Chicago Cubs, one of the most exciting teams in baseball history. Future Hall of Famers Hack Wilson, '29 NL MVP Rogers Hornsby, and Kiki Cuyler, along with Riggs Stephenson formed one of the most potent quartets in baseball history. The magical season came to an ignominious end in the World Series and helped craft the future "lovable loser" image of the team.
Edited by Gregory H. Wolf
$19.95 paperback (ISBN 978-1-933599-89-2)
$9.99 ebook (ISBN 978-1-933599-88-5)
8.5"x11", 314 pages, 59 photos

DETROIT THE UNCONQUERABLE:
THE 1935 WORLD CHAMPION TIGERS
Biographies of every player, coach, and broadcaster involved with the 1935 World Champion Detroit Tigers baseball team, written by members of the Society for American Baseball Research. Also includes a season in review and other articles about the 1935 team. Hank Greenberg, Mickey Cochrane, Charlie Gehringer, Schoolboy Rowe, and more.
Edited by Scott Ferkovich
$19.95 paperback (ISBN 9978-1-933599-78-6)
$9.99 ebook (ISBN 978-1-933599-79-3)
8.5"X11", 230 pages, 52 photos

THE TEAM THAT TIME WON'T FORGET:
THE 1951 NEW YORK GIANTS
Because of Bobby Thomson's dramatic "Shot Heard 'Round the World" in the bottom of the ninth of the decisive playoff game against the Brooklyn Dodgers, the team will forever be in baseball public's consciousness. Includes a foreword by Giants outfielder Monte Irvin.
Edited by Bill Nowlin and C. Paul Rogers III
$19.95 paperback (ISBN 978-1-933599-99-1)
$9.99 ebook (ISBN 978-1-933599-98-4)
8.5"X11", 282 pages, 47 photos

A PENNANT FOR THE TWIN CITIES:
THE 1965 MINNESOTA TWINS
This volume celebrates the 1965 Minnesota Twins, who captured the American League pennant in just their fifth season in the Twin Cities. Led by an All-Star cast, from Harmon Killebrew, Tony Oliva, Zoilo Versalles, and Mudcat Grant to Bob Allison, Jim Kaat, Earl Battey, and Jim Perry, the Twins won 102 games, but bowed to the Los Angeles Dodgers and Sandy Koufax in Game Seven
Edited by Gregory H. Wolf
$19.95 paperback (ISBN 978-1-943816-09-5)
$9.99 ebook (ISBN 978-1-943816-08-8)
8.5"X11", 405 pages, over 80 photos

MUSTACHES AND MAYHEM: CHARLIE O'S THREE TIME CHAMPIONS:
THE OAKLAND ATHLETICS: 1972-74
The Oakland Athletics captured major league baseball's crown each year from 1972 through 1974. Led by future Hall of Famers Reggie Jackson, Catfish Hunter and Rollie Fingers, the Athletics were a largely homegrown group who came of age together. Biographies of every player, coach, manager, and broadcaster (and mascot) from 1972 through 1974 are included, along with season recaps.
Edited by Chip Greene
$29.95 paperback (ISBN 978-1-943816-07-1)
$9.99 ebook (ISBN 978-1-943816-06-4)
8.5"X11", 600 pages, almost 100 photos

SABR Members can purchase each book at a significant discount (often 50% off) and receive the ebook edtions free as a member benefit. Each book is available in a trade paperback edition as well as ebooks suitable for reading on a home computer or Nook, Kindle, or iPad/tablet.
To learn more about becoming a member of SABR, visit the website: sabr.org/join

The SABR Digital Library

The Society for American Baseball Research, the top baseball research organization in the world, disseminates some of the best in baseball history, analysis, and biography through our publishing programs. The SABR Digital Library contains a mix of books old and new, and focuses on a tandem program of paperback and ebook publication, making these materials widely available for both on digital devices and as traditional printed books.

Greatest Games Books

TIGERS BY THE TALE:
GREAT GAMES AT MICHIGAN AND TRUMBULL
For over 100 years, Michigan and Trumbull was the scene of some of the most exciting baseball ever. This book portrays 50 classic games at the corner, spanning the earliest days of Bennett Park until Tiger Stadium's final closing act. From Ty Cobb to Mickey Cochrane, Hank Greenberg to Al Kaline, and Willie Horton to Alan Trammell.
Edited by Scott Ferkovich
$12.95 paperback (ISBN 978-1-943816-21-7)
$6.99 ebook (ISBN 978-1-943816-20-0)
8.5"x11", 160 pages, 22 photos

FROM THE BRAVES TO THE BREWERS: GREAT GAMES AND HISTORY AT MILWAUKEE'S COUNTY STADIUM
The National Pastime provides in-depth articles focused on the geographic region where the national SABR convention is taking place annually. The SABR 45 convention took place in Chicago, and here are 45 articles on baseball in and around the bat-and-ball crazed Windy City: 25 that appeared in the souvenir book of the convention plus another 20 articles available in ebook only.
Edited by Gregory H. Wolf
$19.95 paperback (ISBN 978-1-943816-23-1)
$9.99 ebook (ISBN 978-1-943816-22-4)
8.5"X11", 290 pages, 58 photos

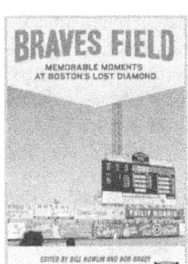

BRAVES FIELD:
MEMORABLE MOMENTS AT BOSTON'S LOST DIAMOND
From its opening on August 18, 1915, to the sudden departure of the Boston Braves to Milwaukee before the 1953 baseball season, Braves Field was home to Boston's National League baseball club and also hosted many other events: from NFL football to championship boxing. The most memorable moments to occur in Braves Field history are portrayed here.
Edited by Bill Nowlin and Bob Brady
$19.95 paperback (ISBN 978-1-933599-93-9)
$9.99 ebook (ISBN 978-1-933599-92-2)
8.5"X11", 282 pages, 182 photos

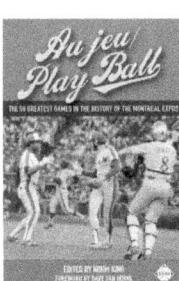

AU JEU/PLAY BALL: THE 50 GREATEST GAMES IN THE HISTORY OF THE MONTREAL EXPOS
The 50 greatest games in Montreal Expos history. The games described here recount the exploits of the many great players who wore Expos uniforms over the years—Bill Stoneman, Gary Carter, Andre Dawson, Steve Rogers, Pedro Martinez, from the earliest days of the franchise, to the glory years of 1979-1981, the what-might-have-been years of the early 1990s, and the sad, final days.and others.
Edited by Norm King
$12.95 paperback (ISBN 978-1-943816-15-6)
$5.99 ebook (ISBN978-1-943816-14-9)
8.5"x11", 162 pages, 50 photos

Original SABR Research

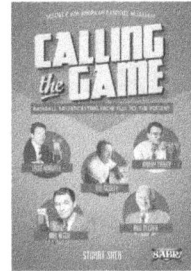

CALLING THE GAME:
BASEBALL BROADCASTING FROM 1920 TO THE PRESENT
An exhaustive, meticulously researched history of bringing the national pastime out of the ballparks and into living rooms via the airwaves. Every play-by-play announcer, color commentator, and ex-ballplayer, every broadcast deal, radio station, and TV network. Plus a foreword by "Voice of the Chicago Cubs" Pat Hughes, and an afterword by Jacques Doucet, the "Voice of the Montreal Expos" 1972-2004.
by Stuart Shea
$24.95 paperback (ISBN 978-1-933599-40-3)
$9.99 ebook (ISBN 978-1-933599-41-0)
7"X10", 712 pages, 40 photos

BioProject Books

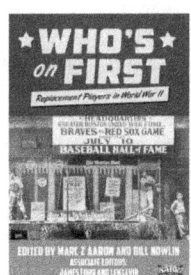

WHO'S ON FIRST:
REPLACEMENT PLAYERS IN WORLD WAR II
During World War II, 533 players made the major league debuts. More than 60% of the players in the 1941 Opening Day lineups departed for the service and were replaced by first-times and oldsters. Hod Lisenbee was 46. POW Bert Shepard had an artificial leg, and Pete Gray had only one arm. The 1944 St. Louis Browns had 13 players classified 4-F. These are their stories.
Edited by Marc Z Aaron and Bill Nowlin
$19.95 paperback (ISBN 978-1-933599-91-5)
$9.99 ebook (ISBN 978-1-933599-90-8)
8.5"X11", 422 pages, 67 photos

VAN LINGLE MUNGO:
THE MAN, THE SONG, THE PLAYERS
40 baseball players with intriguing names have been named in renditions of Dave Frishberg's classic 1969 song, Van Lingle Mungo. This book presents biographies of all 40 players and additional information about one of the greatest baseball novelty songs of all time.
Edited by Bill Nowlin
$19.95 paperback (ISBN 978-1-933599-76-2)
$9.99 ebook (ISBN 978-1-933599-77-9)
8.5"X11", 278 pages, 46 photos

NUCLEAR POWERED BASEBALL
Nuclear Powered Baseball tells the stories of each player—past and present—featured in the classic Simpsons episode "Homer at the Bat." Wade Boggs, Ken Griffey Jr., Ozzie Smith, Nap Lajoie, Don Mattingly, and many more. We've also included a few very entertaining takes on the now-famous episode from prominent baseball writers Jonah Keri, Joe Posnanski, Erik Malinowski, and Bradley Woodrum
Edited by Emily Hawks and Bill Nowlin
$19.95 paperback (ISBN 978-1-943816-11-8)
$9.99 ebook (ISBN 978-1-943816-10-1)
8.5"X11", 250 pages

SABR Members can purchase each book at a significant discount (often 50% off) and receive the ebook edtions free as a member benefit. Each book is available in a trade paperback edition as well as ebooks suitable for reading on a home computer or Nook, Kindle, or iPad/tablet.
To learn more about becoming a member of SABR, visit the website: sabr.org/join

SABR Books on the Negro Leagues and Black Baseball

From Rube to Robinson: SABR's Best Articles on Black Baseball

From Rube to Robinson brings together the best Negro League baseball scholarship that the Society of American Baseball Research (SABR) has ever produced, culled from its journals, Biography Project, and award-winning essays. The book includes a star-studded list of scholars and historians, from the late Jerry Malloy and Jules Tygiel, to award winners Larry Lester, Geri Strecker, and Jeremy Beer, and a host of other talented writers. The essays cover topics ranging over nearly a century, from 1866 and the earliest known Black baseball championship, to 1962 and the end of the Negro American League.

Edited by John Graf; Associate Editors Duke Goldman and Larry Lester
$24.95 paperback (ISBN 978-1-970159-41-7)
$9.99 ebook (ISBN 978-1-970159-40-0)
8.5"X11", 220 pages

Pride of Smoketown: The 1935 Pittsburgh Crawfords

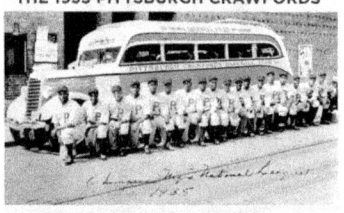

The 1935 Pittsburgh Crawfords team, one of the dominant teams in Negro League history, is often compared to the legendary 1927 "Murderer's Row" New York Yankees. The squad from "Smoketown"—a nickname that the *Pittsburgh Courier* often applied to the metropolis better-known as "Steel City"—boasted four Hall-of-Fame players in outfielder James "Cool Papa" Bell, first baseman/manager Oscar Charleston, catcher Josh Gibson, and third baseman William "Judy" Johnson. This volume contains exhaustively-researched articles about the players, front office personnel, Greenlee Field, and the exciting games and history of the team that were written and edited by 25 SABR members. The inclusion of historical photos about every subject in the book helps to shine a spotlight on the 1935 Pittsburgh Crawfords, who truly were the Pride of Smoketown.

Edited by Frederick C. Bush and Bill Nowlin
$29.95 paperback (ISBN 978-1-970159-25-7)
$9.99 ebook (ISBN 978-1-970159-24-0)
8.5"X11", 340 pages, over 60 photos

The Newark Eagles Take Flight: The Story of the 1946 Negro League Champions

The Newark Eagles won only one Negro National League pennant during the franchise's 15-year tenure in the Garden State, but the 1946 squad that ran away with the NNL and then triumphed over the Kansas City Monarchs in a seven-game World Series was a team for the ages. The returning WWII veterans composed a veritable "Who's Who in the Negro Leagues" and included Leon Day, Larry Doby, Monte Irvin, and Max Manning, as well as numerous role players. Four of the Eagles' stars—Day, Doby, Irvin, and player/manager Raleigh "Biz" Mackey, as well as co-owner Effa Manley—have been enshrined in the National Baseball Hall of Fame in Cooperstown. In addition to biographies of the players, co-owners, and P.A. announcer, there are also articles about Newark's Ruppert Stadium, Leon Day's Opening Day no-hitter, a sensational midseason game, the season's two East-West All-Star Games, and the 1946 Negro League World Series between the Eagles and the renowned Kansas City Monarchs.

Edited by Frederick C. Bush and Bill Nowlin
$24.95 paperback (ISBN 978-1-970159-07-3)
$9.99 ebook (ISBN 978-1-970159-06-6)
8.5"X11", 228 pages, over 60 photos

Bittersweet Goodbye: The Black Barons, The Grays, and the 1948 Negro League World Series

This book was inspired by the last Negro League World Series ever played and presents biographies of the players on the two contending teams in 1948—the Birmingham Black Barons and the Homestead Grays—as well as the managers, the owners, and articles on the ballparks the teams called home. Also included are articles that recap the season's two East-West All-Star Games, the Negro National League and Negro American League playoff series, and the World Series itself. Additional context is provided in essays about the effects of baseball's integration on the Negro Leagues, the exodus of Negro League players to Canada, and the signing away of top Negro League players, specifically Willie Mays. Many of the players' lives and careers have been presented to a much greater extent than previously possible.

Edited by Frederick C. Bush and Bill Nowlin
$21.95 paperback (ISBN 978-1-943816-55-2)
$9.99 ebook (ISBN 978-1-943816-54-5)
8.5"X11", 442 pages, over 100 photos and images

www.ingramcontent.com/pod-product-compliance
Lightning Source LLC
Chambersburg PA
CBHW081343070526
44578CB00005B/710